10 MORE ACTUAL, OFFICIAL
LSAT **PREPTESTS**™

A Publication of the Law School Admission Council,
Newtown, PA

The Law School Admission Council (LSAC) is a nonprofit corporation that provides unique, state-of-the-art admission products and services to ease the admission process for law schools and their applicants worldwide. Currently 219 law schools in the United States, Canada, and Australia are members of the Council and benefit from LSAC's services.

LSAC fees, policies, and procedures relating to, but not limited to, test registration, test administration, test score reporting, misconduct and irregularities, Credential Assembly Service (CAS), and other matters may change without notice at any time. Up-to-date LSAC policies and procedures are available at LSAC.org.

ISBN-13: 978-0-9793050-3-0
ISBN-10: 0-9793050-3-9

Print number
10 9 8 7 6

TABLE OF CONTENTS

INTRODUCTION

The 10 PrepTests in this book are disclosed Law School Admission Tests (LSATs) that were administered between June 1996 and June 1999. Each test in this volume includes actual logical reasoning, reading comprehension, and analytical reasoning items followed by the writing sample, score computation table, and answer key for that test. This publication is designed to be an inexpensive way for you to gain practice and better prepare yourself for taking the LSAT.

The LSAT is a half-day standardized test required for admission to all ABA-approved law schools, most Canadian law schools, and many other law schools. It consists of five 35-minute sections of multiple-choice questions. Four of the five sections contribute to the test taker's score. These sections include one Reading Comprehension section, one Analytical Reasoning section, and two Logical Reasoning sections. The unscored section, commonly referred to as the variable section, typically is used to pretest new test questions or preequate new test forms. The placement of this section in the LSAT will vary.

A 35-minute writing sample is administered at the end of the test. The writing sample is not scored by LSAC, but copies are sent to all law schools to which you apply. The score scale for the LSAT is 120 to 180.

The LSAT is designed to measure skills that are considered essential for success in law school: the reading and comprehension of complex texts with accuracy and insight; the organization and management of information and the ability to draw reasonable inferences from it; the ability to think critically; and the analysis and evaluation of the reasoning and arguments of others.

The LSAT provides a standard measure of acquired reading and verbal reasoning skills that law schools can use as one of several factors in assessing applicants.

For up-to-date information on LSAC's services go to LSAC.org.

SCORING

Your LSAT score is based on the number of questions you answer correctly (the raw score). There is no deduction for incorrect answers, and all questions count equally. In other words, there is no penalty for guessing.

Test Score Accuracy—Reliability and Standard Error of Measurement

Candidates perform at different levels on different occasions for reasons quite unrelated to the characteristics of a test itself. The accuracy of test scores is best described by the use of two related statistical terms: reliability and standard error of measurement.

Reliability is a measure of how consistently a test measures the skills being assessed. The higher the reliability coefficient for a test, the more certain we can be that test takers would get very similar scores if they took the test again.

LSAC reports an internal consistency measure of reliability for every test form. Reliability can vary from 0.00 to 1.00, and a test with no measurement error would have a reliability coefficient of 1.00 (never attained in practice). Reliability coefficients for past LSAT forms have ranged from .90 to .95, indicating a high degree of consistency for these tests. LSAC expects the reliability of the LSAT to continue to fall within the same range.

LSAC also reports the amount of measurement error associated with each test form, a concept known as the standard error of measurement (SEM). The SEM, which is usually about 2.6 points, indicates how close a test taker's observed score is likely to be to his or her true score. True scores are theoretical scores that would be obtained from perfectly reliable tests with no measurement error—scores never known in practice.

Score bands, or ranges of scores that contain a test taker's true score a certain percentage of the time, can be derived using the SEM. LSAT score bands are constructed by adding and subtracting the (rounded) SEM to and from an actual LSAT score (e.g., the LSAT score, plus or minus 3 points). Scores near 120 or 180 have asymmetrical bands. Score bands constructed in this manner will contain an individual's true score approximately 68 percent of the time.

Measurement error also must be taken into account when comparing LSAT scores of two test takers. It is likely that small differences in scores are due to measurement error rather than to meaningful differences in ability. The standard error of score differences provides some guidance as to the importance of differences between two scores. The standard error of score differences is approximately 1.4 times larger than the standard error of measurement for the individual scores.

Thus, a test score should be regarded as a useful but approximate measure of a test taker's abilities as measured by the test, not as an exact determination of his or her abilities. LSAC encourages law schools to examine the range of scores within the interval that probably contains the test taker's true score (e.g., the test taker's score band) rather than solely interpret the reported score alone.

Adjustments for Variation in Test Difficulty

All test forms of the LSAT reported on the same score scale are designed to measure the same abilities, but one test form may be slightly easier or more difficult than another. The scores from different test forms are made comparable through a statistical procedure known as equating. As a result of equating, a given scaled score earned on different test forms reflects the same level of ability.

Research on the LSAT

Summaries of LSAT validity studies and other LSAT research can be found in member law school libraries and at LSAC.org.

To Inquire About Test Questions

If you find what you believe to be an error or ambiguity in a test question that affects your response to the question, contact LSAC by e-mail: LSATTS@LSAC.org, or write to Law School Admission Council, Test Development Group, PO Box 40, Newtown PA 18940-0040.

HOW THESE PREPTESTS DIFFER FROM AN ACTUAL LSAT

These PrepTests are made up of the scored sections and writing samples from the actual disclosed LSATs administered from June 1996 through June 1999. However, in the Analytical Reasoning section the questions are distributed over four pages rather than over eight pages as in more recent versions of the LSAT and the Reading Comprehension sections do not contain a Comparative Reading set (see page 5). Also, these PrepTests do not contain the extra, variable section that is used to pretest new test items of one of the three multiple-choice question types. The three multiple-choice question types may be in a different order in an actual LSAT than in these PrepTests. This is because the order of these question types is intentionally varied for each administration of the test.

THE THREE LSAT MULTIPLE-CHOICE QUESTION TYPES

The multiple-choice questions that make up most of the LSAT reflect a broad range of academic disciplines and are intended to give no advantage to candidates from a particular academic background.

The five sections of the test contain three different question types. The following material presents a general discussion of the nature of each question type and some strategies that can be used in answering them.

Analytical Reasoning Questions

Analytical Reasoning questions are designed to assess the ability to consider a group of facts and rules, and, given those facts and rules, determine what could or must be true. The specific scenarios associated with these questions are usually unrelated to law, since they are intended to be accessible to a wide range of test takers.

However, the skills tested parallel those involved in determining what could or must be the case given a set of regulations, the terms of a contract, or the facts of a legal case in relation to the law. In Analytical Reasoning questions, you are asked to reason deductively from a set of statements and rules or principles that describe relationships among persons, things, or events.

Analytical Reasoning questions appear in sets, with each set based on a single passage. The passage used for each set of questions describes common ordering relationships or grouping relationships, or a combination of both types of relationships. Examples include scheduling employees for work shifts, assigning instructors to class sections, ordering tasks according to priority, and distributing grants for projects.

Analytical Reasoning questions test a range of deductive reasoning skills. These include:

- Comprehending the basic structure of a set of relationships by determining a complete solution to the problem posed (for example, an acceptable seating arrangement of all six diplomats around a table)

- Reasoning with conditional ("if-then") statements and recognizing logically equivalent formulations of such statements

- Inferring what could be true or must be true from given facts and rules

- Inferring what could be true or must be true from given facts and rules together with new information in the form of an additional or substitute fact or rule

- Recognizing when two statements are logically equivalent in context by identifying a condition or rule that could replace one of the original conditions while still resulting in the same possible outcomes

Analytical Reasoning questions reflect the kinds of detailed analyses of relationships and sets of constraints that a law student must perform in legal problem solving. For example, an Analytical Reasoning passage might describe six diplomats being seated around a table, following certain rules of protocol as to who can sit where. You, the test taker, must answer questions about the logical implications of given and new information. For example, you may be asked who can sit between diplomats X and Y, or who cannot sit next to X if W sits next to Y. Similarly, if you were a student in law school, you might be asked to analyze a scenario involving a set of particular circumstances and a set of governing rules in the form of constitutional provisions, statutes, administrative codes, or prior rulings that have been upheld. You might then be asked to determine the legal options in the scenario: what is required given the scenario, what is permissible given the scenario, and what is prohibited given the scenario. Or you might be asked to develop a "theory" for the case: when faced with an incomplete set of facts about the case, you must fill in the picture based on what is implied by the facts that are known. The problem could be elaborated by the addition of new information or hypotheticals. No formal training in logic is required to answer these questions correctly. Analytical Reasoning questions are intended to be answered using knowledge, skills, and reasoning ability generally expected of college students and graduates.

Suggested Approach

Some people may prefer to answer first those questions about a passage that seem less difficult and then those that seem more difficult. In general, it is best to finish one passage before starting on another, because much time can be lost in returning to a passage and reestablishing familiarity with its relationships. However, if you are having great difficulty on one particular set of questions and are spending too much time on them, it may be to your advantage to skip that set of questions and go on to the next passage, returning to the problematic set of questions after you have finished the other questions in the section.

Do not assume that because the conditions for a set of questions look long or complicated, the questions based on those conditions will be especially difficult.

Read the passage carefully. Careful reading and analysis are necessary to determine the exact nature of the relationships involved in an Analytical Reasoning passage. Some relationships are fixed (for example, P and R must always work on the same project). Other relationships are variable (for example, Q must be assigned to either team 1 or team 3). Some relationships that are not stated explicitly in the conditions are implied by and can be deduced from those that are stated (for example, if one condition about paintings in a display specifies that Painting K must be to the left of Painting Y, and another specifies that Painting W must be to the left of Painting K, then it can be deduced that Painting W must be to the left of Painting Y).

In reading the conditions, do not introduce unwarranted assumptions. For instance, in a set of questions establishing relationships of height and weight among the members of a team, do not assume that a person who is taller than another person must weigh more than that person. As another example, suppose a set involves ordering and a question in the set asks what must be true if both X and Y must be earlier than Z; in this case, do not assume that X must be earlier than Y merely because X is mentioned before Y. All the information needed to answer each question is provided in the passage and the question itself.

The conditions are designed to be as clear as possible. Do not interpret the conditions as if they were intended to trick you. For example, if a question asks how many people could be eligible to serve on a committee, consider only those people named in the passage unless directed otherwise. When in doubt, read the conditions in their most obvious sense. Remember, however, that the language in the conditions is intended to be read for precise meaning. It is essential to pay particular attention to words that describe or limit relationships, such as "only," "exactly," "never," "always," "must be," "cannot be," and the like. The result of this careful reading will be a clear picture of the structure of the relationships involved, including the kinds of relationships permitted, the participants in the relationships, and the range of possible actions or attributes for these participants.

Keep in mind question independence. Each question should be considered separately from the other questions in its set. No information, except what is given in the original conditions, should be carried over from one question to another. In some cases a question will simply ask for conclusions to be drawn from the conditions as originally given. Some questions may, however, add information to the original conditions or temporarily suspend or replace one of the original conditions for the purpose of that question only. For example, if Question 1 adds the supposition "if P is sitting at table 2 ...," this supposition should NOT be carried over to any other question in the set.

Consider highlighting text and using diagrams. Many people find it useful to underline key points in the passage and in each question. In addition, it may prove very helpful to draw a diagram to assist you in finding the solution to the problem. In preparing for the test, you may wish to experiment with different types of diagrams. For a scheduling problem, a simple calendar-like diagram may be helpful. For a grouping problem, an array of labeled columns or rows may be useful. Even though most people find diagrams to be very helpful, some people seldom use them, and for some individual questions no one will need a diagram. There is by no means universal agreement on which kind of diagram is best for which problem or in which cases a diagram is most useful. Do not be concerned if a particular problem in the test seems to be best approached without the use of a diagram.

Logical Reasoning Questions

Arguments are a fundamental part of the law, and analyzing arguments is a key element of legal analysis. Training in the law builds on a foundation of basic reasoning skills. Law students must draw on the skills of analyzing, evaluating, constructing, and refuting arguments. They need to be able to identify what information is relevant to an issue or argument and what impact further evidence might have. They need to be able to reconcile opposing positions and use arguments to persuade others.

Logical Reasoning questions evaluate the ability to analyze, critically evaluate, and complete arguments as they occur in ordinary language. The questions are based on short arguments drawn from a wide variety of sources, including newspapers, general interest magazines, scholarly publications, advertisements, and informal discourse. These arguments mirror legal reasoning in the types of arguments presented and in their complexity, though few of the arguments actually have law as a subject matter.

Each Logical Reasoning question requires you to read and comprehend a short passage, then answer one question (or, rarely, two questions) about it. The questions are designed to assess a wide range of skills involved in thinking critically, with an emphasis on skills that are central to legal reasoning.

These skills include:

- Recognizing the parts of an argument and their relationships

- Recognizing similarities and differences between patterns of reasoning

- Drawing well-supported conclusions

- Reasoning by analogy

- Recognizing misunderstandings or points of disagreement

- Determining how additional evidence affects an argument

- Detecting assumptions made by particular arguments

- Identifying and applying principles or rules

- Identifying flaws in arguments

- Identifying explanations

The questions do not presuppose specialized knowledge of logical terminology. For example, you will not be expected to know the meaning of specialized terms such as "ad hominem" or "syllogism." On the other hand, you will be expected to understand and critique the reasoning contained in arguments. This requires that you possess a university-level understanding of widely used concepts such as argument, premise, assumption, and conclusion.

Suggested Approach
Read each question carefully. Make sure that you understand the meaning of each part of the question. Make sure that you understand the meaning of each answer choice and the ways in which it may or may not

relate to the question posed. Do not pick a response simply because it is a true statement. Although true, it may not answer the question posed. Answer each question on the basis of the information that is given, even if you do not agree with it. Work within the context provided by the passage. LSAT questions do not involve any tricks or hidden meanings.

Reading Comprehension Questions

Both law school and the practice of law revolve around extensive reading of highly varied, dense, argumentative, and expository texts (for example, cases, codes, contracts, briefs, decisions, evidence). This reading must be exacting, distinguishing precisely what is said from what is not said. It involves comparison, analysis, synthesis, and application (for example, of principles and rules). It involves drawing appropriate inferences and applying ideas and arguments to new contexts. Law school reading also requires the ability to grasp unfamiliar subject matter and the ability to penetrate difficult and challenging material.

The purpose of LSAT Reading Comprehension questions is to measure the ability to read, with understanding and insight, examples of lengthy and complex materials similar to those commonly encountered in law school. The Reading Comprehension section of the LSAT contains four sets of reading questions, each set consisting of a selection of reading material followed by five to eight questions. The reading selection in three of the four sets consists of a single reading passage; the other set contains two related shorter passages. Sets with two passages are a variant of Reading Comprehension called Comparative Reading, which was introduced in June 2007. (See page 5.)

Reading selections for LSAT Reading Comprehension questions are drawn from a wide range of subjects in the humanities, the social sciences, the biological and physical sciences, and areas related to the law. Generally, the selections are densely written, use high-level vocabulary, and contain sophisticated argument or complex rhetorical structure (for example, multiple points of view). Reading Comprehension questions require you to read carefully and accurately, to determine the relationships among the various parts of the reading selection, and to draw reasonable inferences from the material in the selection. The questions may ask about the following characteristics of a passage or pair of passages:

- The main idea or primary purpose

- Information that is explicitly stated

- Information or ideas that can be inferred

- The meaning or purpose of words or phrases as used in context

- The organization or structure

- The application of information in the selection to a new context

- Principles that function in the selection

- Analogies to claims or arguments in the selection

- An author's attitude as revealed in the tone of a passage or the language used

- The impact of new information on claims or arguments in the selection

Suggested Approach

Since reading selections are drawn from many different disciplines and sources, you should not be discouraged if you encounter material with which you are not familiar. It is important to remember that questions are to be answered exclusively on the basis of the information provided in the selection. There is no particular knowledge that you are expected to bring to the test, and you should not make inferences based on any prior knowledge of a subject that you may have. You may, however, wish to defer working on a set of questions that seems particularly difficult or unfamiliar until after you have dealt with sets you find easier.

Strategies. One question that often arises in connection with Reading Comprehension has to do with the most effective and efficient order in which to read the selections and questions. Possible approaches include:

- reading the selection very closely and then answering the questions;

- reading the questions first, reading the selection closely, and then returning to the questions; or

- skimming the selection and questions very quickly, then rereading the selection closely and answering the questions.

The best strategy for one test taker might not be the best strategy for another. In preparing for the test, therefore, you might want to experiment with the different strategies and decide what works most effectively for you.

Remember that your strategy must be effective under timed conditions. For this reason, the first strategy—reading the selection very closely and then answering the questions—may be the most effective for you. Nonetheless, if you believe that one of the other strategies might be more effective for you, you should try it out and assess your performance using it.

Reading the selection. Whatever strategy you choose, you should give the passage or pair of passages at least one careful reading before answering the questions. Try to distinguish main ideas from supporting ideas, and opinions or attitudes from factual, objective information. Note transitions from one idea to the next and identify the relationships among the different ideas or parts of a passage, or between the two passages in Comparative Reading sets. Consider how and why an author makes points and draws conclusions. Be sensitive to implications of what the passages say.

You may find it helpful to mark key parts of passages. For example, you might underline main ideas or important arguments, and you might circle transitional words—"although," "nevertheless," "correspondingly," and the like—that will help you map the structure of a passage. Also, you might note descriptive words that will help you identify an author's attitude toward a particular idea or person.

Answering the Questions

- Always read all the answer choices before selecting the best answer. The best answer choice is the one that most accurately and completely answers the question.

- Respond to the specific question being asked. Do not pick an answer choice simply because it is a true statement. For example, picking a true statement might yield an incorrect answer to a question in which you are asked to identify an author's position on an issue, since you are not being asked to evaluate the truth of the author's position but only to correctly identify what that position is.

- Answer the questions only on the basis of the information provided in the selection. Your own views, interpretations, or opinions, and those you have heard from others, may sometimes conflict with those expressed in a reading selection; however, you are expected to work within the context provided by the reading selection. You should not expect to agree with everything you encounter in Reading Comprehension passages.

Comparative Reading

Starting with the June 2007 administration, LSAC introduced a new variant of Reading Comprehension, called Comparative Reading, as one of the four sets in the LSAT Reading Comprehension section. In general, Comparative Reading questions are similar to traditional Reading Comprehension questions, except that Comparative Reading questions are based on two shorter passages instead of one longer passage. The two passages together are of roughly the same length as one Reading

Comprehension passage, so the total amount of reading in the Reading Comprehension section will remain essentially the same. A few of the questions that follow a Comparative Reading passage pair might concern only one of the two passages, but most will be about both passages and how they relate to each other.

Comparative Reading questions reflect the nature of some important tasks in law school work, such as understanding arguments from multiple texts by applying skills of comparison, contrast, generalization, and synthesis to the texts. The purpose of comparative reading is to assess this important set of skills directly.

What Comparative Reading Looks Like

The two passages in a Comparative Reading set—labeled "Passage A" and "Passage B"—discuss the same topic or related topics. The topics fall into the same academic categories traditionally used in Reading Comprehension: humanities, natural sciences, social sciences, and issues related to the law. Like traditional Reading Comprehension passages, Comparative Reading passages are complex and generally involve argument. The two passages in a Comparative Reading pair are typically adapted from two different published sources written by two different authors. They are usually independent of each other, with neither author responding directly to the other.

As you read the pair of passages, it is helpful to try to determine what the central idea or main point of each passage is, and to determine how the passages relate to each other. The passage will relate to each other in various ways. In some cases, the authors of the passages will be in general agreement with each other, while in others their views will be directly opposed. Passage pairs may also exhibit more complex types of relationships: for example, one passage might articulate a set of principles, while the other passage applies those or similar principles to a particular situation.

Questions that are concerned with only one of the passages are essentially identical to traditional reading comprehension questions. Questions that address both passages test the same fundamental reading skills as traditional reading comprehension questions, but the skills are applied to two texts instead of one. You may be asked to identify a main purpose shared by both passages, a statement with which both authors would agree, or a similarity or dissimilarity in the structure of the arguments in the two passages. The following are additional examples of comparative reading questions:

- Which one of the following is the central topic of each passage?

- Both passages explicitly mention which one of the following?

- Which one of the following statements is most strongly supported by both passages?

- Which one of the following most accurately describes the attitude expressed by the author of passage B toward the overall argument in passage A?

- The relationship between passage A and passage B is most analogous to the relationship in which one of the following?

This is not a complete list of the sorts of questions you may be asked in a comparative reading set, but it illustrates the range of questions you may be asked.

Eight Sample Comparative Reading Questions and Explanations

The following comparative reading set was administered in field test trials in 2003.

<u>Directions</u>: Each set of questions in this section is based on a single passage or a pair of passages. The questions are to be answered on the basis of what is <u>stated</u> or <u>implied</u> in the passage or pair of passages. For some of the questions, more than one of the choices could conceivably answer the question. However, you are to choose the <u>best</u> answer; that is, the response that most accurately and completely answers the question, and blacken the corresponding space on your answer sheet.

Passage Pair for Questions 1–8

The following passages on freedom of information are adapted from texts published in the United Kingdom.

Passage A

We have made a commitment to openness in government, and now it is essential that we strengthen that commitment with legislation that guarantees public access to government information. This is something
(5) that the previous Government conspicuously failed to do. What resulted was a haphazard approach based largely on nonstatutory arrangements, in particular the Code of Practice on Access to Government Information. Those statutory requirements for openness
(10) that were in place applied only in certain areas, such as environmental information, or were limited to particular sectors of the public service.

We could have scored an early legislative achievement by simply enacting the Code of Practice
(15) into law, but it does not ultimately provide a satisfactory guarantee of openness. Some of its significant drawbacks, which our proposed legislation seeks to remedy, are that:

(20)
- it contains too many exemptions—more than any of the main statutory freedom of information regimes elsewhere in the world. This inevitably makes it complex for applicants to use, and encourages accusations that Departments "trawl" for possible reasons
(25)
  for nondisclosure;
- its wording encourages the use of a "category-based" approach toward exemptions by which whole classes of information or records are protected against disclosure,
(30)
  leaving no scope for partial disclosure of documents of those types (after deletion of sensitive material);
- it often requires assessing the relative weights to be assigned to the harm that a disclosure
(35)
  could cause and the public interest in disclosure. But the "public interest" is not defined, making it difficult for government staff, as well as for those who may be unfamiliar with the Code and with effective
(40)
  disclosure practices, to assess what would constitute harm to that interest.

Passage B

There is, of course, room for disagreement as to how best to achieve freedom of information, but there are a number of features common to all genuinely
(45) successful freedom of information regimes. The statute (or other legal instrument) creating the regime must contain a general presumption in favor of disclosure. There must be a general right of access to information held by public authorities that relates to their public
(50) functions. This right must be made subject to exemptions in order to protect specified public interests such as public health or public safety. These interests must, however, be narrowly drawn and disclosure refused only where it can be shown that disclosure of
(55) the particular piece of information withheld would cause harm to one or more of those interests. Many advocates of freedom of information would add that even where there is potential harm to a specified interest, disclosure should only be refused where the
(60) harm can be shown to outweigh the public's interest in disclosure of the information in question. Lastly, there must be the possibility of appeal to an independent body or official against refusals by public authorities to disclose information. This body or official must have
(65) the power to redetermine applications independently and to make binding decisions.

Question 1

Which one of the following most accurately describes a way in which the two passages are related to each other?

(A) Passage A contains reasoning of a kind that passage B suggests is fallacious.
(B) Passage B presupposes that information given in passage A regarding specific events is accurate.
(C) Passage A contains an explanation that, if valid, helps to resolve a paradox suggested in passage B.
(D) If all of the claims made in passage A are true, then some of the claims made in passage B are false.
(E) If the assertions made in passage B are valid, they strengthen the position expressed in passage A.

Explanation for Question 1

This question asks the test taker to identify a way in which the two passages relate to each other.

The correct response is (E), "If the assertions made in passage B are valid, they strengthen the position expressed in passage A." Passage A argues in favor of the new government's proposed legislation by pointing to alleged flaws in the previous freedom of information regime and pledging that the new regime would avoid those problems. In a nutshell, passage A charges that the previous freedom of information regime contained too many exemptions, that it allowed a category-based approach in which entire classes of information were protected from disclosure, and that it depended on an undefined notion of public interest. These criticisms rely on the presumption that it is good for a freedom of information regime to limit exemptions, to avoid protecting entire classes of information, and to define public interest. Passage B offers general principles that, if valid, justify the particular presumptions and criticisms made in passage A. Passage B allows that exemptions may be necessary to protect other public interests, but states that such exemptions must be limited to cases in which "disclosure of the particular piece of information withheld would cause harm to one or more of those interests" (lines 54–56). Because it permits refusal of disclosure requests only when it can be shown that harm to a specific public interest would result from the disclosure, this same principle also rules out category-based exemptions. Finally, the author of passage B speaks in terms of "specified" (lines 51 and 58) and "narrowly drawn" (line 53) public interests, which indicates a belief that "public interest" can be clearly defined. Thus, if these assertions from passage B are valid, they do in fact strengthen the position taken in passage A.

Response (A) is incorrect because passage B does not suggest that the type of reasoning employed in passage A is fallacious. In fact, as noted in the explanation for response (E), the principles articulated in passage B tend to support passage A.

Response (B) is incorrect because none of the particular details mentioned in passage A, for example, the events surrounding the Code of Practice, play any role in passage B. The assertions made in passage B are couched at a very general level; passage B does not presume anything about the accuracy or inaccuracy of any of the particular information in passage A.

Response (C) is incorrect because passage B does not discuss or otherwise give rise to any paradox, nor does passage A offer an explanation that resolves any paradox.

Response (D) is incorrect because the truth of all the claims in passage A does not imply the falsity of any of the claims in passage B. The two passages are not in conflict with each other.

Difficulty Level: Difficult

Question 2

Which one of the following most accurately expresses the main point of passage A?

(A)   The current government is fully committed to openness in government, whereas the previous government was not.
(B)   The Code of Practice has many weaknesses that the current government's proposed legislation is designed to avoid.
(C)   There must be a general right of access to information held by public authorities that relates to public functions.
(D)   The previous government was more interested in scoring a legislative victory than in providing a suitable approach to openness in government.
(E)   Freedom of information regimes should not depend on nonstatutory arrangements that grant large numbers of exemptions.

Explanation for Question 2

Early in most traditional reading comprehension sets there is a question that asks about the passage's main point or central topic, or the author's main purpose in writing. The same is true of most comparative reading sets. In some cases, these questions might ask about the main point, primary purpose, or central issue of both passages. However, in cases where understanding the main point of one of the passages is particularly important to understanding the broader context of the two passages,

the test taker might be asked about the main point of that individual passage. That is the case here.

The correct response is (B), "The Code of Practice has many weaknesses that the current government's proposed legislation is designed to avoid." Passage A opens with an assertion that it is essential to enact legislative guarantees of public access to government information. The previous government, passage A says, failed to enact such legislative guarantees (note that passage A uses the first person plural pronoun "we" in lines 1, 2, and 13, indicating that its author is affiliated with the current government in the United Kingdom). Because no freedom of information legislation was passed, passage A asserts, the result was a "haphazard approach" to freedom of information that relied on the nonstatutory Code of Practice on Access to Government Information (lines 6–9). The bulk of the passage is then devoted to a description of significant flaws in the Code of Practice, flaws which, the passage says, "our proposed legislation seeks to remedy" (lines 17–18). Thus the main point of the passage is to identify weaknesses in the Code of Practice and to proclaim that the current government's proposed legislation is designed to correct those problems.

Response (A) is incorrect. Although passage A does declare the current government to be committed to openness in government (lines 1–2), it does not claim that the previous government was not committed to openness. Passage A says only that the previous government failed to enact legislation that guarantees public access to government information (lines 4–6). And in any case, the previous government's commitment to openness, or lack thereof, is not the central focus of the passage. The passage is focused on flaws in the Code of Practice and the proposed legislation designed to correct those flaws.

Response (C) is incorrect because passage A does not seek to argue for the principle stated in the response—namely, that there must be a general right of access to information held by public authorities that relates to their public functions. In fact, passage A evidently takes it for granted that this principle—or at least something close to it—is valid, because, rather than seeking to argue for the principle, passage A seeks to show why the current government's proposed legislation offers a better approach to upholding the principle than the Code of Practice does. It is also worth noting that response (C) is taken directly from passage B (lines 48–50). That fact alone is not enough to eliminate response (C) because, though it is unlikely, it is conceivable that a statement from one passage in a comparative reading set could express the main point of the other passage. In this case, response (C) can be eliminated because it fails to accurately state the main point of passage A, not because it is taken from passage B.

Response (D) is incorrect. The phrase "scoring a legislative victory" refers to lines 13–16 in passage A, where it is asserted that the current government "could have scored an early legislative achievement by simply enacting the Code of Practice into law," but did not do so. Passage A does not ascribe this hypothetical goal of seeking a legislative victory to the previous government.

Response (E) is incorrect because it is too narrow in focus to be the main point of passage A. It is true that among the factors identified in passage A as limiting the effectiveness of the Code of Practice are the fact that it is a nonstatutory arrangement (lines 6–9) and that it contains too many exemptions (lines 19–25). But passage A focuses on other flaws in the Code of Practice as well: namely, its "category-based" approach (lines 26–32) and its failure to offer a clear definition for the key term "public interest" (lines 36–41). Because response (E) focuses on the former two flaws while ignoring the latter two, it reflects only part of the main point of passage A.

Difficulty Level: Difficult

Question 3

Which one of the following is identified in passage B, but not in passage A, as a necessary component of an effective guarantee of freedom of information?

(A) a category-based approach in which certain classes of information are declared exempt from disclosure requirements
(B) a mechanism for appealing government denials of requests for specific information
(C) a statutory guarantee of public access to government information
(D) a government agency devoted solely to the processing of requests for government information
(E) a limit to the number of exemptions from requirements to release government information

Explanation for Question 3

This question is designed to test the ability to recognize a notable difference in the contents of the two passages. The test taker is asked to identify a feature that is mentioned in passage B, but not in passage A, as necessary for an effective guarantee of freedom of information.

The correct response is (B), "a mechanism for appealing government denials of requests for specific information." This type of mechanism is identified at the end of passage B as necessary for a successful freedom of information regime: "Lastly, there must be the possibility of appeal to an independent body or official against refusals by public authorities to disclose information" (lines 61–64). Passage A, on the other hand, makes no mention of a mechanism for appealing denials of requests for information.

Response (A) is incorrect because, while passage B does argue that the public's right to information must be subject to exemptions, passage B does not call for a "category-based approach" to such exemptions. Passage B states that public access to information must be subject to exemptions to protect interests such as public health and safety, but it also stipulates that these interests must be "narrowly drawn and disclosure refused only where it can be shown that disclosure of the particular piece of information withheld would cause harm to one or more of those interests" (lines 53–56). This approach would evidently allow for fewer exemptions than would a "category-based approach."

Response (C) is incorrect because, while passage A favors a legislative guarantee of public access to information (lines 2–4), passage B does not specifically call for a statutory guarantee. In fact, passage B refers to "the statute (or other legal instrument) creating the regime" (lines 45–46), suggesting that the author of passage B does not regard a statutory guarantee of access to information as necessary. Thus response (C) is identified in passage A, and not passage B, as essential.

Response (D) is incorrect because neither passage identifies an agency devoted solely to the processing of requests for government information as a necessary component of an effective guarantee of freedom of information.

Response (E) is incorrect because both passages argue in favor of limiting exemptions to disclosure (lines 19–25 in passage A; lines 52–56 in passage B). Moreover, passage B does not call specifically for a limit to the *number* of exemptions but rather for balancing the public's interest in disclosure against other public interests, such as health and safety.

Difficulty Level: Medium difficulty

Question 4

Which one of the following most accurately characterizes how the use of the word "regimes" in passage A (line 21) relates to the use of the word "regimes" in passage B (line 45)?

(A) In passage A it refers to formal hierarchies within a government, whereas in passage B it refers to informal arrangements that evolve over time.
(B) In passage A it refers to governments that have been in power at particular times, whereas in passage B it refers to statutes that are enacted by those governments.
(C) In both passage A and passage B it refers to governments that have been in power at particular times.

(D) In both passage A and passage B it refers to sets of laws or other policy mechanisms that impose particular duties on governments.
(E) In both passage A and passage B it refers to political ideologies underlying the policies followed by various governments.

Explanation for Question 4

In traditional reading comprehension sets, test takers are sometimes asked to determine the meaning of a particular word or phrase in the passage based on the surrounding context. In comparative reading sets, test takers may be asked to identify how the use of a particular word or phrase used in one passage compares to the use of that same word or phrase in the other passage, again based on the surrounding context. That is the case in this question, where test takers are asked how the use of the word "regimes" in passage A relates to the use of the same word in passage B.

The correct answer is (D), "In both passage A and passage B it refers to sets of laws or other policy mechanisms that impose particular duties on governments." The use of the term "regimes" in passage A occurs in lines 19–21, where it is asserted that the Code of Practice contains more exemptions "than any of the main statutory freedom of information regimes elsewhere in the world." The word "regime" often refers to a government, but that is obviously not the case in passage A: it would make little sense to refer to a freedom of information *regime* in that sense of the word. Instead, since these freedom of information regimes determine how many and what kinds of exemptions to disclosure are allowable, it becomes clear from context that these regimes are more like regulations that set out what obligations governments have with respect to public access to information. Meanwhile, passage B opens with the assertion that there are certain features common "to all genuinely successful freedom of information regimes" (lines 44–45). Again, the rest of the passage makes clear that a freedom of information regime determines a government's obligations with respect to freedom of information. Thus response (D) describes how "regimes" is used in both passages.

Responses (A) and (B) are incorrect because they both say that the two passages use the word "regimes" to mean different things, whereas, as noted in the explanation for response (D) above, both passages actually use the term "regimes" to express the same concept.

Response (C) is incorrect because, as noted in the explanation for response (D) above, neither passage uses the term "regimes" to refer to governments.

Response (E) is incorrect because in both passages the term "regimes" is used to refer to laws or regulations that govern freedom of information. Nothing in the context of either passage suggests that "regimes" refers to ideologies.

Difficulty Level: Very difficult

Question 5

If the author of passage B were to read passage A, he or she would be most likely to draw which one of the following conclusions regarding matters addressed in passage A?

(A) The Code of Practice did not allow sufficient public access to information.
(B) It would have been premature for the previous government to have enacted statutory measures to guarantee freedom of information.
(C) The measures recommended by the current government are unnecessarily complex.
(D) Freedom of information laws ought not to allow sensitive material to be deleted from any document before disclosure of the document.
(E) The current government's proposed legislation depends too heavily on the questionable assumption that "public interest" can be clearly defined.

Explanation for Question 5

A significant number of questions for comparative reading passages require an ability to infer what the authors' views are and how they compare. In most cases, questions might ask about points of agreement or disagreement between the authors; in some cases, however, test takers will be asked to infer how one author would be likely to view the other passage or some aspect of the other passage. Here, the test taker is asked to infer how the author of passage B would be likely to regard the matters discussed in passage A.

The correct answer is (A), "The Code of Practice did not allow sufficient public access to information." The key to answering this question lies in the fact that passage B presents a survey of some of the requirements for a successful freedom of information regime. The Code of Practice, as it is described in passage A, fails to conform to several of those requirements. For example, passage B states that there must be a presumption in favor of disclosure (lines 45–47), whereas the Code of Practice encouraged a "category-based" approach in which "whole classes of information or records are protected against disclosure" (lines 26–29). Similarly, passage B argues that exemptions should be limited to cases in which "it can be shown that disclosure of the particular piece of information withheld would cause harm to one or more [public] interests" (lines 54–56), whereas the Code of Practice "contains too many exemptions—more than any of the main statutory freedom of information regimes elsewhere in the world" (lines 19–21). Finally, passage B states that the public interests against which possible disclosures are to be weighed must be narrowly drawn (lines 52–53), whereas the Code of Practice does not define "public interest," which makes it difficult "to assess what would constitute harm to that interest" (lines 40–41). All of this evidence supports the conclusion that the author of passage B would regard the Code of Practice as a freedom of information regime that did not allow sufficient public access to government information.

Response (B) is incorrect because there is nothing in either passage to suggest that the previous government's enacting statutory guarantees of freedom of information would have been premature in any way. In fact, since there are grounds for inferring that the author of passage B would regard the Code of Practice as inadequate (see the explanation of response (A)), it seems likely that the author of passage B would view statutory guarantees, had they been enacted by the previous government, as warranted rather than premature.

Response (C) is incorrect because there is no indication that the legislation advocated in passage A is complex in a way that the author of passage B would find objectionable. In fact, there is evidence that the author of passage B would endorse the measures recommended by the current government insofar as they are designed to "remedy" (line 18) shortcomings of the Code of Practice (see the explanation of response (A)).

Response (D) is incorrect because there is no reason to conclude that the author of passage B would object to the idea, stated in passage A (see lines 30–32), that documents can be partially disclosed with sensitive material deleted. Indeed, given that the author of passage B holds that the public's interest in disclosure must be weighed against other public interests (see lines 50–56), the author of passage B might very well endorse the idea of deleting sensitive material before disclosing documents as a way of balancing those competing interests.

Response (E) is incorrect because there is no indication that the author of passage B regards the assumption that "public interest" can be clearly defined as questionable. In fact, the author of passage B speaks in terms of "specified" (lines 51 and 58) and "narrowly drawn" (line 53) public interests, which indicates a belief that "public interest" can be clearly defined.

Difficulty Level: Difficult

Question 6

Passage A differs from passage B in that passage A displays an attitude that is more

(A) partisan
(B) tentative
(C) analytical
(D) circumspect
(E) pessimistic

Explanation for Question 6

Some traditional reading comprehension questions require test takers to identify the attitude displayed by the author, using cues such as tone and word choice. In comparative reading, test takers may be asked to identify and compare, based on the same types of cues, the attitudes displayed in the two passages. This question asks the test taker to select the adjective that accurately describes an attitude displayed in passage A more than in passage B.

The correct response is (A), "partisan." This is based on the fact that passage A argues in favor of proposed legislation and criticizes the freedom of information regime it is meant to replace. In so doing, it also criticizes the previous government. Passage B, in contrast, speaks in fairly abstract terms about the requirements for any successful freedom of information regime. It does not argue in favor of any particular freedom of information regime, legislation, or government.

Response (B) is incorrect because neither passage can be accurately described as "tentative" in its argument.

Response (C) is incorrect because, if anything, it is passage B that is more analytical than passage A. The bulk of passage B is devoted to distinguishing the features possessed by successful freedom of information regimes; this process of identifying the components of a significant phenomenon is the hallmark of an analytical approach. And while it is true that passage A points to three alleged flaws in the Code of Practice, its purpose in doing so is to tout the advantages of the proposed legislation, rather than to analyze the status quo.

Response (D) is incorrect because passage A is quite direct, rather than circumspect, in its assertions.

Response (E) is incorrect because neither passage A nor passage B displays any pessimism with regard to its subject. The author of passage A identifies flaws in the previous freedom of information regime but seems quite optimistic that the proposed legislation will address those problems. Passage B seems equally optimistic about the possibility that the public's right to information can be adequately guaranteed by means of successful freedom of information regimes.

Difficulty Level: Very difficult

Question 7

It can be inferred from the passages that both authors hold which one of the following views?

(A) Freedom of information laws should not compel governments to comply with all requests for disclosure of information.
(B) "Public interest" is too vague a concept to be cited in justifying freedom of information laws.
(C) Freedom of information laws should unequivocally specify the categories to which they apply, so that case-by-case determinations are unnecessary.
(D) Noncompulsory freedom of information policies are often sufficient to guarantee adequate public access to government information.
(E) There should be a presumption in favor of disclosing government information, but only in explicitly specified branches of government.

Explanation for Question 7

A significant number of questions for comparative reading passages require an ability to infer what the authors' views are and how they compare. Some questions ask about points of disagreement between the authors; others, such as this one, ask about points on which the authors are likely to agree.

The correct response is (A), "Freedom of information laws should not compel governments to comply with all requests for disclosure of information." The evidence that the author of passage B holds this view is quite straightforward. The author states that there must be a general right of access to government information, but this assertion is then qualified: "This right must be made subject to exemptions in order to protect specified public interests such as public health or public safety" (lines 50–52). The evidence that the author of passage A holds this view is more indirect; nonetheless, it can be found in the three bulleted statements in the passage. In line 19, the author of passage A charges that the Code of Practice has too many exemptions, and in lines 26–27, the author states that the Code of Practice "encourages the use of a 'category-based' approach towards exemptions." Both of these claims imply that it is appropriate that there be *some* exemptions to the right of access to government information (if that were not the case, the author of passage A would presumably object to the very existence of the exemptions, rather than to their scope). This inference is further supported by the argument in lines 36–41, where the author objects to a lack of clarity in the Code of Practice's requirements for balancing the public's interest in disclosure against other public interests, rather than objecting to the requirement that those interests be balanced at all. Most directly, the author of passage A endorses "*partial* disclosure" (line 30, emphasis added) of government documents.

Response (B) is incorrect because it expresses a view that neither author endorses. The author of passage A does indeed object that "public interest" is not defined in the Code of Practice (lines 36–41), but this does not support the conclusion that, in the author's eyes, the concept is too vague to be cited in justifying freedom of information laws. Indeed, the lack of definition is something the "proposed legislation seeks to remedy" (lines 17–18). Meanwhile, the author of passage B sees no problem in balancing "the public's interest in disclosure of the information" (lines 60–61) with any other "specified interest" (lines 58–59).

Response (C) is incorrect because it expresses a view that neither author would endorse. The principle expressed in response (C) corresponds closely to the "category-based" approach criticized in passage A. Under the category-based approach, information or documents that belong to certain designated categories are automatically exempted from disclosure requirements (lines 26–29). The problem with this approach, according to passage A, is precisely that it leaves "no scope for partial disclosure of documents" (lines 30–31), thereby making case-by-case determinations unnecessary, if not impossible. Likewise, the general presumption in favor of disclosure called for by passage B (line 47), together with the requirement that disclosure be refused only when it can be demonstrated that disclosure would harm certain "narrowly drawn" public interests (lines 52–56), indicates that the author of passage B would favor case-by-case determinations over the broader category-based approach.

Response (D) is incorrect because it expresses a view that neither author would endorse. The author of passage A writes that it is essential that the government strengthen its commitment to openness in government with "legislation that *guarantees* public access to government information" (lines 2–4, emphasis added). The author of passage B presumes that the freedom of information policy would be created by "statute (or other legal instrument)" (lines 45–46) and argues that disclosure should be refused "only where it can be shown that disclosure of the particular piece of information withheld would cause harm to one or more [public] interests" (lines 54–56). Passage B also states that "there must be the possibility of appeal to an independent body or official against refusals by public authorities to disclose information" (lines 61–64). None of these statements is consistent with a view that noncompulsory (i.e., optional or voluntary) freedom of information policies are sufficient to guarantee adequate public access to information.

Response (E) is incorrect because there is no basis for inferring that either author thinks that there should be a presumption in favor of disclosure, but that the presumption should apply only to certain explicitly identified branches of government. To the extent that either author allows exemptions to disclosure requirements, it is to protect other public interests, not certain branches of government. In fact, according to passage A, one of the flaws of the "haphazard approach" to freedom of information that developed over time is that "those statutory requirements for openness that were in place applied only in certain areas, such as environmental information, or were limited to particular sectors of the public service" (lines 9–12).

Difficulty Level: Very difficult

Question 8

Based on what can be inferred from their titles, the relationship between which one of the following pairs of documents is most analogous to the relationship between passage A and passage B?

(A) "What the Previous Management of the Midtown Health Club Left Undone"
"The New Management of the Crescent Restaurant Has Some Bad Policies"
(B) "A List of Grievances by Tenants of Garden Court Apartments"
"Why the Grievances of the Garden Court Apartments Tenants Are Unfounded"
(C) "How We Plan to Improve the Way in Which This Restaurant Is Managed"
"Standards of Good Restaurant Management"
(D) "Three Alternative Proposals for Our New Advertising Campaign"
"Three Principles to Be Followed in Developing an Effective Sales Team"
(E) "Detailed Instructions for Submitting a Formal Grievance to the Committee"
"Procedures for Adjudicating Grievances"

Explanation for Question 8

The response choices in this question consist of the titles of pairs of hypothetical documents. Based on what can be inferred about the contents of those documents from their titles, the test taker is asked to identify the documents that stand in a relationship to each other that is most analogous to the relationship between passage A and passage B. In order to answer this question, the test taker needs to determine, at least in a general way, what the relationship between passage A and passage B is.

As discussed in the explanation for question 1, passage A argues that the previous freedom of information regime in the United Kingdom was flawed in certain ways, and it claims that the freedom of information legislation proposed by the current government is designed to avoid those flaws. The arguments made in passage A presume certain general principles about what characteristics a freedom of information regime should have. Passage B can be said to support the claims advanced in passage A inasmuch as it articulates those principles directly. The closest analogy to this relationship is found in response (C):

"How We Plan to Improve the Way in Which This Restaurant Is Managed"
"Standards of Good Restaurant Management"

Like passage A, the first of these documents describes a plan for improving the administration of a particular enterprise (a restaurant in response (C), the government's freedom of information regime in passage A). And like passage B, the second document in response (C) articulates general standards that ought to govern the administration of such an enterprise.

Response (A) is incorrect because each document describes how the management of a particular enterprise (a health club in the first case, a restaurant in the second) is flawed. Neither document articulates general standards or principles for management that could be applied in the situation addressed in the other document, as is the case with the principles stated in passage B in relation to the situation addressed in passage A.

Response (B) is incorrect because the documents in it appear to concern a dispute between the tenants and owners of an apartment complex, and the two documents appear to be expressing the opposing sides of the dispute. The second document evidently attempts to deny the validity of the claims made in the first document, whereas passage B can be said to support passage A inasmuch as it articulates principles that strengthen the case made in passage A.

Response (D) is incorrect because the first document describes three possible proposals rather than being committed to one, as passage A is. In addition, while the second document evidently expresses some principles, they are not principles that can be applied to the situation addressed in the first document, as is the case with passage B.

Response (E) is incorrect because both documents are evidently procedural documents describing the steps to be followed at different stages in a grievance procedure. Neither document makes any arguments or claims about what should be done in a particular situation, as passage A does, and neither document expresses any principles that could be applied to the discussion in the other document, as passage B does.

Difficulty Level: Medium difficulty

THE WRITING SAMPLE

On the day of the test, you will be asked to write one sample essay. LSAC does not score the writing sample, but copies are sent to all law schools to which you apply. According to a 2015 LSAC survey of 129 United States and Canadian law schools, almost all use the writing sample in evaluating some applications for admission. Failure to respond to writing sample prompts and frivolous responses have been used by law schools as grounds for rejection of applications for admission.

In developing and implementing the writing sample portion of the LSAT, LSAC has operated on the following premises: First, law schools and the legal profession value highly the ability to communicate effectively in writing. Second, it is important to encourage potential law students to develop effective writing skills. Third, a sample of an applicant's writing, produced under controlled conditions, is a potentially useful indication of that person's writing ability. Fourth, the writing sample can serve as an independent check on other writing submitted by applicants as part of the admission process. Finally, writing samples may be useful for diagnostic purposes related to improving a candidate's writing.

The writing prompt presents a decision problem. You are asked to make a choice between two positions or courses of action. Both of the choices are defensible, and you are given criteria and facts on which to base your decision. There is no "right" or "wrong" position to take on the topic, so the quality of each test taker's response is a function not of which choice is made, but of how well or poorly the choice is supported and how well or poorly the other choice is criticized.

The LSAT writing prompt was designed and validated by legal education professionals. Since it involves writing based on fact sets and criteria, the writing sample gives applicants the opportunity to demonstrate the type of argumentative writing that is required in law school, although the topics are usually nonlegal.

You will have 35 minutes in which to plan and write an essay on the topic you receive. Read the topic and the accompanying directions carefully. You will probably find it best to spend a few minutes considering the topic and organizing your thoughts before you begin writing. In your essay, be sure to develop your ideas fully, leaving time, if possible, to review what you have written. Do not write on a topic other than the one specified. Writing on a topic of your own choice is not acceptable.

No special knowledge is required or expected for this writing exercise. Law schools are interested in the reasoning, clarity, organization, language usage, and writing mechanics displayed in your essay. How well you write is more important than how much you write. Confine your essay to the blocked, lined area on the front and back of the separate Writing Sample Response Sheet. Only that area will be reproduced for law schools. Be sure that your writing is legible.

TAKING THE PREPTEST UNDER SIMULATED LSAT CONDITIONS

One important way to prepare for the LSAT is to take a practice test under actual time constraints. Doing so will help you estimate the amount of time you can afford to spend on each question in a section and to determine the question types on which you may need additional practice.

Since the LSAT is a timed test, it is important to use your allotted time wisely. During the test, you may work only on the section designated by the test supervisor. You cannot devote extra time to a difficult section and make up that time on a section you find easier. In pacing yourself, and checking your answers, you should think of each section of the test as a separate minitest.

Be sure that you answer every question on the test. When you do not know the correct answer to a question, first eliminate the responses that you know are incorrect, then make your best guess among the remaining choices. Do not be afraid to guess as there is no penalty for incorrect answers.

When you take a practice test, abide by all the requirements specified in the directions and keep strictly within the specified time limits. Work without a rest period. When you take an actual test, you will have only a short break—usually 10–15 minutes—after SECTION III.

When taken under conditions as much like actual testing conditions as possible, a practice test provides very useful preparation for taking the LSAT.

Official directions for the four multiple-choice sections and the writing sample are included in the PrepTests so that you can approximate actual testing conditions as you practice. To take the test:

- Set a timer for 35 minutes. Answer all the questions in SECTION I of the PrepTest. Stop working on that section when the 35 minutes have elapsed.

- Repeat, allowing yourself 35 minutes each for sections II, III, and IV.

- Set the timer again for 35 minutes, then prepare your response to the writing sample topic at the end of the PrepTest.

Refer to "Computing Your Score" for the PrepTest for instruction on evaluating your performance. An answer key is provided for that purpose.

The Official LSAT PrepTest

19

- June 1996
- Form 7LSS32

The sample test that follows consists of four sections corresponding to the four scored sections of the June 1996 LSAT.

SECTION I

Time—35 minutes

24 Questions

Directions: Each group of questions in this section is based on a set of conditions. In answering some of the questions, it may be useful to draw a rough diagram. Choose the response that most accurately and completely answers each question and blacken the corresponding space on your answer sheet.

Questions 1–7

During a period of six consecutive days—day 1 through day 6—each of exactly six factories—F, G, H, J, Q, and R—will be inspected. During this period, each of the factories will be inspected exactly once, one factory per day. The schedule for the inspections must conform to the following conditions:

F is inspected on either day 1 or day 6.
J is inspected on an earlier day than Q is inspected.
Q is inspected on the day immediately before R is inspected.
If G is inspected on day 3, Q is inspected on day 5.

1. Which one of the following could be a list of the factories in the order of their scheduled inspections, from day 1 through day 6 ?

   (A)   F, Q, R, H, J, G
   (B)   G, H, J, Q, R, F
   (C)   G, J, Q, H, R, F
   (D)   G, J, Q, R, F, H
   (E)   J, H, G, Q, R, F

2. Which one of the following must be false?

   (A)   The inspection of G is scheduled for day 4.
   (B)   The inspection of H is scheduled for day 6.
   (C)   The inspection of J is scheduled for day 4.
   (D)   The inspection of Q is scheduled for day 3.
   (E)   The inspection of R is scheduled for day 2.

3. The inspection of which one of the following CANNOT be scheduled for day 5 ?

   (A)   G
   (B)   H
   (C)   J
   (D)   Q
   (E)   R

4. The inspections scheduled for day 3 and day 5, respectively, could be those of

   (A)   G and H
   (B)   G and R
   (C)   H and G
   (D)   R and J
   (E)   R and H

5. If the inspection of R is scheduled for the day immediately before the inspection of F, which one of the following must be true about the schedule?

   (A)   The inspection of either G or H is scheduled for day 1.
   (B)   The inspection of either G or J is scheduled for day 1.
   (C)   The inspection of either G or J is scheduled for day 2.
   (D)   The inspection of either H or J is scheduled for day 3.
   (E)   The inspection of either H or J is scheduled for day 4.

6. If the inspections of G and of H are scheduled, not necessarily in that order, for days as far apart as possible, which one of the following is a complete and accurate list of the factories any one of which could be scheduled for inspection for day 1 ?

   (A)   F, J
   (B)   G, H
   (C)   G, H, J
   (D)   F, G, H
   (E)   F, G, H, J

7. If the inspection of G is scheduled for the day immediately before the inspection of Q, which one of the following could be true?

   (A)   The inspection of G is scheduled for day 5.
   (B)   The inspection of H is scheduled for day 6.
   (C)   The inspection of J is scheduled for day 2.
   (D)   The inspection of Q is scheduled for day 4.
   (E)   The inspection of R is scheduled for day 3.

GO ON TO THE NEXT PAGE.

Questions 8–12

In a theater company, four two-day workshops—Lighting, Production, Rehearsals, and Staging—are conducted over the course of five days, Monday through Friday. The workshops are conducted in a manner consistent with the following constraints:

The two days on which a given workshop is in session are consecutive.
On each of the five days, at least one, but no more than two, of the workshops are in session.
The workshops on Production and Rehearsals begin no earlier than the day immediately following the second day of the workshop on Lighting.

8. Which one of the following could be true?

   (A) Only one workshop is in session on Thursday.
   (B) Only one workshop is in session on Friday.
   (C) The workshop on Rehearsals is in session on Tuesday.
   (D) The workshop on Staging is in session on Thursday.
   (E) The workshops in Rehearsals and Production are both in session on Wednesday.

9. Which one of the following could be true?

   (A) The workshop on Lighting is in session on Wednesday, and the workshop on Rehearsals is in session on Tuesday.
   (B) The workshop on Lighting is in session on Wednesday, and the only workshop in session on Thursday is the workshop on Rehearsals.
   (C) The workshop on Lighting is in session on Wednesday, and the only workshop in session on Monday is the workshop on Staging.
   (D) The workshop on Lighting is in session on Monday, and the only workshop in session on Thursday is the workshop on Staging.
   (E) The workshops on Lighting and Production are both in session on Wednesday.

10. If the workshop on Production is in session on Wednesday, which one of the following must be true?

    (A) The workshop on Lighting is in session on Monday.
    (B) The workshop on Rehearsals is in session on Wednesday.
    (C) The workshop on Staging is in session on Thursday.
    (D) The workshop on Staging is in session on Monday.
    (E) The workshop on Staging is in session on Wednesday.

11. If the workshop on Production is the only workshop in session on Friday, which one of the following must be false?

    (A) The workshop on Lighting is in session both on Tuesday and on Wednesday.
    (B) The workshop on Rehearsals is in session both on Wednesday and on Thursday.
    (C) The workshop on Staging is in session both on Monday and on Tuesday.
    (D) The workshop on Lighting is in session on the same two days as is the workshop on Staging.
    (E) The workshop on Rehearsals is in session on a day when the workshop on Staging is also in session.

12. If the workshop on Lighting is the only workshop in session on Monday, which one of the following could be true?

    (A) The workshops on Rehearsals and Staging are both in session on Tuesday.
    (B) The workshop on Rehearsals is the only workshop in session on Wednesday.
    (C) The workshop on Staging is the only workshop in session on Wednesday.
    (D) The workshops on Staging and Rehearsals are both in session on Wednesday and on Thursday.
    (E) The workshops on Staging and Production are both in session on Thursday.

GO ON TO THE NEXT PAGE.

Questions 13–19

Each of two boats, boat 1 and boat 2, will be assigned exactly four people. Exactly eight people, three adults—F, G, and H— and five children—V, W, X, Y, and Z—must be assigned to the boats according to the following conditions:

Each boat is assigned at least one adult.
If F is assigned to boat 2, G is assigned to boat 2.
If V is assigned to boat 1, W is assigned to boat 2.
X and Z are assigned to different boats.

13. Which one of the following is an acceptable assignment of people to boat 1 ?

(A) F, G, H, X
(B) F, H, W, Y
(C) F, H, Y, Z
(D) F, V, W, X
(E) G, H, X, Y

14. If F is assigned to boat 2, which one of the following is a pair of people who could be assigned to the same boat as each other?

(A) F and Y
(B) G and H
(C) G and Y
(D) V and W
(E) Y and Z

15. If exactly three children are assigned to boat 1, which one of the following is a pair of people who could both be assigned to boat 2 ?

(A) F and H
(B) G and Y
(C) H and W
(D) V and W
(E) W and Y

16. If G is assigned to boat 1, which one of the following must be true?

(A) H is assigned to boat 2.
(B) V is assigned to boat 2.
(C) Exactly one adult is assigned to boat 1.
(D) Exactly two adults are assigned to boat 2.
(E) Exactly two children are assigned to boat 2.

17. If V and W are assigned to the same boat as each other, which one of the following is a pair of people who must also be assigned to the same boat as each other?

(A) F and H
(B) F and Y
(C) G and X
(D) W and X
(E) Y and Z

18. If H is assigned to a different boat than Y, which one of the following must be assigned to boat 1 ?

(A) F
(B) G
(C) H
(D) V
(E) Y

19. If exactly one adult is assigned to boat 1, which one of the following must be true?

(A) F is assigned to boat 1.
(B) G is assigned to boat 2.
(C) H is assigned to boat 2.
(D) V is assigned to boat 1.
(E) Z is assigned to boat 2.

GO ON TO THE NEXT PAGE.

Questions 20–24

Each of nine students—Faith, Gregory, Harlan, Jennifer, Kenji, Lisa, Marcus, Nari, and Paul—will be assigned to exactly one of three panels: Oceans, Recycling, and Wetlands. Exactly three of the students will be assigned to each panel. The assignment of students to panels must meet the following conditions:

Faith is assigned to the same panel as Gregory.
Kenji is assigned to the same panel as Marcus.
Faith is not assigned to the same panel as Paul.
Gregory is not assigned to the same panel as Harlan.
Jennifer is not assigned to the same panel as Kenji.
Harlan is not assigned to the Oceans panel if Paul is not assigned to the Oceans panel.

20. Which one of the following is an acceptable assignment of students to the panels?

(A) Oceans: Faith, Gregory, Jennifer
Recycling: Kenji, Lisa, Nari
Wetlands: Harlan, Marcus, Paul
(B) Oceans: Faith, Jennifer, Lisa
Recycling: Harlan, Kenji, Marcus
Wetlands: Gregory, Nari, Paul
(C) Oceans: Harlan, Kenji, Marcus
Recycling: Faith, Gregory, Jennifer
Wetlands: Lisa, Nari, Paul
(D) Oceans: Jennifer, Kenji, Marcus
Recycling: Faith, Gregory, Nari
Wetlands: Harlan, Lisa, Paul
(E) Oceans: Kenji, Marcus, Paul
Recycling: Harlan, Jennifer, Nari
Wetlands: Faith, Gregory, Lisa

21. If Marcus and Paul are both assigned to the Wetlands panel, which one of the following must be true?

(A) Harlan is assigned to the Recycling panel.
(B) Jennifer is assigned to the Oceans panel.
(C) Kenji is assigned to the Recycling panel.
(D) Lisa is assigned to the Wetlands panel.
(E) Nari is assigned to the Oceans panel.

22. Which one of the following is a pair of students who could be assigned to the same panel as each other?

(A) Faith and Harlan
(B) Gregory and Paul
(C) Harlan and Marcus
(D) Faith and Marcus
(E) Jennifer and Marcus

23. If Kenji and Paul are both assigned to the Recycling panel, which one of the following could be true?

(A) Faith is assigned to the Wetlands panel.
(B) Gregory is assigned to the Recycling panel.
(C) Harlan is assigned to the Oceans panel.
(D) Jennifer is assigned to the Wetlands panel.
(E) Lisa is assigned to the Recycling panel.

24. Each of the following is a pair of students who could be assigned to the same panel as each other EXCEPT:

(A) Gregory and Kenji
(B) Gregory and Lisa
(C) Kenji and Nari
(D) Lisa and Marcus
(E) Lisa and Paul

S T O P

IF YOU FINISH BEFORE TIME IS CALLED, YOU MAY CHECK YOUR WORK ON THIS SECTION ONLY.
DO NOT WORK ON ANY OTHER SECTION IN THE TEST.

SECTION II

Time—35 minutes

24 Questions

Directions: The questions in this section are based on the reasoning contained in brief statements or passages. For some questions, more than one of the choices could conceivably answer the question. However, you are to choose the best answer; that is, the response that most accurately and completely answers the question. You should not make assumptions that are by commonsense standards implausible, superfluous, or incompatible with the passage. After you have chosen the best answer, blacken the corresponding space on your answer sheet.

1. Director of Ace Manufacturing Company: Our management consultant proposes that we reassign staff so that all employees are doing both what they like to do and what they do well. This, she says, will "increase productivity by fully exploiting our available resources." But Ace Manufacturing has a long-standing commitment not to exploit its workers. Therefore, implementing her recommendations would cause us to violate our own policy.

The director's argument for rejecting the management consultant's proposal is most vulnerable to criticism on which one of the following grounds?

(A) failing to distinguish two distinct senses of a key term
(B) attempting to defend an action on the ground that it is frequently carried out
(C) defining a term by pointing to an atypical example of something to which the term applies
(D) drawing a conclusion that simply restates one of the premises of the argument
(E) calling something by a less offensive term than the term that is usually used to name that thing

2. A large number of drivers routinely violate highway speed limits. Since driving at speeds that exceed posted limits is a significant factor in most accidents, installing devices in all cars that prevent those cars from traveling faster than the speed limit would prevent most accidents.

Which one of the following is an assumption on which the argument depends?

(A) A person need not be a trained mechanic to install the device properly.
(B) Most accidents are caused by inexperienced drivers.
(C) A driver seldom needs to exceed the speed limit to avoid an accident when none of the other drivers involved are violating the speed limit.
(D) Most drivers who exceed the speed limit do so unintentionally.
(E) Even if the fines for speed-limit violations were increased, the number of such violations would still not be reduced.

3. In a recession, a decrease in consumer spending causes many businesses to lay off workers or even to close. Workers who lose their jobs in a recession usually cannot find new jobs. The result is an increase in the number of people who are jobless. Recovery from a recession is defined by an increase in consumer spending and an expansion of business activity that creates a need for additional workers. But businesspeople generally have little confidence in the economy after a recession and therefore delay hiring additional workers as long as possible.

The statements above, if true, provide most support for which one of the following conclusions?

(A) Recessions are usually caused by a decrease in businesspeople's confidence in the economy.
(B) Governmental intervention is required in order for an economy to recover from a recession.
(C) Employees of businesses that close during a recession make up the majority of the workers who lose their jobs during that recession.
(D) Sometimes recovery from a recession does not promptly result in a decrease in the number of people who are jobless.
(E) Workers who lose their jobs during a recession are likely to get equally good jobs when the economy recovers.

GO ON TO THE NEXT PAGE.

4. Scientists analyzing air bubbles that had been trapped in Antarctic ice during the Earth's last ice age found that the ice-age atmosphere had contained unusually large amounts of ferrous material and surprisingly small amounts of carbon dioxide. One scientist noted that algae absorb carbon dioxide from the atmosphere. The scientist hypothesized that the ferrous material, which was contained in atmospheric dust, had promoted a great increase in the population of Antarctic algae such as diatoms.

Which one of the following, if true, would most seriously undermine the scientist's hypothesis?

(A) Diatoms are a microscopic form of algae that has remained largely unchanged since the last ice age.

(B) Computer models suggest that a large increase in ferrous material today could greatly promote the growth of oceanic algae.

(C) The dust found in the air bubbles trapped in Antarctic ice contained other minerals in addition to the ferrous material.

(D) Sediment from the ocean floor near Antarctica reflects no increase, during the last ice age, in the rate at which the shells that diatoms leave when they die accumulated.

(E) Algae that currently grow in the oceans near Antarctica do not appear to be harmed by even a large increase in exposure to ferrous material.

5. Adults who work outside the home spend, on average, 100 minutes less time each week in preparing dinner than adults who do not work outside the home. But, contrary to expectation, comparisons show that the dinners eaten at home by the two groups of adults do not differ significantly with respect to nutritional value, variety of menus, or number of courses.

Which one of the following, if true, most helps to resolve the apparent discrepancy in the information above?

(A) The fat content of the dinners eaten at home by adults who do not work outside the home is 25 percent higher than national guidelines recommend.

(B) Adults who do not work outside the home tend to prepare breakfast more often than adults who work outside the home.

(C) Adults who work outside the home spend 2 hours less time per day on all household responsibilities, including dinner preparation, than do adults who do not work outside the home.

(D) Adults who work outside the home eat dinner at home 20 percent less often than do adults who do not work outside the home.

(E) Adults who work outside the home are less likely to plan dinner menus well in advance than are adults who do not work outside the home.

6. Legislator: Your agency is responsible for regulating an industry shaken by severe scandals. You were given funds to hire 500 investigators to examine the scandals, but you hired no more than 400. I am forced to conclude that you purposely limited hiring in an attempt to prevent the full extent of the scandals from being revealed.

Regulator: We tried to hire the 500 investigators but the starting salaries for these positions had been frozen so low by the legislature that it was impossible to attract enough qualified applicants.

The regulator responds to the legislator's criticism by

(A) shifting the blame for the scandals to the legislature

(B) providing information that challenges the conclusion drawn by the legislator

(C) claiming that compliance with the legislature's mandate would have been an insufficient response

(D) rephrasing the legislator's conclusion in terms more favorable to the regulator

(E) showing that the legislator's statements are self-contradictory

7. A commonly accepted myth is that left-handed people are more prone to cause accidents than are right-handed people. But this is, in fact, just a myth, as is indicated by the fact that more household accidents are caused by right-handed people than are caused by left-handed people.

The reasoning is flawed because the argument

(A) makes a distinction where there is no real difference between the things distinguished

(B) takes no account of the relative frequency of left-handed people in the population as a whole

(C) uses the word "accidents" in two different senses

(D) ignores the possibility that some household accidents are caused by more than one person

(E) gives wholly irrelevant evidence and simply disparages an opposing position by calling it a "myth"

GO ON TO THE NEXT PAGE.

Questions 8–9

Ornithologist: The curvature of the claws of modern tree-dwelling birds enables them to perch in trees. The claws of Archeopteryx, the earliest known birdlike creature, show similar curvature that must have enabled the creature to perch on tree limbs. Therefore, Archeopteryx was probably a tree-dwelling creature.

Paleontologist: No, the ability to perch in trees is not good evidence that Archeopteryx was a tree-dwelling bird. Chickens also spend time perched in trees, yet chickens are primarily ground-dwelling.

8. In responding to the ornithologist's hypothesis that Archeopteryx was tree-dwelling, the paleontologist

(A)   questions the qualifications of the ornithologist to evaluate the evidence

(B)   denies the truth of the claims the ornithologist makes in support of the hypothesis

(C)   uses a parallel case to illustrate a weakness in the ornithologist's argument

(D)   shows that the hypothesis contradicts one of the pieces of evidence used to support it

(E)   provides additional evidence to support the ornithologist's argument

9. Which one of the following is an assumption on which the ornithologist's reasoning depends?

(A)   Modern tree-dwelling birds are the direct descendants of Archeopteryx.

(B)   Archeopteryx made use of the curvature of its claws.

(C)   There have never been tree-dwelling birds without curved claws.

(D)   Archeopteryx was in fact the earliest birdlike creature.

(E)   The curvature of the claws is the only available evidence for the claim that Archeopteryx was tree-dwelling.

10. There are rumors that the Premier will reshuffle the cabinet this week. However, every previous reshuffle that the Premier has made was preceded by meetings between the Premier and senior cabinet members. No such meetings have occurred or are planned. Therefore the rumors are most likely false.

Which one of the following most accurately expresses a principle of reasoning employed by the argument?

(A)   When a conclusion follows logically from a set of premises, the probability that the conclusion is true cannot be any less than the probability that the premises are all true.

(B)   A hypothesis is undermined when a state of affairs does not obtain that would be expected to obtain if the hypothesis were true.

(C)   It is possible for a hypothesis to be false even though it is supported by all the available data.

(D)   Even if in the past a phenomenon was caused by particular circumstances, it is erroneous to assume that the phenomenon will recur only under the circumstances in which it previously occurred.

(E)   If two statements are known to be inconsistent with each other and if one of the statements is known to be false, it cannot be deduced from these known facts that the other statement is true.

GO ON TO THE NEXT PAGE.

Questions 11–12

Carl: Researchers who perform operations on animals for experimental purposes are legally required to complete detailed pain protocols indicating whether the animals will be at risk of pain and, if so, what steps will be taken to minimize or alleviate it. Yet when human beings undergo operations, such protocols are never required. If lawmakers were as concerned about human beings as they seem to be about animals, there would be pain protocols for human beings too.

Debbie: But consider this: a person for whom a doctor wants to schedule surgery can simply be told what pain to expect and can then decide whether or not to undergo the operation. So you see, pain protocols are unnecessary for human beings.

11. Debbie attempts to counter Carl's argument by

(A) showing that one of the claims on which Carl bases his conclusion is inaccurate

(B) pointing out a relevant difference to undermine an analogy on which Carl bases his conclusion

(C) claiming that Carl's argument should be rejected because it is based on an appeal to sentimentality rather than on reasoned principles

(D) drawing an analogy that illustrates a major flaw in Carl's argument

(E) offering a specific example to demonstrate that Carl's argument is based on a claim that can be neither confirmed nor disproved

12. Which one of the following, if true, most seriously weakens the argument made by Debbie in response to Carl's argument?

(A) Not all operations that are performed on human beings are painful.

(B) Some experimentation that is now done on animals need not be done at all.

(C) Preparing pain protocols is not a time-consuming or costly procedure.

(D) Some surgical operations performed on infants are painful.

(E) Unalleviated pain after an operation tends to delay the healing process.

13. A company with long-outstanding bills owed by its customers can assign those bills to a collection agency that pays the company a fraction of their amount and then tries to collect payment from the customers. Since these agencies pay companies only 15 percent of the total amount of the outstanding bills, a company interested in reducing losses from long-outstanding bills would be well advised to pursue its debtors on its own.

The argument depends on the assumption that

(A) a company that pursues its debtors on its own typically collects more than 15 percent of the total amount of the long-outstanding bills that it is owed

(B) the cost to a company of pursuing its debtors on its own for payment of long-outstanding bills does not exceed 15 percent of the total amount of those bills

(C) collection agencies that are assigned bills for collection by companies are unsuccessful in collecting, on average, only 15 percent of the total amount of those bills

(D) at least 15 percent of the customers that owe money to companies eventually pay their bills whether or not those bills are assigned to a collection agency

(E) unless most of the customers of a company pay their bills, that company in the long run will not be profitable

GO ON TO THE NEXT PAGE.

14. Herbalist: Many of my customers find that their physical coordination improves after drinking juice containing certain herbs. A few doctors assert that the herbs are potentially harmful, but doctors are always trying to maintain a monopoly over medical therapies. So there is no reason not to try my herb juice.

The reasoning in the herbalist's argument is flawed because the argument

(A)   attempts to force acceptance of a claim by inducing fear of the consequences of rejecting that claim

(B)   bases a conclusion on claims that are inconsistent with each other

(C)   rejects a claim by attacking the proponents of the claim rather than addressing the claim itself

(D)   relies on evidence presented in terms that presuppose the truth of the claim for which the evidence is offered

(E)   mistakes the observation that one thing happens after another for proof that the second thing is the result of the first

15. Because of the lucrative but illegal trade in rhinoceros horns, a certain rhinoceros species has been hunted nearly to extinction. Therefore an effective way to ensure the survival of that species would be to periodically trim off the horns of all rhinoceroses, thereby eliminating the motivation for poaching.

Which one of the following is an assumption required by the argument?

(A)   Most poachers who are discouraged from hunting rhinoceroses are not likely to hunt other animals for their horns.

(B)   At least some rhinoceroses whose horns are periodically trimmed off will be able to attract mates.

(C)   Poachers hunt at least some immature rhinoceroses whose horns have not yet started to develop.

(D)   The demand for rhinoceros horns will remain constant even if the supply decreases after the periodic trimming-off of the rhinoceros horns has begun.

(E)   Rhinoceroses whose horns have been trimmed off are unable to defend themselves against predators.

16. Motorcoach driver: Professional drivers spend much more time driving, on average, than do other people and hence are more competent drivers than are other, less experienced drivers. Therefore, the speed limit on major highways should not be reduced, because that action would have the undesirable effect of forcing some people who are now both law-abiding and competent drivers to break the law.

Police officer: All drivers can drive within the legal speed limit if they wish, so it is not true to say that reducing the speed limit would be the cause of such illegal behavior.

The point at issue between the motorcoach driver and the police officer is whether

(A)   it would be desirable to reduce the speed limit on major highways

(B)   professional drivers will drive within the legal speed limit if that limit is reduced

(C)   reducing the speed limit on major highways would cause some professional drivers to break the law

(D)   professional drivers are more competent drivers than are other, less experienced drivers

(E)   all drivers wish to drive within the speed limit

GO ON TO THE NEXT PAGE.

17. People cannot devote themselves to the study of natural processes unless they have leisure, and people have leisure when resources are plentiful, not when resources are scarce. Although some anthropologists claim that agriculture, the cultivation of crops, actually began under conditions of drought and hunger, the early societies that domesticated plants must first have discovered how the plants they cultivated reproduced themselves and grew to maturity. These complex discoveries were the result of the active study of natural processes.

The argument is structured to lead to the conclusion that

(A) whenever a society has plentiful resources, some members of that society devote themselves to the study of natural processes

(B) plants cannot be cultivated by someone lacking theoretical knowledge of the principles of plant generation and growth

(C) agriculture first began in societies that at some time in their history had plentiful resources

(D) early agricultural societies knew more about the natural sciences than did early nonagricultural societies

(E) early societies could have discovered by accident how the plants they cultivated reproduced and grew

18. In the past decade, a decreasing percentage of money spent on treating disease X went to pay for standard methods of treatment, which are known to be effective though they are expensive and painful. An increasing percentage is being spent on nonstandard treatments, which cause little discomfort. Unfortunately, the nonstandard treatments have proved to be ineffective. Obviously, less money is being spent now on effective treatments of disease X than was spent ten years ago.

Which one of the following, if assumed, allows the conclusion above to be properly drawn?

(A) Varieties of disease X requiring expensive special treatment have become less common during the past decade.

(B) Nonstandard methods of treating disease X are more expensive now than they were a decade ago.

(C) Of total medical expenditures, the percentage that is due to treatment of disease X increased during the past decade.

(D) Most of the money spent on treating disease X during the last decade went to pay for nonstandard treatments.

(E) The total amount of money spent on treating disease X slowly declined during the past decade.

19. When an ordinary piece of steel is put under pressure, the steel compresses; that is, its volume slightly decreases. Glass, however, is a fluid, so rather than compressing, it flows when put under pressure; its volume remains unchanged. Any portion of a sheet of glass that is under sustained pressure will very slowly flow to areas under less pressure. Therefore, if a single, extremely heavy object is placed in the middle of a horizontal sheet of glass of uniform thickness and if the glass is able to support the weight without cracking, then the sheet of glass will eventually _____ .

Which one of the following most logically completes the argument?

(A) become larger in size yet still be of uniform thickness

(B) flow toward the point at which the pressure of the object is greatest

(C) compress, although not as much as a piece of steel would

(D) divide into exactly two pieces that are equal in neither size nor shape to the original piece of glass

(E) be thinner in the portion of the glass that is under the pressure of the object than in those portions of the glass that are not under that pressure

GO ON TO THE NEXT PAGE.

20. Anyone who insists that music videos are an art form should also agree that television gave rise to an art form, since television gave rise to music videos.

The pattern of reasoning displayed in the argument above most closely parallels that displayed in which one of the following?

(A) Anyone who claims that all vegetables are nutritious should also agree that some vegetables are harmful if eaten in large quantities.

(B) Anyone who holds that avocados are a fruit should also hold that pound cake is lower in fat than some fruit, since pound cake is lower in fat than avocados.

(C) Anyone who dislikes tomatoes should also agree that some people do like tomatoes, if that person agrees that no taste is universal.

(D) A person who eats a variety of vegetables is probably well nourished, since most people who eat a variety of vegetables generally eat well-balanced meals.

(E) A person who claims to prefer fruit to vegetables should also prefer cake to bread, since fruit is sweeter than vegetables and cake is sweeter than bread.

21. Medieval Arabs had manuscripts of many ancient Greek texts, which were translated into Arabic when there was a demand for them. Medieval Arab philosophers were very interested in Aristotle's *Poetics,* an interest that evidently was not shared by medieval Arab poets, because a poet interested in the *Poetics* would certainly have wanted to read Homer, to whose epics Aristotle frequently refers. But Homer was not translated into Arabic until modern times.

Which one of the following, if true, most strongly supports the argument above?

(A) A number of medieval Arab translators possessed manuscripts of the Homeric epics in their original Greek.

(B) Medieval Arabic story cycles, such as the *Arabian Nights,* are in some ways similar to parts of the Homeric epics.

(C) In addition to translating from Greek, medieval Arab translators produced Arabic editions of many works originally written in Indian languages and in Persian.

(D) Aristotle's *Poetics* has frequently been cited and commented on by modern Arab poets.

(E) Aristotle's *Poetics* is largely concerned with drama, and dramatic works were written and performed by medieval Arabs.

22. Congenial guests and a plentiful supply of good things to eat and drink will ensure a successful dinner party. Since Sylvia has prepared more than enough to eat and drink and her guests are all congenial people, her dinner party is certain to be a success.

The pattern of flawed reasoning exhibited by the argument above is most similar to that exhibited by which one of the following?

(A) The right ingredients, properly combined and baked in a reliable oven will always produce a well-baked cake. Since Emily has properly combined the right ingredients, her cake is certain to come out well if she bakes it in a reliable oven.

(B) If corn is baked with its husks on, the resulting dish will always be moist and sweet. Since George wishes to ensure that the corn he plans to serve is moist, he will be certain both to bake it and to leave its husks on.

(C) Making pie dough using ice water and thoroughly chilling the dough before rolling it out will ensure a flaky crust. Andrew thoroughly chilled his pie dough before rolling it out, so, since he used ice water in making it, his pie is certain to have a flaky crust.

(D) If soup is made with a well-seasoned meat stock and fresh ingredients, it will always be welcome at dinner. Since to his meat stock Arnold added only very fresh ingredients, the resulting soup is certain to be welcome at dinner.

(E) Fresh greens, carefully washed and served with a light dressing, always produce a refreshing salad. Since Tisha has developed an exceptionally light dressing but never washes her fresh greens, no salad she serves will be a refreshing one.

GO ON TO THE NEXT PAGE.

23. A museum director, in order to finance expensive new acquisitions, discreetly sold some paintings by major artists. All of them were paintings that the director privately considered inferior. Critics roundly condemned the sale, charging that the museum had lost first-rate pieces, thereby violating its duty as a trustee of art for future generations. A few months after being sold by the museum, those paintings were resold, in an otherwise stagnant art market, at two to three times the price paid to the museum. Clearly, these prices settle the issue, since they demonstrate the correctness of the critics' evaluation.

The reasoning in the argument is vulnerable to the criticism that the argument does which one of the following?

(A) It concludes that a certain opinion is correct on the grounds that it is held by more people than hold the opposing view.

(B) It rejects the judgment of the experts in an area in which there is no better guide to the truth than expert judgment.

(C) It rejects a proven means of accomplishing an objective without offering any alternative means of accomplishing that objective.

(D) It bases a firm conclusion about a state of affairs in the present on somewhat speculative claims about a future state of affairs.

(E) It bases its conclusion on facts that could, in the given situation, have resulted from causes other than those presupposed by the argument.

24. The United States ranks far behind countries such as Sweden and Canada when it comes to workplace safety. In all three countries, joint labor-management committees that oversee workplace safety conditions have been very successful in reducing occupational injuries. In the United States, such committees are found only in the few companies that have voluntarily established them. However, in Sweden and several Canadian provinces, joint safety committees are required by law and exist in all medium-sized and large workplaces.

Which one of the following is supported by the information above?

(A) The establishment of joint safety committees in all medium-sized and large workplaces in the United States would result in a reduction of occupational injuries.

(B) A joint safety committee that is required by law is more effective at reducing occupational injuries than is a joint safety committee that is voluntarily established.

(C) Workplace safety in Sweden and Canada was superior to that in the United States even prior to the passage of laws requiring joint safety committees in all medium-sized and large workplaces.

(D) Joint safety committees had been voluntarily established in most medium-sized and large workplaces in Sweden and several Canadian provinces prior to the passage of laws requiring such committees.

(E) The United States would surpass Sweden and Canada in workplace safety if joint safety committees were required in all medium-sized and large workplaces in the United States.

S T O P

IF YOU FINISH BEFORE TIME IS CALLED, YOU MAY CHECK YOUR WORK ON THIS SECTION ONLY.
DO NOT WORK ON ANY OTHER SECTION IN THE TEST.

SECTION III

Time—35 minutes

27 Questions

Directions: Each passage in this section is followed by a group of questions to be answered on the basis of what is stated or implied in the passage. For some of the questions, more than one of the choices could conceivably answer the question. However, you are to choose the best answer; that is, the response that most accurately and completely answers the question, and blacken the corresponding space on your answer sheet.

Wherever the crime novels of P. D. James are discussed by critics, there is a tendency on the one hand to exaggerate her merits and on the other to castigate her as a genre writer who is getting above
(5) herself. Perhaps underlying the debate is that familiar, false opposition set up between different kinds of fiction, according to which enjoyable novels are held to be somehow slightly lowbrow, and a novel is not considered true literature unless it is a tiny bit dull.
(10) Those commentators who would elevate James's books to the status of high literature point to her painstakingly constructed characters, her elaborate settings, her sense of place, and her love of abstractions: notions about morality, duty, pain, and
(15) pleasure are never far from the lips of her police officers and murderers. Others find her pretentious and tiresome; an inverted snobbery accuses her of abandoning the time-honored conventions of the detective genre in favor of a highbrow literary style.
(20) The critic Harriet Waugh wants P. D. James to get on with "the more taxing business of laying a tricky trail and then fooling the reader"; Philip Oakes in *The Literary Review* groans, "Could we please proceed with the business of clapping the handcuffs on the
(25) killer?"
James is certainly capable of strikingly good writing. She takes immense trouble to provide her characters with convincing histories and passions. Her descriptive digressions are part of the pleasure of her
(30) books and give them dignity and weight. But it is equally true that they frequently interfere with the story; the patinas and aromas of a country kitchen receive more loving attention than does the plot itself. Her devices to advance the story can be shameless and
(35) thin, and it is often impossible to see how her detective arrives at the truth; one is left to conclude that the detective solves crimes through intuition. At this stage in her career P. D. James seems to be less interested in the specifics of detection than in her characters'
(40) vulnerabilities and perplexities.
However, once the rules of a chosen genre cramp creative thought, there is no reason why an able and interesting writer should accept them. In her latest book, there are signs that James is beginning to feel
(45) constrained by the crime-novel genre. Here her determination to leave areas of ambiguity in the solution of the crime and to distribute guilt among the murderer, victim, and bystanders points to a conscious rebellion against the traditional neatness of detective
(50) fiction. It is fashionable, though reprehensible, for one

writer to prescribe to another. But perhaps the time has come for P. D. James to slide out of her handcuffs and stride into the territory of the mainstream novel.

1. Which one of the following best states the author's main conclusion?

(A) Because P. D. James's potential as a writer is stifled by her chosen genre, she should turn her talents toward writing mainstream novels.

(B) Because the requirements of the popular novel are incompatible with true creative expression, P. D. James's promise as a serious author has been diminished.

(C) The dichotomy between popular and sophisticated literature is well illustrated in the crime novels of P. D. James.

(D) The critics who have condemned P. D. James's lack of attention to the specifics of detection fail to take into account her carefully constructed plots.

(E) Although her plots are not always neatly resolved, the beauty of her descriptive passages justifies P. D. James's decision to write in the crime-novel genre.

2. The author refers to the "patinas and aromas of a country kitchen" (line 32) most probably in order to

(A) illustrate James's gift for innovative phrasing
(B) highlight James's interest in rural society
(C) allow the reader to experience the pleasure of James's books
(D) explain how James typically constructs her plots
(E) exemplify James's preoccupation with descriptive writing

GO ON TO THE NEXT PAGE.

3. The second paragraph serves primarily to

   (A) propose an alternative to two extreme opinions described earlier
   (B) present previously mentioned positions in greater detail
   (C) contradict an assertion cited previously
   (D) introduce a controversial interpretation
   (E) analyze a dilemma in greater depth

4. The passage supports which one of the following statements about detective fiction?

   (A) There are as many different detective-novel conventions as there are writers of crime novels.
   (B) Detective fiction has been characterized by extremely high literary quality.
   (C) Detective fiction has been largely ignored by literary critics.
   (D) There is very little agreement among critics about the basic elements of a typical detective novel.
   (E) Writers of detective fiction have customarily followed certain conventions in constructing their novels.

5. The passage suggests that both Waugh and Oakes consider James's novels to have

   (A) too much material that is extraneous to the solution of the crime
   (B) too little characterization to enable the reader to solve the crime
   (C) too few suspects to generate suspense
   (D) too simple a plot to hold the attention of the reader
   (E) too convoluted a plot for the reader to understand

6. It can be inferred from the passage that, in the author's view, traditional detective fiction is characterized by

   (A) concern for the weaknesses and doubts of the characters
   (B) transparent devices to advance the plot
   (C) the attribution of intuition to the detective
   (D) the straightforward assignment of culpability for the crime
   (E) attention to the concepts of morality and responsibility

7. The author characterizes the position of some critics as "inverted snobbery" (line 17) because they hold which one of the following views?

   (A) Critics of literature must acknowledge that they are less talented than creators of literature.
   (B) Critics should hesitate to disparage popular authors.
   (C) P. D. James's novels should focus less on characters from the English landed gentry.
   (D) Detective fiction should be content to remain an unambitious literary genre.
   (E) P. D. James should be less fastidious about portraying violence.

8. Which one of the following quotations about literature best exemplifies the "familiar" attitude mentioned in lines 5–9?

   (A) "The fantasy and whimsy characteristic of this writer's novels qualify them as truly great works of literature."
   (B) "The greatest work of early English literature happens to be a highly humorous collection of tales."
   (C) "A truly great work of literature should place demands upon its readers, rather than divert them."
   (D) "Although many critics are condescending about best-selling novels, I would not wish to challenge the opinion of millions of readers."
   (E) "A novel need only satisfy the requirements of its particular genre to be considered a true work of literature."

GO ON TO THE NEXT PAGE.

Many Native Americans view the archaeological excavation and museum display of ancestral skeletal remains and items buried with them as a spiritual desecration. A number of legal remedies that either
(5) prohibit or regulate such activities may be available to Native American communities, if they can establish standing in such cases. In disinterment cases, courts have traditionally affirmed the standing of three classes of plaintiffs: the deceased's heirs, the owner of the
(10) property on which the grave is located, and parties, including organizations or distant relatives of the deceased, that have a clear interest in the preservation of a particular grave. If an archaeologically discovered grave is of recent historical origin and associated with
(15) an identifiable Native American community, Native Americans are likely to establish standing in a suit to prevent disinterment of the remains, but in cases where the grave is ancient and located in an area where the community of Native Americans associated with the
(20) grave has not recently lived, they are less likely to be successful in this regard. Indeed, in most cases involving ancient graves, to recognize that Native Americans have standing would represent a significant expansion of common law. In cases where standing can
(25) be achieved, however, common law may provide a basis for some Native American claims against archaeologists and museums.

Property law, for example, can be useful in establishing Native American claims to artifacts that
(30) are retrieved in the excavation of ancient graves and can be considered the communal property of Native American tribes or communities. In *Charrier* v. *Bell,* a United States appellate court ruled that the common law doctrine of abandonment, which allows the finder
(35) of abandoned property to claim ownership, does not apply to objects buried with the deceased. The court ruled that the practice of burying items with the body of the deceased "is not intended as a means of relinquishing ownership to a stranger," and that to
(40) interpret it as such "would render a grave subject to despoliation either immediately after interment or . . . after removal of the descendants of the deceased from the neighborhood of the cemetery." This ruling suggests that artifacts excavated from Native American
(45) ancestral graves should be returned to representatives of tribal groups who can establish standing in such cases.

More generally, United States courts have upheld the distinction between individual and communal
(50) property, holding that an individual Native American does not have title to communal property owned and held for common use by his or her tribe. As a result, museums cannot assume that they have valid title to cultural property merely because they purchased in
(55) good faith an item that was originally sold in good faith by an individual member of a Native American community.

9. The primary purpose of the passage is to provide an answer to which one of the following questions?

(A) How should the legal protection of Native American burial grounds be enhanced?

(B) What characteristics of Native American burial grounds enhance their chances for protection by the law?

(C) In what ways does the law protect the rights of Native Americans in regard to the contents of ancestral graves?

(D) Why are the courts concerned with protecting Native American burial grounds from desecration?

(E) By what means can Native Americans establish their rights to land on which their ancestors are buried?

10. It can be inferred that a court would be most likely to deny standing in a disinterment case to which one of the following Native American plaintiffs?

(A) one who seeks, as one of several beneficiaries of his father's estate, to protect the father's burial site

(B) one who seeks to prevent tenants on her land from taking artifacts from a grave located on the property

(C) one who represents a tribe whose members hope to prevent the disinterment of remains from a distant location from which the tribe recently moved

(D) one who seeks to have artifacts that have been removed from a grave determined to be that of her second cousin returned to the grave

(E) one who seeks the return of artifacts taken from the ancient burial grounds of disparate tribes and now displayed in a museum

GO ON TO THE NEXT PAGE.

11. According to the passage, which one of the following is true of cases involving ancient graves?

(A) Once a plaintiff's standing has been established, such cases are usually more difficult to resolve than are cases involving more recent graves.

(B) The distinction between individual and communal property is usually an issue in such cases.

(C) Even when a plaintiff's standing has been established, property law cannot be used as a basis for the claims of Native Americans in most such cases.

(D) In most such cases, common law does not currently provide a clear basis for establishing that Native Americans have standing.

(E) Common law is rarely used as a basis for the claims of Native Americans who have established standing in such cases.

12. The passage suggests that in making the ruling in *Charrier* v. *Bell* the court is most likely to have considered the answer to which one of the following questions?

(A) Are the descendants of the deceased still alive?

(B) What was the reason for burying the objects in question?

(C) How long after interment had buried objects been claimed by a stranger?

(D) Did the descendants of the deceased remain in the neighborhood of the cemetery?

(E) Could the property on which buried objects were found be legally considered to be abandoned property?

13. The author uses the second paragraph to

(A) illustrate the contention that common law may support the claims of Native Americans to the contents of ancestral graves

(B) exemplify the difficulties that Native Americans are likely to encounter in claiming ancestral remains

(C) introduce a discussion of the distinction between individual and communal property

(D) confirm the contention that cases involving ancient graves present unresolved legal problems

(E) suggest that property law is applicable in most disinterment cases

14. Which one of the following best expresses the main idea of the passage?

(A) Prior to an appellate court's ruling in *Charrier* v. *Bell,* Native Americans had no legal grounds for demanding the return of artifacts excavated from ancient graves.

(B) Property law offers the most promising remedies to Native Americans seeking to recover communally owned artifacts that were sold to museums without tribal authorization.

(C) The older the grave, the more difficult it is for Native Americans to establish standing in cases concerning the disposition of archaeologically excavated ancestral remains.

(D) In cases in which Native Americans can establish standing, common law can be useful in protecting ancestral remains and the artifacts buried with them.

(E) Native Americans are unlikely to make significant progress in the recovery of cultural property until common law is significantly expanded to provide them with standing in cases involving the excavation of ancient graves.

GO ON TO THE NEXT PAGE.

When the same habitat types (forests, oceans, grasslands, etc.) in regions of different latitudes are compared, it becomes apparent that the overall number of species increases from pole to equator. This

(5) latitudinal gradient is probably even more pronounced than current records indicate, since researchers believe that most undiscovered species live in the tropics.

One hypothesis to explain this phenomenon, the "time theory," holds that diverse species adapted to

(10) today's climatic conditions have had more time to emerge in the tropical regions, which, unlike the temperate and arctic zones, have been unaffected by a succession of ice ages. However, ice ages have caused less disruption in some temperate regions than in others

(15) and have not interrupted arctic conditions.

Alternatively, the species-energy hypothesis proposes the following positive correlations: incoming energy from the Sun correlated with rates of growth and reproduction; rates of growth and reproduction

(20) with the amount of living matter (biomass) at a given moment; and the amount of biomass with number of species. However, since organisms may die rapidly, high production rates can exist with low biomass. And high biomass can exist with few species. Moreover, the

(25) mechanism proposed—greater energy influx leading to bigger populations, thereby lowering the probability of local extinction—remains untested.

A third hypothesis centers on the tropics' climatic stability, which provides a more reliable supply of

(30) resources. Species can thus survive even with few types of food, and competing species can tolerate greater overlap between their respective niches. Both capabilities enable more species to exist on the same resources. However, the ecology of local communities

(35) cannot account for the origin of the latitudinal gradient. Localized ecological processes such as competition do not generate regional pools of species, and it is the total number of species available regionally for colonizing any particular area that makes the difference between,

(40) for example, a forest at the equator and one at a higher latitude.

A fourth and most plausible hypothesis focuses on regional speciation, and in particular on rates of speciation and extinction. According to this hypothesis,

(45) if speciation rates become higher toward the tropics, and are not negated by extinction rates, then the latitudinal gradient would result—and become increasingly steep.

The mechanism for this rate-of-speciation

(50) hypothesis is that most new animal species, and perhaps plant species, arise because a population subgroup becomes isolated. This subgroup evolves differently and eventually cannot interbreed with members of the original population. The uneven spread

(55) of a species over a large geographic area promotes this mechanism: at the edges, small populations spread out and form isolated groups. Since subgroups in an arctic environment are more likely to face extinction than those in the tropics, the latter are more likely to survive

(60) long enough to adapt to local conditions and ultimately become new species.

15. Which one of the following most accurately expresses the main idea of the passage?

(A) At present, no single hypothesis explaining the latitudinal gradient in numbers of species is more widely accepted than any other.

(B) The tropical climate is more conducive to promoting species diversity than are arctic or temperate climates.

(C) Several explanations have been suggested for global patterns in species distribution, but a hypothesis involving rates of speciation seems most promising.

(D) Despite their differences, the various hypotheses regarding a latitudinal gradient in species diversity concur in predicting that the gradient can be expected to increase.

(E) In distinguishing among the current hypotheses for distribution of species, the most important criterion is whether a hypothesis proposes a mechanism that can be tested and validated.

16. Which one of the following situations is most consistent with the species-energy hypothesis as described in the passage?

(A) The many plants in a large agricultural tract represent a limited range of species.

(B) An animal species experiences a death rate almost as rapid as its rate of growth and reproduction.

(C) Within the small number of living organisms in a desert habitat, many different species are represented.

(D) In a tropical rain forest, a species with a large population is found to exhibit instances of local extinction.

(E) In an arctic tundra, the plants and animals exhibit a slow rate of growth and reproduction.

GO ON TO THE NEXT PAGE.

17. As presented in the passage, the principles of the time theory most strongly support which one of the following predictions?

 (A) In the absence of additional ice ages, the number of species at high latitudes could eventually increase significantly.

 (B) No future ice ages are likely to change the climatic conditions that currently characterize temperate regions.

 (C) If no further ice ages occur, climatic conditions at high latitudes might eventually resemble those at today's tropical latitudes.

 (D) Researchers will continue to find many more new species in the tropics than in the arctic and temperate zones.

 (E) Future ice ages are likely to interrupt the climatic conditions that now characterize high-latitude regions.

18. Which one of the following, if true, most clearly weakens the rate-of-speciation hypothesis as it is described in the passage?

 (A) A remote subgroup of a tropical species is reunited with the original population and proves unable to interbreed with members of this original population.

 (B) Investigation of a small area of a tropical rain forest reveals that many competing species are able to coexist on the same range of resources.

 (C) A correlation between higher energy influx, larger populations, and lower probability of local extinction is definitively established.

 (D) Researchers find more undiscovered species during an investigation of an arctic region than they had anticipated.

 (E) Most of the isolated subgroups of mammalian life within a tropical zone are found to experience rapid extinction.

19. Which one of the following inferences about the biological characteristics of a temperate-zone grassland is most strongly supported by the passage?

 (A) It has more different species than does a tropical-zone forest.

 (B) Its climatic conditions have been severely interrupted in the past by a succession of ice ages.

 (C) If it has a large amount of biomass, it also has a large number of different species.

 (D) It has a larger regional pool of species than does an arctic grassland.

 (E) If population groups become isolated at its edges, they are likely to adapt to local conditions and become new species.

20. With which one of the following statements concerning possible explanations for the latitudinal gradient in number of species would the author be most likely to agree?

 (A) The time theory is the least plausible of proposed hypotheses, since it does not correctly assess the impact of ice ages upon tropical conditions.

 (B) The rate-of-speciation hypothesis addresses a principal objection to the climatic-stability hypothesis.

 (C) The major objection to the time theory is that it does not accurately reflect the degree to which the latitudinal gradient exists, especially when undiscovered species are taken into account.

 (D) Despite the claims of the species-energy hypothesis, a high rate of biological growth and reproduction is more likely to exist with low biomass than with high biomass.

 (E) An important advantage of the rate-of-speciation theory is that it considers species competition in a regional rather than local context.

GO ON TO THE NEXT PAGE.

Two impressive studies have reexamined Eric Williams' conclusion that Britain's abolition of the slave trade in 1807 and its emancipation of slaves in its colonies in 1834 were driven primarily by economic
(5) rather than humanitarian motives. Blighted by depleted soil, indebtedness, and the inefficiency of coerced labor, these colonies, according to Williams, had by 1807 become an impediment to British economic progress.
(10) Seymour Drescher provides a more balanced view. Rejecting interpretations based either on economic interest or the moral vision of abolitionists, Drescher has reconstructed the populist characteristics of British abolitionism, which appears to have cut across lines of
(15) class, party, and religion. Noting that between 1780 and 1830 antislavery petitions outnumbered those on any other issue, including parliamentary reform, Drescher concludes that such support cannot be explained by economic interest alone, especially when
(20) much of it came from the unenfranchised masses. Yet, aside from demonstrating that such support must have resulted at least in part from widespread literacy and a tradition of political activism, Drescher does not finally explain how England, a nation deeply divided by class
(25) struggles, could mobilize popular support for antislavery measures proposed by otherwise conservative politicians in the House of Lords and approved there with little dissent.
David Eltis' answer to that question actually
(30) supports some of Williams' insights. Eschewing Drescher's idealization of British traditions of liberty, Eltis points to continuing use of low wages and Draconian vagrancy laws in the seventeenth and eighteenth centuries to ensure the industriousness of
(35) British workers. Indeed, certain notables even called for the enslavement of unemployed laborers who roamed the British countryside—an acceptance of coerced labor that Eltis attributes to a preindustrial desire to keep labor costs low and exports competitive.
(40) By the late eighteenth century, however, a growing home market began to alert capitalists to the importance of "want creation" and to incentives such as higher wages as a means of increasing both worker productivity and the number of consumers.
(45) Significantly, it was products grown by slaves, such as sugar, coffee, and tobacco, that stimulated new wants at all levels of British society and were the forerunners of products intended in modern capitalist societies to satisfy what Eltis describes as "nonsubsistence or
(50) psychological needs." Eltis concludes that in an economy that had begun to rely on voluntary labor to satisfy such needs, forced labor necessarily began to appear both inappropriate and counterproductive to employers. Eltis thus concludes that, while Williams
(55) may well have underestimated the economic viability of the British colonies employing forced labor in the early 1800s, his insight into the economic motives for abolition was partly accurate. British leaders became committed to colonial labor reform only when they
(60) became convinced, for reasons other than those cited by Williams, that free labor was more beneficial to the imperial economy.

21. Which one of the following best describes the main idea of the passage?

(A) Although they disagree about the degree to which economic motives influenced Britain's abolition of slavery, Drescher and Eltis both concede that moral persuasion by abolitionists was a significant factor.

(B) Although both Drescher and Eltis have questioned Williams' analysis of the motivation behind Britain's abolition of slavery, there is support for part of Williams' conclusion.

(C) Because he has taken into account the populist characteristics of British abolitionism, Drescher's explanation of what motivated Britain's abolition of slavery is finally more persuasive than that of Eltis.

(D) Neither Eltis nor Drescher has succeeded in explaining why support for Britain's abolition of slavery appears to have cut across lines of party, class, and religion.

(E) Although flawed in certain respects, Williams' conclusions regarding the economic condition of British slave colonies early in the nineteenth century have been largely vindicated.

22. It can be inferred that Eltis cites the views of "certain notables" (line 35) in order to

(A) support the claim that British traditions of liberty were not as strong as Drescher believed them to be

(B) support the contention that a strong labor force was important to Britain's economy

(C) emphasize the importance of slavery as an institution in preindustrial Britain

(D) indicate that the laboring classes provided little support for the abolition of slavery

(E) establish that laborers in preindustrial Britain had few civil rights

GO ON TO THE NEXT PAGE.

23. Which one of the following best states Williams' view of the primary reason for Britain's abolition of the slave trade and the emancipation of slaves in its colonies?

   (A) British populism appealed to people of varied classes, parties, and religions.
   (B) Both capitalists and workers in Britain accepted the moral precepts of abolitionists.
   (C) Forced labor in the colonies could not produce enough goods to satisfy British consumers.
   (D) The operation of colonies based on forced labor was no longer economically advantageous.
   (E) British workers became convinced that forced labor in the colonies prevented paid workers from receiving higher wages.

24. According to Eltis, low wages and Draconian vagrancy laws in Britain in the seventeenth and eighteenth centuries were intended to

   (A) protect laborers against unscrupulous employment practices
   (B) counter the move to enslave unemployed laborers
   (C) ensure a cheap and productive work force
   (D) ensure that the work force experienced no unemployment
   (E) ensure that products produced in British colonies employing forced labor could compete effectively with those produced in Britain

25. It can be inferred that the author of the passage views Drescher's presentation of British traditions concerning liberty as

   (A) accurately stated
   (B) somewhat unrealistic
   (C) carefully researched
   (D) unnecessarily tentative
   (E) superficially convincing

26. The information in the passage suggests that Eltis and Drescher agree that

   (A) people of all classes in Britain supported the abolition of slavery
   (B) the motives behind Britain's abolition of slavery were primarily economic
   (C) the moral vision of abolitionists played a vital part in Britain's abolition of slavery
   (D) British traditions of liberty have been idealized by historians
   (E) Britain's tradition of political activism was primarily responsible for Britain's abolition of slavery

27. According to the passage, Eltis argues against which one of the following contentions?

   (A) Popular support for antislavery measures existed in Britain in the early nineteenth century.
   (B) In the early nineteenth century, colonies that employed forced labor were still economically viable.
   (C) British views concerning personal liberty motivated nineteenth-century British opposition to slavery.
   (D) Widespread literacy in Britain contributed to public opposition to slavery in the early nineteenth century.
   (E) Antislavery measures proposed by conservative politicians in the early nineteenth century met with little opposition.

S T O P

IF YOU FINISH BEFORE TIME IS CALLED, YOU MAY CHECK YOUR WORK ON THIS SECTION ONLY.
DO NOT WORK ON ANY OTHER SECTION IN THE TEST.

SECTION IV
Time—35 minutes
26 Questions

<u>Directions:</u> The questions in this section are based on the reasoning contained in brief statements or passages. For some questions, more than one of the choices could conceivably answer the question. However, you are to choose the <u>best</u> answer; that is, the response that most accurately and completely answers the question. You should not make assumptions that are by commonsense standards implausible, superfluous, or incompatible with the passage. After you have chosen the best answer, blacken the corresponding space on your answer sheet.

1. Three-year-old Sara and her playmate Michael are both ill and have the same symptoms. Since they play together every afternoon, Sara probably has the same illness as Michael does. Since Michael definitely does not have a streptococcal infection, despite his having some symptoms of one, the illness that Sara has is definitely not a streptococcal infection either.

The reasoning in the argument is flawed because the argument

(A) presupposes what it sets out to prove
(B) mistakes the cause of a particular phenomenon for the effect of that phenomenon
(C) fails to distinguish between acute streptococcal infections on the one hand, and less severe streptococcal infections on the other
(D) treats evidence that the conclusion is probably true as if that evidence establishes the certainty of the conclusion
(E) makes a general claim based on particular examples that do not adequately represent the respective groups that they are each intended to represent

2. Lambert: The proposal to raise gasoline taxes to support mass transit networks is unfair. Why should drivers who will never use train or bus lines be forced to pay for them?

Keziah: You have misunderstood. The government has always spent far more, per user, from general revenue sources to fund highways than to fund mass transit. The additional revenue from the gasoline tax will simply allow the government to make its distribution of transportation funds more equitable.

Keziah uses which one of the following argumentative strategies in replying to Lambert?

(A) elaborating the context of the issue in order to place the proposal in a more favorable light
(B) appealing to the principle that what benefits society as a whole benefits all individuals within that society
(C) challenging the presupposition that fairness is an appropriate criterion on which to judge the matter
(D) demonstrating that the proposed tax increase will not result in increased expenses for drivers
(E) declining to argue a point with someone who is poorly informed on the matter under discussion

3. The number of calories in a gram of refined cane sugar is the same as in an equal amount of fructose, the natural sugar found in fruits and vegetables. Therefore, a piece of candy made with a given amount of refined cane sugar is no higher in calories than a piece of fruit that contains an equal amount of fructose.

The reasoning in the argument is flawed because the argument

(A) fails to consider the possibility that fruit might contain noncaloric nutrients that candy does not contain
(B) presupposes that all candy is made with similar amounts of sugar
(C) confuses one kind of sugar with another
(D) presupposes what it sets out to establish, that fruit does not differ from sugar-based candy in the number of calories each contains
(E) overlooks the possibility that sugar might not be the only calorie-containing ingredient in candy or fruit

4. In order to increase production, ABC Company should implement a flextime schedule, which would allow individual employees some flexibility in deciding when to begin and end their workday. Studies have shown that working under flextime schedules is associated with increased employee morale.

The argument depends on the assumption that

(A) the employees who prefer a flextime schedule are the most productive employees at ABC Company
(B) an increase in the morale of ABC Company's employees could lead to increased production
(C) flextime schedules tend to be associated with reduced lateness and absenteeism
(D) employees are most productive during the part of the day when all employees are present
(E) companies that are in competition with ABC Company also use a flextime schedule

GO ON TO THE NEXT PAGE.

5. Attorneys for a criminal defendant charged that the government, in a coverup, had destroyed evidence that would have supported the defendant in a case. The government replied that there is no evidence that would even tend to support the defendant in the case.

Which one of the following is the most accurate evaluation of the government's reply?

(A) It leaves open the question of whether the government had destroyed such evidence.
(B) It establishes that the attorneys' charge is an exaggeration.
(C) It shows that the attorneys did not know whether their charge was true.
(D) It demonstrates the government's failure to search for evidence in its files.
(E) If true, it effectively disproves the charge made on behalf of the defendant.

6. Videocassette recorders (VCRs) enable people to watch movies at home on videotape. People who own VCRs go to movie theaters more often than do people who do not own VCRs. Contrary to popular belief, therefore, owning a VCR actually stimulates people to go to movie theaters more often than they otherwise would.

The argument is most vulnerable to criticism on the grounds that it

(A) concludes that a claim must be false because of the mere absence of evidence in its favor
(B) cites, in support of the conclusion, evidence that is inconsistent with other information that is provided
(C) fails to establish that the phenomena interpreted as cause and effect are not both direct effects of some other factor
(D) takes a condition that by itself guarantees the occurrence of a certain phenomenon to be a condition that therefore must be met for that phenomenon to occur
(E) bases a broad claim about the behavior of people in general on a comparison between two groups of people that together include only a small proportion of people overall

7. The cumbersome spears that were the principal weapons used by certain tribes in the early Bronze Age precluded widespread casualties during intertribal conflicts. But the comparatively high number of warrior tombs found in recent excavations of the same tribes' late Bronze Age settlements indicates that in the late Bronze Age, wars between these tribes were frequent, and the casualty rate was high. Hence some archaeologists claim that by the late Bronze Age, these tribes had developed new methods of warfare designed to inflict many casualties.

Which one of the following, if true, most supports the archaeologists' claim?

(A) A royal tomb dating to the early Bronze Age contained pottery depicting battle scenes in which warriors use spears.
(B) There is evidence that many buildings dating to the late Bronze Age were built by prisoners of war taken in battles between enemy tribes.
(C) Scenes of violent warfare, painted in bright hues, frequently appear on pottery that has been found in some early Bronze Age tombs of warriors.
(D) Some tombs of warriors dating to the late Bronze Age contain armor and weapons that anthropologists believe were trophies taken from enemies in battle.
(E) The marks on the bones of many of the late Bronze Age warriors whose tombs were excavated are consistent with the kind of wounds inflicted by arrowheads also found in many late Bronze Age settlements.

GO ON TO THE NEXT PAGE.

8. Based on data collected from policyholders, life insurance companies have developed tables that list standard weight ranges for various heights. Policyholders whose weight fell within the range given for their height lived longer than those whose weight fell outside their given range. Therefore, if people whose weight falls outside their given range modified their weight to fall within that range, their overall life expectancies would improve.

Which one of the following is an assumption on which the argument relies?

(A) Some people would be unwilling to modify their weights solely to increase the general population's overall life expectancies.

(B) Life insurance companies intended their tables to guide individuals in adjusting their weights in order to increase their life spans.

(C) The tables include data gathered from policyholders whose deaths resulted from accidents in addition to those whose deaths resulted from natural causes.

(D) Holders of life insurance policies do not have longer overall life expectancies than the general population.

(E) People's efforts to modify their weight to conform to a given range would not damage their health enough to decrease their overall life expectancies.

9. Measurements of the motion of the planet Uranus seem to show Uranus being tugged by a force pulling it away from the Sun and the inner planets. Neptune and Pluto, the two known planets whose orbits are farther from the Sun than is the orbit of Uranus, do not have enough mass to exert the force that the measurements indicate. Therefore, in addition to the known planets, there must be at least one planet in our solar system that we have yet to discover.

Which one of the following, if true, most seriously weakens the argument?

(A) Pluto was not discovered until 1930.

(B) There is a belt of comets beyond the orbit of Pluto with powerful gravitational pull.

(C) Neither Neptune nor Pluto is as massive as Uranus.

(D) The force the Sun exerts on Uranus is weaker than the force it exerts on the inner planets.

(E) Uranus' orbit is closer to Neptune's orbit than it is to Pluto's.

10. Audiences find a speaker more convincing if the speaker begins a speech by arguing briefly against his or her position before providing reasons for accepting it. The reason this technique is so effective is that it makes the speaker appear fair-minded and trustworthy. Therefore, candidates for national political office who wish to be successful in winning votes should use this argumentative technique in their speeches.

Which one of the following, if true, most seriously limits the effectiveness of adopting the argument's recommendation?

(A) Political candidates typically have no control over which excerpts from their speeches will be reported by the news media.

(B) Many people do not find arguments made by politicians convincing, since the arguments are often one-sided or oversimplify the issues.

(C) People decide which political candidate to vote for more on the basis of their opinions of the candidate's character than on the exact positions of the candidate.

(D) People regard a political candidate more favorably if they think that the candidate respects an opponent's position even while disagreeing with it.

(E) Political candidates have to address audiences of many different sizes and at many different locations in the course of a political campaign.

11. Five thousand of the 50,000 books published in country Z in 1991 were novels. Exactly 25 of the films released in country Z in 1992 were based on those novels. Since 100 films were released in country Z in 1992, no more than one-quarter of them were based on books published in country Z in 1991.

Which one of the following, if assumed, allows the conclusion above to be properly drawn?

(A) None of the scripts used in films released in 1992 were written by professional novelists.

(B) None of the films released in country Z in 1992 were based on books other than novels.

(C) None of the books that were published in country Z in 1992 were based on plots of films released in 1991.

(D) Some of the films released in country Z in 1992 were based on older films that had been released for the first time many years earlier.

(E) Some of the films released in 1991 in country Z were based on novels that were published in 1991.

GO ON TO THE NEXT PAGE.

12. On their way from their nest to a food source, ants of most species leave a trail of chemicals called pheromones. The ants use the scent of the pheromones to guide themselves between the food and their nest. All pheromones evaporate without a trace almost immediately when temperatures rise above 45 degrees Celsius (113 degrees Fahrenheit), as is typical during afternoons in places such as the Sahara Desert.

The statements above, if true, most strongly support which one of the following?

(A) Most ants forage for food either only in the morning or only during the night.
(B) Most ants that do not use pheromones to mark the paths they take between their nest and food live in the Sahara Desert.
(C) If any ants live in the Sahara Desert and forage for food at no time but in the afternoon, those ants generally do not use pheromones to guide themselves between food and their nest.
(D) If any ants do not use pheromones to navigate between food and their nest, those ants use a different substance that does not evaporate in temperatures above 45 degrees Celsius.
(E) If any Saharan ants forage for food in the afternoon, those ants forage for food less efficiently when temperatures are above 45 degrees Celsius than they do when temperatures are lower.

13. Some people think that in every barrel of politicians there are only a few rotten ones. But if deceit is a quality of rottenness, I believe all effective politicians are rotten. They must be deceitful in order to do the job properly. Someone who is scrupulously honest about obeying the rules of society will never be an effective politician.

Assuming that the author's statements are accurate, which one of the following statements CANNOT be true?

(A) Some people think all politicians are rotten.
(B) Some politicians are scrupulously honest.
(C) Some people define a politician's job as obeying the rules of society.
(D) Some deceitful politicians are ineffective.
(E) Some scrupulously honest politicians are effective.

14. The Biocarb Company wants to build a sterilization plant to treat contaminated medical waste in a city neighborhood where residents and environmental activists fear that such a facility will pollute the area. Biocarb's president argues that the operation of the plant cannot cause pollution because the waste would be sterile after processing by the plant. He claims that after exposure for an hour to superheated steam in the autoclave, such refuse would be far cleaner than food prepared in the cleanest kitchen.

The president's argument depends on which one of the following assumptions?

(A) Environmental activists believe that waste treated with steam will not pollute.
(B) Handling of the waste before treatment in the proposed facility will not pose a threat of pollution to the area.
(C) Fear of pollution is the only argument against construction of an autoclave facility for medical waste.
(D) No others besides environmental activists are concerned about pollution hazards that can result from processing medical waste.
(E) Treatment by superheated steam represents the surest method of sterilization.

15. Grow-Again ointment is a proven treatment for reversing male hereditary baldness. Five drops daily is the recommended dose, and exceeding this quantity does not increase the product's effectiveness. Therefore, offering a manufacturer's rebate on the purchase price of Grow-Again will not increase sales and consequently would be unprofitable for the manufacturer.

Which one of the following, if true, would most strengthen the argument?

(A) When using an ointment, people tend to believe that applying it in greater quantities can make it more effective.
(B) Grow-Again is more effective on some of the men who use it than it is on others.
(C) The rebate, if offered, would not attract purchasers who otherwise might not use Grow-Again.
(D) Baldness in men can be caused by a variety of factors, only one of which is heredity.
(E) Grow-Again is a product whose per-unit manufacturing cost does not fall significantly when the product is produced in large quantities.

GO ON TO THE NEXT PAGE.

Questions 16–17

Henry: Some scientists explain the dance of honeybees as the means by which honeybees communicate the location of whatever food source they have just visited to other members of the hive. But honeybees do not need so complicated a mechanism to communicate that information. Forager honeybees returning to their hive simply leave a scent trail from the food source they have just visited. There must therefore be some other explanation for the honeybees' dance.

Winifred: Not necessarily. Most animals have several ways of accomplishing critical tasks. Bees of some species can navigate using either the position of the Sun or the memory of landmarks. Similarly, for honeybees, scent trails are a supplementary not an exclusive means of communicating.

16.   The point at issue between Henry and Winifred is whether

(A)   theories of animal behavior can be established on the basis of evidence about only one species of animal

(B)   there is more than one valid explanation for the dance of honeybees

(C)   honeybees communicate the location of food sources through their dance

(D)   the honeybee is the only species of bee that is capable of communicating navigational information to other hive members

(E)   the honeybee's sense of smell plays a role in its foraging strategies

17.   In Winifred's response to Henry, the statement about how bees of some species navigate plays which one of the following roles?

(A)   It addresses an ambiguity in Henry's use of the expression "communicate the location."

(B)   It provides evidence in support of a general claim.

(C)   It calls into question the accuracy of key evidence cited by Henry.

(D)   It points out that Henry's conclusion directly contradicts one of his premises.

(E)   It proposes an alternative explanation for the honeybees' dance.

18.   Politician: A government that taxes incomes at a rate of 100 percent will generate no revenue because all economic activity will cease. So it follows that the lower the rate of income tax, the more revenue the government will generate by that tax.

Economist: Your conclusion cannot be correct, since it would mean that an income tax of 0 percent would generate the maximum revenue.

Which one of the following argumentative strategies is used by the economist in responding to the politician?

(A)   stating a general principle that is incompatible with the conclusion the politician derives

(B)   providing evidence that where the politician's advice has been adopted, the results have been disappointing

(C)   arguing that the principle derived by the politician, if applied in the limiting case, leads to an absurdly false conclusion

(D)   undermining the credibility of the politician by openly questioning the politician's understanding of economics

(E)   attacking the politician's argument by giving reason to doubt the truth of a premise

GO ON TO THE NEXT PAGE.

19. Sponges attach to the ocean floor, continually filtering seawater for food and ejecting water they have just filtered to avoid reingesting it. Tubular and vase-shaped sponges can eject filtered water without assistance from surrounding ocean currents and thus are adapted to slow-moving, quiet waters. Because of their shape, however, these sponges cannot live in strong currents, since strong currents would dislodge them. Both of these varieties of sponge were widespread during the late Jurassic period.

The statements above, if true, most strongly support which one of the following claims?

(A) Few tubular or vase-shaped sponges lived before the late Jurassic period.
(B) Tubular and vase-shaped sponges were more common during the late Jurassic period than in succeeding geological eras.
(C) During the late Jurassic period there were many areas of the ocean floor where currents were weak.
(D) All sponges that are neither tubular nor vase-shaped inhabit areas of the ocean floor where there are extremely strong currents.
(E) No types of sponge live in large colonies, since sponges do not flourish in areas where much of the water has been filtered by other sponges.

20. There is strong evidence that the cause of migraines (severe recurrent headaches) is not psychological but instead is purely physiological. Yet several studies have found that people being professionally treated for migraines rate higher on a standard psychological scale of anxiety than do people not being professionally treated for migraines.

Which one of the following, if true, most helps to resolve the apparent discrepancy in the information above?

(A) People who have migraine headaches tend to have relatives who also have migraine headaches.
(B) People who have migraine headaches often suffer these headaches when under emotional stress.
(C) People who rate higher on the standard psychological scale of anxiety are more likely to seek professional treatment than are people who rate lower on the scale.
(D) Of the many studies done on the cause of migraine headaches, most of those that suggest that psychological factors such as anxiety cause migraines have been widely publicized.
(E) Most people who have migraines and who seek professional treatment remain in treatment until they stop having migraines, whether their doctors consider the cause to be physiological or psychological.

21. Not all tenured faculty are full professors. Therefore, although every faculty member in the linguistics department has tenure, it must be the case that not all of the faculty members in the linguistics department are full professors.

The flawed pattern of reasoning exhibited by the argument above is most similar to that exhibited by which one of the following?

(A) Although all modern office towers are climate-controlled buildings, not all office buildings are climate-controlled. Therefore, it must be the case that not all office buildings are modern office towers.
(B) All municipal hospital buildings are massive, but not all municipal hospital buildings are forbidding in appearance. Therefore, massive buildings need not present a forbidding appearance.
(C) Although some buildings designed by famous architects are not well proportioned, all government buildings are designed by famous architects. Therefore, some government buildings are not well proportioned.
(D) Not all public buildings are well designed, but some poorly designed public buildings were originally intended for private use. Therefore, the poorly designed public buildings were all originally designed for private use.
(E) Although some cathedrals are not built of stone, every cathedral is impressive. Therefore, buildings can be impressive even though they are not built of stone.

GO ON TO THE NEXT PAGE.

22. When a planetary system forms, the chances that a planet capable of supporting life will be formed are high. The chances that a large planet the size of Jupiter or Saturn will be formed, however, are low. Without Jupiter and Saturn, whose gravitational forces have prevented Earth from being frequently struck by large comets, intelligent life would never have arisen on Earth. Since planetary systems are unlikely to contain any large planets, the chances that intelligent life will emerge on a planet are, therefore, low.

Knowing which one of the following would be most useful in evaluating the argument?

(A) whether all planetary systems are formed from similar amounts of matter

(B) whether intelligent species would be likely to survive if a comet struck their planet

(C) whether large comets could be deflected by only one large planet rather than by two

(D) how high the chances are that planetary systems will contain many large comets

(E) how likely it is that planetary systems containing large planets will also contain planets the size of Earth

23. Construction contractors working on the cutting edge of technology nearly always work on a "cost-plus" basis only. One kind of cost-plus contract stipulates the contractor's profit as a fixed percentage of the contractor's costs; the other kind stipulates a fixed amount of profit over and above costs. Under the first kind of contract, higher costs yield higher profits for the contractor, so this is where one might expect final costs in excess of original cost estimates to be more common. Paradoxically, such cost overruns are actually more common if the contract is of the fixed-profit kind.

Which one of the following, if true, most helps to resolve the apparent paradox in the situation described above?

(A) Clients are much less likely to agree to a fixed-profit type of cost-plus contract when it is understood that under certain conditions the project will be scuttled than they are when there is no such understanding.

(B) On long-term contracts, cost projections take future inflation into account, but since the figures used are provided by the government, they are usually underestimates.

(C) On any sizable construction project, the contractor bills the client monthly or quarterly, so any tendency for original cost estimates to be exceeded can be detected early.

(D) Clients billed under a cost-plus contract are free to review individual billings in order to uncover wasteful expenditures, but they do so only when the contractor's profit varies with cost.

(E) The practice of submitting deliberately exaggerated cost estimates is most common in the case of fixed-profit contracts, because it makes the profit, as a percentage of estimated cost, appear modest.

GO ON TO THE NEXT PAGE.

24. That wall is supported by several joists. The only thing that can have caused the bulge that the wall now has is a broken joist. Therefore, at least one of the joists is broken.

Which one of the following arguments is most similar in its logical features to the argument above?

(A) At least one of the players in the orchestra must have made a mistake, since nothing else would have made the conductor grimace in the way she just did.

(B) The first piece must have been the easiest, since it was the only piece in the entire concert in which the orchestra did not make many mistakes.

(C) The players play well only when they like the music, since they tend to make mistakes when they play something they do not like.

(D) One of the orchestra's players must be able to play the harp, since in one of the pieces they are playing at next week's concert the composer specified that a harp should be played.

(E) The emotion of the music is the only thing that can have caused the conductor to look so angry just then, since the orchestra was playing perfectly.

Questions 25–26

Sasha: Handwriting analysis should be banned in court as evidence of a person's character: handwriting analysts called as witnesses habitually exaggerate the reliability of their analyses.

Gregory: You are right that the current use of handwriting analysis as evidence is problematic. But this problem exists only because there is no licensing board to set professional standards and thus deter irresponsible analysts from making exaggerated claims. When such a board is established, however, handwriting analysis by licensed practitioners will be a legitimate courtroom tool for character assessment.

25. Gregory does which one of the following in responding to Sasha's argument?

(A) He ignores evidence introduced as support for Sasha's recommendation.

(B) He defends a principle by restricting the class to which it is to be applied.

(C) He abstracts a general principle from specific evidence.

(D) He identifies a self-contradictory statement in Sasha's argument.

(E) He shows that Sasha's argument itself manifests the undesirable characteristic that it condemns.

26. Which one of the following, if true, would provide Sasha with the strongest counter to Gregory's response?

(A) Courts routinely use means other than handwriting analysis to provide evidence of a person's character.

(B) Many people can provide two samples of their handwriting so different that only a highly trained professional could identify them as having been written by the same person.

(C) A licensing board would inevitably refuse to grant licenses to some responsible handwriting analysts for reasons having nothing to do with their reliability.

(D) The only handwriting analysts who claim that handwriting provides reliable evidence of a person's character are irresponsible.

(E) The number of handwriting analysts who could conform to professional standards set by a licensing board is very small.

S T O P

IF YOU FINISH BEFORE TIME IS CALLED, YOU MAY CHECK YOUR WORK ON THIS SECTION ONLY.
DO NOT WORK ON ANY OTHER SECTION IN THE TEST.

LSAT® Writing Sample Topic

Directions: The scenario presented below describes two choices, either one of which can be supported on the basis of the information given. Your essay should consider both choices and argue for one over the other, based on the two specified criteria and the facts provided. There is no "right" or "wrong" choice: a reasonable argument can be made for either.

Elstar, a manufacturer of video games for children, has sufficient funds to promote one of two games for the coming season. Write an argument in support of promoting one game rather than the other based on the following criteria:

- Elstar must reverse a recent decline in sales.
- Elstar has received a good deal of criticism for its excessively violent video games and wants to improve its image.

"Peacekeepers" was developed by the creators of "Warlords of the Cosmos," the game that put Elstar at the top of the industry. In this game, as in "Warlords," the player engages in battles against a succession of adversaries. In "Warlords," the battles involve alien enemies; in "Peacekeepers," they are drawn from actual historical situations. In one sequence, the player confronts a tyrannical leader's threat to world peace by progressing through a series of diplomatic and military confrontations until the leader is defeated. This game ends with a review of key historical military leaders.

"Guardians of Gaia" was developed by Techwise, the leading maker of educational videos that have sold well to schools but have not been extensively marketed to the general public. Players contend with natural and human-made obstacles as they attempt, using their knowledge of science and geography, to reach a destination or solve an environmental problem. Players travel everywhere from the Galapagos Islands to the Arctic Circle, journeying over geographically accurate maps displayed on Veratope, Techwise's cutting edge video display system, never before used in commercial video games. It will run on existing commercial systems. In one sequence, the player must brave Veratopic wild rivers and greedy poachers in order to find and relocate the last remaining pair of a rare bird species.

Directions:

1. Use the Answer Key on the next page to check your answers.

2. Use the Scoring Worksheet below to compute your raw score.

3. Use the Score Conversion Chart to convert your raw score into the 120-180 scale.

Scoring Worksheet

1. Enter the number of questions you answered correctly in each section.

Number Correct

SECTION I . . . . . . _____
SECTION II . . . . . _____
SECTION III . . . . . _____
SECTION IV . . . . . _____

2. Enter the sum here: _____
This is your Raw Score.

Conversion Chart

For Converting Raw Score to the 120-180 LSAT Scaled Score
LSAT Form 7LSS32

Reported Score	Raw Score Lowest	Highest
180	99	101
179	98	98
178	97	97
177	—*	—*
176	96	96
175	95	95
174	94	94
173	93	93
172	92	92
171	90	91
170	89	89
169	88	88
168	86	87
167	85	85
166	83	84
165	82	82
164	80	81
163	79	79
162	77	78
161	75	76
160	74	74
159	72	73
158	70	71
157	68	69
156	66	67
155	65	65
154	63	64
153	61	62
152	59	60
151	57	58
150	55	56
149	54	54
148	52	53
147	50	51
146	48	49
145	47	47
144	45	46
143	43	44
142	42	42
141	40	41
140	38	39
139	37	37
138	35	36
137	34	34
136	32	33
135	31	31
134	30	30
133	28	29
132	27	27
131	26	26
130	25	25
129	24	24
128	23	23
127	22	22
126	21	21
125	20	20
124	19	19
123	18	18
122	17	17
121	16	16
120	0	15

*There is no raw score that will produce this scaled score for this form.

SECTION I

1.	B	8.	B	15.	C	22.	C
2.	E	9.	C	16.	A	23.	D
3.	C	10.	A	17.	B	24.	A
4.	E	11.	A	18.	A		
5.	D	12.	C	19.	B		
6.	D	13.	C	20.	E		
7.	C	14.	E	21.	A		

SECTION II

1.	A	8.	C	15.	B	22.	D
2.	C	9.	B	16.	C	23.	E
3.	D	10.	B	17.	C	24.	A
4.	D	11.	B	18.	E		
5.	D	12.	D	19.	E		
6.	B	13.	A	20.	B		
7.	B	14.	C	21.	A		

SECTION III

1.	A	8.	C	15.	C	22.	A
2.	E	9.	C	16.	E	23.	D
3.	B	10.	E	17.	A	24.	C
4.	E	11.	D	18.	E	25.	B
5.	A	12.	B	19.	D	26.	A
6.	D	13.	A	20.	B	27.	C
7.	D	14.	D	21.	B		

SECTION IV

1.	D	8.	E	15.	C	22.	D
2.	A	9.	B	16.	C	23.	D
3.	E	10.	A	17.	B	24.	A
4.	B	11.	B	18.	C	25.	B
5.	A	12.	C	19.	C	26.	D
6.	C	13.	E	20.	C		
7.	E	14.	B	21.	C		

The Official LSAT PrepTest

20

- October 1996
- Form 7LSS33

The sample test that follows consists of four sections corresponding to the four scored sections of the October 1996 LSAT.

SECTION I
Time—35 minutes

25 Questions

Directions: The questions in this section are based on the reasoning contained in brief statements or passages. For some questions, more than one of the choices could conceivably answer the question. However, you are to choose the best answer; that is, the response that most accurately and completely answers the question. You should not make assumptions that are by commonsense standards implausible, superfluous, or incompatible with the passage. After you have chosen the best answer, blacken the corresponding space on your answer sheet.

1. French divers recently found a large cave along the coast of the Mediterranean Sea. The cave is accessible only through an underwater tunnel. The interior of the cave is completely filled with seawater and contains numerous large stalagmites, which are stony pillars that form when drops of water fall repeatedly on a single spot on a cave floor, leaving behind mineral deposits that accumulate over time.

   The information above most strongly supports which one of the following?

   (A) The Mediterranean Sea was at a higher level in the past than it is now.
   (B) The water level within the cave is higher now than it once was.
   (C) The French divers were the first people who knew that the tunnel leading to the cave existed.
   (D) There was once an entrance to the cave besides the underwater tunnel.
   (E) Seawater in the Mediterranean has a lower mineral content now than it had when the stalagmites were being formed.

2. A director of the Rexx Pharmaceutical Company argued that the development costs for new vaccines that the health department has requested should be subsidized by the government, since the marketing of vaccines promised to be less profitable than the marketing of any other pharmaceutical product. In support of this claim the director argued that sales of vaccines are likely to be lower since each vaccine is administered to a patient only once, whereas medicines that combat diseases and chronic illnesses are administered many times to each patient.

   Which one of the following, if true, most weakens the support offered by the company director for the claim concerning the marketing of vaccines?

   (A) Vaccines are administered to many more people than are most other pharmaceutical products.
   (B) Many of the diseases that vaccines are designed to prevent can be successfully treated by medicines.
   (C) Pharmaceutical companies occasionally market products that are neither medicines nor vaccines.
   (D) Pharmaceutical companies other than the Rexx Pharmaceutical Company produce vaccines.
   (E) The cost of administering a vaccine is rarely borne by the pharmaceutical company that manufactures that vaccine.

3. Manager: Our new computer network, the purpose of which is to increase productivity, can be installed during the day, which would disrupt our employees' work, or else at night, which would entail much higher installation charges. Since saving money is important, we should have the network installed during the day.

   The manager's argument assumes which one of the following?

   (A) The monetary value of the network equipment would not exceed the cost of having the equipment installed at night.
   (B) The monetary value of any productivity lost during a daytime installation would be less than the difference between daytime and nighttime installation costs.
   (C) A daytime installation would be completed by no larger a crew and would take the crew no more time than would a nighttime installation.
   (D) Once the network has been installed, most of the company's employees will be able to use it immediately to increase their productivity.
   (E) Most of the company's employees would be able to work productively while a daytime installation is in progress.

GO ON TO THE NEXT PAGE.

4. An ingredient in marijuana known as THC has been found to inactivate herpesviruses in experiments. In previous experiments researchers found that inactivated herpesviruses can convert healthy cells into cancer cells. It can be concluded that the use of marijuana can cause cancer.

Which one of the following, if true, most seriously weakens the argument?

(A) Several teams of scientists performed the various experiments and all of the teams had similar results.
(B) The carcinogenic effect of THC could be neutralized by the other ingredients found in marijuana.
(C) When THC kills herpesviruses it weakens the immune system, and it might thus diminish the body's ability to fight other viruses, including viruses linked to cancers.
(D) If chemists modify the structure of THC, THC can be safely incorporated into medications to prevent herpes.
(E) To lessen the undesirable side effects of chemotherapy, the use of marijuana has been recommended for cancer patients who are free of the herpesvirus.

5. Archaeologist: A large corporation has recently offered to provide funding to restore an archaeological site and to construct facilities to make the site readily accessible to the general public. The restoration will conform to the best current theories about how the site appeared at the height of the ancient civilization that occupied it. This offer should be rejected, however, because many parts of the site contain unexamined evidence.

Which one of the following principles, if valid, justifies the archaeologist's argument?

(A) The ownership of archaeological sites should not be under the control of business interests.
(B) Any restoration of an archaeological site should represent only the most ancient period of that site's history.
(C) No one should make judgments about what constitutes the height of another civilization.
(D) Only those with a true concern for an archaeological site's history should be involved in the restoration of that site.
(E) The risk of losing evidence relevant to possible future theories should outweigh any advantages of displaying the results of theories already developed.

6. Besides laying eggs in her own nest, any female wood duck will lay an egg in the nest of another female wood duck if she sees the other duck leaving her nest. Under natural nesting conditions, this parasitic behavior is relatively rare because the ducks' nests are well hidden. However, when people put up nesting boxes to help the ducks breed, they actually undercut the ducks' reproductive efforts. These nesting boxes become so crowded with extra eggs that few, if any, of the eggs in those boxes hatch.

The statements above, if true, most strongly support which one of the following?

(A) Female wood ducks will establish nests in nest boxes only when natural nesting sites are not available.
(B) Nesting female wood ducks who often see other female wood ducks are the most successful in their breeding efforts.
(C) The nesting boxes for wood ducks have less space for eggs than do natural nesting sites.
(D) The nesting boxes would be more effective in helping wood ducks breed if they were less visible to other wood ducks than they currently are.
(E) Nesting boxes are needed to supplement the natural nesting sites of wood ducks because of the destruction of much of the ducks' habitat.

7. The crux of creativity resides in the ability to manufacture variations on a theme. If we look at the history of science, for instance, we see that every idea is built upon a thousand related ideas. Careful analysis leads us to understand that what we choose to call a new theme or a new discovery is itself always and without exception some sort of variation, on a deep level, of previous themes.

If all of the statements in the passage are true, each of the following must also be true EXCEPT:

(A) A lack of ability to manufacture a variation on a previous theme connotes a lack of creativity.
(B) No scientific idea is entirely independent of all other ideas.
(C) Careful analysis of a specific variation can reveal previous themes of which it is a variation.
(D) All great scientific discoverers have been able to manufacture a variation on a theme.
(E) Some new scientific discoveries do not represent, on a deep level, a variation on previous themes.

GO ON TO THE NEXT PAGE.

8. Millions of female bats rear their pups in Bracken Cave. Although the mothers all leave the cave nightly, on their return each mother is almost always swiftly reunited with her own pup. Since the bats' calls are their only means of finding one another, and a bat pup cannot distinguish the call of its mother from that of any other adult bat, it is clear that each mother bat can recognize the call of her pup.

The argument seeks to do which one of the following?

(A) derive a general conclusion about all members of a group from facts known about representative members of that group

(B) establish the validity of one explanation for a phenomenon by excluding alternative explanations

(C) support, by describing a suitable mechanism, the hypothesis that a certain phenomenon can occur

(D) conclude that members of two groups are likely to share a certain ability because of other characteristics they share

(E) demonstrate that a general rule applies in a particular case

9. Someone who gets sick from eating a meal will often develop a strong distaste for the one food in the meal that had the most distinctive flavor, whether or not that food caused the sickness. This phenomenon explains why children are especially likely to develop strong aversions to some foods.

Which one of the following, if true, provides the strongest support for the explanation?

(A) Children are more likely than adults to be given meals composed of foods lacking especially distinctive flavors.

(B) Children are less likely than adults to see a connection between their health and the foods they eat.

(C) Children tend to have more acute taste and to become sick more often than adults do.

(D) Children typically recover more slowly than adults do from sickness caused by food.

(E) Children are more likely than are adults to refuse to eat unfamiliar foods.

10. Premiums for automobile accident insurance are often higher for red cars than for cars of other colors. To justify these higher charges, insurance companies claim that, overall, a greater percentage of red cars are involved in accidents than are cars of any other color. If this claim is true, then lives could undoubtedly be saved by banning red cars from the roads altogether.

The reasoning in the argument is flawed because the argument

(A) accepts without question that insurance companies have the right to charge higher premiums for higher-risk clients

(B) fails to consider whether red cars cost the same to repair as cars of other colors

(C) ignores the possibility that drivers who drive recklessly have a preference for red cars

(D) does not specify precisely what percentage of red cars are involved in accidents

(E) makes an unsupported assumption that every automobile accident results in some loss of life

11. A certain credit-card company awards its customers bonus points for using its credit card. Customers can use accumulated points in the purchase of brand name merchandise by mail at prices lower than the manufacturers' suggested retail prices. At any given time, therefore, customers who purchase merchandise using the bonus points spend less than they would spend if they purchased the same merchandise in retail stores.

Which one of the following is an assumption on which the argument depends?

(A) The merchandise that can be ordered by mail using the bonus points is not offered at lower prices by other credit-card companies that award bonus points.

(B) The bonus points cannot be used by the credit-card customers in the purchase of brand name merchandise that is not available for purchase in retail stores.

(C) The credit-card company does not require its customers to accumulate a large number of bonus points before becoming eligible to order merchandise at prices lower than the manufacturers' suggested retail price.

(D) The amount credit-card customers pay for shipping the merchandise ordered by mail does not increase the amount customers spend to an amount greater than they would spend if they purchased the same merchandise in retail stores.

(E) The merchandise available to the company's credit-card customers using the bonus points is frequently sold in retail stores at prices that are higher than the manufacturers' suggested retail prices.

GO ON TO THE NEXT PAGE.

12. It is probably not true that colic in infants is caused by the inability of those infants to tolerate certain antibodies found in cow's milk, since it is often the case that symptoms of colic are shown by infants that are fed breast milk exclusively.

Which one of the following, if true, most seriously weakens the argument?

(A)   A study involving 500 sets of twins has found that if one infant has colic, its twin will probably also have colic.

(B)   Symptoms of colic generally disappear as infants grow older, whether the infants have been fed breast milk exclusively or have been fed infant formula containing cow's milk.

(C)   In a study of 5,000 infants who were fed only infant formula containing cow's milk, over 4,000 of the infants never displayed any symptoms of colic.

(D)   When mothers of infants that are fed only breast milk eliminate cow's milk and all products made from cow's milk from their own diets, any colic symptoms that their infants have manifested quickly disappear.

(E)   Infants that are fed breast milk develop mature digestive systems at an earlier age than do those that are fed infant formulas, and infants with mature digestive systems are better able to tolerate certain proteins and antibodies found in cow's milk.

Questions 13–14

Yolanda: Gaining access to computers without authorization and manipulating the data and programs they contain is comparable to joyriding in stolen cars; both involve breaking into private property and treating it recklessly. Joyriding, however, is the more dangerous crime because it physically endangers people, whereas only intellectual property is harmed in the case of computer crimes.

Arjun: I disagree! For example, unauthorized use of medical records systems in hospitals could damage data systems on which human lives depend, and therefore computer crimes also cause physical harm to people.

13. An issue in dispute between Yolanda and Arjun is

(A)   whether joyriding physically endangers human lives

(B)   whether the unauthorized manipulation of computer data involves damage to private property

(C)   whether damage to physical property is more criminal than damage to intellectual property

(D)   whether the unauthorized use of computers is as dangerous to people as is joyriding

(E)   whether treating private property recklessly is ever a dangerous crime

14. The reasoning in Arjun's response is flawed because he

(A)   fails to maintain a distinction made in Yolanda's argument

(B)   denies Yolanda's conclusion without providing evidence against it

(C)   relies on the actuality of a phenomenon that he has only shown to be possible

(D)   mistakes something that leads to his conclusion for something that is necessary for his conclusion

(E)   uses as evidence a phenomenon that is inconsistent with his own conclusion

GO ON TO THE NEXT PAGE.

15. A report of a government survey concluded that Center City was among the ten cities in the nation with the highest dropout rate from its schools. The survey data were obtained by asking all city residents over the age of 19 whether they were high school graduates and computing the proportion who were not. A city school official objected that the result did not seem accurate according to the schools' figures.

The school official can most properly criticize the reasoning by which the survey report reached its result for failure to do which one of the following?

(A) take into account instances of respondents' dropping out that occurred before the respondents reached high school

(B) ask residents whether they had completed their high school work in fewer than the usual number of years

(C) distinguish between residents who had attended the city's schools and those who had received their schooling elsewhere

(D) predict the effect of the information contained in the report on future high school dropout rates for the city

(E) consider whether a diploma from the city's high schools signaled the same level of achievement over time

16. Brown dwarfs—dim red stars that are too cool to burn hydrogen—are very similar in appearance to red dwarf stars, which are just hot enough to burn hydrogen. Stars, when first formed, contain substantial amounts of the element lithium. All stars but the coolest of the brown dwarfs are hot enough to destroy lithium completely by converting it to helium. Accordingly, any star found that contains no lithium is not one of these coolest brown dwarfs.

The argument depends on assuming which one of the following?

(A) None of the coolest brown dwarfs has ever been hot enough to destroy lithium.

(B) Most stars that are too cool to burn hydrogen are too cool to destroy lithium completely.

(C) Brown dwarfs that are not hot enough to destroy lithium are hot enough to destroy helium.

(D) Most stars, when first formed, contain roughly the same percentage of lithium.

(E) No stars are more similar in appearance to red dwarfs than are brown dwarfs.

17. Whenever a company loses a major product-liability lawsuit, the value of the company's stocks falls significantly within hours after the announcement. Cotoy has long been involved in a major product-liability lawsuit, and its stocks fell significantly in value today. Therefore, we can be sure that an unfavorable judgment against Cotoy in that lawsuit was announced earlier today.

Which one of the following contains flawed reasoning that most closely parallels that in the argument above?

(A) Whenever a business treats its customers discourteously, its customers begin to shop elsewhere. Shopwell wants to keep all of its customers; therefore, its employees will never treat customers discourteously.

(B) Whenever the large airlines decrease fares, the financial stability of smaller competing airlines is adversely affected. Therefore, the smaller competing airlines' financial stability must be seriously threatened when the large airlines announce a large price decrease.

(C) Whenever a country shows a lack of leadership on international issues, respect for the country's policies begins to decline. Therefore, to gain respect for its policies, a country should show leadership on international issues.

(D) Whenever an entering student at Cashman College wins the Performance Fellowship, he or she receives $10,000. Therefore, Eula, a student who has enrolled at Cashman, must have won the Performance Fellowship, because she just received $10,000 from the college.

(E) Whenever a company advertises its products effectively, the company's sales increase. Oroco's sales have not increased; therefore, it is likely that the company did not advertise its products effectively.

GO ON TO THE NEXT PAGE.

18. In recent years the climate has been generally cool in northern Asia. But during periods when the average daily temperature and humidity in northern Asia were slightly higher than their normal levels the yields of most crops grown there increased significantly. In the next century, the increased average daily temperature and humidity attained during those periods are expected to become the norm. Yet scientists predict that the yearly yields of most of the region's crops will decrease during the next century.

Which one of the following, if true, most helps to resolve the apparent paradox in the information above?

(A) Crop yields in southern Asia are expected to remain constant even after the average daily temperature and humidity there increase from recent levels.

(B) Any increases in temperature and humidity would be accompanied by higher levels of atmospheric carbon dioxide, which is vital to plant respiration.

(C) The climate in northern Asia has generally been too cool and dry in recent years for populations of many crop insect pests to become established.

(D) In many parts of Asia, the increased annual precipitation that would result from warmer and wetter climates would cause most edible plant species to flourish.

(E) The recent climate of northern Asia prevents many crops from being farmed there during the winter.

19. No one in the French department to which Professor Alban belongs is allowed to teach more than one introductory level class in any one term. Moreover, the only language classes being taught next term are advanced ones. So it is untrue that both of the French classes Professor Alban will be teaching next term will be introductory level classes.

The pattern of reasoning displayed in the argument above is most closely paralleled by that in which one of the following arguments?

(A) The Morrison Building will be fully occupied by May and since if a building is occupied by May the new tax rates apply to it, the Morrison Building will be taxed according to the new rates.

(B) The revised tax code does not apply at all to buildings built before 1900, and only the first section of the revised code applies to buildings built between 1900 and 1920, so the revised code does not apply to the Norton Building, since it was built in 1873.

(C) All property on Overton Road will be reassessed for tax purposes by the end of the year and the Elnor Company headquarters is on Overton Road, so Elnor's property taxes will be higher next year.

(D) New buildings that include public space are exempt from city taxes for two years and all new buildings in the city's Alton district are exempt for five years, so the building with the large public space that was recently completed in Alton will not be subject to city taxes next year.

(E) Since according to recent statute, a building that is exempt from property taxes is charged for city water at a special rate, and hospitals are exempt from property taxes, Founder's Hospital will be charged for city water at the special rate.

GO ON TO THE NEXT PAGE.

Questions 20–21

Some people have been promoting a new herbal mixture as a remedy for the common cold. The mixture contains, among other things, extracts of the plants purple coneflower and goldenseal. A cold sufferer, skeptical of the claim that the mixture is an effective cold remedy, argued, "Suppose that the mixture were an effective cold remedy. Since most people with colds wish to recover quickly, it follows that almost everybody with a cold would be using it. Therefore, since there are many people who have colds but do not use the mixture, it is obviously not effective."

20. Each of the following is an assumption required by the skeptical cold sufferer's argument EXCEPT:

(A) Enough of the mixture is produced to provide the required doses to almost everybody with a cold.

(B) The mixture does not have side effects severe enough to make many people who have colds avoid using it.

(C) The mixture is powerful enough to prevent almost everybody who uses it from contracting any further colds.

(D) The mixture is widely enough known that almost everybody with a cold is aware of it.

(E) There are no effective cold remedies available that many people who have colds prefer to the mixture.

21. Which one of the following most accurately describes the method of reasoning the cold sufferer uses to reach the conclusion of the argument?

(A) finding a claim to be false on the grounds that it would if true have consequences that are false

(B) accepting a claim on the basis of public opinion of the claim

(C) showing that conditions necessary to establish the truth of a claim are met

(D) basing a generalization on a representative group of instances

(E) showing that a measure claimed to be effective in achieving a certain effect would actually make achieving the effect more difficult

22. To hold criminals responsible for their crimes involves a failure to recognize that criminal actions, like all actions, are ultimately products of the environment that forged the agent's character. It is not criminals but people in the law-abiding majority who by their actions do most to create and maintain this environment. Therefore, it is law-abiding people whose actions, and nothing else, make them alone truly responsible for crime.

The reasoning in the argument is most vulnerable to criticism on the grounds that

(A) it exploits an ambiguity in the term "environment" by treating two different meanings of the word as though they were equivalent

(B) it fails to distinguish between actions that are socially acceptable and actions that are socially unacceptable

(C) the way it distinguishes criminals from crimes implicitly denies that someone becomes a criminal solely in virtue of having committed a crime

(D) its conclusion is a generalization of statistical evidence drawn from only a small minority of the population

(E) its conclusion contradicts an implicit principle on which an earlier part of the argument is based

GO ON TO THE NEXT PAGE.

23. Chronic back pain is usually caused by a herniated or degenerated spinal disk. In most cases the disk will have been damaged years before chronic pain develops, and in fact an estimated one in five people over the age of 30 has a herniated or degenerated disk that shows no chronic symptoms. If chronic pain later develops in such a case, it is generally brought about by a deterioration of the abdominal and spinal muscles caused by insufficient exercise.

The statements above, if true, most strongly support which one of the following?

(A) Four out of five people over the age of 30 can be sure they will never develop chronic back pain.

(B) People who exercise their abdominal and spinal muscles regularly are sure to be free from chronic back pain.

(C) Patients rarely suffer even mild and fleeting back pain at the time that a spinal disk first becomes herniated or degenerated.

(D) Doctors can accurately predict which people who do not have chronic back pain will develop it in the future.

(E) There is a strategy that can be effective in delaying or preventing the onset of pain from a currently asymptomatic herniated or degenerated spinal disk.

24. Each December 31 in Country Q, a tally is made of the country's total available coal supplies—that is, the total amount of coal that has been mined throughout the country but not consumed. In 1991 that amount was considerably lower than it had been in 1990. Furthermore, Country Q has not imported or exported coal since 1970.

If the statements above are true, which one of the following must also be true on the basis of them?

(A) In Country Q, more coal was mined in 1990 than was mined in 1991.

(B) In Country Q, the amount of coal consumed in 1991 was greater than the amount of coal mined in 1991.

(C) In Country Q, the amount of coal consumed in 1990 was greater than the amount of coal consumed in 1991.

(D) In Country Q, the amount of coal consumed in 1991 was greater than the amount of coal consumed in 1990.

(E) In Country Q, more coal was consumed during the first half of 1991 than was consumed during the first half of 1990.

25. Tom: Employers complain that people graduating from high school too often lack the vocational skills required for full-time employment. Therefore, since these skills are best acquired on the job, we should require high school students to work at part-time jobs so that they acquire the skills needed for today's job market.

Mary: There are already too few part-time jobs for students who want to work, and simply requiring students to work will not create jobs for them.

Which one of the following most accurately describes how Mary's response is related to Tom's argument?

(A) It analyzes an undesirable result of undertaking the course of action that Tom recommends.

(B) It argues that Tom has mistaken an unavoidable trend for an avoidable one.

(C) It provides information that is inconsistent with an explicitly stated premise in Tom's argument.

(D) It presents a consideration that undercuts an assumption on which Tom's argument depends.

(E) It defends an alternative solution to the problem that Tom describes.

S T O P

IF YOU FINISH BEFORE TIME IS CALLED, YOU MAY CHECK YOUR WORK ON THIS SECTION ONLY.
DO NOT WORK ON ANY OTHER SECTION IN THE TEST.

SECTION II

Time—35 minutes

26 Questions

Directions: Each passage in this section is followed by a group of questions to be answered on the basis of what is <u>stated</u> or <u>implied</u> in the passage. For some of the questions, more than one of the choices could conceivably answer the question. However, you are to choose the <u>best</u> answer; that is, the response that most accurately and completely answers the question, and blacken the corresponding space on your answer sheet.

The career of trumpeter Miles Davis was one of the most astonishingly productive that jazz music has ever seen. Yet his genius has never received its due. The impatience and artistic restlessness that characterized
(5) his work spawned one stylistic turn after another and made Davis anathema to many critics, who deplored his abandonment first of bebop and then of "cool" acoustic jazz for ever more innovative sounds.

Having begun his career studying bebop, Davis
(10) pulled the first of many stylistic surprises when, in 1948, he became a member of an impromptu musical think tank that gathered in a New York City apartment. The work of this group not only slowed down tempos and featured ensemble playing as much as or even
(15) more than solos—in direct reaction to bebop—it also became the seedbed for the "West Coast cool" jazz style.

In what would become a characteristic zigzag, Davis didn't follow up on these innovations himself.
(20) Instead, in the late 1950s he formed a new band that broke free from jazz's restrictive pattern of chord changes. Soloists could determine the shapes of their melodies without referring back to the same unvarying repetition of chords. In this period, Davis attempted to
(25) join jazz phrasings, harmonies, and tonal qualities with a unified and integrated sound similar to that of a classical orchestral piece: in his recordings the rhythms, no matter how jazzlike, are always understated, and the instrumental voicings seem muted.
(30) Davis's recordings from the late 1960s signal that, once again, his direction was changing. On *Filles de Kilimanjaro,* Davis's request that keyboardist Herbie Hancock play electric rather than acoustic piano caused consternation among jazz purists of the time. Other
(35) albums featured rock-style beats, heavily electronic instrumentation, a loose improvisational attack and a growing use of studio editing to create jagged soundscapes. By 1969 Davis's typical studio procedure was to have musicians improvise from a base script of
(40) material and then to build finished pieces out of tape, like a movie director. Rock groups had pioneered the process; to jazz lovers, raised on the ideal of live improvisation, that approach was a violation of the premise that recordings should simply document the
(45) musicians' thought processes in real time. Davis again became the target of fierce polemics by purist jazz critics, who have continued to belittle his contributions to jazz.

What probably underlies the intensity of the
(50) reactions against Davis is fear of the broadening of

possibilities that he exemplified. Ironically, he was simply doing what jazz explorers have always done: reaching for something new that was his own. But because his career endured, because he didn't die
(55) young or record only sporadically, and because he refused to dwell in whatever niche he had previously carved out, critics find it difficult to definitively rank Davis in the aesthetic hierarchy to which they cling.

1. Which one of the following best states the main point of the passage?

    (A)   Because the career of Miles Davis was characterized by frequent shifts in styles, he never fulfilled his musical potential.

    (B)   Because the career of Miles Davis does not fit neatly into their preconceptions about the life and music of jazz musicians, jazz critics have not accorded him the appreciation he deserves.

    (C)   Because the career of Miles Davis was unusually long and productive, he never received the popular acclaim generally reserved for artists with more tragic life histories.

    (D)   The long and productive career of Miles Davis spawned most of the major stylistic changes affecting twentieth-century jazz.

    (E)   Miles Davis's versatility and openness have inspired the admiration of most jazz critics.

2. According to the passage, which one of the following is true of the "West Coast cool" jazz style?

    (A)   It was popularized by Miles Davis.
    (B)   It was characterized by a unified and integrated sound.
    (C)   It was played primarily by large ensembles.
    (D)   It introduced a wide variety of chord change patterns.
    (E)   It grew out of innovations developed in New York City.

GO ON TO THE NEXT PAGE.

3. The passage suggests which one of the following about the kind of jazz played by Miles Davis prior to 1948 ?

    (A)   It was characterized by rapid tempos and an emphasis on solo playing.
    (B)   It equally balanced ensemble and solo playing.
    (C)   It was a reaction against more restrictive jazz styles.
    (D)   It is regarded by purist jazz critics as the only authentic jazz style.
    (E)   It was played primarily in New York City jazz clubs.

4. Which one of the following best describes the author's attitude toward Miles Davis's music?

    (A)   uneasy ambivalence
    (B)   cautious neutrality
    (C)   grudging respect
    (D)   moderate commendation
    (E)   appreciative advocacy

5. Which one of the following creative processes is most similar to Miles Davis's typical studio procedure of the late 1960s, as described in the fourth paragraph of the passage?

    (A)   The producer of a television comedy show suggests a setting and general topic for a comedy sketch and then lets the comedians write their own script.
    (B)   An actor digresses from the written script and improvises during a monologue in order to introduce a feeling of spontaneity to the performance.
    (C)   A conductor rehearses each section of the orchestra separately before assembling them to rehearse the entire piece together.
    (D)   An artist has several photographers take pictures pertaining to a certain assigned theme and then assembles them into a pictorial collage.
    (E)   A teacher has each student in a writing class write an essay on an assigned topic and then submits the best essays to be considered for publication in a journal.

6. Which one of the following, if true, would most undermine the author's explanation for the way Miles Davis is regarded by jazz critics?

    (A)   Many jazz musicians who specialize in improvisational playing are greatly admired by jazz critics.
    (B)   Many jazz musicians whose careers have been characterized by several radical changes in style are greatly admired by jazz critics.
    (C)   Several jazz musicians who perform exclusively on electronic instruments are very highly regarded by jazz critics.
    (D)   The jazz innovators who are held in the highest regard by jazz critics had brief yet brilliant careers.
    (E)   Jazz critics are known to have a higher regard for musicality than for mere technical virtuosity.

GO ON TO THE NEXT PAGE.

By the mid-fourteenth century, professional associations of canon lawyers (legal advocates in Christian ecclesiastical courts, which dealt with cases involving marriage, inheritance, and other issues) had
(5) appeared in most of Western Europe, and a body of professional standards had been defined for them. One might expect that the professional associations would play a prominent role in enforcing these standards of conduct, as other guilds often did, and as modern
(10) professional associations do, but that seems not to have happened. Advocates' professional organizations showed little fervor for disciplining their erring members. Some even attempted to hobble efforts at enforcement. The Florentine guild of lawyers, for
(15) example, forbade its members to play any role in disciplinary proceedings against other guild members. In the few recorded episodes of disciplinary enforcement, the initiative for disciplinary action apparently came from a dissatisfied client, not from
(20) fellow lawyers.

At first glance, there seem to be two possible explanations for the rarity of disciplinary proceedings. Medieval canon lawyers may have generally observed the standards of professional conduct scrupulously.
(25) Alternatively, it is possible that deviations from the established standards of behavior were not uncommon, but that canonical disciplinary mechanisms were so inefficient that most delinquents escaped detection and punishment.

(30) Two considerations make it clear that the second of these explanations is more plausible. First, the English civil law courts, whose ethical standards were similar to those of ecclesiastical courts, show many more examples of disciplinary actions against legal
(35) practitioners than do the records of church courts. This discrepancy could well indicate that the disciplinary mechanisms of the civil courts functioned more efficiently than those of the church courts. The alternative inference, namely, that ecclesiastical
(40) advocates were less prone to ethical lapses than their counterparts in the civil courts, seems inherently weak, especially since there was some overlap of personnel between the civil bar and the ecclesiastical bar.

Second, church authorities themselves complained
(45) about the failure of advocates to measure up to ethical standards and deplored the shortcomings of the disciplinary system. Thus the Council of Basel declared that canon lawyers failed to adhere to the ethical prescriptions laid down in numerous papal
(50) constitutions and directed Cardinal Cesarini to address the problem. In England, where medieval church records are extraordinarily rich, similar complaints about the failure of the disciplinary system to reform unethical practices were very common.

(55) Such criticisms seem to have had a paradoxical result, for they apparently reinforced the professional solidarity of lawyers at the expense of the enforcement of ethical standards. Thus the profession's critics may actually have induced advocates to organize
(60) professional associations for self-defense. The critics'

attacks may also have persuaded lawyers to assign a higher priority to defending themselves against attacks by nonprofessionals than to disciplining wayward members within their own ranks.

7. Which one of the following best states the main conclusion of the passage?

(A) Professional organizations of medieval canon lawyers probably only enforced ethical standards among their own members when provoked to do so by outside criticisms.

(B) Professional organizations of medieval civil lawyers seem to have maintained stricter ethical standards for their own members than did professional organizations of medieval canon lawyers.

(C) Professional organizations of medieval canon lawyers apparently served to defend their members against critics' attacks rather than to enforce ethical standards.

(D) The ethical standards maintained by professional associations of medieval canon lawyers were chiefly laid down in papal constitutions.

(E) Ethical standards for medieval canon lawyers were not laid down until professional organizations for these lawyers had been formed.

8. According to the passage, which one of the following statements about law courts in medieval England is true?

(A) Some English lawyers who practiced in civil courts also practiced in church courts, but others served exclusively in one court or the other.

(B) English canon lawyers were more likely to initiate disciplinary proceedings against their colleagues than were English civil lawyers.

(C) English civil lawyers maintained more stringent ethical standards than did civil lawyers in the rest of Europe.

(D) English ecclesiastical courts had originally been modeled upon English civil courts.

(E) English ecclesiastical courts kept richer and more thorough records than did English civil courts.

GO ON TO THE NEXT PAGE.

9. The author refers to the Florentine guild of lawyers in the first paragraph most probably in order to

(A) introduce a theory about to be promoted
(B) illustrate the type of action referred to in the previous sentence
(C) underline the universality of a method discussed throughout the paragraph
(D) point out a flaw in an argument presented earlier in the paragraph
(E) rebut an anticipated objection to a thesis just proposed

10. The author refers to the Council of Basel (line 47) primarily in order to

(A) provide an example of the type of action needed to establish professional standards for canon lawyers
(B) contrast the reactions of English church authorities with the reactions of other bodies to violations of professional standards by canon lawyers
(C) bolster the argument that violations of professional standards by canon lawyers did take place
(D) explain how rules of conduct for canon lawyers were established
(E) describe the development of a disciplinary system to enforce professional standards among canon lawyers

11. According to the information in the passage, for which one of the following ethical violations would documentation of disciplinary action against a canon lawyer be most likely to exist?

(A) betraying a client's secrets to the opposing party
(B) bribing the judge to rule in favor of a client
(C) misrepresenting credentials in order to gain admission to the lawyers' guild
(D) spreading rumors in order to discredit an opposing lawyer
(E) knowingly helping a client to misrepresent the truth

12. Which one of the following is most analogous to the "professional solidarity" referred to in lines 56–57?

(A) Members of a teachers' union go on strike when they believe one of their colleagues to be falsely accused of using an inappropriate textbook.
(B) In order to protect the reputation of the press in the face of a largely hostile public, a journalist conceals distortions in a colleague's news article.
(C) Several dozen recording artists agree to participate in a concert to benefit an endangered environmental habitat.
(D) In order to expedite governmental approval of a drug, a government official is persuaded to look the other way when a pharmaceutical manufacturer conceals evidence that the drug may have minor side effects.
(E) A popular politician agrees to campaign for another, less popular politician belonging to the same political party.

13. The passage suggests that which one of the following is most likely to have been true of medieval guilds?

(A) Few guilds of any importance existed before the mid-fourteenth century.
(B) Many medieval guilds exercised influence over the actions of their members.
(C) Most medieval guilds maintained more exacting ethical standards than did the associations of canon lawyers.
(D) Medieval guilds found it difficult to enforce discipline among their members.
(E) The ethical standards of medieval guilds varied from one city to another.

14. The author would be most likely to agree with which one of the following regarding the hypothesis that medieval canon lawyers observed standards of professional conduct scrupulously?

(A) It is untrue because it is contradicted by documents obtained from the ecclesiastical courts.
(B) It is unlikely because it describes behavior markedly different from behavior observed in the same situation in modern society.
(C) It is unlikely because it describes behavior markedly different from behavior observed in a similar area of medieval society.
(D) It is impossible to assess intelligently because of the dearth of civil and ecclesiastical documents.
(E) It is directly supported by documents obtained from civil and ecclesiastical courts.

GO ON TO THE NEXT PAGE.

Many birds that form flocks compete through aggressive interaction for priority of access to resources such as food and shelter. The result of repeated interactions between flock members is that (5) each bird gains a particular social status related to its fighting ability, with priority of access to resources increasing with higher status. As the number and intensity of interactions between birds increase, however, so increase the costs to each bird in terms of (10) energy expenditure, time, and risk of injury. Thus, birds possessing attributes that reduce the number of costly interactions in which they must be involved, without leading to a reduction in status, are at an advantage. An external signal, such as a plumage type, (15) announcing fighting ability and thereby obviating the actual need to fight, could be one such attribute.

The zoologist Rohwer asserted that plumage variations in "Harris sparrows" support the status signaling hypothesis (SSH). He reported that almost (20) without exception birds with darker throats win conflicts with individuals having lighter plumage. He claimed that even among birds of the same age and sex the amount of dark plumage predicts relative dominance status.

(25) However, Rohwer's data do not support his assertions: in one of his studies darker birds won only 57 out of 75 conflicts; within another, focusing on conflicts between birds of the same age group or sex, darker birds won 63 and lost 62. There are indications (30) that plumage probably does signal broad age-related differences in status among Harris sparrows: adults, usually dark throated, have higher status than juveniles, who are usually light throated; moreover, juveniles dyed to resemble adults are dominant over undyed (35) juveniles. However, the Harris sparrows' age-related plumage differences do not signal the status of *individual* birds within an age class, and thus cannot be included under the term "status signaling."

The best evidence for status signaling is from the (40) greater titmouse. Experiments show a strong correlation between the width of the black breast-plumage stripe and status as measured by success in aggressive interactions. An analysis of factors likely to be associated with breast-stripe width (sex, age, wing (45) length, body weight) has demonstrated social status to be the only variable that correlates with stripe width when the other variables are held constant.

An ingenious experiment provided further evidence for status signaling in the greater titmouse. One of (50) three stuffed titmouse dummies was mounted on a feeding tray. When a live bird approached, the dummy was turned by radio control to face the bird and present its breast stripe in "display." When presented with a dummy having a narrower breast stripe than their own, (55) birds approached closely and behaved aggressively. However, when presented with a dummy having a broader breast stripe than their own, live birds acted submissive and did not approach.

15. According to the passage, the status signaling hypothesis holds that the ability to display a recognizable external signal would have the effect on an individual bird of

(A) enabling it to attract a mate of high status
(B) allowing it to avoid costly aggressive interactions
(C) decreasing its access to limited resources
(D) making it less attractive to predatory species
(E) increasing its fighting ability

16. The author refers to the fact that adult Harris sparrows are usually dark throated (lines 31–32), in order to do which one of the following?

(A) support the conclusion that plumage variation among Harris sparrows probably does not signal individual status
(B) argue that plumage variation among Harris sparrows helps to confirm the status signaling hypothesis
(C) indicate that in light of plumage variation patterns among Harris sparrows, the status signaling hypothesis should probably be modified
(D) demonstrate that Harris sparrows are the most appropriate subjects for the study of status signaling among birds
(E) suggest that the signaling of age-related differences in status is widespread among birds that form flocks

GO ON TO THE NEXT PAGE.

17. Which one of the following, if true, would most seriously undermine the validity of the results of the experiment discussed in the last paragraph?

 (A) The live birds all came from different titmouse flocks.
 (B) The physical characteristics of the stuffed dummies varied in ways other than just breast-stripe width.
 (C) No live juvenile birds were included in the experiment.
 (D) The food placed in the feeding tray was not the kind of food normally eaten by titmice in the wild.
 (E) Even the live birds that acted aggressively did not actually physically attack the stuffed dummies.

18. Which one of the following best describes the organization of the passage?

 (A) A hypothesis is introduced and studies relevant to the hypothesis are discussed and evaluated.
 (B) A natural phenomenon is presented and several explanations for the phenomenon are examined in detail.
 (C) Behavior is described, possible underlying causes for the behavior are reported, and the likelihood of each cause is assessed.
 (D) A scientific conundrum is explained and the history of the issue is recounted.
 (E) A scientific theory is outlined and opinions for and against its validity as well as experiments supporting each side are compared.

19. According to the passage, which one of the following is true of Rohwer's relationship to the status signaling hypothesis (SSH)?

 (A) Although his research was designed to test the SSH, his data proved to be more relevant to other issues.
 (B) He set out to confirm the SSH, but ended up revising it.
 (C) He set out to disprove the SSH, but ended up accepting it.
 (D) He altered the SSH by expanding it to encompass various types of signals.
 (E) He advocated the SSH, but his research data failed to confirm it.

20. The passage suggests that among birds that form flocks, a bird of high status is most likely to have which one of the following?

 (A) dark throat plumage
 (B) greater-than-average body weight
 (C) offspring of high status
 (D) strong fighting ability
 (E) frequent injuries

21. Which one of the following can be inferred about Harris sparrows from the passage?

 (A) Among Harris sparrows, plumage differences signal individual status only within age groups.
 (B) Among Harris sparrows, adults have priority of access to food over juveniles.
 (C) Among Harris sparrows, juveniles with relatively dark plumage have status equal to that of adults with relatively light plumage.
 (D) Juvenile Harris sparrows engage in aggressive interaction more frequently than do adult Harris sparrows.
 (E) Harris sparrows engage in aggressive interaction less frequently than do greater titmice.

GO ON TO THE NEXT PAGE.

In *The Dynamics of Apocalypse,* John Lowe attempts to solve the mystery of the collapse of the Classic Mayan civilization. Lowe bases his study on a detailed examination of the known archaeological
(5) record. Like previous investigators, Lowe relies on dated monuments to construct a step-by-step account of the actual collapse. Using the erection of new monuments as a means to determine a site's occupation span, Lowe assumes that once new monuments ceased
(10) to be built, a site had been abandoned. Lowe's analysis of the evidence suggests that construction of new monuments continued to increase between A.D. 672 and 751, but that the civilization stopped expanding geographically; new construction took place almost
(15) exclusively in established settlements. The first signs of trouble followed. Monument inscriptions indicate that between 751 and 790, long-standing alliances started to break down. Evidence also indicates that between 790 and 830, the death rate in Classic Mayan
(20) cities outstripped the birthrate. After approximately 830, construction stopped throughout the area, and within a hundred years, the Classic Mayan civilization all but vanished.

Having established this chronology, Lowe sets
(25) forth a plausible explanation of the collapse that accommodates the available archaeological evidence. He theorizes that Classic Mayan civilization was brought down by the interaction of several factors, set in motion by population growth. An increase in
(30) population, particularly within the elite segment of society, necessitated ever more intense farming. Agricultural intensification exerted stress on the soil and led to a decline in productivity (the amount of food produced through each unit of labor invested). At the
(35) same time, the growth of the elite class created increasing demands for ceremonial monuments and luxuries, diverting needed labor from the fields. The theory holds that these stresses were communicated— and amplified—throughout the area as Mayan states
(40) engaged in warfare to acquire laborers and food, and refugees fled impoverished areas. The most vulnerable states thus began to break down, and each downfall triggered others, until the entire civilization collapsed.

If there is a central flaw in Lowe's explanation, it is
(45) that the entire edifice rests on the assumption that the available evidence paints a true picture of how the collapse proceeded. However, it is difficult to know how accurately the archaeological record reflects historic activity, especially of a complex civilization
(50) such as the Mayans', and a hypothesis can be tested only against the best available data. It is quite possible that our understanding of the collapse might be radically altered by better data. For example, Lowe's assumption about monument construction and the
(55) occupation span of a site might well be disproved if further investigations of Classic Mayan sites established that some remained heavily settled long after the custom of carving dynastic monuments had ceased.

22. Which one of the following best describes the organization of the passage?

(A) A method used to analyze evidence is described, an explanation of the evidence is suggested, and then a conclusion is drawn from the evidence.

(B) A hypothesis is presented, evidence supporting the hypothesis is provided, and then the hypothesis is affirmed.

(C) An analysis of a study is presented, contradictory evidence is examined, and then a direction for future studies is suggested.

(D) The basis of a study is described, a theory that explains the available evidence is presented, and a possible flaw in the study is pointed out.

(E) An observation is made, evidence supporting the observation is presented, and then contradictions in the evidence are discussed.

23. Which one of the following best expresses the main idea of the passage?

(A) In *The Dynamics of Apocalypse,* John Lowe successfully proves that the collapse of Classic Mayan civilization was set in motion by increasing population and decreasing productivity.

(B) In *The Dynamics of Apocalypse,* John Lowe breaks new ground in solving the mystery of the collapse of Classic Mayan civilization through his use of dated monuments to create a step-by-step account of the collapse.

(C) In *The Dynamics of Apocalypse,* John Lowe successfully uses existing data to document the reduction and then cessation of new construction throughout Classic Mayan civilization.

(D) Although John Lowe's study is based on a careful examination of the historical record, it does not accurately reflect the circumstances surrounding the collapse of Classic Mayan civilization.

(E) While John Lowe's theory about the collapse of Classic Mayan civilization appears credible, it is based on an assumption that cannot be verified using the archaeological record.

GO ON TO THE NEXT PAGE.

24. Which one of the following is most closely analogous to the assumption Lowe makes about the relationship between monument construction and Classic Mayan cities?

(A) A person assumes that the shortage of fresh produce on the shelves of a grocery store is due to the effects of poor weather conditions during the growing season.

(B) A person assumes that a movie theater only shows foreign films because the titles of the films shown there are not familiar to the person.

(C) A person assumes that a restaurant is under new ownership because the restaurant's menu has changed drastically since the last time the person ate there.

(D) A person assumes that a corporation has been sold because there is a new name for the corporation on the sign outside the building where the company is located.

(E) A person assumes a friend has sold her stamp collection because the friend has stopped purchasing new stamps.

25. It can be inferred from the passage that the author would describe the method Lowe used to construct a step-by-step chronology of the actual collapse of Classic Mayan civilization as

(A) daringly innovative but flawed
(B) generally accepted but questionable
(C) very reliable but outdated
(D) unscientific but effective
(E) unconventional but brilliant

26. The author of the passage would most likely agree with which one of the following statements about the use of the archaeological record to reconstruct historic activity?

(A) With careful analysis, archaeological evidence can be used to reconstruct accurately the historic activity of a past civilization.

(B) Archaeological evidence is more useful for reconstructing the day-to-day activities of a culture than its long-term trends.

(C) The accuracy of the archaeological record for reconstructing historic activity is dependent on the duration of the particular civilization.

(D) The archaeological record is not an appropriate source of data for reconstructing historic activity.

(E) Historic activity can be reconstructed from archaeological evidence, but it is ultimately impossible to confirm the accuracy of the reconstruction.

S T O P

IF YOU FINISH BEFORE TIME IS CALLED, YOU MAY CHECK YOUR WORK ON THIS SECTION ONLY.
DO NOT WORK ON ANY OTHER SECTION IN THE TEST.

SECTION III

Time—35 minutes

24 Questions

Directions: Each group of questions in this section is based on a set of conditions. In answering some of the questions, it may be useful to draw a rough diagram. Choose the response that most accurately and completely answers each question and blacken the corresponding space on your answer sheet.

Questions 1–5

Each of seven travelers—Norris, Oribe, Paulsen, Rosen, Semonelli, Tan, and Underwood—will be assigned to exactly one of nine airplane seats. The seats are numbered from 1 through 9 and arranged in rows as follows:

    Front row: 1 2 3
    Middle row: 4 5 6
    Last row: 7 8 9

Only seats in the same row as each other are immediately beside each other. Seat assignments must meet the following conditions:

    Oribe's seat is in the last row.
    Paulsen's seat is immediately beside Rosen's seat and also immediately beside an unassigned seat.
    Rosen's seat is in the row immediately behind the row in which Norris' seat is located.
    Neither Semonelli nor Underwood is seated immediately beside Norris.

1. Which one of the following is a pair of travelers who could be assigned to seats 2 and 8, respectively?

    (A)   Norris, Semonelli
    (B)   Oribe, Underwood
    (C)   Paulsen, Oribe
    (D)   Rosen, Semonelli
    (E)   Underwood, Tan

2. If Semonelli and Underwood are not assigned to seats in the same row as each other, which one of the following must be false?

    (A)   Norris is assigned to seat 2.
    (B)   Paulsen is assigned to seat 5.
    (C)   Rosen is assigned to seat 4.
    (D)   Tan is assigned to seat 2.
    (E)   Underwood is assigned to seat 1.

3. If Semonelli is assigned to a seat in the same row as Underwood, which one of the following travelers could be assigned to a seat immediately beside one of the unassigned seats?

    (A)   Oribe
    (B)   Rosen
    (C)   Semonelli
    (D)   Tan
    (E)   Underwood

4. If the seat to which Tan is assigned is immediately beside a seat assigned to another traveler and also immediately beside one of the unassigned seats, which one of the following must be true?

    (A)   Tan is assigned to a seat in the front row.
    (B)   Tan is assigned to a seat in the last row.
    (C)   Oribe is assigned to a seat immediately beside Semonelli.
    (D)   Oribe is assigned to a seat immediately beside Tan.
    (E)   Semonelli is assigned to a seat immediately beside Underwood.

5. If Oribe is assigned to a seat immediately beside one of the unassigned seats, which one of the following must be true?

    (A)   Oribe is assigned to seat 8.
    (B)   Tan is assigned to seat 2.
    (C)   Underwood is assigned to seat 1.
    (D)   Seat 4 is unassigned.
    (E)   Seat 9 is unassigned.

GO ON TO THE NEXT PAGE.

Questions 6–12

A university library budget committee must reduce exactly five of eight areas of expenditure—G, L, M, N, P, R, S, and W—in accordance with the following conditions:
  If both G and S are reduced, W is also reduced.
  If N is reduced, neither R nor S is reduced.
  If P is reduced, L is not reduced.
  Of the three areas L, M, and R, exactly two are reduced.

6. Which one of the following could be a complete and accurate list of the areas of expenditure reduced by the committee?

  (A) G, L, M, N, W
  (B) G, L, M, P, W
  (C) G, M, N, R, W
  (D) G, M, P, R, S
  (E) L, M, R, S, W

7. If W is reduced, which one of the following could be a complete and accurate list of the four other areas of expenditure to be reduced?

  (A) G, M, P, S
  (B) L, M, N, R
  (C) L, M, P, S
  (D) M, N, P, S
  (E) M, P, R, S

8. If P is reduced, which one of the following is a pair of areas of expenditure both of which must be reduced?

  (A) G, M
  (B) M, R
  (C) N, R
  (D) R, S
  (E) S, W

9. If both L and S are reduced, which one of the following could be a pair of areas of expenditure both of which are reduced?

  (A) G, M
  (B) G, P
  (C) N, R
  (D) N, W
  (E) P, S

10. If R is not reduced, which one of the following must be true?

  (A) G is reduced.
  (B) N is not reduced.
  (C) P is reduced.
  (D) S is reduced.
  (E) W is not reduced.

11. If both M and R are reduced, which one of the following is a pair of areas neither of which could be reduced?

  (A) G, L
  (B) G, N
  (C) L, N
  (D) L, P
  (E) P, S

12. Which one of the following areas must be reduced?

  (A) G
  (B) L
  (C) N
  (D) P
  (E) W

GO ON TO THE NEXT PAGE.

Questions 13–18

A jeweler makes a single strand of beads by threading onto a string in a single direction from a clasp a series of solid-colored beads. Each bead is either green, orange, purple, red, or yellow. The resulting strand satisfies the following specifications:

If a purple bead is adjacent to a yellow bead, any bead that immediately follows and any bead that immediately precedes that pair must be red.

Any pair of beads adjacent to each other that are the same color as each other must be green.

No orange bead can be adjacent to any red bead.

Any portion of the strand containing eight consecutive beads must include at least one bead of each color.

13. If the strand has exactly eight beads, which one of the following is an acceptable order, starting from the clasp, for the eight beads?

  (A) green, red, purple, yellow, red, orange, green, purple
  (B) orange, yellow, red, red, yellow, purple, red, green
  (C) purple, yellow, red, green, green, orange, yellow, orange
  (D) red, orange, red, yellow, purple, green, yellow, green
  (E) red, yellow, purple, red, green, red, green, green

14. If an orange bead is the fourth bead from the clasp, which one of the following is a pair that could be the second and third beads, respectively?

  (A) green, orange
  (B) green, red
  (C) purple, purple
  (D) yellow, green
  (E) yellow, purple

15. If on an eight-bead strand the second, third, and fourth beads from the clasp are red, green, and yellow, respectively, and the sixth and seventh beads are purple and red, respectively, then which one of the following must be true?

  (A) The first bead is purple.
  (B) The fifth bead is green.
  (C) The fifth bead is orange.
  (D) The eighth bead is orange.
  (E) The eighth bead is yellow.

16. If on a six-bead strand the first and second beads from the clasp are purple and yellow, respectively, then the fifth and sixth beads CANNOT be

  (A) green and orange, respectively
  (B) orange and green, respectively
  (C) orange and yellow, respectively
  (D) purple and orange, respectively
  (E) yellow and purple, respectively

17. If on a nine-bead strand the first and fourth beads from the clasp are purple, and the second and fifth beads are yellow, which one of the following could be true?

  (A) The seventh bead is orange.
  (B) The eighth bead is green.
  (C) The eighth bead is red.
  (D) The ninth bead is red.
  (E) The ninth bead is yellow.

18. If on an eight-bead strand the first, second, third, and fourth beads from the clasp are red, yellow, green, and red, respectively, then the fifth and sixth beads CANNOT be

  (A) green and orange, respectively
  (B) green and purple, respectively
  (C) purple and orange, respectively
  (D) purple and yellow, respectively
  (E) yellow and orange, respectively

GO ON TO THE NEXT PAGE.

Questions 19–24

At an evening concert, a total of six songs—O, P, T, X, Y, and Z—will be performed by three vocalists—George, Helen, and Leslie. The songs will be sung consecutively as solos, and each will be performed exactly once. The following constraints govern the composition of the concert program:

    Y must be performed earlier than T and earlier than O.
    P must be performed earlier than Z and later than O.
    George can perform only X, Y, and Z.
    Helen can perform only T, P, and X.
    Leslie can perform only O, P, and X.
    The vocalist who performs first must be different from the vocalist who performs last.

19. Which one of the following is an acceptable schedule for the performance of the songs, in order from the first to last song performed?

    (A)   X, T, Y, O, P, Z
    (B)   X, Z, Y, T, O, P
    (C)   Y, O, P, X, T, Z
    (D)   Y, P, O, Z, T, X
    (E)   Y, X, O, P, Z, T

20. Which one of the following must be true about the program?

    (A)   George performs X.
    (B)   Helen performs O.
    (C)   Helen performs T.
    (D)   Leslie performs P.
    (E)   Leslie performs X.

21. Which one of the following is a complete and accurate list of the songs any one of which could be the last song performed at the concert?

    (A)   O, P, Z
    (B)   O, T, X
    (C)   T, P, Z
    (D)   T, X, Z
    (E)   X, P, Z

22. If X is performed first, which one of the following must be true?

    (A)   X is performed by George.
    (B)   X is performed by Helen.
    (C)   P is the fourth song performed.
    (D)   Y is the second song performed.
    (E)   Y is the third song performed.

23. Each of the following is an acceptable schedule for the performance of the songs, in order from the first to last song performed, EXCEPT:

    (A)   Y, O, P, T, Z, X
    (B)   Y, T, O, P, X, Z
    (C)   Y, X, O, P, Z, T
    (D)   X, Y, O, P, Z, T
    (E)   X, Y, O, T, P, Z

24. If Y is performed first, the songs performed second, third, and fourth, respectively, could be

    (A)   T, X, and O
    (B)   T, Z, and O
    (C)   X, O, and P
    (D)   X, P, and Z
    (E)   X, T, and O

S T O P

IF YOU FINISH BEFORE TIME IS CALLED, YOU MAY CHECK YOUR WORK ON THIS SECTION ONLY.
DO NOT WORK ON ANY OTHER SECTION IN THE TEST.

SECTION IV

Time—35 minutes

26 Questions

Directions: The questions in this section are based on the reasoning contained in brief statements or passages. For some questions, more than one of the choices could conceivably answer the question. However, you are to choose the best answer; that is, the response that most accurately and completely answers the question. You should not make assumptions that are by commonsense standards implausible, superfluous, or incompatible with the passage. After you have chosen the best answer, blacken the corresponding space on your answer sheet.

1. Critic: People today place an especially high value on respect for others; yet, in their comedy acts, many of today's most popular comedians display blatant disrespect for others. But when people fail to live up to the very ideals they hold in highest esteem, exaggeration of such failings often forms the basis of successful comedy. Thus the current popularity of comedians who display disrespect in their acts is hardly surprising.

The critic's argument depends on which one of the following assumptions?

(A)   People who enjoy comedians who display disrespect in their acts do not place a high value on respect for others.

(B)   Only comedians who display blatant disrespect in their acts are currently successful.

(C)   Many people disapprove of the portrayal of blatant disrespect for others in comedy acts.

(D)   People who value an ideal especially highly do not always succeed in living up to this ideal.

(E)   People today fail to live up to their own ideals more frequently than was the case in the past.

2. The law firm of Sutherlin, Pérez, and Associates is one of the most successful law firms whose primary specialization is in criminal defense cases. In fact, the firm has a better than 90 percent acquittal rate in such cases. Dalton is an attorney whose primary specialization is in divorce cases, so Dalton certainly cannot be a member of Sutherlin, Pérez, and Associates.

The reasoning in the argument is flawed because the argument

(A)   offers in support of its conclusion pieces of evidence that are mutually contradictory

(B)   overlooks the possibility that a person can practice law without being a member of a law firm

(C)   concludes that someone is not a member of a group on the grounds that that person does not have a characteristic that the group as a whole has

(D)   takes a high rate of success among the members of a group to indicate that the successes are evenly spread among the members

(E)   states a generalization based on a selection that is not representative of the group about which the generalization is supposed to hold true

3. Opponents of allowing triple-trailer trucks to use the national highway system are wrong in claiming that these trucks are more dangerous than other commercial vehicles. In the western part of the country, in areas where triple-trailers are now permitted on some highways, for these vehicles the rate of road accident fatalities per mile of travel is lower than the national rate for other types of commercial vehicles. Clearly, triple-trailers are safer than other commercial vehicles.

Which one of the following, if true, most substantially weakens the argument?

(A)   It takes two smaller semitrailers to haul as much weight as a single triple-trailer can.

(B)   Highways in the sparsely populated West are much less heavily traveled and consequently are far safer than highways in the national system as a whole.

(C)   Opponents of the triple-trailers also once opposed the shorter twin-trailers, which are now common on the nation's highways.

(D)   In areas where the triple-trailers are permitted, drivers need a special license to operate them.

(E)   For triple-trailers the rate of road accident fatalities per mile of travel was higher last year than in the two previous years.

4. Whittaker: There can be no such thing as the number of medical school students who drop out before their second year, because if they drop out, they never have a second year.

Hudson: By your reasoning I cannot help but become rich, because there is similarly no such thing as my dying before my first million dollars is in the bank.

Hudson responds to Whittaker by

(A)   showing that a relevantly analogous argument leads to an untenable conclusion

(B)   citing a specific example to counter Whittaker's general claim

(C)   pointing out that Whittaker mistakes a necessary situation for a possible situation

(D)   claiming that what Whittaker says cannot be true because Whittaker acts as if it were false

(E)   showing that Whittaker's argument relies on analyzing an extreme and unrepresentative case

GO ON TO THE NEXT PAGE.

5. A newly developed light bulb is much more cost-effective than conventional light bulbs: it costs only about 3 times what a conventional light bulb costs but it lasts up to 10 times as long as a conventional light bulb. Despite the manufacturer's intense efforts to publicize the advantages of the new bulb, one analyst predicts that these new bulbs will prove to sell very poorly.

Each of the following, if true, provides support for the analyst's prediction EXCEPT:

(A) The light generated by the new bulb is in the yellow range of the spectrum, a type of artificial light most people find unappealing.

(B) Most people who purchase light bulbs prefer to buy inexpensive light bulbs rather than more durable but expensive light bulbs.

(C) A manufacturer of one brand of conventional light bulb has advertised claims that the new light bulb uses more electricity than do conventional light bulbs.

(D) The new bulb is to be marketed in several different quantities, ranging from packages containing one bulb to packages containing four bulbs.

(E) A competing manufacturer is about to introduce a light bulb that lasts 10 times as long as a conventional bulb but costs less than a conventional bulb.

6. The *Rienzi,* a passenger ship, sank as a result of a hole in its hull, possibly caused by sabotage. Normally, when a holed ship sinks as rapidly as the *Rienzi* did, water does not enter the ship quickly enough for the ship to be fully flooded when it reaches the ocean floor. Full flooding can be achieved, however, by sabotage. Any ship that sinks deep into the ocean when not fully flooded will implode. Deep-sea photographs, taken of the sunken *Rienzi* where it rests on the ocean floor, reveal that the *Rienzi* did not implode.

Which one of the following must be true on the basis of the information above?

(A) The *Rienzi* was so constructed as to reduce the risk of sinking by impact.

(B) If the *Rienzi* became fully flooded, it did so only after it reached the ocean floor.

(C) If the *Rienzi* was not sunk by sabotage, water flooded into it unusually fast.

(D) If the *Rienzi* had sunk more slowly, it would have imploded.

(E) The *Rienzi* was so strongly constructed as to resist imploding under deep-sea pressure.

7. For every 50 dogs that contract a certain disease, one will die from it. A vaccine exists that is virtually 100 percent effective in preventing this disease. Since the risk of death from complications of vaccination is one death per 5,000 vaccinations, it is therefore safer for a dog to receive the vaccine than not to receive it.

Which one of the following would it be most helpful to know in order to evaluate the argument?

(A) the total number of dogs that die each year from all causes taken together

(B) whether the vaccine is effective against the disease in household pets other than dogs

(C) the number of dogs that die each year from diseases other than the disease in question

(D) the likelihood that a dog will contract another disease such as rabies

(E) the likelihood that an unvaccinated dog will contract the disease in question

8. The symptoms of mental disorders are behavioral, cognitive, or emotional problems. Some patients with mental disorders can be effectively treated with psychotherapy. But it is now known that in some patients mental disorders result from chemical imbalances affecting the brain. Thus these patients can be effectively treated only with medication that will reduce or correct the imbalance.

The argument depends on assuming which one of the following?

(A) Treatment by psychotherapy can produce no effective reduction in or correction of chemical imbalances that cause mental disorders.

(B) Treatment with medication always shows faster results for patients with mental disorders than does treatment with psychotherapy.

(C) Most mental disorders are not the result of chemical imbalances affecting the brain.

(D) Medication is always more effective in treating patients with mental disorders than is psychotherapy.

(E) Treatment with psychotherapy has no effect on mental disorders other than a reduction of the symptoms.

GO ON TO THE NEXT PAGE.

Questions 9–10

Curator: The decision to restore the cloak of the central figure in Veronese's painting from its present red to the green found underneath is fully justified. Reliable x-ray and chemical tests show that the red pigment was applied after the painting had been completed, and that the red paint was not mixed in Veronese's workshop. Hence it appears likely that an artist other than Veronese tampered with Veronese's painting after its completion.

Art critic: But in a copy of Veronese's painting made shortly after Veronese died, the cloak is red. It is highly unlikely that a copyist would have made so major a change so soon after Veronese's death.

9. The assertion that a later artist tampered with Veronese's painting serves which one of the following functions in the curator's argument?

   (A) It is the main point toward which the argument as a whole is directed.
   (B) It is a subsidiary conclusion that supports the argument's main conclusion.
   (C) It is a clarification of a key term of the argument.
   (D) It is a particular instance of the general position to be defended.
   (E) It is a reiteration of the main point that is made for the sake of emphasis.

10. The art critic's response to the curator would provide the strongest support for which one of the following conclusions?

    (A) The copy of Veronese's painting that was made soon after the painter's death is indistinguishable from the original.
    (B) No painting should be restored before the painting is tested with technologically sophisticated equipment.
    (C) The proposed restoration will fail to restore Veronese's painting to the appearance it had at the end of the artist's lifetime.
    (D) The value of an artist's work is not necessarily compromised when that work is tampered with by later artists.
    (E) Veronese did not originally intend the central figure's cloak to be green.

11. John works five days each week except when on vacation or during weeks in which national holidays occur. Four days a week he works in an insurance company; on Fridays he works as a blacksmith. Last week there were no holidays, and John was not on vacation. Therefore, he must have worked in the insurance company on Monday, Tuesday, Wednesday, and Thursday last week.

    Which one of the following is an assumption on which the argument depends?

    (A) John never takes a vacation of more than one week in length.
    (B) Every day last week that John worked, he worked for an entire workday.
    (C) John does not take vacations in weeks in which national holidays occur.
    (D) Last week John worked neither on Saturday nor on Sunday.
    (E) There were no days last week on which John both worked in the insurance company and also worked as a blacksmith.

12. After several attempts to distract his young parrot from chewing on furniture, George reluctantly took an expert's advice and gently hit the parrot's beak whenever the bird started to chew furniture. The bird stopped chewing furniture, but it is now afraid of hands and will sometimes bite. Since chewing on the furniture would not have hurt the bird, George should not have hit it.

    When Carla's puppy escaped from her yard, it bounded into a busy street. Although Carla does not generally approve of physical discipline, she hit the puppy sharply with her hand. Now the puppy enters the street only when accompanied by Carla, so Carla was justified in disciplining the puppy.

    Which one of the following principles, if established, would justify the judgments about George's and Carla's actions?

    (A) When disciplining an animal physically, a trainer should use an object such as a rolled up newspaper to avoid making the animal frightened of hands.
    (B) When training an animal, physical discipline should be used only when such discipline is necessary to correct behavior that could result in serious harm to the animal.
    (C) Using physical discipline to train an animal is justified only when all alternative strategies for correcting undesirable behavior have failed.
    (D) Physical discipline should not be used on immature animals.
    (E) Physical discipline should not be used by an animal trainer except to correct persistent behavior problems.

GO ON TO THE NEXT PAGE.

13. Mature white pines intercept almost all the sunlight that shines on them. They leave a deep litter that dries readily, and they grow to prodigious height so that, even when there are large gaps in a stand of such trees, little light reaches the forest floor. For this reason white pines cannot regenerate in their own shade. Thus, when in a dense forest a stand of trees consists of nothing but mature white pines, it is a fair bet that _____ .

Which one of the following most logically concludes the argument?

(A) the ages of the trees in the stand do not differ from each other by much more than the length of time it takes a white pine to grow to maturity

(B) the land on which the stand is now growing had been cleared of all trees at the time when the first of the white pines started growing

(C) competition among the trees in the stand for sunlight will soon result in some trees' dying and the stand thus becoming thinner

(D) other species of trees will soon begin to colonize the stand, eventually replacing all of the white pines

(E) any differences in the heights of the trees in the stand are attributable solely to differences in the ages of the trees

14. Advertisement: A leading economist has determined that among people who used computers at their place of employment last year, those who also owned portable ("laptop") computers earned 25 percent more on average than those who did not. It is obvious from this that owning a laptop computer led to a higher-paying job.

Which one of the following identifies a reasoning error in the argument?

(A) It attempts to support a sweeping generalization on the basis of information about only a small number of individuals.

(B) Its conclusion merely restates a claim made earlier in the argument.

(C) It concludes that one thing was caused by another although the evidence given is consistent with the first thing's having caused the second.

(D) It offers information as support for a conclusion when that information actually shows that the conclusion is false.

(E) It uncritically projects currently existing trends indefinitely into the future.

15. Rhonda will see the movie tomorrow afternoon only if Paul goes to the concert in the afternoon. Paul will not go to the concert unless Ted agrees to go to the concert. However, Ted refuses to go to the concert. So Rhonda will not see the movie tomorrow afternoon.

The pattern of reasoning displayed above is most closely paralleled in which one of the following?

(A) If Janice comes to visit, Mary will not pay the bills tomorrow. Janice will not come to visit unless she locates a babysitter. However, Janice has located a babysitter, so she will visit Mary.

(B) Gary will do his laundry tomorrow only if Peter has to go to work. Unless Cathy is ill, Peter will not have to go to work. Since Cathy is not ill, Gary will not do his laundry tomorrow.

(C) Kelly will barbecue fish tonight if it does not rain and the market has fresh trout. Although the forecast does not call for rain, the market does not have fresh trout. So Kelly will not barbecue fish tonight.

(D) Lisa will attend the family reunion next week only if one of her brothers, Jared or Karl, also attends. Karl will not attend the reunion, but Jared will. So Lisa will attend the reunion.

(E) George will not go to the museum tomorrow unless Mark agrees to go. Mark will go to the museum only if he can postpone most of his appointments. Mark has postponed some of his appointments, so he will go to the museum.

GO ON TO THE NEXT PAGE.

16. Private industry is trying to attract skilled research scientists by offering them high salaries. As a result, most research scientists employed in private industry now earn 50 percent more than do comparably skilled research scientists employed by the government. So, unless government-employed research scientists are motivated more by a sense of public duty than by their own interests, the government is likely to lose its most skilled research scientists to private industry, since none of these scientists would have problems finding private-sector jobs.

Which one of the following is an assumption on which the argument depends?

(A) Government research scientists are less likely to receive acknowledgment for their research contributions than are research scientists in the private sector.

(B) None of the research scientists currently employed by the government earns more than the highest-paid researchers employed in the private sector.

(C) The government does not employ as many research scientists who are highly skilled as does any large company in the private sector which employs research scientists.

(D) The government does not provide its research scientists with unusually good working conditions or fringe benefits that more than compensate for the lower salaries they receive.

(E) Research scientists employed in the private sector generally work longer hours than do researchers employed by the government.

17. Using fossil energy more efficiently is in the interest of the nation and the global environment, but major improvements are unlikely unless proposed government standards are implemented to eliminate products or practices that are among the least efficient in their class.

Objection: Decisions on energy use are best left to the operation of the market.

Which one of the following, if true, most directly undermines the objection above?

(A) It would be unrealistic to expect society to make the changes necessary to achieve maximum energy efficiency all at once.

(B) There are products, such as automobiles, that consume energy at a sufficient rate that persons who purchase and use them will become conscious of any unusual energy inefficiency in comparison with other products in the same class.

(C) Whenever a new mode of generating energy, such as a new fuel, is introduced, a number of support systems, such as a fuel-distribution system, must be created or adapted.

(D) When energy prices rise, consumers of energy tend to look for new ways to increase energy efficiency, such as by adding insulation to their houses.

(E) Often the purchaser of a product, such as a landlord buying an appliance, chooses on the basis of purchase price because the purchaser is not the person who will pay for energy used by the product.

GO ON TO THE NEXT PAGE.

18. Dobson: Some historians claim that the people who built a ring of stones thousands of years ago in Britain were knowledgeable about celestial events. The ground for this claim is that two of the stones determine a line pointing directly to the position of the sun at sunrise at the spring equinox. There are many stones in the ring, however, so the chance that one pair will point in a celestially significant direction is large. Therefore, the people who built the ring were not knowledgeable about celestial events.

Which one of the following is an error of reasoning in Dobson's argument?

(A) The failure of cited evidence to establish a statement is taken as evidence that that statement is false.

(B) Dobson's conclusion logically contradicts some of the evidence presented in support of it.

(C) Statements that absolutely establish Dobson's conclusion are treated as if they merely give some support to that conclusion.

(D) Something that is merely a matter of opinion is treated as if it were subject to verification as a matter of fact.

(E) Dobson's drawing the conclusion relies on interpreting a key term in two different ways.

19. Nearly all mail that is correctly addressed arrives at its destination within two business days of being sent. In fact, correctly addressed mail takes longer than this only when it is damaged in transit. Overall, however, most mail arrives three business days or more after being sent.

If the statements above are true, which one of the following must be true?

(A) A large proportion of the mail that is correctly addressed is damaged in transit.

(B) No incorrectly addressed mail arrives within two business days of being sent.

(C) Most mail that arrives within two business days of being sent is correctly addressed.

(D) A large proportion of mail is incorrectly addressed.

(E) More mail arrives within two business days of being sent than arrives between two and three business days after being sent.

20. The report released by the interior ministry states that within the past 5 years the national land-reclamation program has resulted in a 19 percent increase in the amount of arable land within the country. If these figures are accurate, the program has been a resounding success. Senator Armand, a distinguished mathematician and a woman of indisputable brilliance, maintains, however, that the reclamation program could not possibly have been successful. Clearly, therefore, the figures cited in the report cannot be accurate.

The argument above exhibits an erroneous pattern of reasoning most similar to that exhibited by which one of the following?

(A) Albert's father claims that Albert does not know where the spare car keys are hidden. Yesterday, however, Albert reported that he had discovered the spare car keys in the garage toolbox, so his father's claim cannot be true.

(B) Gloria's drama teacher claims that her policy is to give each student the opportunity to act in at least one play during the year but, since Gloria, who attended every class, reports that she was not given such an opportunity, the teacher's claim cannot be true.

(C) Amos claims that he can hold his breath under water for a full hour. Dr. Treviso, a cardiopulmonary specialist, has stated that humans are physiologically incapable of holding their breath for even half that long; so Amos' claim cannot be true.

(D) Evelyn reports that she got home before midnight. Robert, who always knows the time, insists that she did not. If Robert is right, Evelyn could not possibly have listened to the late news; since she admits not having listened to the late news, her report cannot be true.

(E) Moira, after observing the finish of the 60-kilometer bicycle race, reports that Lee won with Adams a distant third. Lomas, a bicycle engineering expert, insists, however, that Lee could not have won a race in which Adams competed; so Moira's report cannot be true.

GO ON TO THE NEXT PAGE.

Questions 21–22

Wirth: All efforts to identify a gene responsible for predisposing people to manic-depression have failed. In fact, nearly all researchers now agree that there is no "manic-depression gene." Therefore, if these researchers are right, any claim that some people are genetically predisposed to manic-depression is simply false.

Chang: I do not dispute your evidence, but I take issue with your conclusion. Many of the researchers you refer to have found evidence that a set of several genes is involved and that complex interactions among these genes produce a predisposition to manic-depression.

21. The point at issue between Wirth and Chang is whether

(A)   efforts to identify a gene or set of several genes responsible for predisposing people to manic-depression have all failed

(B)   it is likely that researchers will ever be able to find a single gene that predisposes people to manic-depression

(C)   nearly all researchers now agree that there is no manic-depression gene

(D)   current research supports the claim that no one is genetically predisposed to manic-depression

(E)   the efforts made to find a gene that can produce a predisposition to manic-depression were thorough

22. Which one of the following most accurately expresses Chang's criticism of Wirth's argument?

(A)   It presupposes only one possibility where more than one exists.

(B)   It depends on separate pieces of evidence that contradict each other.

(C)   It relies on the opinion of experts in an area outside the experts' field of expertise.

(D)   It disallows in principle any evidence that would disconfirm its conclusion.

(E)   It treats something that is merely unlikely as though it were impossible.

23. Garbage dumps do not harm wildlife. Evidence is furnished by the Masai-Mara reserve in Kenya, where baboons that use the garbage dumps on the reserve as a food source mature faster and have more offspring than do baboons on the reserve that do not scavenge on garbage.

Each of the following statements, if true, casts doubt on the argument EXCEPT:

(A)   The baboons that feed on the garbage dump are of a different species from those that do not.

(B)   The life expectancy of baboons that eat garbage is significantly lower than that of baboons that do not eat garbage.

(C)   The cholesterol level of garbage-eating baboons is dangerously higher than that of baboons that do not eat garbage.

(D)   The population of hyenas that live near unregulated garbage landfills north of the reserve has doubled in the last two years.

(E)   The rate of birth defects for the baboon population on the reserve has doubled since the first landfills were opened.

GO ON TO THE NEXT PAGE.

Questions 24–25

Marianne is a professional chess player who hums audibly while playing her matches, thereby distracting her opponents. When ordered by chess officials to cease humming or else be disqualified from professional chess, Marianne protested the order. She argued that since she was unaware of her humming, her humming was involuntary and that therefore she should not be held responsible for it.

24. Which one of the following principles, if valid, most helps to support Marianne's argument against the order?

(A) Chess players who hum audibly while playing their matches should not protest if their opponents also hum.

(B) Of a player's actions, only those that are voluntary should be used as justification for disqualifying that player from professional chess.

(C) A person should be held responsible for those involuntary actions that serve that person's interests.

(D) Types of behavior that are not considered voluntary in everyday circumstances should be considered voluntary if they occur in the context of a professional chess match.

(E) Chess players should be disqualified from professional chess matches if they regularly attempt to distract their opponents.

25. Which one of the following, if true, most undermines Marianne's argument against the order?

(A) The officials of chess have little or no authority to control the behavior of its professional players outside of matches.

(B) Many of the customs of amateur chess matches are not observed by professional chess players.

(C) Not all of a person's involuntary actions are actions of which that person is unaware.

(D) A person who hums involuntarily can easily learn to notice it and can thereby come to control it.

(E) Not all of Marianne's opponents are distracted by her humming during chess matches.

26. Smoking in bed has long been the main cause of home fires. Despite a significant decline in cigarette smoking in the last two decades, however, there has been no comparable decline in the number of people killed in home fires.

Each one of the following statements, if true over the last two decades, helps to resolve the apparent discrepancy above EXCEPT:

(A) Compared to other types of home fires, home fires caused by smoking in bed usually cause relatively little damage before they are extinguished.

(B) Home fires caused by smoking in bed often break out after the home's occupants have fallen asleep.

(C) Smokers who smoke in bed tend to be heavy smokers who are less likely to quit smoking than are smokers who do not smoke in bed.

(D) An increasing number of people have been killed in home fires that started in the kitchen.

(E) Population densities have increased, with the result that one home fire can cause more deaths than in previous decades.

S T O P

IF YOU FINISH BEFORE TIME IS CALLED, YOU MAY CHECK YOUR WORK ON THIS SECTION ONLY.
DO NOT WORK ON ANY OTHER SECTION IN THE TEST.

LSAT® Writing Sample Topic

Roberto Martinez, owner of a small used book store, has recently purchased an adjacent store and is deciding how best to use it to expand his business. Write an argument in support of one plan over the other based on the following criteria:

- Martinez wants to attract a significant number of new customers.
- Martinez wants to retain the loyal clientele who look to him for out-of-print books and first editions.

One plan is for Martinez to begin carrying best-sellers and popular fiction. Because of his downtown location, publishers of these works are likely to put his store on their book tours; although the large bookstore chains have taken hold in the suburbs, none has yet located in the downtown area. Under this plan, however, Martinez would have enough room to keep only the best books from his current inventory. To capitalize on this collection, he is considering an occasional evening series called "Rediscoveries," featuring discussions of authors whose out-of-print books he carries, particularly several authors who are currently enjoying a resurgence of critical attention.

An alternative plan is for Martinez to use the new space to open a small coffeehouse with a limited menu. He would furnish the area as a sitting room with couches and chairs and a few regular dining tables. Although there are several restaurants nearby, they offer primarily full meals in more formal settings. Retaining much of his inventory of used books, he would add novels, poetry, and nonfiction published by small presses to feature lesser-known writers whose work is difficult to find in this community. These small presses include a number of local authors who are eager to read and discuss their work in the coffeehouse.

Directions:

1. Use the Answer Key on the next page to check your answers.

2. Use the Scoring Worksheet below to compute your raw score.

3. Use the Score Conversion Chart to convert your raw score into the 120-180 scale.

Scoring Worksheet

1. Enter the number of questions you answered correctly in each section.

Number Correct

SECTION I . . . . . . _____
SECTION II . . . . . _____
SECTION III . . . . . _____
SECTION IV . . . . . _____

2. Enter the sum here: _____
This is your Raw Score.

Conversion Chart
For Converting Raw Score to the 120-180 LSAT Scaled Score
LSAT Form 7LSS33

Reported Score	Raw Score Lowest	Raw Score Highest
180	99	101
179	98	98
178	97	97
177	96	96
176	95	95
175	94	94
174	93	93
173	92	92
172	91	91
171	90	90
170	89	89
169	88	88
168	86	87
167	85	85
166	84	84
165	82	83
164	81	81
163	79	80
162	78	78
161	76	77
160	75	75
159	73	74
158	71	72
157	69	70
156	68	68
155	66	67
154	64	65
153	63	63
152	61	62
151	59	60
150	57	58
149	55	56
148	54	54
147	52	53
146	50	51
145	49	49
144	47	48
143	45	46
142	44	44
141	42	43
140	40	41
139	39	39
138	37	38
137	36	36
136	34	35
135	33	33
134	31	32
133	30	30
132	29	29
131	27	28
130	26	26
129	25	25
128	23	24
127	22	22
126	21	21
125	20	20
124	19	19
123	18	18
122	17	17
121	16	16
120	0	15

SECTION I

1.	B	8.	B	15.	C	22.	E
2.	A	9.	C	16.	A	23.	E
3.	B	10.	C	17.	D	24.	B
4.	B	11.	D	18.	C	25.	D
5.	E	12.	D	19.	D		
6.	D	13.	D	20.	C		
7.	E	14.	C	21.	A		

SECTION II

1.	B	8.	A	15.	B	22.	D
2.	E	9.	B	16.	A	23.	E
3.	A	10.	C	17.	B	24.	E
4.	E	11.	A	18.	A	25.	B
5.	D	12.	B	19.	E	26.	E
6.	B	13.	B	20.	D		
7.	C	14.	C	21.	B		

SECTION III

1.	A	8.	B	15.	C	22.	D
2.	A	9.	A	16.	E	23.	B
3.	D	10.	A	17.	E	24.	C
4.	A	11.	C	18.	D		
5.	B	12.	E	19.	E		
6.	A	13.	C	20.	C		
7.	E	14.	D	21.	D		

SECTION IV

1.	D	8.	A	15.	B	22.	A
2.	C	9.	B	16.	D	23.	D
3.	B	10.	C	17.	E	24.	B
4.	A	11.	D	18.	A	25.	D
5.	D	12.	B	19.	D	26.	B
6.	C	13.	A	20.	E		
7.	E	14.	C	21.	D		

The Official LSAT PrepTest 2

- December 1996
- Form 6LSS30

The sample test that follows consists of four sections corresponding to the four scored sections of the December 1996 LSAT.

SECTION I

Time—35 minutes

24 Questions

<u>Directions:</u> Each group of questions in this section is based on a set of conditions. In answering some of the questions, it may be useful to draw a rough diagram. Choose the response that most accurately and completely answers each question and blacken the corresponding space on your answer sheet.

<u>Questions 1–6</u>

Seven students—fourth-year students Kim and Lee; third-year students Pat and Robin; and second-year students Sandy, Terry, and Val—and only those seven, are being assigned to rooms of equal size in a dormitory. Each room assigned must have either one, or two, or three students assigned to it, and will accordingly be called either a single, or a double, or a triple. The seven students are assigned to rooms in accordance with the following conditions:

No fourth-year student can be assigned to a triple.
No second-year student can be assigned to a single.
Lee and Robin must not share the same room.
Kim and Pat must share the same room.

1. Which one of the following is a combination of rooms to which the seven students could be assigned?

    (A)   two triples and one single
    (B)   one triple and four singles
    (C)   three doubles and a single
    (D)   two doubles and three singles
    (E)   one double and five singles

2. If the room assigned to Robin is a single, which one of the following could be true?

    (A)   There is exactly one double that has a second-year student assigned to it.
    (B)   Lee is assigned to a single.
    (C)   Sandy, Pat, and one other student are assigned to a triple together.
    (D)   Exactly three of the rooms assigned to the students are singles.
    (E)   Exactly two of the rooms assigned to the students are doubles.

3. Which one of the following must be true?

    (A)   Lee is assigned to a single.
    (B)   Pat shares a double with another student.
    (C)   Robin shares a double with another student.
    (D)   Two of the second-year students share a double with each other.
    (E)   Neither of the third-year students is assigned to a single.

4. If Robin is assigned to a triple, which one of the following must be true?

    (A)   Lee is assigned to a single.
    (B)   Two second-year students share a double with each other.
    (C)   None of the rooms assigned to the students is a single.
    (D)   Two of the rooms assigned to the students are singles.
    (E)   Three of the rooms assigned to the students are singles.

5. If Terry and Val are assigned to different doubles from each other, then it must be true of the students' rooms that exactly

    (A)   one is a single
    (B)   two are singles
    (C)   two are doubles
    (D)   one is a triple
    (E)   two are triples

6. Which one of the following could be true?

    (A)   The two fourth-year students are assigned to singles.
    (B)   The two fourth-year students share a double with each other.
    (C)   Lee shares a room with a second-year student.
    (D)   Lee shares a room with a third-year student.
    (E)   Pat shares a triple with two other students.

GO ON TO THE NEXT PAGE.

Questions 7–11

A worker will insert colored light bulbs into a billboard equipped with exactly three light sockets, which are labeled lights 1, 2, and 3. The worker has three green bulbs, three purple bulbs, and three yellow bulbs. Selection of bulbs for the sockets is governed by the following conditions:

Whenever light 1 is purple, light 2 must be yellow.
Whenever light 2 is green, light 1 must be green.
Whenever light 3 is either purple or yellow, light 2 must be purple.

7. Which one of the following could be an accurate list of the colors of light bulbs selected for lights 1, 2, and 3, respectively?

(A) green, green, yellow
(B) purple, green, green
(C) purple, purple, green
(D) yellow, purple, green
(E) yellow, yellow, yellow

8. If light 1 is yellow, then any of the following can be true, EXCEPT:

(A) Light 2 is green.
(B) Light 2 is purple.
(C) Light 3 is green.
(D) Light 3 is purple.
(E) Light 3 is yellow.

9. There is exactly one possible color sequence of the three lights if which one of the following is true?

(A) Light 1 is purple.
(B) Light 2 is purple.
(C) Light 2 is yellow.
(D) Light 3 is purple.
(E) Light 3 is yellow.

10. If no green bulbs are selected, there are exactly how many possible different color sequences of the three lights?

(A) one
(B) two
(C) three
(D) four
(E) five

11. If no two lights are assigned light bulbs that are the same color as each other, then which one of the following could be true?

(A) Light 1 is green, and light 2 is purple.
(B) Light 1 is green, and light 2 is yellow.
(C) Light 1 is purple, and light 3 is yellow.
(D) Light 1 is yellow, and light 2 is green.
(E) Light 1 is yellow, and light 3 is purple.

GO ON TO THE NEXT PAGE.

Questions 12–17

An attorney is scheduling interviews with witnesses for a given week, Monday through Saturday. Two full consecutive days of the week must be reserved for interviewing hostile witnesses. In addition, nonhostile witnesses Q, R, U, X, Y, and Z will each be interviewed exactly once for a full morning or afternoon. The only witnesses who will be interviewed simultaneously with each other are Q and R. The following conditions apply:

X must be interviewed on Thursday morning.
Q must be interviewed at some time before X.
U must be interviewed at some time before R.
Z must be interviewed at some time after X and at some time after Y.

12. Which one of the following is a sequence, from first to last, in which the nonhostile witnesses could be interviewed?

(A)   Q with R, U, X, Y, Z
(B)   Q, U, R, X with Y, Z
(C)   U, X, Q with R, Y, Z
(D)   U, Y, Q with R, X, Z
(E)   X, Q with U, Z, R, Y

13. Which one of the following is acceptable as a complete schedule of witnesses for Tuesday morning, Tuesday afternoon, and Wednesday morning, respectively?

(A)   Q, R, none
(B)   R, none, Y
(C)   U, none, X
(D)   U, Y, none
(E)   Y, Z, none

14. If Y is interviewed at some time after X, which one of the following must be a day reserved for interviewing hostile witnesses?

(A)   Monday
(B)   Tuesday
(C)   Wednesday
(D)   Friday
(E)   Saturday

15. If R is interviewed at some time after Y, which one of the following must be a day reserved for interviewing hostile witnesses?

(A)   Monday
(B)   Tuesday
(C)   Wednesday
(D)   Thursday
(E)   Friday

16. If on Wednesday afternoon and on Monday the attorney conducts no interviews, which one of the following must be true?

(A)   Q is interviewed on the same day as U.
(B)   R is interviewed on the same day as Y.
(C)   Y is interviewed at some time before U.
(D)   Y is interviewed at some time before Wednesday.
(E)   Z is interviewed at some time before Friday.

17. If Z is interviewed on Saturday morning, which one of the following can be true?

(A)   Wednesday is a day reserved for interviewing hostile witnesses.
(B)   Friday is a day reserved for interviewing hostile witnesses.
(C)   R is interviewed on Thursday.
(D)   U is interviewed on Tuesday.
(E)   Y is interviewed at some time before Thursday.

GO ON TO THE NEXT PAGE.

Questions 18–24

During a four-week period, each of seven previously unadvertised products—G, H, J, K, L, M, and O—will be advertised. A different pair of these products will be advertised each week. Exactly one of the products will be a member of two of these four pairs. The following constraints must be observed:

J is not advertised during a given week unless H is advertised during the immediately preceding week.

The product that is advertised during two of the weeks is advertised during week 4 but is not advertised during week 3.

G is not advertised during a given week unless either J or else O is also advertised that week.

K is advertised during one of the first two weeks.

O is one of the products advertised during week 3.

18. Which one of the following could be the schedule of advertisements?

   (A)   week 1: G, J; week 2: K, L; week 3: O, M; week 4: H, L

   (B)   week 1: H, K; week 2: J, G; week 3: O, L; week 4: M, K

   (C)   week 1: H, K; week 2: J, M; week 3: O, L; week 4: G, M

   (D)   week 1: H, L; week 2: J, M; week 3: O, G; week 4: K, L

   (E)   week 1: K, M; week 2: H, J; week 3: O, G; week 4: L, M

19. Which one of the following is a pair of products that CANNOT be advertised during the same week as each other?

   (A)   H and K
   (B)   H and M
   (C)   J and O
   (D)   K and L
   (E)   L and M

20. Which one of the following must be advertised during week 2 ?

   (A)   G
   (B)   J
   (C)   K
   (D)   L
   (E)   M

21. Which one of the following CANNOT be the product that is advertised during two of the weeks?

   (A)   G
   (B)   H
   (C)   K
   (D)   L
   (E)   M

22. If L is the product that is advertised during two of the weeks, which one of the following is a product that must be advertised during one of the weeks in which L is advertised?

   (A)   G
   (B)   H
   (C)   J
   (D)   K
   (E)   M

23. Which one of the following is a product that could be advertised in any of the four weeks?

   (A)   H
   (B)   J
   (C)   K
   (D)   L
   (E)   O

24. Which one of the following is a pair of products that could be advertised during the same week as each other?

   (A)   G and H
   (B)   H and J
   (C)   H and O
   (D)   K and O
   (E)   M and O

S T O P

IF YOU FINISH BEFORE TIME IS CALLED, YOU MAY CHECK YOUR WORK ON THIS SECTION ONLY.
DO NOT WORK ON ANY OTHER SECTION IN THE TEST.

SECTION II

Time—35 minutes

25 Questions

Directions: The questions in this section are based on the reasoning contained in brief statements or passages. For some questions, more than one of the choices could conceivably answer the question. However, you are to choose the best answer; that is, the response that most accurately and completely answers the question. You should not make assumptions that are by commonsense standards implausible, superfluous, or incompatible with the passage. After you have chosen the best answer, blacken the corresponding space on your answer sheet.

1. When politicians resort to personal attacks, many editorialists criticize these attacks but most voters pay them scant attention. Everyone knows such attacks will end after election day, and politicians can be excused for mudslinging. Political commentators, however, cannot be. Political commentators should be engaged in sustained and serious debate about ideas and policies. In such a context, personal attacks on opponents serve not to beat those opponents but to cut off the debate.

   Which one of the following most accurately states the main point of the argument?

   (A) Personal attacks on opponents serve a useful purpose for politicians.
   (B) Political commentators should not resort to personal attacks on their opponents.
   (C) Editorialists are right to criticize politicians who resort to personal attacks on their opponents.
   (D) The purpose of serious debate about ideas and policies is to counteract the effect of personal attacks by politicians.
   (E) Voters should be concerned about the personal attacks politicians make on each other.

2. Throughout the Popoya Islands community pressure is exerted on people who win the national lottery to share their good fortune with their neighbors. When people living in rural areas win the lottery they invariably throw elaborate neighborhood feasts, often wiping out all of their lottery winnings. However, in the cities, lottery winners frequently use their winnings for their own personal investment rather than sharing their good fortune with their neighbors.

   Which one of the following, if true, contributes most to an explanation of the difference between the behavior of lottery winners in rural areas and those in cities?

   (A) Twice as many Popoyans live in rural areas as live in the city.
   (B) Popoyan city dwellers tend to buy several lottery tickets at a time, but they buy tickets less frequently than do rural dwellers.
   (C) Lottery winners in rural areas are notified of winning by public posting of lists of winners, but notification in the city is by private mail.
   (D) Families in rural areas in the Popoyas may contain twelve or fourteen people, but city families average six or seven.
   (E) Twice as many lottery tickets are sold in rural areas as are sold in the city.

GO ON TO THE NEXT PAGE.

3. A new medication for migraine seems effective, but there is concern that the medication might exacerbate heart disease. If patients with heart disease take the medication under careful medical supervision, however, harmful side effects can definitely be averted. The concern about those side effects is thus unfounded.

The argument depends on which one of the following assumptions?

(A) The new medication actually is effective when taken by patients with heart disease.

(B) No migraine sufferers with heart disease will take the new medication except under careful medical supervision.

(C) Most migraine sufferers who have taken the new medication in trials also had heart disease.

(D) The new medication has various other side effects, but none as serious as that of exacerbating heart disease.

(E) The new medication will displace all migraine medications currently being used.

4. The highest-ranking detectives in the city's police department are also the most adept at solving crimes. Yet in each of the past ten years, the average success rate for the city's highest-ranking detectives in solving criminal cases has been no higher than the average success rate for its lowest-ranking detectives.

Which one of the following, if true, most helps to resolve the apparent paradox?

(A) The detectives who have the highest success rate in solving criminal cases are those who have worked as detectives the longest.

(B) It generally takes at least ten years for a detective to rise from the lowest to the highest ranks of the city's detective force.

(C) Those detectives in the police department who are the most adept at solving criminal cases are also those most likely to remain in the police department.

(D) The police department generally gives the criminal cases that it expects to be the easiest to solve to its lowest-ranking detectives.

(E) None of the lowest-ranking detectives in the police department had experience in solving criminal cases prior to joining the police department.

5. Irrigation runoff from neighboring farms may well have increased the concentration of phosphorus in the local swamp above previous levels, but the claim that the increase in phosphorus is harming the swamp's native aquatic wildlife is false; the phosphorus concentration in the swamp is actually less than that found in certain kinds of bottled water that some people drink every day.

The argument is vulnerable to criticism on the ground that it

(A) makes exaggerations in formulating the claim against which it argues

(B) bases its conclusion on two contradictory claims

(C) relies on evidence the relevance of which has not been established

(D) concedes the very point that it argues against

(E) makes a generalization that is unwarranted because the sources of the data on which it is based have not been specified

6. Copyright laws protect the rights of writers to profits earned from their writings, whereas patent laws protect inventors' rights to profits earned from their inventions. In Jawade, when computer-software writers demanded that their rights to profit be protected, the courts determined that information written for a machine does not fit into either the copyright or the patent category. Clearly, therefore, the profit rights of computer-software writers remain unprotected in Jawade.

Which one of the following is an assumption on which the argument depends?

(A) Computer-software writers are not an influential enough group in Jawade for the government to consider modifying existing copyright laws in order to protect this group's profit rights.

(B) No laws exist, other than copyright laws and patent laws, that would protect the profit rights of computer-software writers in Jawade.

(C) Most of the computer software used in Jawade is imported from other countries.

(D) Computer software is more similar to writings covered by copyright laws than it is to inventions covered by patent laws.

(E) Copyright laws and patent laws in Jawade have not been modified since their original adoption.

GO ON TO THE NEXT PAGE.

7. Brownlea's post office must be replaced with a larger one. The present one cannot be expanded. Land near the present location in the center of town is more expensive than land on the outskirts of town. Since the cost of acquiring a site is a significant part of the total construction cost, the post office clearly could be built more cheaply on the outskirts of town.

Which one of the following, if true, most seriously undermines the argument's stated conclusion?

(A) The new post office will have to be built in accordance with a demanding new citywide building code.

(B) If the new post office is built on the outskirts of town, it will require a parking lot, but if sited near the present post office it will not.

(C) If the new post office is built on the outskirts of town, current city bus routes will have to be expanded to provide access.

(D) If the new post office is built on the outskirts of town, residents will make decreased use of post office boxes, with the result that mail carriers will have to deliver more mail to homes.

(E) If the new post office is built near the center of town, disruptions to city traffic would have to be minimized by taking such steps as doing some construction work in stages at night and on weekends.

8. In the past, the railroads in Ostronia were run as regional monopolies and operated with little regard for what customers wanted. In recent years, with improvements to the Ostronian national highway network, the railroad companies have faced heavy competition from long-distance trucking companies. But because of government subsidies that have permitted Ostronian railroad companies to operate even while incurring substantial losses, the companies continue to disregard customers' needs and desires.

If the statements above are true, which one of the following must also be true on the basis of them?

(A) If the government of Ostronia ceases to subsidize railroad companies, few of those companies will continue to operate.

(B) Few companies in Ostronia that have received subsidies from the government have taken the needs and desires of their customers into account.

(C) Without government subsidies, railroad companies in Ostronia would have to increase the prices they charge their customers.

(D) The transportation system in Ostronia is no more efficient today than it was in the past.

(E) In recent years, some companies in Ostronia that have had little regard for the desires of their customers have nonetheless survived.

9. Although Damon had ample time earlier in the month to complete the paper he is scheduled to present at a professional conference tomorrow morning, he repeatedly put off doing it. Damon could still get the paper ready in time, but only if he works on it all evening without interruption. However, his seven-year-old daughter's tap-dance recital takes place this evening, and Damon had promised both to attend and to take his daughter and her friends out for ice cream afterward. Thus, because of his procrastination, Damon will be forced to choose between his professional and his family responsibilities.

The argument proceeds by

(A) providing evidence that one event will occur in order to establish that an alternative event cannot occur

(B) showing that two situations are similar in order to justify the claim that someone with certain responsibilities in the first situation has similar responsibilities in the second situation

(C) invoking sympathy for someone who finds himself in a dilemma in order to excuse that person's failure to meet all of his responsibilities

(D) making clear the extent to which someone's actions resulted in harm to others in order to support the claim that those actions were irresponsible

(E) demonstrating that two situations cannot both occur by showing that something necessary for one of those situations is incompatible with something necessary for the other situation

10. The increase in the price of jet fuel is due to a sharp decrease over the past year in the supply of jet fuel available relative to demand. Nonetheless, the amount of jet fuel available for sale is larger today than it was last year.

If the statements above are true, which one of the following conclusions can be properly drawn on the basis of them?

(A) The demand for jet fuel has increased over the past year.

(B) The fuel efficiency of jet engines has increased over the past year.

(C) The number of jet airline flights has decreased over the past year.

(D) The cost of refining petroleum for jet fuel has increased over the past year.

(E) The supply of petroleum available for jet fuel has decreased over the past year.

GO ON TO THE NEXT PAGE.

Questions 11–12

Alan: Government subsidies have been proposed in Cariana to encourage farmers in Rochelle, the country's principal agricultural region, to implement certain new farming techniques. Unless these techniques are implemented, erosion of productive topsoil cannot be controlled. Unfortunately, farmers cannot afford to shoulder the entire cost of the new techniques, which are more expensive than those currently used. Therefore, without subsidies, agricultural output in Rochelle will inevitably decline.

Betty: But erosion in Rochelle is caused by recurring floods, which will end next year once Cariana completes the hydroelectric dam it is building across the region's major river. Therefore, Rochelle's total agricultural output will stabilize at its present level even without subsidies.

11. Which one of the following is an assumption on which Betty's argument depends?

(A) Building a dam across Rochelle's major river will not reduce any recurrent flooding that occurs in regions of Cariana other than Rochelle.

(B) The new farming techniques that must be implemented to control soil erosion in Rochelle are not well suited to other regions of Cariana.

(C) The current yearly output, if any, from Rochelle's land that will be permanently under water once the dam is completed will at least be matched by additional yearly output from Rochelle's remaining land.

(D) The cost to the government of Cariana to operate the hydroelectric dam will not be greater than the projected cost of subsidizing the farmers of Rochelle in the implementation of the new farming techniques.

(E) The government of Cariana has sufficient financial resources both to subsidize its farmers' implementation of new farming techniques and to operate a hydroelectric dam.

12. Betty uses which one of the following argumentative techniques in countering Alan's argument?

(A) showing that one premise in Alan's argument is inconsistent with another premise in his argument

(B) making additional claims that, if correct, undermine a premise in Alan's argument

(C) demonstrating that Alan's conclusion is true but not for the reasons Alan gives to support it

(D) presenting evidence indicating that the policy Alan argues in favor of would have damaging consequences that outweigh its positive consequences

(E) pointing out that Alan's argument mistakenly identifies something as the cause of a trend when it is really an effect of that trend

13. Astronomers have long thought that the irregularity in the orbit of the planet Neptune was adequately explained by the gravitational pull exerted on Neptune by the planet Pluto. The most recent observations of Pluto, however, indicate that this planet is much too small to exert the amount of gravitational pull on Neptune that astronomers once thought it did.

If the statements above are true, they provide the most support for which one of the following?

(A) Neptune is somewhat larger than scientists once believed it to be.

(B) The orbit of Neptune is considerably more irregular than scientists once thought it was.

(C) There exists another, as yet undiscovered planet with an orbit beyond that of Pluto.

(D) The gravitational pull of Pluto is not the sole cause of Neptune's irregular orbit.

(E) Further observations of Pluto will eventually show it to be even smaller than it is now thought to be.

GO ON TO THE NEXT PAGE.

Questions 14–15

In most corporations the salaries of executives are set by a group from the corporation's board of directors. Since the board's primary mission is to safeguard the economic health of the corporation rather than to make its executives rich, this way of setting executives' salaries is expected to prevent excessively large salaries. But, clearly, this expectation is based on poor reasoning. After all, most members of a corporation's board are themselves executives of some corporation and can expect to benefit from setting generous benchmarks for executives' salaries.

14. The point made by the author is that the most common way of setting executives' salaries might not keep those salaries in bounds because

(A) most corporate executives, thanks to their generous salaries, are not financially dependent on money earned as board members

(B) most corporate executives might be less generous in setting their own salaries than the board members actually setting them are

(C) many board members might let their self-interest as executives interfere with properly discharging their role, as board members, in setting executives' salaries

(D) many board members who set executives' salaries unreasonably high do so because they happen to be on the board of a corporation of which they expect later to become executives

(E) many board members are remunerated generously and wish to protect this source of income by pleasing the executives to whom they owe their appointments on the board

15. Which one of the following practices is vulnerable to a line of criticism most parallel to that used in the argument in the passage?

(A) in medical malpractice suits, giving physicians not directly involved in a suit a major role in determining the damages due to successful plaintiffs

(B) in a legislature, allowing the legislators to increase their own salaries only if at least two-thirds of them vote in favor of an increase

(C) on a factory floor, giving workers an incentive to work both fast and accurately by paying them by the piece but counting only pieces of acceptable quality

(D) in a sports competition decided by judges' scores, selecting the judges from among people retired from that sport after successful careers

(E) in a business organization, distributing a group bonus among the members of a task force on the basis of a confidential evaluation, by each member, of the contribution made by each of the others

16. Consumer advocate: One advertisement that is deceptive, and thus morally wrong, states that "gram for gram, the refined sugar used in our chocolate pies is no more fattening than the sugars found in fruits and vegetables." This is like trying to persuade someone that chocolate pies are not fattening by saying that, calorie for calorie, they are no more fattening than celery. True, but it would take a whole shopping cart full of celery to equal a chocolate pie's worth of calories.

Advertiser: This advertisement cannot be called deceptive. It is, after all, true.

Which one of the following principles, if established, would do most to support the consumer advocate's position against the advertiser's response?

(A) It is morally wrong to seek to persuade by use of deceptive statements.

(B) A true statement should be regarded as deceptive only if the person making the statement believes it to be false, and thus intends the people reading or hearing it to acquire a false belief.

(C) To make statements that impart only a small proportion of the information in one's possession should not necessarily be regarded as deceptive.

(D) It is morally wrong to make a true statement in a manner that will deceive hearers or readers of the statement into believing that it is false.

(E) A true statement should be regarded as deceptive if it is made with the expectation that people hearing or reading the statement will draw a false conclusion from it.

GO ON TO THE NEXT PAGE.

17. Members of the Amazonian Akabe people commonly take an early-morning drink of a tea made from the leaves of a forest plant. Although they greatly enjoy this drink, at dawn they drink it only in small amounts. Anthropologists hypothesize that since this tea is extraordinarily high in caffeine, the explanation for the Akabe's not drinking more of it at dawn is that high caffeine intake would destroy the surefootedness that their daily tasks require.

Which one of the following, if true, most seriously calls the anthropologists' explanation into question?

(A) The drink is full of nutrients otherwise absent from the Akabe diet.
(B) The Akabe also drink the tea in the evening, after their day's work is done.
(C) The leaves used for the tea contain a soluble narcotic.
(D) Akabe children are introduced to the tea in only a very weak form.
(E) When celebrating, the Akabe drink the tea in large quantities.

18. All of the cargo ships of the Blue Star Line are over 100 meters long, and all of its passenger ships are under 100 meters long. Most of the ships of the Blue Star Line were built before 1980. All of the passenger and cargo ships of the Gold Star Line were built after 1980, and all are under 100 meters long. The dockside facilities of Port Tropica, which is open only to ships of these two lines, can accommodate only those ships that are less than 100 meters long. The S.S. Coral is a cargo ship that is currently docked at Port Tropica.

If the statements above are true, which one of the following must be true on the basis of them?

(A) The S.S. Coral was built after 1980.
(B) The S.S. Coral belongs to the Blue Star Line.
(C) Port Tropica is served only by cargo ships.
(D) Port Tropica is not served by ships of the Blue Star Line.
(E) All of the ships of the Blue Star Line are older than any of the ships of the Gold Star Line.

19. Spectroscopic analysis has revealed the existence of frozen nitrogen, methane, and carbon monoxide on the surface of Pluto. Such ices have a tendency to vaporize, producing an atmosphere. Since the proportion of any gas in such an atmosphere depends directly on how readily the corresponding ice vaporizes, astronomers have concluded that the components of Pluto's atmosphere are nitrogen, carbon monoxide, and methane, in order of decreasing abundance.

The astronomers' argument relies on which one of the following assumptions?

(A) There is no more frozen nitrogen on the surface of Pluto than there is either frozen carbon monoxide or methane.
(B) Until space probes reach Pluto, direct analysis of the atmosphere is impossible.
(C) There is no frozen substance on the surface of Pluto that vaporizes more readily than methane but less readily than carbon monoxide.
(D) Nitrogen is found in the atmosphere of a planet only if nitrogen ice is found on the surface of that planet.
(E) A mixture of nitrogen, carbon monoxide, and methane is characteristic of the substances from which the Solar System formed.

GO ON TO THE NEXT PAGE.

20. Ann will either take a leave of absence from Technocomp and return in a year or else she will quit her job there; but she would not do either one unless she were offered a one-year teaching fellowship at a prestigious university. Technocomp will allow her to take a leave of absence if it does not find out that she has been offered the fellowship, but not otherwise. Therefore, Ann will quit her job at Technocomp only if Technocomp finds out she has been offered the fellowship.

Which one of the following, if assumed, allows the conclusion above to be properly drawn?

(A) Technocomp will find out about Ann being offered the fellowship only if someone informs on her.

(B) The reason Ann wants the fellowship is so she can quit her job at Technocomp.

(C) Technocomp does not allow any of its employees to take a leave of absence in order to work for one of its competitors.

(D) Ann will take a leave of absence if Technocomp allows her to take a leave of absence.

(E) Ann would be offered the fellowship only if she quit her job at Technocomp.

21. If a mechanical aerator is installed in a fish pool, the water in the pool can be properly aerated. So, since John's fish pool does not have a mechanical aerator, it must be that his pool is not properly aerated. Without properly aerated water, fish cannot thrive. Therefore, any fish in John's fish pool will not thrive.

Which one of the following arguments contains an error of reasoning that is also contained in the argument above?

(A) If alum is added to pickle brine, brine can replace the water in the pickles. Therefore, since Paula does not add alum to her pickle brine, the water in the pickles cannot be replaced by brine. Unless their water is replaced with brine, pickles will not stay crisp. Thus, Paula's pickles will not stay crisp.

(B) If pectin is added to jam, the jam will gel. Without a setting agent such as pectin, jam will not gel. So in order to make his jam gel, Harry should add a setting agent such as pectin to the jam.

(C) If stored potatoes are not exposed to ethylene, the potatoes will not sprout. Beets do not release ethylene. Therefore, if Sara stores her potatoes together with beets, the potatoes will not sprout.

(D) If a carrot patch is covered with mulch in the fall, the carrots can be left in the ground until spring. Without a mulch cover, carrots stored in the ground can suffer frost damage. Thus, since Kevin covers his carrot patch with mulch in the fall, the carrots can safely be left in the ground.

(E) If tomatoes are not stored in a dark place, their seeds sometimes sprout. Sprouted seeds can make tomatoes inedible. Therefore, since Maria does not store her tomatoes in a dark place, some of Maria's tomatoes could be inedible.

GO ON TO THE NEXT PAGE.

Questions 22–23

Antinuclear activist: The closing of the nuclear power plant is a victory for the antinuclear cause. It also represents a belated acknowledgment by the power industry that they cannot operate such plants safely.

Nuclear power plant manager: It represents no such thing. The availability of cheap power from nonnuclear sources, together with the cost of mandated safety inspections and safety repairs, made continued operation uneconomic. Thus it was not safety considerations but economic considerations that dictated the plant's closing.

22. The reasoning in the manager's argument is flawed because the argument

(A) fails to acknowledge that the power industry might now believe nuclear power plants to be unsafe even though this plant was not closed for safety reasons

(B) overlooks the possibility that the sources from which cheap power is available might themselves be subject to safety concerns

(C) mistakes the issue of what the closure of the plant represents to the public for the issue of what the managers' reasons for the closure were

(D) takes as one of its premises a view about the power industry's attitude toward nuclear safety that contradicts the activist's view

(E) counts as purely economic considerations some expenses that arise as a result of the need to take safety precautions

23. Which one of the following, if true, most strongly supports the activist's claim of victory?

(A) The plant had reached the age at which its operating license expired.

(B) The mandate for inspections and repairs mentioned by the manager was recently enacted as a result of pressure from antinuclear groups.

(C) The plant would not have closed if cheap power from nonnuclear sources had not been available.

(D) Per unit of electricity produced, the plant had the highest operating costs of any nuclear power plant.

(E) The plant that closed had been able to provide backup power to an electrical network when parts of the network became overloaded.

Questions 24–25

Statistician: Changes in the Sun's luminosity correlate exceedingly well with average land temperatures on Earth. Clearly—and contrary to accepted opinion among meteorologists—the Sun's luminosity essentially controls land temperatures on Earth.

Meteorologist: I disagree. Any professional meteorologist will tell you that in a system as complicated as that giving rise to the climate, no significant aspect can be controlled by a single variable.

24. The rejection by the meteorologist of the statistician's conclusion employs which one of the following techniques of argumentation?

(A) supporting a conclusion about a specific case by invoking a relevant generalization

(B) producing a single counterexample that establishes that a generalization is false as stated

(C) reanalyzing a correlation as reflecting the multiple effects of a single cause

(D) rejecting a conclusion because it is a proposition that cannot be experimentally tested

(E) pointing out that potentially unfavorable evidence has been systematically neglected

25. The reasoning in the meteorologist's counterargument is questionable because that argument

(A) rejects a partial explanation, not because it is incorrect, but only because it is not complete

(B) fails to distinguish phenomena that exist independently of a particular system from phenomena that exist only as part of the system

(C) calls into question the existence of a correlation when the only real issue is that of how to interpret the correlation

(D) dismisses a hypothesis on the grounds that it fails to deal with any matters of scientific significance

(E) appeals to the authoritativeness of an opinion without evaluating the merit of a putative counterexample

S T O P

IF YOU FINISH BEFORE TIME IS CALLED, YOU MAY CHECK YOUR WORK ON THIS SECTION ONLY.
DO NOT WORK ON ANY OTHER SECTION IN THE TEST.

SECTION III

Time—35 minutes

25 Questions

Directions: The questions in this section are based on the reasoning contained in brief statements or passages. For some questions, more than one of the choices could conceivably answer the question. However, you are to choose the best answer; that is, the response that most accurately and completely answers the question. You should not make assumptions that are by commonsense standards implausible, superfluous, or incompatible with the passage. After you have chosen the best answer, blacken the corresponding space on your answer sheet.

1. Everyone sitting in the waiting room of the school's athletic office this morning at nine o'clock had just registered for a beginners tennis clinic. John, Mary, and Teresa were all sitting in the waiting room this morning at nine o'clock. No accomplished tennis player would register for a beginners tennis clinic.

   If the statements above are true, which one of the following must also be true on the basis of them?

   (A) None of the people sitting in the school's athletic office this morning at nine o'clock had ever played tennis.
   (B) Everyone sitting in the school's athletic office this morning at nine o'clock registered only for a beginners tennis clinic.
   (C) John, Mary, and Teresa were the only people who registered for a beginners tennis clinic this morning.
   (D) John, Mary, and Teresa were the only people sitting in the waiting room of the school's athletic office this morning at nine o'clock.
   (E) Neither John nor Teresa is an accomplished tennis player.

2. Most people who ride bicycles for pleasure do not ride until the warm weather of spring and summer arrives. Yet it is probably more effective to advertise bicycles earlier in the year. Most bicycles are purchased in the spring, but once shoppers are ready to shop for a bicycle, they usually have already decided which brand and model of bicycle they will purchase. By then it is generally too late to induce them to change their minds.

   The main point of the argument is that

   (A) bicycle advertisements are probably more effective if they appear before the arrival of warm spring weather
   (B) most bicycle purchasers decide on the brand and model of bicycle that they will buy before beginning to shop for a bicycle
   (C) more bicycles are purchased in the spring than at any other time of year
   (D) in general, once a bicycle purchaser has decided which bicycle he or she intends to purchase, it is difficult to bring about a change in that decision
   (E) spring and summer are the time of year in which bicycle riding as a leisure activity is most popular

3. During 1991 the number of people in the town of Bayburg who received municipal food assistance doubled, even though the number of people in Bayburg whose incomes were low enough to qualify for such assistance remained unchanged.

   Which one of the following, if true, most helps to resolve the apparent discrepancy in the information above?

   (A) In 1990 the Bayburg Town Council debated whether or not to alter the eligibility requirements for the food assistance program but ultimately decided not to change them.
   (B) In 1990 the Bayburg social service department estimated the number of people in Bayburg who might be eligible for the food assistance program and then informed the Bayburg Town Council of the total amount of assistance likely to be needed.
   (C) During 1991 many residents of a nearby city lost their jobs and moved to Bayburg in search of work.
   (D) During 1991 the number of applicants for food assistance in Bayburg who were rejected on the basis that their incomes were above the maximum allowable limit was approximately the same as it had been in 1990.
   (E) During 1991 Bayburg's program of rent assistance for low-income tenants advertised widely and then informed all applicants about other assistance programs for which they would be qualified.

GO ON TO THE NEXT PAGE.

4. Campaigning for election to provincial or state office frequently requires that a candidate spend much time and energy catering to the interests of national party officials who can help the candidate to win office. The elected officials who campaign for reelection while they are in office thus often fail to serve the interests of their local constituencies.

Which one of the following is an assumption made by the argument?

(A) Catering to the interests of national party officials sometimes conflicts with serving the interests of a provincial or state official's local constituencies.

(B) Only by catering to the interests of national party officials can those who hold provincial or state office win reelection.

(C) The interests of local constituencies are well served only by elected officials who do not cater to the interests of national party officials.

(D) Officials elected to provincial or state office are obligated to serve only the interests of constituents who belong to the same party as do the officials.

(E) All elected officials are likely to seek reelection to those offices that are not limited to one term.

5. Since Professor Smythe has been head of the department, the most distinguished member of the faculty has resigned, fewer new courses have been developed, student enrollment has dropped, and the reputation of the department has gone down. These facts provide conclusive evidence that Professor Smythe was appointed to undermine the department.

The reasoning in the argument is flawed because the argument

(A) overlooks the fact that something can have the reputation for being of poor quality without being of poor quality

(B) bases a general claim on a few exceptional instances

(C) assumes that because an action was followed by a change, the action was undertaken to bring about that change

(D) fails to distinguish between a decline in quantity and a decline in quality

(E) presupposes what it purports to establish

6. Books about architectural works, unless they are not intended for a general audience, ought to include discussions of both the utility and the aesthetic appeal of each of the buildings they consider. If they do not, they are flawed. Morton's book on Italian Baroque palaces describes these palaces' functional aspects, but fails to mention that the main hall of a palace he discusses at length has a ceiling that is one of the truly breathtaking masterpieces of Western art.

If the statements above are true, it would be necessary to establish which one of the following in order to conclude that Morton's book is flawed?

(A) Morton's description of the palaces' utility is inaccurate.

(B) Morton's book does not discuss aspects of the palaces other than utility and aesthetic appeal.

(C) Morton's book is intended for a general audience.

(D) The passage discussing the palace plays a very important role in helping to establish the overall argument of Morton's book.

(E) The palace discussed at length is one of the most aesthetically important of those treated in Morton's book.

7. Of all the photographs taken of him at his wedding, there was one that John and his friends sharply disagreed about. His friends all said that this particular picture did not much resemble him, but John said that on the contrary it was the only photograph that did.

Which one of the following, if true about the photograph, most helps to explain John's disagreement with his friends?

(A) It, unlike the other photographs of John, showed him in the style of dress he and his friends usually wear rather than the formal clothes he wore at the ceremony.

(B) It was the only photograph taken of John at his wedding for which the photographer had used a flash.

(C) It was a black-and-white photograph, whereas the other photographs that showed John were mostly color photographs.

(D) It was unique in showing John's face reflected in a mirror, the photographer having taken the photograph over John's shoulder.

(E) It was one of only a few taken at the wedding that showed no one but John.

GO ON TO THE NEXT PAGE.

Questions 8–9

Eva: A "smart highway" system should be installed, one that would monitor areawide traffic patterns and communicate with computers in vehicles or with programmable highway signs to give drivers information about traffic congestion and alternate routes. Such a system, we can infer, would result in improved traffic flow in and around cities that would do more than improve drivers' tempers; it would decrease the considerable loss of money and productivity that now results from traffic congestion.

Luis: There are already traffic reports on the radio. Why would a "smart highway" system be any better?

8. Eva's argument depends on the assumption that

(A) on "smart highways" there would not be the breakdowns of vehicles that currently cause traffic congestion

(B) traffic lights, if coordinated by the system, would assure a free flow of traffic

(C) traffic flow in and around cities is not now so congested that significant improvement is impossible

(D) the type of equipment used in "smart highway" systems would vary from one city to another

(E) older vehicles could not be fitted with equipment to receive signals sent by a "smart highway" system

9. If Eva responded to Luis by saying that the current one-minute radio reports are too short to give a sufficient description of overall patterns of traffic congestion, which one of the following, if true, would most strengthen Luis's challenge?

(A) Bad weather, which radio stations report, would cause traffic to slow down whether or not a "smart highway" system was in operation.

(B) It would be less costly to have radio stations that give continual, lengthier traffic reports than to install a "smart highway" system.

(C) Radio reports can take note of congestion once it occurs, but a "smart highway" system could anticipate and forestall it in many instances.

(D) The proposed traffic monitoring would not reduce the privacy of drivers.

(E) Toll collection booths, which constitute traffic bottlenecks, would largely be replaced in the "smart highway" system by electronic debiting of commuters' accounts while traffic proceeded at full speed.

10. The terms "sex" and "gender" are often used interchangeably. But "sex" more properly refers to biological differences of male and female, while "gender" refers to society's construction of a system that identifies what is masculine and feminine. Unlike the set of characteristics defining biological sex, the set of traits that are associated with gender does not sort people into two nonoverlapping groups. The traits characterize people in a complex way, so that a person may have both "masculine" and "feminine" traits.

Which one of the following statements best expresses a main point of the argument?

(A) Distinctions based on gender are frequently arbitrary.

(B) Gender traits are not determined at birth.

(C) Masculine gender traits are highly correlated with maleness.

(D) The terms "sex" and "gender" are not properly interchangeable.

(E) Society rather than the individual decides what is considered proper behavior.

11. Raising the tax rate on essential goods—a traditional means of increasing government revenues—invariably turns low- and middle-income taxpayers against the government. Hence government officials have proposed adding a new tax on purchases of luxury items such as yachts, private planes, jewels, and furs. The officials claim that this tax will result in a substantial increase in government revenues while affecting only the wealthy individuals and corporations who can afford to purchase such items.

The answer to which one of the following questions would be most relevant in evaluating the accuracy of the government officials' prediction?

(A) Will luxury goods be taxed at a higher rate than that at which essential goods are currently taxed?

(B) Will the revenues generated by the proposed tax be comparable to those that are currently being generated by taxes on essential goods?

(C) Will sales of the luxury items subject to the proposed tax occur at current rates once the proposed tax on luxury items has been passed?

(D) Will the proposed tax on luxury items win support for the government in the eyes of low- and middle-income taxpayers?

(E) Will purchases of luxury items by corporations account for more of the revenue generated by the proposed tax than will purchases of luxury items by wealthy individuals?

GO ON TO THE NEXT PAGE.

12. In a study of the relationship between aggression and television viewing in nursery school children, many interesting interactions among family styles, aggression, and television viewing were found. High aggression occurred in both high-viewing and low-viewing children and this seemed to be related to parental lifestyle. High-achieving, competitive, middle-class parents, whose children did not watch much television, had more aggressive children than parents who planned their lives in an organized, child-centered way, which included larger amounts of television viewing.

Which one of the following conclusions is best supported by the passage?

(A) Low levels of television viewing often lead to high levels of aggression among children.
(B) The level of aggression of a child cannot be predicted from levels of television viewing alone.
(C) If high-achieving, competitive parents were more child-centered, their children would be less aggressive.
(D) High levels of television viewing can explain high levels of aggression among children only when the parents are not child-centered.
(E) Parental lifestyle is less important than the amount of television viewing in determining the aggressiveness of children.

13. One of the effects of lead poisoning is an inflammation of the optic nerve, which causes those who have it to see bright haloes around light sources. In order to produce the striking yellow effects in his "Sunflowers" paintings, Van Gogh used Naples yellow, a pigment containing lead. Since in his later paintings, Van Gogh painted bright haloes around the stars and sun, it is likely that he was suffering from lead poisoning caused by ingesting the pigments he used.

Which one of the following is an assumption on which the argument relies?

(A) In Van Gogh's later paintings he painted some things as he saw them.
(B) Van Gogh continued to use paints containing lead after having painted the "Sunflowers" paintings.
(C) Van Gogh did not have symptoms of lead poisoning aside from seeing bright haloes around light sources.
(D) The paints Van Gogh used in the "Sunflowers" paintings had no toxic ingredients other than lead.
(E) The effects of Naples yellow could not have been achieved using other pigments.

Questions 14–15

Politician: The mandatory jail sentences that became law two years ago for certain crimes have enhanced the integrity of our system of justice, for no longer are there two kinds of justice, the kind dispensed by lenient judges and the kind dispensed by severe ones.

Public advocate: But with judges stripped of discretionary powers, there can be no leniency even where it would be appropriate. So juries now sometimes acquit a given defendant solely because the jurors feel that the mandatory sentence would be too harsh. Those juries, then, do not return an accurate verdict on the defendant's guilt. This is why it is imperative that the legislation instituting mandatory jail sentences be repealed.

14. The public advocate responds to the politician's argument by doing which one of the following?

(A) trying to show that the politician's conclusion merely paraphrases the politician's evidence
(B) claiming that the politician's evidence, properly analyzed, has no bearing on the conclusion the politician derives from it
(C) arguing that leniency is not a trait of individuals but that, rather, it is a property of certain kinds of decisions
(D) arguing that an analysis of the consequences of certain legislation undermines the politician's conclusion
(E) charging that the politician exaggerated the severity of a problem in order to justify a sweeping solution

15. Which one of the following principles, if valid, provides the politician with the strongest basis for countering the public advocate's argument?

(A) Juries should always consider whether the sum of the evidence leaves any reasonable doubt concerning the defendant's guilt, and in all cases in which it does, they should acquit the defendant.
(B) A system of justice should clearly define what the specific actions are that judges are to perform within the system.
(C) A system of justice should not require any legal expertise on the part of the people selected to serve on juries.
(D) Changes in a system of justice in response to some undesirable feature of the system should be made as soon as possible once that feature has been recognized as undesirable.
(E) Changes in a system of justice that produce undesirable consequences should be reversed only if it is not feasible to ameliorate those undesirable consequences through further modification.

GO ON TO THE NEXT PAGE.

16. Researchers studying artificial sweeteners have long claimed that the perception of sweetness is determined by the activation of a single type of receptor on the tongue, called a sweetness receptor. They have also claimed that any given individual molecule of substance can activate at most one sweetness receptor and that the fewer molecules that are required to activate a receptor, the sweeter that substance will be perceived to be. Now, the researchers claim to have discovered a substance of which only one molecule is needed to activate any sweetness receptor.

Which one of the following conclusions is most strongly supported by the researchers' claims, if all of those claims are true?

(A) The more sweetness receptors a person has on his or her tongue, the more likely it is that that person will find sweet sensations pleasurable.

(B) In sufficient quantity, the molecules of any substance can activate a sweetness receptor.

(C) No substance will be found that is perceived to be sweeter than the substance the researchers have discovered.

(D) A substance that does not activate a sweetness receptor will activate a taste receptor of another type.

(E) The more molecules of a substance that are required to activate a single sweetness receptor, the more bitter that substance will be perceived to be.

17. An editorial in the *Grandburg Daily Herald* claims that Grandburg's voters would generally welcome the defeat of the political party now in control of the Grandburg City Council. The editorial bases its claim on a recent survey that found that 59 percent of Grandburg's registered voters think that the party will definitely be out of power after next year's city council elections.

Which one of the following is a principle that, if established, would provide the strongest justification for the editorial's conclusion?

(A) The way voters feel about a political party at a given time can reasonably be considered a reliable indicator of the way they will continue to feel about that party, barring unforeseeable political developments.

(B) The results of surveys that gauge current voter sentiment toward a given political party can legitimately be used as the basis for making claims about the likely future prospects of that political party.

(C) An increase in ill-feeling toward a political party that is in power can reasonably be expected to result in a corresponding increase in support for rival political parties.

(D) The proportion of voters who expect a given political possibility to be realized can legitimately be assumed to approximate the proportion of voters who are in favor of that possibility being realized.

(E) It can reasonably be assumed that registered voters who respond to a survey regarding the outcome of a future election will exercise their right to vote in that election.

GO ON TO THE NEXT PAGE.

18. Prolonged exposure to nonionizing radiation—electromagnetic radiation at or below the frequency of visible light—increases a person's chances of developing soft-tissue cancer. Electric power lines as well as such electrical appliances as electric blankets and video-display terminals are sources of nonionizing radiation.

Which one of the following conclusions is best supported by the statements above?

(A) People with short-term exposure to nonionizing radiation are not at risk of developing soft-tissue cancers.

(B) Soft-tissue cancers are more common than other cancers.

(C) Soft-tissue cancers are frequently cured spontaneously when sources of nonionizing radiation are removed from the patient's home.

(D) Certain electrical devices can pose health risks for their users.

(E) Devices producing electromagnetic radiation at frequencies higher than that of visible light do not increase a person's risk of developing soft-tissue cancers.

19. In the first decade following the founding of the British Labour party, the number of people regularly voting for Labour increased fivefold. The number of committed Labour voters increased a further fivefold during the party's second decade. Since the increase was thus the same in the first as in the second decade, the often-made claim that the Labour party gained more voters in the party's second decade than in its first is clearly false.

The reasoning in the argument is flawed because the argument

(A) fails to specify dates necessary to evaluate the truth of the conclusion, even though the argument depends on distinguishing between two time periods

(B) draws a conclusion that cannot be true if all the data advanced in its support are true

(C) relies on statistical evidence that, strictly speaking, is irrelevant to establishing the conclusion drawn

(D) fails to allow for the possibility that the policy positions advocated by the Labour party changed during the period in question

(E) overlooks the possibility that more elections were held in one of the two decades than were held in the other

Questions 20–21

A number of seriously interested amateur astronomers have tested the new Exodus refractor telescope. With it, they were able to observe in crisp detail planetary features that were seen only as fuzzy images in their 8-inch (approximately 20-centimeter) Newtonian telescopes, even though the 8-inch telescopes, with their wider apertures, gather more light than the 4-inch (approximately 10-centimeter) Exodus. Given these amateur astronomers' observational findings, any serious amateur astronomer ought to choose the Exodus if she or he is buying a telescope for planetary observation.

20. The argument proceeds by

(A) evaluating the credibility of claims made by a particular group

(B) detailing the ways in which a testing situation approximates the conditions of ordinary use

(C) placing a phenomenon in a wider context in order to explain it

(D) supporting a recommendation to a group on the basis of the experience of a subset of that group

(E) distinguishing between the actual reasons why a certain group did a particular thing and the best reasons for doing that thing

21. Which one of the following most seriously weakens the argument?

(A) Telescopes of certain types will not perform well unless they have been precisely collimated, a delicate adjustment requiring deftness.

(B) Image quality is only one of several different factors that, taken together, should determine the choice of a telescope for planetary observation.

(C) Many serious amateur astronomers have no intention of buying a telescope for planetary observation.

(D) The comparisons made by the amateur astronomers were based on observations made during several different observation sessions.

(E) The substance used to make the lenses of Exodus telescopes differs from that used in the lenses of other telescopes.

GO ON TO THE NEXT PAGE.

22. Anatomical bilateral symmetry is a common trait. It follows, therefore, that it confers survival advantages on organisms. After all, if bilateral symmetry did not confer such advantages, it would not be common.

The pattern of reasoning in which one of the following arguments is most similar to that in the argument above?

(A) Since it is Sawyer who is negotiating for the city government, it must be true that the city takes the matter seriously. After all, if Sawyer had not been available, the city would have insisted that the negotiations be deferred.

(B) Clearly, no candidate is better qualified for the job than Trumbull. In fact, even to suggest that there might be a more highly qualified candidate seems absurd to those who have seen Trumbull at work.

(C) If Powell lacked superior negotiating skills, she would not have been appointed arbitrator in this case. As everyone knows, she is the appointed arbitrator, so her negotiating skills are, detractors notwithstanding, bound to be superior.

(D) Since Varga was away on vacation at the time, it must have been Rivers who conducted the secret negotiations. Any other scenario makes little sense, for Rivers never does the negotiating unless Varga is unavailable.

(E) If Wong is appointed arbitrator, a decision will be reached promptly. Since it would be absurd to appoint anyone other than Wong as arbitrator, a prompt decision can reasonably be expected.

23. Electrical engineers have repeatedly demonstrated that the best solid-state amplifiers are indistinguishable from the best vacuum-tube amplifiers with respect to the characteristics commonly measured in evaluating the quality of an amplifier's musical reproduction. Therefore, those music lovers who insist that recorded music sounds better when played with the best vacuum-tube amplifier than when played with the best solid-state amplifier must be imagining the difference in quality that they claim to hear.

Which one of the following, if true, most seriously weakens the argument?

(A) Many people cannot tell from listening to it whether a recording is being played with a very good solid-state amplifier or a very good vacuum-tube amplifier.

(B) The range of variation with respect to the quality of musical reproduction is greater for vacuum-tube amplifiers than for solid-state amplifiers.

(C) Some of the characteristics that are important in determining how music sounds to a listener cannot be measured.

(D) Solid-state amplifiers are more compact, use less power, and generate less heat than vacuum-tube amplifiers that produce a comparable volume of sound.

(E) Some vacuum-tube amplifiers are clearly superior to some solid-state amplifiers with respect to the characteristics commonly measured in the laboratory to evaluate the quality of an amplifier's musical reproduction.

GO ON TO THE NEXT PAGE.

24. Explanation must be distinguished from justification. Every human action potentially has an explanation; that is, with sufficient knowledge it would be possible to give an accurate description of the causes of that action. An action is justified only when the person performing the action has sufficient reasons for the action. According to many psychologists, even when there is a justification for an action, that justification often forms no part of the explanation. The general principle, however, is that only an action whose justification, that is, the reasons for the action, forms an essential part of its explanation is rational.

If the statements in the passage are correct, which one of the following can be properly concluded from them?

(A) When a human action is justified, that action has no explanation.

(B) If there are any reasons among the causes of an action, then that action is rational.

(C) Some psychologists believe that the justification for an action never forms an essential part of its explanation.

(D) There are actions whose causes cannot be discovered.

(E) If any human actions are rational, then reasons must sometimes be causes of actions.

25. At the company picnic, all of the employees who participated in more than four of the scheduled events, and only those employees, were eligible for the raffle held at the end of the day. Since only a small proportion of the employees were eligible for the raffle, most of the employees must have participated in fewer than four of the scheduled events.

Which one of the following arguments exhibits a flawed pattern of reasoning most like that exhibited by the argument above?

(A) Only third- and fourth-year students are allowed to keep cars on campus. Since one quarter of the third-year students keep cars on campus and one half of the fourth-year students keep cars on campus, it must be that fewer third-year students than fourth-year students keep cars on campus.

(B) Only those violin students who attended extra rehearsal sessions were eligible for selection as soloists. Since two of the violin students were selected as soloists, those two must have been the only violin students who attended the extra sessions.

(C) The only students honored at a special banquet were the band members who made the dean's list last semester. Since most of the band members were honored, most of the band members must have made the dean's list.

(D) All of the members of the service club who volunteered at the hospital last summer were biology majors. Since ten of the club members are biology majors, those ten members must have volunteered at the hospital last summer.

(E) All of the swim team members who had decreased their racing times during the season were given awards that no other members were given. Since fewer than half the team members were given such awards, the racing times of more than half the team members must have increased during the season.

S T O P

IF YOU FINISH BEFORE TIME IS CALLED, YOU MAY CHECK YOUR WORK ON THIS SECTION ONLY.
DO NOT WORK ON ANY OTHER SECTION IN THE TEST.

SECTION IV

Time—35 minutes

27 Questions

Directions: Each passage in this section is followed by a group of questions to be answered on the basis of what is stated or implied in the passage. For some of the questions, more than one of the choices could conceivably answer the question. However, you are to choose the best answer; that is, the response that most accurately and completely answers the question, and blacken the corresponding space on your answer sheet.

Musicologists concerned with the "London Pianoforte school," the group of composers, pedagogues, pianists, publishers, and builders who contributed to the development of the piano in London
(5) at the turn of the nineteenth century, have long encountered a formidable obstacle in the general unavailability of music of this "school" in modern scholarly editions. Indeed, much of this repertory has more or less vanished from our historical
(10) consciousness. Granted, the sonatas and *Gradus ad Parnassum* of Muzio Clementi and the nocturnes of John Field have remained familiar enough (though more often than not in editions lacking scholarly rigor), but the work of other leading representatives, like
(15) Johann Baptist Cramer and Jan Ladislav Dussek, has eluded serious attempts at revival.

Nicholas Temperley's ambitious new anthology decisively overcomes this deficiency. What underscores the intrinsic value of Temperley's editions
(20) is that the anthology reproduces nearly all of the original music in facsimile. Making available this cross section of English musical life—some 800 works by 49 composers—should encourage new critical perspectives about how piano music evolved in
(25) England, an issue of considerable relevance to our understanding of how piano music developed on the European continent, and of how, finally, the instrument was transformed from the fortepiano to what we know today as the piano.
(30) To be sure, the concept of the London Pianoforte school itself calls for review. "School" may well be too strong a word for what was arguably a group unified not so much by stylistic principles or aesthetic creed as by the geographical circumstance that they worked at
(35) various times in London and produced pianos and piano music for English pianos and English markets. Indeed, Temperley concedes that their "variety may be so great as to cast doubt on the notion of a 'school.'"

The notion of a school was first propounded by
(40) Alexander Ringer, who argued that laws of artistic survival forced the young, progressive Beethoven to turn outside Austria for creative models, and that he found inspiration in a group of pianists connected with Clementi in London. Ringer's proposed London
(45) Pianoforte school did suggest a circumscribed and fairly unified group—for want of a better term, a school—of musicians whose influence was felt primarily in the decades just before and after 1800. After all, Beethoven did respond to the advances of the
(50) Broadwood piano—its reinforced frame, extended

compass, triple stringing, and pedals, for example—and it is reasonable to suppose that London pianists who composed music for such an instrument during the critical phase of its development exercised no small
(55) degree of influence on Continental musicians. Nevertheless, perhaps the most sensible approach to this issue is to define the school by the period (c. 1766–1873) during which it flourished, as Temperley has done in the anthology.

1. Which one of the following most accurately states the author's main point?

(A) Temperley has recently called into question the designation of a group of composers, pedagogues, pianists, publishers, and builders as the London Pianoforte school.

(B) Temperley's anthology of the music of the London Pianoforte school contributes significantly to an understanding of an influential period in the history of music.

(C) The music of the London Pianoforte school has been revived by the publication of Temperley's new anthology.

(D) Primary sources for musical manuscripts provide the most reliable basis for musicological research.

(E) The development of the modern piano in England influenced composers and other musicians throughout Europe.

2. It can be inferred that which one of the following is true of the piano music of the London Pianoforte school?

(A) The nocturnes of John Field typify the London Pianoforte school style.

(B) The *Gradus ad Parnassum* of Muzio Clementi is the best-known work of these composers.

(C) No original scores for this music are extant.

(D) Prior to Temperley's edition, no attempts to issue new editions of this music had been made.

(E) In modern times much of the music of this school has been little known even to musicians.

GO ON TO THE NEXT PAGE.

3. The author mentions the sonatas of Muzio Clementi and the nocturnes of John Field as examples of which one of the following?

   (A)   works by composers of the London Pianoforte school that have been preserved in rigorous scholarly editions

   (B)   works that are no longer remembered by most people

   (C)   works acclaimed by the leaders of the London Pianoforte school

   (D)   works by composers of the London Pianoforte school that are relatively well known

   (E)   works by composers of the London Pianoforte school that have been revived by Temperley in his anthology

4. Which one of the following, if true, would most clearly undermine a portion of Ringer's argument as the argument is described in the passage?

   (A)   Musicians in Austria composed innovative music for the Broadwood piano as soon as the instrument became available.

   (B)   Clementi and his followers produced most of their compositions between 1790 and 1810.

   (C)   The influence of Continental musicians is apparent in some of the works of Beethoven.

   (D)   The pianist-composers of the London Pianoforte school shared many of the same stylistic principles.

   (E)   Most composers of the London Pianoforte school were born on the Continent and were drawn to London by the work of Clementi and his followers.

5. It can be inferred that the author uses the word "advances" (line 49) to refer to

   (A)   enticements offered musicians by instrument manufacturers

   (B)   improvements in the structure of a particular instrument

   (C)   innovations in the forms of music produced for a particular instrument

   (D)   stylistic elaborations made possible by changes in a particular instrument

   (E)   changes in musicians' opinions about a particular instrument

6. It can be inferred from the passage as a whole that the author's purpose in the third paragraph is primarily to

   (A)   cast doubt on the usefulness of Temperley's study of the London Pianoforte school

   (B)   introduce a discussion of the coherency of the London Pianoforte school

   (C)   summarize Ringer's argument about the London Pianoforte school

   (D)   emphasize the complex nature of the musicological elements shared by members of the London Pianoforte school

   (E)   identify the unique contributions made to music by the London Pianoforte school

7. The author of the passage is primarily concerned with

   (A)   explaining the influence of the development of the pianoforte on the music of Beethoven

   (B)   describing Temperley's view of the contrast between the development of piano music in England and the development of piano music elsewhere in Europe

   (C)   presenting Temperley's evaluation of the impact of changes in piano construction on styles and forms of music composed in the era of the London Pianoforte school

   (D)   considering an alternative theory to that proposed by Ringer concerning the London Pianoforte school

   (E)   discussing the contribution of Temperley's anthology to what is known of the history of the London Pianoforte school

8. It can be inferred that Temperley's anthology treats the London Pianoforte school as

   (A)   a group of pianist-composers who shared certain stylistic principles and artistic creeds

   (B)   a group of people who contributed to the development of piano music between 1766 and 1873

   (C)   a group of composers who influenced the music of Beethoven in the decades just before and just after 1800

   (D)   a series of compositions for the pianoforte published in the decades just before and just after 1800

   (E)   a series of compositions that had a significant influence on the music of the Continent in the eighteenth and nineteenth centuries

GO ON TO THE NEXT PAGE.

What is "law"? By what processes do judges arrive at opinions, those documents that justify their belief that the "law" dictates a conclusion one way or the other? These are among the oldest questions in
(5) jurisprudence, debate about which has traditionally been dominated by representatives of two schools of thought: proponents of natural law, who see law as intertwined with a moral order independent of society's rules and mores, and legal positivists, who see law
(10) solely as embodying the commands of a society's ruling authority.

Since the early 1970s, these familiar questions have received some new and surprising answers in the legal academy. This novelty is in part a consequence of the
(15) increasing influence there of academic disciplines and intellectual traditions previously unconnected with the study of law. Perhaps the most influential have been the answers given by the Law and Economics school. According to these legal economists, law consists and
(20) ought to consist of those rules that maximize a society's material wealth and that abet the efficient operation of markets designed to generate wealth. More controversial have been the various answers provided by members of the Critical Legal Studies movement,
(25) according to whom law is one among several cultural mechanisms by which holders of power seek to legitimate their domination. Drawing on related arguments developed in anthropology, sociology, and history, the critical legal scholars contend that law is an
(30) expression of power, but not, as held by the positivists, the power of the legitimate sovereign government. Rather, it is an expression of the power of elites who may have no legitimate authority, but who are intent on preserving the privileges of their race, class, or gender.
(35) In the mid-1970s, James Boyd White began to articulate yet another interdisciplinary response to the traditional questions, and in so doing spawned what is now known as the Law and Literature movement. White has insisted that law, particularly as it is
(40) interpreted in judicial opinions, should be understood as an essentially literary activity. Judicial opinions should be read and evaluated not primarily as political acts or as attempts to maximize society's wealth through efficient rules, but rather as artistic
(45) performances. And like all such performances, White argues, each judicial opinion attempts in its own way to promote a particular political or ethical value.

In the recent *Justice as Translation*, White argues that opinion-writing should be regarded as an act of
(50) "translation," and judges as "translators." As such, judges find themselves mediating between the authoritative legal text and the pressing legal problem that demands resolution. A judge must essentially "re-constitute" that text by fashioning a new one, which
(55) is faithful to the old text but also responsive to and informed by the conditions, constraints, and aspirations of the world in which the new legal problem has arisen.

9. Which one of the following best states the main idea of the passage?

(A) Within the last few decades, a number of novel approaches to jurisprudence have defined the nature of the law in diverse ways.

(B) Within the last few decades, changes in society and in the number and type of cases brought to court have necessitated new methods of interpreting the law.

(C) Of the many interdisciplinary approaches to jurisprudence that have surfaced in the last two decades, the Law and Literature movement is the most intellectually coherent.

(D) The Law and Literature movement, first articulated by James Boyd White in the mid-1970s, represents a synthesis of the many theories of jurisprudence inspired by the social sciences.

(E) Such traditional legal scholars as legal positivists and natural lawyers are increasingly on the defensive against attacks from younger, more progressive theorists.

10. According to the passage, judicial opinions have been described as each of the following EXCEPT:

(A) political statements
(B) arcane statements
(C) economic statements
(D) artistic performances
(E) acts of translation

GO ON TO THE NEXT PAGE.

11. Which one of the following statements is most compatible with the principles of the Critical Legal Studies movement as that movement is described in the passage?

  (A) Laws governing the succession of power at the death of a head of state represent a synthesis of legal precedents, specific situations, and the values of lawmakers.
  (B) Laws allowing income tax deductions for charitable contributions, though ostensibly passed by lawmakers, were devised by and are perpetuated by the rich.
  (C) Laws governing the tariffs placed on imported goods must favor the continuation of mutually beneficial trade arrangements, even at the expense of long-standing legal precedent.
  (D) Laws governing the treatment of the disadvantaged and powerless members of a given society are an accurate indication of that society's moral state.
  (E) Laws controlling the electoral processes of a representative democracy have been devised by lawmakers to ensure the continuation of that governmental system.

12. Which one of the following does the passage mention as a similarity between the Critical Legal Studies movement and the Law and Literature movement?

  (A) Both offer explanations of how elites maintain their hold on power.
  (B) Both are logical extensions of either natural law or legal positivism.
  (C) Both see economic and political primacy as the basis of all legitimate power.
  (D) Both rely on disciplines not traditionally connected with the study of law.
  (E) Both see the practice of opinion-writing as a mediating activity.

13. Which one of the following can be inferred from the passage about the academic study of jurisprudence before the 1970s?

  (A) It was concerned primarily with codifying and maintaining the privileges of elites.
  (B) It rejected theories that interpreted law as an expression of a group's power.
  (C) It seldom focused on how and by what authority judges arrived at opinions.
  (D) It was concerned primarily with the study of law as an economic and moral agent.
  (E) It was not concerned with such disciplines as anthropology and sociology.

14. Proponents of the Law and Literature movement would most likely agree with which one of the following statements concerning the relationship between the law and judges' written opinions?

  (A) The once-stable relationship between law and opinion-writing has been undermined by new and radical theoretical developments.
  (B) Only the most politically conservative of judges continue to base their opinions on natural law or on legal positivism.
  (C) The occurrence of different legal situations requires a judge to adopt diverse theoretical approaches to opinion-writing.
  (D) Different judges will not necessarily write the same sorts of opinions when confronted with the same legal situation.
  (E) Judges who subscribe to divergent theories of jurisprudence will necessarily render divergent opinions.

15. Which one of the following phrases best describes the meaning of "re-constitute" as that word is used in line 54 of the passage?

  (A) categorize and rephrase
  (B) investigate and summarize
  (C) interpret and refashion
  (D) paraphrase and announce
  (E) negotiate and synthesize

16. The primary purpose of the passage is to

  (A) identify differing approaches
  (B) discount a novel trend
  (C) advocate traditional methods
  (D) correct misinterpretations
  (E) reconcile seeming inconsistencies

GO ON TO THE NEXT PAGE.

Since the early 1920s, most petroleum geologists
have favored a biogenic theory for the formation of oil.
According to this theory, organic matter became buried
in sediments, and subsequent conditions of temperature
(5) and pressure over time transformed it into oil.

Since 1979 an opposing abiogenic theory about the
origin of oil has been promulgated. According to this
theory, what is now oil began as hydrocarbon
compounds within the earth's mantle (the region
(10) between the core and the crust) during the formation of
the earth. Oil was created when gases rich in methane,
the lightest of the hydrocarbons, rose from the mantle
through fractures and faults in the crust, carrying a
significant amount of heavier hydrocarbons with them.
(15) As the gases encountered intermittent drops in pressure,
the heavier hydrocarbons condensed, forming oil, and
were deposited in reservoirs throughout the crust. Rock
regions deformed by motions of the crustal plates
provided the conduits and fractures necessary for the
(20) gases to rise through the crust.

Opponents of the abiogenic theory charge that
hydrocarbons could not exist in the mantle, because
high temperatures would destroy or break them down.
Advocates of the theory, however, point out that other
(25) types of carbon exist in the mantle: unoxidized carbon
must exist there, because diamonds are formed within
the mantle before being brought to the surface by
eruptive processes. Proponents of the abiogenic theory
also point to recent experimental work that suggests
(30) that the higher pressures within the mantle tend to
offset the higher temperatures, allowing hydrocarbons,
like unoxidized carbon, to continue to exist in the
mantle.

If the abiogenic theory is correct, vast undiscovered
(35) reservoirs of oil and gas—undiscovered because the
biogenic model precludes their existence—may in
actuality exist. One company owned by the Swedish
government has found the abiogenic theory so
persuasive that it has started exploratory drilling for gas
(40) or oil in a granite formation called the Siljan Ring—not
the best place to look for gas or oil if one believes they
are derived from organic compounds, because granite
forms from magma (molten rock) and contains no
organic sediments. The ring was formed about 360
(45) million years ago when a large meteorite hit the 600-
million-year-old granite that forms the base of the
continental crust. The impact fractured the granite, and
the Swedes believe that if oil comes from the mantle, it
could have risen with methane gas through this now
(50) permeable rock. Fueling their optimism further is the
fact that prior to the start of drilling, methane gas had
been detected rising through the granite.

17. Which one of the following statements best expresses the
main idea of the passage?

(A) Although the new abiogenic theory about the
origin of oil is derived from the conventional
biogenic theory, it suggests new types of
locations for oil drilling.

(B) The small number of drilling companies that have
responded to the new abiogenic theory about the
origin of oil reflects the minimal level of
acceptance the theory has met with in the
scientific community.

(C) Although the new abiogenic theory about the
origin of oil fails to explain several enigmas
about oil reservoirs, it is superior to the
conventional biogenic theory.

(D) Although it has yet to receive either support or
refutation by data gathered from a drilling
project, the new abiogenic theory about the
origin of oil offers a plausible alternative to the
conventional biogenic theory.

(E) Having answered objections about higher
pressures in the earth's core, proponents of the
new abiogenic theory have gained broad
acceptance for their theory in the scientific
community.

GO ON TO THE NEXT PAGE.

18. Which one of the following best describes the function of the third paragraph?

   (A) It presents a view opposed to a theory and points out an internal contradiction in that opposing view.
   (B) It describes a criticism of a theory and provides countervailing evidence to the criticism.
   (C) It identifies a conflict between two views of a theory and revises both views.
   (D) It explains an argument against a theory and shows it to be a valid criticism.
   (E) It points out the correspondence between an argument against one theory and arguments against similar theories.

19. The passage suggests that the opponents of the abiogenic theory mentioned in the third paragraph would most probably agree with which one of the following statements?

   (A) The formation of oil does not involve the condensation of hydrocarbons released from the earth's mantle.
   (B) Large oil reserves are often found in locations that contain small amounts of organic matter.
   (C) The eruptive processes by which diamonds are brought to the earth's surface are similar to those that aid in the formation of oil.
   (D) Motions of the crustal plates often create the pressure necessary to transform organic matter into oil.
   (E) The largest known oil reserves may have resulted from organic matter combining with heavier hydrocarbons carried by methane gas.

20. Which one of the following is most analogous to the situation described in the final paragraph?

   (A) A new theory about the annual cycles of breeding and migration of the monarch butterfly has led scientists to look for similar patterns in other butterfly species.
   (B) A new theory about the stage at which a star collapses into a black hole has led astronomers to search for evidence of black holes in parts of the universe where they had not previously searched.
   (C) A new theory about how the emission of sulfur dioxide during coal-burning can be reduced has led several companies to develop desulfurization systems.
   (D) A new theory about photosynthesis has convinced a research team to explore in new ways the various functions of the cell membrane in plant cells.
   (E) A new theory about the distribution of metals in rock formations has convinced a silver-mining company to keep different types of records of its operations.

21. According to the passage, all of the following are true of the Siljan Ring EXCEPT:

   (A) It was formed from magma.
   (B) It does not contain organic sediments.
   (C) Its ring shape existed 500 million years ago.
   (D) Methane gas has been detected rising through it.
   (E) It was shaped from the granite that makes up the base of the continental crust.

GO ON TO THE NEXT PAGE.

Most studies of recent Southeast Asian immigrants to the United States have focused on their adjustment to life in their adopted country and on the effects of leaving their homelands. James Tollefson's *Alien*
(5) *Winds* examines the resettlement process from a different perspective by investigating the educational programs offered in immigrant processing centers. Based on interviews, transcripts from classes, essays by immigrants, personal visits to a teacher-training unit,
(10) and official government documents, Tollefson relies on an impressive amount and variety of documentation in making his arguments about processing centers' educational programs.

Tollefson's main contention is that the emphasis
(15) placed on immediate employment and on teaching the values, attitudes, and behaviors that the training personnel think will help the immigrants adjust more easily to life in the United States is often counterproductive and demoralizing. Because of
(20) concerns that the immigrants be self-supporting as soon as possible, they are trained almost exclusively for low-level jobs that do not require English proficiency. In this respect, Tollefson claims, the processing centers suit the needs of employers more than they suit the
(25) long-term needs of the immigrant community. Tollefson also detects a fundamental flaw in the attempts by program educators to instill in the immigrants the traditionally Western principles of self-sufficiency and individual success. These efforts often
(30) have the effect of undermining the immigrants' sense of community and, in doing so, sometimes isolate them from the moral support and even from business opportunities afforded by the immigrant community. The programs also encourage the immigrants to shed
(35) their cultural traditions and ethnic identity and adopt the lifestyles, beliefs, and characteristics of their adopted country if they wish to enter fully into the national life.

Tollefson notes that the ideological nature of these
(40) educational programs has roots in the turn-of-the-century educational programs designed to assimilate European immigrants into United States society. Tollefson provides a concise history of the assimilationist movement in immigrant education, in
(45) which European immigrants were encouraged to leave behind the ways of the Old World and to adopt instead the principles and practices of the New World.

Tollefson ably shows that the issues demanding real attention in the educational programs for Southeast
(50) Asian immigrants are not merely employment rates and government funding, but also the assumptions underpinning the educational values in the programs. He recommends many improvements for the programs, including giving the immigrants a stronger voice in
(55) determining their needs and how to meet them, redesigning the curricula, and emphasizing long-term language education and job training over immediate employment and the avoiding of public assistance. Unfortunately, though, Tollefson does not offer enough
(60) concrete solutions as to how these reforms could be carried out, despite his own descriptions of the complicated bureaucratic nature of the programs.

22. Which one of the following statements best expresses the main idea of the passage?

(A) Tollefson's focus on the economic and cultural factors involved in adjusting to a new country offers a significant departure from most studies of Southeast Asian immigration.

(B) In his analysis of educational programs for Southeast Asian immigrants, Tollefson fails to acknowledge many of the positive effects the programs have had on immigrants' lives.

(C) Tollefson convincingly blames the philosophy underlying immigrant educational programs for some of the adjustment problems afflicting Southeast Asian immigrants.

(D) Tollefson's most significant contribution is his analysis of how Southeast Asian immigrants overcome the obstacles they encounter in immigrant educational programs.

(E) Tollefson traces a gradual yet significant change in the attitudes held by processing center educators toward Southeast Asian immigrants.

23. With which one of the following statements concerning the educational programs of the immigration centers would Tollefson most probably agree?

(A) Although the programs offer adequate job training, they offer inadequate English training.

(B) Some of the programs' attempts to improve the earning power of the immigrants cut them off from potential sources of income.

(C) Inclusion of the history of immigration in the United States in the programs' curricula facilitates adjustment for the immigrants.

(D) Immigrants would benefit if instructors in the programs were better prepared to teach the curricula developed in the teacher-training courses.

(E) The programs' curricula should be redesigned to include greater emphasis on the shared values, beliefs, and practices in the United States.

GO ON TO THE NEXT PAGE.

24. Which one of the following best describes the opinion of the author of the passage with respect to Tollefson's work?

   (A) thorough but misguided
   (B) innovative but incomplete
   (C) novel but contradictory
   (D) illuminating but unappreciated
   (E) well documented but unoriginal

25. The passage suggests that which one of the following is an assumption underlying the educational approach in immigrant processing centers?

   (A) There is a set of values and behaviors that, if adopted by immigrants, facilitate adjustment to United States society.
   (B) When recent immigrants are self-supporting rather than supported by public assistance, they tend to gain English proficiency more quickly.
   (C) Immediate employment tends to undermine the immigrants' sense of community with each other.
   (D) Long-term success for immigrants is best achieved by encouraging the immigrants to maintain a strong sense of community.
   (E) The principles of self-sufficiency and individual success are central to Southeast Asian culture and ethnicity.

26. Which one of the following best describes the function of the first paragraph of the passage?

   (A) It provides the scholarly context for Tollefson's study and a description of his methodology.
   (B) It compares Tollefson's study to other works and presents the main argument of his study.
   (C) It compares the types of documents Tollefson uses to those used in other studies.
   (D) It presents the accepted theory on Tollefson's topic and the method by which Tollefson challenges it.
   (E) It argues for the analytical and technical superiority of Tollefson's study over other works on the topic.

27. The author of the passage refers to Tollefson's descriptions of the bureaucratic nature of the immigrant educational programs in the fourth paragraph most probably in order to

   (A) criticize Tollefson's decision to combine a description of the bureaucracies with suggestions for improvement
   (B) emphasize the author's disappointment in Tollefson's overly general recommendations for improvements to the programs
   (C) point out the irony of Tollefson concluding his study with suggestions for drastic changes in the programs
   (D) support a contention that Tollefson's recommendations for improvements do not focus on the real sources of the programs' problems
   (E) suggest a parallel between the complexity of the bureaucracies and the complexity of Tollefson's arguments

S T O P

IF YOU FINISH BEFORE TIME IS CALLED, YOU MAY CHECK YOUR WORK ON THIS SECTION ONLY.
DO NOT WORK ON ANY OTHER SECTION IN THE TEST.

LSAT® Writing Sample Topic

To celebrate the June completion of its downtown renovation project, the Rockland Merchants Association must decide between a street festival and a benefit auction. Write an argument supporting one event over the other based on the following criteria:

- Merchants in the downtown area want the event to showcase the entertainment, dining, and shopping opportunities available in the downtown area.
- The Merchants Association wants to establish the event as an annual tradition that builds a sense of community and civic cooperation among all of Rockland's residents.

The street festival would have the Main Street area of downtown blocked off for an entire Saturday. In addition to the stores and restaurants that would be open all day, booths would feature the work of local artisans and craftspersons. At one end of the street, a farmer's market would sell produce and flowers. At the other end, in the community center, local bands would volunteer their services and a space would be provided for dancing. A group of actors from City Stage, the resident theater in the downtown area, would perform comedy routines every other hour with no admission charge.

The auction would be held one Saturday evening to benefit Rockland General, the city's only hospital, located in the downtown area. Owners of the stores, galleries, and restaurants in the area would donate merchandise or gift certificates for the auction, in addition to keeping their businesses open for the evening. The nominal admission fee for the auction would entitle the buyer to a buffet supper, catered by downtown restaurants, to be held in the community center. Students from local schools would provide entertainment in the form of music, dance, and dramatic readings at City Stage. Proceeds from both the admission fee and the auction would go to the hospital.

Directions:

1. Use the Answer Key on the next page to check your answers.

2. Use the Scoring Worksheet below to compute your raw score.

3. Use the Score Conversion Chart to convert your raw score into the 120-180 scale.

Scoring Worksheet

1. Enter the number of questions you answered correctly in each section.

	Number Correct
SECTION I	_____
SECTION II	_____
SECTION III	_____
SECTION IV	_____

2. Enter the sum here: _____
   This is your Raw Score.

Conversion Chart

For Converting Raw Score to the 120-180 LSAT Scaled Score
LSAT Form 6LSS30

Reported Score	Raw Score Lowest	Raw Score Highest
180	98	101
179	97	97
178	96	96
177	95	95
176	94	94
175	93	93
174	92	92
173	91	91
172	90	90
171	88	89
170	87	87
169	86	86
168	85	85
167	83	84
166	82	82
165	80	81
164	79	79
163	77	78
162	76	76
161	74	75
160	72	73
159	71	71
158	69	70
157	67	68
156	66	66
155	64	65
154	62	63
153	61	61
152	59	60
151	57	58
150	55	56
149	54	54
148	52	53
147	50	51
146	49	49
145	47	48
144	45	46
143	44	44
142	42	43
141	41	41
140	39	40
139	37	38
138	36	36
137	34	35
136	33	33
135	32	32
134	30	31
133	29	29
132	28	28
131	26	27
130	25	25
129	24	24
128	23	23
127	22	22
126	21	21
125	20	20
124	19	19
123	18	18
122	17	17
121	–*	–*
120	0	16

*There is no raw score that will produce this scaled score for this form.

SECTION I

1.	C	8.	A	15.	E	22.	E
2.	B	9.	A	16.	E	23.	D
3.	B	10.	B	17.	A	24.	E
4.	C	11.	A	18.	B		
5.	A	12.	D	19.	C		
6.	C	13.	D	20.	B		
7.	D	14.	B	21.	A		

SECTION II

1.	B	8.	E	15.	A	22.	E
2.	C	9.	E	16.	E	23.	B
3.	B	10.	A	17.	C	24.	A
4.	D	11.	C	18.	A	25.	E
5.	C	12.	B	19.	C		
6.	B	13.	D	20.	D		
7.	B	14.	C	21.	A		

SECTION III

1.	E	8.	C	15.	E	22.	C
2.	A	9.	B	16.	C	23.	C
3.	E	10.	D	17.	D	24.	E
4.	A	11.	C	18.	D	25.	E
5.	C	12.	B	19.	B		
6.	C	13.	A	20.	D		
7.	D	14.	D	21.	B		

SECTION IV

1.	B	8.	B	15.	C	22.	C
2.	E	9.	A	16.	A	23.	B
3.	D	10.	B	17.	D	24.	B
4.	A	11.	B	18.	B	25.	A
5.	B	12.	D	19.	A	26.	A
6.	B	13.	E	20.	B	27.	B
7.	E	14.	D	21.	C		

The Official LSAT PrepTest

2

- June 1997
- Form 8LSS36

The sample test that follows consists of four sections corresponding to the four scored sections of the June 1997 LSAT.

SECTION I

Time—35 minutes

26 Questions

Directions: Each passage in this section is followed by a group of questions to be answered on the basis of what is <u>stated</u> or <u>implied</u> in the passage. For some of the questions, more than one of the choices could conceivably answer the question. However, you are to choose the <u>best</u> answer; that is, the response that most accurately and completely answers the question, and blacken the corresponding space on your answer sheet.

Painter Frida Kahlo (1910–1954) often used harrowing images derived from her Mexican heritage to express suffering caused by a disabling accident and a stormy marriage. Suggesting much personal and
(5) emotional content, her works—many of them self-portraits—have been exhaustively psychoanalyzed, while their political content has been less studied. Yet Kahlo was an ardent political activist who in her art sought not only to explore her own roots, but also to
(10) champion Mexico's struggle for an independent political and cultural identity.

Kahlo was influenced by Marxism, which appealed to many intellectuals in the 1920s and 1930s, and by Mexican nationalism. Interest in Mexico's culture and
(15) history had revived in the nineteenth century, and by the early 1900s, Mexican *indigenista* tendencies ranged from a violently anti-Spanish idealization of Aztec Mexico to an emphasis on contemporary Mexican Indians as the key to authentic Mexican culture.
(20) Mexican nationalism, reacting against contemporary United States political intervention in labor disputes as well as against past domination by Spain, identified the Aztecs as the last independent rulers of an indigenous political unit. Kahlo's form of *Mexicanidad*, a romantic
(25) nationalism that focused upon traditional art uniting all *indigenistas*, revered the Aztecs as a powerful pre-Columbian society that had united a large area of the Middle Americas and that was thought to have been based on communal labor, the Marxist ideal.
(30) In her paintings, Kahlo repeatedly employed Aztec symbols, such as skeletons or bleeding hearts, that were traditionally related to the emanation of life from death and light from darkness. These images of destruction coupled with creation speak not only to
(35) Kahlo's personal battle for life, but also to the Mexican struggle to emerge as a nation—by implication, to emerge with the political and cultural strength admired in the Aztec civilization. *Self-Portrait on the Border between Mexico and the United States* (1932), for
(40) example, shows Kahlo wearing a bone necklace, holding a Mexican flag, and standing between a highly industrialized United States and an agricultural, preindustrial Mexico. On the United States side are mechanistic and modern images such as smokestacks,
(45) light bulbs, and robots. In contrast, the organic and ancient symbols on the Mexican side—a blood-drenched Sun, lush vegetation, an Aztec sculpture, a pre-Columbian temple, and a skull alluding to those that lined the walls of Aztec temples—emphasize the
(50) interrelation of life, death, the earth, and the cosmos.

Kahlo portrayed Aztec images in the folkloric style of traditional Mexican paintings, thereby heightening the clash between modern materialism and indigenous tradition; similarly, she favored planned economic
(55) development, but not at the expense of cultural identity. Her use of familiar symbols in a readily accessible style also served her goal of being popularly understood; in turn, Kahlo is viewed by some Mexicans as a mythic figure representative of
(60) nationalism itself.

1. Which one of the following best expresses the main point of the passage?

(A) The doctrines of Marxist ideology and Mexican nationalism heavily influenced Mexican painters of Kahlo's generation.

(B) Kahlo's paintings contain numerous references to the Aztecs as an indigenous Mexican people predating European influence.

(C) An important element of Kahlo's work is conveyed by symbols that reflect her advocacy of indigenous Mexican culture and Mexican political autonomy.

(D) The use of Aztec images and symbols in Kahlo's art can be traced to the late nineteenth-century revival of interest in Mexican history and culture.

(E) Kahlo used Aztec imagery in her paintings primarily in order to foster contemporary appreciation for the authentic art of traditional Mexican culture.

GO ON TO THE NEXT PAGE.

2. With which one of the following statements concerning psychoanalytic and political interpretations of Kahlo's work would the author be most likely to agree?

    (A) The psychoanalytic interpretations of Kahlo's work tend to challenge the political interpretations.
    (B) Political and psychoanalytic interpretations are complementary approaches to Kahlo's work.
    (C) Recent political interpretations of Kahlo's work are causing psychoanalytic critics to revise their own interpretations.
    (D) Unlike the political interpretations, the psychoanalytic interpretations make use of biographical facts of Kahlo's life.
    (E) Kahlo's mythic status among the audience Kahlo most wanted to reach is based upon the psychoanalytic rather than the political content of her work.

3. Which one of the following stances toward the United States does the passage mention as characterizing Mexican nationalists in the early twentieth century?

    (A) opposition to United States involvement in internal Mexican affairs
    (B) desire to decrease emigration of the Mexican labor force to the United States
    (C) desire to improve Mexico's economic competitiveness with the United States
    (D) reluctance to imitate the United States model of rapid industrialization
    (E) advocacy of a government based upon that of the Marxist Soviet Union rather than that of the United States

4. In the context of the passage, which one of the following phrases could best be substituted for the word "romantic" (line 24) without substantially changing the author's meaning?

    (A) dreamy and escapist
    (B) nostalgic and idealistic
    (C) fanciful and imaginative
    (D) transcendental and impractical
    (E) overwrought and sentimental

5. The passage mentions each of the following as an Aztec symbol or image found in Kahlo's paintings EXCEPT a

    (A) skeleton
    (B) sculpture
    (C) serpent
    (D) skull
    (E) bleeding heart

6. Which one of the following best describes the organization of the third paragraph?

    (A) contrast of opposing ideas
    (B) reconciliation of conflicting concepts
    (C) interrelation of complementary themes
    (D) explication of a principle's implications
    (E) support for a generalization by means of an example

7. The passage implies that Kahlo's attitude toward the economic development of Mexico was

    (A) enthusiastic
    (B) condemnatory
    (C) cautious
    (D) noncommittal
    (E) uncertain

8. The main purpose of the passage is to

    (A) critique an artist's style
    (B) evaluate opposing theories
    (C) reconcile conflicting arguments
    (D) advocate an additional interpretation
    (E) reconsider an artist in light of new discoveries

GO ON TO THE NEXT PAGE.

In recent years, a growing belief that the way society decides what to treat as true is controlled through largely unrecognized discursive practices has led legal reformers to examine the complex
(5) interconnections between narrative and law. In many legal systems, legal judgments are based on competing stories about events. Without having witnessed these events, judges and juries must validate some stories as true and reject others as false. This procedure is rooted
(10) in objectivism, a philosophical approach that has supported most Western legal and intellectual systems for centuries. Objectivism holds that there is a single neutral description of each event that is unskewed by any particular point of view and that has a privileged
(15) position over all other accounts. The law's quest for truth, therefore, consists of locating this objective description, the one that tells what really happened, as opposed to what those involved thought happened. The serious flaw in objectivism is that there is no such thing
(20) as the neutral, objective observer. As psychologists have demonstrated, all observers bring to a situation a set of expectations, values, and beliefs that determine what the observers are able to see and hear. Two individuals listening to the same story will hear
(25) different things, because they emphasize those aspects that accord with their learned experiences and ignore those aspects that are dissonant with their view of the world. Hence there is never any escape in life or in law from selective perception, or from subjective
(30) judgments based on prior experiences, values, and beliefs.
       The societal harm caused by the assumption of objectivist principles in traditional legal discourse is that, historically, the stories judged to be objectively
(35) true are those told by people who are trained in legal discourse, while the stories of those who are not fluent in the language of the law are rejected as false.
       Legal scholars such as Patricia Williams, Derrick Bell, and Mari Matsuda have sought empowerment for
(40) the latter group of people through the construction of alternative legal narratives. Objectivist legal discourse systematically disallows the language of emotion and experience by focusing on cognition in its narrowest sense. These legal reformers propose replacing such
(45) abstract discourse with powerful personal stories. They argue that the absorbing, nonthreatening structure and tone of personal stories may convince legal insiders for the first time to listen to those not fluent in legal language. The compelling force of personal narrative
(50) can create a sense of empathy between legal insiders and people traditionally excluded from legal discourse and, hence, from power. Such alternative narratives can shatter the complacency of the legal establishment and disturb its tranquility. Thus, the engaging power of
(55) narrative might play a crucial, positive role in the process of legal reconstruction by overcoming differences in background and training and forming a new collectivity based on emotional empathy.

9. Which one of the following best states the main idea of the passage?

(A) Some legal scholars have sought to empower people historically excluded from traditional legal discourse by instructing them in the forms of discourse favored by legal insiders.

(B) Some legal scholars have begun to realize the social harm caused by the adversarial atmosphere that has pervaded many legal systems for centuries.

(C) Some legal scholars have proposed alleviating the harm caused by the prominence of objectivist principles within legal discourse by replacing that discourse with alternative forms of legal narrative.

(D) Some legal scholars have contended that those who feel excluded from objectivist legal systems would be empowered by the construction of a new legal language that better reflected objectivist principles.

(E) Some legal scholars have argued that the basic flaw inherent in objectivist theory can be remedied by recognizing that it is not possible to obtain a single neutral description of a particular event.

10. According to the passage, which one of the following is true about the intellectual systems mentioned in line 11 ?

(A) They have long assumed the possibility of a neutral depiction of events.

(B) They have generally remained unskewed by particular points of view.

(C) Their discursive practices have yet to be analyzed by legal scholars.

(D) They accord a privileged position to the language of emotion and experience.

(E) The accuracy of their basic tenets has been confirmed by psychologists.

11. Which one of the following best describes the sense of "cognition" referred to in line 43 of the passage?

(A) logical thinking uninfluenced by passion

(B) the interpretation of visual cues

(C) human thought that encompasses all emotion and experience

(D) the reasoning actually employed by judges to arrive at legal judgments

(E) sudden insights inspired by the power of personal stories

GO ON TO THE NEXT PAGE.

12. It can be inferred from the passage that Williams, Bell, and Matsuda believe which one of the following to be a central component of legal reform?

    (A) incorporating into the law the latest developments in the fields of psychology and philosophy
    (B) eradicating from legal judgments discourse with a particular point of view
    (C) granting all participants in legal proceedings equal access to training in the forms and manipulation of legal discourse
    (D) making the law more responsive to the discursive practices of a wider variety of people
    (E) instilling an appreciation of legal history and methodology in all the participants in a legal proceeding

13. Which one of the following most accurately describes the author's attitude toward proposals to introduce personal stories into legal discourse?

    (A) strongly opposed
    (B) somewhat skeptical
    (C) ambivalent
    (D) strongly supportive
    (E) unreservedly optimistic

14. The passage suggests that Williams, Bell, and Matsuda would most likely agree with which one of the following statements regarding personal stories?

    (A) Personal stories are more likely to adhere to the principles of objectivism than are other forms of discourse.
    (B) Personal stories are more likely to deemphasize differences in background and training than are traditional forms of legal discourse.
    (C) Personal stories are more likely to restore tranquility to the legal establishment than are more adversarial forms of discourse.
    (D) Personal stories are more likely to lead to the accurate reconstruction of facts than are traditional forms of legal narrative.
    (E) Personal stories are more likely to be influenced by a person's expectations, values, and beliefs than are other forms of discourse.

15. Which one of the following statements about legal discourse in legal systems based on objectivism can be inferred from the passage?

    (A) In most Western societies, the legal establishment controls access to training in legal discourse.
    (B) Expertise in legal discourse affords power in most Western societies.
    (C) Legal discourse has become progressively more abstract for some centuries.
    (D) Legal discourse has traditionally denied the existence of neutral, objective observers.
    (E) Traditional legal discourse seeks to reconcile dissonant world views.

16. Those who reject objectivism would regard "the law's quest for truth" (lines 15–16) as most similar to which one of the following?

    (A) a hunt for an imaginary animal
    (B) the search for a valuable mineral among worthless stones
    (C) the painstaking assembly of a jigsaw puzzle
    (D) comparing an apple with an orange
    (E) the scientific analysis of a chemical compound

GO ON TO THE NEXT PAGE.

Many people complain about corporations, but there are also those whose criticism goes further and who hold corporations morally to blame for many of the problems in Western society. Their criticism is not
(5) reserved solely for fraudulent or illegal business activities, but extends to the basic corporate practice of making decisions based on what will maximize profits without regard to whether such decisions will contribute to the public good. Others, mainly
(10) economists, have responded that this criticism is flawed because it inappropriately applies ethical principles to economic relationships.

It is only by extension that we attribute the quality of morality to corporations, for corporations are not
(15) persons. Corporate responsibility is an aggregation of the responsibilities of those persons employed by the corporation when they act in and on behalf of the corporation. Some corporations are owner operated, but in many corporations and in most larger ones there
(20) is a syndicate of owners to whom the chief executive officer, or CEO, who runs the corporation is said to have a fiduciary obligation.

The economists argue that a CEO's sole responsibility is to the owners, whose primary interest,
(25) except in charitable institutions, is the protection of their profits. CEOs are bound, as a condition of their employment, to seek a profit for the owners. But suppose a noncharitable organization is owner operated, or, for some other reason, its CEO is not
(30) obligated to maximize profits. The economists' view is that even if such a CEO's purpose is to look to the public good and nothing else, the CEO should still work to maximize profits, because that will turn out best for the public anyway.
(35) But the economists' position does not hold up under careful scrutiny. For one thing, although there are, no doubt, strong underlying dynamics in national and international economies that tend to make the pursuit of corporate interest contribute to the public
(40) good, there is no guarantee—either theoretically or in practice—that a given CEO will benefit the public by maximizing corporate profit. It is absurd to deny the possibility, say, of a paper mill legally maximizing its profits over a five-year period by decimating a forest
(45) for its wood or polluting a lake with its industrial waste. Furthermore, while obligations such as those of corporate CEOs to corporate owners are binding in a business or legal sense, they are not morally paramount. The CEO could make a case to the owners
(50) that certain profitable courses of action should not be taken because they are likely to detract from the public good. The economic consequences that may befall the CEO for doing so, such as penalty or dismissal, ultimately do not excuse the individual from the
(55) responsibility for acting morally.

17. Which one of the following most accurately states the main point of the passage?

(A) Although CEOs may be legally obligated to maximize their corporations' profits, this obligation does not free them from the moral responsibility of considering the implications of the corporations' actions for the public good.

(B) Although morality is not easily ascribed to nonhuman entities, corporations can be said to have an obligation to act morally in the sense that they are made up of individuals who must act morally.

(C) Although economists argue that maximizing a corporation's profits is likely to turn out best for the public, a CEO's true obligation is still to seek a profit for the corporation's owners.

(D) Although some people criticize corporations for making unethical decisions, economists argue that such criticisms are unfounded because ethical considerations cannot be applied to economics.

(E) Although critics of corporations argue that CEOs ought to consider the public good when making financial decisions, the results of such decisions in fact always benefit the public.

18. The discussion of the paper mill in lines 42–46 is intended primarily to

(A) offer an actual case of unethical corporate behavior

(B) refute the contention that maximization of profits necessarily benefits the public

(C) illustrate that ethical restrictions on corporations would be difficult to enforce

(D) demonstrate that corporations are responsible for many social ills

(E) deny that corporations are capable of acting morally

GO ON TO THE NEXT PAGE.

19. With which one of the following would the economists mentioned in the passage be most likely to agree?

 (A) Even CEOs of charitable organizations are obligated to maximize profits.
 (B) CEOs of owner-operated noncharitable corporations should make decisions based primarily on maximizing profits.
 (C) Owner-operated noncharitable corporations are less likely to be profitable than other corporations.
 (D) It is highly unlikely that the actions of any particular CEO will benefit the public.
 (E) CEOs should attempt to maximize profits unless such attempts result in harm to the environment.

20. The conception of morality that underlies the author's argument in the passage is best expressed by which one of the following principles?

 (A) What makes actions morally right is their contribution to the public good.
 (B) An action is morally right if it carries the risk of personal penalty.
 (C) Actions are morally right if they are not fraudulent or illegal.
 (D) It is morally wrong to try to maximize one's personal benefit.
 (E) Actions are not morally wrong unless they harm others.

21. The primary purpose of the passage is to

 (A) illustrate a paradox
 (B) argue for legal reform
 (C) refute a claim
 (D) explain a decision
 (E) define a concept

GO ON TO THE NEXT PAGE.

What it means to "explain" something in science often comes down to the application of mathematics. Some thinkers hold that mathematics is a kind of language—a systematic contrivance of signs, the

(5) criteria for the authority of which are internal coherence, elegance, and depth. The application of such a highly artificial system to the physical world, they claim, results in the creation of a kind of statement about the world. Accordingly, what matters in the

(10) sciences is finding a mathematical concept that attempts, as other language does, to accurately describe the functioning of some aspect of the world.

At the center of the issue of scientific knowledge can thus be found questions about the relationship

(15) between language and what it refers to. A discussion about the role played by language in the pursuit of knowledge has been going on among linguists for several decades. The debate centers around whether language corresponds in some essential way to objects

(20) and behaviors, making knowledge a solid and reliable commodity; or, on the other hand, whether the relationship between language and things is purely a matter of agreed-upon conventions, making knowledge tenuous, relative, and inexact.

(25) Lately the latter theory has been gaining wider acceptance. According to linguists who support this theory, the way language is used varies depending upon changes in accepted practices and theories among those who work in a particular discipline. These

(30) linguists argue that, in the pursuit of knowledge, a statement is true only when there are no promising alternatives that might lead one to question it. Certainly this characterization would seem to be applicable to the sciences. In science, a mathematical statement may be

(35) taken to account for every aspect of a phenomenon it is applied to, but, some would argue, there is nothing inherent in mathematical language that guarantees such a correspondence. Under this view, acceptance of a mathematical statement by the scientific community—

(40) by virtue of the statement's predictive power or methodological efficiency—transforms what is basically an analogy or metaphor into an explanation of the physical process in question, to be held as true until another, more compelling analogy takes its place.

(45) In pursuing the implications of this theory, linguists have reached the point at which they must ask: If words or sentences do not correspond in an essential way to life or to our ideas about life, then just what are they capable of telling us about the world? In science

(50) and mathematics, then, it would seem equally necessary to ask: If models of electrolytes or $E = mc^2$, say, do not correspond essentially to the physical world, then just what functions do they perform in the acquisition of scientific knowledge? But this question

(55) has yet to be significantly addressed in the sciences.

22. Which one of the following statements most accurately expresses the passage's main point?

(A) Although scientists must rely on both language and mathematics in their pursuit of scientific knowledge, each is an imperfect tool for perceiving and interpreting aspects of the physical world.

(B) The acquisition of scientific knowledge depends on an agreement among scientists to accept some mathematical statements as more precise than others while acknowledging that all mathematics is inexact.

(C) If science is truly to progress, scientists must temporarily abandon the pursuit of new knowledge in favor of a systematic analysis of how the knowledge they already possess came to be accepted as true.

(D) In order to better understand the acquisition of scientific knowledge, scientists must investigate mathematical statements' relationship to the world just as linguists study language's relationship to the world.

(E) Without the debates among linguists that preceded them, it is unlikely that scientists would ever have begun to explore the essential role played by mathematics in the acquisition of scientific knowledge.

23. Which one of the following statements, if true, lends the most support to the view that language has an essential correspondence to the things it describes?

(A) The categories of physical objects employed by one language correspond remarkably to the categories employed by another language that developed independently of the first.

(B) The categories of physical objects employed by one language correspond remarkably to the categories employed by another language that derives from the first.

(C) The categories of physical objects employed by speakers of a language correspond remarkably to the categories employed by other speakers of the same language.

(D) The sentence structures of languages in scientifically sophisticated societies vary little from language to language.

(E) Native speakers of many languages believe that the categories of physical objects employed by their language correspond to natural categories of objects in the world.

GO ON TO THE NEXT PAGE.

24. According to the passage, mathematics can be considered a language because it

(A) conveys meaning in the same way that metaphors do
(B) constitutes a systematic collection of signs
(C) corresponds exactly to aspects of physical phenomena
(D) confers explanatory power on scientific theories
(E) relies on previously agreed-upon conventions

25. The primary purpose of the third paragraph is to

(A) offer support for the view of linguists who believe that language has an essential correspondence to things
(B) elaborate the position of linguists who believe that truth is merely a matter of convention
(C) illustrate the differences between the essentialist and conventionalist positions in the linguists' debate
(D) demonstrate the similarity of the linguists' debate to a current debate among scientists about the nature of explanation
(E) explain the theory that mathematical statements are a kind of language

26. Based on the passage, linguists who subscribe to the theory described in lines 21–24 would hold that the statement "The ball is red" is true because

(A) speakers of English have accepted that "The ball is red" applies to the particular physical relationship being described
(B) speakers of English do not accept that synonyms for "ball" and "red" express these concepts as elegantly
(C) "The ball is red" corresponds essentially to every aspect of the particular physical relationship being described
(D) "ball" and "red" actually refer to an entity and a property respectively
(E) "ball" and "red" are mathematical concepts that attempt to accurately describe some particular physical relationship in the world

S T O P

IF YOU FINISH BEFORE TIME IS CALLED, YOU MAY CHECK YOUR WORK ON THIS SECTION ONLY.
DO NOT WORK ON ANY OTHER SECTION IN THE TEST.

SECTION II

Time—35 minutes

25 Questions

Directions: The questions in this section are based on the reasoning contained in brief statements or passages. For some questions, more than one of the choices could conceivably answer the question. However, you are to choose the best answer; that is, the response that most accurately and completely answers the question. You should not make assumptions that are by commonsense standards implausible, superfluous, or incompatible with the passage. After you have chosen the best answer, blacken the corresponding space on your answer sheet.

1. Braille is a method of producing text by means of raised dots that can be read by touch. A recent development in technology will allow flat computer screens to be made of a material that can be heated in patterns that replicate the patterns used in braille. Since the thermal device will utilize the same symbol system as braille, it follows that anyone who is accustomed to reading braille can easily adapt to the use of this electronic system.

    Which one of the following is an assumption on which the conclusion depends?

    (A) Braille is the only symbol system that can be readily adapted for use with the new thermal screen.
    (B) Only people who currently use braille as their sole medium for reading text will have the capacity to adapt to the use of the thermal screen.
    (C) People with the tactile ability to discriminate symbols in braille have an ability to discriminate similar patterns on a flat heated surface.
    (D) Some symbol systems encode a piece of text by using dots that replicate the shape of letters of the alphabet.
    (E) Eventually it will be possible to train people to read braille by first training them in the use of the thermal screen.

2. Mayor of Outerville, a suburb of Center City:
    Outerville must grow if it is to survive, so, as we have agreed, efforts should be made to attract more residents. The best strategy for attracting residents is to renovate the train station. The numbers of jobs in Center City and of people who prefer to live in suburban towns are increasing. With the rise in tolls, driving into the city is becoming more expensive than train travel. Therefore, people want to live in towns where train travel is convenient and pleasant.

    The argument leads to the conclusion that

    (A) the town of Outerville should attract more residents
    (B) the train station in Outerville should be renovated
    (C) residents of Outerville who are in need of work should look for jobs in Center City
    (D) people who work in Center City but live in Outerville should commute by train rather than driving
    (E) people who want to live where train travel is convenient and pleasant should live in Outerville

3. Land developer: By attempting to preserve endangered species that otherwise would become extinct during our lifetime, we are wasting money on species that will disappear over time regardless of our efforts. Paleontologists have established that extinction is the normal fate of species on the geological time scale of millions of years.

    Environmentalist: To claim that we should let species disappear because all species eventually die out makes about as much sense as arguing that we should not spend money to find a cure for cancer because all humans are inevitably mortal.

    The method the environmentalist uses to object to the land developer's argument is to

    (A) clarify a dilemma that is embedded in the land developer's argument
    (B) attack the character of the land developer rather than the position the land developer is taking
    (C) show that more evidence is needed to substantiate the land developer's conclusion
    (D) show that the land developer's line of reasoning would lead to an unacceptable conclusion if applied to a different situation
    (E) argue that there are problems that money, however judiciously spent, cannot solve

GO ON TO THE NEXT PAGE.

4. Most small children are flat-footed. This failure of the foot to assume its natural arch, if it persists past early childhood, can sometimes result in discomfort and even pain later in life. Traditionally, flat-footedness in children has been treated by having the children wear special shoes that give extra support to the foot, in order to foster the development of the arch.

Which one of the following, if true, most calls into question the efficacy of the traditional treatment described above?

(A) Many small children who have normal feet wear the same special shoes as those worn by flat-footed children.

(B) Studies of flat-footed adults show that flat feet are subject to fewer stress fractures than are feet with unusually high arches.

(C) Although most children's flat-footedness is corrected by the time the children reach puberty, some people remain flat-footed for life.

(D) Flat-footed children who do not wear the special shoes are as likely to develop natural arches as are flat-footed children who wear the special shoes.

(E) Some children who are not flat-footed have hip and lower leg bones that are rotated excessively either inward or outward.

5. The chances that tropical storms will develop in a given area increase whenever the temperature of a large body of water in that area exceeds 26 degrees Celsius to a depth of about 60 meters. If the amount of carbon dioxide in the Earth's atmosphere continues to increase, the temperatures of all of the Earth's waters will rise, with the result that the number of large bodies of water whose temperatures exceed 26 degrees Celsius to a depth of about 60 meters will eventually be greater than it is today.

The statements above, if true, most strongly support which one of the following conclusions?

(A) There are likely to be more tropical storms if the amount of carbon dioxide in the Earth's atmosphere continues to increase.

(B) Tropical storms can occur only when the air temperature exceeds 26 degrees Celsius.

(C) The number of large bodies of water whose temperatures exceed 26 degrees Celsius to a depth of about 60 meters is greater today than it ever was.

(D) The ferocity of tropical storms does not depend on the amount of carbon dioxide in the Earth's atmosphere.

(E) Any increase in the temperatures of the Earth's oceans would cause the amount of carbon dioxide in the atmosphere to increase as well.

6. Astorga's campaign promises are apparently just an attempt to please voters. What she says she will do if elected mayor is simply what she has learned from opinion polls that voters want the new mayor to do. Therefore, voters are not being told what Astorga actually intends to do if she becomes mayor.

Which one of the following is a questionable assumption on which the argument relies?

(A) If she is elected mayor, Astorga will not be capable of carrying out the campaign promises she has made.

(B) The opinion polls on which Astorga's promises are based do not accurately reflect what voters want the new mayor to do.

(C) Most voters are unlikely to be persuaded by Astorga's campaign promises to vote for her in the mayoral election.

(D) Astorga has no strong opinions of her own about what the new mayor ought to do in office.

(E) Astorga does not actually intend, if elected, to do what she has learned from the public opinion polls that voters want the new mayor to do.

7. Newsletter for community-center volunteers: Retired persons who regularly volunteer their time to help others generally display fewer and milder effects of aging than their nonvolunteering contemporaries: in social resources, mental outlook, physical health, economic resources, and overall functioning, they are found to be substantially stronger than nonvolunteers. Volunteering is often described as doing good works to improve the lives of others. How good to know that there is evidence that it can equally benefit your own well-being!

The inference drawn above is unwarranted because

(A) the center has a self-interested motive to attract new volunteers

(B) it interprets "well-being" as including the factors of social and economic resources, mental outlook, physical health, and overall functioning

(C) some of those who do not volunteer might be older than some volunteers and so could not be considered their peers

(D) growing older might not necessarily result in a change in mental outlook

(E) those with better resources, health, outlook, and functioning are more able to work as volunteers

GO ON TO THE NEXT PAGE.

Questions 8–9

The local agricultural official gave the fruit growers of the District 10 Farmers' Cooperative a new pesticide that they applied for a period of three years to their pear orchards in place of the pesticide they had formerly applied. During those three years, the proportion of pears lost to insects was significantly less than it had been during the previous three-year period. On the basis of these results, the official concluded that the new pesticide was more effective than the old pesticide, at least in the short term, in limiting the loss of certain fruit to insects.

8. Each of the following, if true, weakens the official's argument EXCEPT:

(A)   The amount of fruit that an orchard can potentially produce depends in part on how many mature trees it contains, and the number of mature pear trees in District 10 has declined steadily over the past eight years.

(B)   During the past five years, the farmers of the District 10 Farmers' Cooperative have been gradually implementing a variety of insect-abatement programs, and some of these programs have proven successful.

(C)   Over the past five years, one of the several species of birds that typically prey on the insects that feed on pears has gradually shifted its migratory patterns, spending more and more months each year in the region that contains District 10.

(D)   Some of the species of insects in District 10 that infest pear trees are water breeders, and the reservoirs and marshlands in this district have been shrinking rapidly over the past three years.

(E)   The effects of certain pesticides, including the pesticide that had formerly been used in District 10, are cumulative and persist for several years after the pesticide is no longer applied.

9. The official's conclusion is most strongly supported if which one of the following groups of trees did not show a reduction in losses of fruit to insects?

(A)   peach trees grown in the district that were treated with the new pesticide instead of the old pesticide

(B)   peach trees grown in the district that were treated with the new pesticide in addition to the old pesticide

(C)   pear trees grown in the district that were treated with the old pesticide instead of the new pesticide

(D)   pear trees grown in a neighboring district that were treated with neither the old nor the new pesticide

(E)   pear trees grown in a neighboring district that were treated with the new pesticide instead of the old pesticide

10. The only motives that influence all human actions arise from self-interest. It is clear, therefore, that self-interest is the chief influence on human action.

The reasoning in the argument is fallacious because the argument

(A)   denies that an observation that a trait is common to all the events in a pattern can contribute to a causal explanation of the pattern

(B)   takes the occurrence of one particular influence on a pattern or class of events as showing that its influence outweighs any other influence on those events

(C)   concludes that a characteristic of a pattern or class of events at one time is characteristic of similar patterns or classes of events at all times

(D)   concludes that, because an influence is the paramount influence on a particular pattern or class of events, that influence is the only influence on that pattern or class of events

(E)   undermines its own premise that a particular attribute is present in all instances of a certain pattern or class of events

11. Astronomer: Astronomical observatories in many areas have become useless because light from nearby cities obscures the stars. Many people argue that since streetlights are needed for safety, such interference from lights is inevitable. Here in Sandsville, however, the local observatory's view remains relatively clear, since the city has restricted unnecessary lighting and installed special street lamps that direct all their light downward. It is therefore possible to have both well-lighted streets and relatively dark skies.

The astronomer's argument proceeds by

(A)   appealing to a scientific authority to challenge a widely held belief

(B)   questioning the accuracy of evidence given in support of the opposing position

(C)   proposing an alternative scientific explanation for a natural phenomenon

(D)   making a distinction between terms

(E)   offering a counterexample to a general claim

GO ON TO THE NEXT PAGE.

12. Music critic: Some people argue that, unlike certain works of Handel, which set to music familiar religious texts, the organ symphonies of Louis Vierne are not religious music. Quite the contrary. Sitting in Notre Dame cathedral in Paris and hearing his organ symphonies demonstrates that Vierne's works are divinely inspired.

The music critic's reasoning is vulnerable to criticism on the ground that it

(A)   takes for granted that all religious music is inspiring
(B)   confuses two different meanings of the term "religious"
(C)   overlooks the possibility that some organ music is not divinely inspired
(D)   confuses two different meanings of the term "symphonies"
(E)   takes for granted that all organ symphonies are religious music

Questions 13–14

Charles: During recessions unemployment typically rises. Thus, during a recession air pollution due to automobile exhaust decreases, since fewer people commute in cars to jobs and so cars emitting pollutants into the air are used less.

Darla: Why think that air pollution would decrease? During a recession fewer people can afford to buy new cars, and cars tend to emit more pollutants as they get older.

13. Which one of the following most accurately describes how Darla's response is related to Charles's argument?

(A)   It calls into question the truth of the premises that Charles uses to support his conclusion.
(B)   It makes an additional claim that can be true only if Charles's conclusion is false.
(C)   It presents an additional consideration that weakens the support given to Charles's conclusion by his evidence.
(D)   It argues that Charles's conclusion is true, although not for the reasons Charles gives to support that conclusion.
(E)   It presents an argument showing that the premises in Charles's argument support an absurd conclusion that Charles has overlooked.

14. Which one of the following is an assumption on which Charles's argument depends?

(A)   People who have never been employed drive no less frequently during a recession than they would otherwise.
(B)   Most air pollution is caused by automobile exhaust emitted by cars used by people commuting to jobs.
(C)   Most people who are employed do not use any form of public transportation to commute to their jobs.
(D)   During a recession, decreases in the use of cars resulting from reductions in commuting to jobs are not offset by increased use of cars for other reasons.
(E)   During a recession, a higher proportion of people who commute in cars to their jobs lose those jobs than do people who do not use cars to commute to their jobs.

GO ON TO THE NEXT PAGE.

15. For the condor to survive in the wild, its breeding population must be greatly increased. But because only a few eggs can be produced by a breeding pair over their lifetime, any significant increase in the number of birds depends upon most of these eggs hatching, which is extremely unlikely in the wild due to environmental dangers. One possible way to eliminate the effects of these factors is to breed the birds in captivity and subsequently return them to the wild.

Which one of the following is most strongly supported by the information above?

(A) The condor as a species will eventually become extinct in the wild.
(B) The best way to save the condor from extinction is to breed it in captivity.
(C) It is almost impossible to eliminate all the environmental threats to the eggs of condors.
(D) If more condor eggs do not hatch, the condor as a species will not survive in the wild.
(E) The most feasible way to save the condor from extinction is to increase egg production.

16. Allowing more steel imports would depress domestic steel prices and harm domestic steel manufacturers. Since the present government will not do anything that would harm the domestic steel industry, it will not lift restrictions on steel imports.

The pattern of reasoning in the argument above is most similar to that in which one of the following?

(A) Building construction increases only when people are confident that the economy is doing well. Therefore, since people are now confident in the economy we can expect building construction to increase.
(B) Since workers are already guaranteed the right to a safe and healthful workplace by law, there is no need for the government to establish further costly health regulations for people who work all day at computer terminals.
(C) In countries that have deregulated their airline industry, many airlines have gone bankrupt. Since many companies in other transportation industries are in weaker economic condition than were those airlines, deregulating other transportation industries will probably result in bankruptcies as well.
(D) The chief executive officer of Silicon, Inc., will probably not accept stock in the company as a bonus next year, since next year's tax laws will require companies to pay a new tax on stock given to executives.
(E) The installation of bright floodlights on campus would render the astronomy department's telescope useless. The astronomy department will not support any proposal that would render its telescope useless; it will therefore not support proposals to install bright floodlights on campus.

17. Wild cheetahs live in the African grasslands. Previous estimates of the size that the wild cheetah population must be in order for these animals to survive a natural disaster in the African grasslands region were too small, and the current population barely meets the previous estimates. At present, however, there is not enough African grassland to support a wild cheetah population larger than the current population.

The statements above, if true, most strongly support which one of the following conclusions?

(A) Previous estimates of the size of the existing wild cheetah population were inaccurate.
(B) The cheetah's natural habitat is decreasing in size at a faster rate than is the size of the wild cheetah population.
(C) The principal threat to the endangered wild cheetah population is neither pollution nor hunting, but a natural disaster.
(D) In the short term, the wild cheetah population will be incapable of surviving a natural disaster in the African grasslands.
(E) In regions where land is suitable for cheetah habitation, more natural disasters are expected to occur during the next decade than occurred during the past decade.

18. To classify a work of art as truly great, it is necessary that the work have both originality and far-reaching influence upon the artistic community.

The principle above, if valid, most strongly supports which one of the following arguments?

(A) By breaking down traditional schemes of representation, Picasso redefined painting. It is this extreme originality that warrants his work being considered truly great.
(B) Some of the most original art being produced today is found in isolated communities, but because of this isolation these works have only minor influence, and hence cannot be considered truly great.
(C) Certain examples of the drumming practiced in parts of Africa's west coast employ a musical vocabulary that resists representation in Western notational schemes. This tremendous originality, coupled with the profound impact these pieces are having on musicians everywhere, is enough to consider these works to be truly great.
(D) The piece of art in the lobby is clearly not classified as truly great, so it follows that it fails to be original.
(E) Since Bach's music is truly great, it not only has both originality and a major influence on musicians, it has broad popular appeal as well.

GO ON TO THE NEXT PAGE.

19. Professor Robinson: A large meteorite impact crater in a certain region was thought to be the clue to explaining the mass extinction of plant and animal species that occurred at the end of the Mesozoic era. However, the crystalline structure of rocks recovered at the site indicates that the impact that formed this crater was not the culprit. When molten rocks crystallize, they display the polarity of Earth's magnetic field at that time. But the recrystallized rocks recovered at the site display normal magnetic polarity, even though Earth's magnetic field was reversed at the time of the mass extinction.

Each of the following is an assumption on which Professor Robinson's argument depends EXCEPT:

(A) The crater indicates an impact of more than sufficient size to have caused the mass extinction.

(B) The recovered rocks recrystallized shortly after they melted.

(C) No other event caused the rocks to melt after the impact formed the crater.

(D) The recovered rocks melted as a result of the impact that formed the crater.

(E) The mass extinction would have occurred soon after the impact that supposedly caused it.

20. Pieces of music consist of sounds and silences presented to the listener in a temporal order. A painting, in contrast, is not presented one part at a time to the viewer; there is thus no particular path that the viewer's eye must follow in order to "read" the painting. Therefore, an essential distinction between the experiences of hearing music and of viewing paintings is that hearing music has a temporal dimension but viewing a painting has none.

The reasoning in the argument is flawed because

(A) the argument does not allow for the possibility of being immersed in experiencing a painting without being conscious of the passage of time

(B) the argument is based on a very general definition of music that does not incorporate any distinctions among particular styles

(C) the argument fails to bring out the aspects of music and painting that are common to both as forms of artistic expression

(D) relying on the metaphor of "reading" to characterize how a painting is viewed presupposes the correctness of the conclusion to be drawn on the basis of that characterization

(E) the absence of a particular path that the eye must follow does not entail that the eye follows no path

21. A study of the difference in earnings between men and women in the country of Naota found that the average annual earnings of women who are employed full time is 80 percent of the average annual earnings of men who are employed full time. However, other research consistently shows that, in Naota, the average annual earnings of all employed women is 65 percent of the average annual earnings of all employed men.

Which one of the following, if also established by research, most helps explain the apparent discrepancy between the research results described above?

(A) In Naota, the difference between the average annual earnings of all female workers and the average annual earnings of all male workers has been gradually increasing over the past 30 years.

(B) In Naota, the average annual earnings of women who work full time in exactly the same occupations and under exactly the same conditions as men is almost the same as the men's average annual earnings.

(C) In Naota, a growing proportion of female workers hold full-time managerial, supervisory, or professional positions, and such positions typically pay more than other types of positions pay.

(D) In Naota, a larger proportion of female workers than male workers are part-time workers, and part-time workers typically earn less than full-time workers earn.

(E) In ten other countries where the proportion of women in the work force is similar to that of Naota, the average annual earnings of women who work full time ranges from a low of 50 percent to a high of 90 percent of the average annual earnings of men who work full time.

GO ON TO THE NEXT PAGE.

22. Biologist: Some speculate that the unusually high frequency of small goats found in island populations is a response to evolutionary pressure to increase the number of goats so as to ensure a diverse gene pool. However, only the reproductive success of a trait influences its frequency in a population. So, the only kind of evolutionary pressure that can reduce the average size of the members of a goat population is that resulting from small goats achieving greater reproductive success than their larger cousins.

The biologist's view, if true, provides the most support for which one of the following?

(A) The evolutionary pressure to ensure a diverse gene pool could have the effect of increasing the frequency of a gene for small size.

(B) The unusual frequency of small goats in island populations is not a result of the greater reproductive success small goats possess when space is limited.

(C) Contrary to what some believe, large goats achieve greater reproductive success than small goats even when space is limited.

(D) The evolutionary pressure to ensure a diverse gene pool does not have the effect of increasing the frequency of a gene for small size.

(E) A diverse gene pool cannot be achieved in a goat population unless the average size of its members is reduced.

23. Several carefully conducted studies showed that 75 percent of strict vegetarians reached age 50 without developing serious heart disease. We can conclude from this that avoiding meat increases one's chances of avoiding serious heart disease. Therefore, people who want to reduce the risk of serious heart disease should not eat meat.

The flawed pattern of reasoning exhibited by which one of the following is most similar to that exhibited by the argument above?

(A) The majority of people who regularly drive over the speed limit will become involved in traffic accidents. To avoid harm to people who do not drive over the speed limit, we should hire more police officers to enforce the speed laws.

(B) Studies have shown that cigarette smokers have a greater chance of incurring heart disease than people who do not smoke. Since cigarette smoking increases one's chances of incurring heart disease, people who want to try to avoid heart disease should give up cigarette smoking.

(C) The majority of people who regularly drink coffee experience dental problems in the latter part of their lives. Since there is this correlation between drinking coffee and incurring dental problems, the government should make coffee less accessible to the general public.

(D) Studies show that people who do not exercise regularly have a shorter life expectancy than those who exercise regularly. To help increase their patients' life expectancy, doctors should recommend regular exercise to their patients.

(E) Most people who exercise regularly are able to handle stress. This shows that exercising regularly decreases one's chances of being overwhelmed by stress. So people who want to be able to handle stress should regularly engage in exercise.

GO ON TO THE NEXT PAGE.

24. Mr. Nance: Ms. Chan said that she retired from Quad Cities Corporation, and had received a watch and a wonderful party as thanks for her 40 years of loyal service. But I overheard a colleague of hers say that Ms. Chan will be gone for much of the next year on business trips and is now working harder than she ever did before; that does not sound like retirement to me. At least one of them is not telling the truth.

Mr. Nance's reasoning is flawed because it

(A) is based in part on hearsay
(B) criticizes Ms. Chan rather than the claims she made
(C) draws a conclusion based on equivocal language
(D) fails to consider that Ms. Chan's colleague may have been deceived by her
(E) fails to infer that Ms. Chan must be a person of superior character, given her long loyal service

25. A recent survey showed that 50 percent of people polled believe that elected officials should resign if indicted for a crime, whereas 35 percent believe that elected officials should resign only if they are convicted of a crime. Therefore, more people believe that elected officials should resign if indicted than believe that they should resign if convicted.

The reasoning above is flawed because it

(A) draws a conclusion about the population in general based only on a sample of that population
(B) confuses a sufficient condition with a required condition
(C) is based on an ambiguity of one of its terms
(D) draws a conclusion about a specific belief based on responses to queries about two different specific beliefs
(E) contains premises that cannot all be true

S T O P

IF YOU FINISH BEFORE TIME IS CALLED, YOU MAY CHECK YOUR WORK ON THIS SECTION ONLY.
DO NOT WORK ON ANY OTHER SECTION IN THE TEST.

SECTION III

Time—35 minutes

24 Questions

<u>Directions:</u> Each group of questions in this section is based on a set of conditions. In answering some of the questions, it may be useful to draw a rough diagram. Choose the response that most accurately and completely answers each question and blacken the corresponding space on your answer sheet.

<u>Questions 1–7</u>

At a benefit dinner, a community theater's seven sponsors—
K, L, M, P, Q, V, and Z—will be seated at three tables—1, 2, and 3. Of the sponsors, only K, L, and M will receive honors, and only M, P, and Q will give a speech. The sponsors' seating assignments must conform to the following conditions:
  Each table has at least two sponsors seated at it, and each sponsor is seated at exactly one table.
  Any sponsor receiving honors is seated at table 1 or table 2.
  L is seated at the same table as V.

1. Which one of the following is an acceptable assignment of sponsors to tables?

   (A) Table 1: K, P; Table 2: M, Q; Table 3: L, V, Z
   (B) Table 1: K, Q, Z; Table 2: L, V; Table 3: M, P
   (C) Table 1: L, P; Table 2: K, M; Table 3: Q, V, Z
   (D) Table 1: L, Q, V; Table 2: K, M; Table 3: P, Z
   (E) Table 1: L, V, Z; Table 2: K, M, P; Table 3: Q

2. Which one of the following is a list of all and only those sponsors any one of whom could be among the sponsors assigned to table 3 ?

   (A) P, Q
   (B) Q, Z
   (C) P, Q, Z
   (D) Q, V, Z
   (E) P, Q, V, Z

3. If K is assigned to a different table than M, which one of the following must be true of the seating assignment?

   (A) K is seated at the same table as L.
   (B) L is seated at the same table as Q.
   (C) M is seated at the same table as V.
   (D) Exactly two sponsors are seated at table 1.
   (E) Exactly two sponsors are seated at table 3.

4. If Q is assigned to table 1 along with two other sponsors, which one of the following could be true of the seating assignment?

   (A) K is seated at the same table as L.
   (B) K is seated at the same table as Q.
   (C) M is seated at the same table as V.
   (D) M is seated at the same table as Z.
   (E) P is seated at the same table as Q.

5. If the sponsors assigned to table 3 include exactly one of the sponsors who will give a speech, then the sponsors assigned to table 1 could include any of the following EXCEPT:

   (A) K
   (B) M
   (C) P
   (D) Q
   (E) Z

6. If three sponsors, exactly two of whom are receiving honors, are assigned to table 2, which one of the following could be the list of sponsors assigned to table 1 ?

   (A) K, M
   (B) K, Z
   (C) P, V
   (D) P, Z
   (E) Q, Z

7. Which one of the following conditions, if added to the existing conditions, results in a set of conditions to which no seating assignment for the sponsors can conform?

   (A) At most two sponsors are seated at table 1.
   (B) Any sponsor giving a speech is seated at table 1 or else table 2.
   (C) Any sponsor giving a speech is seated at table 2 or else table 3.
   (D) Exactly three of the sponsors are seated at table 1.
   (E) Any table at which both L and V are seated also has a third sponsor seated at it.

GO ON TO THE NEXT PAGE.

Questions 8–14

Exactly four medical training sessions—M, O, R, and S—will be scheduled for four consecutive days—day 1 through day 4—one session each day. Six professionals—three nurses and three psychologists—will teach the sessions. The nurses are Fine, Johnson, and Leopold; the psychologists are Tyler, Vitale, and Wong. Each session will be taught by exactly one nurse and exactly one psychologist. The schedule must conform to the following conditions:

Each professional teaches at least once.
Day 3 is a day on which Leopold teaches.
Neither Fine nor Leopold teaches with Tyler.
Johnson teaches session S only.
Session M is taught on the day after the day on which session S is taught.

8. If session R is the only session for which Leopold is scheduled, which one of the following is a pair of professionals who could be scheduled for day 2 together?

(A) Fine and Tyler
(B) Fine and Wong
(C) Johnson and Tyler
(D) Johnson and Wong
(E) Leopold and Wong

9. Which one of the following must be false?

(A) Session O is scheduled for day 1.
(B) Session S is scheduled for day 3.
(C) Leopold is scheduled for day 1.
(D) Vitale is scheduled for day 4.
(E) Wong is scheduled for day 1.

10. Which one of the following could be the session and the professionals scheduled for day 4 ?

(A) session M, Fine, Wong
(B) session O, Fine, Tyler
(C) session O, Johnson, Tyler
(D) session R, Fine, Wong
(E) session S, Fine, Vitale

11. If session S is scheduled for day 2, which one of the following is a professional who must be scheduled to teach session M ?

(A) Fine
(B) Leopold
(C) Tyler
(D) Vitale
(E) Wong

12. If session O and session R are scheduled for consecutive days, which one of the following is a pair of professionals who could be scheduled for day 2 together?

(A) Fine and Leopold
(B) Fine and Wong
(C) Johnson and Tyler
(D) Johnson and Vitale
(E) Leopold and Tyler

13. Which one of the following could be the order in which the nurses teach the sessions, listed from day 1 through day 4 ?

(A) Fine, Johnson, Leopold, Leopold
(B) Fine, Leopold, Leopold, Johnson
(C) Johnson, Johnson, Leopold, Fine
(D) Johnson, Leopold, Leopold, Johnson
(E) Leopold, Leopold, Fine, Fine

14. If session O is scheduled for day 3, which one of the following must be scheduled for day 4 ?

(A) session R
(B) session S
(C) Fine
(D) Leopold
(E) Vitale

GO ON TO THE NEXT PAGE.

Questions 15–19

Six paintings hang next to each other as shown below:

1	2	3
4	5	6

Each of the paintings is an oil or else a watercolor.
Each oil is directly beside, directly above, or directly
  below another oil.
Each watercolor is directly beside, directly above, or
  directly below another watercolor.
Each painting is a nineteenth-century painting or else a
  twentieth-century painting.
Each painting is directly beside, directly above, or directly
  below another painting painted in the same century.
Painting 2 is a nineteenth-century painting.
Painting 3 is an oil.
Painting 5 is a twentieth-century painting.

15. If all of the nineteenth-century paintings are watercolors,
    which one of the following must be true?

    (A)   Painting 1 is an oil.
    (B)   Painting 3 is a nineteenth-century painting.
    (C)   Painting 4 is a watercolor.
    (D)   Painting 5 is an oil.
    (E)   Painting 6 is a twentieth-century painting.

16. It is possible that the only two watercolors among the six
    paintings are

    (A)   paintings 1 and 5
    (B)   paintings 1 and 6
    (C)   paintings 2 and 4
    (D)   paintings 4 and 5
    (E)   paintings 4 and 6

17. If there are exactly three oils and three watercolors,
    which one of the following must be true?

    (A)   Painting 1 is a watercolor.
    (B)   Painting 2 is a watercolor.
    (C)   Painting 4 is a watercolor.
    (D)   Painting 5 is a watercolor.
    (E)   Painting 6 is a watercolor.

18. If exactly two paintings are oils and exactly two
    paintings are nineteenth-century paintings, which one of
    the following must be false?

    (A)   Painting 1 is a nineteenth-century painting, and
          painting 6 is an oil.
    (B)   Painting 2 is both a nineteenth-century painting
          and an oil.
    (C)   Painting 3 is a nineteenth-century painting.
    (D)   Paintings 1 and 2 are both nineteenth-century
          paintings.
    (E)   Painting 2 is an oil, and painting 4 is a nineteenth-
          century painting.

19. Which one of the following could be true?

    (A)   Paintings 1 and 4 are two of exactly three
          twentieth-century paintings.
    (B)   Paintings 1 and 6 are two of exactly three
          twentieth-century paintings.
    (C)   Paintings 1 and 6 are two of exactly three
          nineteenth-century paintings.
    (D)   Paintings 3 and 4 are two of exactly three
          nineteenth-century paintings.
    (E)   Paintings 4 and 6 are two of exactly three
          nineteenth-century paintings.

GO ON TO THE NEXT PAGE.

Questions 20–24

Exactly six of seven jugglers—G, H, K, L, N, P, and Q—are
each assigned to exactly one of three positions—front, middle,
and rear—on one of two teams—team 1 and team 2. For each
team, exactly one juggler must be assigned to each position
according to the following conditions:

　If either G or H or both are assigned to teams, they are
　　assigned to front positions.
　If assigned to a team, K is assigned to a middle position.
　If assigned to a team, L is assigned to team 1.
　Neither P nor K is on the same team as N.
　P is not on the same team as Q.
　If H is on team 2, then Q is assigned to the middle position
　　on team 1.

20. Which one of the following is an acceptable list of
assignments of jugglers to team 2 ?

(A) front: Q; middle: K; rear: N
(B) front: H; middle: P; rear: K
(C) front: H; middle: L; rear: N
(D) front: G; middle: Q; rear: P
(E) front: G; middle: Q; rear: N

21. If H is assigned to team 2, which one of the following is
an acceptable assignment of jugglers to team 1 ?

(A) front: G; middle: K; rear: L
(B) front: G; middle: K; rear: N
(C) front: L; middle: K; rear: P
(D) front: L; middle: Q; rear: G
(E) front: L; middle: Q; rear: N

22. Which one of the following is an acceptable list of
assignments of jugglers to team 1 ?

(A) front: G; middle: K; rear: L
(B) front: G; middle: K; rear: P
(C) front: L; middle: K; rear: Q
(D) front: Q; middle: K; rear: P
(E) front: Q; middle: L; rear: N

23. If G is assigned to team 1, which one of the following is
a pair of jugglers who could also be assigned to team 1 ?

(A) H and N
(B) K and L
(C) K and P
(D) L and N
(E) L and Q

24. If G is assigned to team 1 and K is assigned to team 2,
which one of the following must be assigned the rear
position on team 2 ?

(A) H
(B) L
(C) N
(D) P
(E) Q

S T O P

IF YOU FINISH BEFORE TIME IS CALLED, YOU MAY CHECK YOUR WORK ON THIS SECTION ONLY.
DO NOT WORK ON ANY OTHER SECTION IN THE TEST.

SECTION IV

Time—35 minutes

26 Questions

<u>Directions:</u> The questions in this section are based on the reasoning contained in brief statements or passages. For some questions, more than one of the choices could conceivably answer the question. However, you are to choose the <u>best</u> answer; that is, the response that most accurately and completely answers the question. You should not make assumptions that are by commonsense standards implausible, superfluous, or incompatible with the passage. After you have chosen the best answer, blacken the corresponding space on your answer sheet.

1. Advertisement: Among popular automobiles, Sturdimades stand apart. Around the world, hundreds of longtime Sturdimade owners have signed up for Sturdimade's "long distance" club, members of which must have a Sturdimade they have driven for a total of at least 100,000 miles or 160,000 kilometers. Some members boast of having driven their Sturdimades for a total of 300,000 miles (480,000 kilometers)! Clearly, if you buy a Sturdimade you can rely on being able to drive it for a very long distance.

Construed as an argument, the advertisement's reasoning is most vulnerable to criticism on which one of the following grounds?

(A)   It draws a general conclusion from cases selected only on the basis of having a characteristic that favors that conclusion.

(B)   Its conclusion merely restates the evidence given to support it.

(C)   It fails to clarify in which of two possible ways an ambiguous term is being used in the premises.

(D)   The evidence given to support the conclusion actually undermines that conclusion.

(E)   It treats popular opinion as if it constituted conclusive evidence for a claim.

2. Faced with a financial crisis, Upland University's board of trustees reduced the budget for the university's computer center from last year's $4 million to $1.5 million for the coming year. However, the center cannot operate on less than $2.5 million. Since the board cannot divert funds from other programs to the computer center, there is no way that the center can be kept operating for the coming year.

The conclusion of the argument is properly drawn if which one of the following is assumed?

(A)   The computer center did not use all of the $4 million that was budgeted to it last year.

(B)   The budgets of other programs at the university were also reduced.

(C)   The computer center has no source of funds other than those budgeted to it for the coming year by the university's board of trustees.

(D)   No funds from any program at the university can be diverted to other programs.

(E)   The board of trustees at the university value other programs at the university more highly than they do the computer center.

GO ON TO THE NEXT PAGE.

Questions 3–4

Muriel: I admire Favilla's novels, but she does not deserve to be considered a great writer. The point is that, no matter how distinctive her style may be, her subject matter is simply not varied enough.

John: I think you are wrong to use that criterion. A great writer does not need any diversity in subject matter; however, a great writer must at least have the ability to explore a particular theme deeply.

3. Which one of the following is a point at issue between Muriel and John?

(A) whether Favilla has treated a wide variety of subjects in her novels

(B) whether Favilla should be considered a great writer because her style is distinctive

(C) whether treating a variety of subjects should be a prerequisite for someone to be considered a great writer

(D) whether the number of novels that a novelist has written should be a factor in judging whether that novelist is great

(E) whether there are many novelists who are considered to be great but do not deserve to be so considered

4. John's statements commit him to which one of the following positions?

(A) Even if the subject matter in Favilla's writings is not particularly varied, she should not thereby be excluded from being considered a great writer.

(B) Even if Favilla cannot explore any particular theme deeply in her writings, she should not thereby be excluded from being considered a great writer.

(C) If Favilla has explored some particular theme exceptionally deeply in her writings, she deserves to be considered a great writer.

(D) If the subject matter in Favilla's writings were exceptionally varied, she would not deserve to be considered a great writer.

(E) If Favilla's writings show no evidence of a distinctive style, she does not deserve to be considered a great writer.

5. Astronaut: Any moon, by definition, orbits some planet in a solar system. So, the moons in solar system S4 all orbit the planet Alpha.

The astronaut's conclusion follows logically if which one of the following is assumed?

(A) There is only one moon in S4.

(B) Every moon in S4 orbits the same planet.

(C) Alpha is the only planet in S4.

(D) Every planet in S4 is orbited by more than one moon.

(E) There is at least one moon that orbits Alpha.

6. A worker for a power company trims the branches of trees that overhang power lines as a prevention against damage to the lines anticipated because of the impending stormy season. The worker reasons that there will be no need for her to trim the overhanging branches of a certain tree because the owners of the tree have indicated that they might cut it down anyway.

Which one of the following decisions is based on flawed reasoning that is most similar to the worker's flawed reasoning?

(A) A well inspector has a limited amount of time to inspect the wells of a town. The inspector reasons that the wells should be inspected in the order of most used to least used, because there might not be enough time to inspect them all.

(B) All sewage and incoming water pipes in a house must be replaced. The plumber reasons that the cheaper polyvinyl chloride pipes should be used for sewage rather than copper pipes, since the money saved might be used to replace worn fixtures.

(C) A mechanic must replace the worn brakes on a company's vans that are used each weekday. The mechanic reasons that since one of the vans is tentatively scheduled to be junked, he will not have to replace its brakes.

(D) A candidate decides to campaign in the areas of the city where the most new votes are concentrated. The candidate reasons that campaigning in other areas is unnecessary because in those areas the candidate's message is actually liable to alienate voters.

(E) None of the children in a certain kindergarten class will take responsibility for the crayon drawing on the classroom wall. The teacher reasons that it is best to keep all the kindergarten children in during recess in order to be certain to punish the one who did the drawing on the wall.

GO ON TO THE NEXT PAGE.

7. Currently, the city of Grimchester is liable for any injury incurred because of a city sidewalk in need of repair or maintenance. However, Grimchester's sidewalks are so extensive that it is impossible to hire enough employees to locate and eliminate every potential danger in its sidewalks. Governments should be liable for injuries incurred on public property only if they knew about the danger beforehand and negligently failed to eliminate it.

Which one of the following describes an injury for which the city of Grimchester is now liable, but should not be according to the principle cited above?

(A) A person is injured after tripping on a badly uneven city sidewalk, and the city administration had been repeatedly informed of the need to repair the sidewalk for several years.

(B) A person is injured after tripping over a shopping bag that someone had left lying in the middle of the sidewalk.

(C) A person is injured after stepping in a large hole in a city sidewalk, and the city administration had first learned of the need to repair that sidewalk minutes before.

(D) A person who is heavily intoxicated is injured after falling on a perfectly even city sidewalk with no visible defects.

(E) A person riding a bicycle on a city sidewalk is injured after swerving to avoid a pedestrian who had walked in front of the bicycle without looking.

8. Early in the development of a new product line, the critical resource is talent. New marketing ventures require a degree of managerial skill disproportionate to their short-term revenue prospects. Usually, however, talented managers are assigned only to established high-revenue product lines and, as a result, most new marketing ventures fail. Contrary to current practice, the best managers in a company should be assigned to development projects.

Which one of the following, if true, most strengthens the author's argument?

(A) On average, new ventures under the direction of managers at executive level survive no longer than those managed by lower-ranking managers.

(B) For most established companies, the development of new product lines is a relatively small part of the company's total expenditure.

(C) The more talented a manager is, the less likely he or she is to be interested in undertaking the development of a new product line.

(D) The current revenue and profitability of an established product line can be maintained even if the company's best managers are assigned elsewhere.

(E) Early short-term revenue prospects of a new product line are usually a good predictor of how successful a product line will ultimately be.

9. Television news coverage gives viewers a sense of direct involvement with current events but does not provide the depth of coverage needed for the significance of those events to be appreciated. Newspapers, on the other hand, provide depth of coverage but no sense of direct involvement. Unfortunately, a full understanding of current events requires both an appreciation of their significance and a sense of direct involvement with them. Therefore, since few people seek out news sources other than newspapers and television, few people ever fully understand current events.

The reasoning in the argument is flawed because the argument

(A) treats two things, neither one of which can plausibly be seen as excluding the other, as though they were mutually exclusive

(B) ignores the possibility that people read newspapers or watch television for reasons other than gaining a full understanding of current events

(C) makes crucial use of the term "depth of coverage" without defining it

(D) fails to consider the possible disadvantages of having a sense of direct involvement with tragic or violent events

(E) mistakenly reasons that just because something has the capacity to perform a given function it actually does so

10. Critic: Some writers have questioned Stalin's sanity during his last years. They typically characterized his vindictiveness and secrecy as "paranoia" and "morbid suspiciousness," the latter almost a standard term applied by the Soviet writers under *glasnost* to explain this extraordinary man's misdeeds. But Stalin's cruelty and deviousness are not more apparent during those years than in earlier periods of his rule. "Morbid suspiciousness" has to be a characteristic of tyrants. Without it they would not remain long in power.

Which one of the following most accurately expresses a point of disagreement between the critic and the writers?

(A) whether Stalin should be held guilty of the cruel deeds attributed to him

(B) whether Stalin's cruel misdeeds provide evidence of morbid suspiciousness

(C) whether it is Stalin's state of paranoia or rather his cruelty that gives the stronger reason for doubting his sanity

(D) whether tyranny tends to lead to cruelty

(E) whether it was Stalin's psychological state or rather his political condition that was the primary cause of his cruel misdeeds

GO ON TO THE NEXT PAGE.

11. Even though apes are the only nonhuman creatures able to learn human language, no ape has ever used its human language skills to ask such philosophical questions as, "How am I different from all other creatures?" Therefore, philosophical thought is unique to humans.

The conclusion in the passage above relies on which one of the following assumptions?

(A) Human language is unique to humans.
(B) Apes are incapable of thinking in human language.
(C) Philosophical thought can be expressed only in human language.
(D) Speaking in human language is easier than thinking in human language.
(E) It is more difficult to learn human language than to express philosophical questions.

12. Most adults in country X consume an increasing amount of fat as they grow older. However, for nearly all adults in country X, the percentage of fat in a person's diet stays the same throughout adult life.

The statements above, if true, most strongly support which one of the following conclusions about adults in country X?

(A) They generally consume more fat than do people of the same age in other countries.
(B) They generally eat more when they are older than they did earlier in their adulthood.
(C) They generally have diets that contain a lower percentage of fat than do the diets of children in country X.
(D) They tend to eat more varied kinds of food as they become older.
(E) They tend to lose weight as they become older.

13. Politician: The bill that makes using car phones while driving illegal should be adopted. My support of this bill is motivated by a concern for public safety. Using a car phone seriously distracts the driver, which in turn poses a threat to safe driving. People would be deterred from using their car phones while driving if it were illegal to do so.

The argument's main conclusion follows logically if which one of the following is assumed?

(A) The more attention one pays to driving, the safer a driver one is.
(B) The only way to reduce the threat to public safety posed by car phones is through legislation.
(C) Some distractions interfere with one's ability to safely operate an automobile.
(D) Any proposed law that would reduce a threat to public safety should be adopted.
(E) Car phone use by passengers does not distract the driver of the car.

14. When soil is plowed in the spring, pigweed seeds that have been buried in the soil all winter are churned up to the surface and redeposited just under the surface. The brief exposure of the seeds to sunlight stimulates receptors, which have become highly sensitive to sunlight during the months the seeds were buried in the soil, and the stimulated receptors trigger germination. Without the prolonged darkness, followed by exposure to sunlight, the seeds do not germinate.

The statements above, if true, most strongly support which one of the following statements about a field that will be plowed in the spring and in which pigweed seeds have been buried in the soil all winter?

(A) Fewer pigweed plants will grow in the field if it is plowed only at night than if it is plowed during the day.
(B) Fewer pigweed plants will grow in the field if it is not plowed at all than if it is plowed only at night.
(C) Fewer pigweed plants will grow in the field if it is plowed just before sunrise than if it is plowed just after sunset.
(D) The pigweed seeds that are churned up to the surface of the soil during the plowing will not germinate unless they are redeposited under the surface of the soil.
(E) All of the pigweed seeds that are already on the surface of the soil before the field is plowed will germinate.

GO ON TO THE NEXT PAGE.

15. In 1992, there were over 250 rescues of mountain climbers, costing the government almost 3 million dollars. More than 25 people died in climbing mishaps that year. Many new climbers enter the sport each year. Members of a task force have proposed a bonding arrangement requiring all climbers to post a large sum of money to be forfeited to the government in case of calamity.

Each of the following principles, if valid, supports the task force members' proposal EXCEPT:

(A) Taxpayers should not subsidize a freely chosen hobby and athletic endeavor of individuals.
(B) The government is obliged to take measures to deter people from risking their lives.
(C) For physically risky sports the government should issue permits only to people who have had at least minimal training in the sport.
(D) Citizens who use publicly subsidized rescue services should be required to pay more toward the cost of these services than citizens who do not.
(E) People who engage in physically risky behavior that is not essential to anyone's welfare should be held responsible for the cost of treating any resulting injuries.

16. The familiar slogan "survival of the fittest" is popularly used to express the claim, often mistakenly attributed to evolutionary biologists, that the fittest are most likely to survive. However, biologists use the term "fittest" to mean "most likely to survive," so the slogan is merely claiming that the most likely to survive are the most likely to survive. While this claim is clearly true, it is a tautology and so is neither informative nor of scientific interest.

The argument above depends on assuming which one of the following?

(A) All claims that are of scientific interest are informative.
(B) Only claims that are true are of scientific interest.
(C) Popular slogans are seldom informative or of scientific interest.
(D) Informative scientific claims cannot use terms in the way they are popularly used.
(E) The truth of a purported scientific claim is not sufficient for it to be of scientific interest.

17. Council member: The preservation of individual property rights is of the utmost importance to the city council. Yet, in this city, property owners are restricted to little more than cutting grass and weeding. Anything more extensive, such as remodeling, is prohibited by our zoning laws.

Which one of the following provides a resolution to the apparent inconsistency described by the council member?

(A) Property owners are sometimes allowed exemptions from restrictive zoning laws.
(B) It is in the best interest of property owners to maintain current laws in order to prevent an increase in their property taxes.
(C) The city council places less importance on property rights than do property owners.
(D) An individual's property rights may be infringed upon by other people altering their own property.
(E) Zoning laws ensure that property rights are not overly extensive.

18. Coach: Our team has often been criticized for our enthusiasm in response to both our successes and our opponents' failures. But this behavior is hardly unprofessional, as our critics have claimed. On the contrary, if one looks at the professionals in this sport, one will find that they are even more effusive. Our critics should leave the team alone and let the players enjoy the game.

The coach's argument is most vulnerable to the charge that it

(A) misleadingly equates enthusiasm with unethical play
(B) misinterprets the critics' claim that the team is unprofessional
(C) too quickly generalizes from the sport at one level to the sport at a different level
(D) shifts the blame for the team's behavior to professional players
(E) takes everyone on the team to have performed the actions of a few

GO ON TO THE NEXT PAGE.

19. Speaker: Contemporary business firms need to recognize that avoiding social responsibility leads to the gradual erosion of power. This is Davis and Blomstrom's Iron Law of Responsibility: "In the long run, those who do not use power in a manner which society considers responsible will tend to lose it." The law's application to human institutions certainly stands confirmed by history. Though the "long run" may require decades or even centuries in some instances, society ultimately acts to reduce power when society thinks it is not being used responsibly. Therefore, a business that wishes to retain its power as long as it can must act responsibly.

Which one of the following statements, if true, most weakens the speaker's argument?

(A) Government institutions are as subject to the Iron Law of Responsibility as business institutions.
(B) Public relations programs can cause society to consider an institution socially responsible even when it is not.
(C) The power of some institutions erodes more slowly than the power of others, whether they are socially responsible or not.
(D) Since no institution is eternal, every business will eventually fail.
(E) Some businesses that have used power in socially responsible ways have lost it.

20. It would be wrong to conclude that a person has a *Streptococcus* infection if there is no other evidence than the fact that *Streptococcus* bacilli are present in the person's throat; after all, infection does not occur unless the host is physically run down.

The reasoning in which one of the following is most similar to the reasoning in the argument above?

(A) When a person experiences blurred vision, it does not follow that a physical defect in the person's eyes is the cause, since blurring of a person's vision also can be induced by certain drugs.
(B) Even if a healthy lavender plant receives six or more hours of direct sunlight each day, one cannot predict on that basis alone that the plant will bloom, because lavender requires both six or more hours of sunlight per day and slightly alkaline soil to bloom.
(C) When a bee colony fails to survive the winter, it would be wrong to conclude that low temperatures were the cause. Bees have very good defense mechanisms against extreme cold, which are designed to ensure survival of the colony, though not of individual bees.
(D) A female holly plant cannot produce berries without a male plant nearby to provide pollen. But it does not follow that two or more male hollies in the vicinity will cause a female plant to bear more berries than it would with only a single male holly nearby.
(E) A person cannot be presumed to be hypertensive on the basis of a high reading for blood pressure that is exceptional for that person, since only people with chronically high blood pressure are properly called hypertensive.

GO ON TO THE NEXT PAGE.

21. Terry: Some actions considered to be bad by our society have favorable consequences. But an action is good only if it has favorable consequences. So, some actions considered to be bad by our society are actually good.

    Pat: I agree with your conclusion, but not with the reasons you give for it. Some good actions actually do not have favorable consequences. But no actions considered to be bad by our society have favorable consequences, so your conclusion, that some actions our society considers bad are actually good, still holds.

    Which one of the following correctly describes both an error in Terry's reasoning and an error in Pat's reasoning?

    (A) presupposing that if a certain property distinguishes one type of action from another type of action, then that property is one of many properties distinguishing the two types of action
    (B) presupposing that if most actions of a certain type share a certain property, then all actions of that type share that property
    (C) presupposing that if a certain property is shared by actions of a certain type in a given society, then that property is shared by actions of that type in every society
    (D) presupposing that if an action's having a certain property is necessary for its being a certain type of action, then having that property is sufficient for being that type of action
    (E) presupposing that if a certain property is shared by two types of action, then that property is the only property distinguishing the two types of action from actions of other types

22. Dinosaur expert: Some paleontologists have claimed that birds are descendants of a group of dinosaurs called dromeosaurs. They appeal to the fossil record, which indicates that dromeosaurs have characteristics more similar to birds than do most dinosaurs. But there is a fatal flaw in their argument; the earliest bird fossils that have been discovered date back tens of millions of years farther than the oldest known dromeosaur fossils. Thus the paleontologists' claim is false.

    The expert's argument depends on assuming which one of the following?

    (A) Having similar characteristics is not a sign that types of animals are evolutionarily related.
    (B) Dromeosaurs and birds could have common ancestors.
    (C) Knowledge of dromeosaur fossils and the earliest bird fossils is complete.
    (D) Known fossils indicate the relative dates of origin of birds and dromeosaurs.
    (E) Dromeosaurs are dissimilar to birds in many significant ways.

Questions 23–24

Party spokesperson: The opposition party's proposal to stimulate economic activity in the province by refunding $600 million in provincial taxes to taxpayers, who could be expected to spend the money, envisions an illusory benefit. Since the province's budget is required to be in balance, either new taxes would be needed to make up the shortfall, in which case the purpose of the refund would be defeated, or else workers for the province would be dismissed. So either the province's taxpayers or its workers, who are also residents of the province, will have the $600 million to spend, but there can be no resulting net increase in spending to stimulate the province's economy.

23. The spokesperson proceeds by

    (A) reinterpreting a term that is central to an opposing argument
    (B) arguing that a predicted advantage would be offset by an accompanying disadvantage
    (C) casting doubt on the motives of opponents
    (D) drawing a distinction between different kinds of economic activity
    (E) seeking to show that the assumption that taxpayers would spend money that might be refunded to them is dubious

24. The conclusion about whether there would be a resulting net increase in spending would not follow if the

    (A) taxpayers of the province would spend outside the province at least $300 million of any $600 million refunded to them
    (B) taxpayers of the province would receive any refund in partial payments during the year rather than in a lump sum
    (C) province could assess new taxes in a way that would avoid angering taxpayers
    (D) province could, instead of refunding the money, stimulate its economy by redirecting its spending to use the $600 million for construction projects creating jobs around the province
    (E) province could keep its workers and use them more effectively, with a resulting savings of $600 million in its out-of-province expenditures

GO ON TO THE NEXT PAGE.

25. Essayist: Every contract negotiator has been lied to by
                someone or other, and whoever lies to anyone is
                practicing deception. But, of course, anyone who
                has been lied to has also lied to someone or other.

    If the essayist's statements are true, which one of the
    following must also be true?

    (A)   Every contract negotiator has practiced deception.
    (B)   Not everyone who practices deception is lying to
           someone.
    (C)   Not everyone who lies to someone is practicing
           deception.
    (D)   Whoever lies to a contract negotiator has been
           lied to by a contract negotiator.
    (E)   Whoever lies to anyone is lied to by someone.

26. A member of the British Parliament is reputed to have
    said, "The first purpose of good social reform is to
    increase the sum total of human happiness. So, any
    reform which makes somebody happy is achieving its
    purpose. Since the reform I propose would make my
    constituents happy, it is a good social reform."

    Which one of the following, if true, most seriously
    weakens the argument attributed to the member of
    Parliament?

    (A)   Different things make different people happy.
    (B)   The proposed reform would make a few people
           happy, but would not increase the happiness of
           most other people.
    (C)   The proposed reform would affect only the
           member of Parliament's constituents and would
           make them happy.
    (D)   Increasing some people's happiness might not
           increase the sum total of human happiness if
           others are made unhappy.
    (E)   Good social reforms usually have widespread
           support.

S T O P

IF YOU FINISH BEFORE TIME IS CALLED, YOU MAY CHECK YOUR WORK ON THIS SECTION ONLY.
DO NOT WORK ON ANY OTHER SECTION IN THE TEST.

LSAT® Writing Sample Topic

To fill the position left by the retirement of the only physician in the rural township of Oakley, the town's medical advisory board is deciding between Chris Sandor and Pat Harrison. Write an argument in support of one candidate over the other based on the following criteria:

- The board wants an experienced physician able to work with patients who have a variety of problems and concerns.
- The board wants a physician who will help expand health education and preventative medicine efforts in the community.

Dr. Sandor is a cardiologist who has practiced for the past decade in a major city, where she has lived all her life. Now she is willing to take a lower salary in order to leave the fast pace of the city and spend more time with her two young children. She has been active in professional organizations, and her frequent volunteer activities include working in a nursing home and a high school clinic. During interviews, she proved herself a skillful negotiator; she convinced the advisory board of the need to raise funds for a mobile unit to serve those unable to get to the clinic.

Dr. Harrison completed his medical training as a generalist. He has worked for the past five years in a neighborhood clinic in the same city where Dr. Sandor practices. Prior to that, he did his residency in the student health center at a large university. Dr. Harrison, who grew up on a farm, says that he wants to return to small-town life. He has written articles on health issues for popular magazines, often focusing on the doctor-patient relationship. During interviews he established an immediate rapport with several members of the advisory board, who were particularly impressed by his idea of writing a weekly column on medical topics for the *Oakley Gazette*.

Directions:

1. Use the Answer Key on the next page to check your answers.

2. Use the Scoring Worksheet below to compute your raw score.

3. Use the Score Conversion Chart to convert your raw score into the 120-180 scale.

Scoring Worksheet

1. Enter the number of questions you answered correctly in each section.

Number Correct

SECTION I . . . . . . _____
SECTION II . . . . . _____
SECTION III . . . . . _____
SECTION IV . . . . . _____

2. Enter the sum here: _____
   This is your Raw Score.

Conversion Chart

For Converting Raw Score to the 120-180 LSAT Scaled Score
LSAT Form 8LSS36

Reported Score	Raw Score Lowest	Raw Score Highest
180	99	101
179	98	98
178	97	97
177	96	96
176	95	95
175	94	94
174	93	93
173	92	92
172	91	91
171	90	90
170	89	89
169	88	88
168	86	87
167	85	85
166	84	84
165	82	83
164	80	81
163	79	79
162	77	78
161	76	76
160	74	75
159	72	73
158	70	71
157	69	69
156	67	68
155	65	66
154	63	64
153	61	62
152	59	60
151	58	58
150	56	57
149	54	55
148	52	53
147	50	51
146	49	49
145	47	48
144	45	46
143	43	44
142	42	42
141	40	41
140	39	39
139	37	38
138	36	36
137	34	35
136	33	33
135	31	32
134	30	30
133	29	29
132	27	28
131	26	26
130	25	25
129	24	24
128	23	23
127	22	22
126	21	21
125	20	20
124	19	19
123	18	18
122	17	17
121	16	16
120	0	15

SECTION I

1.	C	8.	D	15.	B	22.	D
2.	B	9.	C	16.	A	23.	A
3.	A	10.	A	17.	A	24.	B
4.	B	11.	A	18.	B	25.	B
5.	C	12.	D	19.	B	26.	A
6.	E	13.	D	20.	A		
7.	C	14.	B	21.	C		

SECTION II

1.	C	8.	A	15.	D	22.	D
2.	B	9.	C	16.	E	23.	E
3.	D	10.	B	17.	D	24.	C
4.	D	11.	E	18.	B	25.	B
5.	A	12.	B	19.	A		
6.	E	13.	C	20.	E		
7.	E	14.	D	21.	D		

SECTION III

1.	D	8.	B	15.	E	22.	E
2.	C	9.	B	16.	D	23.	E
3.	E	10.	D	17.	C	24.	D
4.	B	11.	B	18.	E		
5.	E	12.	B	19.	A		
6.	B	13.	A	20.	E		
7.	B	14.	A	21.	E		

SECTION IV

1.	A	8.	D	15.	C	22.	D
2.	C	9.	A	16.	E	23.	B
3.	C	10.	E	17.	D	24.	E
4.	A	11.	C	18.	B	25.	A
5.	C	12.	B	19.	B	26.	D
6.	C	13.	D	20.	B		
7.	C	14.	A	21.	D		

The Official LSAT PrepTest

23

- October 1997
- Form 7LSS34

The sample test that follows consists of four sections corresponding to the four scored sections of the October 1997 LSAT.

SECTION I

Time—35 minutes

24 Questions

Directions: Each group of questions in this section is based on a set of conditions. In answering some of the questions, it may be useful to draw a rough diagram. Choose the response that most accurately and completely answers each question and blacken the corresponding space on your answer sheet.

Questions 1–5

A producer is positioning exactly seven music pieces—F, G, H, J, K, L, and M—one after another on a music recording, not necessarily in that order. Each piece will fill exactly one of the seven sequential tracks on the recording, according to the following conditions:

F must be second.
J cannot be seventh.
G can come neither immediately before nor immediately after H.
H must be in some track before that of L.
L must be in some track before that of M.

1. Which one of the following could be the order, from first to seventh, of the pieces on the recording?

   (A)   F, K, G, J, H, L, M
   (B)   G, F, H, K, L, J, M
   (C)   G, F, H, K, L, M, J
   (D)   K, F, G, H, J, L, M
   (E)   K, F, L, J, H, M, G

2. If M fills some track before that of J and also before that of K on the recording, which one of the following must be true?

   (A)   G is first.
   (B)   K is seventh.
   (C)   L is third.
   (D)   H comes either immediately before or immediately after F.
   (E)   L comes either immediately before or immediately after G.

3. Which one of the following is a complete and accurate list of the pieces any of which could be first on the recording?

   (A)   G, J, K
   (B)   G, H, J, K
   (C)   G, H, J, L
   (D)   G, J, K, L
   (E)   H, J, K, L, M

4. The earliest track that M can fill is the

   (A)   first
   (B)   third
   (C)   fourth
   (D)   fifth
   (E)   sixth

5. If G is to come immediately before H but all the other conditions remain in effect, any of the following could be true EXCEPT:

   (A)   J comes immediately before F.
   (B)   K comes immediately before G.
   (C)   J comes immediately after L.
   (D)   J comes immediately after K.
   (E)   K comes immediately after M.

GO ON TO THE NEXT PAGE.

Questions 6–11

Fu, Gunsel, Jackson, Kowalski, Lee, Mayer, and Ordoveza are the only applicants being considered for some positions at a nonprofit organization. Only applicants who are interviewed will be hired. The hiring process must meet the following constraints:

If Gunsel is interviewed, Jackson is interviewed.
If Jackson is interviewed, Lee is interviewed.
Fu is interviewed.
Fu is not hired, unless Kowalski is interviewed.
Kowalski is not hired, unless Mayer is interviewed.
If Mayer is hired, and Lee is interviewed, Ordoveza is hired.

6. Which one of the following could be a complete and accurate list of the applicants that are interviewed?

(A) Fu, Gunsel
(B) Fu, Jackson
(C) Fu, Lee
(D) Fu, Gunsel, Lee
(E) Fu, Gunsel, Jackson

7. Which one of the following could be true?

(A) Lee and Mayer are the only applicants interviewed.
(B) Fu, Jackson, and Kowalski are the only applicants interviewed.
(C) Gunsel and one other applicant are the only applicants interviewed.
(D) Gunsel and two other applicants are the only applicants interviewed.
(E) Gunsel and three other applicants are the only applicants interviewed.

8. If Mayer is not interviewed, which one of the following must be true?

(A) Kowalski is not interviewed.
(B) Kowalski is interviewed but not hired.
(C) Fu is not hired.
(D) Fu is hired but Kowalski is not hired.
(E) Fu is interviewed but Kowalski is not hired.

9. If Gunsel and five other applicants are the only applicants interviewed, and if exactly three applicants are hired, then which one of the following could be an accurate list of the applicants hired?

(A) Fu, Lee, Mayer
(B) Fu, Kowalski, Mayer
(C) Kowalski, Lee, Ordoveza
(D) Gunsel, Jackson, Mayer
(E) Gunsel, Jackson, Lee

10. If every applicant that is interviewed is hired, and if Lee is hired, then each of the following applicants must be interviewed EXCEPT:

(A) Fu
(B) Jackson
(C) Kowalski
(D) Mayer
(E) Ordoveza

11. If Ordoveza is not interviewed, and if exactly four applicants are hired, then which one of the following must be false?

(A) Lee is hired.
(B) Mayer is hired.
(C) Jackson is interviewed.
(D) Kowalski is interviewed.
(E) Gunsel is interviewed.

GO ON TO THE NEXT PAGE.

Questions 12–18

Exactly six of seven researchers—three anthropologists: Franklin, Jones, and Marquez; and four linguists: Neil, Osborne, Rice, and Samuels—will be included in two three-person teams—team 1 and team 2. No researcher will be included in more than one team. Each team must include at least one anthropologist and at least one linguist. The teams composition must conform to the following conditions:

Neither team includes both Franklin and Samuels.
Neither team includes both Neil and Rice.
If a team includes Marquez, it includes neither Rice nor Samuels.
If team 1 includes Jones, team 2 includes Rice.

12. Which one of the following could be the list of the researchers on the two teams?

(A) team 1: Franklin, Marquez, Osborne
team 2: Jones, Neil, Rice
(B) team 1: Franklin, Neil, Samuels
team 2: Jones, Osborne, Rice
(C) team 1: Franklin, Osborne, Rice
team 2: Jones, Neil, Samuels
(D) team 1: Jones, Marquez, Neil
team 2: Osborne, Rice, Samuels
(E) team 1: Jones, Osborne, Rice
team 2: Franklin, Marquez, Neil

13. If Jones is on team 1, which one of the following is a pair of researchers that must be on team 2 together?

(A) Franklin and Rice
(B) Marquez and Osborne
(C) Neil and Osborne
(D) Osborne and Samuels
(E) Rice and Samuels

14. If Neil is on team 1, which one of the following is a pair of researchers that could be on team 1 together with Neil?

(A) Franklin and Jones
(B) Jones and Osborne
(C) Jones and Rice
(D) Jones and Samuels
(E) Osborne and Samuels

15. If Franklin is on the same team as Marquez, which one of the following could be true?

(A) Jones is on team 1.
(B) Rice is on team 1.
(C) Samuels is on team 2.
(D) Both Neil and Osborne are on team 1.
(E) Both Neil and Osborne are on team 2.

16. Each of the following is a pair of researchers that could be on team 2 together EXCEPT:

(A) Franklin and Jones
(B) Franklin and Marquez
(C) Franklin and Rice
(D) Jones and Marquez
(E) Jones and Rice

17. Which one of the following could be true?

(A) Franklin is on team 1 and Neil is on team 2.
(B) Franklin is on team 2 and Jones is not on any team.
(C) Franklin is on team 2 and Marquez is on team 2.
(D) Franklin is not on any team and Jones is on team 1.
(E) Jones is on team 1 and Neil is on team 2.

18. If Marquez is on team 2, which one of the following must also be on team 2 ?

(A) Franklin
(B) Jones
(C) Osborne
(D) Rice
(E) Samuels

GO ON TO THE NEXT PAGE.

Questions 19–24

Five candidates for mayor—Q, R, S, T, and U—will each speak exactly once at each of three town meetings—meetings 1, 2, and 3. At each meeting, each candidate will speak in one of five consecutive time slots. No two candidates will speak in the same time slot as each other at any meeting. The order in which the candidates will speak will meet the following conditions:

Each candidate must speak either first or second at at least one of the meetings.

Any candidate who speaks fifth at any of the meetings must speak first at at least one of the other meetings.

No candidate can speak fourth at more than one of the meetings.

19. Which one of the following could be the order, from first to fifth, in which the candidates speak at the meetings?

(A)   meeting 1: Q, U, R, T, S
      meeting 2: S, T, R, U, Q
      meeting 3: T, U, Q, R, S
(B)   meeting 1: R, S, Q, T, U
      meeting 2: U, T, S, R, Q
      meeting 3: Q, R, T, U, S
(C)   meeting 1: S, Q, U, T, R
      meeting 2: U, T, Q, R, S
      meeting 3: R, Q, S, T, U
(D)   meeting 1: T, R, S, U, Q
      meeting 2: Q, R, S, T, U
      meeting 3: U, S, R, Q, T
(E)   meeting 1: U, T, R, S, Q
      meeting 2: Q, R, S, T, U
      meeting 3: S, T, U, Q, R

20. If R speaks second at meeting 2 and first at meeting 3, which one of the following is a complete and accurate list of those time slots any one of which could be the time slot in which R speaks at meeting 1 ?

(A)   fourth, fifth
(B)   first, second, fifth
(C)   second, third, fifth
(D)   third, fourth, fifth
(E)   second, third, fourth, fifth

21. If the order in which the candidates speak at meeting 1 is R, U, S, T, Q, and the order in which they speak at meeting 2 is Q, R, U, S, T, which one of the following could be true of meeting 3 ?

(A)   Q speaks first.
(B)   R speaks third.
(C)   S speaks first.
(D)   T speaks second.
(E)   U speaks fifth.

22. If R speaks first at meetings 1 and 2, and S speaks first at meeting 3, which one of the following must be true?

(A)   R speaks second at meeting 3.
(B)   R speaks fourth at meeting 3.
(C)   S speaks second at at least one of the meetings.
(D)   S speaks fifth at exactly one of the meetings.
(E)   S speaks fifth at exactly two of the meetings.

23. It could be true that at all three meetings T speaks

(A)   first
(B)   second
(C)   in some time slot after the time slot in which R speaks
(D)   in some time slot after the time slots in which S and U speak
(E)   in some time slot before the time slots in which R and U speak

24. If S, T, and U speak second at meetings 1, 2, and 3, respectively, which one of the following must be true?

(A)   The fifth speaker at at least one of the meetings is either Q or R.
(B)   Either Q speaks first at exactly two of the meetings or else R does so.
(C)   Neither S nor T speaks fifth at any of the meetings.
(D)   Q speaks third at one of the meetings, and R speaks third at another of the meetings.
(E)   Q speaks fourth at one of the meetings, and R speaks fourth at another of the meetings.

S T O P

IF YOU FINISH BEFORE TIME IS CALLED, YOU MAY CHECK YOUR WORK ON THIS SECTION ONLY.
DO NOT WORK ON ANY OTHER SECTION IN THE TEST.

SECTION II

Time—35 minutes

26 Questions

Directions: The questions in this section are based on the reasoning contained in brief statements or passages. For some questions, more than one of the choices could conceivably answer the question. However, you are to choose the best answer; that is, the response that most accurately and completely answers the question. You should not make assumptions that are by commonsense standards implausible, superfluous, or incompatible with the passage. After you have chosen the best answer, blacken the corresponding space on your answer sheet.

1. Anita: Since 1960 the spotted owl population has declined alarmingly. Timber companies that have been clearing the old-growth forests where the spotted owl lives are responsible for this.

    Jean: No, the spotted owl's decline is due not to the timber companies but to a rival species. For the past three decades, the more prolific barred owl has been moving steadily into the spotted owl's habitat and replacing the spotted owl.

    Jean does which one of the following in her response to Anita?

    (A)   denies the truth of Anita's premise that timber companies have been clearing old-growth forests

    (B)   challenges Anita's assumption that the decline in the population of the spotted owl poses a threat to the species' continued survival

    (C)   proposes an alternative explanation for the decline in the spotted owl population

    (D)   argues that Anita's conclusion is not valid because she has failed to consider the spotted owl population over a long enough time period

    (E)   suggests that Anita overlooked the possibility that spotted owls are able to live in forests that are not old-growth forests

Questions 2–3

Veterinarian: A disease of purebred racehorses that is caused by a genetic defect prevents afflicted horses from racing and can cause paralysis and death. Some horse breeders conclude that because the disease can have such serious consequences, horses with this defect should not be bred. But they are wrong because, in most cases, the severity of the disease can be controlled by diet and medication, and the defect also produces horses of extreme beauty that are in great demand in the horse show industry.

2. The point of the veterinarian's response to the horse breeders is most accurately expressed by which one of the following?

    (A)   Racehorses that have the genetic defect need not be prevented from racing.

    (B)   There should not be an absolute ban on breeding racehorses that have the genetic defect.

    (C)   Racehorses that are severely afflicted with the disease have not been provided with the proper diet.

    (D)   The best way to produce racehorses of extreme beauty is to breed horses that have the genetic defect.

    (E)   There should be no prohibition against breeding racehorses that have any disease that can be controlled by diet and exercise.

3. The veterinarian's argument employs which one of the following techniques?

    (A)   calling into question the motives of the horse breeders cited

    (B)   demonstrating that the horse breeders' conclusion is inconsistent with evidence advanced to support it

    (C)   providing evidence that contradicts the horse breeders' evidence

    (D)   disputing the accuracy of evidence on which the horse breeders' argument depends

    (E)   introducing considerations that lead to a conclusion different from that of the horse breeders' argument

GO ON TO THE NEXT PAGE.

4. Political scientist: The concept of freedom is hopelessly vague. Any definition of freedom will either exclude some acts that intuitively qualify as free, or admit some acts that intuitively fall outside the concept. The notions of justice, fairness, and equality are equally indeterminate. This is why political organization should be disavowed as futile.

    The reasoning in the argument is questionable because the argument

    (A) generalizes from an unrepresentative sample to every political idea
    (B) makes the unsupported claim that the concept of freedom is hopelessly vague
    (C) ignores the fact that some people view freedom as indispensable
    (D) fails to show any specific link between the vagueness of concepts such as freedom and the rejection of political organization
    (E) is mounted by someone who has a vested interest in the rejection of political organization

5. A recently passed law requires all places of public accommodation to eliminate discrimination against persons with disabilities by removing all physical barriers to accessibility. Private schools, therefore, are legally obligated to make their campuses physically accessible to persons with disabilities.

    The conclusion above follows logically if which one of the following is assumed?

    (A) No private school can legally deny admission to a person with a disability.
    (B) Private schools have historically been resistant to changes in government policy on discrimination.
    (C) Private schools, like public schools, are places of public accommodation.
    (D) Private schools have enough funds to make their campuses barrier-free.
    (E) Private property is often considered to be public space by groups that have historically been subjects of discrimination.

6. Prehistoric chimpanzee species used tools similar to those used by prehistoric humans; prehistoric tools recently found in East Africa are of a type used by both species. The area where the tools were found, however, is a savanna, and whereas there were prehistoric humans who lived in savanna habitats, prehistoric chimpanzees lived only in forests. Therefore, the tools must have been used by humans rather than by chimpanzees.

    Which one of the following is an assumption on which the argument depends?

    (A) Prehistoric humans did not carry their tools with them when they traveled from one place to another.
    (B) Since the evolution of the first primates, East Africa has been predominantly savanna.
    (C) Prehistoric humans never ventured into areas of the forest that were inhabited by prehistoric chimpanzees.
    (D) The area where the tools were found was not a forest at the time the tools were in use.
    (E) The prehistoric ancestors of modern chimpanzees were not capable of using tools more sophisticated than those found recently in East Africa.

7. Computers perform actions that are closer to thinking than anything nonhuman animals do. But computers do not have volitional powers, although some nonhuman animals do.

    Which one of the following is most strongly supported by the information above?

    (A) Having volitional powers need not involve thinking.
    (B) Things that are not animals do not have volitional powers.
    (C) Computers possess none of the attributes of living things.
    (D) It is necessary to have volitional powers in order to think.
    (E) Computers will never be able to think as human beings do.

GO ON TO THE NEXT PAGE.

8. The caterpillar of the monarch butterfly feeds on milkweed plants, whose toxins make the adult monarch poisonous to many predators. The viceroy butterfly, whose caterpillars do not feed on milkweed plants, is very similar in appearance to the monarch. Therefore, it can be concluded that the viceroy is so seldom preyed on because of its visual resemblance to the monarch.

Which one of the following, if it were discovered to be true, would most seriously undermine the argument?

(A) Some predators do not have a toxic reaction to insects that feed on milkweed plants.

(B) Being toxic to predators will not protect individual butterflies unless most members of the species to which such butterflies belong are similarly toxic.

(C) Some of the predators of the monarch butterfly also prey on viceroys.

(D) The viceroy butterfly is toxic to most predators.

(E) Toxicity to predators is the principal means of protection for only a few butterfly species.

9. Every action has consequences, and among the consequences of any action are other actions. And knowing whether an action is good requires knowing whether its consequences are good, but we cannot know the future, so good actions are impossible.

Which one of the following is an assumption on which the argument depends?

(A) Some actions have only other actions as consequences.

(B) We can know that past actions were good.

(C) To know that an action is good requires knowing that refraining from performing it is bad.

(D) Only actions can be the consequences of other actions.

(E) For an action to be good we must be able to know that it is good.

10. All bridges built from 1950 to 1960 are in serious need of rehabilitation. Some bridges constructed in this period, however, were built according to faulty engineering design. That is the bad news. The good news is that at least some bridges in serious need of rehabilitation are not suspension bridges, since no suspension bridges are among the bridges that were built according to faulty engineering design.

If the statements above are true, then, on the basis of those statements, which one of the following must also be true?

(A) Some suspension bridges are not in serious need of rehabilitation.

(B) Some suspension bridges are in serious need of rehabilitation.

(C) Some bridges that were built according to faulty engineering design are in serious need of rehabilitation.

(D) Some bridges built from 1950 to 1960 are not in serious need of rehabilitation.

(E) Some bridges that were built according to faulty engineering design are not bridges other than suspension bridges.

11. A severe blow to the head can cause one to lose consciousness; from this some people infer that consciousness is a product of the brain and cannot survive bodily death. But a radio that becomes damaged may suddenly cease to broadcast the program it had been receiving, and we do not conclude from this that the program itself has ceased to exist. Similarly, more substantial evidence would be needed to conclude that consciousness does not survive bodily death.

Which one of the following most accurately describes the role played in the argument by the example of the damaged radio?

(A) It is cited as evidence that consciousness does in fact survive bodily death.

(B) It is cited as a counterexample to a widely accepted belief about the nature of consciousness.

(C) It is cited as a case analogous to loss of consciousness in which people do not draw the same sort of conclusion that some people draw about consciousness.

(D) It is cited as the primary piece of evidence for the conclusion that the relationship of consciousness to the brain is analogous to that of a radio program to the radio that receives it.

(E) It is cited as an example of a case in which something consisting purely of energy depends on the existence of something material to provide evidence of its existence.

GO ON TO THE NEXT PAGE.

12. Political theorist: The vast majority of countries that have a single political party have corrupt national governments, but some countries with a plurality of parties also have corrupt national governments. What all countries with corrupt national governments have in common, however, is the weakness of local governments.

If all of the political theorist's statements are true, which one of the following must also be true?

(A) Every country with weak local government has a single political party.
(B) Some countries with weak local governments have a plurality of political parties.
(C) Some countries with weak local governments do not have corrupt national governments.
(D) The majority of countries with weak local governments have a single political party.
(E) Fewer multiparty countries than single-party countries have weak local governments.

13. Committee member: We should not vote to put at the top of the military's chain of command an individual whose history of excessive drinking is such that that person would be barred from commanding a missile wing, a bomber squadron, or a contingent of fighter jets. Leadership must be established from the top down.

The committee member's argument conforms most closely to which one of the following principles?

(A) No one who would be barred from important jobs in an organization should lead that organization.
(B) Whoever leads an organization must have served at every level in the organization.
(C) Whoever leads an organization must be qualified to hold each important job in the organization.
(D) No one who drinks excessively should hold a leadership position anywhere along the military's chain of command.
(E) No one who cannot command a missile wing should be at the top of the military's chain of command.

Questions 14–15

Kim: In northern Europe during the eighteenth century a change of attitude occurred that found expression both in the adoption of less solemn and elaborate death rites by the population at large and in a more optimistic view of the human condition as articulated by philosophers. This change can be explained as the result of a dramatic increase in life expectancy that occurred in northern Europe early in the eighteenth century.

Lee: Your explanation seems unlikely, because it could not be correct unless the people of the time were aware that their life expectancy had increased.

14. Which one of the following, if true, provides the strongest defense of Kim's explanation against Lee's criticism?

(A) An increase in life expectancy in a population often gives rise to economic changes that, in turn, directly influence people's attitudes.
(B) Present-day psychologists have noted that people's attitudes toward life can change in response to information about their life expectancy.
(C) Philosophers in northern Europe during the eighteenth century made many conjectures that did not affect the ideas of the population at large.
(D) The concept of life expectancy is based on statistical theories that had not been developed in the eighteenth century.
(E) Before the eighteenth century the attitudes of northern Europeans were more likely to be determined by religious teaching than by demographic phenomena.

15. Which one of the following most accurately describes Lee's criticism of Kim's explanation?

(A) It refers to sources of additional data that cannot easily be reconciled with the facts Kim cites.
(B) It offers an alternative explanation that is equally supported by the evidence Kim cites.
(C) It cites an analogous case in which Kim's explanation clearly cannot hold.
(D) It suggests that Kim's explanation depends on a questionable assumption.
(E) It points out that Kim's explanation is based on two hypotheses that contradict each other.

GO ON TO THE NEXT PAGE.

16. Some health officials are concerned about the current sustained increase in reported deaths from alcohol-related conditions, attributing this increase to a rise in alcoholism. What these health officials are overlooking, however, is that attitudes toward alcoholism have changed radically. Alcoholism is now widely viewed as a disease, whereas in the past it was considered a moral failing. It is therefore likely that more deaths are being reported as alcohol-related because physicians are more likely to identify these deaths as alcohol-related.

Which one of the following, if true, provides the most support for the argument?

(A) The frequent use of alcohol by young people is being reported as occurring at increasingly early ages.

(B) In some places and times, susceptibility to any kind of disease has been viewed as a moral failing.

(C) More physicians now than in the past are trained to recognize the physical effects of alcoholism.

(D) Even though alcoholism is considered to be a disease, most doctors recommend psychological counseling and support groups as the best treatment.

(E) Many health officials are not physicians.

17. Studies show that the most creative engineers get their best and most useful ideas only after doodling and jotting down what turn out to be outlandish ideas. Now that many engineers do their work with computers instead of on paper, however, doodling is becoming much less common, and some experts fear that the result will be fewer creative and useful engineering ideas. These experts argue that this undesirable consequence would be avoided if computer programs for engineering work included simulated notepads that would allow engineers to suspend their "serious" work on the computer, type up outlandish ideas, and then quickly return to their original work.

Which one of the following is an assumption on which the experts' reasoning depends?

(A) Most creative engineers who work with paper and pencil spend about as much time doodling as they spend on what they consider serious work.

(B) Simulated notepads would not be used by engineers for any purpose other than typing up outlandish ideas.

(C) No engineers who work with computers keep paper and pencils near their computers in order to doodle and jot down ideas.

(D) The physical act of working on paper is not essential in providing engineers with the benefits that can be gained by doodling.

(E) Most of the outlandish ideas engineers jot down while doodling are later incorporated into projects that have practical applications.

18. Columnist: The advent of television helps to explain why the growth in homicide rates in urban areas began significantly earlier than the growth in homicide rates in rural areas. Television sets became popular in urban households about five years earlier than in rural households. Urban homicide rates began increasing in 1958, about four years earlier than a similar increase in rural homicide rates began.

Which one of the following, if true, most supports the columnist's argument?

(A) In places where the number of violent television programs is low, the homicide rates are also low.

(B) The portrayal of violence on television is a cause, not an effect, of the violence in society.

(C) There were no violent television programs during the early years of television.

(D) The earlier one is exposed to violence on television, the more profound the effect.

(E) Increasing one's amount of leisure time increases one's inclination to act violently.

19. Even in ancient times, specialized farms (farms that grow a single type of crop or livestock) existed only where there were large commercial markets for farm products, and such markets presuppose urban populations. Therefore the extensive ruins in the archaeological site at Kadshim are probably the remains of a largely uninhabited ceremonial structure rather than of a densely populated city, since the land in the region of Kadshim could never have supported any farms except mixed farms, which grow a variety of crops and livestock.

Which one of the following is an error of reasoning in the argument?

(A) taking the fact that something is true of one sample of a class of things as evidence that the same is true of the entire class of things

(B) taking the nonexistence of something as evidence that a necessary precondition for that thing also did not exist

(C) interpreting an ambiguous claim in one way in one part of the argument and in another way in another part of the argument

(D) supposing that because two things usually occur in conjunction with one another, one of them must be the cause of the other

(E) drawing a conclusion that is simply a restatement of one of the premises on which the argument is based

GO ON TO THE NEXT PAGE.

20. It has recently been found that job prospects for college graduates have never been better. The trend is likely to continue over the next decade. A recent survey found that most employers simply did not know that the number of students graduating would drop by 25 percent over the past ten years, and had not anticipated or planned for this trend. Most employers were not aware that, although the supply of graduates currently meets demand, this situation could change. The same survey revealed that the number of undergraduates choosing to study subjects in high demand, like mathematics and engineering, has dropped substantially. This trend is likely to continue over the next decade.

Which one of the following can properly be concluded from the passage above?

(A) Soon, more graduates are likely to be competing for fewer jobs.

(B) Soon, there is likely to be a shortage of graduates to fill certain vacancies.

(C) Employers are aware of changing trends in subjects studied by undergraduates.

(D) Soon, fewer graduates are likely to be competing for fewer available jobs.

(E) Employers who are well-informed about future trends have anticipated and planned for them.

21. The cities of Oldtown and Spoonville are the same in area and size of population. Since certain health problems that are caused by crowded living conditions are widespread in Oldtown, such problems must be as widespread in Spoonville.

The reasoning in the argument is most vulnerable to criticism on the grounds that the argument

(A) presupposes without warrant that the health problems that are widespread in any particular city cannot be caused by the living conditions in that city

(B) fails to distinguish between the size of the total population of a city and the size of the geographic region covered by that city

(C) fails to indicate whether average life expectancy is lowered as a result of living in crowded conditions

(D) fails to distinguish between those health problems that are easily treatable and those that are not

(E) fails to take into account that having identical overall population density is consistent with great disparity in living conditions

22. Shortly after the Persian Gulf War, investigators reported that the area, which had been subjected to hundreds of smoky oil fires and deliberate oil spills when regular oil production slowed down during the war, displayed less oil contamination than they had witnessed in prewar surveys of the same area. They also reported that the levels of polycyclic aromatic hydrocarbons (PAHs)—used as a marker of combustion products spewed from oil wells ignited during the war—were also relatively low, comparable to those recorded in the temperate oil-producing areas of the Baltic Sea.

Which one of the following, if true, does most to resolve the apparent discrepancy in the information above?

(A) Oil contaminants have greater environmental effects in temperate regions than in desert regions.

(B) Oil contamination and PAH pollution dissipate more rapidly in temperate regions than in desert regions.

(C) Oil contamination and PAH pollution dissipate more rapidly in desert regions than in temperate regions.

(D) Peacetime oil production and transport in the Persian Gulf result in high levels of PAHs and massive oil dumping.

(E) The Persian Gulf War ended before the oil fires and spills caused as much damage as originally expected.

GO ON TO THE NEXT PAGE.

23. An independent audit found no indication of tax avoidance on the part of the firm in the firm's accounts; therefore, no such problem exists.

The questionable reasoning in the argument above is most closely paralleled by that in which one of the following?

(A) The plan for the introduction of the new product has been unmodified so far; therefore, it will not be modified in the future.

(B) The overall budget for the projects has been exceeded by a large amount; therefore, at least one of the projects has exceeded its budget by a large amount.

(C) A compilation of the best student essays of the year includes no essays on current events; therefore, students have become apathetic toward current events.

(D) A survey of schools in the district found no school without a need for building repair; therefore, the education provided to students in the district is substandard.

(E) An examination of the index of the book found no listing for the most prominent critic of the theory the book advocates; therefore, the book fails to refer to that critic.

24. One of the great difficulties in establishing animal rights based merely on the fact that animals are living things concerns scope. If one construes the term "living things" broadly, one is bound to bestow rights on organisms that are not animals (e.g., plants). But if this term is construed narrowly, one is apt to refuse rights to organisms that, at least biologically, are considered members of the animal kingdom.

If the statements above are true, which one of the following can be most reasonably inferred from them?

(A) Not all animals should be given rights.

(B) One cannot bestow rights on animals without also bestowing rights on at least some plants.

(C) The problem of delineating the boundary of the set of living things interferes with every attempt to establish animal rights.

(D) Successful attempts to establish rights for all animals are likely either to establish rights for some plants or not to depend solely on the observation that animals are living things.

(E) The fact that animals are living things is irrelevant to the question of whether animals should or should not be accorded rights, because plants are living things too.

GO ON TO THE NEXT PAGE.

25. Economist: No economic system that is centrally planned can efficiently allocate resources, and efficient allocation of resources is a necessary condition for achieving a national debt of less than 5 percent of Gross Domestic Product (GDP). It follows that any nation with a centrally planned economy has a national debt that is at least 5 percent of GDP.

The pattern of reasoning exhibited by the economist's argument is most similar to that exhibited by which one of the following?

(A) Not all mammals are without wings, because bats are mammals and bats have wings.

(B) All of the rural districts are free of major air pollution problems because such problems occur only where there is a large concentration of automobiles, and there are no such places in the rural districts.

(C) All of the ungulates are herbivores, and most herbivores would not attack a human being. It follows that any animal that would attack a human being is unlikely to be an ungulate.

(D) All rock stars who are famous have their own record companies, and all rock stars with their own record companies receive company profits over and above their regular royalties. This implies that receiving large regular royalties is a necessary condition of being a famous rock star.

(E) Every mutual fund manager knows someone who trades on inside information, and no one who trades on inside information is unknown to every mutual fund manager. One must conclude that no mutual fund manager is unknown to everyone who trades on inside information.

26. Editorialist: Additional restrictions should be placed on driver's licenses of teenagers because teenagers lack basic driving skills. Even though drivers of age nineteen and younger make up only 7 percent of registered drivers, they are responsible for over 14 percent of traffic fatalities.

Each of the following, if true, weakens the argument that teenagers lack basic driving skills EXCEPT:

(A) Teenagers tend to drive older and less stable cars than other drivers.

(B) Teenagers and their passengers are less likely to use seat belts and shoulder straps than others.

(C) Teenagers drive, on average, over twice as far each year as other drivers.

(D) Teenagers cause car accidents that are more serious than those caused by others.

(E) Teenagers are likely to drive with more passengers than the average driver.

S T O P

IF YOU FINISH BEFORE TIME IS CALLED, YOU MAY CHECK YOUR WORK ON THIS SECTION ONLY.
DO NOT WORK ON ANY OTHER SECTION IN THE TEST.

SECTION III

Time—35 minutes

25 Questions

Directions: The questions in this section are based on the reasoning contained in brief statements or passages. For some questions, more than one of the choices could conceivably answer the question. However, you are to choose the best answer; that is, the response that most accurately and completely answers the question. You should not make assumptions that are by commonsense standards implausible, superfluous, or incompatible with the passage. After you have chosen the best answer, blacken the corresponding space on your answer sheet.

1. Question withheld from scoring.

2. Owners of deeply indebted and chronically unprofitable small businesses sometimes try to convince others to invest money in their companies. Since the money thus acquired will inevitably be used to pay off debts, rather than to expand operations, this money will not stimulate sales growth in such companies. Thus, most people are reluctant to make these investments. Surprisingly, however, such investments often earn handsome returns in the very first year they are made.

   Which one of the following, if true, most helps to explain the surprising results of such investments?

   (A) Investors usually choose to reinvest their returns on such investments.
   (B) Expanding production in such companies would usually require more funds than would paying off debts.
   (C) Paying off debts, by saving a company the money it would otherwise owe in interest, decreases the company's overall expenses and thereby increases its profits.
   (D) Banks are reluctant to lend money to any company that is already heavily in debt and chronically unprofitable.
   (E) If the sales of a company do not grow, there is usually little need to devote a large share of company resources to expanding production.

3. After purchasing a pot-bellied pig at the pet store in Springfield, Amy was informed by a Springfield city official that she would not be allowed to keep the pig as a pet, since city codes classify pigs as livestock, and individuals may not keep livestock in Springfield.

   The city official's argument depends on assuming which one of the following?

   (A) Amy lives in Springfield.
   (B) Pigs are not classified as pets in Springfield.
   (C) Any animal not classified as livestock may be kept in Springfield.
   (D) Dogs and cats are not classified as livestock in Springfield.
   (E) It is legal for pet stores to sell pigs in Springfield.

GO ON TO THE NEXT PAGE.

4. Historian: The central claim of the "end-of-history" theory is that history has reached its final stage of development. According to its adherents, democratic ideals have triumphed over their rivals, and history is effectively at an ideological end. But, this view fails to consider that it is impossible to stand outside all of history to judge whether history is really at an end.

Which one of the following can be most reasonably inferred from the historian's statements?

(A) We can never know whether the end-of-history theory is true.
(B) Advocates of the end-of-history theory have too ideological an understanding of history.
(C) If we were at the end of history, we would automatically know whether the end-of-history theory is true.
(D) It is impossible for the end-of-history theory to be true.
(E) Ideological developments are the essential elements of history.

5. John: As I was driving to work this morning, I was stopped by a police officer and ticketed for speeding. Since there were many other cars around me that were going as fast as I was, the police officer clearly treated me unfairly.

Mary: You were not treated unfairly, since the police officer was obviously unable to stop all the drivers who were speeding. Everyone who was speeding at that time and place had an equal chance of being stopped.

Which one of the following principles, if established, would most help to justify Mary's position?

(A) If all of those who violate a traffic law on a particular occasion are equally likely to be penalized for violating it, then the law is fairly applied to whoever among them is then penalized.
(B) The penalties attached to traffic laws should be applied not as punishments for breaking the law, but rather as deterrents to unsafe driving.
(C) The penalties attached to traffic laws should be imposed on all people who violate those laws, and only those people.
(D) It is fairer not to enforce a traffic law at all than it is to enforce it in some, but not all, of the cases to which it applies.
(E) Fairness in the application of a traffic law is ensured not by all violators' having an equal chance of being penalized for their violation of the law, but rather by penalizing all known violators to the same extent.

6. A purse containing 32 ancient gold coins that had been minted in Morocco was discovered in the ruins of an ancient Jordanian city some 4,000 kilometers to the east of Morocco. In its time the Jordanian city was an important trading center along the trade route linking China and Europe, and it was also a popular stopover for pilgrims on the route between Morocco and Mecca. The purse of a trader in the city would probably have contained a more diverse set of coins.

The statements above, if true, most strongly support which one of the following hypotheses?

(A) Moroccan coins were more valuable in the ancient city than were Jordanian coins.
(B) Most gold coins available during the time when the ancient city thrived were minted in Morocco.
(C) The purse with the gold coins had been brought to the ancient city by a pilgrim on the route between Morocco and Mecca.
(D) Gold coins were the only medium of exchange used in the ancient city.
(E) Pilgrims and traders in the ancient city were unlikely to have interacted with one another.

7. Studies indicate that the rate at which water pollution is increasing is leveling off: the amount of water pollution caused this year is almost identical to the amount caused last year. If this trend continues, the water pollution problem will no longer be getting more serious.

The reasoning is questionable because it ignores the possibility that

(A) some types of water pollution have no noticeable effect on organisms that use the water
(B) the types of water pollution caused this year are less dangerous than those caused last year
(C) the leveling-off trend of water pollution will not continue
(D) air and soil pollution are becoming more serious
(E) the effects of water pollution are cumulative

GO ON TO THE NEXT PAGE.

8. One researcher writes, "Human beings are innately aggressive." As evidence, the researcher cites the prevalence of warfare in history, and then discounts any current disinclination to fight: "The most peaceable peoples of today were often ravagers of yesteryear and will probably fight again in the future." But if some peoples are peaceable now, then aggression itself cannot be coded in our genes, only the potential for it. If "innate" only means *possible*, or even *likely in certain environments*, then everything we do is innate and the word has no meaning.

Which one of the following most accurately describes the technique used in the passage to weaken the argument for the claim that aggressiveness is innate to human beings?

(A) The accuracy of the historical data cited in the argument for innate aggressiveness is called into question.

(B) The force of the concept of innateness used in the argument for innate aggressiveness is called into question.

(C) An attempt is made to undermine the argument for innate aggressiveness by arguing that there are no genetically based traits.

(D) An attempt is made to undermine the argument for innate aggressiveness by suggesting that it appeals to emotional considerations rather than to reason.

(E) An attempt is made to undermine the argument for innate aggressiveness by arguing that all peoples are peaceable.

Questions 9–10

If a person chooses to walk rather than drive, there is one less vehicle emitting pollution into the air than there would be otherwise. Therefore if people would walk whenever it is feasible for them to do so, then pollution will be greatly reduced.

9. Which one of the following is an assumption on which the argument depends?

(A) Cutting down on pollution can be achieved in a variety of ways.

(B) Taking public transportation rather than driving is not always feasible.

(C) Walking is the only feasible alternative to driving that results in a reduction in pollution.

(D) There are people who never drive but who often walk.

(E) People sometimes drive when it is feasible to walk instead.

10. Which one of the following, if true, most strengthens the argument?

(A) If automobile passengers who never drive walk instead of ride, there will not be fewer vehicles on the road as a result.

(B) Nonmoving running vehicles, on average, emit half as much pollution per second as moving vehicles, but the greater congestion is, the more nonmoving running vehicles there are.

(C) Since different vehicles can pollute at different rates, it is possible for one driver who walks to make a greater contribution to pollution prevention than another driver who walks.

(D) On average, buses pollute more than cars do, but buses usually carry more passengers than cars do.

(E) Those who previously rode as passengers in a vehicle whose driver decides to walk instead of drive might themselves decide to drive.

GO ON TO THE NEXT PAGE.

11. Editorial: The most vocal proponents of the proposed law are not permanent residents of this island but rather a few of the wealthiest summer residents, who leave when the vacation months have passed. These people will benefit from passage of this law while not having to deal with the problems associated with its adoption. Therefore, anyone who supports the proposed law is serving only the interests of a few outsiders at the cost of creating problems for the island's permanent residents.

Which one of the following is an assumption on which the argument depends?

(A) The average income of the island's summer residents is greater than the average income of its permanent residents.

(B) The problems associated with this law outweigh any benefits it might provide the island's permanent residents.

(C) Most of the island's summer residents would benefit from passage of this law.

(D) Most of the island's summer residents support passage of this law.

(E) Most of the island's permanent residents oppose passage of this law.

12. Vitamin XYZ has long been a favorite among health food enthusiasts. In a recent large study, those who took large amounts of vitamin XYZ daily for two years showed on average a 40 percent lower risk of heart disease than did members of a control group. Researchers corrected for differences in relevant health habits, such as diet.

Which one of the following inferences is most supported by the passage?

(A) Taking large amounts of vitamins is probably worth risking the side effects.

(B) Those who take large doses of vitamin XYZ daily for the next two years will exhibit on average an increase in the likelihood of avoiding heart disease.

(C) Li, who has taken large amounts of vitamin XYZ daily for the past two years, has a 40 percent lower risk of heart disease than she did two years ago.

(D) Taking large amounts of vitamin XYZ daily over the course of one's adult life should be recommended to most adults.

(E) Health food enthusiasts are probably correct in believing that large daily doses of multiple vitamins promote good health.

13. In 1988, a significant percentage of seals in the Baltic Sea died from viral diseases; off the coast of Scotland, however, the death rate due to viral diseases was approximately half what it was for the Baltic seals. The Baltic seals had significantly higher levels of pollutants in their blood than did the Scottish seals. Since pollutants are known to impair marine mammals' ability to fight off viral infection, it is likely that the higher death rate among the Baltic seals was due to the higher levels of pollutants in their blood.

Which one of the following, if true, provides the most additional support for the argument?

(A) The large majority of Scottish seals that died were either old or unhealthy animals.

(B) The strain of virus that killed Scottish seals overwhelms impaired immune systems much more quickly than it does healthy immune systems.

(C) There were slight fluctuations in the levels of pollutants found in the blood of Baltic seals.

(D) The kinds of pollutants found in the Baltic Sea are significantly different from those that have been detected in the waters off the coast of Scotland.

(E) Among marine mammals other than seals, the death rate due to viral diseases in 1988 was higher in the Baltic Sea than it was off the Scottish coast.

14. If the proposed tax reduction package is adopted this year, the library will be forced to discontinue its daily story hours for children. But if the daily story hours are discontinued, many parents will be greatly inconvenienced. So the proposed tax reduction package will not be adopted this year.

Which one of the following, if assumed, allows the argument's conclusion to be properly drawn?

(A) Any tax reduction package that will not force the library to discontinue daily story hours will be adopted this year.

(B) Every tax reduction package that would force the library to discontinue daily story hours would greatly inconvenience parents.

(C) No tax reduction package that would greatly inconvenience parents would fail to force the library to discontinue daily story hours.

(D) No tax reduction package that would greatly inconvenience parents will be adopted this year.

(E) Any tax reduction package that will not greatly inconvenience parents will be adopted this year.

GO ON TO THE NEXT PAGE.

15. Funding opponent: Some people favor city funding for the spaying and neutering of pets at the owners' request. They claim that the decrease in the number of stray animals to contend with will offset the cost of the funding. These people fail to realize that over 80 percent of pet owners already pay to spay or neuter their animals, so there will not be a significant decrease in the number of stray animals in the city if this funding is provided.

Each of the following, if true, strengthens the argument of the funding opponent EXCEPT:

(A)   Very few of the stray animals in the city are offspring of pets.
(B)   Many pet owners would have their animals spayed or neutered sooner if funding were provided by the city.
(C)   The only way the number of stray animals can decrease is if existing strays are spayed or neutered.
(D)   Most pet owners who do not have their pets spayed or neutered believe that spaying and neutering are morally wrong.
(E)   The majority of pets that are not spayed or neutered are used for breeding purposes, and are not likely to produce stray animals.

16. Research indicates that college professors generally were raised in economically advantaged households. For it was discovered that, overall, college professors grew up in communities with average household incomes that were higher than the average household income for the nation as a whole.

The reasoning in the argument is flawed because the argument

(A)   inappropriately assumes a correlation between household income and economic advantage
(B)   fails to note there are some communities with high average household incomes in which no college professors grew up
(C)   presumes without justification that college professors generally were raised in households with incomes that are average or above average for their communities
(D)   does not take into account the fact that college professors generally have lower salaries than their counterparts in the private sector
(E)   fails to take into account the fact that many college professors live in rural communities, which generally have low average household incomes

17. Magazine article: Punishment for crimes is justified if it actually deters people from committing them. But a great deal of carefully assembled and analyzed empirical data show clearly that punishment is not a deterrent. So punishment is never justified.

The reasoning in the magazine article's argument is flawed because the argument

(A)   depends on data that there is reason to suspect may be biased
(B)   mistakenly allows the key term "punishment" to shift in meaning
(C)   mistakes being sufficient to justify punishment for being required to justify it
(D)   ignores the problem of mistakenly punishing the innocent
(E)   attempts to be more precise than its subject matter properly allows

18. If the recording now playing on the jazz program is really "Louis Armstrong recorded in concert in 1989," as the announcer said, then Louis Armstrong was playing some of the best jazz of his career years after his death. Since the trumpeter was definitely Louis Armstrong, somehow the announcer must have gotten the date of the recording wrong.

The pattern of reasoning in the argument above is most similar to that in which one of the following arguments?

(A)   The museum is reported as having acquired a painting "by Malvina Hoffman, an artist who died in 1966." But Hoffman was a sculptor, not a painter, so the report must be wrong about the acquisition being a painting.
(B)   This painting titled *La Toilette* is Berthe Morisot's *La Toilette* only if a painting can be in two museums at the same time. Since nothing can be in two places at once, this painting must somehow have been mistitled.
(C)   Only if a twentieth-century Mexican artist painted in Japan during the seventeenth century can this work both be "by Frida Kahlo" as labeled and the seventeenth-century Japanese landscape it appears to be. Since it is what it appears to be, the label is wrong.
(D)   Unless Käthe Kollwitz was both a sculptor and a printmaker, the volunteer museum guide is wrong in his attribution of this sculpture. Since what Kollwitz is known for is her prints, the guide must be wrong.
(E)   If this painting is a portrait done in acrylic, it cannot be by Elisabeth Vigée-Lebrun, since acrylic paint was developed only after her death. Thus, since it is definitely a portrait, the paint must not be acrylic.

GO ON TO THE NEXT PAGE.

19. When a stone is trimmed by a mason and exposed to the elements, a coating of clay and other minerals, called rock varnish, gradually accumulates on the freshly trimmed surface. Organic matter trapped beneath the varnish on stones of an Andean monument was found to be over 1,000 years old. Since the organic matter must have grown on the stone shortly after it was trimmed, it follows that the monument was built long before the arrival of Europeans in the Americas in 1492.

Which one of the following, if true, most seriously weakens the argument?

(A) Rock varnish itself contains some organic matter.
(B) The reuse of ancient trimmed stones was common in the Andes both before and after 1492.
(C) The Andean monument bears a striking resemblance to monuments found in ancient sites in western Asia.
(D) The earliest written reference to the Andean monument dates from 1778.
(E) Rock varnish forms very slowly, if at all, on trimmed stones that are stored in a dry, sheltered place.

20. Legal rules are expressed in general terms. They concern classifications of persons and actions and they prescribe legal consequences for persons and actions falling into the relevant categories. The application of a rule to a particular case, therefore, involves a decision on whether the facts of that case fall within the categories mentioned in the rule. This decision establishes the legal effect of what happened rather than any matter of fact.

The passage provides the most support for which one of the following?

(A) Legal rules, like matters of fact, are concerned with classifications of things such as actions.
(B) Matters of fact, like legal rules, can sometimes be expressed in general terms.
(C) Making a legal decision does not involve matters of fact.
(D) The application of a rule to a particular case need not be left to a judge.
(E) Whether the facts of a case fall into a relevant category is not itself a matter of fact.

Questions 21–22

Helen: It was wrong of my brother Mark to tell our mother that the reason he had missed her birthday party the evening before was that he had been in a traffic accident and that by the time he was released from the hospital emergency room the party was long over. Saying something that is false can never be other than morally wrong, and there had been no such accident—Mark had simply forgotten all about the party.

21. The main conclusion drawn in Helen's argument is that

(A) Mark did not tell his mother the truth
(B) the real reason Mark missed his mother's birthday party was that he had forgotten all about it
(C) it is wrong to attempt to avoid blame for one's failure to do something by claiming that one was prevented from doing that thing by events outside one's control
(D) it was wrong of Mark to tell his mother that he had missed her birthday party as a result of having been in a traffic accident
(E) it is always wrong not to tell the truth

22. The justification Helen offers for her judgment of Mark's behavior is most vulnerable to criticism on the grounds that the justification

(A) ignores an important moral distinction between saying something that is false and failing to say something that one knows to be true
(B) confuses having identified one cause of a given effect with having eliminated the possibility of there being any other causes of that effect
(C) judges behavior that is outside an individual's control according to moral standards that can properly be applied only to behavior that is within such control
(D) relies on an illegitimate appeal to pity to obscure the fact that the conclusion does not logically follow from the premises advanced
(E) attempts to justify a judgment about a particular case by citing a general principle that stands in far greater need of support than does the particular judgment

GO ON TO THE NEXT PAGE.

23. Candidate: The government spends $500 million more each year promoting highway safety than it spends combating cigarette smoking. But each year many more people die from smoking-related diseases than die in highway accidents. So the government would save lives by shifting funds from highway safety programs to antismoking programs.

The flawed reasoning in which one of the following arguments most closely parallels the flawed reasoning in the candidate's argument?

(A) The government enforces the speed limit on freeways much more closely than on tollways. But many more people die each year in auto accidents on freeways than die in auto accidents on tollways. So the government would save lives by shifting funds from enforcement of speed limits on freeways to enforcement of speed limits on tollways.

(B) A certain professional musician spends several times as many hours practicing guitar as she spends practicing saxophone. But she is hired much more often to play saxophone than to play guitar, so she would increase her number of playing engagements by spending less time practicing guitar and more time practicing saxophone.

(C) Automobiles burn more gas per minute on highways than on residential streets. But they get fewer miles per gallon on residential streets. Therefore, gas would be saved by driving less on residential streets and more on highways.

(D) The local swim team spends many more hours practicing the backstroke than it spends practicing the breaststroke. But the team's lap times for the breaststroke are much better than its times for the backstroke, so the team would win more swim meets if it spent less time practicing the backstroke and more time practicing the breaststroke.

(E) Banks have a higher profit margin on loans that have a high interest rate than on loans that have a low interest rate. But borrowers are willing to borrow larger sums at low rates than at high rates. Therefore, banks would be more profitable if they gave more loans at low rates and fewer loans at high rates.

24. A person's failure to keep a promise is wrong only if, first, doing so harms the one to whom the promise is made and, second, all of those who discover the failure to keep the promise lose confidence in the person's ability to keep promises.

Which one of the following judgments most closely conforms to the principle above?

(A) Ann kept her promise to repay Felicia the money she owed her. Further, this convinced everyone who knew Ann that she is trustworthy. Thus, Ann's keeping her promise was not wrong.

(B) Jonathan took an oath of secrecy concerning the corporation's technical secrets, but he sold them to a competitor. His action was wrong even though the corporation intended that he leak these secrets to its competitors.

(C) George promised to repay Reiko the money he owed her. However, George was unable to keep his promise to Reiko and as a result, Reiko suffered a serious financial loss. Thus, George's failure to keep his promise was wrong.

(D) Because he lost his job, Carlo was unable to repay the money he promised to Miriam. However, Miriam did not need this money nor did she lose confidence in Carlo's ability to keep promises. So, Carlo's failure to keep his promise to Miriam was not wrong.

(E) Elizabeth promised to return the book she borrowed from Steven within a week, but she was unable to do so because she became acutely ill. Not knowing this, Steven lost confidence in her ability to keep a promise. So, Elizabeth's failure to return the book to Steven was wrong.

GO ON TO THE NEXT PAGE.

25. The end of an action is the intended outcome of the action and not a mere by-product of the action, and the end's value is thus the only reason for the action. So while it is true that not every end's value will justify any means, and even, perhaps, that there is no end whose value will justify every means, it is clear that nothing will justify a means except an end's value.

Which one of the following most accurately expresses the main conclusion of the argument?

(A) The value of some ends may justify any means.
(B) One can always justify a given action by appeal to the value of its intended outcome.
(C) One can justify an action only by appeal to the value of its intended outcome.
(D) Only the value of the by-products of an action can justify that action.
(E) Nothing can justify the intended outcome of an action except the value of that action's actual outcomes.

S T O P

IF YOU FINISH BEFORE TIME IS CALLED, YOU MAY CHECK YOUR WORK ON THIS SECTION ONLY.
DO NOT WORK ON ANY OTHER SECTION IN THE TEST.

SECTION IV

Time—35 minutes

26 Questions

Directions: Each passage in this section is followed by a group of questions to be answered on the basis of what is <u>stated</u> or <u>implied</u> in the passage. For some of the questions, more than one of the choices could conceivably answer the question. However, you are to choose the <u>best</u> answer; that is, the response that most accurately and completely answers the question, and blacken the corresponding space on your answer sheet.

It has recently been discovered that many attributions of paintings to the seventeenth-century Dutch artist Rembrandt may be false. The contested paintings are not minor works, whose removal from the
(5) Rembrandt corpus would leave it relatively unaffected: they are at its very center. In her recent book, Svetlana Alpers uses these cases of disputed attribution as a point of departure for her provocative discussion of the radical distinctiveness of Rembrandt's approach to
(10) painting.

Alpers argues that Rembrandt exercised an unprecedentedly firm control over his art, his students, and the distribution of his works. Despite Gary Schwartz's brilliant documentation of Rembrandt's
(15) complicated relations with a wide circle of patrons, Alpers takes the view that Rembrandt refused to submit to the prevailing patronage system. He preferred, she claims, to sell his works on the open market and to play the entrepreneur. At a time when Dutch artists were
(20) organizing into professional brotherhoods and academies, Rembrandt stood apart. In fact, Alpers' portrait of Rembrandt shows virtually every aspect of his art pervaded by economic motives. Indeed, so complete was Rembrandt's involvement with the
(25) market, she argues, that he even presented himself as a commodity, viewing his studio's products as extensions of himself, sent out into the world to earn money. Alpers asserts that Rembrandt's enterprise is found not just in his paintings, but in his refusal to limit
(30) his enterprise to those paintings he actually painted. He marketed Rembrandt.

Although there may be some truth in the view that Rembrandt was an entrepreneur who made some aesthetic decisions on the basis of what he knew the
(35) market wanted, Alpers' emphasis on economic factors sacrifices discussion of the aesthetic qualities that make Rembrandt's work unique. For example, Alpers asserts that Rembrandt deliberately left his works unfinished so as to get more money for their revision and
(40) completion. She implies that Rembrandt actually wished the Council of Amsterdam to refuse the great *Claudius Civilis*, which they had commissioned for their new town hall, and she argues that "he must have calculated that he would be able to get more money by
(45) retouching [the] painting." Certainly the picture is painted with very broad strokes, but there is no evidence that it was deliberately left unfinished. The fact is that the look of a work like *Claudius Civilis* must also be understood as the consequence of
(50) Rembrandt's powerful and profound meditations on

painting itself. Alpers makes no mention of the pictorial dialectic that can be discerned between, say, the lessons Rembrandt absorbed from the Haarlem school of painters and the styles of his native Leiden.
(55) The trouble is that while Rembrandt's artistic enterprise may indeed not be reducible to the works he himself painted, it is not reducible to marketing practices either.

1. Which one of the following best summarizes the main conclusion of the author of the passage?

   (A) Rembrandt differed from other artists of his time both in his aesthetic techniques and in his desire to meet the demands of the marketplace.

   (B) The aesthetic qualities of Rembrandt's work cannot be understood without consideration of how economic motives pervaded decisions he made about his art.

   (C) Rembrandt was one of the first artists to develop the notion of a work of art as a commodity that could be sold in an open marketplace.

   (D) Rembrandt's artistic achievement cannot be understood solely in terms of decisions he made on the basis of what would sell in the marketplace.

   (E) Rembrandt was an entrepreneur whose artistic enterprise was not limited to the paintings he actually painted himself.

2. According to the passage, Alpers and Schwartz disagree about which one of the following?

   (A) the degree of control Rembrandt exercised over the production of his art

   (B) the role that Rembrandt played in organizing professional brotherhoods and academies

   (C) the kinds of relationships Rembrandt had with his students

   (D) the degree of Rembrandt's involvement in the patronage system

   (E) the role of the patronage system in seventeenth-century Holland

GO ON TO THE NEXT PAGE.

3. In the third paragraph, the author of the passage discusses aesthetic influences on Rembrandt's work most probably in order to

(A) suggest that many critics have neglected to study the influence of the Haarlem school of painters on Rembrandt's work

(B) suggest that *Claudius Civilis* is similar in style to many paintings from the seventeenth century

(C) suggest that Rembrandt's style was not affected by the aesthetic influences that Alpers points out

(D) argue that Rembrandt's style can best be understood as a result of the influences of his native Leiden

(E) indicate that Alpers has not taken into account some important aspects of Rembrandt's work

4. Which one of the following, if true, would provide the most support for Alpers' argument about *Claudius Civilis*?

(A) Rembrandt was constantly revising his prints and paintings because he was never fully satisfied with stylistic aspects of his earlier drafts.

(B) The works of many seventeenth-century Dutch artists were painted with broad strokes and had an unfinished look.

(C) Many of Rembrandt's contemporaries eschewed the patronage system and sold their works on the open market.

(D) Artists were frequently able to raise the price of a painting if the buyer wanted the work revised in some way.

(E) Rembrandt did not allow his students to work on paintings that were commissioned by public officials.

5. It can be inferred that the author of the passage and Alpers would be most likely to agree on which one of the following?

(A) Rembrandt made certain aesthetic decisions on the basis of what he understood about the demands of the marketplace.

(B) The Rembrandt corpus will not be affected if attributions of paintings to Rembrandt are found to be false.

(C) Stylistic aspects of Rembrandt's painting can be better explained in economic terms than in historical or aesthetic terms.

(D) Certain aesthetic aspects of Rembrandt's art are the result of his experimentation with different painting techniques.

(E) Most of Rembrandt's best-known works were painted by his students, but were sold under Rembrandt's name.

GO ON TO THE NEXT PAGE.

Medievalists usually distinguish medieval public law from private law: the former was concerned with government and military affairs and the latter with the family, social status, and land transactions.
(5) Examination of medieval women's lives shows this distinction to be overly simplistic. Although medieval women were legally excluded from roles thus categorized as public, such as soldier, justice, jury member, or professional administrative official,
(10) women's control of land—usually considered a private or domestic phenomenon—had important political implications in the feudal system of thirteenth-century England. Since land equaled wealth and wealth equaled power, certain women exercised influence by
(15) controlling land. Unlike unmarried women (who were legally subject to their guardians) or married women (who had no legal identity separate from their husbands), women who were widows had autonomy with respect to acquiring or disposing of certain
(20) property, suing in court, incurring liability for their own debts, and making wills.

Although feudal lands were normally transferred through primogeniture (the eldest son inheriting all), when no sons survived, the surviving daughters
(25) inherited equal shares under what was known as partible inheritance. In addition to controlling any such land inherited from her parents and any bridal dowry—property a woman brought to the marriage from her own family—a widow was entitled to use of one-third
(30) of her late husband's lands. Called "dower" in England, this grant had greater legal importance under common law than did the bridal dowry; no marriage was legal unless the groom endowed the bride with this property at the wedding ceremony. In 1215 Magna
(35) Carta guaranteed a widow's right to claim her dower without paying a fine; this document also strengthened widows' ability to control land by prohibiting forced remarriage. After 1272 women could also benefit from jointure: the groom could agree to hold part or all of
(40) his lands jointly with the bride, so that if one spouse died, the other received these lands.

Since many widows had inheritances as well as dowers, widows were frequently the financial heads of the family; even though legal theory assumed the
(45) maintenance of the principle of primogeniture, the amount of land the widow controlled could exceed that of her son or of other male heirs. Anyone who held feudal land exercised authority over the people attached to the land—knights, rental tenants, and
(50) peasants—and had to hire estate administrators, oversee accounts, receive rents, protect tenants from outside encroachment, punish tenants for not paying rents, appoint priests to local parishes, and act as guardians of tenants' children and executors of their
(55) wills. Many married women fulfilled these duties as deputies for husbands away at court or at war, but widows could act on their own behalf. Widows' legal independence is suggested by their frequent appearance in thirteenth-century English legal records. Moreover,
(60) the scope of their sway is indicated by the fact that some controlled not merely single estates, but multiple counties.

6. Which one of the following best expresses the main idea of the passage?

(A) The traditional view of medieval women as legally excluded from many public offices fails to consider thirteenth-century women in England who were exempted from such restrictions because of their wealth and social status.

(B) The economic independence of women in thirteenth-century England was primarily determined not by their marital status, but by their status as heirs to their parents' estates.

(C) The laws and customs of the feudal system in thirteenth-century England enabled some women to exercise a certain amount of power despite their legal exclusion from most public roles.

(D) During the thirteenth century in England, widows gained greater autonomy and legal rights to their property than they had had in previous centuries.

(E) Widows in thirteenth-century England were able to acquire and dispose of lands through a number of different legal processes.

7. With which one of the following statements about the views held by the medievalists mentioned in line 1 would the author of the passage most probably agree?

(A) The medieval role of landowner was less affected by thirteenth-century changes in law than these medievalists customarily have recognized.

(B) The realm of law labeled public by these medievalists ultimately had greater political implications than that labeled private.

(C) The amount of wealth controlled by medieval women was greater than these medievalists have recorded.

(D) The distinction made by these medievalists between private law and public law fails to consider some of the actual legal cases of the period.

(E) The distinction made by these medievalists between private and public law fails to address the political importance of control over land in the medieval era.

GO ON TO THE NEXT PAGE.

8. Which one of the following most accurately expresses the meaning of the word "sway" as it is used in line 60 of the passage?

    (A) vacillation
    (B) dominion
    (C) predisposition
    (D) inclination
    (E) mediation

9. Which one of the following most accurately describes the function of the second paragraph of the passage?

    (A) providing examples of specific historical events as support for the conclusion drawn in the third paragraph
    (B) narrating a sequence of events whose outcome is discussed in the third paragraph
    (C) explaining how circumstances described in the first paragraph could have occurred
    (D) describing the effects of an event mentioned in the first paragraph
    (E) evaluating the arguments of a group mentioned in the first paragraph

10. According to information in the passage, a widow in early thirteenth-century England could control more land than did her eldest son if

    (A) the widow had been granted the customary amount of dower land and the eldest son inherited the rest of the land
    (B) the widow had three daughters in addition to her eldest son
    (C) the principle of primogeniture had been applied in transferring the lands owned by the widow's late husband
    (D) none of the lands held by the widow's late husband had been placed in jointure
    (E) the combined amount of land the widow had acquired from her own family and from dower was greater than the amount inherited by her son

11. Which one of the following is mentioned in the passage as a reason why a married woman might have fulfilled certain duties associated with holding feudal land in thirteenth-century England?

    (A) the legal statutes set forth by Magna Carta
    (B) the rights a woman held over her inheritance during her marriage
    (C) the customary division of duties between husbands and wives
    (D) the absence of the woman's husband
    (E) the terms specified by the woman's jointure agreement

12. The phrase "in England" (lines 30–31) does which one of the following?

    (A) It suggests that women in other countries also received grants of their husbands' lands.
    (B) It identifies a particular code of law affecting women who were surviving daughters.
    (C) It demonstrates that dower had greater legal importance in one European country than in others.
    (D) It emphasizes that women in one European country had more means of controlling property than did women in other European countries.
    (E) It traces a legal term back to the time at which it entered the language.

13. The primary purpose of the passage is to

    (A) explain a legal controversy of the past in light of modern theory
    (B) evaluate the economic and legal status of a particular historical group
    (C) resolve a scholarly debate about legal history
    (D) trace the historical origins of a modern economic situation
    (E) provide new evidence about a historical event

GO ON TO THE NEXT PAGE.

The debate over the environmental crisis is not
new; anxiety about industry's impact on the
environment has existed for over a century. What is
new is the extreme polarization of views. Mounting
(5)   evidence of humanity's capacity to damage the
environment irreversibly coupled with suspicions that
government, industry, and even science might be
impotent to prevent environmental destruction have
provoked accusatory polemics on the part of
(10) environmentalists. In turn, these polemics have elicited
a corresponding backlash from industry. The sad effect
of this polarization is that it is now even more difficult
for industry than it was a hundred years ago to respond
appropriately to impact analyses that demand action.
(15)   Unlike today's adversaries, earlier ecological
reformers shared with advocates of industrial growth a
confidence in timely corrective action. George P.
Marsh's pioneering conservation tract *Man and Nature*
(1864) elicited wide acclaim without embittered
(20) denials. *Man and Nature* castigated Earth's despoilers
for heedless greed, declaring that humanity "has
brought the face of the Earth to a desolation almost as
complete as that of the Moon." But no entrepreneur or
industrialist sought to refute Marsh's accusations, to
(25) defend the gutting of forests or the slaughter of wildlife
as economically essential, or to dismiss his ecological
warnings as hysterical. To the contrary, they generally
agreed with him.
        Why? Marsh and his followers took environmental
(30) improvement and economic progress as givens; they
disputed not the desirability of conquering nature but
the bungling way in which the conquest was carried
out. Blame was not personalized; Marsh denounced
general greed rather than particular entrepreneurs, and
(35) the media did not hound malefactors. Further,
corrective measures seemed to entail no sacrifice, to
demand no draconian remedies. Self-interest
underwrote most prescribed reforms. Marsh's emphasis
on future stewardship was then a widely accepted ideal
(40) (if not practice). His ecological admonitions were in
keeping with the Enlightenment premise that
humanity's mission was to subdue and transform
nature.
        Not until the 1960s did a gloomier perspective gain
(45) popular ground. Frederic Clements' equilibrium model
of ecology, developed in the 1930s, seemed consistent
with mounting environmental disasters. In this view,
nature was most fruitful when least altered. Left
undisturbed, flora and fauna gradually attained
(50) maximum diversity and stability. Despoliation
thwarted the culmination or shortened the duration of
this beneficent climax; technology did not improve
nature but destroyed it.
        The equilibrium model became an ecological
(55) mystique: environmental interference was now taboo,
wilderness adored. Nature as unfinished fabric
perfected by human ingenuity gave way to the image of
nature debased and endangered by technology. In
contrast to the Enlightenment vision of nature,
(60) according to which rational managers construct an ever

more improved environment, twentieth-century
reformers' vision of nature calls for a reduction of
human interference in order to restore environmental
stability.

14.   Which one of the following most accurately states the
      main idea of the passage?

      (A)   Mounting evidence of humanity's capacity to
            damage the environment should motivate action
            to prevent further damage.
      (B)   The ecological mystique identified with Frederic
            Clements has become a religious conviction
            among ecological reformers.
      (C)   George P. Marsh's ideas about conservation and
            stewardship have heavily influenced the present
            debate over the environment.
      (D)   The views of ecologists and industrial growth
            advocates concerning the environment have only
            recently become polarized.
      (E)   General greed, rather than particular individuals
            or industries, should be blamed for the
            environmental crisis.

GO ON TO THE NEXT PAGE.

15. The author refers to the equilibrium model of ecology as an "ecological mystique" (lines 54–55) most likely in order to do which one of the following?

(A) underscore the fervor with which twentieth-century reformers adhere to the equilibrium model

(B) point out that the equilibrium model of ecology has recently been supported by empirical scientific research

(C) express appreciation for how plants and animals attain maximum diversity and stability when left alone

(D) indicate that the ideas of twentieth-century ecological reformers are often so theoretical as to be difficult to understand

(E) indicate how widespread support is for the equilibrium model of ecology in the scientific community

16. Which one of the following practices is most clearly an application of Frederic Clements' equilibrium model of ecology?

(A) introducing a species into an environment to which it is not native to help control the spread of another species that no longer has any natural predators

(B) developing incentives for industries to take corrective measures to protect the environment

(C) using scientific methods to increase the stability of plants and animals in areas where species are in danger of becoming extinct

(D) using technology to develop plant and animal resources but balancing that development with stringent restrictions on technology

(E) setting areas of land aside to be maintained as wilderness from which the use or extraction of natural resources is prohibited

17. The passage suggests that George P. Marsh and today's ecological reformers would be most likely to agree with which one of the following statements?

(A) Regulating industries in order to protect the environment does not conflict with the self-interest of those industries.

(B) Solving the environmental crisis does not require drastic and costly remedies.

(C) Human despoliation of the Earth has caused widespread environmental damage.

(D) Environmental improvement and economic progress are equally important goals.

(E) Rather than blaming specific industries, general greed should be denounced as the cause of environmental destruction.

18. The passage is primarily concerned with which one of the following?

(A) providing examples of possible solutions to a current crisis

(B) explaining how conflicting viewpoints in a current debate are equally valid

(C) determining which of two conflicting viewpoints in a current debate is more persuasive

(D) outlining the background and development of conflicting viewpoints in a current debate

(E) demonstrating weaknesses in the arguments made by one side in a current debate

GO ON TO THE NEXT PAGE.

Recently the focus of historical studies of different ethnic groups in the United States has shifted from the transformation of ethnic identity to its preservation.
(5) Whereas earlier historians argued that the ethnic identity of various immigrant groups to the United States blended to form an American national character, the new scholarship has focused on the transplantation of ethnic cultures to the United States. Fugita and O'Brien's *Japanese American Ethnicity* provides an
(10) example of this recent trend; it also exemplifies a problem that is common to such scholarship.

In comparing the first three generations of Japanese Americans (the Issei, Nisei, and Sansei), Fugita and O'Brien conclude that assimilation to United States
(15) culture increased among Japanese Americans over three generations, but that a sense of ethnic community endured. Although the persistence of community is stressed by the authors, their emphasis in the book could just as easily have been on the high degree of
(20) assimilation of the Japanese American population in the late twentieth century, which Fugita and O'Brien believe is demonstrated by the high levels of education, income, and occupational mobility achieved by Japanese Americans. In addition, their data reveal that
(25) the character of the ethnic community itself changed: the integration of Sanseis into new professional communities and nonethnic voluntary associations meant at the very least that ethnic ties had to accommodate multiple and layered identities. Fugita
(30) and O'Brien themselves acknowledge that there has been a "weakening of Japanese American ethnic community life."

Because of the social changes weakening the bonds of community, Fugita and O'Brien maintain that the
(35) community cohesion of Japanese Americans is notable not for its initial intensity but because "there remains a degree of involvement in the ethnic community surpassing that found in most other ethnic groups at similar points in their ethnic group life cycle." This
(40) comparative difference is important to Fugita and O'Brien, and they hypothesize that the Japanese American community persisted in the face of assimilation because of a particularly strong preexisting sense of "peoplehood." They argue that this
(45) sense of peoplehood extended beyond local and family ties.

Fugita and O'Brien's hypothesis illustrates a common problem in studies that investigate the history of ethnic community. Like historians who have studied
(50) European ethnic cultures in the United States, Fugita and O'Brien have explained persistence of ethnic community by citing a preexisting sense of national consciousness that is independent of how a group adapts to United States culture. However, it is difficult
(55) to prove, as Fugita and O'Brien have attempted to do, that a sense of peoplehood is a distinct phenomenon. Historians should instead attempt to identify directly the factors that sustain community cohesion in generations that have adapted to United States culture
(60) and been exposed to the pluralism of American life.

19. Which one of the following best summarizes the main point of the author of the passage?

(A) Fugita and O'Brien's study provides a comparison of the degree of involvement in ethnic community of different groups in the United States.

(B) Fugita and O'Brien's study describes the assimilation of three generations of Japanese Americans to United States culture.

(C) Fugita and O'Brien's study illustrates both a recent trend in historical studies of ethnic groups and a problem typical of that trend.

(D) Historical studies of ethnic preservation among Japanese Americans have done much to define the interpretive framework for studies of other ethnic groups.

(E) Historical studies are more concerned with the recent development of ethnic communities in the United States than with the process of adaptation to United States culture.

20. According to the passage, Fugita and O'Brien's data indicate which one of the following about the Japanese American ethnic community?

(A) Community bonds have weakened primarily as a result of occupational mobility by Japanese Americans.

(B) The community is notable because it has accommodated multiple and layered identities without losing its traditional intensity.

(C) Community cohesion is similar in intensity to the community cohesion of other ethnic groups that have been in the United States for the same period of time.

(D) Community involvement weakened during the second generation, but strengthened as the third generation regained an interest in cultural traditions.

(E) The nature of the community has been altered by Japanese American participation in new professional communities and nonethnic voluntary associations.

GO ON TO THE NEXT PAGE.

21. Which one of the following provides an example of a research study that has a conclusion most analogous to that argued for by the historians mentioned in line 4?

 (A) a study showing how musical forms brought from other countries have persisted in the United States

 (B) a study showing the organization and function of ethnic associations in the United States

 (C) a study showing how architectural styles brought from other countries have merged to form an American style

 (D) a study showing how cultural traditions have been preserved for generations in American ethnic neighborhoods

 (E) a study showing how different religious practices brought from other countries have been sustained in the United States

22. According to the passage, which one of the following is true about the focus of historical studies on ethnic groups in the United States?

 (A) Current studies are similar to earlier studies in claiming that a sense of peoplehood helps preserve ethnic community.

 (B) Current studies have clearly identified factors that sustain ethnic community in generations that have been exposed to the pluralism of American life.

 (C) Current studies examine the cultural practices that make up the American national character.

 (D) Earlier studies focused on how ethnic identities became transformed in the United States.

 (E) Earlier studies focused on the factors that led people to immigrate to the United States.

23. The author of the passage quotes Fugita and O'Brien in lines 36–39 most probably in order to

 (A) point out a weakness in their hypothesis about the strength of community ties among Japanese Americans

 (B) show how they support their claim about the notability of community cohesion for Japanese Americans

 (C) indicate how they demonstrate the high degree of adaptation of Japanese Americans to United States culture

 (D) suggest that they have inaccurately compared Japanese Americans to other ethnic groups in the United States

 (E) emphasize their contention that the Japanese American sense of peoplehood extended beyond local and family ties

24. The passage suggests that the author would be most likely to describe the hypothesis mentioned in line 47 as

 (A) highly persuasive
 (B) original but poorly developed
 (C) difficult to substantiate
 (D) illogical and uninteresting
 (E) too similar to earlier theories

25. The passage suggests which one of the following about the historians mentioned in line 49?

 (A) They have been unable to provide satisfactory explanations for the persistence of European ethnic communities in the United States.

 (B) They have suggested that European cultural practices have survived although the community ties of European ethnic groups have weakened.

 (C) They have hypothesized that European ethnic communities are based on family ties rather than on a sense of national consciousness.

 (D) They have argued that European cultural traditions have been transformed in the United States because of the pluralism of American life.

 (E) They have claimed that the community ties of European Americans are still as strong as they were when the immigrants first arrived.

26. As their views are discussed in the passage, Fugita and O'Brien would be most likely to agree with which one of the following?

 (A) The community cohesion of an ethnic group is not affected by the length of time it has been in the United States.

 (B) An ethnic group in the United States can have a high degree of adaptation to United States culture and still sustain strong community ties.

 (C) The strength of an ethnic community in the United States is primarily dependent on the strength of local and family ties.

 (D) High levels of education and occupational mobility necessarily erode the community cohesion of an ethnic group in the United States.

 (E) It has become increasingly difficult for ethnic groups to sustain any sense of ethnic identity in the pluralism of United States life.

S T O P

**IF YOU FINISH BEFORE TIME IS CALLED, YOU MAY CHECK YOUR WORK ON THIS SECTION ONLY.
DO NOT WORK ON ANY OTHER SECTION IN THE TEST.**

LSAT® Writing Sample Topic

Directions: The scenario presented below describes two choices, either one of which can be supported on the basis of the information given. Your essay should consider both choices and argue for one over the other, based on the two specified criteria and the facts provided. There is no "right" or "wrong" choice: a reasonable argument can be made for either.

To support efforts to treat congenital nervous disorders, Lifetime Foundation is funding a two-year grant, for which BioSearch and Hanson Pharmaceutical are the two finalists. Write an argument in support of one company over the other based on the following criteria:

- The grant money must be used to develop projects that will provide relief to persons currently suffering from these disorders.
- The grant must be awarded to a company that has the financial resources to continue such projects after the grant has expired.

BioSearch, a small company with a strong reputation for pure medical research, has been facing financial difficulty for the last two years. Recently, its scientists developed a chemical compound that can, according to many researchers unconnected to the company, treat certain congenital nervous disorders and may lead to a new family of drugs useful in the treatment of a wide range of these disorders. BioSearch plans to use part of this grant to hire one of the leading scientists in the field, Dr. Ruth Sherman. Dr. Sherman has identified another funding source that will match Lifetime's grant, should it be awarded to BioSearch.

Hanson Pharmaceutical is a profitable drug manufacturer. It has recently purchased the rights to a drug, originally developed by researchers at a medical school, that could have immediate application in the treatment of one fairly common nervous disorder. At this time, however, there is no commercially viable method to produce the drug. Hanson is seeking this grant to help defray the cost of researching a new production method, one that will make this drug cost-effective. Hanson has in the past successfully developed streamlined production methods that made certain prescription drugs more affordable.

Directions:

1. Use the Answer Key on the next page to check your answers.

2. Use the Scoring Worksheet below to compute your raw score.

3. Use the Score Conversion Chart to convert your raw score into the 120-180 scale.

Scoring Worksheet

1. Enter the number of questions you answered correctly in each section.

	Number Correct
SECTION I	_____
SECTION II	_____
SECTION III	_____
SECTION IV	_____

2. Enter the sum here: _____
   This is your Raw Score.

Conversion Chart
For Converting Raw Score to the 120-180 LSAT Scaled Score
LSAT Form 7LSS34

Reported Score	Raw Score Lowest	Raw Score Highest
180	96	100
179	94	95
178	93	93
177	92	92
176	91	91
175	90	90
174	89	89
173	88	88
172	87	87
171	86	86
170	84	85
169	83	83
168	82	82
167	81	81
166	79	80
165	78	78
164	76	77
163	75	75
162	74	74
161	72	73
160	71	71
159	69	70
158	68	68
157	66	67
156	65	65
155	63	64
154	62	62
153	60	61
152	58	59
151	57	57
150	55	56
149	54	54
148	52	53
147	51	51
146	49	50
145	48	48
144	46	47
143	45	45
142	43	44
141	41	42
140	40	40
139	38	39
138	37	37
137	36	36
136	34	35
135	33	33
134	31	32
133	30	30
132	29	29
131	28	28
130	26	27
129	25	25
128	24	24
127	23	23
126	22	22
125	21	21
124	19	20
123	18	18
122	17	17
121	16	16
120	0	15

SECTION I

1.	B	8.	E	15.	C	22.	E
2.	D	9.	E	16.	B	23.	C
3.	B	10.	B	17.	A	24.	A
4.	C	11.	B	18.	B		
5.	D	12.	C	19.	D		
6.	C	13.	A	20.	D		
7.	E	14.	D	21.	B		

SECTION II

1.	C	8.	D	15.	D	22.	D
2.	B	9.	E	16.	C	23.	E
3.	E	10.	C	17.	D	24.	D
4.	D	11.	C	18.	B	25.	B
5.	C	12.	B	19.	B	26.	D
6.	D	13.	A	20.	B		
7.	A	14.	A	21.	E		

SECTION III

1.	*	8.	B	15.	B	22.	E
2.	C	9.	E	16.	C	23.	B
3.	A	10.	B	17.	C	24.	D
4.	A	11.	B	18.	C	25.	C
5.	A	12.	B	19.	B		
6.	C	13.	E	20.	E		
7.	E	14.	D	21.	D		

SECTION IV

1.	D	8.	B	15.	A	22.	D
2.	D	9.	C	16.	E	23.	B
3.	E	10.	E	17.	C	24.	C
4.	D	11.	D	18.	D	25.	A
5.	A	12.	A	19.	C	26.	B
6.	C	13.	B	20.	E		
7.	E	14.	D	21.	C		

*Withdrawn

The Official LSAT PrepTest

24

- December 1997
- Form 7LSS35

The sample test that follows consists of four sections corresponding to the four scored sections of the December 1997 LSAT.

SECTION I

Time—35 minutes

27 Questions

Directions: Each passage in this section is followed by a group of questions to be answered on the basis of what is stated or implied in the passage. For some of the questions, more than one of the choices could conceivably answer the question. However, you are to choose the best answer; that is, the response that most accurately and completely answers the question, and blacken the corresponding space on your answer sheet.

To many developers of technologies that affect public health or the environment, "risk communication" means persuading the public that the potential risks of such technologies are small and
(5) should be ignored. Those who communicate risks in this way seem to believe that lay people do not understand the actual nature of technological risk, and they can cite studies asserting that, although people apparently ignore mundane hazards that pose
(10) significant danger, they get upset about exotic hazards that pose little chance of death or injury. Because some risk communicators take this persuasive stance, many lay people see "risk communication" as a euphemism for brainwashing done by experts.
(15) Since, however, the goal of risk communication should be to enable people to make informed decisions about technological risks, a clear understanding about how the public perceives risk is needed. Lay people's definitions of "risk" are more likely to reflect
(20) subjective ethical concerns than are experts' definitions. Lay people, for example, tend to perceive a small risk to children as more significant than a larger risk to consenting adults who benefit from the risk-creating technology. However, if asked to rank hazards
(25) by the number of annual fatalities, without reference to ethical judgments, lay people provide quite reasonable estimates, demonstrating that they have substantial knowledge about many risks. Although some studies claim to demonstrate that lay people have inappropriate
(30) concerns about exotic hazards, these studies often use questionable methods, such as asking lay people to rank risks that are hard to compare. In contrast, a recent study showed that when lay people were given the necessary facts and time, they understood the specific
(35) risks of electromagnetic fields produced by high-voltage power transmission well enough to make informed decisions.
Risk communication should therefore be based on the principle that people process new information in
(40) the context of their existing beliefs. If people know nothing about a topic, they will find messages about that topic incomprehensible. If they have erroneous beliefs, they are likely to misconstrue the messages. Thus, communicators need to know the nature and
(45) extent of recipients' knowledge and beliefs in order to design messages that will not be dismissed or misinterpreted. This need was demonstrated in a research project concerning the public's level of knowledge about risks posed by the presence of radon
(50) in the home. Researchers used open-ended interviews

and questionnaires to determine what information should be included in their brochure on radon. Subjects who read the researchers' brochure performed significantly better in understanding radon risks than
(55) did a control group who read a brochure that was written using a different approach by a government agency. Thus, careful preparation can help risk communicators to produce balanced material that tells people what they need to know to make decisions
(60) about technological risks.

1. Which one of the following best expresses the main point of the passage?

   (A)   Risk communicators are effectively addressing the proliferation of complex technologies that have increasing impact on public health and safety.

   (B)   Risk communicators should assess lay people's understanding of technologies in order to be able to give them the information they need to make reasonable decisions.

   (C)   Experts who want to communicate to the public about the possible risks of complex technologies must simplify their message to ensure that it is understandable.

   (D)   Risk communication can be perceived as the task of persuading lay people to accept the impact of a particular technology on their lives.

   (E)   Lay people can be unduly influenced by subjective concerns when making decisions about technological risks.

2. The authors of the passage would be most likely to agree that the primary purpose of risk communication should be to

   (A)   explain rather than to persuade

   (B)   promote rather than to justify

   (C)   influence experts rather than to influence lay people

   (D)   allay people's fears about mundane hazards rather than about exotic hazards

   (E)   foster public acceptance of new technologies rather than to acknowledge people's ethical concerns

GO ON TO THE NEXT PAGE.

3. According to the passage, it is probable that which one of the following will occur when risk communicators attempt to communicate with lay people who have mistaken ideas about a particular technology?

   (A) The lay people, perceiving that the risk communicators have provided more-reliable information, will discard their mistaken notions.

   (B) The lay people will only partially revise their ideas on the basis of the new information.

   (C) The lay people, fitting the new information into their existing framework, will interpret the communication differently than the risk communicators had intended.

   (D) The lay people, misunderstanding the new information, will further distort the information when they communicate it to other lay people.

   (E) The lay people will ignore any communication about a technology they consider potentially dangerous.

4. Which one of the following is most clearly an example of the kind of risk perception discussed in the "studies" mentioned in line 8?

   (A) A skydiver checks the lines on her parachute several times before a jump because tangled lines often keep the parachutes from opening properly.

   (B) A person decides to quit smoking in order to lessen the probability of lung damage to himself and his family.

   (C) A homeowner who decides to have her house tested for radon also decides not to allow anyone to smoke in her house.

   (D) A person who often weaves in and out of traffic while driving his car at excessive speeds worries about meteorites hitting his house.

   (E) A group of townspeople opposes the building of a nuclear waste dump outside their town and proposes that the dump be placed in another town.

5. It can be inferred that the authors of the passage would be more likely than would the risk communicators discussed in the first paragraph to emphasize which one of the following?

   (A) lay people's tendency to become alarmed about technologies that they find new or strange

   (B) lay people's tendency to compare risks that experts would not consider comparable

   (C) the need for lay people to adopt scientists' advice about technological risk

   (D) the inability of lay people to rank hazards by the number of fatalities caused annually

   (E) the impact of lay people's value systems on their perceptions of risk

6. According to the passage, many lay people believe which one of the following about risk communication?

   (A) It focuses excessively on mundane hazards.
   (B) It is a tool used to manipulate the public.
   (C) It is a major cause of inaccuracies in public knowledge about science.
   (D) It most often functions to help people make informed decisions.
   (E) Its level of effectiveness depends on the level of knowledge its audience already has.

GO ON TO THE NEXT PAGE.

In April 1990 representatives of the Pico Korea Union of electronics workers in Buchon City, South Korea, traveled to the United States in order to demand just settlement of their claims from the parent company
(5) of their employer, who upon the formation of the union had shut down operations without paying the workers. From the beginning, the union cause was championed by an unprecedented coalition of Korean American groups and deeply affected the Korean American
(10) community on several levels.

First, it served as a rallying focus for a diverse community often divided by generation, class, and political ideologies. Most notably, the Pico cause mobilized many young second-generation Korean
(15) Americans, many of whom had never been part of a political campaign before, let alone one involving Korean issues. Members of this generation, unlike first-generation Korean Americans, generally fall within the more privileged sectors of the Korean American
(20) community and often feel alienated from their Korean roots. In addition to raising the political consciousness of young Korean Americans, the Pico struggle sparked among them new interest in their cultural identity. The Pico workers also suggested new roles that can be
(25) played by recent immigrants, particularly working-class immigrants. These immigrants' knowledge of working conditions overseas can help to globalize the perspective of their communities and can help to establish international ties on a more personal level, as
(30) witnessed in the especially warm exchange between the Pico workers and recent working-class immigrants from China. In addition to broadening the political base within the Korean American community, the Pico struggle also led to new alliances between the Korean
(35) American community and progressive labor and social justice groups within the larger society—as evidenced in the support received from the Coalition of Labor Union Women and leading African American unionists.
(40) The reasons for these effects lie in the nature of the cause. The issues raised by the Pico unionists had such a strong human component that differences within the community became secondary to larger concerns for social justice and workers' rights. The workers'
(45) demands for compensation and respect were unencumbered with strong ideological trappings. The economic exploitation faced by the Pico workers underscored the common interests of Korean workers, Korean Americans, the working class more inclusively,
(50) and a broad spectrum of community leaders.

The Pico workers' campaign thus offers an important lesson. It demonstrates that ethnic communities need more than just a knowledge of history and culture as artifacts of the past in order to
(55) strengthen their ethnic identity. It shows that perhaps the most effective means of empowerment for many ethnic communities of immigrant derivation may be an identification with and participation in current struggles for economic and social justice in their
(60) countries of origin.

7. Which one of the following best describes the main topic of the passage?

(A) the contribution of the Korean American community to improving the working conditions of Koreans employed by United States companies

(B) the change brought about in the Korean American community by contacts with Koreans visiting the United States

(C) the contribution of recent immigrants from Korea to strengthening ethnic identity in the Korean American community

(D) the effects on the Korean American community of a dispute between Korean union workers and a United States company

(E) the effect of the politicization of second-generation Korean Americans on the Korean American community as a whole

8. The passage suggests that which one of the following was a significant factor in the decision to shut down the Pico plant in Buchon City?

(A) the decreasing profitability of maintaining operations in Korea

(B) the failure to resolve long-standing disputes between the Pico workers and management

(C) the creation of a union by the Pico workers

(D) the withholding of workers' wages by the parent company

(E) the finding of an alternate site for operations

GO ON TO THE NEXT PAGE.

9. Which one of the following is NOT mentioned in the passage as a recent development in the Korean American community?

(A) Young second-generation Korean Americans have begun to take an interest in their Korean heritage.

(B) Recent Korean American immigrants of working-class backgrounds have begun to enter the more privileged sectors of the Korean American community.

(C) Korean Americans have developed closer ties with activist groups from other sectors of the population.

(D) Previously nonpolitical members of the Korean American community have become more politically active.

(E) The Korean American community has been able to set aside political and generational disparities in order to support a common cause.

10. It can be inferred that the author of the passage would most likely agree with which one of the following statements about ethnic communities of immigrant derivation?

(A) Such communities can derive important benefits from maintaining ties with their countries of origin.

(B) Such communities should focus primarily on promoting study of the history and culture of their people in order to strengthen their ethnic identity.

(C) Such communities can most successfully mobilize and politicize their young people by addressing the problems of young people of all backgrounds.

(D) The more privileged sectors of such communities are most likely to maintain a sense of closeness to their cultural roots.

(E) The politicization of such a community is unlikely to affect relations with other groups within the larger society.

11. In the second paragraph, the author refers to immigrants from China most probably in order to do which one of the following?

(A) highlight the contrast between working conditions in the United States and in Korea

(B) demonstrate the uniqueness of the problem faced by the Pico workers

(C) offer an example of the type of role that can be played by recent working-class immigrants

(D) provide an analogy for the type of activism displayed by the Korean American community

(E) compare the disparate responses of two immigrant communities to similar problems

12. The primary purpose of the passage is to

(A) describe recent developments in the Korean American community that have strongly affected other ethnic communities of immigrant derivation

(B) describe a situation in the Korean American community that presents a model for the empowerment of ethnic communities of immigrant derivation

(C) detail the problems faced by the Korean American community in order to illustrate the need for the empowerment of ethnic communities of immigrant derivation

(D) argue against economic and social injustice in the countries of origin of ethnic communities of immigrant derivation

(E) assess the impact of the unionization movement on ethnic communities of immigrant derivation

13. Which one of the following most accurately states the function of the third paragraph?

(A) It explains why the Pico workers brought their cause to the United States.

(B) It explains how the Pico cause differed from other causes that had previously mobilized the Korean American community.

(C) It explains why the Pico workers were accorded such broad support.

(D) It explains how other ethnic groups of immigrant derivation in the United States have profited from the example of the Pico workers.

(E) It explains why different generations of Korean Americans reacted in different ways to the Pico cause.

GO ON TO THE NEXT PAGE.

In recent years, scholars have begun to use social science tools to analyze court opinions. These scholars have justifiably criticized traditional legal research for its focus on a few cases that may not be representative
(5) and its fascination with arcane matters that do not affect real people with real legal problems. Zirkel and Schoenfeld, for example, have championed the application of social science tools to the analysis of case law surrounding discrimination against women in
(10) higher education employment. Their studies have demonstrated how these social science tools may be used to serve the interests of scholars, lawyers, and prospective plaintiffs as well. However, their enthusiasm for the "outcomes analysis" technique
(15) seems misguided.

Of fundamental concern is the outcomes analysts' assumption that simply counting the number of successful and unsuccessful plaintiffs will be useful to prospective plaintiffs. Although the odds are clearly
(20) against the plaintiff in sex discrimination cases, plaintiffs who believe that their cause is just and that they will prevail are not swayed by such evidence. In addition, because lawsuits are so different in the details of the case, in the quality of the evidence the plaintiff
(25) presents, and in the attitude of the judge toward academic plaintiffs, giving prospective plaintiffs statistics about overall outcomes without analyzing the reason for these outcomes is of marginal assistance. Outcomes analysis, for example, ignores the fact that in
(30) certain academic sex discrimination cases—those involving serious procedural violations or incriminating evidence in the form of written admissions of discriminatory practices—plaintiffs are much more likely to prevail.

(35) Two different approaches offer more useful applications of social science tools in analyzing sex discrimination cases. One is a process called "policy capturing," in which the researcher reads each opinion; identifies variables discussed in the opinion, such as
(40) the regularity of employer evaluations of the plaintiff's performance, training of evaluators, and the kind of evaluation instrument used; and then uses multivariate analysis to determine whether these variables predict the outcome of the lawsuit. The advantage of policy-
(45) capturing research is that it attempts to explain the reason for the outcome, rather than simply reporting the outcome, and identifies factors that contribute to a plaintiff's success or failure. Taking a slightly different approach, other scholars have adopted a technique that
(50) requires reading complete transcripts of all sex discrimination cases litigated during a certain time period to identify variables such as the nature of the allegedly illegal conduct, the consequences for employers, and the nature of the remedy, as well as the
(55) factors that contributed to the verdict and the kind of evidence necessary for the plaintiff to prevail. While the findings of these studies are limited to the period covered, they assist potential plaintiffs and defendants in assessing their cases.

14. Which one of the following best expresses the main idea of the passage?

(A) The analysis of a limited number of atypical discrimination suits is of little value to potential plaintiffs.

(B) When the number of factors analyzed in a sex discrimination suit is increased, the validity of the conclusions drawn becomes suspect.

(C) Scholars who are critical of traditional legal research frequently offer alternative approaches that are also seriously flawed.

(D) Outcomes analysis has less predictive value in sex discrimination cases than do certain other social science techniques.

(E) Given adequate information, it is possible to predict with considerable certainty whether a plaintiff will be successful in a discrimination suit.

15. It can be inferred from the author's discussion of traditional legal research that the author is

(A) frustrated because traditional legal research has not achieved its full potential

(B) critical because traditional legal research has little relevance to those actually involved in cases

(C) appreciative of the role traditional legal research played in developing later, more efficient approaches

(D) derisive because traditional legal research has outlasted its previously significant role

(E) grateful for the ability of traditional legal research to develop unique types of evidence

GO ON TO THE NEXT PAGE.

16. Which one of the following statements about Zirkel and Schoenfeld can be inferred from the passage?

 (A) They were the first scholars to use social science tools in analyzing legal cases.
 (B) They confined their studies to the outcomes analysis technique.
 (C) They saw no value in the analysis provided by traditional legal research.
 (D) They rejected policy capturing as being too limited in scope.
 (E) They believed that the information generated by outcomes analysis would be relevant for plaintiffs.

17. The author's characterization of traditional legal research in the first paragraph is intended to

 (A) provide background information for the subsequent discussion
 (B) summarize an opponent's position
 (C) argue against the use of social science tools in the analysis of sex discrimination cases
 (D) emphasize the fact that legal researchers act to the detriment of potential plaintiffs
 (E) reconcile traditional legal researchers to the use of social science tools

18. The information in the passage suggests that plaintiffs who pursue sex discrimination cases despite the statistics provided by outcomes analysis can best be likened to

 (A) athletes who continue to employ training techniques despite their knowledge of statistical evidence indicating that these techniques are unlikely to be effective
 (B) lawyers who handle lawsuits for a large number of clients in the hope that some percentage will be successful
 (C) candidates for public office who are more interested in making a political statement than in winning an election
 (D) supporters of a cause who recruit individuals sympathetic to it in the belief that large numbers of supporters will lend the cause legitimacy
 (E) purchasers of a charity's raffle tickets who consider the purchase a contribution because the likelihood of winning is remote

19. The policy-capturing approach differs from the approach described in lines 48–59 in that the latter approach

 (A) makes use of detailed information on a greater number of cases
 (B) focuses more directly on issues of concern to litigants
 (C) analyzes information that is more recent and therefore reflects current trends
 (D) allows assessment of aspects of a case that are not specifically mentioned in a judge's opinion
 (E) eliminates any distortion due to personal bias on the part of the researcher

20. Which one of the following best describes the organization of the passage?

 (A) A technique is introduced, its shortcomings are summarized, and alternatives are described.
 (B) A debate is introduced, evidence is presented, and a compromise is reached.
 (C) A theory is presented, clarification is provided, and a plan of further evaluation is suggested.
 (D) Standards are established, hypothetical examples are analyzed, and the criteria are amended.
 (E) A position is challenged, its shortcomings are categorized, and the challenge is revised.

GO ON TO THE NEXT PAGE.

A fake can be defined as an artwork intended to deceive. The motives of its creator are decisive, and the merit of the object itself is a separate issue. The question mark in the title of Mark Jones's *Fake? The*
(5) *Art of Deception* reveals the study's broader concerns. Indeed, it might equally be entitled *Original?*, and the text begins by noting a variety of possibilities somewhere between the two extremes. These include works by an artist's followers in the style of the master,
(10) deliberate archaism, copying for pedagogical purposes, and the production of commercial facsimiles.

The greater part of *Fake?* is devoted to a chronological survey suggesting that faking feeds on the many different motives people have for collecting
(15) art, and that, on the whole, the faking of art flourishes whenever art collecting flourishes. In imperial Rome there was a widespread interest in collecting earlier Greek art, and therefore in faking it. No doubt many of the sculptures now exhibited as "Roman copies" were
(20) originally passed off as Greek. In medieval Europe, because art was celebrated more for its devotional uses than for its provenance or the ingenuity of its creators, the faking of art was virtually nonexistent. The modern age of faking began in the Italian Renaissance, with
(25) two linked developments: a passionate identification with the world of antiquity and a growing sense of individual artistic identity. A patron of the young Michelangelo prevailed upon the artist to make his sculpture *Sleeping Cupid* look as though it had been
(30) buried in the earth so that "it will be taken for antique, and you will sell it much better." Within a few years, however, beginning with his first masterpiece, the *Bacchus*, Michelangelo had shown his contemporaries that great art can assimilate and transcend what came
(35) before, resulting in a wholly original work. Soon his genius made him the object of imitators.

Fake? also reminds us that in certain cultures authenticity is a foreign concept. This is true of much African art, where the authenticity of an object is
(40) considered by collectors to depend on its function. As an illustration, the study compares two versions of a *chi wara* mask made by the Bambara people of Mali. One has pegs allowing it to be attached to a cap for its intended ceremonial purpose. The second, otherwise
(45) identical, lacks the pegs and is a replica made for sale. African carving is notoriously difficult to date, but even if the ritual mask is recent, made perhaps to replace a damaged predecessor, and the replica much older, only the ritual mask should be seen as authentic,
(50) for it is tied to the form's original function. That, at least, is the consensus of the so-called experts. One wonders whether the Bambaran artists would agree.

21. The passage can best be described as doing which one of the following?

(A) reconciling varied points of view
(B) chronicling the evolution of a phenomenon
(C) exploring a complex question
(D) advocating a new approach
(E) rejecting an inadequate explanation

22. Which one of the following best expresses the author's main point?

(A) The faking of art has occurred throughout history and in virtually every culture.
(B) Whether a work of art is fake or not is less important than whether it has artistic merit.
(C) It is possible to show that a work of art is fake, but the authenticity of a work cannot be proved conclusively.
(D) A variety of circumstances make it difficult to determine whether a work of art can appropriately be called a fake.
(E) Without an international market to support it, the faking of art would cease.

23. According to the passage, an artwork can be definitively classified as a fake if the person who created it

(A) consciously adopted the artistic style of an influential mentor
(B) deliberately imitated a famous work of art as a learning exercise
(C) wanted other people to be fooled by its appearance
(D) made multiple, identical copies of the work available for sale
(E) made the work resemble the art of an earlier era

GO ON TO THE NEXT PAGE.

24. The author provides at least one example of each of the following EXCEPT:

    (A) categories of art that are neither wholly fake nor wholly original
    (B) cultures in which the faking of art flourished
    (C) qualities that art collectors have prized in their acquisitions
    (D) cultures in which the categories "fake" and "original" do not apply
    (E) contemporary artists whose works have inspired fakes

25. The author implies which one of the following about the artistic merits of fakes?

    (A) Because of the circumstances of its production, a fake cannot be said to have true artistic merit.
    (B) A fake can be said to have artistic merit only if the attempted deception is successful.
    (C) A fake may or may not have artistic merit in its own right, regardless of the circumstances of its production.
    (D) Whether a fake has artistic merit depends on whether its creator is accomplished as an artist.
    (E) The artistic merit of a fake depends on the merit of the original work that inspired the fake.

26. By the standard described in the last paragraph of the passage, which one of the following would be considered authentic?

    (A) an ancient Roman copy of an ancient Greek sculpture
    (B) a painting begun by a Renaissance master and finished by his assistants after his death
    (C) a print of a painting signed by the artist who painted the original
    (D) a faithful replica of a ceremonial crown that preserves all the details of, and is indistinguishable from, the original
    (E) a modern reconstruction of a medieval altarpiece designed to serve its traditional role in a service of worship

27. Which one of the following best describes how the last paragraph functions in the context of the passage?

    (A) It offers a tentative answer to a question posed by the author in the opening paragraph.
    (B) It summarizes an account provided in detail in the preceding paragraph.
    (C) It provides additional support for an argument advanced by the author in the preceding paragraph.
    (D) It examines another facet of a distinction developed in the preceding paragraphs.
    (E) It affirms the general principle enunciated at the beginning of the passage.

S T O P

IF YOU FINISH BEFORE TIME IS CALLED, YOU MAY CHECK YOUR WORK ON THIS SECTION ONLY.
DO NOT WORK ON ANY OTHER SECTION IN THE TEST.

SECTION II

Time—35 minutes

25 Questions

Directions: The questions in this section are based on the reasoning contained in brief statements or passages. For some questions, more than one of the choices could conceivably answer the question. However, you are to choose the best answer; that is, the response that most accurately and completely answers the question. You should not make assumptions that are by commonsense standards implausible, superfluous, or incompatible with the passage. After you have chosen the best answer, blacken the corresponding space on your answer sheet.

1. Press release: A comprehensive review evaluating the medical studies done up to the present time has found no reason to think that drinking coffee in normal amounts harms the coffee-drinker's heart. So coffee drinkers can relax and enjoy their beverage—it is safe to drink coffee.

Which one of the following points to a weakness in the reasoning in the press release's argument?

(A)   The review was only an evaluation of studies and did not itself undertake to study patients.
(B)   The health of the heart is not identical with the general health of the body.
(C)   Coffee drinkers might choose to eat, along with their coffee, foods containing substances that harm the heart.
(D)   Other beverages besides coffee might contain stimulants that have some effect on the heart.
(E)   Drinking unusually large amounts of coffee could be caused by stress that itself directly harms the heart.

2. All people prefer colors that they can distinguish easily to colors that they have difficulty distinguishing. Infants can easily distinguish bright colors but, unlike adults, have difficulty distinguishing subtle shades. A brightly colored toy for infants sells better than the same toy in subtle shades at the same price.

Which one of the following conclusions is most strongly supported by the information in the passage?

(A)   Infants prefer bright primary colors to bright secondary colors.
(B)   Color is the most important factor in determining which toys an infant will prefer to play with.
(C)   Individual infants do not have strong preferences for one particular bright color over other bright colors.
(D)   The sales of toys for infants reflect the preferences of infants in at least one respect.
(E)   Toy makers study infants to determine what colors the infants can distinguish easily.

3. A group of unusual meteorites was found in Shergotty, India. Their structure indicates that they originated on one of the geologically active planets, Mercury, Venus, or Mars. Because of Mercury's proximity to the Sun, any material dislodged from that planet's surface would have been captured by the Sun, rather than falling to Earth as meteorites. Nor could Venus be the source of the meteorites, because its gravity would have prevented dislodged material from escaping into space. The meteorites, therefore, probably fell to Earth after being dislodged from Mars, perhaps as the result of a collision with a large object.

The argument derives its conclusion by

(A)   offering a counterexample to a theory
(B)   eliminating competing alternative explanations
(C)   contrasting present circumstances with past circumstances
(D)   questioning an assumption
(E)   abstracting a general principle from specific data

4. Because quitting smoking is very stressful and leads to weight gain, it is difficult to do. The key to quitting, however, may be as simple as replacing an unhealthy activity with a healthy one. In one study, half of those attempting to quit were assigned to a smoking-cessation program alone, and the other half were assigned to the same program plus fifteen weeks of aerobic exercise. At the one-month mark, none in the first group had quit, but 40 percent of those in the second group had not smoked.

Each of the following, if true, provides some support for the argument EXCEPT:

(A)   Regular exercise prevents weight gain.
(B)   Each group in the study included four hundred randomly selected participants.
(C)   Nonsmokers accustomed to regular exercise do not gain weight when they stop exercising.
(D)   Aerobic exercise can stimulate the brain's production of endorphins, which reduce tension.
(E)   Of those in the second group in the study, 38 percent had not smoked at the one-year mark.

GO ON TO THE NEXT PAGE.

5. Altogether, the students in Ms. Tarnowski's Milton Elementary School class collected more aluminum cans than did the students in any of the school's other classes. Therefore, the Milton student who collected the most aluminum cans was in Ms. Tarnowski's class.

Which one of the following arguments contains flawed reasoning that is most parallel to that in the argument above?

(A) Altogether, more trees were planted by the students in Mr. Kelly's class than were planted by those in Mr. Liang's class and Ms. Jackson's class combined. Therefore, Mr. Kelly's students planted more trees than Ms. Jackson's students planted.

(B) More than half of Milton Elementary School's students play in the band and more than half of the school's students sing in the choir. Therefore, every student at Milton Elementary School either plays in the band or sings in the choir.

(C) Mr. Rowe's Milton Elementary School class raised more money by selling candy bars than Ms. Hunt's class raised by holding a raffle. Therefore, the number of candy bars sold by Mr. Rowe's class was greater than the number of raffle tickets sold by Ms. Hunt's class.

(D) The total number of tickets to the school fair sold by the students in Ms. Ramirez's Milton Elementary School class was greater than the number sold by Milton students from any other class. Therefore, the Milton student who sold the most tickets to the school fair was a student in Ms. Ramirez's class.

(E) Ms. Ventura's Milton Elementary School class assembled more birdhouses than did any of the school's other classes. Since Ms. Ventura's class had fewer students than any other Milton class, her students assembled more birdhouses, on average, than did the students in any other Milton class.

6. Several excellent candidates have been proposed for the presidency of United Wire, and each candidate would bring to the job different talents and experience. If the others are compared with Jones, however, it will be apparent that none of them has her unique set of qualifications. Jones, therefore, is best qualified to be the new president of United Wire.

The argument is vulnerable to criticism on the ground that it

(A) uses flattery to win over those who hold an opposing position

(B) refutes a distorted version of an opposing position

(C) seeks to distinguish one member of a group on the basis of something that applies to all

(D) supports a universal claim on the basis of a single example

(E) describes an individual in terms that appropriately refer only to the group as a whole

7. A neighborhood group plans to protest the closing of the neighborhood's only recreation center on the grounds that to do so would leave the neighborhood without local access to a recreation center. "Our neighborhood already has the most residents per center of any neighborhood in the city," complained one resident, "and closing this center would make the situation unacceptable since access to recreational facilities is a necessity for this neighborhood."

Each of the following, if true, weakens the resident's argument EXCEPT:

(A) A large number of the neighborhood's residents are unable to travel outside their locality to gain access to recreational facilities.

(B) Children, the main users of recreational facilities, make up a disproportionately small segment of the neighborhood's population.

(C) Often the recreation center in the neighborhood is open but not being used.

(D) Programs that are routinely filled at other recreation centers must be canceled at the neighborhood's recreation center due to lack of interest.

(E) As people become more involved in computers and computer games, recreation centers are becoming increasingly less important.

GO ON TO THE NEXT PAGE.

8. Sociologist: The claim that there is a large number of violent crimes in our society is false, for this claim is based upon the large number of stories in newspapers about violent crimes. But since violent crimes are very rare occurrences, newspapers are likely to print stories about them.

The sociologist's argument is flawed because it

(A) presupposes that most newspaper stories are about violent crime
(B) presupposes the truth of the conclusion it is attempting to establish
(C) assumes without warrant that the newspaper stories in question are not biased
(D) mistakes a property of each member of a group taken as an individual for a property of the group taken as a whole
(E) uncritically draws an inference from what has been true in the past to what will be true in the future

9. Historian: Anyone who thinks that the terrors of the ancient regime of Q were exclusively the work of fanatics is overlooking a basic truth: the regime was made up primarily of ordinary people enthusiastically seeking paradise. The regime executed many people in pursuit of its goal; but it later became clear that paradise, as they defined it, is unrealizable. So at least some of the ordinary people of Q were in fact murderers.

Which one of the following principles, if valid, provides the most support for the historian's argumentation?

(A) The pursuit of paradise does not justify murder.
(B) The pursuit of paradise justifies fanaticism.
(C) Execution in pursuit of what is later found to be unattainable constitutes murder.
(D) Fanaticism in pursuit of paradise constitutes inhumanity.
(E) Enthusiasm in pursuit of what is eventually found to be unattainable constitutes fanaticism.

10. Economist: The economy seems to be heading out of recession. Recent figures show that consumers are buying more durable goods than before, indicating that they expect economic growth in the near future.

That consumers are buying more durable goods than before figures in the economist's argument in which one of the following ways?

(A) It is the phenomenon that the argument seeks to explain.
(B) Its truth is required in order for the argument's conclusion to be true.
(C) It is an inference drawn from the premise that the recession seems to be ending.
(D) It is an inference drawn from the premise that consumers expect economic growth in the near future.
(E) It is the primary evidence from which the argument's conclusion is drawn.

11. Not surprisingly, there are no professors under the age of eighteen. And, as is well known, no one under eighteen can vote legally. Finally, some brilliant people are professors, some are legal voters, and some are under eighteen.

If the statements above are true, then on the basis of them which one of the following must also be true?

(A) No professors are eighteen-year-olds.
(B) All brilliant people are either professors, legal voters, or under eighteen.
(C) Some legal voters are not professors.
(D) Some professors are neither legal voters nor brilliant people.
(E) Some brilliant people are neither professors nor legal voters.

GO ON TO THE NEXT PAGE.

12. For years scientists have been scanning the skies in the hope of finding life on other planets. But in spite of the ever-increasing sophistication of the equipment they employ, some of it costing hundreds of millions of dollars, not the first shred of evidence of such life has been forthcoming. And there is no reason to think that these scientists will be any more successful in the future, no matter how much money is invested in the search. The dream of finding extraterrestrial life is destined to remain a dream, as science's experience up to this point should indicate.

Which one of the following most accurately states the main point of the argument?

(A) There is no reason to believe that life exists on other planets.

(B) The equipment that scientists employ is not as sophisticated as it should be.

(C) Scientists searching for extraterrestrial life will not find it.

(D) Only if scientists had already found evidence of life on other planets would continued search be justified.

(E) We should not spend money on sophisticated equipment to aid in the search for extraterrestrial life.

13. Carl's Coffee Emporium stocks only two decaffeinated coffees: French Roast and Mocha Java. Yusef only serves decaffeinated coffee, and the coffee he served after dinner last night was far too smooth and mellow to have been French Roast. So, if Yusef still gets all his coffee from Carl's, what he served last night was Mocha Java.

The argument above is most similar in its logical structure to which one of the following?

(A) Samuel wants to take three friends to the beach. His mother owns both a sedan and a convertible. The convertible holds four people so, although the sedan has a more powerful engine, if Samuel borrows a vehicle from his mother, he will borrow the convertible.

(B) If Anna wants to walk from her house to the office where she works, she must either go through the park or take the overpass across the railroad tracks. The park paths are muddy, and Anna does not like using the overpass, so she never walks to work.

(C) Rose can either take a two-week vacation in July or wait until October and take a three-week vacation. The trail she had planned to hike requires three weeks to complete but is closed by October, so if Rose takes a vacation, it will not be the one she had planned.

(D) Werdix, Inc., has offered Arno a choice between a job in sales and a job in research. Arno would like to work at Werdix but he would never take a job in sales when another job is available, so if he accepts one of these jobs, it will be the one in research.

(E) If Teresa does not fire her assistant, her staff will rebel and her department's efficiency will decline. Losing her assistant would also reduce its efficiency, so, if no alternative solution can be found, Teresa's department will become less efficient.

GO ON TO THE NEXT PAGE.

14. Steven: The allowable blood alcohol level for drivers should be cut in half. With this reduced limit, social drinkers will be deterred from drinking and driving, resulting in significantly increased highway safety.

    Miguel: No, lowering the current allowable blood alcohol level would have little effect on highway safety, because it would not address the most important aspect of the drunken driving problem, which is the danger to the public posed by heavy drinkers, who often drive with a blood alcohol level of twice the current legal limit.

    Steven and Miguel's statements provide the most support for holding that they would disagree about the truth of which one of the following statements?

    (A) Social drinkers who drink and drive pose a substantial threat to the public.
    (B) There is a direct correlation between a driver's blood alcohol level and the driver's ability to drive safely.
    (C) A driver with a blood alcohol level above the current legal limit poses a substantial danger to the public.
    (D) Some drivers whose blood alcohol level is lower than the current legal limit pose a danger to the public.
    (E) A driver with a blood alcohol level slightly greater than half the current legal limit poses no danger to the public.

Questions 15–16

The authors of a recent article examined warnings of an impending wave of extinctions of animal species within the next 100 years. These authors say that no evidence exists to support the idea that the rate of extinction of animal species is now accelerating. They are wrong, however. Consider only the data on fishes: 40 species and subspecies of North American fishes have vanished in the twentieth century, 13 between 1900 and 1950, and 27 since 1950.

15. Which one of the following is the main point of the argument?

    (A) There is evidence that the rate of extinction of animal species is accelerating.
    (B) The future rate of extinction of animal species cannot be determined from available evidence.
    (C) The rate of extinction of North American fishes is parallel to the rate of extinction of all animal species taken together.
    (D) Forty species and subspecies of North American fishes have vanished in the twentieth century.
    (E) A substantial number of fish species are in danger of imminent extinction.

16. The answer to which one of the following questions would contribute most to an evaluation of the argument?

    (A) Were the fish species and subspecies that became extinct unrepresentative of animal species in general with regard to their pattern of extinction?
    (B) How numerous were the populations in 1950 of the species and subspecies of North American fishes that have become extinct since 1950?
    (C) Did any of the species or subspecies of North American fishes that became extinct in the twentieth century originate in regions outside of North America?
    (D) What proportion of North American fish species and subspecies whose populations were endangered in 1950 are now thriving?
    (E) Were any of the species or subspecies of North American fishes that became extinct in the twentieth century commercially important?

GO ON TO THE NEXT PAGE.

17. After the Second World War, the charter of the newly formed United Nations established an eleven-member Security Council and charged it with taking collective action in response to threats to world peace. The charter further provided that the five nations that were then the major powers would permanently have sole authority to cast vetoes. The reason given for this arrangement was that the burden of maintaining world peace would rest on the world's major powers, and no nation should be required to assume the burden of enforcing a decision it found repugnant.

The reasoning given for the structure of the Security Council assumes that

(A) it does not make sense to provide for democracy among nations when nations themselves are not all democracies

(B) no nation that was not among the major powers at the end of the Second World War would become a major power

(C) nations would not eventually gravitate into large geographical blocs, each containing minor powers as well as at least one major power

(D) minor powers would not ally themselves with major powers to gain the protection of the veto exercised by major powers

(E) decisions reached by a majority of nations in response to threats to world peace would be biased in favor of one or more major powers

18. Environmental scientist: It is true that over the past ten years, there has been a sixfold increase in government funding for the preservation of wetlands, while the total area of wetlands needing such preservation has increased only twofold (although this area was already large ten years ago). Even when inflation is taken into account, the amount of funding now is at least three times what it was ten years ago. Nevertheless, the current amount of government funding for the preservation of wetlands is inadequate and should be augmented.

Which one of the following, if true, most helps to reconcile the environmental scientist's conclusion with the evidence cited above?

(A) The governmental agency responsible for administering wetland-preservation funds has been consistently mismanaged and run inefficiently over the past ten years.

(B) Over the past ten years, the salaries of scientists employed by the government to work on the preservation of wetlands have increased at a rate higher than the inflation rate.

(C) Research over the past ten years has enabled scientists today to identify wetlands in need of preservation well before the areas are at serious risk of destruction.

(D) More people today, scientists and nonscientists alike, are working to preserve all natural resources, including wetlands.

(E) Unlike today, funding for the preservation of wetlands was almost nonexistent ten years ago.

GO ON TO THE NEXT PAGE.

19. In Australia the population that is of driving age has grown larger over the last five years, but the annual number of traffic fatalities has declined. This leads to the conclusion that, overall, the driving-age population of Australia consists of more skillful drivers now than five years ago.

Each of the statements below, if true, weakens the argument EXCEPT:

(A) Three years ago, a mandatory seat-belt law went into effect throughout Australia.

(B) Five years ago, Australia began a major road repair project.

(C) Because of increases in the price of fuel, Australians on average drive less each year than in the preceding year.

(D) The number of hospital emergency facilities in Australia has doubled in the last five years.

(E) In response to an increase in traffic fatalities, Australia instituted a program of mandatory driver education five years ago.

20. Anthropological studies indicate that distinct cultures differ in their moral codes. Thus, as long as there are distinct cultures, there are no values shared across cultures.

Each of the following, if true, would weaken the argument EXCEPT:

(A) Anthropologists rely on inadequate translation techniques to investigate the values of cultures that use languages different from the anthropologists' languages.

(B) As a result of advancing technology and global communication, we will someday all share the same culture and the same values.

(C) Although specific moral values differ across cultures, more general moral principles, such as "Friendship is good," are common to all cultures.

(D) The anthropologists who have studied various cultures have been biased in favor of finding differences rather than similarities between distinct cultures.

(E) What appear to be differences in values between distinct cultures are nothing more than differences in beliefs about how to live in accordance with shared values.

21. Newspaper editor: Law enforcement experts, as well as most citizens, have finally come to recognize that legal prohibitions against gambling all share a common flaw: no matter how diligent the effort, the laws are impossible to enforce. Ethical qualms notwithstanding, when a law fails to be effective, it should not be a law. That is why there should be no legal prohibition against gambling.

Which one of the following, if assumed, allows the argument's conclusion to be properly drawn?

(A) No effective law is unenforceable.

(B) All enforceable laws are effective.

(C) No legal prohibitions against gambling are enforceable.

(D) Most citizens must agree with a law for the law to be effective.

(E) Most citizens must agree with a law for the law to be enforceable.

22. Copernicus's astronomical system is superior to Ptolemy's and was so at the time it was proposed, even though at that time all observational evidence was equally consistent with both theories. Ptolemy believed that the stars revolved around the earth at great speeds. This struck Copernicus as unlikely; he correctly thought that a simpler theory is that the earth rotates on its axis.

The argument most closely conforms to which one of the following principles?

(A) Simplicity should be the sole deciding factor in choosing among competing scientific theories.

(B) If one theory is likely to be true, and another competing theory is likely to be false, then the one likely to be true is the superior of the two.

(C) If all observational evidence is consistent with two competing theories, the one that is more intuitively true is the more practical theory to adopt.

(D) Other things being equal, the more complex of two competing theories is the inferior theory.

(E) Other things being equal, the simpler of two competing theories is the more scientifically important theory.

GO ON TO THE NEXT PAGE.

23. Essayist: The existence of a moral order in the universe—i.e., an order in which bad is always eventually punished and good rewarded—depends upon human souls being immortal. In some cultures this moral order is regarded as the result of a karma that controls how one is reincarnated, in others it results from the actions of a supreme being who metes out justice to people after their death. But however a moral order is represented, if human souls are immortal, then it follows that the bad will be punished.

Which one of the following most accurately describes a flaw in the essayist's reasoning?

(A) From the assertion that something is necessary to a moral order, the argument concludes that that thing is sufficient for an element of the moral order to be realized.

(B) The argument takes mere beliefs to be established facts.

(C) From the claim that the immortality of human souls implies that there is a moral order in the universe, the argument concludes that there being a moral order in the universe implies that human souls are immortal.

(D) The argument treats two fundamentally different conceptions of a moral order as essentially the same.

(E) The argument's conclusion is presupposed in the definition it gives of a moral order.

24. No mathematical proposition can be proven true by observation. It follows that it is impossible to know any mathematical proposition to be true.

The conclusion follows logically if which one of the following is assumed?

(A) Only propositions that can be proven true can be known to be true.

(B) Observation alone cannot be used to prove the truth of any proposition.

(C) If a proposition can be proven true by observation, then it can be known to be true.

(D) Knowing a proposition to be true is impossible only if it cannot be proven true by observation.

(E) Knowing a proposition to be true requires proving it true by observation.

25. The publisher of a best-selling self-help book had, in some promotional material, claimed that it showed readers how to become exceptionally successful. Of course, everyone knows that no book can deliver to the many what, by definition, must remain limited to the few: exceptional success. Thus, although it is clear that the publisher knowingly made a false claim, doing so should not be considered unethical in this case.

Which one of the following principles, if valid, most strongly supports the reasoning above?

(A) Knowingly making a false claim is unethical only if it is reasonable for people to accept the claim as true.

(B) Knowingly making a false claim is unethical if those making it derive a gain at the expense of those acting as if the claim were true.

(C) Knowingly making a false claim is unethical in only those cases in which those who accept the claim as true suffer a hardship greater than the gain they were anticipating.

(D) Knowingly making a false claim is unethical only if there is a possibility that someone will act as if the claim might be true.

(E) Knowingly making a false claim is unethical in at least those cases in which for someone else to discover that the claim is false, that person must have acted as if the claim were true.

S   T   O   P

IF YOU FINISH BEFORE TIME IS CALLED, YOU MAY CHECK YOUR WORK ON THIS SECTION ONLY.
DO NOT WORK ON ANY OTHER SECTION IN THE TEST.

SECTION III

Time—35 minutes

26 Questions

Directions: The questions in this section are based on the reasoning contained in brief statements or passages. For some questions, more than one of the choices could conceivably answer the question. However, you are to choose the <u>best</u> answer; that is, the response that most accurately and completely answers the question. You should not make assumptions that are by commonsense standards implausible, superfluous, or incompatible with the passage. After you have chosen the best answer, blacken the corresponding space on your answer sheet.

1. Francis: Failure to become properly registered to vote prevents one-third of the voting-age citizens of Lagonia from voting. If local election boards made the excessively cumbersome registration process easier, more people would register and vote.

    Sharon: The high number of citizens not registered to vote has persisted despite many attempts to make registering easier. Surveys show that most of these citizens believe that their votes would not make a difference. Until that belief is changed, simplifying the registration process will not increase the percentage of citizens registering to vote.

    The main issue in dispute between Francis and Sharon is

    (A)   whether changing the voter registration process would be cumbersome
    (B)   why so many citizens do not register to vote
    (C)   what percentage of those registered to vote actually vote
    (D)   whether local election boards have simplified the registration process
    (E)   why the public lacks confidence in the effects of voting

2. Advertisement: Anyone who thinks moisturizers are not important for beautiful skin should consider what happens to the earth, the skin of the world, in times of drought. Without regular infusions of moisture the ground becomes lined and cracked and its lush loveliness fades away. Thus your skin, too, should be protected from the ravages caused by lack of moisture; give it the protection provided by regular infusions of Dewyfresh, the drought-defying moisturizer.

    The Dewyfresh advertisement exhibits which one of the following errors of reasoning?

    (A)   It treats something that is necessary for bringing about a state of affairs as something that is sufficient to bring about that state of affairs.
    (B)   It treats the fact that two things regularly occur together as proof that there is a single thing that is the cause of them both.
    (C)   It overlooks the fact that changing what people think is the case does not necessarily change what is the case.
    (D)   It relies on the ambiguity of the term "infusion," which can designate either a process or the product of that process.
    (E)   It relies on an analogy between two things that are insufficiently alike in the respects in which they would have to be alike for the conclusion to be supported.

GO ON TO THE NEXT PAGE.

Questions 3–4

M: The Greek alphabet must have been invented by some individual who knew the Phoenician writing system and who wanted to have some way of recording Homeric epics and thereby preserving expressions of a highly developed tradition of oral poetry.

P: Your hypothesis is laughable! What would have been the point of such a person's writing Homeric epics down? Surely a person who knew them well enough to write them down would not need to read them; and no one else could read them, according to your hypothesis.

3. Which one of the following is an argumentative strategy that P uses in responding to M?

(A) attacking M's understanding of the literary value of oral poetry
(B) disagreeing with M's thesis without attempting to refute it
(C) challenging M's knowledge of the Phoenician writing system
(D) attempting to undermine M's hypothesis by making it appear absurd
(E) providing an alternative interpretation of evidence put forward by M

4. P's argument is vulnerable to which one of the following criticisms?

(A) It fails to demonstrate that the Phoenician alphabet alone could have provided the basis for the Greek alphabet.
(B) It incorrectly assumes that the first text ever written in Greek was a Homeric poem.
(C) It confuses the requirements for a complex oral tradition with the requirements of a written language.
(D) It attempts to demonstrate the truth of a hypothesis merely by showing that it is possible.
(E) It overlooks the possibility that the person who invented the Greek alphabet did so with the intention of teaching it to others.

5. Bacteria from food can survive for several days on the surface of plastic cutting boards, but bacteria can penetrate wooden cutting boards almost immediately, leaving the surface free of contamination. Therefore, wooden cutting boards, unlike plastic cutting boards, need not be washed in order to prevent their contaminating food that is cut on them; wiping them off to remove food debris is sufficient.

Which one of the following is an assumption on which the argument depends?

(A) Washing plastic cutting boards does not remove all bacteria from the surface.
(B) Prevention of bacterial contamination is the only respect in which wooden cutting boards are superior to plastic cutting boards.
(C) Food that is not already contaminated with bacteria can be contaminated only by being cut on contaminated cutting boards.
(D) Bacteria that penetrate into wooden cutting boards do not reemerge on the surface after the cutting boards have been used.
(E) Washing wooden cutting boards kills bacteria below the surface of the cutting boards.

6. Asthmagon was long considered the most effective of the drugs known as beta-2 agonists, designed to alleviate asthma attacks. However, studies conducted in Rhiago between 1981 and 1987 revealed that nearly one out of every five of the asthma patients under observation who took asthmagon suffered serious side effects after taking the drug. Citing this statistic, some doctors argue that asthmagon should be banned as an anti-asthma drug.

Which one of the following, if true, most weakens the case for the proposed ban of asthmagon?

(A) In Rhiago, where asthmagon had been the most widely prescribed of the beta-2 agonists, the number of asthma deaths increased between 1981 and 1987.
(B) Many of the patients under observation to whom asthmagon was administered had not previously taken a beta-2 agonist.
(C) Despite the growing concern about the drug, many physicians in Rhiago still prescribe asthmagon to asthma sufferers.
(D) Among the patients observed, only those who had very high cholesterol counts suffered side effects after taking asthmagon.
(E) Asthmagon increases the severity of asthma attacks in some people because the drug can cause damage to heart tissues.

GO ON TO THE NEXT PAGE.

7. In response to requests made by the dairy industry the government is considering whether to approve the synthetic hormone BST for use in dairy cows. BST increases milk production but also leads to recurring udder inflammation, decreased fertility, and symptoms of stress in cows who receive the hormone. All of these problems can be kept under control with constant veterinary care, but such levels of veterinary help would cost big farms far less per cow than they would small farms.

If the statements above are true, which one of the following claims is most strongly supported by them?

(A) The government is unlikely to approve the synthetic hormone BST for use in cows.
(B) The proportion of cows that suffer from udder inflammation, decreased fertility, and symptoms of stress is currently greater on big dairy farms than on small ones.
(C) At the present time milk from cows raised on small farms is safer to drink than milk from cows raised on big farms.
(D) The milk from cows who receive BST will not be safe for people to drink.
(E) Owners of big farms stand to gain more from government approval of BST than do owners of small farms.

8. Jones is selling a house to Smith. The contract between the two specifies that for up to a year after ownership is transferred, Jones will be responsible for repairing any "major structural defects," defined as defects in the roof or roof-supporting components of the house, that might be found. Jones is not responsible for any other repairs. The house has a truss roof, which means that the only walls that support the roof are the exterior walls.

It can be properly concluded from the information above that

(A) Jones did not know of any defects in the roof or roof-supporting components of the house at the time the contract was written
(B) although other components of the house may contain defects, the roof and roof-supporting components of the house are currently free from such defects
(C) the contract does not oblige Jones to repair any defects in the house's nonexterior walls after ownership of the house has been transferred
(D) Smith will be obliged to repair all structural defects in the house within a year after ownership is transferred, except those for which Jones is responsible
(E) in the past Jones has had to make repairs to some of the house's exterior walls

9. The play *Mankind* must have been written between 1431 and 1471. It cannot have been written before 1431, for in that year the rose noble, a coin mentioned in the play, was first circulated. The play cannot have been written after 1471, since in that year King Henry VI died, and he is mentioned as a living monarch in the play's dedication.

The argument would be most seriously weakened if which one of the following were discovered?

(A) The Royal Theatre Company includes the play on a list of those performed in 1480.
(B) Another coin mentioned in the play was first minted in 1422.
(C) The rose noble was neither minted nor circulated after 1468.
(D) Although Henry VI was deposed in 1461, he was briefly restored to the throne in 1470.
(E) In a letter written in early 1428, a merchant told of having seen the design for a much-discussed new coin called the "rose noble."

10. All material bodies are divisible into parts, and everything divisible is imperfect. It follows that all material bodies are imperfect. It likewise follows that the spirit is not a material body.

The final conclusion above follows logically if which one of the following is assumed?

(A) Everything divisible is a material body.
(B) Nothing imperfect is indivisible.
(C) The spirit is divisible.
(D) The spirit is perfect.
(E) The spirit is either indivisible or imperfect.

11. Special kinds of cotton that grow fibers of green or brown have been around since the 1930s but only recently became commercially feasible when a long-fibered variety that can be spun by machine was finally bred. Since the cotton need not be dyed, processing plants avoid the expense of dyeing and the ecological hazards of getting rid of leftover dye and by-products.

Which one of the following can be properly inferred from the passage?

(A) It is ecologically safer to process long-fibered cotton than short-fibered cotton.
(B) Green and brown cottons that can be spun only by hand are not commercially viable.
(C) Hand-spun cotton is more ecologically safe than machine-spun cotton.
(D) Short-fibered regular cottons are economically competitive with synthetic fabrics.
(E) Garments made of green and brown cottons are less expensive than garments made of regular cotton.

GO ON TO THE NEXT PAGE.

12. People in the tourist industry know that excessive development of seaside areas by the industry damages the environment. Such development also hurts the tourist industry by making these areas unattractive to tourists, a fact of which people in the tourist industry are well aware. People in the tourist industry would never knowingly do anything to damage the industry. Therefore, they would never knowingly damage the seaside environment, and people who are concerned about damage to the seaside environment thus have nothing to fear from the tourist industry.

The reasoning in the argument is most vulnerable to criticism on which one of the following grounds?

(A) No support is provided for the claim that excessive development hurts the tourist industry.
(B) That something is not the cause of a problem is used as evidence that it never coexists with that problem.
(C) The argument shifts from applying a characteristic to a few members of a group to applying the characteristic to all members of that group.
(D) The possibility that the tourist industry would unintentionally harm the environment is ignored.
(E) The argument establishes that a certain state of affairs is likely and then treats that as evidence that the state of affairs is inevitable.

13. Health officials claim that because the foods and beverages mentioned or consumed on many television programs are extremely low in nutritional value, watching television has a bad influence on the dietary habits of television viewers.

The claim by health officials depends on the presupposition that

(A) the eating and drinking habits of people on television programs are designed to mirror the eating and drinking habits of television viewers
(B) seeing some foods and beverages being consumed on, or hearing them mentioned on, television programs increases the likelihood that viewers will consume similar kinds of foods and beverages
(C) the food and beverage industry finances television programs so that the foods and beverages that have recently appeared on the market can be advertised on those programs
(D) television viewers are only interested in the people on television programs who have the same eating and drinking habits as they do
(E) the eating and drinking habits of people on television programs provide health officials with accurate predictions about the foods and beverages that will become popular among television viewers

14. In an effort to boost sales during the summer months, which are typically the best for soft-drink sales, Foamy Soda lowered its prices. In spite of this, however, the sales of Foamy Soda dropped during the summer months.

Each of the following, if true, contributes to reconciling the apparent discrepancy indicated above EXCEPT:

(A) The soft-drink industry as a whole experienced depressed sales during the summer months.
(B) Foamy Soda's competitors lowered their prices even more drastically during the summer months.
(C) Because of an increase in the price of sweeteners, the production costs of Foamy Soda rose during the summer months.
(D) A strike at Foamy Soda's main plant forced production cutbacks that resulted in many stores not receiving their normal shipments during the summer months.
(E) The weather during the summer months was unseasonably cool, decreasing the demand for soft drinks.

15. Dr. Z: Many of the characterizations of my work offered by Dr. Q are imprecise, and such characterizations do not provide an adequate basis for sound criticism of my work.

Which one of the following can be properly inferred from Dr. Z's statement?

(A) Some of Dr. Q's characterizations of Dr. Z's work provide an adequate basis for sound criticism of Dr. Z's work.
(B) All of Dr. Q's characterizations of Dr. Z's work that are not imprecise provide an adequate basis for sound criticism of Dr. Z's work.
(C) All of the characterizations of Dr. Z's work by Dr. Q that do not provide an adequate basis for sound criticism of Dr. Z's work are imprecise.
(D) If the characterization of someone's work is precise, then it provides a sound basis for criticizing that work.
(E) At least one of Dr. Q's characterizations of Dr. Z's work fails to provide an adequate basis for sound criticism of that work.

GO ON TO THE NEXT PAGE.

16. K, a research scientist, was accused of having falsified laboratory data. Although the original data in question have disappeared, data from K's more recent experiments have been examined and clearly none of them were falsified. Therefore, the accusation should be dismissed.

Which one of the following contains questionable reasoning that is most similar to that in the argument above?

(A) L, an accountant, was charged with having embezzled funds from a client. The charge should be ignored, however, because although the records that might reveal this embezzlement have been destroyed, records of L's current clients show clearly that there has never been any embezzlement from them.

(B) M, a factory supervisor, was accused of failing to enforce safety standards. This accusation should be discussed, because although the identity of the accuser was not revealed, a survey of factory personnel revealed that some violations of the standards have occurred.

(C) N, a social scientist, was charged with plagiarism. The charge is without foundation because although strong similarities between N's book and the work of another scholar have been discovered, the other scholar's work was written after N's work was published.

(D) O, an auto mechanic, has been accused of selling stolen auto parts. The accusation seems to be justified since although no evidence links O directly to these sales, the pattern of distribution of the auto parts points to O as the source.

(E) P, a politician, has been accused of failing to protect the public interest. From at least some points of view, however, the accusation will undoubtedly be considered false, because there is clearly disagreement about where the public interest lies.

Questions 17–18

The widespread staff reductions in a certain region's economy are said to be causing people who still have their jobs to cut back on new purchases as though they, too, had become economically distressed. Clearly, however, actual spending by such people is undiminished, because there has been no unusual increase in the amount of money held by those people in savings accounts.

17. The argument in the passage proceeds by doing which one of the following?

(A) concluding that since an expected consequence of a supposed development did not occur, that development itself did not take place

(B) concluding that since only one of the two predictable consequences of a certain kind of behavior is observed to occur, this observed occurrence cannot, in the current situation, be a consequence of such behavior

(C) arguing that since people's economic behavior is guided by economic self-interest, only misinformation or error will cause people to engage in economic behavior that harms them economically

(D) arguing that since two alternative developments exhaust all the plausible possibilities, one of those developments occurred and the other did not

(E) concluding that since the evidence concerning a supposed change is ambiguous, it is most likely that no change is actually taking place

18. Which one of the following is an assumption on which the argument relies?

(A) If people in the region who continue to be employed have debts, they are not now paying them off at an accelerated rate.

(B) People in the region who continue to be employed and who have relatives who have lost their jobs commonly assist those relatives financially.

(C) If people in the region who have lost jobs get new jobs, the new jobs generally pay less well than the ones they lost.

(D) People in the region who continue to be employed are pessimistic about their prospects for increasing their incomes.

(E) There exist no statistics about sales of goods in the region as a whole.

GO ON TO THE NEXT PAGE.

19. Every student who walks to school goes home for lunch. It follows that some students who have part-time jobs do not walk to school.

The conclusion of the argument follows logically if which one of the following is assumed?

(A) Some students who do not have part-time jobs go home for lunch.
(B) Every student who goes home for lunch has a part-time job.
(C) Some students who do not have part-time jobs do not go home for lunch.
(D) Some students who do not go home for lunch have part-time jobs.
(E) Every student who goes home for lunch walks to school.

20. When the Pinecrest Animal Shelter, a charitable organization, was in danger of closing because it could not pay for important repairs, its directors appealed to the townspeople to donate money that would be earmarked to pay for those repairs. Since more funds were ultimately donated than were used for the repairs, the directors plan to donate the surplus funds to other animal shelters. But before doing so, the directors should obtain permission from those who made the donations.

Which one of the following principles, if valid, most helps to justify the position advocated above and yet places the least restriction on the allocation of funds by directors of charitable organizations?

(A) The directors of charitable organizations cannot allocate publicly solicited funds to any purposes for which the directors had not specifically earmarked the funds in advance.
(B) People who solicit charitable donations from the public for a specific cause should spend the funds only on that cause or, if that becomes impossible, should dispose of the funds according to the express wishes of the donors.
(C) Directors of charitable organizations who solicit money from the public must return all the money received from an appeal if more money is received than can practicably be used for the purposes specified in the appeal.
(D) Donors of money to charitable organizations cannot delegate to the directors of those organizations the responsibility of allocating the funds received to various purposes consonant with the purposes of the organization as the directors of the organization see fit.
(E) People who contribute money to charitable organizations should be considered to be placing their trust in the directors of those organizations to use the money wisely according to whatever circumstance might arise.

21. The amount of electricity consumed in Millville on any day in August is directly proportional to peak humidity on that day. Since the average peak humidity this August was three points higher than the average peak humidity last August, it follows that more energy was consumed in Millville this August than last August.

Which one of the following arguments has a pattern of reasoning most similar to the one in the argument above?

(A) The amount of art supplies used in any of the Aesthetic Institute's 25 classes is directly proportional to the number of students in that class. Since in these classes the institute enrolled 20 percent more students overall last year than in the previous year, more art supplies were used in the institute's classes last year than in the previous year.
(B) The number of courses in painting offered by the Aesthetic Institute in any term is directly proportional to the number of students enrolled in the institute in that term. But the institute offers the same number of courses in sculpture each term. Hence, the institute usually offers more courses in painting than in sculpture.
(C) The number of new students enrolled at the Aesthetic Institute in any given year is directly proportional to the amount of advertising the institute has done in the previous year. Hence, if the institute seeks to increase its student body it must increase the amount it spends on advertising.
(D) The fees paid by a student at the Aesthetic Institute are directly proportional to the number of classes in which that student enrolls. Since the number of students at the Aesthetic Institute is increasing, it follows that the institute is collecting a greater amount in fees paid by students than it used to.
(E) The number of instructors employed by the Aesthetic Institute in any term is directly proportional to the number of classes offered in that term and also directly proportional to the number of students enrolled at the institute. Thus, the number of classes offered by the institute in any term is directly proportional to the number of students enrolled in that term.

GO ON TO THE NEXT PAGE.

22. Letter to the editor: After Baerton's factory closed, there was a sharp increase in the number of claims filed for job-related injury compensation by the factory's former employees. Hence there is reason to believe that most of those who filed for compensation after the factory closed were just out to gain benefits they did not deserve, and filed only to help them weather their job loss.

Each of the following, if true, weakens the argument above EXCEPT:

(A) Workers cannot file for compensation for many job-related injuries, such as hearing loss from factory noise, until they have left the job.

(B) In the years before the factory closed, the factory's managers dismissed several employees who had filed injury claims.

(C) Most workers who receive an injury on the job file for compensation on the day they suffer the injury.

(D) Workers who incur partial disabilities due to injuries on the job often do not file for compensation because they would have to stop working to receive compensation but cannot afford to live on that compensation alone.

(E) Workers who are aware that they will soon be laid off from a job often become depressed, making them more prone to job-related injuries.

23. Historians of North American architecture who have studied early nineteenth-century houses with wooden floors have observed that the boards used on the floors of bigger houses were generally much narrower than those used on the floors of smaller houses. These historians have argued that, since the people for whom the bigger houses were built were generally richer than the people for whom the smaller houses were built, floors made out of narrow floorboards were probably once a status symbol, designed to proclaim the owner's wealth.

Which one of the following, if true, most helps to strengthen the historians' argument?

(A) More original floorboards have survived from big early nineteenth-century houses than from small early nineteenth-century houses.

(B) In the early nineteenth century, a piece of narrow floorboard was not significantly less expensive than a piece of wide floorboard of the same length.

(C) In the early nineteenth century, smaller houses generally had fewer rooms than did bigger houses.

(D) Some early nineteenth-century houses had wide floorboards near the walls of each room and narrower floorboards in the center, where the floors were usually carpeted.

(E) Many of the biggest early nineteenth-century houses but very few small houses from that period had some floors that were made of materials that were considerably more expensive than wood, such as marble.

24. Ethicist: A society is just when, and only when, first, each person has an equal right to basic liberties, and second, inequalities in the distribution of income and wealth are not tolerated unless these inequalities are to everyone's advantage and are attached to jobs open to everyone.

Which one of the following judgments most closely conforms to the principle described above?

(A) Society S guarantees everyone an equal right to basic liberties, while allowing inequalities in the distribution of income and wealth that are to the advantage of everyone. Further, the jobs to which these inequalities are attached are open to most people. Thus, society S is just.

(B) Society S gives everyone an equal right to basic liberties, but at the expense of creating inequalities in the distribution of income and wealth. Thus, society S is not just.

(C) Society S allows inequalities in the distribution of income and wealth, although everyone benefits, and these inequalities are attached to jobs that are open to everyone. Thus, society S is just.

(D) Society S distributes income and wealth to everyone equally, but at the expense of creating inequalities in the right to basic liberties. Thus, society S is not just.

(E) Society S gives everyone an equal right to basic liberties, and although there is an inequality in the distribution of income and wealth, the jobs to which these inequalities are attached are open to all. Thus, society S is just.

GO ON TO THE NEXT PAGE.

25. Economist: In order to decide what to do about protecting the ozone layer, we must determine the monetary amount of the economic resources that we would willingly expend to protect it. Such a determination amounts to a calculation of the monetary value of the ozone layer. Environmentalists argue that the ozone layer does not have a calculable monetary value. However, we would not willingly expend an amount equal to all of the world's economic resources to protect the ozone layer, so the ozone layer is demonstrably worth less than that amount. Thus, the ozone layer has a calculable monetary value.

The reasoning in the economist's argument is flawed in that the argument

(A) uses evidence that the monetary value of a particular natural resource is less than a certain amount in order to establish that the monetary value of any natural resource is less than that amount

(B) presupposes that the ozone layer should not be protected and then argues to that claim as a conclusion

(C) takes advantage of an ambiguity in the term "value" to deflect the environmentalists' charge

(D) gives no reason for thinking that merely establishing an upper limit on a certain monetary value would allow the calculation of that monetary value

(E) does not directly address the argument of the environmentalists

26. Columnist on the arts: My elected government representatives were within their rights to vote to support the arts with tax dollars. While funded by the government, however, some artists have produced works of art that are morally or aesthetically offensive to many taxpayers. Nonetheless, my conclusion is that no taxpayers have been treated unjustly whose tax dollars are used to fund some particular work of art that they may find abominable.

Which one of the following principles, if valid, most supports the columnist's argument?

(A) Taxpayers should be allowed to decide whether a portion of their tax dollars is to be used to fund the arts.

(B) The funding of a particular activity is warranted if it is funded by elected representatives who legitimately fund that activity in general.

(C) Elected representatives are within their rights to fund any activity that is supported by a majority of their constituents.

(D) Those who resent taxation to subsidize offensive art should vote against their incumbent government representatives.

(E) Since taxpayers are free to leave their country if they disapprove of their representatives' decisions, they have no right to complain about arts funding.

S T O P

IF YOU FINISH BEFORE TIME IS CALLED, YOU MAY CHECK YOUR WORK ON THIS SECTION ONLY.
DO NOT WORK ON ANY OTHER SECTION IN THE TEST.

SECTION IV

Time—35 minutes

23 Questions

Directions: Each group of questions in this section is based on a set of conditions. In answering some of the questions, it may be useful to draw a rough diagram. Choose the response that most accurately and completely answers each question and blacken the corresponding space on your answer sheet.

Questions 1–5

In a certain recipe contest, each contestant submits two recipes, one for an appetizer and one for a main dish. Together the two recipes must include exactly seven flavorings—fenugreek, ginger, lemongrass, nutmeg, paprika, saffron, and turmeric—with no flavoring included in more than one of the two recipes. Each contestant's recipes must satisfy the following conditions:

The appetizer recipe includes at most three of the flavorings.
Fenugreek is not included in the same recipe as nutmeg.
Saffron is not included in the same recipe as turmeric.
Ginger is included in the same recipe as nutmeg.

1. Which one of the following could be a complete and accurate list of the flavorings included in one contestant's main-dish recipe?

    (A) fenugreek, lemongrass, saffron
    (B) fenugreek, ginger, nutmeg, turmeric
    (C) ginger, lemongrass, nutmeg, paprika
    (D) ginger, nutmeg, paprika, turmeric
    (E) lemongrass, nutmeg, saffron, turmeric

2. If a contestant's appetizer recipe does not include fenugreek, then the contestant's appetizer recipe must include

    (A) ginger
    (B) lemongrass
    (C) paprika
    (D) saffron
    (E) turmeric

3. Which one of the following could be a list of all of the flavorings included in one contestant's appetizer recipe?

    (A) fenugreek, saffron
    (B) ginger, nutmeg
    (C) fenugreek, nutmeg, turmeric
    (D) lemongrass, nutmeg, saffron
    (E) fenugreek, lemongrass, paprika, turmeric

4. If a contestant includes lemongrass in the same recipe as paprika, which one of the following is a flavoring that must be included in the contestant's main-dish recipe?

    (A) ginger
    (B) lemongrass
    (C) nutmeg
    (D) saffron
    (E) turmeric

5. If the condition that requires ginger to be included in the same recipe as nutmeg is suspended but all of the other original conditions remain in effect, then which one of the following could be a list of all of the flavorings included in one contestant's main-dish recipe?

    (A) ginger, lemongrass, nutmeg, paprika
    (B) ginger, lemongrass, paprika, turmeric
    (C) fenugreek, ginger, lemongrass, paprika, saffron
    (D) fenugreek, ginger, lemongrass, saffron, turmeric
    (E) fenugreek, lemongrass, nutmeg, paprika, saffron

GO ON TO THE NEXT PAGE.

Questions 6–10

Seven singers—Jamie, Ken, Lalitha, Maya, Norton, Olive, and Patrick—will be scheduled to perform in the finals of a singing competition. During the evening of the competition, each singer, performing alone, will give exactly one performance. The schedule for the evening must conform to the following requirements:

Jamie performs immediately after Ken.
Patrick performs at some time after Maya.
Lalitha performs third only if Norton performs fifth.
If Patrick does not perform second, he performs fifth.

6. Which one of the following is an acceptable schedule for the evening's performers, from first through seventh?

   (A) Ken, Jamie, Maya, Lalitha, Patrick, Norton, Olive
   (B) Lalitha, Patrick, Norton, Olive, Maya, Ken, Jamie
   (C) Norton, Olive, Ken, Jamie, Maya, Patrick, Lalitha
   (D) Olive, Maya, Ken, Lalitha, Patrick, Norton, Jamie
   (E) Olive, Maya, Lalitha, Norton, Patrick, Ken, Jamie

7. If Lalitha is scheduled for the third performance, which one of the following must be scheduled for the sixth performance?

   (A) Jamie
   (B) Ken
   (C) Norton
   (D) Olive
   (E) Patrick

8. If Norton is scheduled for the fifth performance, which one of the following could be true?

   (A) Jamie is scheduled for the sixth performance.
   (B) Ken is scheduled for the second performance.
   (C) Lalitha is scheduled for the fourth performance.
   (D) Maya is scheduled for the third performance.
   (E) Olive is scheduled for the first performance.

9. If Maya is scheduled for the second performance, which one of the following could be true?

   (A) Jamie is scheduled for the sixth performance.
   (B) Ken is scheduled for the fourth performance.
   (C) Lalitha is scheduled for the third performance.
   (D) Norton is scheduled for the fifth performance.
   (E) Olive is scheduled for the fourth performance.

10. If Jamie's performance is scheduled to be immediately before Lalitha's performance, Jamie's performance CANNOT be scheduled to be

   (A) second
   (B) third
   (C) fourth
   (D) fifth
   (E) sixth

GO ON TO THE NEXT PAGE.

Questions 11–17

At a small press, six textbooks, three introductory—F, G, and H—and three advanced—X, Y, and Z—will each be evaluated once by the editor, Juarez, and once by the publisher, Rosenberg, during six consecutive weeks—week 1 through week 6. Each evaluator evaluates exactly one textbook per week. No textbook will be evaluated by Juarez and Rosenberg during the same week. The following additional constraints apply:

    Rosenberg cannot evaluate any introductory textbook until Juarez has evaluated that textbook.
    Juarez cannot evaluate any advanced textbook until Rosenberg has evaluated that textbook.
    Rosenberg cannot evaluate any two introductory textbooks consecutively.
    Juarez must evaluate X during week 4.

11. Which one of the following is an acceptable evaluation schedule, with the textbooks listed in order of evaluation from week 1 through week 6 ?

  (A) Juarez: F, G, X, Z, H, Y
         Rosenberg: X, F, Z, G, Y, H
  (B) Juarez: F, Y, G, X, H, Z
         Rosenberg: Y, F, X, G, Z, H
  (C) Juarez: G, H, F, X, Y, Z
         Rosenberg: X, G, H, Y, Z, F
  (D) Juarez: G, Z, F, X, H, Y
         Rosenberg: Z, F, X, G, Y, H
  (E) Juarez: H, Y, F, X, G, Z
         Rosenberg: X, H, Z, F, Y, G

12. If Juarez evaluates H during week 3 and Rosenberg evaluates G during week 6, which one of the following must be true?

  (A) Juarez evaluates F during week 1.
  (B) Juarez evaluates G during week 2.
  (C) Juarez evaluates Z during week 6.
  (D) Rosenberg evaluates X during week 1.
  (E) Rosenberg evaluates Y during week 5.

13. If Juarez evaluates Z during week 2, then Rosenberg must evaluate which one of the following textbooks during week 5 ?

  (A) F
  (B) H
  (C) X
  (D) Y
  (E) Z

14. Which one of the following must be true?

  (A) Rosenberg evaluates H during week 6.
  (B) Rosenberg evaluates an advanced textbook during week 3.
  (C) Juarez evaluates an advanced textbook during week 2.
  (D) Juarez evaluates Y before evaluating G.
  (E) Juarez does not evaluate any two introductory textbooks consecutively.

15. If Rosenberg evaluates X during week 1 and F during week 2, which one of the following could be true?

  (A) X is the third of the advanced textbooks to be evaluated by Juarez.
  (B) Y is the first of the advanced textbooks to be evaluated by Juarez.
  (C) Juarez does not evaluate any two introductory textbooks in a row.
  (D) Juarez evaluates G during week 5.
  (E) Juarez evaluates Z during week 6.

16. Which one of the following is a complete and accurate list of those weeks during which Juarez must evaluate an introductory textbook?

  (A) week 1
  (B) week 6
  (C) week 1, week 5
  (D) week 1, week 2, week 3
  (E) week 1, week 3, week 5

17. Which one of the following could be true?

  (A) Juarez evaluates F during week 6.
  (B) Juarez evaluates Z during week 1.
  (C) Rosenberg evaluates F during week 3.
  (D) Rosenberg evaluates H during week 2.
  (E) Rosenberg evaluates X during week 5.

GO ON TO THE NEXT PAGE.

Questions 18–23

Nine different treatments are available for a certain illness: three antibiotics—F, G, and H—three dietary regimens—M, N, and O—and three physical therapies—U, V, and W. For each case of the illness, a doctor will prescribe exactly five of the treatments, in accordance with the following conditions:

If two of the antibiotics are prescribed, the remaining antibiotic cannot be prescribed.
There must be exactly one dietary regimen prescribed.
If O is not prescribed, F cannot be prescribed.
If W is prescribed, F cannot be prescribed.
G cannot be prescribed if both N and U are prescribed.
V cannot be prescribed unless both H and M are prescribed.

18. Which one of the following could be the five treatments prescribed for a given case?

   (A)   F, G, H, M, V
   (B)   F, G, M, O, V
   (C)   F, H, M, O, W
   (D)   G, H, N, U, W
   (E)   G, H, O, U, W

19. Which one of the following could be the antibiotics and physical therapies prescribed for a given case?

   (A)   F, G, H, W
   (B)   F, G, U, V
   (C)   F, U, V, W
   (D)   G, U, V, W
   (E)   H, U, V, W

20. If O is prescribed for a given case, which one of the following is a pair of treatments both of which must also be prescribed for that case?

   (A)   F, M
   (B)   G, V
   (C)   N, U
   (D)   U, V
   (E)   U, W

21. If G is prescribed for a given case, which one of the following is a pair of treatments both of which could also be prescribed for that case?

   (A)   F, M
   (B)   F, N
   (C)   N, V
   (D)   O, V
   (E)   V, W

22. Which one of the following is a list of three treatments that could be prescribed together for a given case?

   (A)   F, M, U
   (B)   F, O, W
   (C)   G, N, V
   (D)   G, V, W
   (E)   H, N, V

23. Which one of the following treatments CANNOT be prescribed for any case?

   (A)   G
   (B)   M
   (C)   N
   (D)   U
   (E)   W

S T O P

IF YOU FINISH BEFORE TIME IS CALLED, YOU MAY CHECK YOUR WORK ON THIS SECTION ONLY.
DO NOT WORK ON ANY OTHER SECTION IN THE TEST.

LSAT® Writing Sample Topic

Directions: The scenario presented below describes two choices, either one of which can be supported on the basis of the information given. Your essay should consider both choices and argue for one over the other, based on the two specified criteria and the facts provided. There is no "right" or "wrong" choice: a reasonable argument can be made for either.

For the past five years, Martin Shreve has been the head chef in a popular resort in a small town. He has decided to move to a large city, where he has received two job offers. Write an argument for his accepting one offer over the other based on the following considerations:

- Shreve wants to learn as much as possible about the restaurant business.
- Shreve likes being his own boss and wants to have as much control as possible over his working environment.

For nearly a generation, Chez Marie was known as the premier restaurant in the city and still has a loyal and influential clientele. In recent years, however, the restaurant has declined in popularity. Lars Ginacres, the strong-willed owner and founder, has insisted on micromanaging every aspect of the restaurant and has lately resisted changing trends in dining preferences. Now that the last manager and several experienced employees have quit, Ginacres admits that he knows the time for a more collaborative management style has come. He has offered to make Shreve the manager in charge of hiring staff and developing a new menu.

A new restaurant in an affluent suburb, Cafe Caribe is owned and operated by Nicole Lawson. Known for her high standards and demanding style, Lawson opened her first restaurant a decade ago and quickly turned it into one of the most popular establishments in the area. She currently owns a chain of over a dozen cafes throughout the region, all featuring a house specialty characteristic of the area or neighborhood where it is located. Each is run by an on-site manager, who reports directly to her. After learning Lawson's formula for success in a six-month training period at one of her cafes, Shreve would be expected to adhere to that formula in managing Cafe Caribe, though he would have the opportunity to develop the specialty that would distinguish his restaurant.

Directions:

1. Use the Answer Key on the next page to check your answers.

2. Use the Scoring Worksheet below to compute your raw score.

3. Use the Score Conversion Chart to convert your raw score into the 120-180 scale.

Scoring Worksheet

1. Enter the number of questions you answered correctly in each section.

Number Correct

SECTION I . . . . . . _____
SECTION II . . . . . _____
SECTION III . . . . . _____
SECTION IV . . . . . _____

2. Enter the sum here: _____
   This is your Raw Score.

Conversion Chart

For Converting Raw Score to the 120-180 LSAT Scaled Score
LSAT Form 7LSS35

Reported Score	Raw Score Lowest	Raw Score Highest
180	99	101
179	97	98
178	96	96
177	95	95
176	94	94
175	93	93
174	92	92
173	91	91
172	90	90
171	88	89
170	87	87
169	86	86
168	84	85
167	83	83
166	81	82
165	80	80
164	78	79
163	77	77
162	75	76
161	74	74
160	72	73
159	70	71
158	69	69
157	67	68
156	65	66
155	64	64
154	62	63
153	60	61
152	59	59
151	57	58
150	56	56
149	54	55
148	52	53
147	51	51
146	49	50
145	47	48
144	46	46
143	44	45
142	43	43
141	41	42
140	39	40
139	38	38
138	36	37
137	35	35
136	33	34
135	32	32
134	30	31
133	29	29
132	28	28
131	26	27
130	25	25
129	24	24
128	22	23
127	21	21
126	20	20
125	19	19
124	18	18
123	17	17
122	16	16
121	15	15
120	0	14

SECTION I

1.	B	8.	C	15.	B	22.	D
2.	A	9.	B	16.	E	23.	C
3.	C	10.	A	17.	A	24.	E
4.	D	11.	C	18.	A	25.	C
5.	E	12.	B	19.	D	26.	E
6.	B	13.	C	20.	A	27.	D
7.	D	14.	D	21.	C		

SECTION II

1.	B	8.	B	15.	A	22.	D
2.	D	9.	C	16.	A	23.	A
3.	B	10.	E	17.	B	24.	E
4.	C	11.	E	18.	E	25.	A
5.	D	12.	C	19.	E		
6.	C	13.	D	20.	B		
7.	A	14.	A	21.	A		

SECTION III

1.	B	8.	C	15.	E	22.	C
2.	E	9.	E	16.	A	23.	B
3.	D	10.	D	17.	A	24.	D
4.	E	11.	B	18.	A	25.	D
5.	D	12.	D	19.	D	26.	B
6.	D	13.	B	20.	B		
7.	E	14.	C	21.	A		

SECTION IV

1.	D	8.	C	15.	E	22.	D
2.	A	9.	E	16.	A	23.	C
3.	A	10.	A	17.	D		
4.	B	11.	B	18.	E		
5.	C	12.	A	19.	E		
6.	A	13.	D	20.	E		
7.	B	14.	B	21.	E		

The Official LSAT PrepTest

25

- June 1998
- Form 9LSS37

The sample test that follows consists of four sections corresponding to the four scored sections of the June 1998 LSAT.

SECTION I

Time—35 minutes

26 Questions

Directions: Each passage in this section is followed by a group of questions to be answered on the basis of what is <u>stated</u> or <u>implied</u> in the passage. For some of the questions, more than one of the choices could conceivably answer the question. However, you are to choose the <u>best</u> answer; that is, the response that most accurately and completely answers the question, and blacken the corresponding space on your answer sheet.

Most office workers assume that the messages they send to each other via electronic mail are as private as a telephone call or a face-to-face meeting. That assumption is wrong. Although it is illegal in many
(5) areas for an employer to eavesdrop on private conversations or telephone calls—even if they take place on a company-owned telephone—there are no clear rules governing electronic mail. In fact, the question of how private electronic mail transmissions
(10) should be has emerged as one of the more complicated legal issues of the electronic age.

People's opinions about the degree of privacy that electronic mail should have vary depending on whose electronic mail system is being used and who is reading
(15) the messages. Does a government office, for example, have the right to destroy electronic messages created in the course of running the government, thereby denying public access to such documents? Some hold that government offices should issue guidelines that allow
(20) their staff to delete such electronic records, and defend this practice by claiming that the messages thus deleted already exist in paper versions whose destruction is forbidden. Opponents of such practices argue that the paper versions often omit such information as who
(25) received the messages and when they received them, information commonly carried on electronic mail systems. Government officials, opponents maintain, are civil servants; the public should thus have the right to review any documents created during the conducting of
(30) government business.

Questions about electronic mail privacy have also arisen in the private sector. Recently, two employees of an automotive company were discovered to have been communicating disparaging information about their
(35) supervisor via electronic mail. The supervisor, who had been monitoring the communication, threatened to fire the employees. When the employees filed a grievance complaining that their privacy had been violated, they were let go. Later, their court case for unlawful
(40) termination was dismissed; the company's lawyers successfully argued that because the company owned the computer system, its supervisors had the right to read anything created on it.

In some areas, laws prohibit outside interception of
(45) electronic mail by a third party without proper authorization such as a search warrant. However, these laws do not cover "inside" interception such as occurred at the automotive company. In the past, courts have ruled that interoffice communications may be
(50) considered private only if employees have a

"reasonable expectation" of privacy when they send the messages. The fact is that no absolute guarantee of privacy exists in any computer system. The only solution may be for users to scramble their own
(55) messages with encryption codes; unfortunately, such complex codes are likely to undermine the principal virtue of electronic mail: its convenience.

1. Which one of the following statements most accurately summarizes the main point of the passage?

(A) Until the legal questions surrounding the privacy of electronic mail in both the public and private sectors have been resolved, office workers will need to scramble their electronic mail messages with encryption codes.

(B) The legal questions surrounding the privacy of electronic mail in the workplace can best be resolved by treating such communications as if they were as private as telephone conversations or face-to-face meetings.

(C) Any attempt to resolve the legal questions surrounding the privacy of electronic mail in the workplace must take into account the essential difference between public-sector and private-sector business.

(D) At present, in both the public and private sectors, there seem to be no clear general answers to the legal questions surrounding the privacy of electronic mail in the workplace.

(E) The legal questions surrounding the privacy of electronic mail in the workplace can best be resolved by allowing supervisors in public-sector but not private-sector offices to monitor their employees' communications.

GO ON TO THE NEXT PAGE.

2. According to the passage, which one of the following best expresses the reason some people use to oppose the deletion of electronic mail records at government offices?

(A) Such deletion reveals the extent of government's unhealthy obsession with secrecy.

(B) Such deletion runs counter to the notion of government's accountability to its constituency.

(C) Such deletion clearly violates the legal requirement that government offices keep duplicate copies of all their transactions.

(D) Such deletion violates the government's own guidelines against destruction of electronic records.

(E) Such deletion harms relations between government employees and their supervisors.

3. Which one of the following most accurately states the organization of the passage?

(A) A problem is introduced, followed by specific examples illustrating the problem; a possible solution is suggested, followed by an acknowledgment of its shortcomings.

(B) A problem is introduced, followed by explications of two possible solutions to the problem; the first solution is preferred to the second, and reasons are given for why it is the better alternative.

(C) A problem is introduced, followed by analysis of the historical circumstances that helped bring the problem about; a possible solution is offered and rejected as being only a partial remedy.

(D) A problem is introduced, followed by enumeration of various questions that need to be answered before a solution can be found; one possible solution is proposed and argued for.

(E) A problem is introduced, followed by descriptions of two contrasting approaches to thinking about the problem; the second approach is preferred to the first, and reasons are given for why it is more likely to yield a successful solution.

4. Based on the passage, the author's attitude toward interception of electronic mail can most accurately be described as

(A) outright disapproval of the practice
(B) support for employers who engage in it
(C) support for employees who lose their jobs because of it
(D) intellectual interest in its legal issues
(E) cynicism about the motives behind the practice

5. It can be inferred from the passage that the author would most likely hold which one of the following opinions about an encryption system that could encode and decode electronic mail messages with a single keystroke?

(A) It would be an unreasonable burden on a company's ability to monitor electronic mail created by its employees.

(B) It would significantly reduce the difficulty of attempting to safeguard the privacy of electronic mail.

(C) It would create substantial legal complications for companies trying to prevent employees from revealing trade secrets to competitors.

(D) It would guarantee only a minimal level of employee privacy, and so would not be worth the cost involved in installing such a system.

(E) It would require a change in the legal definition of "reasonable expectation of privacy" as it applies to employer-employee relations.

6. Given the information in the passage, which one of the following hypothetical events is LEAST likely to occur?

(A) A court rules that a government office's practice of deleting its electronic mail is not in the public's best interests.

(B) A private-sector employer is found liable for wiretapping an office telephone conversation in which two employees exchanged disparaging information about their supervisor.

(C) A court upholds the right of a government office to destroy both paper and electronic versions of its in-house documents.

(D) A court upholds a private-sector employer's right to monitor messages sent between employees over the company's in-house electronic mail system.

(E) A court rules in favor of a private-sector employee whose supervisor stated that in-house electronic mail would not be monitored but later fired the employee for communicating disparaging information via electronic mail.

7. The author's primary purpose in writing the passage is to

(A) demonstrate that the individual right to privacy has been eroded by advances in computer technology

(B) compare the legal status of electronic mail in the public and private sectors

(C) draw an extended analogy between the privacy of electronic mail and the privacy of telephone conversations or face-to-face meetings

(D) illustrate the complexities of the privacy issues surrounding electronic mail in the workplace

(E) explain why the courts have not been able to rule definitively on the issue of the privacy of electronic mail

GO ON TO THE NEXT PAGE.

While a new surge of critical interest in the ancient Greek poems conventionally ascribed to Homer has taken place in the last twenty years or so, it was nonspecialists rather than professional scholars who (5) studied the poetic aspects of the *Iliad* and the *Odyssey* between, roughly, 1935 and 1970. During these years, while such nonacademic intellectuals as Simone Weil and Erich Auerbach were trying to define the qualities that made these epic accounts of the Trojan War and its (10) aftermath great poetry, the questions that occupied the specialists were directed elsewhere: "Did the Trojan War really happen?" "Does the bard preserve Indo-European folk memories?" "How did the poems get written down?" Something was driving scholars away (15) from the actual works to peripheral issues. Scholars produced books about archaeology, about gift-exchange in ancient societies, about the development of oral poetry, about virtually anything except the *Iliad* and the *Odyssey* themselves as unique reflections or (20) distillations of life itself—as, in short, great poetry. The observations of the English poet Alexander Pope seemed as applicable in 1970 as they had been when he wrote them in 1715: according to Pope, the remarks of critics "are rather Philosophical, Historical, (25) Geographical . . . or rather anything than Critical and Poetical."

Ironically, the modern manifestation of this "nonpoetical" emphasis can be traced to the profoundly influential work of Milman Parry, who attempted to (30) demonstrate in detail how the Homeric poems, believed to have been recorded nearly three thousand years ago, were the products of a long and highly developed tradition of oral poetry about the Trojan War. Parry proposed that this tradition built up its (35) diction and its content by a process of constant accumulation and refinement over many generations of storytellers. But after Parry's death in 1935, his legacy was taken up by scholars who, unlike Parry, forsook intensive analysis of the poetry itself and focused (40) instead on only one element of Parry's work: the creative limitations and possibilities of oral composition, concentrating on fixed elements and inflexibilities, focusing on the things that oral poetry allegedly can and cannot do. The dryness of this kind (45) of study drove many of the more inventive scholars away from the poems into the rapidly developing field of Homer's archaeological and historical background.

Appropriately, Milman Parry's son Adam was among those scholars responsible for a renewed (50) interest in Homer's poetry as literary art. Building on his father's work, the younger Parry argued that the Homeric poems exist both within and against a tradition. The *Iliad* and the *Odyssey* were, Adam Parry thought, the beneficiaries of an inherited store of (55) diction, scenes, and concepts, and at the same time highly individual works that surpassed these conventions. Adam Parry helped prepare the ground for the recent Homeric revival by affirming his father's belief in a strong inherited tradition, but also by (60) emphasizing Homer's unique contributions within that tradition.

8. Which one of the following best states the main idea of the passage?

(A) The Homeric poems are most fruitfully studied as records of the time and place in which they were written.

(B) The Homeric poems are the products of a highly developed and complicated tradition of oral poetry.

(C) The Homeric poems are currently enjoying a resurgence of critical interest after an age of scholarship largely devoted to the poems' nonpoetic elements.

(D) The Homeric poems are currently enjoying a resurgence of scholarly interest after an age during which most studies were authored by nonacademic writers.

(E) Before Milman Parry published his pioneering work in the early twentieth century, it was difficult to assign a date or an author to the Homeric poems.

9. According to the passage, the work of Simone Weil and Erich Auerbach on Homer was primarily concerned with which one of the following?

(A) considerations of why criticism of Homer had moved to peripheral issues

(B) analyses of the poetry itself in terms of its literary qualities

(C) studies in the history and nature of oral poetry

(D) analyses of the already ancient epic tradition inherited by Homer

(E) critiques of the highly technical analyses of academic critics

GO ON TO THE NEXT PAGE.

10. The passage suggests which one of the following about scholarship on Homer that has appeared since 1970?

(A) It has dealt extensively with the Homeric poems as literary art.
(B) It is more incisive than the work of the Parrys.
(C) It has rejected as irrelevant the scholarship produced by specialists between 1935 and 1970.
(D) It has ignored the work of Simone Weil and Erich Auerbach.
(E) It has attempted to confirm that the *Iliad* and the *Odyssey* were written by Homer.

11. The author of the passage most probably quotes Alexander Pope (lines 24–26) in order to

(A) indicate that the Homeric poems have generally received poor treatment at the hands of English critics
(B) prove that poets as well as critics have emphasized elements peripheral to the poems
(C) illustrate that the nonpoetical emphasis also existed in an earlier century
(D) emphasize the problems inherent in rendering classical Greek poetry into modern English
(E) argue that poets and literary critics have seldom agreed about the interpretation of poetry

12. According to the passage, which one of the following is true of Milman Parry's immediate successors in the field of Homeric studies?

(A) They reconciled Homer's poetry with archaeological and historical concerns.
(B) They acknowledged the tradition of oral poetry, but focused on the uniqueness of Homer's poetry within the tradition.
(C) They occupied themselves with the question of what qualities made for great poetry.
(D) They emphasized the boundaries of oral poetry.
(E) They called for a revival of Homer's popularity.

13. Which one of the following best describes the organization of the passage?

(A) A situation is identified and its origins are examined.
(B) A series of hypotheses is reviewed and one is advocated.
(C) The works of two influential scholars are summarized.
(D) Several issues contributing to a current debate are summarized.
(E) Three possible solutions to a long-standing problem are posed.

GO ON TO THE NEXT PAGE.

Even in the midst of its resurgence as a vital tradition, many sociologists have viewed the current form of the powwow, a ceremonial gathering of native Americans, as a sign that tribal culture is in decline.
(5) Focusing on the dances and rituals that have recently come to be shared by most tribes, they suggest that an intertribal movement is now in ascension and claim the inevitable outcome of this tendency is the eventual dissolution of tribes and the complete assimilation of
(10) native Americans into Euroamerican society. Proponents of this "Pan-Indian" theory point to the greater frequency of travel and communication between reservations, the greater urbanization of native Americans, and, most recently, their increasing
(15) politicization in response to common grievances as the chief causes of the shift toward intertribalism.

Indeed, the rapid diffusion of dance styles, outfits, and songs from one reservation to another offers compelling evidence that intertribalism has been
(20) increasing. However, these sociologists have failed to note the concurrent revitalization of many traditions unique to individual tribes. Among the Lakota, for instance, the Sun Dance was revived, after a forty-year hiatus, during the 1950s. Similarly, the Black Legging
(25) Society of the Kiowa and the Hethuska Society of the Ponca—both traditional groups within their respective tribes—have gained new popularity. Obviously, a more complex societal shift is taking place than the theory of Pan-Indianism can account for.

(30) An examination of the theory's underpinnings may be critical at this point, especially given that native Americans themselves chafe most against the Pan-Indian classification. Like other assimilationist theories with which it is associated, the Pan-Indian view is
(35) predicated upon an a priori assumption about the nature of cultural contact: that upon contact minority societies immediately begin to succumb in every respect—biologically, linguistically, and culturally—to the majority society. However, there is no evidence
(40) that this is happening to native American groups.

Yet the fact remains that intertribal activities are a major facet of native American culture today. Certain dances at powwows, for instance, are announced as intertribal, others as traditional. Likewise, speeches
(45) given at the beginnings of powwows are often delivered in English, while the prayer that follows is usually spoken in a native language. Cultural borrowing is, of course, old news. What is important to note is the conscious distinction native Americans
(50) make between tribal and intertribal tendencies.

Tribalism, although greatly altered by modern history, remains a potent force among native Americans. It forms a basis for tribal identity, and aligns music and dance with other social and cultural
(55) activities important to individual tribes. Intertribal activities, on the other hand, reinforce native American identity along a broader front, where this identity is directly threatened by outside influences.

14. Which one of the following best summarizes the main idea of the passage?

(A) Despite the fact that sociologists have only recently begun to understand its importance, intertribalism has always been an influential factor in native American culture.

(B) Native Americans are currently struggling with an identity crisis caused primarily by the two competing forces of tribalism and intertribalism.

(C) The recent growth of intertribalism is unlikely to eliminate tribalism because the two forces do not oppose one another but instead reinforce distinct elements of native American identity.

(D) The tendency toward intertribalism, although prevalent within native American culture, has had a minimal effect on the way native Americans interact with the broader community around them.

(E) Despite the recent revival of many native American tribal traditions, the recent trend toward intertribalism is likely to erode cultural differences among the various native American tribes.

15. The author most likely states that "cultural borrowing is, of course, old news" (lines 47–48) primarily to

(A) acknowledge that in itself the existence of intertribal tendencies at powwows is unsurprising

(B) suggest that native Americans' use of English in powwows should be accepted as unavoidable

(C) argue that the deliberate distinction of intertribal and traditional dances is not a recent development

(D) suggest that the recent increase in intertribal activity is the result of native Americans borrowing from non-native American cultures

(E) indicate that the powwow itself could have originated by combining practices drawn from both native and non-native American cultures

16. The author of the passage would most likely agree with which one of the following assertions?

(A) Though some believe the current form of the powwow signals the decline of tribal culture, the powwow contains elements that indicate the continuing strength of tribalism.

(B) The logical outcome of the recent increase in intertribal activity is the eventual disappearance of tribal culture.

(C) Native Americans who participate in both tribal and intertribal activities usually base their identities on intertribal rather than tribal affiliations.

(D) The conclusions of some sociologists about the health of native American cultures show that these sociologists are in fact biased against such cultures.

(E) Until it is balanced by revitalization of tribal customs, intertribalism will continue to weaken the native American sense of identity.

GO ON TO THE NEXT PAGE.

17. The primary function of the third paragraph is to

(A) search for evidence to corroborate the basic assumption of the theory of Pan-Indianism

(B) demonstrate the incorrectness of the theory of Pan-Indianism by pointing out that native American groups themselves disagree with the theory

(C) explain the origin of the theory of Pan-Indianism by showing how it evolved from other assimilationist theories

(D) examine several assimilationist theories in order to demonstrate that they rest on a common assumption

(E) criticize the theory of Pan-Indianism by pointing out that it rests upon an assumption for which there is no supporting evidence

18. Which one of the following most accurately describes the author's attitude toward the theory of Pan-Indianism?

(A) critical of its tendency to attribute political motives to cultural practices

(B) discomfort at its negative characterization of cultural borrowing by native Americans

(C) hopeful about its chances for preserving tribal culture

(D) offended by its claim that assimilation is a desirable consequence of cultural contact

(E) skeptical that it is a complete explanation of recent changes in native American society

19. With which one of the following statements would the author of the passage be most likely to agree?

(A) The resurgence of the powwow is a sign that native American customs are beginning to have an important influence on Euroamerican society.

(B) Although native Americans draw conscious distinctions between tribal and intertribal activities, there is no difference in how the two types of activity actually function within the context of native American society.

(C) Without intertribal activities, it would be more difficult for native Americans to maintain the cultural differences between native American and Euroamerican society.

(D) The powwow was recently revived, after an extended hiatus, in order to strengthen native Americans' sense of ethnic identity.

(E) The degree of urbanization, intertribal communication, and politicization among native Americans has been exaggerated by proponents of the theory of Pan-Indianism.

20. Which one of the following situations most clearly illustrates the phenomenon of intertribalism, as that phenomenon is described in the passage?

(A) a native American tribe in which a number of powerful societies attempt to prevent the revival of a traditional dance

(B) a native American tribe whose members attempt to learn the native languages of several other tribes

(C) a native American tribe whose members attempt to form a political organization in order to redress several grievances important to that tribe

(D) a native American tribe in which a significant percentage of the members have forsaken their tribal identity and become assimilated into Euroamerican society

(E) a native American tribe whose members often travel to other parts of the reservation in order to visit friends and relatives

21. In the passage, the author is primarily concerned with doing which one of the following?

(A) identifying an assumption common to various assimilationist theories and then criticizing these theories by showing this assumption to be false

(B) arguing that the recent revival of a number of tribal practices shows sociologists are mistaken in believing intertribalism to be a potent force among native American societies

(C) questioning the belief that native American societies will eventually be assimilated into Euroamerican society by arguing that intertribalism helps strengthen native American identity

(D) showing how the recent resurgence of tribal activities is a deliberate attempt to counteract the growing influence of intertribalism

(E) proposing an explanation of why the ascension of intertribalism could result in the eventual dissolution of tribes and complete assimilation of native Americans into Euroamerican society

GO ON TO THE NEXT PAGE.

Scientists typically advocate the analytic method of studying complex systems: systems are divided into component parts that are investigated separately. But nineteenth-century critics of this method claimed that (5) when a system's parts are isolated its complexity tends to be lost. To address the perceived weaknesses of the analytic method these critics put forward a concept called organicism, which posited that the whole determines the nature of its parts and that the parts of a (10) whole are interdependent.

Organicism depended upon the theory of internal relations, which states that relations between entities are possible only within some whole that embraces them, and that entities are altered by the relationships (15) into which they enter. If an entity stands in a relationship with another entity, it has some property as a consequence. Without this relationship, and hence without the property, the entity would be different— and so would be another entity. Thus, the property is (20) one of the entity's defining characteristics. Each of an entity's relationships likewise determines a defining characteristic of the entity.

One problem with the theory of internal relations is that not all properties of an entity are defining (25) characteristics: numerous properties are accompanying characteristics—even if they are always present, their presence does not influence the entity's identity. Thus, even if it is admitted that every relationship into which an entity enters determines some characteristic of the (30) entity, it is not necessarily true that such characteristics will define the entity; it is possible for the entity to enter into a relationship yet remain essentially unchanged.

The ultimate difficulty with the theory of internal (35) relations is that it renders the acquisition of knowledge impossible. To truly know an entity, we must know all of its relationships; but because the entity is related to everything in each whole of which it is a part, these wholes must be known completely before the entity (40) can be known. This seems to be a prerequisite impossible to satisfy.

Organicists' criticism of the analytic method arose from their failure to fully comprehend the method. In rejecting the analytic method, organicists overlooked (45) the fact that before the proponents of the method analyzed the component parts of a system, they first determined both the laws applicable to the whole system and the initial conditions of the system; proponents of the method thus did not study parts of a (50) system in full isolation from the system as a whole. Since organicists failed to recognize this, they never advanced any argument to show that laws and initial conditions of complex systems cannot be discovered. Hence, organicists offered no valid reason for rejecting (55) the analytic method or for adopting organicism as a replacement for it.

22. Which one of the following most completely and accurately summarizes the argument of the passage?

(A) By calling into question the possibility that complex systems can be studied in their entirety, organicists offered an alternative to the analytic method favored by nineteenth-century scientists.

(B) Organicists did not offer a useful method of studying complex systems because they did not acknowledge that there are relationships into which an entity may enter that do not alter the entity's identity.

(C) Organicism is flawed because it relies on a theory that both ignores the fact that not all characteristics of entities are defining and ultimately makes the acquisition of knowledge impossible.

(D) Organicism does not offer a valid challenge to the analytic method both because it relies on faulty theory and because it is based on a misrepresentation of the analytic method.

(E) In criticizing the analytic method, organicists neglected to disprove that scientists who employ the method are able to discover the laws and initial conditions of the systems they study.

23. According to the passage, organicists' chief objection to the analytic method was that the method

(A) oversimplified systems by isolating their components

(B) assumed that a system can be divided into component parts

(C) ignored the laws applicable to the system as a whole

(D) claimed that the parts of a system are more important than the system as a whole

(E) denied the claim that entities enter into relationships

GO ON TO THE NEXT PAGE.

24. The passage offers information to help answer each of the following questions EXCEPT:

(A) Why does the theory of internal relations appear to make the acquisition of knowledge impossible?

(B) Why did the organicists propose replacing the analytic method?

(C) What is the difference between a defining characteristic and an accompanying characteristic?

(D) What did organicists claim are the effects of an entity's entering into a relationship with another entity?

(E) What are some of the advantages of separating out the parts of a system for study?

25. The passage most strongly supports the ascription of which one of the following views to scientists who use the analytic method?

(A) A complex system is best understood by studying its component parts in full isolation from the system as a whole.

(B) The parts of a system should be studied with an awareness of the laws and initial conditions that govern the system.

(C) It is not possible to determine the laws governing a system until the system's parts are separated from one another.

(D) Because the parts of a system are interdependent, they cannot be studied separately without destroying the system's complexity.

(E) Studying the parts of a system individually eliminates the need to determine which characteristics of the parts are defining characteristics.

26. Which one of the following is a principle upon which the author bases an argument against the theory of internal relations?

(A) An adequate theory of complex systems must define the entities of which the system is composed.

(B) An acceptable theory cannot have consequences that contradict its basic purpose.

(C) An adequate method of study of complex systems should reveal the actual complexity of the systems it studies.

(D) An acceptable theory must describe the laws and initial conditions of a complex system.

(E) An acceptable method of studying complex systems should not study parts of the system in isolation from the system as a whole.

S T O P

IF YOU FINISH BEFORE TIME IS CALLED, YOU MAY CHECK YOUR WORK ON THIS SECTION ONLY.
DO NOT WORK ON ANY OTHER SECTION IN THE TEST.

SECTION II

Time—35 minutes

25 Questions

<u>Directions:</u> The questions in this section are based on the reasoning contained in brief statements or passages. For some questions, more than one of the choices could conceivably answer the question. However, you are to choose the <u>best</u> answer; that is, the response that most accurately and completely answers the question. You should not make assumptions that are by commonsense standards implausible, superfluous, or incompatible with the passage. After you have chosen the best answer, blacken the corresponding space on your answer sheet.

1. Psychiatrist: We are learning that neurochemical imbalances can cause behavior ranging from extreme mental illness to less serious but irritating behavior such as obsessive fantasizing, petulance, or embarrassment. These findings will promote compassion and tolerance when looking at a mental illness, quirk, or mere difference between two persons, since being mentally healthy can now begin to be seen as simply having the same neurochemical balances as most people.

Which one of the following most accurately expresses the conclusion of the psychiatrist's argument?

(A)   Understanding the role of the neurochemical in behavior will foster empathy toward others.

(B)   Neurochemical imbalances can cause mental illness and other behaviors.

(C)   Neurochemical balances and imbalances are the main determinants of mental behavior.

(D)   Being mentally healthy is a matter of having the same neurochemical balances as most people.

(E)   Advances in neurochemistry enhance our theories of mental illness.

2. No one wants this job as much as Joshua does, but he is not applying for it. It follows that there will not be any applicants, no matter how high the salary that is being offered.

The flawed reasoning in the argument above most closely parallels that in which one of the following?

(A)   Beth knows better than anyone else how to spot errors in a computer program, yet even she has not found any in this program so far. So it is clear that the errors must all be in the rest of the program.

(B)   If anyone can decipher this inscription, it is Professor Alvárez, but she is so involved with her new research that it will be impossible to interest her in this sort of task. Therefore, all we can do now is hope to find someone else.

(C)   Although he has the strongest motive of anyone for buying Anna's plot of land, Manfred is not pursuing the matter. Therefore, regardless of how low a price Anna is prepared to accept, she will be looking for a buyer in vain.

(D)   The person initially most interested in obtaining the contract was Mr. Moore, but he of all people suddenly withdrew his bid. This means that, no matter how discouraged the other bidders had been, they will now redouble their efforts.

(E)   Three times Paul would have liked to take advantage of a special vacation package for himself and his family, but each time he was indispensable at the factory just then. So the more seniority Paul acquires, the greater are the constraints on his personal life.

GO ON TO THE NEXT PAGE.

3. Many people limit the intake of calories and cholesterol in their diet in order to lose weight and reduce the level of cholesterol in their blood. When a person loses weight, the fat cells in that person's body decrease in size but not in number. As they decrease in size, fat cells spill the cholesterol they contain into the bloodstream. Therefore, a person who goes on a low-calorie, low-cholesterol diet ___

Which one of the following most logically completes the argument?

(A) might at first have an increased level of cholesterol in his or her blood
(B) will not lose weight any faster than will a person whose diet is high in calories
(C) might lose more weight by going on a low-calorie, high-cholesterol diet than by going on the low-calorie, low-cholesterol diet
(D) will not decrease the size of his or her fat cells
(E) will both decrease the level of cholesterol in his or her blood and gain weight

Questions 4–5

Advances in photocopying technology allow criminals with no printing expertise to counterfeit paper currency. One standard anticounterfeiting technique, microprinting, prints paper currency with tiny designs that cannot be photocopied distinctly. Although counterfeits of microprinted currency can be detected easily by experts, such counterfeits often circulate widely before being detected. An alternative, though more costly, printing technique would print currency with a special ink. Currency printed with the ink would change color depending on how ordinary light strikes it, whereas photocopied counterfeits of such currency would not. Because this technique would allow anyone to detect photocopied counterfeit currency easily, it should be adopted instead of microprinting, despite the expense.

4. Which one of the following, if true, provides the most support for the recommendation made by the argument?

(A) When an anticounterfeiting technique depends on the detection of counterfeits by experts, the cost of inspection by experts adds significantly to the cost to society of that technique.
(B) For any anticounterfeiting technique to be effective, the existence of anticounterfeiting techniques should be widely broadcast, but the method by which counterfeits are detected should be kept secret.
(C) The process of microprinting paper currency involves fewer steps than does the printing of paper currency with the special ink.
(D) Before photocopying technology existed, most counterfeits of paper currency were accomplished by master engravers.
(E) Many criminals do not have access to the advanced photocopiers that are needed to produce counterfeits of microprinted paper currency that cashiers will accept as real.

5. Which one of the following, if true, most seriously undermines the argument?

(A) The longer the interval between the time a counterfeit bill passes into circulation and the time the counterfeit is detected, the more difficult it is for law enforcement officials to apprehend the counterfeiter.
(B) Sophisticated counterfeiters could produce currency printed with the special ink but cannot duplicate microprinted currency exactly.
(C) Further advances in photocopying technology will dramatically increase the level of detail that photocopies can reproduce.
(D) The largest quantities of counterfeit currency now entering circulation are produced by ordinary criminals who engage in counterfeiting only briefly.
(E) It is very difficult to make accurate estimates of what the costs to society would be if large amounts of counterfeit currency circulated widely.

GO ON TO THE NEXT PAGE.

6. One test to determine whether a person has been infected with tuberculosis consists of injecting the person with proteins extracted from the tuberculosis bacterium. Once a person has been infected by a bacterium, the person's immune system subsequently recognizes certain proteins present in that bacterium and attacks the bacterium. This recognition also takes place in the test and results in a skin irritation at the injection site. Hence the physicians who designed the test reasoned that anyone who reacts in this manner to an injection with the tuberculosis proteins has been infected with tuberculosis.

Which one of the following is an assumption on which the physicians' reasoning depends?

(A) All of the proteins present in disease-causing bacteria can be recognized by the body's immune system.

(B) Localized skin irritations are a characteristic symptom of tuberculosis in most people.

(C) The ability of the proteins present in the tuberculosis bacterium to trigger the skin irritation is exclusive to that bacterium.

(D) Some people who have been injected with proteins extracted from the tuberculosis bacterium will contract tuberculosis as a result of the injection.

(E) The body's immune system cannot recognize infectious bacteria unless there are sufficient quantities of the bacteria to cause overt symptoms of disease.

7. Generations of European-history students have been taught that a political assassination caused the First World War. Without some qualification, however, this teaching is bound to mislead, since the war would not have happened without the treaties and alliances that were already in effect and the military force that was already amassed. These were the deeper causes of the war, whereas the assassination was a cause only in a trivial sense. It was like the individual spark that happens to ignite a conflagration that was, in the prevailing conditions, inevitable.

Which one of the following most accurately restates the main point of the passage?

(A) The assassination did not cause the war, since the assassination was only the last in a chain of events leading up to the war, each of which had equal claim to being called its "cause."

(B) The war was destined to happen, since the course of history up to that point could not have been altered.

(C) Though the statement that the assassination caused the war is true, the term "cause" more fundamentally applies to the conditions that made it possible for that event to start the war.

(D) If the assassination had occurred when it did but less military force had at that time been amassed, then the war's outbreak might have been considerably delayed or the war might not have occurred at all.

(E) Although the conditions prevailing at the time the war started made war inevitable, if the war had not been triggered by the assassination it would not have taken the course with which students of history are familiar.

GO ON TO THE NEXT PAGE.

8. Toddlers are not being malicious when they bite people. For example, a child may want a toy, and feel that the person he or she bites is preventing him or her from having it.

The situation as described above most closely conforms to which one of the following generalizations?

(A) Biting people is sometimes a way for toddlers to try to solve problems.

(B) Toddlers sometimes engage in biting people in order to get attention from adults.

(C) Toddlers mistakenly believe that biting people is viewed as acceptable behavior by adults.

(D) Toddlers do not recognize that by biting people they often thwart their own ends.

(E) Resorting to biting people is in some cases an effective way for toddlers to get what they want.

9. Consumer advocate: Last year's worldwide alarm about a computer "virus"—a surreptitiously introduced computer program that can destroy other programs and data—was a fraud. Companies selling programs to protect computers against such viruses raised worldwide concern about the possibility that a destructive virus would be activated on a certain date. There was more smoke than fire, however; only about a thousand cases of damage were reported around the world. Multitudes of antivirus programs were sold, so the companies' warning was clearly only an effort to stimulate sales.

The reasoning in the consumer advocate's argument is flawed because this argument

(A) restates its conclusion without attempting to offer a reason to accept it

(B) fails to acknowledge that antivirus programs might protect against viruses other than the particular one described

(C) asserts that the occurrence of one event after another shows that the earlier event was the cause of the later one

(D) uses inflammatory language as a substitute for providing any evidence

(E) overlooks the possibility that the protective steps taken did work and, for many computers, prevented the virus from causing damage

10. Insects can see ultraviolet light and are known to identify important food sources and mating sites by sensing the characteristic patterns of ultraviolet light that these things reflect. Insects are also attracted to *Glomosus* spiderwebs, which reflect ultraviolet light. Thus, insects are probably attracted to these webs because of the specific patterns of ultraviolet light that these webs reflect.

Which one of the following, if true, most strongly supports the argument?

(A) When webs of many different species of spider were illuminated with a uniform source of white light containing an ultraviolet component, many of these webs did not reflect the ultraviolet light.

(B) When the silks of spiders that spin silk only for lining burrows and covering eggs were illuminated with white light containing an ultraviolet component, the silks of these spiders reflected ultraviolet light.

(C) When webs of the comparatively recently evolved common garden spider were illuminated with white light containing an ultraviolet component, only certain portions of these webs reflected ultraviolet light.

(D) When *Drosophila* fruit flies were placed before a *Glomosus* web and a synthetic web of similar pattern that also reflected ultraviolet light and both webs were illuminated with white light containing an ultraviolet component, many of the fruit flies flew to the *Glomosus* web.

(E) When *Drosophila* fruit flies were placed before two *Glomosus* webs, one illuminated with white light containing an ultraviolet component and one illuminated with white light without an ultraviolet component, the majority flew to the ultraviolet reflecting web.

GO ON TO THE NEXT PAGE.

11. A Habitat Conservation Plan (HCP) is based on a law that allows developers to use land inhabited by endangered species in exchange for a promise to preserve critical habitat or provide replacement land nearby. Some individuals of endangered species are lost in return for assurances by the owner or developer that habitat for those remaining animals will be protected. Environmentalists are pleased that HCPs allow them to win concessions from developers who would otherwise ignore rarely enforced environmental laws. Satisfied property owners prefer HCPs to more restrictive prohibitions of land use.

The situation described above most closely conforms to which one of the following principles?

(A) In order to avoid protracted legal battles environmentalists should compromise with developers.

(B) Developers should adhere only to those environmental laws that are not overburdensome.

(C) Laws should not be designed to serve the interests of all the parties concerned since they are often so weak that no one's interest is served well.

(D) Laws should be fashioned in such a way as to reconcile the interests of developers and environmentalists.

(E) The most effective means of preserving endangered species is to refrain from alienating property owners.

12. It has long been thought that lizards evolved from a group of amphibians called anthracosaurs, no fossils of which have been found in any rocks older than 300 million years. However, a fossil of a lizard was recently found that is estimated to be 340 million years old. Lizards could not have evolved from creatures that did not exist until after the first lizards. Therefore, lizards could not have evolved from anthracosaurs.

An assumption made in the argument is that there are no

(A) unknown anthracosaur fossils older than 340 million years

(B) unknown lizard fossils older than 340 million years

(C) known lizard fossils that predate some anthracosaur fossils

(D) known anthracosaur fossils that predate some lizard fossils

(E) known lizard fossils whose age is uncertain

Questions 13–14

Numismatist: In medieval Spain, most gold coins were minted from gold mined in West Africa, in the area that is now Senegal. The gold mined in this region was the purest known. Its gold content of 92 percent allowed coins to be minted without refining the gold, and indeed coins minted from this source of gold can be recognized because they have that gold content. The mints could refine gold and produced other kinds of coins that had much purer gold content, but the Senegalese gold was never refined.

13. Which one of the following inferences about gold coins minted in medieval Spain is most strongly supported by the information the numismatist gives?

(A) Coins minted from Senegalese gold all contained the same weight, as well as the same proportion, of gold.

(B) The source of some refined gold from which coins were minted was unrefined gold with a gold content of less than 92 percent.

(C) Two coins could have the same monetary value even though they differed from each other in the percentage of gold they contained.

(D) No gold coins were minted that had a gold content of less than 92 percent.

(E) The only unrefined gold from which coins could be minted was Senegalese gold.

14. As a preliminary to negotiating prices, merchants selling goods often specified that payment should be in the coins minted from Senegalese gold. Which one of the following, if true, most helps to explain this preference?

(A) Because refined gold varied considerably in purity, specifying a price as a number of refined-gold coins did not fix the quantity of gold received in payment.

(B) During this period most day-to-day trading was conducted using silver coins, though gold coins were used for costly transactions and long-distance commerce.

(C) The mints were able to determine the purity, and hence the value, of gold coins by measuring their density.

(D) Since gold coins' monetary value rested on the gold they contained, payments were frequently made using coins minted in several different countries.

(E) Merchants obtaining gold to resell for use in jewelry could not sell the metal unless it was first refined.

GO ON TO THE NEXT PAGE.

15. Some plants have extremely sensitive biological thermometers. For example, the leaves of rhododendrons curl when the temperature of the air around them is below 0°C (Celsius). Similarly, mature crocus blossoms open in temperatures above 2°C. So someone who simultaneously observed rhododendrons with uncurled leaves, crocuses with mature but unopened blossoms, and a thermometer showing 1°C could determine that the thermometer's reading was accurate to within plus or minus 1°C.

Which one of the following, if true, most seriously undermines the reasoning above?

(A) Neither rhododendrons nor crocuses bloom for more than a few weeks each year, and the blossoms of rhododendrons growing in any area do not appear until at least several weeks after crocuses growing in that area have ceased to bloom.

(B) Many people find it unpleasant to be outdoors for long periods when the temperature is at or about 1°C.

(C) The climate and soil conditions that favor the growth of rhododendrons are also favorable to the growth of crocuses.

(D) Air temperature surrounding rhododendrons, which can grow 12 feet tall, is likely to differ from air temperature surrounding crocuses, which are normally only a few inches high, by more than 2°C, even if the two plants are growing side by side.

(E) Certain types of thermometers that are commonly used to measure outdoor temperatures can be extremely accurate in moderate temperature ranges but much less accurate in warmer or colder temperature ranges.

16. Political scientist: The dissemination of political theories is in principle able to cause change in existing social structures. However, all political theories are formulated in the educationally privileged setting of the university, leading to convoluted language that is alienating to many individuals outside academia who would be important agents of change. It follows that, with respect to political theory, there is a special role for those outside the university context to render it into accessible, clear language.

Which one of the following is an assumption on which the argument depends?

(A) Persons outside academic settings are the most important agents of change to the social structure.

(B) Persons within academic settings who formulate political theories attempt to change existing social structures.

(C) Persons outside academic settings are better left out of the initial formulation of political theories.

(D) Persons outside academic settings stand to gain more from the dissemination of political theories than persons inside.

(E) Persons within academic settings are less willing or less able than persons outside to write in a straightforward way.

17. Nicotine has long been known to cause heart attacks and high blood pressure. Yet a recent study has shown that the incidence of heart attacks and high blood pressure is significantly higher among cigarette smokers who do not chew tobacco than among nonsmokers exposed to an equal amount of nicotine through tobacco chewing.

Which one of the following, if true, helps LEAST to resolve the apparent discrepancy described above?

(A) People who smoke but do not chew tobacco tend to exercise less than those who chew tobacco but do not smoke.

(B) Chemicals other than nicotine present in chewing tobacco but not present in cigarette smoke mitigate the effects that nicotine has on the cardiovascular system.

(C) People who chew tobacco but do not smoke tend to have healthier diets than those who smoke but do not chew tobacco.

(D) Chemicals other than nicotine present in chewing tobacco but not present in cigarette smoke can cause cancer.

(E) Chemicals other than nicotine present in cigarette smoke but not present in chewing tobacco raise blood pressure.

GO ON TO THE NEXT PAGE.

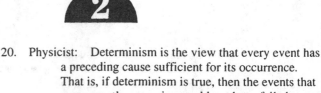

18. President of Central Supply Company: Profits are at an all-time low this fiscal year because of decreased demand for our products. If this situation continues, the company may have to declare bankruptcy. So it is important to prevent any further decrease in profits. Consequently, the only options are to reduce planned expansion or to eliminate some less profitable existing operations.

Which one of the following most accurately describes a flaw in the company president's reasoning?

(A) It presumes without giving justification that survival of the company has been a good thing.
(B) It does not take into account that there are alternatives to declaring bankruptcy.
(C) It presumes without giving justification that only decreased demand can ever be the cause of decreased profits.
(D) It does not allow for the possibility that profits will decrease only slightly during the next fiscal year.
(E) It does not take into account that there may be other ways to stop the decrease in profits.

19. In all mammalian species, the period of a young mammal's life in which it is most frequently playful coincides with the period of most rapid growth of the neural connections in the mammal's brain that give rise to various complex patterns of movement, posture, and social response. Indeed, the neural connections created by frequent play during this period later become indispensable for the mammal's survival and well-being as an adult.

The statements above, if true, serve LEAST well as evidence for which one of the following?

(A) Young mammals of species that are preyed on by other animals are likely to engage in forms of sudden mock flight, bolting away from locations where no predators are to be found.
(B) The young of nonmammalian species such as fish, reptiles, and birds do not normally engage in playful behavior that serves the function served by play in the development of young mammals.
(C) Adult mammals are more likely to engage in interactive play with their young if they engaged in similar forms of play when they themselves were young.
(D) Mammals that cannot engage in certain common forms of play when young are likely to show certain deficits that limit their subsequent success as adults.
(E) Young mammals of predatory species tend to practice in their play inoffensive versions of motions and actions that are useful in finding and catching prey when these mammals become adults.

20. Physicist: Determinism is the view that every event has a preceding cause sufficient for its occurrence. That is, if determinism is true, then the events that are presently occurring could not have failed to occur given the state of the universe a moment ago. Determinism, however, is false because it is impossible to know the complete state of the universe at any given time since it is impossible to measure accurately both the position and velocity of any given subatomic particle at a particular time.

The physicist's reasoning is most vulnerable to criticism on which one of the following grounds?

(A) That it is impossible to measure accurately both the position and velocity of any given subatomic particle does not imply that it is impossible to know either the position or velocity of all subatomic particles.
(B) That the complete state of the universe at any given time is unknowable does not imply that the states at that time of the individual subatomic particles making it up are unknowable.
(C) That it is impossible to measure accurately both the position and velocity of any given subatomic particle at a particular time does not imply that its position or velocity cannot be accurately measured separately.
(D) That it is impossible to know the complete state of the universe at any given time does not imply that there is no complete state of the universe at that time.
(E) That the position and velocity of any given subatomic particle cannot be jointly measured with accuracy does not imply that this is the case for the position and velocity of all subatomic particles.

21. If this parking policy is unpopular with the faculty, then we should modify it. If it is unpopular among students, we should adopt a new policy. And, it is bound to be unpopular either with the faculty or among students.

If the statements above are true, which one of the following must also be true?

(A) We should attempt to popularize this parking policy among either the faculty or students.
(B) We should modify this parking policy only if this will not reduce its popularity among students.
(C) We should modify this parking policy if modification will not reduce its popularity with the faculty.
(D) If this parking policy is popular among students, then we should adopt a new policy.
(E) If this parking policy is popular with the faculty, then we should adopt a new policy.

GO ON TO THE NEXT PAGE.

22. It is an absurd idea that whatever artistic endeavor the government refuses to support it does not allow, as one can see by rephrasing the statement to read: No one is allowed to create art without a government subsidy.

The pattern of reasoning in which one of the following is most similar to that in the argument above?

(A) The claim that any driver who is not arrested does not break the law is absurd, as one can see by rewording it: Every driver who breaks the law gets arrested.

(B) The claim that any driver who is not arrested does not break the law is absurd, as one can see by rewording it: Every driver who gets arrested has broken the law.

(C) The notion that every scientist who is supported by a government grant will be successful is absurd, as one can see by rewording it: No scientist who is successful is so without a government grant.

(D) The notion that every scientist who is supported by a government grant will be successful is absurd, as one can see by rewording it: No scientist lacking governmental support will be successful.

(E) The notion that every scientist who has been supported by a government grant will be successful is absurd, as one can see by rewording it: No scientist is allowed to do research without a government grant.

23. Politician: Nobody can deny that homelessness is a problem, yet there seems to be little agreement on how to solve it. One thing, however, is clear: ignoring the problem will not make it go away. Only if the government steps in and provides the homeless with housing will this problem disappear, and this necessitates increased taxation. For this reason, we should raise taxes.

Which one of the following principles, if valid, most supports the politician's argument?

(A) Only if a measure is required to solve a problem should it be adopted.

(B) Only if a measure is sufficient to solve a problem should it be adopted.

(C) If a measure is required to solve a problem, then it should be adopted.

(D) If a measure is sufficient to solve a problem, then it should be adopted.

(E) If a measure is sufficient to solve a problem, any steps necessitated by that measure should be adopted.

24. Trade official: Country X deserves economic retribution for its protectionism. However, it is crucial that we recognize that there are overriding considerations in this case. We should still sell to X the agricultural equipment it ordered; there is high demand in our country for agricultural imports from X.

The argument depends on assuming which one of the following principles?

(A) Agricultural components of international trade are more important than nonagricultural commodities.

(B) The ability to keep popular products available domestically is less important than our being able to enter international markets.

(C) We should never jeopardize the interests of our people to punish a protectionist country.

(D) In most cases, punishing a protectionist country should have priority over the interests of our people.

(E) We should balance the justice of an action with the consequences for our interests of undertaking that action.

25. Jack's aunt gave him her will, asking him to make it public when she died; he promised to do so. After her death, Jack looked at the will; it stipulated that all her money go to her friend George. Jack knew that if he made the will public, George would squander the money, benefiting neither George nor anyone else. Jack also knew that if he did not make the will public, the money would go to his own mother, who would use it to benefit herself and others, harming no one. After reflection, he decided not to make the will public.

Which one of the following principles, if valid, would require Jack to act as he did in the situation described?

(A) Duties to family members take priority over duties to people who are not family members.

(B) Violating a promise is impermissible whenever doing so would become known by others.

(C) One must choose an alternative that benefits some and harms no one over an alternative that harms some and benefits no one.

(D) When faced with alternatives it is obligatory to choose whichever one will benefit the greatest number of people.

(E) A promise becomes nonbinding when the person to whom the promise was made is no longer living.

S T O P

IF YOU FINISH BEFORE TIME IS CALLED, YOU MAY CHECK YOUR WORK ON THIS SECTION ONLY.
DO NOT WORK ON ANY OTHER SECTION IN THE TEST.

SECTION III

Time—35 minutes

24 Questions

Directions: Each group of questions in this section is based on a set of conditions. In answering some of the questions, it may be useful to draw a rough diagram. Choose the response that most accurately and completely answers each question and blacken the corresponding space on your answer sheet.

Questions 1–5

The members of two committees, a planting committee and a trails committee, are to be selected from among seven volunteers—F, G, H, J, K, L, and M. The following conditions govern the composition of the committees:
Each committee must have at least three members.
F cannot be on the same committee as K.
If K is on a committee, J must also be on that committee.
M must be on at least one of the committees.
The two committees must have at least one member in common.

1. Which one of the following represents an acceptable selection of volunteers for the committees?

   (A) planting: F, G, H;   trails: G, J, K, L
   (B) planting: F, H, J;   trails: G, H, L, M
   (C) planting: F, H, M;   trails: G, K, L, M
   (D) planting: F, G, L, M;   trails: F, H
   (E) planting: F, H, J, K;   trails: H, L, M

2. If the planting committee consists of F, H, L, and M, and if the trails committee consists of G, H, and J, then K could replace which one of the following committee members on a committee without violating any of the conditions governing the composition of the committees?

   (A) F
   (B) G
   (C) H
   (D) L
   (E) M

3. If the only members of the planting committee are G, H, and L and if the two committees are to have as many members in common as the conditions allow, then which one of the following must be true?

   (A) The trails committee and the planting committee have exactly one member in common.
   (B) The trails committee and the planting committee have exactly two members in common.
   (C) The trails committee and the planting committee have an equal number of members.
   (D) The trails committee has at least one more member than the planting committee.
   (E) The planting committee has exactly two more members than the trails committee.

4. If K is on both committees and L is also on both committees and if the planting committee has exactly three members, then which one of the following must be true?

   (A) F is on the planting committee.
   (B) F is on the trails committee.
   (C) G is on the planting committee.
   (D) M is on the planting committee.
   (E) M is on the trails committee.

5. The largest number of members that the planting committee and the trails committee could have in common is

   (A) three
   (B) four
   (C) five
   (D) six
   (E) seven

GO ON TO THE NEXT PAGE.

 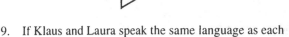
Questions 6–12

Exactly six tourists—Harry, Irene, Klaus, Laura, Michael, Norma—are to be assigned to four guides: Valois, Xerxes, Yossarian, Zalamea. Each tourist is assigned to exactly one guide, with at least one tourist assigned to each guide. Valois speaks only French. Xerxes speaks only Turkish and Spanish. Yossarian speaks only French and Turkish. Zalamea speaks only Spanish and Russian. Each tourist speaks exactly one of the languages spoken by his or her guide and speaks no other language.

The following rules govern the assignment of the tourists to the guides:

At least Harry and Irene are assigned to Yossarian.
At least Laura is assigned to Zalamea.
If Klaus is assigned to Xerxes, then Michael speaks French.

6. Each of the following could be true EXCEPT:

   (A) Both Klaus and Harry speak Turkish.
   (B) Both Klaus and Michael speak French.
   (C) Both Klaus and Michael speak Russian.
   (D) Both Klaus and Norma speak French.
   (E) Both Klaus and Norma speak Spanish.

7. Which one of the following must be true?

   (A) Zalamea is assigned fewer than three of the tourists.
   (B) Xerxes is assigned fewer than two of the tourists.
   (C) Yossarian is assigned exactly two of the tourists.
   (D) Valois is assigned exactly one of the tourists.
   (E) Zalamea is assigned exactly one of the tourists.

8. Each of the following could be true of the assignment of tourists to guides EXCEPT:

   (A) It assigns Klaus to Valois and Michael to Xerxes.
   (B) It assigns Klaus to Yossarian and Norma to Zalamea.
   (C) It assigns Laura to Zalamea and Michael to Zalamea.
   (D) It assigns Michael to Valois and Klaus to Zalamea.
   (E) It assigns Michael to Xerxes and Klaus to Zalamea.

9. If Klaus and Laura speak the same language as each other, then which one of the following must be true?

   (A) At least one of Michael and Norma speaks Spanish.
   (B) At least two tourists speak Russian.
   (C) Klaus and Laura speak Russian.
   (D) At least two tourists speak French.
   (E) At least one of Michael and Norma speaks French.

10. If Laura and Norma speak the same language as each other, then the maximum number of the tourists who could speak Turkish is

    (A) two
    (B) three
    (C) four
    (D) five
    (E) six

11. If exactly two tourists are assigned to Xerxes, then which one of the following could be true?

    (A) Norma speaks Russian and Laura speaks Russian.
    (B) Norma speaks French and Michael speaks French.
    (C) Norma speaks French and Klaus speaks Turkish.
    (D) Michael speaks Spanish and Klaus speaks Spanish.
    (E) Michael speaks French and Klaus speaks Spanish.

12. If Harry, Irene, Michael, and Norma all speak the same language as each other, then which one of the following could be true?

    (A) Klaus speaks Russian.
    (B) Exactly two of the tourists speak Russian.
    (C) Exactly three of the tourists speak Spanish.
    (D) Exactly two of the tourists speak Turkish.
    (E) Klaus speaks French.

GO ON TO THE NEXT PAGE.

Questions 13–18

Each of six people—Kim, Lina, Maricella, Oliver, Paulo, and Shigeru—plays exactly one of two sports—golf and tennis. If a sport is played by more than one of the six people, then the people who play that sport are ranked in order of ability from highest to lowest, with no ties. The following conditions must apply:

Oliver plays tennis.
Lina plays golf.
There is no golf player ranked higher than Lina.
If Maricella plays golf, then Paulo and Shigeru play golf, Paulo ranking lower than Maricella but higher than Shigeru.
If Maricella plays tennis, then Shigeru plays tennis, Shigeru ranking lower than Oliver but higher than Maricella.
If Paulo plays tennis, then Kim plays tennis, Oliver ranking lower than Kim but higher than Paulo.

13. Which one of the following could be true?

   (A) Maricella plays tennis and Shigeru plays golf.
   (B) Paulo plays tennis and Kim plays golf.
   (C) Kim plays tennis and Paulo plays golf.
   (D) Paulo and Oliver play tennis, Paulo ranking higher than Oliver.
   (E) Maricella and Shigeru play tennis, Maricella ranking higher than Shigeru.

14. Each of the following could be the lowest-ranking tennis player EXCEPT:

   (A) Shigeru
   (B) Kim
   (C) Oliver
   (D) Paulo
   (E) Maricella

15. Which one of the following could be a complete and accurate list of the people who play tennis, listed in order of rank from highest to lowest?

   (A) Shigeru, Paulo, Oliver
   (B) Oliver, Paulo, Kim
   (C) Shigeru, Oliver, Maricella
   (D) Oliver, Shigeru, Kim, Maricella
   (E) Paulo, Maricella, Shigeru, Kim

16. If Shigeru plays golf, then each of the following are pairs of people who must play the same sport as each other EXCEPT:

   (A) Paulo and Maricella
   (B) Paulo and Shigeru
   (C) Kim and Maricella
   (D) Paulo and Lina
   (E) Maricella and Shigeru

17. If Oliver is the highest-ranking tennis player, which one of the following must be true?

   (A) Oliver and Maricella play the same sport as each other.
   (B) Paulo and Lina play the same sport as each other.
   (C) Paulo and Oliver play the same sport as each other.
   (D) Kim and Lina do not play the same sport as each other.
   (E) Kim and Paulo do not play the same sport as each other.

18. Suppose that the condition is added that Shigeru and Paulo do not play the same sport as each other. If all the other conditions remain in effect, then each of the following could be true EXCEPT:

   (A) Maricella and Kim play the same sport as each other.
   (B) Paulo and Kim play the same sport as each other.
   (C) Paulo and Maricella play the same sport as each other.
   (D) Kim and Paulo do not play the same sport as each other.
   (E) Maricella and Kim do not play the same sport as each other.

GO ON TO THE NEXT PAGE.

Questions 19–24

A disc jockey will play a sequence consisting of exactly seven different songs: three ballads—F, G, and H—and four dance tunes—R, S, V, and X. The following conditions must be met:

No dance tune can be played immediately after another dance tune.

H must be played earlier in the sequence than V.

V and S must be separated from each other by exactly one song.

S must be played immediately before or immediately after F.

F must be played immediately after R, unless G is played earlier than R.

19. Which one of the following could be the order of the songs in the sequence?

(A) G, H, S, X, V, F, R
(B) R, H, X, G, S, F, V
(C) S, F, X, G, R, H, V
(D) V, F, S, H, X, G, R
(E) X, G, R, H, S, F, V

20. Which one of the following must be true about the sequence?

(A) The first song is X.
(B) The fifth song is S.
(C) No ballad is played immediately after a dance tune.
(D) No ballad is played immediately after another ballad.
(E) No dance tune is played immediately after a ballad.

21. Which one of the following could be the fourth song in the sequence?

(A) G
(B) R
(C) S
(D) V
(E) X

22. Which one of the following could be the first song in the sequence?

(A) R
(B) S
(C) V
(D) F
(E) G

23. If the third song in the sequence is S, which one of the following must be the sixth song?

(A) G
(B) H
(C) R
(D) V
(E) X

24. If the seventh song in the sequence is R, which one of the following could be the fifth song?

(A) F
(B) G
(C) H
(D) V
(E) X

S T O P

IF YOU FINISH BEFORE TIME IS CALLED, YOU MAY CHECK YOUR WORK ON THIS SECTION ONLY.
DO NOT WORK ON ANY OTHER SECTION IN THE TEST.

SECTION IV

Time—35 minutes

26 Questions

Directions: The questions in this section are based on the reasoning contained in brief statements or passages. For some questions, more than one of the choices could conceivably answer the question. However, you are to choose the best answer; that is, the response that most accurately and completely answers the question. You should not make assumptions that are by commonsense standards implausible, superfluous, or incompatible with the passage. After you have chosen the best answer, blacken the corresponding space on your answer sheet.

1. Taxpayer: For the last ten years, Metro City's bridge-maintenance budget of $1 million annually has been a prime example of fiscal irresponsibility. In a well-run bridge program, the city would spend $15 million a year on maintenance, which would prevent severe deterioration, thus limiting capital expenses for needed bridge reconstruction to $10 million. However, as a result of its attempt to economize, the city is now faced with spending $400 million over two years on emergency reconstruction of its bridges.

The main point of the taxpayer's argument is that Metro City

(A) should have budgeted substantially more money for maintenance of its bridges

(B) would have had a well-run bridge program if it had spent more money for reconstruction of its bridges

(C) is spending more than it needs to on maintenance of its bridges

(D) is economizing on its bridge program to save money in case of emergencies

(E) has bridges that are more expensive to maintain than they were to build

2. Twenty professional income-tax advisors were given identical records from which to prepare an income-tax return. The advisors were not aware that they were dealing with fictitious records compiled by a financial magazine. No two of the completed tax returns agreed with each other, and only one was technically correct.

If the information above is correct, which one of the following conclusions can be properly drawn on the basis of it?

(A) Only one out of every twenty income-tax returns prepared by any given professional income-tax advisor will be correct.

(B) The fact that a tax return has been prepared by a professional income-tax advisor provides no guarantee that the tax return has been correctly prepared.

(C) In order to ensure that tax returns are correct, it is necessary to hire professional income-tax advisors to prepare them.

(D) All professional income-tax advisors make mistakes on at least some of the tax returns they prepare.

(E) People are more likely to have an incorrectly prepared tax return if they prepare their own tax returns than if they hire a professional income-tax advisor.

GO ON TO THE NEXT PAGE.

3. The manager of a nuclear power plant defended the claim that the plant was safe by revealing its rate of injury for current workers: only 3.2 injuries per 200,000 hours of work, a rate less than half the national average for all industrial plants. The manager claimed that, therefore, by the standard of how many injuries occur, the plant was safer than most other plants where the employees could work.

Which one of the following, if true, most calls into question the manager's claim?

(A) Workers at nuclear power plants are required to receive extra training in safety precautions on their own time and at their own expense.

(B) Workers at nuclear power plants are required to report to the manager any cases of accidental exposure to radiation.

(C) The exposure of the workers to radiation at nuclear power plants was within levels the government considers safe.

(D) Workers at nuclear power plants have filed only a few lawsuits against the management concerning unsafe working conditions.

(E) Medical problems arising from work at a nuclear power plant are unusual in that they are not likely to appear until after an employee has left employment at the plant.

4. Columnist: The country is presently debating legislation that, if passed, would force manufacturers to increase the number of paid vacation days for employees, to pay higher overtime wages, and to pay all day-care expenses for children of each employee. This legislation is being supported by members of groups that have resorted to violent tactics in the past, and by individuals who are facing indictment on tax-evasion charges. We must defeat this legislation and what it stands for.

The columnist's argument is flawed because it

(A) attacks legislation by calling into question the integrity of the originators of the legislation

(B) assails legislation on the basis of the questionable character of supporters of the legislation

(C) attempts to discredit legislation by appealing to public sentiment for those who would be adversely affected

(D) presupposes that legislation is bad legislation whenever it has only a small number of supporters outside the country's national legislative body

(E) rejects legislation on the grounds that its supporters act inconsistently in seeking to place burdens on manufacturers upon whose business success the supporters depend

5. If the ivory trade continues, experts believe, the elephant will soon become extinct in Africa, because poaching is rife in many areas. A total ban on ivory trading would probably prevent the extinction. However, the country of Zimbabwe—which has virtually eliminated poaching within its borders and which relies on income from carefully culling elephant herds that threaten to become too big—objects to such a ban. Zimbabwe holds that the problem lies not with the ivory trade but with the conservation policies of other countries.

Which one of the following principles forms a logical basis for Zimbabwe's objection to a ban?

(A) International measures to correct a problem should not adversely affect countries that are not responsible for the problem.

(B) Freedom of trade is not a right but a consequence of agreements among nations.

(C) Respecting a country's sovereignty is more important than preventing the extinction of a species.

(D) Prohibitions affecting several countries should be enforced by a supranational agency.

(E) Effective conservation cannot be achieved without eliminating poaching.

6. The male sage grouse has air sacs that, when not inflated, lie hidden beneath the grouse's neck feathers. During its spring courtship ritual, the male sage grouse inflates these air sacs and displays them to the female sage grouse. Some scientists hypothesize that this courtship ritual serves as a means for female sage grouse to select healthy mates.

Which one of the following, if true, most strongly supports the scientists' hypothesis?

(A) Some female sage grouse mate with unhealthy male sage grouse.

(B) When diseased male sage grouse were treated with antibiotics, they were not selected by female sage grouse during the courtship ritual.

(C) Some healthy male sage grouse do not inflate their air sacs as part of the courtship ritual.

(D) Male sage grouse are prone to parasitic infections that exhibit symptoms visible on the birds' air sacs.

(E) The sage grouse is commonly afflicted with a strain of malaria that tends to change as the organism that causes it undergoes mutation.

GO ON TO THE NEXT PAGE.

7. Consumers will be hurt by the new lower ceilings on halibut catches. Given the law of supply and demand these restrictions are likely to result in an increase in the price of the fish.

Which one of the following, if assumed, would do most to justify the claim that the price of halibut will increase?

(A) The demand for halibut will not decrease substantially after the new restrictions are imposed.
(B) There is a connection between the supply of halibut and the demand for it.
(C) The lost production of halibut will not be replaced by increased production of other fish.
(D) The demand for other fish will be affected by the new restrictions.
(E) The amount of halibut consumed represents a very small proportion of all fish consumed.

8. Knowledge of an ancient language is essential for reading original ancient documents. Most ancient historical documents, however, have been translated into modern languages, so scholars of ancient history can read them for their research without learning ancient languages. Therefore, aspirants to careers as ancient-history scholars no longer need to take the time to learn ancient languages.

The argument is vulnerable to criticism on which one of the following grounds?

(A) It concludes that something is never necessary on the grounds that it is not always necessary.
(B) A statement of fact is treated as if it were merely a statement of opinion.
(C) The conclusion is no more than a restatement of the evidence provided as support of that conclusion.
(D) The judgment of experts is applied to a matter in which their expertise is irrelevant.
(E) Some of the evidence presented in support of the conclusion is inconsistent with other evidence provided.

Questions 9–10

The Board of Trustees of the Federici Art Museum has decided to sell some works from its collection in order to raise the funds necessary to refurbish its galleries. Although this may seem like a drastic remedy, the curator has long maintained that among the paintings that the late Ms. Federici collected for the museum were several unsuccessful immature works by Renoir and Cézanne that should be sold because they are of inferior quality and so add nothing to the overall quality of the museum's collection. Hence, the board's action will not detract from the quality of the museum's collection.

9. The conclusion drawn depends on which one of the following assumptions?

(A) Art speculators are unable to distinguish an inferior painting by Renoir from a masterpiece by him.
(B) All of the paintings that the board of trustees sells will be among those that the curator recommends selling.
(C) All of the paintings by Renoir and Cézanne that are owned by the Federici Art Museum were purchased by Ms. Federici herself.
(D) Only an avid collector of paintings by Cézanne would be willing to pay a high price for early works by this artist.
(E) A great work of art can be truly appreciated only if it is displayed in a carefully designed and well-maintained gallery.

10. Which one of the following, if true, most weakens the argument?

(A) The directors of an art museum can generally raise funds for refurbishing the building in which the museum's collection is housed by means other than selling part of its collection.
(B) The quality of an art collection is determined not just by the quality of its paintings, but by what its collection demonstrates about the development of the artistic talent and ideas of the artists represented.
(C) The immature works by Renoir and Cézanne that were purchased by Ms. Federici were at that time thought by some critics to be unimportant juvenile works.
(D) Those people who speculate in art by purchasing artworks merely to sell them at much higher prices welcome inflation in the art market, but curators of art museums regret the inflation in the art market.
(E) The best work of a great artist demands much higher prices in the art market than the worst work of that same artist.

GO ON TO THE NEXT PAGE.

11. Taken together, some 2,000 stocks recommended on a popular television show over the course of the past 12 years by the show's guests, most of whom are successful consultants for multibillion-dollar stock portfolios, performed less successfully than the market as a whole for this 12-year period. So clearly, no one should ever follow any recommendations by these so-called experts.

Each of the following, if true, weakens the argument EXCEPT:

(A) Taken together, the stocks recommended on the television show performed better than the market as a whole for the past year.

(B) Taken together, the stocks recommended on the television show performed better for the past 12-year period than stock portfolios that were actually selected by any other means.

(C) Performance of the stocks recommended on the television show was measured by stock dividends, whereas the performance of the market as a whole was measured by change in share value.

(D) Performance of the stocks recommended on the television show was measured independently by a number of analysts, and the results of all the measurements concurred.

(E) The stock portfolios for which the guests were consultants performed better for the past 12-year period than the market as a whole.

12. The school principal insisted that student failures are caused by bad teaching. In a relatively short time failing grades disappeared from the school. The principal happily recognized this as evidence that the teaching had improved at the school.

The flawed pattern of reasoning in the above is most similar to that in which one of the following?

(A) The nutritionist insisted that the weight gain that team members complained of was caused by overeating. In a brief time all the members stopped overeating. The nutritionist was pleased to conclude that they had stopped gaining weight.

(B) The manager insisted that the workers who filed complaints had too many different tasks. The manager simplified the jobs, and complaints stopped. The manager happily concluded that the working environment had been improved.

(C) The nutritionist insisted that the weight gain that team members complained of was merely in their imagination. Members were given weight charts for the last three months. The nutritionist was pleased to conclude that the complaints of weight gain had stopped.

(D) The manager insisted that the workers who filed complaints did not have enough to do. Soon there were no more complaints filed. The manager was pleased to conclude that the workers were now productively filling their time.

(E) The nutritionist insisted that the weight gain that team members complained of was caused by their thinking of food too often. The nutritionist was happy to conclude that the weight gain had stopped once the team members reported that they had stopped thinking of food so often.

GO ON TO THE NEXT PAGE.

13. Unlike other primroses, self-pollinating primroses do not need to rely on insects for pollination. In many years insect pollinators are scarce, and in those years a typical non-self-pollinating primrose produces fewer seeds than does a typical self-pollinating primrose. In other years, seed production is approximately equal. Thus, self-pollinating primroses have the advantage of higher average seed production. Aside from seed production, these self-pollinating primroses are indistinguishable from non-self-pollinating primroses. Nevertheless, self-pollinating primrose plants remain rare among primroses.

Which one of the following, if true, most helps to resolve the apparent discrepancy in the information above?

(A) Insects that collect pollen from primroses do not discriminate between self-pollinating primroses and non-self-pollinating primroses.

(B) When insect pollinators are scarce, non-self-pollinating primroses produce larger seeds that are more likely to germinate than are seeds from self-pollinating primroses.

(C) Self-pollinating primroses that are located in areas with few insects produce no fewer seeds than do self-pollinating primroses that are located in areas with many insects.

(D) Many primroses are located in areas in which the soil conditions that are optimal for seed germination are not present.

(E) Self-pollinating primroses can be assisted by insects during pollination but do not require the assistance of insects to be pollinated.

14. We have a moral obligation not to destroy books, even if they belong to us. The reason is quite simple: If preserved, books will almost certainly contribute to the intellectual and emotional enrichment of future generations.

Which one of the following most accurately expresses the principle underlying the argument?

(A) It is morally incumbent upon us to devote effort to performing actions that have at least some chance of improving other people's lives.

(B) We are morally obligated to preserve anything that past generations had preserved for our intellectual and emotional enrichment.

(C) The moral commitments we have to future generations supersede the moral commitments we have to the present generation.

(D) We are morally obligated not to destroy anything that will most likely enrich, either intellectually or emotionally, our posterity.

(E) Being morally obligated not to destroy something requires that we be reasonably assured that that thing will lead to the betterment of someone we know.

15. The southern half of a certain region of the earth was covered entirely by water during the Cretaceous period, the last 75 million years of the Mesozoic era, the era when dinosaurs roamed the earth. Dinosaurs lived only on land. Thus, plesiosaurs—swimming reptiles that lived during the Cretaceous period exclusively—were not dinosaurs. No single species of dinosaur lived throughout the entire Mesozoic era.

If the statements in the passage are true, each of the following could be true EXCEPT:

(A) Dinosaurs inhabited the northern half of the region throughout the entire Mesozoic era.

(B) Plesiosaurs did not inhabit the southern half of the region during the Cretaceous period.

(C) Plesiosaurs did not inhabit the southern half of the region before the Cretaceous period.

(D) Dinosaurs did not inhabit the northern half of the region during the Cretaceous period.

(E) Dinosaurs inhabited the southern half of the region throughout the entire Mesozoic era.

16. Essayist: Wisdom and intelligence are desirable qualities. However, being intelligent does not imply that one is wise, nor does being wise imply that one is intelligent. In my own experience, the people I meet have one or the other of these qualities but not both.

If the essayist's statements are true, then each of the following could be true EXCEPT:

(A) Most people are neither intelligent nor wise.
(B) Most people are both intelligent and wise.
(C) No one is both wise and intelligent.
(D) No one is either wise or intelligent.
(E) Many people are intelligent and yet lack wisdom.

GO ON TO THE NEXT PAGE.

17. Concerned citizen: The mayor, an outspoken critic of the proposed restoration of city hall, is right when he notes that the building is outdated, but that the restoration would be expensive at a time when the budget is already tight. We cannot afford such a luxury item in this time of financial restraint, he says. However, I respectfully disagree. The building provides the last remaining link to the days of the city's founding, and preserving a sense of municipal history is crucial to maintaining respect for our city government and its authority. So to the question, "Can we really afford to?" I can only respond, "Can we afford not to?"

Which one of the following most accurately characterizes a flaw in the concerned citizen's argument?

(A) The argument is solely an emotional appeal to history.
(B) The argument ambiguously uses the word "afford."
(C) The argument inappropriately appeals to the authority of the mayor.
(D) The argument incorrectly presumes that the restoration would be expensive.
(E) The argument inappropriately relies on the emotional connotations of words such as "outdated" and "luxury."

18. Obviously, we cannot in any real sense mistreat plants. Plants do not have nervous systems, and having a nervous system is necessary to experience pain.

The conclusion above follows logically if which one of the following is assumed?

(A) Any organism that can experience pain can be mistreated.
(B) Only organisms that have nervous systems can experience pain.
(C) Any organism that has a nervous system can experience pain.
(D) Only organisms that can experience pain can be mistreated.
(E) Any organism that has a nervous system can be mistreated.

19. Inez: In these poor economic times, people want to be sure they are getting good value for their money. I predict people would be more willing to buy antiques at our fair if we first have the objects inspected by professional appraisers who would remove any objects of questionable authenticity.

Anika: I disagree with your prediction. Our customers already are antiques experts. Furthermore, hiring professional appraisers would push up our costs considerably, thus forcing us to raise the prices on all our antiques.

Anika's response proceeds by

(A) indicating that a particular plan would have an effect contrary to the anticipated effect
(B) claiming that a particular plan should not be adopted because, while effective, it would have at least one undesirable consequence
(C) arguing that an alternative plan could achieve a desired result more easily than the plan originally proposed
(D) questioning the assumption that authorities are available who have special knowledge of the problem under discussion
(E) offering a counterexample in order to show that a particular general claim is too broadly stated

20. In some ill-considered popularizations of interesting current research, it is argued that higher apes have the capacity for language but have never put it to use—a remarkable biological miracle, given the enormous selectional advantage of even minimal linguistic skills. It is rather like claiming that some animal has wings adequate for flight but has never thought to fly.

Which one of the following is most similar in its reasoning to the argument above?

(A) Arguing that there are some humans who never sleep is rather like discovering a species of lion that does not eat meat.
(B) Arguing that Earth has been visited by aliens from outer space is rather like claiming that early explorers had visited North America but never founded cities.
(C) Arguing that the human brain has telekinetic powers that no humans have ever exercised is rather like arguing that some insect has legs but never uses them to walk.
(D) Claiming that some people raised tobacco but did not smoke it is rather like claiming that a society that knew how to brew alcohol never drank it.
(E) Arguing that not all people with cars will drive them is rather like claiming that humans invented gasoline long before they used it as fuel for transportation.

GO ON TO THE NEXT PAGE.

Questions 21–22

Sarah: Some schools seek to foster a habit of volunteering in their students by requiring them to perform community service. But since a person who has been forced to do something has not really volunteered and since the habit of volunteering cannot be said to have been fostered in a person who has not yet volunteered for anything, there is no way this policy can succeed by itself.

Paul: I disagree. Some students forced to perform community service have enjoyed it so much that they subsequently actually volunteer to do something similar. In such cases, the policy can clearly be said to have fostered a habit of volunteering.

21. Paul responds to Sarah's argument using which one of the following argumentative techniques?

(A) He argues that Sarah is assuming just what she sets out to prove.
(B) He argues that Sarah's conception of what it means to volunteer excludes certain activities that ought to be considered instances of volunteering.
(C) He introduces considerations that call into question one of Sarah's assumptions.
(D) He questions Sarah's motives for advancing an argument against the school policy.
(E) He argues that a policy Sarah fails to consider could accomplish the same aim as the policy that Sarah considers.

22. The main point at issue between Sarah and Paul is whether

(A) there are any circumstances under which an individual forced to perform a task can correctly be said to have genuinely volunteered to perform that task
(B) being forced to perform community service can provide enjoyment to the individual who is forced to perform such service
(C) being forced to perform community service can by itself encourage a genuine habit of volunteering in those students who are forced to perform such service
(D) it is possible for schools to develop policies that foster the habit of volunteering in their students
(E) students who develop a habit of volunteering while in school are inclined to perform community service later in their lives

23. Only computer scientists understand the architecture of personal computers, and only those who understand the architecture of personal computers appreciate the advances in technology made in the last decade. It follows that only those who appreciate these advances are computer scientists.

Which one of the following most accurately describes a flaw in the reasoning in the argument?

(A) The argument contains no stated or implied relationship between computer scientists and those who appreciate the advances in technology in the last decade.
(B) The argument ignores the fact that some computer scientists may not appreciate the advances in technology made in the last decade.
(C) The argument ignores the fact that computer scientists may appreciate other things besides the advances in technology made in the last decade.
(D) The premises of the argument are stated in such a way that they exclude the possibility of drawing any logical conclusion.
(E) The premises of the argument presuppose that everyone understands the architecture of personal computers.

24. Sociologist: Research shows, contrary to popular opinion, that, all other things being equal, most people who have pets are less happy than most people who do not. Therefore, any person who wants to be as happy as possible would do well to consider not having a pet.

Which one of the following, if true, most seriously weakens the sociologist's argument?

(A) Some people who have pets are happier than most people who do not.
(B) Most people who have no pets occasionally wish that they had pets.
(C) Most people who have pets are reasonably happy.
(D) Most people who have pets feel happier because they have pets.
(E) All people who have no pets admit to feeling unhappy sometimes.

GO ON TO THE NEXT PAGE.

25. The dwarf masked owl, a rare migratory bird of prey, normally makes its winter home on the Baja peninsula, where it nests in the spiny cactus. In fact, there are no other suitable nesting sites for the dwarf masked owl on the Baja peninsula. But a blight last spring destroyed all of the spiny cacti on the Baja peninsula. So unless steps are taken to reestablish the spiny cactus population, the dwarf masked owl will not make its home on the Baja peninsula this winter.

The argument depends on assuming which one of the following?

(A) No birds of prey other than the dwarf masked owl nest in the spiny cactus.

(B) If the Baja peninsula contains spiny cacti, then the dwarf masked owl makes its winter home there.

(C) On occasion the dwarf masked owl has been known to make its winter home far from its normal migratory route.

(D) The dwarf masked owl will not make its winter home on the Baja peninsula only if that region contains no spiny cacti.

(E) Suitable nesting sites must be present where the dwarf masked owl makes its winter home.

26. At night, a flock of crows will generally perch close together in a small place—often a piece of wooded land—called a roost. Each morning, the crows leave the roost and fan out in small groups to hunt and scavenge the surrounding area. For most flocks, the crows' hunting extends as far as 100 to 130 kilometers (60 to 80 miles) from the roost. Normally, a flock will continue to occupy the same roost for several consecutive years, and when it abandons a roost site for a new one, the new roost is usually less than eight kilometers (five miles) away.

Of the following claims, which one can most justifiably be rejected on the basis of the statements above?

(A) Crows will abandon their roost site only in response to increases in the population of the flock.

(B) When there is a shortage of food in the area in which a flock of crows normally hunts and scavenges, some members of the flock will begin to hunt and scavenge outside that area.

(C) Most of the hunting and scavenging that crows do occurs more than eight kilometers (five miles) from their roost.

(D) Once a flock of crows has settled on a new roost site, it is extremely difficult to force it to abandon that site for another.

(E) When a flock of crows moves to a new roost site, it generally does so because the area in which it has hunted and scavenged has been depleted of food sources.

S T O P

IF YOU FINISH BEFORE TIME IS CALLED, YOU MAY CHECK YOUR WORK ON THIS SECTION ONLY.
DO NOT WORK ON ANY OTHER SECTION IN THE TEST.

LSAT® Writing Sample Topic

Directions: The scenario presented below describes two choices, either one of which can be supported on the basis of the information given. Your essay should consider both choices and argue for one over the other, based on the two specified criteria and the facts provided. There is no "right" or "wrong" choice: a reasonable argument can be made for either.

The Transit Authority of Metropolitan Yorkville (TAMY) is plagued by various problems. Its fares are the highest in the nation. Because of declining ridership, a significant shortfall in TAMY's budget for next year is projected. TAMY receives limited financial support through government subsidies, but taxpayers are increasingly reluctant to endorse even this limited support because of a widespread perception that TAMY wastes money. Given the severity of TAMY's crisis, TAMY's governing board has concluded that a radical restructuring is necessary. It has decided to hire a management consulting firm to study the situation and recommend changes. The board has narrowed its choices to two firms, Transit Analysts and DeWitt Consulting. Using the following criteria, write an argument in favor of the board's hiring one firm rather than the other:

- The board wants to hire a firm with expertise particularly relevant to TAMY.
- The board wants to hire a firm with a proven record of success in devising radical business restructurings.

Transit Analysts specializes in public transportation. It has far more experience analyzing troubled transit authorities than any other management consulting firm in the nation. Most of Transit Analysts's consultants are former officials of various transit authorities. A sizable majority of the transit authorities that have employed Transit Analysts have subsequently experienced satisfactory recoveries. But Transit Analysts has never recommended dramatic changes to any of the transit authorities it has analyzed. The newest member of Transit Analysts's team of consultants, however, is a former airline executive who is known for advocating a radical overhaul of the nation's public transportation system.

DeWitt Consulting has experience in many industries but not in public transportation. All of its consultants have backgrounds in the private sector; none has worked in any industry closely related to public transportation. But DeWitt Consulting does have experience analyzing several troubled municipal utilities. After evaluating each of these utilities, DeWitt Consulting recommended radical changes in their operations, and as a result each utility rapidly achieved dramatic gains. Additionally, DeWitt Consulting has typically advised the private companies it has analyzed to completely restructure their businesses, resulting in comparable successes.

Directions:

1. Use the Answer Key on the next page to check your answers.

2. Use the Scoring Worksheet below to compute your raw score.

3. Use the Score Conversion Chart to convert your raw score into the 120-180 scale.

Scoring Worksheet

1. Enter the number of questions you answered correctly in each section.

	Number Correct
SECTION I	_____
SECTION II	_____
SECTION III	_____
SECTION IV	_____

2. Enter the sum here: _____
   This is your Raw Score.

Conversion Chart
For Converting Raw Score to the 120-180 LSAT Scaled Score
LSAT Form 9LSS37

Reported Score	Raw Score Lowest	Raw Score Highest
180	99	101
179	98	98
178	97	97
177	96	96
176	95	95
175	94	94
174	93	93
173	92	92
172	91	91
171	90	90
170	89	89
169	87	88
168	86	86
167	85	85
166	83	84
165	82	82
164	80	81
163	78	79
162	77	77
161	75	76
160	73	74
159	72	72
158	70	71
157	68	69
156	66	67
155	65	65
154	63	64
153	61	62
152	59	60
151	58	58
150	56	57
149	54	55
148	52	53
147	51	51
146	49	50
145	47	48
144	46	46
143	44	45
142	42	43
141	41	41
140	39	40
139	37	38
138	36	36
137	34	35
136	33	33
135	31	32
134	30	30
133	29	29
132	27	28
131	26	26
130	24	25
129	23	23
128	22	22
127	21	21
126	19	20
125	18	18
124	17	17
123	16	16
122	15	15
121	14	14
120	0	13

SECTION I

1.	D	8.	C	15.	A	22.	D
2.	B	9.	B	16.	A	23.	A
3.	A	10.	A	17.	E	24.	E
4.	D	11.	C	18.	E	25.	B
5.	B	12.	D	19.	C	26.	B
6.	C	13.	A	20.	B		
7.	D	14.	C	21.	C		

SECTION II

1.	A	8.	A	15.	D	22.	A
2.	C	9.	E	16.	E	23.	C
3.	A	10.	E	17.	D	24.	E
4.	A	11.	D	18.	E	25.	D
5.	B	12.	A	19.	B		
6.	C	13.	B	20.	D		
7.	C	14.	A	21.	E		

SECTION III

1.	B	8.	B	15.	D	22.	A
2.	B	9.	E	16.	C	23.	A
3.	D	10.	B	17.	B	24.	D
4.	E	11.	E	18.	C		
5.	D	12.	E	19.	E		
6.	C	13.	C	20.	D		
7.	A	14.	A	21.	A		

SECTION IV

1.	A	8.	A	15.	E	22.	C
2.	B	9.	B	16.	D	23.	B
3.	E	10.	B	17.	B	24.	D
4.	B	11.	D	18.	D	25.	E
5.	A	12.	D	19.	A	26.	E
6.	D	13.	B	20.	C		
7.	A	14.	D	21.	C		

The Official LSAT PrepTest

26

- **September 1998**
- **Form 8LSS39**

The sample test that follows consists of four sections corresponding to the four scored sections of the September 1998 LSAT.

SECTION I

Time—35 minutes

24 Questions

<u>Directions:</u> Each group of questions in this section is based on a set of conditions. In answering some of the questions, it may be useful to draw a rough diagram. Choose the response that most accurately and completely answers each question and blacken the corresponding space on your answer sheet.

Questions 1–7

Eight physics students—four majors: Frank, Gwen, Henry, and Joan; and four nonmajors: Victor, Wanda, Xavier, and Yvette—are being assigned to four laboratory benches, numbered 1 through 4. Each student is assigned to exactly one bench, and exactly two students are assigned to each bench. Assignments of students to benches must conform to the following conditions:

　Exactly one major is assigned to each bench.
　Frank and Joan are assigned to consecutively numbered benches, with Frank assigned to the lower-numbered bench.
　Frank is assigned to the same bench as Victor.
　Gwen is not assigned to the same bench as Wanda.

1. Which one of the following could be the assignment of students to benches?

　(A)　1: Frank, Victor; 2: Joan, Gwen; 3: Henry, Wanda; 4: Xavier, Yvette
　(B)　1: Gwen, Yvette; 2: Frank, Xavier; 3: Joan, Wanda; 4: Henry, Victor
　(C)　1: Henry, Wanda; 2: Gwen, Xavier; 3: Frank, Victor; 4: Joan, Yvette
　(D)　1: Henry, Xavier; 2: Joan, Wanda; 3: Frank, Victor; 4: Gwen, Yvette
　(E)　1: Henry, Yvette; 2: Gwen, Wanda; 3: Frank, Victor; 4: Joan, Xavier

2. If Victor is assigned to bench 2 and Wanda is assigned to bench 4, which one of the following must be true?

　(A)　Frank is assigned to bench 1.
　(B)　Gwen is assigned to bench 1.
　(C)　Henry is assigned to bench 3.
　(D)　Xavier is assigned to bench 1.
　(E)　Yvette is assigned to bench 3.

3. If Gwen and Henry are not assigned to consecutively numbered benches, which one of the following must be true?

　(A)　Victor is assigned to bench 2.
　(B)　Victor is assigned to bench 3.
　(C)　Wanda is assigned to bench 1.
　(D)　Wanda is assigned to bench 3.
　(E)　Wanda is assigned to bench 4.

4. If Henry and Yvette are both assigned to bench 1, which one of the following could be true?

　(A)　Gwen is assigned to bench 3.
　(B)　Joan is assigned to bench 2.
　(C)　Wanda is assigned to bench 2.
　(D)　Wanda is assigned to bench 3.
　(E)　Xavier is assigned to bench 3.

5. If Gwen is assigned to bench 4 and Xavier is assigned to bench 3, then any one of the following could be true EXCEPT:

　(A)　Gwen is assigned to the same bench as Yvette.
　(B)　Henry is assigned to the same bench as Wanda.
　(C)　Henry is assigned to the same bench as Xavier.
　(D)　Joan is assigned to the same bench as Xavier.
　(E)　Joan is assigned to the same bench as Yvette.

6. If Wanda is assigned to a lower-numbered bench than is Joan, then Henry must be assigned to a

　(A)　lower-numbered bench than is Frank
　(B)　lower-numbered bench than is Gwen
　(C)　lower-numbered bench than is Xavier
　(D)　higher-numbered bench than is Victor
　(E)　higher-numbered bench than is Yvette

7. Which one of the following could be the assignments for bench 2 and bench 4 ?

　(A)　2: Gwen, Xavier
　　　　4: Henry, Yvette
　(B)　2: Henry, Yvette
　　　　4: Joan, Xavier
　(C)　2: Joan, Victor
　　　　4: Gwen, Xavier
　(D)　2: Joan, Wanda
　　　　4: Gwen, Xavier
　(E)　2: Joan, Xavier
　　　　4: Henry, Yvette

GO ON TO THE NEXT PAGE.

Questions 8–12

A messenger will deliver exactly seven packages—L, M, N, O, P, S, and T—one at a time, not necessarily in that order. The seven deliveries must be made according to the following conditions:

P is delivered either first or seventh.

The messenger delivers N at some time after delivering L.

The messenger delivers T at some time after delivering M.

The messenger delivers exactly one package between delivering L and delivering O, whether or not L is delivered before O.

The messenger delivers exactly one package between delivering M and delivering P, whether or not M is delivered before P.

8. Which one of the following is an order in which the messenger could make the deliveries, from first to seventh?

(A)   L, N, S, O, M, T, P
(B)   M, T, P, S, L, N, O
(C)   O, S, L, N, M, T, P
(D)   P, N, M, S, O, T, L
(E)   P, T, M, S, L, N, O

9. Which one of the following could be true?

(A)   N is delivered first.
(B)   T is delivered first.
(C)   T is delivered second.
(D)   M is delivered fourth.
(E)   S is delivered seventh.

10. If N is delivered fourth, which one of the following could be true?

(A)   L is delivered first.
(B)   L is delivered second.
(C)   M is delivered third.
(D)   O is delivered fifth.
(E)   S is delivered first.

11. If T is delivered fourth, the seventh package delivered must be

(A)   L
(B)   N
(C)   O
(D)   P
(E)   S

12. If the messenger delivers M at some time after delivering O, the fifth package delivered could be any one of the following EXCEPT:

(A)   L
(B)   M
(C)   N
(D)   S
(E)   T

GO ON TO THE NEXT PAGE.

Questions 13–18

Each of exactly five persons—Nguyen, Olson, Pike, Tyner, and Valdez—participates in exactly one of three activities: going to a movie, going to a soccer game, or going to a restaurant. The following conditions must apply:

Nguyen and Olson do not participate in the same activity as each other, nor does either one of them participate in the same activity as Pike.

Exactly two persons go to a soccer game.

Tyner and Pike do not participate in the same activity as each other.

If Nguyen or Valdez goes to a movie, they both go to a movie.

13. Which one of the following could be an accurate list of the activities participated in by Nguyen, Olson, Pike, Tyner, and Valdez, respectively?

(A) movie, soccer game, soccer game, restaurant, movie
(B) movie, restaurant, soccer game, soccer game, movie
(C) soccer game, restaurant, movie, soccer game, movie
(D) soccer game, restaurant, movie, soccer game, restaurant
(E) soccer game, restaurant, movie, soccer game, soccer game

14. If Valdez goes to a soccer game, then each of the following could be true EXCEPT:

(A) Olson goes to a movie.
(B) Nguyen goes to a restaurant.
(C) Nguyen goes to a soccer game.
(D) Tyner goes to a soccer game.
(E) Tyner goes to a movie.

15. Which one of the following is a pair of persons who could go to a movie together?

(A) Nguyen and Tyner
(B) Olson and Tyner
(C) Olson and Valdez
(D) Pike and Olson
(E) Pike and Tyner

16. Each of the following statements must be false EXCEPT:

(A) Only Olson goes to a restaurant.
(B) Only Pike goes to a restaurant.
(C) Only Tyner goes to a restaurant.
(D) Only Valdez goes to a restaurant.
(E) Tyner and Valdez go to a restaurant together.

17. If Nguyen goes to a soccer game, then which one of the following is a complete and accurate list of the persons any one of whom could go to a movie?

(A) Olson
(B) Pike, Valdez
(C) Olson, Tyner
(D) Pike, Tyner, Valdez
(E) Olson, Pike, Tyner

18. If the condition that exactly two persons go to a soccer game is changed to require that exactly three persons go to a soccer game, but all other conditions remain the same, then which one of the following persons must participate in an activity other than going to a soccer game?

(A) Nguyen
(B) Olson
(C) Pike
(D) Tyner
(E) Valdez

GO ON TO THE NEXT PAGE.

Questions 19–24

In each of two years exactly two of four lawmakers—Feld, Gibson, Hsu, and Ivins—and exactly two of three scientists—Vega, Young, and Zapora—will serve as members of a four-person panel. In each year, one of the members will be chairperson. The chairperson in the first year cannot serve on the panel in the second year. The chairperson in the second year must have served on the panel in the first year. Service on the panel must obey the following conditions:

    Gibson and Vega do not serve on the panel in the same year as each other.

    Hsu and Young do not serve on the panel in the same year as each other.

    Each year, either Ivins or Vega, but not both, serves on the panel.

19. Which one of the following could be the list of the people who serve on the panel in the first year?

    (A)   Feld, Gibson, Vega, Zapora
    (B)   Feld, Hsu, Vega, Zapora
    (C)   Feld, Ivins, Vega, Zapora
    (D)   Gibson, Hsu, Ivins, Zapora
    (E)   Hsu, Ivins, Young, Zapora

20. If Vega is the chairperson in the first year, which one of the following is a pair of people who must serve on the panel in the second year?

    (A)   Gibson and Young
    (B)   Gibson and Zapora
    (C)   Hsu and Ivins
    (D)   Ivins and Young
    (E)   Vega and Young

21. If Hsu is the chairperson in the first year, which one of the following could be the chairperson in the second year?

    (A)   Feld
    (B)   Gibson
    (C)   Hsu
    (D)   Ivins
    (E)   Young

22. If Feld serves on the panel in a given year, any one of the following could serve on the panel that year EXCEPT:

    (A)   Gibson
    (B)   Hsu
    (C)   Ivins
    (D)   Vega
    (E)   Young

23. If Ivins is the chairperson in the first year, which one of the following could be the chairperson in the second year?

    (A)   Feld
    (B)   Gibson
    (C)   Hsu
    (D)   Vega
    (E)   Young

24. Which one of the following must be true?

    (A)   Feld is on the panel in the second year.
    (B)   Hsu is on the panel in the first year.
    (C)   Ivins is on the panel in both years.
    (D)   Young is on the panel in both years.
    (E)   Zapora is on the panel in the second year.

S T O P

IF YOU FINISH BEFORE TIME IS CALLED, YOU MAY CHECK YOUR WORK ON THIS SECTION ONLY.
DO NOT WORK ON ANY OTHER SECTION IN THE TEST.

SECTION II

Time—35 minutes

25 Questions

<u>Directions:</u> The questions in this section are based on the reasoning contained in brief statements or passages. For some questions, more than one of the choices could conceivably answer the question. However, you are to choose the <u>best</u> answer; that is, the response that most accurately and completely answers the question. You should not make assumptions that are by commonsense standards implausible, superfluous, or incompatible with the passage. After you have chosen the best answer, blacken the corresponding space on your answer sheet.

1. Insurance that was to become effective at 9 A.M. on a certain date was taken out on the life of a flight attendant. He died on that date at 10 A.M. local time, which was two hours before 9 A.M. in the time zone where the policy had been purchased. The insurance company contended that the policy had not become effective; a representative of the flight attendant's beneficiary, his mother, countered by arguing that the policy amount should be paid because the attendant had been his mother's sole support, and she was ill.

   The representative's argument is flawed as a counter to the insurance company's contention because

   (A) the conclusion is no more than a paraphrase of the evidence offered in support of it
   (B) it appeals to the emotion of pity rather than addressing the issue raised
   (C) it makes an unwarranted distinction between family obligations and business obligations
   (D) it substitutes an attack on a person for the giving of reasons
   (E) a cause and its effect are mistaken for each other

2. Once a child's imagination becomes developed, a host of imaginary creatures may torment the child. But this newly developed cognitive capacity may also be used to render these creatures harmless. For instance, a child's new toy may be imagined as an ally, powerful enough to ward off any imaginary threats.

   The type of situation described above most closely conforms to which one of the following propositions?

   (A) Some newly developed capacities only give rise to problems.
   (B) Sometimes the cause of a problem may also provide its solution.
   (C) Children are not able to distinguish between real and imaginary threats.
   (D) The most effective way for children to address their fears is to acknowledge them.
   (E) Most problems associated with child-rearing can be solved with a little imagination.

3. Trisha: Today's family is declining in its ability to carry out its functions of child-rearing and providing stability for adult life. There must be a return to the traditional values of commitment and responsibility.

   Jerod: We ought to leave what is good enough alone. Contemporary families may be less stable than traditionally, but most people do not find that to be bad. Contemporary criticisms of the family are overblown and destructive.

   Trisha and Jerod disagree over whether the institution of the family is

   (A) adequate as it is
   (B) changing over time
   (C) valued by most people
   (D) not going to survive
   (E) no longer traditional

4. Politician P: My opponent claims that the government is obligated to raise taxes to increase funding for schools and health care. Because raising taxes to increase funding for schools and health care would make taxpayers upset over their loss of buying power, my opponent is simply mistaken.

   Politician P's reasoning is questionable because it involves

   (A) presupposing that a claim is mistaken on the grounds that the person defending it advocates other unpopular views
   (B) assuming that a claim is false on the grounds that the person defending it is of questionable character
   (C) concluding that a view is false on the grounds that its implementation would lead to unhappiness
   (D) appealing to wholly irrelevant issues to deflect attention away from the real issue
   (E) insisting that an obligation exists without offering any evidence that it exists

GO ON TO THE NEXT PAGE.

5. In defending the Hyperion School of Journalism from charges that its program is of little or no value to its students, the dean of the school pointed to its recent success in placing students: 65 percent of its graduates went on to internships or jobs in print or broadcast journalism.

Which one of the following, if true, most seriously undermines the defense offered by the dean?

(A) More than half of the school's students came from jobs in journalism to improve their skills.

(B) Some newspaper editors do not regard journalism school as a necessary part of the training of a journalist.

(C) The number of cities with more than one major newspaper has declined sharply over the last 25 years.

(D) The program offered by the Hyperion School of Journalism is similar in quality and content to those offered by its peer institutions.

(E) The proportion of applicants to the Hyperion School of Journalism that are admitted is lower than it was ten years ago.

6. The largest volcano on Mars rises 27 kilometers above the surrounding plain and covers an area roughly the size of Romania. Even if the Earth's gravity were as low as the gravity of Mars is, no volcano of such size could exist on Earth, for the Earth's crust, although of essentially the same composition as that of Mars, is too thin to support even a small fraction of that mass and would buckle under it, causing the mountain to sink.

If the statements above are true, which one of the following must also be true on the basis of them?

(A) The surface of Mars is less subject to forces of erosion than is the surface of the Earth.

(B) The highest volcanoes on Mars occur where its crust is thickest.

(C) On average, volcanoes on Mars are higher than those on Earth.

(D) The crust of Mars, at least at certain points on the planet, is thicker than the crust of the Earth.

(E) At least some of the Earth's volcanoes would be larger than they actually are if the Earth's crust were thicker than it is.

7. Speakers of the Caronian language constitute a minority of the population in several large countries. An international body has recommended that the regions where Caronian-speakers live be granted autonomy as an independent nation in which Caronian-speakers would form a majority. But Caronian-speakers live in several, widely scattered areas that cannot be united within a single continuous boundary while at the same time allowing Caronian-speakers to be the majority population. Hence, the recommendation cannot be satisfied.

The argument relies on which one of the following assumptions?

(A) A nation once existed in which Caronian-speakers formed the majority of the population.

(B) Caronian-speakers tend to perceive themselves as constituting a single community.

(C) The recommendation would not be satisfied by the creation of a nation formed of disconnected regions.

(D) The new Caronian nation will not include as citizens anyone who does not speak Caronian.

(E) In most nations several different languages are spoken.

8. Sociologist: The welfare state cannot be successfully implemented because it rests on the assumption that human beings are unselfish—a seemingly false assumption. The welfare state is feasible only if wage earners are prepared to have their hard-earned funds used to help others in greater need, and that requires an unselfish attitude. But people innately seek their own well-being, especially when the interests of others threaten it.

Which one of the following most accurately expresses the main conclusion of the sociologist's argument?

(A) The welfare state will not work.

(B) The welfare state unfairly asks those who work hard to help those in greater need.

(C) The assumption that human beings are unselfish is false.

(D) The interests of the less fortunate impinge on the interests of others.

(E) The welfare state relies on the generosity of wage earners.

GO ON TO THE NEXT PAGE.

9. Early pencil leads were made of solid graphite mined in Cumberland, in Britain. Modern methods of manufacturing pencil leads from powdered graphite are the result of research sponsored by the government of France in the 1790s, when France was at war with Britain and thus had no access to Cumberland graphite.

The information above most strongly supports which one of the following?

(A) The world's only deposit of graphite suitable for manufacture of pencils is in Cumberland, in Britain.

(B) In the 1790s, France's government did not know of any accessible source of solid graphite appropriate to meet France's need for pencils.

(C) One of the causes of war between France and Britain in the 1790s was the British government's attempt to limit the amount of Cumberland graphite being exported to France.

(D) Government-sponsored research frequently gives rise to inventions that are of great benefit to society.

(E) Even today, all pencil leads contain Cumberland graphite.

Questions 10–11

Commercial passenger airplanes can be equipped with a collision-avoidance radar system that provides pilots with information about the proximity of other airplanes. Because the system warns pilots to take evasive action when it indicates a possible collision, passengers are safer on airplanes equipped with the system than on comparable airplanes not so equipped, even though the system frequently warns pilots to evade phantom airplanes.

10. Which one of the following is an assumption on which the argument depends?

(A) Passengers feel no safer on airplanes equipped with the radar system than on comparable airplanes not so equipped.

(B) Warnings given by a collision-avoidance system about phantom airplanes are not caused by distorted radar signals.

(C) The frequency of invalid warnings will not cause pilots routinely to disregard the system's warnings.

(D) Commercial passenger airplanes are not the only planes that can be equipped with a collision-avoidance system.

(E) The greatest safety risk for passengers traveling on commercial passenger airplanes is that of a midair collision.

11. Which one of the following, if true, most strengthens the argument?

(A) Evasive action taken in response to the system's warnings poses no risk to the passengers.

(B) Commercial passenger airplanes are in greater danger of colliding with other airplanes while on the ground than they are while in flight.

(C) Commercial passenger airplanes are rarely involved in collisions while in flight.

(D) A study by ground-based air traffic controllers found that 63 percent of the warnings by the system were invalid.

(E) The collision-avoidance radar system is run by a computerized device on the plane that scans the sky and calculates the distances between planes.

GO ON TO THE NEXT PAGE.

12. The higher the average fat intake among the residents of a country, the higher the incidence of cancer in that country; the lower the average fat intake, the lower the incidence of cancer. So individuals who want to reduce their risk of cancer should reduce their fat intake.

Which one of the following, if true, most weakens the argument?

(A) The differences in average fat intake between countries are often due to the varying makeup of traditional diets.

(B) The countries with a high average fat intake tend to be among the wealthiest in the world.

(C) Cancer is a prominent cause of death in countries with a low average fat intake.

(D) The countries with high average fat intake are also the countries with the highest levels of environmental pollution.

(E) An individual resident of a country whose population has a high average fat intake may have a diet with a low fat intake.

13. A local television station is considering a plan to create a panel of child psychologists to review programs in advance of their airing and rate the level of violence. A program that portrays a high level of violence would be listed in newspapers with four guns after the title. On the other hand, if a show has little violence, one gun would appear after its listing. The station believes that this remedy would forewarn parents about the level of violence in any given program.

Which one of the following must the television station assume in order to conclude that the plan will meet its stated purpose?

(A) Parents would read and pay attention to the ratings listed in the newspapers.

(B) There would be fewer shows rated with one gun than with four guns.

(C) The rating system described in the passage is the most effective system available.

(D) The local television station has an obligation to forewarn parents of the level of violence in television shows.

(E) Television producers of programs rated as having high levels of violence would make an effort to reduce those levels.

14. The common ancestors of Australian land- and tree-dwelling kangaroos had prehensile (grasping) tails and long opposable thumbs, attributes that are well-adapted to tree-dwelling but offer kangaroos few advantages on land. It is hardly surprising, therefore, that land-dwelling kangaroos eventually lost these attributes; what is puzzling is the fact that all modern tree-dwelling kangaroos now lack them as well.

Which one of the following, if true, most helps explain the puzzling fact cited above?

(A) Modern tree-dwelling kangaroos must back down tree trunks slowly and carefully, but the common ancestors of modern tree- and land-dwelling kangaroos used their opposable thumbs to descend trees quickly headfirst.

(B) Modern tree-dwelling kangaroos are smaller than most modern land-dwelling kangaroos but larger than their common ancestors.

(C) Modern tree-dwelling kangaroos' tails cannot grasp branches, but they are somewhat longer and more flexible than those of modern land-dwelling kangaroos.

(D) Modern tree-dwelling kangaroos are descended from species of land-dwelling kangaroos that had been land-dwellers for many generations before modern tree-dwelling kangaroos started to develop.

(E) Modern tree-dwelling kangaroos have smaller and weaker hind legs than modern land-dwelling kangaroos, and they move more slowly on land than do modern land-dwelling kangaroos.

GO ON TO THE NEXT PAGE.

15. Editorialist: Society is obliged to bestow the privileges of adulthood upon its members once they are mature enough to accept the corresponding responsibilities. But science has established that physiological development is completed in most persons by age seventeen. Since this maturing process has been completed by most seventeen-year-olds, there is no reason not to grant these citizens all of the privileges of adulthood.

The editorialist's argument is most vulnerable to criticism on the ground that it

(A) assumes what it is trying to prove
(B) too hastily reaches a general conclusion on the basis of a few examples
(C) equivocates with respect to a central concept
(D) too readily accepts a claim by appeal to inappropriate authority
(E) ignores the fact that some people are mature at age sixteen

16. Every new play that runs for more than three months is either a commercial or a critical success. Last year, all new plays that were critical successes were also commercial successes. Therefore, every new play that ran for more than three months last year was a commercial success.

The pattern of reasoning in which one of the following arguments is most similar to that in the argument above?

(A) Most new restaurants require either good publicity or a good location in order to succeed. But most restaurants with a good location also receive good publicity. Hence, a restaurant that has a good location is guaranteed to succeed.
(B) Every best-selling cookbook published last year is both well written and contains beautiful photographs. The cookbook Cynthia Cleveland published last year is well written and contains beautiful photographs. Therefore, Cleveland's cookbook is a best seller.
(C) All students at the Freeman School of Cooking study either desserts or soups in their second year. This year, all Freeman students studying soups are also studying desserts. Therefore, every second-year student at Freeman is studying desserts this year.
(D) Chefs who become celebrities either open their own restaurants or write books about their craft, but not both. John Endicott is a celebrated chef who opened his own restaurant. Therefore, Endicott does not write books about his craft.
(E) Every catering service in Woodside Township will accept both residential and business catering assignments. Peggy's Fine Foods is a catering service that will not accept business catering assignments. Hence, Peggy's Fine Foods is not in Woodside Township.

17. Commissioner: I have been incorrectly criticized for having made my decision on the power plant issue prematurely. I based my decision on the report prepared by the neighborhood association and, although I have not studied it thoroughly, I am sure that the information it contains is accurate. Moreover, you may recall that when I received input from the neighborhood association on jail relocation, I agreed with its recommendation.

The commissioner's argument is LEAST vulnerable to which one of the following criticisms?

(A) It takes for granted that the association's information is not distorted by bias.
(B) It draws a conclusion about the recommendations of the association from incomplete recollections.
(C) It takes for granted that the association's report is the only direct evidence that needed to be considered.
(D) It hastily concludes that the association's report is accurate, without having studied it in detail.
(E) It takes for granted that agreeing with the association's past recommendation helps to justify agreeing with its current recommendation.

GO ON TO THE NEXT PAGE.

18. Each child in a group of young children read aloud both a short paragraph and a list of randomly ordered words from the paragraph. The more experienced readers among them made fewer pronunciation errors in whichever task they performed second, whether it was the list or the paragraph. The order in which the two tasks were performed, however, had no effect on the performance of beginning readers, who always made fewer pronunciation errors when reading the paragraph than when reading the list.

Which one of the following, if true, most helps to explain why the order in which the tasks were performed was not significant for the beginning readers?

(A) Because several words were used more than once in the paragraph but only once in the list, the list was shorter than the paragraph.

(B) In reading the paragraph, the more experienced readers were better at using context to guess at difficult words than were the beginning readers.

(C) The more experienced readers sounded out difficult words, while the beginning readers relied solely on context to guess at difficult words.

(D) Both tasks used the same words, so that the words the children read in whichever task was performed first would be recognized in the second task.

(E) The beginning readers made more pronunciation errors than the more experienced readers did in reading both the paragraph and the list.

19. Anthropologist: Violence is an extreme form of aggression, and is distinct from the self-expression sufficient for survival under normal conditions. Human beings in certain situations react to unpleasant stimuli with violence—but only because they are conditioned by their culture to react in this manner.

Each of the following can be logically inferred from the anthropologist's statements EXCEPT:

(A) Not all aggression is violent.

(B) The self-expression required for survival is generally nonaggressive.

(C) Some behaviors are influenced by the cultures in which human beings live.

(D) In normal circumstances, human beings can survive by responding nonviolently.

(E) Violent behavior is a product of one's cultural environment.

20. Martha's friend, who is very knowledgeable about edible flowers, told Martha that there are no edible daisies, at least not any that are palatable. Martha, however, reasons that since there are daisies that are a kind of chrysanthemum and since there are edible chrysanthemums that are quite palatable, what her friend told her must be incorrect.

Which one of the following has a flawed pattern of reasoning most like that in Martha's reasoning?

(A) Jeanne is a member of the city chorus, and the city chorus is renowned. So Jeanne is an excellent singer.

(B) Rolfe belongs to the library reading group, and all members of that group are avid readers. So Rolfe is an avid reader.

(C) Some of Noriko's sisters are on the debate team, and some members of the debate team are poor students. So at least one of Noriko's sisters must be a poor student.

(D) Most of Leon's friends are good swimmers, and good swimmers are quite strong. So it is likely that at least some of Leon's friends are quite strong.

(E) Many of Teresa's colleagues have written books. Most of the books they have written are on good writing. So some of Teresa's colleagues are good writers.

GO ON TO THE NEXT PAGE.

21. Attorney for Ziegler: My client continued to do consulting work between the time of his arrest for attempted murder and the start of this trial. But I contend that Ziegler was insane at the time that he fired the shot. This is the only reasonable conclusion to draw from the fact that the accusers have submitted no evidence that he was sane at the time he pulled the trigger, only that he was sane some time after he did so.

Which one of the following most accurately describes a flaw in the reasoning of Ziegler's attorney?

(A)   It presumes that being a well-educated professional is relevant to being guilty or innocent.

(B)   It concludes on the basis of evidence against Ziegler's being sane that there is a lack of evidence for Ziegler's being sane.

(C)   It fails to consider that Ziegler might have been insane when he worked as a consultant.

(D)   It presumes that whether one is sane is relevant to whether one is morally responsible for one's actions.

(E)   It fails to consider the possibility that Ziegler's being sane after the shooting is an indication that he was sane at the time of the shooting.

22. Most students are bored by history courses as they are usually taught, primarily because a large amount of time is spent teaching dates and statistics. The best way to teach history, therefore, is to spend most class time recounting the lives of historical figures and very little on dates and statistics.

Each of the following is an assumption on which the argument depends EXCEPT:

(A)   One should avoid boring one's students when teaching a history course.

(B)   It is not incompatible with the attainable goals of teaching history to spend very little class time on dates and statistics.

(C)   It is possible to recount the lives of historical figures without referring to dates and statistics.

(D)   It is compatible with the attainable goals of teaching history to spend most class time recounting the lives of historical figures.

(E)   Students are more bored by history courses as they are usually taught than they would be by courses that spend most class time recounting the lives of historical figures.

23. In a certain municipality, a judge overturned a suspect's conviction for possession of an illegal weapon. The suspect had fled upon seeing police and subsequently discarded the illegal weapon after the police gave chase. The judge reasoned as follows: the only cause for the police giving chase was the suspect's flight; by itself, flight from the police does not create a reasonable suspicion of a criminal act; evidence collected during an illegal chase is inadmissible; therefore, the evidence in this case was inadmissible.

Which one of the following principles, if valid, most helps to justify the judge's decision that the evidence was inadmissible?

(A)   Flight from the police could create a reasonable suspicion of a criminal act as long as other significant factors are involved.

(B)   People can legally flee from the police only when those people are not involved in a criminal act at the time.

(C)   Police can legally give chase to a person only when the person's actions have created a reasonable suspicion of a criminal act.

(D)   Flight from the police should not itself be considered a criminal act.

(E)   In all cases in which a person's actions have created a reasonable suspicion of a criminal act, police can legally give chase to that person.

GO ON TO THE NEXT PAGE.

Questions 24–25

Monica: The sculpture commissioned for our town plaza has been scorned by the public ever since it went up. But since the people in our town do not know very much about contemporary art, the unpopularity of the work says nothing about its artistic merit and thus gives no reason for removing it.

Hector: You may be right about what the sculpture's popularity means about its artistic merit. However, a work of art that was commissioned for a public space ought to benefit the public, and popular opinion is ultimately the only way of determining what the public feels is to its benefit. Thus, if public opinion of this sculpture is what you say, then it certainly ought to be removed.

24. Monica's and Hector's statements commit them to disagreeing about which one of the following principles?

(A) Public opinion of a work of art is an important consideration in determining the work's artistic merit.

(B) Works of art commissioned for public spaces ought at least to have sufficient artistic merit to benefit the public.

(C) The only reason for removing a work of art commissioned for a public space would be that the balance of public opinion is against the work.

(D) The sculpture cannot benefit the public by remaining in the town plaza unless the sculpture has artistic merit.

(E) In determining whether the sculpture should remain in the town plaza, the artistic merit of the sculpture should be a central consideration.

25. The argument Hector makes in responding to Monica depends on the assumption that

(A) no matter what the public's opinion is on an issue affecting the public good, that public opinion ought to be acted on, even though the opinion may not be a knowledgeable one

(B) Monica's assessment of the public's opinion of the sculpture is accurate

(C) if the sculpture had artistic merit, then even a public that was not knowledgeable about modern art would not scorn the sculpture

(D) works of art commissioned for public spaces ought not to be expected to have artistic merit

(E) if the public feels that it does not benefit from the sculpture, this shows that the public does not in fact benefit from the sculpture

S T O P

IF YOU FINISH BEFORE TIME IS CALLED, YOU MAY CHECK YOUR WORK ON THIS SECTION ONLY.
DO NOT WORK ON ANY OTHER SECTION IN THE TEST.

SECTION III

Time—35 minutes

25 Questions

Directions: The questions in this section are based on the reasoning contained in brief statements or passages. For some questions, more than one of the choices could conceivably answer the question. However, you are to choose the best answer; that is, the response that most accurately and completely answers the question. You should not make assumptions that are by commonsense standards implausible, superfluous, or incompatible with the passage. After you have chosen the best answer, blacken the corresponding space on your answer sheet.

Questions 1–2

From the tenth century until around the year 1500, there were Norse settlers living in Greenland. During that time, average yearly temperatures fell slightly worldwide, and some people claim that this temperature drop wiped out the Norse settlements by rendering Greenland too cold for human habitation. But this explanation cannot be correct, because Inuit settlers from North America, who were living in Greenland during the time the Norse settlers were there, continued to thrive long after 1500.

1. Which one of the following, if true, most helps explain why the Norse settlements in Greenland disappeared while the Inuit settlements survived?

    (A)   The drop in average yearly temperature was smaller in Greenland than it was in the world as a whole.
    (B)   The Norse settlers' diet, unlike that of the Inuit, was based primarily on livestock and crops that were unable to survive the temperature drop.
    (C)   There were settlements in North America during the fifteenth century that were most likely founded by Norse settlers who had come from Greenland.
    (D)   The Inuit and the Norse settlements were typically established in coastal areas.
    (E)   The Norse community in Norway continued to thrive long after 1500.

2. Which one of the following is a technique of reasoning used in the argument?

    (A)   denying the relevance of an analogy
    (B)   producing evidence that is inconsistent with the claim being opposed
    (C)   presenting an alternative explanation that purports to account for more of the known facts
    (D)   citing a general rule that undermines the claim being opposed
    (E)   redefining a term in a way that is favorable to the argument's conclusion

3. Even though trading in ivory has been outlawed by international agreement, some piano makers still use ivory, often obtained illegally, to cover piano keys. Recently, experts have devised a synthetic ivory that, unlike earlier ivory substitutes, has found favor with concert pianists throughout the world. But because piano makers have never been major consumers of ivory, the development of the synthetic ivory will therefore probably do little to help curb the killing of elephants, from whose tusks most natural ivory is obtained.

Which one of the following, if true, most helps to strengthen the argument?

    (A)   Most people who play the piano but are not concert pianists can nonetheless easily distinguish between the new synthetic ivory and inferior ivory substitutes.
    (B)   The new synthetic ivory can be manufactured to resemble in color and surface texture any of the various types of natural ivory that have commercial uses.
    (C)   Other natural products such as bone or tortoise shell have not proven to be acceptable substitutes for natural ivory in piano keys.
    (D)   The most common use for natural ivory is in ornamental carvings, which are prized not only for the quality of their workmanship but also for the authenticity of their materials.
    (E)   It costs significantly less to produce the new synthetic ivory than it does to produce any of the ivory substitutes that scientists had developed previously.

GO ON TO THE NEXT PAGE.

4. The government has spent heavily to clean groundwater contaminated by toxic chemical spills. Yet not even one spill site has been completely cleaned, and industrial accidents are spilling more toxic chemicals annually than are being cleaned up. More of the government's budget should be redirected to preventing spills. Since prevention is far more effective than cleanup, it makes little sense that the entire annual budget for prevention is less than the amount spent annually on one typical cleanup site.

The proposal about how the government's budget should be redirected plays which one of the following roles in the argument?

(A) It represents an unsupported speculation.
(B) It both supports another claim in the argument and is supported by others.
(C) It is the claim that the argument as a whole is structured to support.
(D) It is a presupposition on which the argument is explicitly based.
(E) It presents an objection to another proposal mentioned in the argument.

5. Consumer: I would like to have the features contained in the latest upgrade to your computer software package, but I am leery of installing the upgrade because a friend has told me he had a problem with it.

Company representative: We have distributed nearly 3,000 copies of the upgrade and we have received fewer than 100 calls saying that it has caused problems. So it is very unlikely that you will experience any problems with the upgrade.

The reasoning in the company representative's argument is most vulnerable to criticism because it fails to consider the possibility that

(A) the company will issue another upgrade that corrects the problems with the current upgrade
(B) some of the problems people have experienced with the upgrade have been quite serious
(C) a significant number of people have experienced problems with the upgrade but have not reported them
(D) the consumer will experience software problems if the upgrade is not installed
(E) some of the reported problems were a result of users failing to follow instructions

6. First legislator: Medical research is predominantly done on groups of patients that include only men. For example, the effects of coffee drinking on health are evaluated only for men, and studies are lacking on hormone treatments for older women. Government-sponsored medical research should be required to include studies of women.

Second legislator: Considerations of male/female balance such as this are inappropriate with respect to research; they have no place in science.

Which one of the following rejoinders, if true, most directly counters the second legislator's objection?

(A) Government-sponsored research is supported by all taxpayers, both male and female.
(B) Serving as a subject for medical research can provide a patient access to new treatments but also can subject the patient to risks.
(C) Government-sponsored medical research is often done in military hospitals or prisons that hold only male residents.
(D) The training of male and female scientists does not differ according to their sex.
(E) Restriction to males of the patient base on which data are collected results in inadequate science.

7. Lack of exercise produces the same or similar bodily effects as aging. In fact, the physical changes that accompany aging can often be slowed down by appropriate exercise. No drug, however, holds any promise for slowing down the changes associated with aging. Therefore, _____.

Which one of the following provides a logical completion to the passage above?

(A) taking drugs has the same effect on aging as does a lack of exercise
(B) people who do not exercise are likely to need drugs to sustain their health
(C) appropriate exercise can prevent the physical changes associated with aging
(D) people who do not exercise when they are young will gain few benefits from beginning to exercise at a later age
(E) if the physical changes of aging are to be slowed, it is more practical to rely on exercise than on drugs

GO ON TO THE NEXT PAGE.

8. Grasses and woody plants are planted on dirt embankments to keep the embankments from eroding. The embankments are mowed to keep the grasses from growing too tall; as a result, clippings pile up. These piles of clippings smother the woody plants, causing their roots, which serve to keep the embankments from eroding, to rot; they also attract rodents that burrow into the dirt and damage the woody plants' roots. Therefore, bringing in predators to eradicate the rodents will prevent erosion of the embankments.

Which one of the following is an error of reasoning in the argument?

(A) Two events that merely co-occur are treated as if one caused the other.

(B) A highly general proposal is based only on an unrepresentative set of facts.

(C) The conclusion is no more than a restatement of one of the pieces of evidence provided to support it.

(D) One possible solution to a problem is claimed to be the only possible solution to that problem.

(E) An action that would eliminate one cause of a problem is treated as if it would solve the entire problem.

9. Scientific and technological discoveries have considerable effects on the development of any society. It follows that predictions of the future condition of societies in which scientific and technological discovery is particularly frequent are particularly untrustworthy.

The argument depends on assuming which one of the following?

(A) Predictions of scientific and technological discoveries, or predictions of their effects, have harmful consequences in some societies.

(B) The development of a society requires scientific and technological discoveries.

(C) Forecasts of scientific and technological discoveries, or forecasts of their effects, are not entirely reliable.

(D) An advanced scientific and technological society frequently benefits from new discoveries.

(E) It is not as difficult to predict scientific and technological discoveries in a technologically more advanced society as it is in a technologically less advanced society.

10. Tires may be either underinflated, overinflated, or neither. We are pretty safe in assuming that underinflation or overinflation of tires harms their tread. After all, no one has been able to show that these do not harm tire tread.

Which one of the following most accurately describes a flaw in the argument's reasoning?

(A) The argument assumes what it is attempting to demonstrate.

(B) The argument overlooks that what is not in principle susceptible to proof might be false.

(C) The argument fails to specify how it is that underinflation or overinflation harms tire tread.

(D) The argument rejects the possibility that what has not been proven is nevertheless true.

(E) The argument fails to precisely define the terms "underinflation" and "overinflation."

11. Linsey has been judged to be a bad songwriter simply because her lyrics typically are disjointed and subjective. This judgment is ill founded, however, since the writings of many modern novelists typically are disjointed and subjective and yet these novelists are widely held to be good writers.

Which one of the following is an assumption on which the argument depends?

(A) Disjointed and subjective writing has a comparable effect in modern novels and in songs.

(B) Some readers do not appreciate the subtleties of the disjointed and subjective style adopted by modern novelists.

(C) Song lyrics that are disjointed and subjective have at least as much narrative structure as any other song lyrics do.

(D) A disjointed and subjective style of writing is usually more suitable for novels and song lyrics than it is for any other written works.

(E) The quality of Linsey's songs is better judged by the quality of their lyrics than by the quality of their musical form.

GO ON TO THE NEXT PAGE.

12. The Levant—the area that borders the eastern Mediterranean—was heavily populated in prehistoric times. The southern Levant was abandoned about 6,000 years ago, although the northern Levant, which shared the same climate, remained heavily populated. Recently archaeologists have hypothesized that the sudden depopulation in the southern Levant was due to an economic collapse resulting from deforestation.

If the statements above are true and the archaeologists' hypothesis is correct, which one of the following CANNOT be true?

(A) The sheep and goats herded by the peoples of the southern Levant until 6,000 years ago grazed extensively on the seedlings and saplings of indigenous tree species.

(B) Trees were used in the production of lime plaster, a building material used extensively throughout the southern Levant until 6,000 years ago.

(C) Organic remains from the northern Levant reliably indicate that tree species flourished there without interruption during the period when the southern Levant was being abandoned.

(D) Carbon dating of organic remains from the southern Levant reliably demonstrates that there were no forests present in that area prior to 6,000 years ago.

(E) Since there are few traces of either quarried stone or of mud brick in buildings excavated in the southern Levant, it is likely that the buildings built there prior to 6,000 years ago were made almost entirely of timber.

13. Using rational argument in advertisements does not persuade people to buy the products being advertised. Therefore, advertisers who replace rational argument with nonrational appeals to emotion in advertisements will persuade people to buy the products being advertised.

Which one of the following contains flawed reasoning most similar to the flawed reasoning in the argument above?

(A) People who ask others for favors are refused. Therefore, anyone who has not had the experience of being refused has never asked for a favor.

(B) In the past, people who have tried to solve their problems by discussing them have often failed. Therefore, in the future, people who try to solve their problems by discussing them will often fail.

(C) Using a computer has not improved students' writing skills. Thus, students should not try to improve their writing skills by using a computer.

(D) A person who does not have positive letters of reference cannot get a good job. Therefore, the better the letters of reference a person has, the better the job that person will get.

(E) People never learn to program a computer by reading poorly written directions. Therefore, if people read well-written directions, they will learn to program a computer.

GO ON TO THE NEXT PAGE.

14. A commercial insect trap consists of a small box containing pesticide mixed with glucose, a sweet substance known to attract insect pests. Yet in households where this type of trap has been used regularly for the past several years, recently installed traps are far less effective in eliminating insect pests than were traps of that type installed several years ago. Research scientists have hypothesized that traps in those households decreased in effectiveness because successive generations of the pests developed a resistance to the pesticide in the traps.

Which one of the following, if true, most seriously undermines the hypothesis?

(A) In households where the traps have been used regularly, the proportion of insect pests that have a natural aversion to eating glucose has increased with each successive generation.

(B) Even when only a few individuals out of an entire generation of insects survive the effects of a pesticide, the offspring of those individuals are usually resistant to that pesticide.

(C) After eating glucose mixed with the pesticide, insects that live in households that do not use the trap tend to die in greater numbers than do insects from households where the traps have been used regularly.

(D) After the manufacturer of the traps increased the concentration of the pesticide used in the traps, the traps were no more effective in eliminating household insect pests than were the original traps.

(E) The kind of glucose used to bait the traps is one of several different kinds of glucose that occur naturally.

15. A person's dietary consumption of cholesterol and fat is one of the most important factors determining the level of cholesterol in the person's blood (serum cholesterol). Serum cholesterol levels rise proportionally to increased cholesterol and fat consumption until that consumption reaches a threshold, but once consumption of these substances exceeds that threshold, serum cholesterol levels rise only gradually, even with dramatic increases in consumption. The threshold is one fourth the consumption level of cholesterol and fat in today's average North American diet.

The statements above, if true, most strongly support which one of the following?

(A) The threshold can be lowered by lowering the dietary consumption of cholesterol and fat.

(B) People who consume an average North American diet cannot increase their consumption of cholesterol and fat without dramatically increasing their serum cholesterol levels.

(C) People who consume half as much cholesterol and fat as in the average North American diet will not necessarily have half the average serum cholesterol level.

(D) Serum cholesterol levels cannot be affected by nondietary modifications in behavior, such as exercising more or smoking less.

(E) People who consume less cholesterol and fat than the threshold cannot reduce their serum cholesterol levels.

16. The recently negotiated North American Free Trade Agreement among Canada, Mexico, and the United States is misnamed, because it would not result in truly free trade. Adam Smith, the economist who first articulated the principles of free trade, held that any obstacle placed in the way of the free movement of goods, investment, or labor would defeat free trade. So since under the agreement workers would be restricted by national boundaries from seeking the best conditions they could find, the resulting obstruction of the flow of trade would, from a free-trade perspective, be harmful.

The argument proceeds by

(A) ruling out alternatives
(B) using a term in two different senses
(C) citing a nonrepresentative instance
(D) appealing to a relevant authority
(E) responding to a different issue from the one posed

GO ON TO THE NEXT PAGE.

17. Parents who wish to provide a strong foundation for the musical ability of their children should provide them with a good musical education. Since formal instruction is often a part of a good musical education, parents who wish to provide this strong foundation need to ensure that their children receive formal instruction.

The reasoning is most vulnerable to criticism on the grounds that it fails to consider that

(A) parents might not be the only source of a child's musical education

(B) some children might not be interested in receiving a strong foundation for their musical ability

(C) there are many examples of people with formal instruction whose musical ability is poor

(D) formal instruction might not always be a part of a good musical education

(E) some children might become good musicians even if they have not had good musical educations

18. A stingray without parasites is healthier than it would be if it had parasites. Nevertheless, the lack of parasites in stingrays is an indicator that the ecosystem in which the stingrays live is under environmental stress such as pollution.

Which one of the following, if true, most helps to reconcile the discrepancy indicated above?

(A) During part of their life cycles, the parasites of stingrays require as hosts shrimp or oysters, which are environmentally vulnerable organisms.

(B) A stingray is a free-ranging predator that feeds on smaller organisms but has few predators itself.

(C) A parasite drains part of the vitality of its host by drawing nourishment from the host.

(D) An ecosystem can be considered stressed if only a few species of very simple organisms can live there.

(E) Since the life of parasites depends on that of their host, they need to live without killing their host or else to reproduce and infect other individuals before their own host dies.

19. Over the past 20 years, skiing has become a relatively safe sport due to improvements in ski equipment. There has been a 50 percent drop in the number of ski injuries over the last 20 years. Clearly, however, there have not been decreases in the number of injuries in all categories, as statistical data readily show, for although broken legs and ankle injuries have decreased by an astounding 90 percent, knee injuries now represent 16 percent of all ski injuries, up significantly from the 11 percent of 20 years ago.

The reasoning in the argument is flawed because the argument does which one of the following?

(A) It fails to allow for there being ski injuries other than broken legs, ankle injuries, and knee injuries.

(B) It infers disparate effects from the same single cause.

(C) It ignores the possibility that the number of skiers has increased over the past 20 years.

(D) It assumes that an increase in the proportion of knee injuries rules out a decrease in the number of knee injuries.

(E) It proceeds as though there could be a greater decrease in injuries in each category of injury than there is in injuries overall.

GO ON TO THE NEXT PAGE.

20. Only poetry cannot be translated well, and therefore it is poets who preserve languages, for we would not bother to learn a language if we could get everything written in it from translation. So, since we cannot witness the beauty of poetry except in the language in which it is composed, we have motivation to learn the language.

The information above provides the LEAST support for which one of the following?

(A) All nonpoetic literature can be translated well.
(B) One purpose of writing poetry is to preserve the language in which it is written.
(C) Some translations do not capture all that was expressed in the original language.
(D) The beauty of poetry is not immediately accessible to people who do not understand the language in which the poetry was written.
(E) Perfect translation from one language to another is sometimes impossible.

21. The companies that are the prime purchasers of computer software will not buy a software package if the costs of training staff to use it are high, and we know that it is expensive to teach people a software package that demands the memorization of unfamiliar commands. As a result, to be successful, commercial computer software cannot require users to memorize unfamiliar commands.

The conclusion above follows logically if which one of the following is assumed?

(A) If most prime purchasers of computer software buy a software product, that product will be successful.
(B) Commercial computer software that does not require users to memorize unfamiliar commands is no more expensive than software that does.
(C) Commercial computer software will not be successful unless prime purchasers buy it.
(D) If the initial cost of computer software is high, but the cost of training users is low, prime purchasers will still buy that software.
(E) The more difficult it is to learn how to use a piece of software, the more expensive it is to teach a person to use that software.

Questions 22–23

Whenever she considers voting in an election to select one candidate for a position and there is at least one issue important to her, Kay uses the following principle in choosing which course of action to take: it is acceptable for me to vote for a candidate whose opinions differ from mine on at least one issue important to me whenever I disagree with each of the other candidates on even more such issues; it is otherwise unacceptable to vote for that candidate. In the upcoming mayoral election, the three candidates are Legrand, Medina, and Norton. There is only one issue important to Kay, and only Medina shares her opinion on that issue.

22. If the statements in the passage are true, which one of the following must also be true about Kay's course of action in any election to select one candidate for a position?

(A) If there are no issues important to her, it is unacceptable for her to vote for any candidate in the election.
(B) If she agrees with each of the candidates on most of the issues important to her, it is unacceptable for her to vote for any candidate in the election.
(C) If she agrees with a particular candidate on only one issue important to her, it is unacceptable for her to vote for that candidate.
(D) If she disagrees with each of the candidates on exactly three issues important to her, it is unacceptable for her to vote for any candidate in the election.
(E) If there are more issues important to her on which she disagrees with a particular candidate than there are such issues on which she agrees with that candidate, it is unacceptable for her to vote for that candidate.

23. According to the principle stated in the passage, in the upcoming mayoral election

(A) it is acceptable for Kay to vote for either Medina or Legrand, but it is unacceptable for her to vote for Norton
(B) the only unacceptable courses of action are for Kay to vote for Norton and for her to vote for Legrand
(C) it is unacceptable for Kay to vote for any of the candidates
(D) the only unacceptable course of action is for Kay to vote for Medina
(E) it is acceptable for Kay to vote for any of the candidates

GO ON TO THE NEXT PAGE.

24. Over the last 25 years, the average price paid for a new car has steadily increased in relation to average individual income. This increase indicates that individuals who buy new cars today spend, on average, a larger amount relative to their incomes buying a car than their counterparts did 25 years ago.

Which one of the following, if true, most weakens the argument?

(A) There has been a significant increase over the last 25 years in the proportion of individuals in households with more than one wage earner.

(B) The number of used cars sold annually is the same as it was 25 years ago.

(C) Allowing for inflation, average individual income has significantly declined over the last 25 years.

(D) During the last 25 years, annual new-car sales and the population have both increased, but new-car sales have increased by a greater percentage.

(E) Sales to individuals make up a smaller proportion of all new-car sales than they did 25 years ago.

25. Credit card companies justify charging cardholders additional fees for late payments by asserting the principle that those who expose other individuals, companies, or institutions to financial risk should pay for that risk, and by pointing out that late-paying cardholders present a greater risk of default than other cardholders. Without late fees, the companies argue, they would have to spread the cost of the risk over all cardholders.

The principle invoked by the credit card companies would, if established, be most usefully invoked in which one of the following arguments?

(A) School authorities should use student activity funds to pay for student-caused damages to school property since, even though only a few students cause any significant damage, authorities cannot in most instances determine which students caused the damage.

(B) Insurance companies should demand higher insurance rates of drivers of sports cars than of other drivers, since sports car drivers are more likely to cause accidents and thus are more likely to require the companies to pay out money in claims.

(C) Libraries should charge high fines for overdue books, since if they did not do so some people would keep books out indefinitely, risking inconvenience to other library users who might want to use the books.

(D) Cities should impose high fines for littering. The risk of being caught littering is quite low, so the fine for those who are caught must be correspondingly high in order to deter people from littering.

(E) Municipalities should use tax money to pay for the maintenance of municipal roads, since if individuals paid for only those roads they used, some important roads in remote areas would be inadequately maintained.

S T O P

IF YOU FINISH BEFORE TIME IS CALLED, YOU MAY CHECK YOUR WORK ON THIS SECTION ONLY.
DO NOT WORK ON ANY OTHER SECTION IN THE TEST.

SECTION IV

Time—35 minutes

27 Questions

Directions: Each passage in this section is followed by a group of questions to be answered on the basis of what is stated or implied in the passage. For some of the questions, more than one of the choices could conceivably answer the question. However, you are to choose the best answer; that is, the response that most accurately and completely answers the question, and blacken the corresponding space on your answer sheet.

Opponents of compulsory national service claim that such a program is not in keeping with the liberal principles upon which Western democracies are founded. This reasoning is reminiscent of the argument
(5) that a tax on one's income is undemocratic because it violates one's right to property. Such conceptions of the liberal state fail to take into account the intricate character of the social agreement that undergirds our liberties. It is only in the context of a community that
(10) the notion of individual rights has any application; individual rights are meant to define the limits of people's actions with respect to other people. Implicit in such a context is the concept of shared sacrifice. Were no taxes paid, there could be no law enforcement,
(15) and the enforcement of law is of benefit to everyone in society. Thus, each of us must bear a share of the burden to ensure that the community is protected.

The responsibility to defend one's nation against outside aggression is surely no less than the
(20) responsibility to help pay for law enforcement within the nation. Therefore, the state is certainly within its rights to compel citizens to perform national service when it is needed for the benefit of society.

It might be objected that the cases of taxation and
(25) national service are not analogous: While taxation must be coerced, the military is quite able to find recruits without resorting to conscription. Furthermore, proponents of national service do not limit its scope to only those duties absolutely necessary to the defense of
(30) the nation. Therefore, it may be contended, compulsory national service oversteps the acceptable boundaries of governmental interference in the lives of its citizens.

By responding thus, the opponent of national service has already allowed that it is a right of
(35) government to demand service when it is needed. But what is the true scope of the term "need"? If it is granted, say, that present tax policies are legitimate intrusions on the right to property, then it must also be granted that need involves more than just what is
(40) necessary for a sound national defense. Even the most conservative of politicians admits that tax money is rightly spent on programs that, while not necessary for the survival of the state, are nevertheless of great benefit to society. Can the opponent of national service
(45) truly claim that activities of the military such as quelling civil disorders, rebuilding dams and bridges, or assisting the victims of natural disasters—all extraneous to the defense of society against outside aggression—do not provide a similar benefit to the
(50) nation? Upon reflection, opponents of national service

must concede that such a broadened conception of what is necessary is in keeping with the ideas of shared sacrifice and community benefit that are essential to the functioning of a liberal democratic state.

1. Which one of the following most accurately describes the author's attitude toward the relationship between citizenship and individual rights in a democracy?

   (A) confidence that individual rights are citizens' most important guarantees of personal freedom
   (B) satisfaction at how individual rights have protected citizens from unwarranted government intrusion
   (C) alarm that so many citizens use individual rights as an excuse to take advantage of one another
   (D) concern that individual rights represent citizens' only defense against government interference
   (E) dissatisfaction at how some citizens cite individual rights as a way of avoiding certain obligations to their government

GO ON TO THE NEXT PAGE.

2. The author indicates that all politicians agree about the

(A) legitimacy of funding certain programs that serve the national good
(B) use of the military to prevent domestic disorders
(C) similarity of conscription and compulsory taxation
(D) importance of broadening the definition of necessity
(E) compatibility of compulsion with democratic principles

3. Which one of the following most accurately characterizes what the author means by the term "social agreement" (line 8)?

(A) an agreement among members of a community that the scope of their individual liberties is limited somewhat by their obligations to one another
(B) an agreement among members of a community that they will not act in ways that infringe upon each other's pursuit of individual liberty
(C) an agreement among members of a community that they will petition the government for redress when government actions limit their rights
(D) an agreement between citizens and their government detailing which government actions do or do not infringe upon citizens' personal freedoms
(E) an agreement between citizens and their government stating that the government has the right to suspend individual liberties whenever it sees fit

4. According to the author, national service and taxation are analogous in the sense that both

(A) do not require that citizens be compelled to help bring them about
(B) are at odds with the notion of individual rights in a democracy
(C) require different degrees of sacrifice from different citizens
(D) allow the government to overstep its boundaries and interfere in the lives of citizens
(E) serve ends beyond those related to the basic survival of the state

5. Based on the information in the passage, which one of the following would most likely be found objectionable by those who oppose compulsory national service?

(A) the use of tax revenues to prevent the theft of national secrets by foreign agents
(B) the use of tax revenues to fund relief efforts for victims of natural disasters in other nations
(C) the use of tax revenues to support the upkeep of the nation's standing army
(D) the use of tax revenues to fund programs for the maintenance of domestic dams and bridges
(E) the use of tax revenues to aid citizens who are victims of natural disasters

GO ON TO THE NEXT PAGE.

James Porter (1905–1970) was the first scholar to identify the African influence on visual art in the Americas, and much of what is known about the cultural legacy that African-American artists inherited

(5) from their African forebears has come to us by way of his work. Porter, a painter and art historian, began by studying African-American crafts of the eighteenth and nineteenth centuries. This research revealed that many of the household items created by African-American

(10) men and women—walking sticks, jugs, and textiles— displayed characteristics that linked them iconographically to artifacts of West Africa. Porter then went on to establish clearly the range of the cultural territory inherited by later African-American

(15) artists.

An example of this aspect of Porter's research occurs in his essay "Robert S. Duncanson, Midwestern Romantic-Realist." The work of Duncanson, a nineteenth-century painter of the Hudson River school,

(20) like that of his predecessor in the movement, Joshua Johnston, was commonly thought to have been created by a Euro-American artist. Porter proved definitively that both Duncanson and Johnston were of African ancestry. Porter published this finding and thousands of

(25) others in a comprehensive volume tracing the history of African-American art. At the time of its first printing in 1943, only two other books devoted exclusively to the accomplishments of African-American artists existed. Both of these books were written by Alain

(30) LeRoy Locke, a professor at the university where Porter also taught. While these earlier studies by Locke are interesting for being the first to survey the field, neither addressed the critical issue of African precursors; Porter's book addressed this issue,

(35) painstakingly integrating the history of African-American art into the larger history of art in the Americas without separating it from those qualities that gave it its unique ties to African artisanship. Porter may have been especially attuned to these ties because

(40) of his conscious effort to maintain them in his own paintings, many of which combine the style of the genre portrait with evidence of an extensive knowledge of the cultural history of various African peoples.

In his later years, Porter wrote additional chapters

(45) for later editions of his book, constantly revising and correcting his findings, some of which had been based of necessity on fragmentary evidence. Among his later achievements were his definitive reckoning of the birth year of the painter Patrick Reason, long a point of

(50) scholarly uncertainty, and his identification of an unmarked grave in San Francisco as that of the sculptor Edmonia Lewis. At his death, Porter left extensive notes for an unfinished project aimed at exploring the influence of African art on the art of the Western world

(55) generally, a body of research whose riches scholars still have not exhausted.

6. Which one of the following most accurately states the main idea of the passage?

(A) Because the connections between African-American art and other art in the Americas had been established by earlier scholars, Porter's work focused on showing African-American art's connections to African artisanship.

(B) In addition to showing the connections between African-American art and African artisanship, Porter's most important achievement was illustrating the links between African-American art and other art in the Americas.

(C) Despite the fact that his last book remains unfinished, Porter's work was the first to devote its attention exclusively to the accomplishments of African-American artists.

(D) Although showing the connections between African-American art and African artisanship, Porter's work concentrated primarily on placing African-American art in the context of Western art in general.

(E) While not the first body of scholarship to treat the subject of African-American art, Porter's work was the first to show the connections between African-American art and African artisanship.

7. The discussion of Locke's books is intended primarily to

(A) argue that Porter's book depended upon Locke's pioneering scholarship

(B) highlight an important way in which Porter's work differed from previous work in his field

(C) suggest an explanation for why Porter's book was little known outside academic circles

(D) support the claim that Porter was not the first to notice African influences in African-American art

(E) argue that Locke's example was a major influence on Porter's decision to publish his findings

8. The passage states which one of the following about the 1943 edition of Porter's book on African-American art?

(A) It received little scholarly attention at first.

(B) It was revised and improved upon in later editions.

(C) It took issue with several of Locke's conclusions.

(D) It is considered the definitive version of Porter's work.

(E) It explored the influence of African art on Western art in general.

GO ON TO THE NEXT PAGE.

9. Given the information in the passage, Porter's identification of the ancestry of Duncanson and Johnston provides conclusive evidence for which one of the following statements?

(A) Some of the characteristics defining the Hudson River school are iconographically linked to West African artisanship.

(B) Some of the works of Duncanson and Johnston are not in the style of the Hudson River school.

(C) Some of the work of Euro-American painters displays similarities to African-American crafts of the eighteenth and nineteenth centuries.

(D) Some of the works of the Hudson River school were done by African-American painters.

(E) Some of the works of Duncanson and Johnston were influenced by West African artifacts.

10. Which one of the following can most reasonably be inferred from the passage about the study that Porter left unfinished at his death?

(A) If completed, it would have contradicted some of the conclusions contained in his earlier book.

(B) If completed, it would have amended some of the conclusions contained in his earlier book.

(C) If completed, it would have brought up to date the comprehensive history of African-American art begun in his earlier book.

(D) If completed, it would have expanded upon the project of his earlier book by broadening the scope of inquiry found in the earlier book.

(E) If completed, it would have supported some of the theories put forth by Porter's contemporaries since the publication of his earlier book.

11. Which one of the following hypothetical observations is most closely analogous to the discoveries Porter made about African-American crafts of the eighteenth and nineteenth centuries?

(A) Contemporary Haitian social customs have a unique character dependent on but different from both their African and French origins.

(B) Popular music in the United States, some of which is based on African musical traditions, often influences music being composed on the African continent.

(C) Many novels written in Canada by Chinese immigrants exhibit narrative themes very similar to those found in Chinese folktales.

(D) Extensive Indian immigration to England has made traditional Indian foods nearly as popular there as the traditional English foods that had been popular there before Indian immigration.

(E) Some Mexican muralists of the early twentieth century consciously imitated the art of native peoples as a response to the Spanish influences that had predominated in Mexican art.

12. The passage most strongly supports which one of the following inferences about Porter's own paintings?

(A) They often contained figures or images derived from the work of African artisans.

(B) They fueled his interest in pursuing a career in art history.

(C) They were used in Porter's book to show the extent of African influence on African-American art.

(D) They were a deliberate attempt to prove his theories about art history.

(E) They were done after all of his academic work had been completed.

13. Based on the passage, which one of the following, if true, would have been most relevant to the project Porter was working on at the time of his death?

(A) African-American crafts of the eighteenth and nineteenth centuries have certain resemblances to European folk crafts of earlier periods.

(B) The paintings of some twentieth-century European artists prefigured certain stylistic developments in North African graphic art.

(C) The designs of many of the quilts made by African-American women in the nineteenth century reflect designs of European trade goods.

(D) After the movement of large numbers of African Americans to cities, the African influences in the work of many African-American painters increased.

(E) Several portraits by certain twentieth-century European painters were modeled after examples of Central African ceremonial masks.

GO ON TO THE NEXT PAGE.

Between June 1987 and May 1988, the bodies of at least 740 bottlenose dolphins out of a total coastal population of 3,000 to 5,000 washed ashore on the Atlantic coast of the United States. Since some of the
(5) dead animals never washed ashore, the overall disaster was presumably worse; perhaps 50 percent of the population died. A dolphin die-off of this character and magnitude had never before been observed; furthermore, the dolphins exhibited a startling range of
(10) symptoms. The research team that examined the die-off noted the presence of both skin lesions and internal lesions in the liver, lung, pancreas, and heart, which suggested a massive opportunistic bacterial infection of already weakened animals.
(15) Tissues from the stricken dolphins were analyzed for a variety of toxins. Brevetoxin, a toxin produced by the blooming of the alga *Ptychodiscus brevis*, was present in eight out of seventeen dolphins tested. Tests for synthetic pollutants revealed that polychlorinated
(20) biphenyls (PCBs) were present in almost all animals tested.
The research team concluded that brevetoxin poisoning was the most likely cause of the illnesses that killed the dolphins. Although *P. brevis* is
(25) ordinarily not found along the Atlantic coast, an unusual bloom of this organism—such blooms are called "red tides" because of the reddish color imparted by the blooming algae—did occur in the middle of the affected coastline in October 1987. These researchers
(30) believe the toxin accumulated in the tissue of fish and then was ingested by dolphins that preyed on them. The emaciated appearance of many dolphins indicated that they were metabolizing their blubber reserves, thereby reducing their buoyancy and insulation (and
(35) adding to overall stress) as well as releasing stores of previously accumulated synthetic pollutants, such as PCBs, which further exacerbated their condition. The combined impact made the dolphins vulnerable to opportunistic bacterial infection, the ultimate cause of
(40) death.
For several reasons, however, this explanation is not entirely plausible. First, bottlenose dolphins and *P. brevis* red tides are both common in the Gulf of Mexico, yet no dolphin die-off of a similar magnitude
(45) has been noted there. Second, dolphins began dying in June, hundreds of miles north of and some months earlier than the October red tide bloom. Finally, the specific effects of brevetoxin on dolphins are unknown, whereas PCB poisoning is known to impair functioning
(50) of the immune system and liver and to cause skin lesions; all of these problems were observed in the diseased animals. An alternative hypothesis, which accounts for these facts, is that a sudden influx of pollutants, perhaps from offshore dumping, triggered a
(55) cascade of disorders in animals whose systems were already heavily laden with pollutants. Although brevetoxin may have been a contributing factor, the event that actually precipitated the die-off was a sharp increase in the dolphins' exposure to synthetic
(60) pollutants.

14. The passage is primarily concerned with assessing

(A) the effects of a devastating bacterial infection in Atlantic coast bottlenose dolphins
(B) the process by which illnesses in Atlantic coast bottlenose dolphins were correctly diagnosed
(C) the weaknesses in the research methodology used to explore the dolphin die-off
(D) possible alternative explanations for the massive dolphin die-off
(E) relative effects of various marine pollutants on dolphin mortality

15. Which one of the following is mentioned in the passage as evidence for the explanation of the dolphin die-off offered in the final paragraph?

(A) the release of stored brevetoxins from the dolphins' blubber reserves
(B) the date on which offshore dumping was known to have occurred nearby
(C) the presence of dumping sites for PCBs in the area
(D) the synthetic pollutants that were present in the fish eaten by the dolphins
(E) the effects of PCBs on liver function in dolphins

16. Which one of the following is most analogous to the approach taken by the author of the passage with regard to the research described in the third paragraph?

(A) A physics teacher accepts the data from a student's experiment but questions the student's conclusions.
(B) An astronomer provides additional observations to support another astronomer's theory.
(C) A cook revises a traditional recipe by substituting modern ingredients for those used in the original.
(D) A doctor prescribes medication for a patient whose illness was misdiagnosed by another doctor.
(E) A microbiologist sets out to replicate the experiment that yielded a classic theory of cell structure.

GO ON TO THE NEXT PAGE.

17. Which one of the following most accurately describes the organization of the last paragraph?

(A) One explanation is criticized and a different explanation is proposed.

(B) An argument is advanced and then refuted by means of an opposing argument.

(C) Objections against a hypothesis are advanced, the hypothesis is explained more fully, and then the objections are rejected.

(D) New evidence in favor of a theory is described, and then the theory is reaffirmed.

(E) Discrepancies between two explanations are noted, and a third explanation is proposed.

18. It can be inferred from the passage that the author would most probably agree with which one of the following statements about brevetoxin?

(A) It may have been responsible for the dolphins' skin lesions but could not have contributed to the bacterial infection.

(B) It forms more easily when both *P. brevis* and synthetic pollutants are present in the environment simultaneously.

(C) It damages liver function and immune system responses in bottlenose dolphins but may not have triggered this particular dolphin die-off.

(D) It is unlikely to be among the factors that contributed to the dolphin die-off.

(E) It is unlikely to have caused the die-off because it was not present in the dolphins' environment when the die-off began.

19. The explanation for the dolphin die-off given by the research team most strongly supports which one of the following?

(A) The biological mechanism by which brevetoxin affects dolphins is probably different from that by which it affects other marine animals.

(B) When *P. brevis* blooms in an area where it does not usually exist, it is more toxic than it is in its usual habitat.

(C) Opportunistic bacterial infection is usually associated with brevetoxin poisoning in bottlenose dolphins.

(D) The dolphins' emaciated state was probably a symptom of PCB poisoning rather than of brevetoxin poisoning.

(E) When a dolphin metabolizes its blubber, the PCBs released may be more dangerous to the dolphin than they were when stored in the blubber.

20. The author refers to dolphins in the Gulf of Mexico in the last paragraph in order to

(A) refute the assertion that dolphins tend not to inhabit areas where *P. brevis* is common

(B) compare the effects of synthetic pollutants on these dolphins and on Atlantic coast dolphins

(C) cast doubt on the belief that *P. brevis* contributes substantially to dolphin die-offs

(D) illustrate the fact that dolphins in relatively pollution-free waters are healthier than dolphins in polluted waters

(E) provide evidence for the argument that *P. brevis* was probably responsible for the dolphins' deaths

21. Which one of the following factors is explicitly cited as contributing to the dolphins' deaths in both theories discussed in the passage?

(A) the dolphins' diet

(B) the presence of *P. brevis* in the Gulf of Mexico

(C) the wide variety of toxins released by the red tide bloom of October 1987

(D) the presence of synthetic pollutants in the dolphins' bodies

(E) the bacterial infection caused by a generalized failure of the dolphins' immune systems

GO ON TO THE NEXT PAGE.

In England before 1660, a husband controlled his wife's property. In the late seventeenth and eighteenth centuries, with the shift from land-based to commercial wealth, marriage began to incorporate certain features (5) of a contract. Historians have traditionally argued that this trend represented a gain for women, one that reflects changing views about democracy and property following the English Restoration in 1660. Susan Staves contests this view; she argues that whatever (10) gains marriage contracts may briefly have represented for women were undermined by judicial decisions about women's contractual rights.

Sifting through the tangled details of court cases, Staves demonstrates that, despite surface changes, a (15) rhetoric of equality, and occasional decisions supporting women's financial power, definitions of men's and women's property remained inconsistent—generally to women's detriment. For example, dower lands (property inherited by wives after their husbands' (20) deaths) could not be sold, but "curtesy" property (inherited by husbands from their wives) could be sold. Furthermore, comparatively new concepts that developed in conjunction with the marriage contract, such as jointure, pin money, and separate maintenance, (25) were compromised by peculiar rules. For instance, if a woman spent her pin money (money paid by the husband according to the marriage contract for the wife's personal items) on possessions other than clothes she could not sell them; in effect they belonged (30) to her husband. In addition, a wife could sue for pin money only up to a year in arrears—which rendered a suit impractical. Similarly, separate maintenance allowances (stated sums of money for the wife's support if husband and wife agreed to live apart) were (35) complicated by the fact that if a couple tried to agree in a marriage contract on an amount, they were admitting that a supposedly indissoluble bond could be dissolved, an assumption courts could not recognize. Eighteenth-century historians underplayed these inconsistencies, (40) calling them "little contrarieties" that would soon vanish. Staves shows, however, that as judges gained power over decisions on marriage contracts, they tended to fall back on pre-1660 assumptions about property.
(45) Staves' work on women's property has general implications for other studies about women in eighteenth-century England. Staves revises her previous claim that separate maintenance allowances proved the weakening of patriarchy; she now finds that (50) an oversimplification. She also challenges the contention by historians Jeanne and Lawrence Stone that in the late eighteenth century wealthy men married widows less often than before because couples began marrying for love rather than for financial reasons. (55) Staves does not completely undermine their contention, but she does counter their assumption that widows had more money than never-married women. She points out that jointure property (a widow's lifetime use of an amount of money specified in the marriage contract) (60) was often lost on remarriage.

22. Which one of the following best expresses the main idea of the passage?

(A) As notions of property and democracy changed in late seventeenth- and eighteenth-century England, marriage settlements began to incorporate contractual features designed to protect women's property rights.

(B) Traditional historians have incorrectly identified the contractual features that were incorporated into marriage contracts in late seventeenth- and eighteenth-century England.

(C) The incorporation of contractual features into marriage settlements in late seventeenth- and eighteenth-century England did not represent a significant gain for women.

(D) An examination of late seventeenth- and eighteenth-century English court cases indicates that most marriage settlements did not incorporate contractual features designed to protect women's property rights.

(E) Before marriage settlements incorporated contractual features protecting women's property rights, women were unable to gain any financial power in England.

23. Which one of the following best describes the function of the last paragraph in the context of the passage as a whole?

(A) It suggests that Staves' recent work has caused significant revision of theories about the rights of women in eighteenth-century England.

(B) It discusses research that may qualify Staves' work on women's property in eighteenth-century England.

(C) It provides further support for Staves' argument by describing more recent research on women's property in eighteenth-century England.

(D) It asserts that Staves' recent work has provided support for two other hypotheses developed by historians of eighteenth-century England.

(E) It suggests the implications Staves' recent research has for other theories about women in eighteenth-century England.

GO ON TO THE NEXT PAGE.

24. The primary purpose of the passage is to

   (A) compare two explanations for the same phenomenon
   (B) summarize research that refutes an argument
   (C) resolve a long-standing controversy
   (D) suggest that a recent hypothesis should be reevaluated
   (E) provide support for a traditional theory

25. According to the passage, Staves' research has which one of the following effects on the Stones' contention about marriage in late eighteenth-century England?

   (A) Staves' research undermines one of the Stones' assumptions but does not effectively invalidate their contention.
   (B) Staves' research refutes the Stones' contention by providing additional data overlooked by the Stones.
   (C) Staves' research shows that the Stones' contention cannot be correct, and that a number of their assumptions are mistaken.
   (D) Staves' research indicates that the Stones' contention is incorrect because it is based on contradictory data.
   (E) Staves' research qualifies the Stones' contention by indicating that it is based on accurate but incomplete data.

26. According to the passage, Staves indicates that which one of the following was true of judicial decisions on contractual rights?

   (A) Judges frequently misunderstood and misapplied laws regarding married women's property.
   (B) Judges were aware of inconsistencies in laws concerning women's contractual rights but claimed that such inconsistencies would soon vanish.
   (C) Judges' decisions about marriage contracts tended to reflect assumptions about property that had been common before 1660.
   (D) Judges had little influence on the development and application of laws concerning married women's property.
   (E) Judges recognized the patriarchal assumptions underlying laws concerning married women's property and tried to interpret the laws in ways that would protect women.

27. The passage suggests that the historians mentioned in line 5 would be most likely to agree with which one of the following statements?

   (A) The shift from land-based to commercial wealth changed views about property but did not significantly benefit married women until the late eighteenth century.
   (B) Despite initial judicial resistance to women's contractual rights, marriage contracts represented a significant gain for married women.
   (C) Although marriage contracts incorporated a series of surface changes and a rhetoric of equality, they did not ultimately benefit married women.
   (D) Changing views about property and democracy in post-Restoration England had an effect on property laws that was beneficial to women.
   (E) Although contractual rights protecting women's property represented a small gain for married women, most laws continued to be more beneficial for men than for women.

S T O P

IF YOU FINISH BEFORE TIME IS CALLED, YOU MAY CHECK YOUR WORK ON THIS SECTION ONLY.
DO NOT WORK ON ANY OTHER SECTION IN THE TEST.

LSAT® Writing Sample Topic

Directions: The scenario presented below describes two choices, either one of which can be supported on the basis of the information given. Your essay should consider both choices and argue for one over the other, based on the two specified criteria and the facts provided. There is no "right" or "wrong" choice: a reasonable argument can be made for either.

The city of Williamsville is considering two proposals to develop a large vacant lot on the northern end of its downtown area. Write an argument in support of one proposal over the other based on the following criteria:

- The city wants to reduce its unemployment rate, which is very high.
- The city wants to improve the appearance of its downtown area, which has deteriorated substantially over the past two decades.

The owner of the Owls, a major league baseball team, has offered to move the team to Williamsville, which currently has no major league baseball team, if the city agrees to build a stadium for the team. The stadium would give the downtown area a major attraction and could, some city officials believe, promote enough interest in downtown to reverse the trend of deterioration. However, in order to pay for the new stadium, the city would need to borrow so much money that it would have to eliminate a job creation program and would be unable to restart the program during the fifteen years it would take to repay the loan. Construction of the stadium would create jobs in the short term, but once the stadium was constructed, it would employ only about 100 local residents.

The Acme Tire Company proposes to build a factory in Williamsville. The factory would employ 2,000 people, only a few of whom would be transferred from other Acme locations. Acme has a reputation as a dependable employer; it has never closed a factory and has a policy of laying off workers only as a last resort. Acme factories in other cities produce unpleasant odors and large quantities of air pollution. However, in order to help beautify downtown, Acme has offered to build a small park next to the factory.

Directions:

1. Use the Answer Key on the next page to check your answers.

2. Use the Scoring Worksheet below to compute your raw score.

3. Use the Score Conversion Chart to convert your raw score into the 120-180 scale.

Scoring Worksheet

1. Enter the number of questions you answered correctly in each section.

Number Correct

SECTION I. . . . . . _____
SECTION II . . . . . _____
SECTION III. . . . . _____
SECTION IV. . . . . _____

2. Enter the sum here: _____
   This is your Raw Score.

Conversion Chart

For Converting Raw Score to the 120-180 LSAT Scaled Score
LSAT Form 8LSS39

Reported Score	Raw Score Lowest	Raw Score Highest
180	98	101
179	97	97
178	96	96
177	95	95
176	94	94
175	93	93
174	92	92
173	91	91
172	90	90
171	89	89
170	87	88
169	86	86
168	85	85
167	83	84
166	82	82
165	80	81
164	79	79
163	77	78
162	76	76
161	74	75
160	72	73
159	71	71
158	69	70
157	68	68
156	66	67
155	64	65
154	63	63
153	61	62
152	59	60
151	58	58
150	56	57
149	54	55
148	53	53
147	51	52
146	49	50
145	48	48
144	46	47
143	44	45
142	43	43
141	41	42
140	40	40
139	38	39
138	36	37
137	35	35
136	33	34
135	32	32
134	31	31
133	29	30
132	28	28
131	26	27
130	25	25
129	24	24
128	23	23
127	21	22
126	20	20
125	19	19
124	18	18
123	17	17
122	16	16
121	15	15
120	0	14

SECTION I

1.	C	8.	C	15.	B	22.	A
2.	B	9.	E	16.	B	23.	A
3.	A	10.	A	17.	E	24.	E
4.	D	11.	C	18.	C		
5.	E	12.	A	19.	B		
6.	A	13.	D	20.	D		
7.	D	14.	D	21.	A		

SECTION II

1.	B	8.	A	15.	C	22.	C
2.	B	9.	B	16.	C	23.	C
3.	A	10.	C	17.	B	24.	E
4.	C	11.	A	18.	C	25.	E
5.	A	12.	D	19.	B		
6.	D	13.	A	20.	C		
7.	C	14.	D	21.	E		

SECTION III

1.	B	8.	E	15.	C	22.	D
2.	B	9.	C	16.	D	23.	B
3.	D	10.	D	17.	D	24.	E
4.	C	11.	A	18.	A	25.	B
5.	C	12.	D	19.	D		
6.	E	13.	E	20.	B		
7.	E	14.	A	21.	C		

SECTION IV

1.	E	8.	B	15.	E	22.	C
2.	A	9.	D	16.	A	23.	E
3.	A	10.	D	17.	A	24.	B
4.	E	11.	C	18.	E	25.	A
5.	B	12.	A	19.	E	26.	C
6.	E	13.	E	20.	C	27.	D
7.	B	14.	D	21.	D		

The Official LSAT PrepTest

27

- December 1998
- Form 8LSS38

The sample test that follows consists of four sections corresponding to the four scored sections of the December 1998 LSAT.

SECTION I
Time—35 minutes

26 Questions

<u>Directions:</u> The questions in this section are based on the reasoning contained in brief statements or passages. For some questions, more than one of the choices could conceivably answer the question. However, you are to choose the <u>best</u> answer; that is, the response that most accurately and completely answers the question. You should not make assumptions that are by commonsense standards implausible, superfluous, or incompatible with the passage. After you have chosen the best answer, blacken the corresponding space on your answer sheet.

1. Powell: Private waste-removal companies spend 60 percent of what public waste-removal companies spend per customer, yet give their customers at least as good service. Private waste-removal companies, therefore, work more efficiently.

   Freeman: Your conclusion is unwarranted. Different customers have different waste-removal needs. Since private companies, unlike their public counterparts, can select which customers to serve, they choose to exclude the potential customers whom they judge to be the most costly to serve.

   The issue in dispute between Powell and Freeman is the

   (A)   accuracy of the figure of 60 percent with regard to the difference in service costs between private and public waste-removal companies
   (B)   reason private waste-removal companies are able to offer service comparable to that offered by public ones while spending less money per customer
   (C)   ability of private versus public waste-removal companies to select which customers to serve
   (D)   likelihood of the local authorities' turning public waste-removal companies into private ones so that the companies can operate with lower service costs than they now incur
   (E)   relationship between the needs of a waste-removal customer and the amount of money it takes to serve that customer

2. Although 90 percent of the population believes itself to be well informed about health care, only 20 percent knows enough about DNA to understand a news story about DNA. So apparently at least 80 percent of the population does not know enough about medical concepts to make well-informed personal medical choices or to make good public policy decisions about health care.

   The argument's reasoning is questionable because the argument fails to demonstrate that

   (A)   those people who can understand news stories about DNA are able to make well-informed personal medical choices
   (B)   more than 20 percent of the population needs to be well informed about health care for good public policy decisions about health care to be made
   (C)   one's being able to make well-informed personal medical choices ensures that one makes good public policy decisions about health care
   (D)   an understanding of DNA is essential to making well-informed personal medical choices or to making good public policy decisions about health care
   (E)   since 90 percent of the population believes itself to be well informed about health care, at least 70 percent of the population is mistaken in that belief

GO ON TO THE NEXT PAGE.

Questions 3–4

In Yasukawa's month-long study of blackbirds, the percentage of smaller birds that survived the duration of the study exceeded the percentage of larger birds that survived. However, Yasukawa's conclusion that size is a determinant of a blackbird's chances of survival over a month-long period is probably mistaken, since smaller blackbirds are generally younger than larger ones.

3. The statements above, if true, support which one of the following inferences?

(A) Among the blackbirds that survived the month-long study, there was no relation between size and age.

(B) Larger blackbirds of a given age are actually more likely to survive over a one-month period than are smaller blackbirds of the same age.

(C) Among blackbirds of the same size, a difference in age probably does not indicate a difference in chances of survival over a one-month period.

(D) Among blackbirds of the same age, a difference in size may not indicate a difference in chances of survival over a month-long period.

(E) With a larger sample of blackbirds, the percentage of smaller birds that survive a one-month period would be the same as the percentage of larger birds that survive.

4. Which one of the following, if true, indicates that the criticism of Yasukawa's research is based on a misunderstanding of it?

(A) Yasukawa compared the survival chances of two different species of blackbirds, a larger and a smaller species, rather than of different sizes of birds within one species.

(B) Yasukawa examined blackbirds in their natural habitat rather than in captivity.

(C) Yasukawa did not compare the survival chances of blackbirds with those of other kinds of birds.

(D) Yasukawa noted that the larger blackbirds had more success in fights than did the smaller blackbirds.

(E) Yasukawa noted that the larger blackbirds tended to have more firmly established social hierarchies than did the smaller blackbirds.

5. During the 1980s, Japanese collectors were very active in the market for European art, especially as purchasers of nineteenth-century Impressionist paintings. This striking pattern surely reflects a specific preference on the part of many Japanese collectors for certain aesthetic attributes they found in nineteenth-century Impressionist paintings.

Which one of the following, if true, most strongly supports the explanation above?

(A) Impressionist paintings first became popular among art collectors in Europe at the beginning of the twentieth century.

(B) During the 1980s, the Japanese economy underwent a sustained expansion that was unprecedented in the country's recent history.

(C) Several nineteenth-century Impressionist painters adopted certain techniques and visual effects found in Japanese prints that are highly esteemed in Japan.

(D) During the 1960s and 1970s, the prices of nineteenth-century Impressionist paintings often exceeded the prices of paintings by older European masters.

(E) During the 1980s, collectors from Japan and around the world purchased many paintings and prints by well-known twentieth-century Japanese artists.

GO ON TO THE NEXT PAGE.

6. Frankie: If jelly makers were given incentives to make a certain percentage of their jellies from cloudberries, income for cloudberry gatherers would increase.

   Anna: That plan would fail. Cacao, like cloudberries, was once harvested from wild plants. When chocolate became popular in Europe, the cacao gatherers could not supply enough to meet the increased demand, and farmers began to grow large quantities of it at low cost. Now all cacao used in commercial chocolate production is grown on farms. Likewise, if the demand for cloudberries increases, domesticated berries grown on farms will completely supplant berries gathered in the wild.

   Anna's argument proceeds by

   (A) giving a reason why a proposed course of action would be beneficial to all those affected by it
   (B) reinterpreting evidence presented in support of a proposal as a reason to reject the proposal
   (C) projecting the result of following a proposal in a given situation by comparing that situation with a past situation
   (D) proposing a general theory as a way of explaining a specific market situation
   (E) contending that the uses for one product are similar to the uses for another product

7. Because of the recent recession in Country A, most magazines published there have experienced decreases in advertising revenue, so much so that the survival of the most widely read magazines is in grave doubt. At the same time, however, more people in Country A are reading more magazines than ever before, and the number of financially successful magazines in Country A is greater than ever.

   Which one of the following, if true, most helps to resolve the apparent discrepancy in the information above?

   (A) Most magazines reduce the amount they charge for advertisements during a recession.
   (B) The audience for a successful television show far exceeds the readership of even the most widely read magazine.
   (C) Advertising is the main source of revenue only for the most widely read magazines; other magazines rely on circulation for their revenue.
   (D) Because of the recession, people in Country A have cut back on magazine subscriptions and are reading borrowed magazines.
   (E) More of the new general interest magazines that were launched this year in Country A have survived than survived in previous years.

8. The gray squirrel, introduced into local woodlands ten years ago, threatens the indigenous population of an endangered owl species, because the squirrels' habitual stripping of tree bark destroys the trees in which the owls nest. Some local officials have advocated setting out poison for the gray squirrels. The officials argue that this measure, while eliminating the squirrels, would pose no threat to the owl population, since the poison would be placed in containers accessible only to squirrels and other rodents.

   Which one of the following, if true, most calls into question the officials' argument?

   (A) One of the species whose members are likely to eat the poison is the red squirrel, a species on which owls do not prey.
   (B) The owls whose nesting sites are currently being destroyed by the gray squirrels feed primarily on rodents.
   (C) No indigenous population of any other bird species apart from the endangered owls is threatened by the gray squirrels.
   (D) The owls that are threatened build their nests in the tops of trees, but the gray squirrels strip away bark from the trunks.
   (E) The officials' plan entails adding the poison to food sources that are usually eaten by rodents but not by other animals.

GO ON TO THE NEXT PAGE.

Sales manager: Last year the total number of meals sold in our company's restaurants was much higher than it was the year before. Obviously consumers find our meals desirable.

Accountant: If you look at individual restaurants, however, you find that the number of meals sold actually decreased substantially at every one of our restaurants that was in operation both last year and the year before. The desirability of our meals to consumers has clearly decreased, given that this group of restaurants—the only ones for which we have sales figures that permit a comparison between last year and the year before—demonstrates a trend toward fewer sales.

9. If the sales figures cited by the accountant and the sales manager are both accurate, which one of the following must be true?

(A)   The company opened at least one new restaurant in the last two years.

(B)   The company's meals are less competitive than they once were.

(C)   The quality of the company's meals has not improved over the past two years.

(D)   The prices of the company's meals have changed over the past two years.

(E)   The market share captured by the company's restaurants fell last year.

10. Which one of the following, if true, most seriously calls into question the accountant's argument?

(A)   The company's restaurants last year dropped from their menus most of the new dishes that had been introduced the year before.

(B)   Prior to last year there was an overall downward trend in the company's sales.

(C)   Those of the company's restaurants that did increase their sales last year did not offer large discounts on prices to attract customers.

(D)   Sales of the company's most expensive meal contributed little to the overall two-year sales increase.

(E)   Most of the company's restaurants that were in operation throughout both last year and the year before are located in areas where residents experienced a severe overall decline in income last year.

11. A local chemical plant produces pesticides that can cause sterility in small mammals such as otters. Soon after the plant began operating, the incidence of sterility among the otters that swim in a nearby river increased dramatically. Therefore, pesticides are definitely contaminating the river.

Which one of the following arguments contains a flaw in reasoning that is similar to one in the argument above?

(A)   The bacteria that cause tetanus live in the digestive tract of horses. Tetanus is a highly infectious disease. Consequently it must be that horses contract tetanus more frequently than do most other animals.

(B)   A diet low in calcium can cause a drop in egg production in poultry. When chickens on a local farm were let out in the spring to forage for food, their egg production dropped noticeably. So the food found and eaten by the chickens is undeniably low in calcium.

(C)   Animals that are undernourished are very susceptible to infection. Animals in the largest metropolitan zoos are not undernourished, so they surely must not be very susceptible to disease.

(D)   Apes are defined by having, among other characteristics, opposable thumbs and no external tail. Recently, fossil remains of a previously unknown animal were found. Because this animal had opposable thumbs, it must have been an ape.

(E)   The only animal that could have produced a track similar to this one is a bear. But there are no bears in this area of the country, so this animal track is a fake.

GO ON TO THE NEXT PAGE.

12. Clothes made from natural fibers such as cotton, unlike clothes made from artificial fibers such as polyester, often shrink when washed at high temperatures. The reason for this shrinkage is that natural fibers are tightly curled in their original state. Since the manufacture of cloth requires straight fibers, natural fibers are artificially straightened prior to being made into cloth. High temperatures cause all fibers in cloth to return to their original states.

Which one of the following is most strongly supported by the information above?

(A) Washing clothes made from natural fibers at low temperatures causes the fibers to straighten slightly.
(B) High temperatures have no effect on the straightness of fibers in clothes made from a blend of natural and artificial fibers.
(C) Clothes made from natural fibers stretch more easily than do clothes made from artificial fibers.
(D) If natural fibers that have been straightened and used for cloth are curled up again by high temperatures, they cannot be straightened again.
(E) Artificial fibers are straight in their original state.

13. Problems caused by the leaching of pollutants from dumps and landfills are worst in countries with an annual per capita economic output of $4,000 to $5,000, and less severe for considerably poorer and considerably richer countries. This is so because pollution problems increase during the early stages of a country's industrial development but then diminish as increasing industrial development generates adequate resources to tackle such problems. Therefore, problems caused by such leaching in Country X, where the annual per capita economic output is now $5,000, should begin to diminish in the next few years.

Which one of the following is an assumption on which the argument depends?

(A) Within the next few years, Country X will impose a system of fines for illegal waste disposal by its industrial companies.
(B) Countries surrounding Country X will reduce the amount of pollution that their factories release into the air and water.
(C) Industrial development in Country X will increase in the next few years.
(D) Country X will begin the process of industrialization in the next few years.
(E) No other country with a similar amount of industrial development has pollution problems that are as severe as those in Country X.

14. Critic: Many popular psychological theories are poor theories in that they are inelegant and do not help to dispel the mystery that surrounds our psyche. However, this is not really important. The theories produce the right results: therapeutically, they tend to have greater success than their more scientific rivals.

The statement about the relative therapeutic success of many popular psychological theories plays which one of the following roles in the critic's argument?

(A) It is used to disprove evidence against these theories.
(B) It is used to override some considerations against these theories.
(C) It is used to suggest that popular psychological theories are actually better scientific explanations than are their rivals.
(D) It is used to illustrate what the critic takes to be the most important aspect of scientific theories.
(E) It is used to suggest that the popular theories may not be as devoid of explanatory power as one may be led to believe.

15. Tony: Few anarchists have ever performed violent actions. These few are vastly outnumbered by the violent adherents of other political ideologies. Therefore, the special association in the public mind between anarchism and political violence is unwarranted.

Keisha: Anarchists have always been few in number, whereas other ideologies have often spawned mass movements. Therefore, the proportion of anarchists who are violent is possibly greater than the proportion of adherents of other ideologies who are violent.

Keisha responds to Tony's argument in which one of the following ways?

(A) She shows that Tony's conclusion is questionable because Tony bases it on a comparison that inappropriately involves absolute numbers rather than proportions.
(B) She attempts to undermine Tony's conclusion by introducing plausible evidence that is incompatible with the evidence Tony offers in support of that conclusion.
(C) She questions the accuracy of the claims on which Tony bases his conclusion.
(D) She presents evidence that the two groups Tony has compared have no significant qualities in common.
(E) She indicates that Tony has adopted questionable criteria for including certain people in the groups he is comparing.

16. Recent research shows that sound change (pronunciation shift) in a language is not gradual. New sounds often emerge suddenly. This confounds the classical account of sound change, whose central tenet is gradualness. Since this classical account must be discarded, sound-change theory in general must also be.

Which one of the following, if assumed, does most to justify the argument's conclusion?

(A) The data on which the classical account of sound-change theory was based are now known to be inaccurate.
(B) The emergence of new sounds appears to be random.
(C) The meeting of linguistically disparate cultures can affect the sounds of their languages in unpredictable ways.
(D) All theories of sound change rely heavily on the classical theory.
(E) For most languages, historical records of their earlier stages are scarce or nonexistent.

17. The stable functioning of a society depends upon the relatively long-term stability of the goals of its citizens. This is clear from the fact that unless the majority of individuals have a predictable and enduring set of aspirations, it will be impossible for a legislature to craft laws that will augment the satisfaction of the citizenry, and it should be obvious that a society is stable only if its laws tend to increase the happiness of its citizens.

The claim that a society is stable only if its laws tend to increase the happiness of its citizens plays which one of the following roles in the argument?

(A) It is the conclusion of the argument.
(B) It helps to support the conclusion of the argument.
(C) It is a claim that must be refuted if the conclusion is to be established.
(D) It is a consequence of the argument.
(E) It is used to illustrate the general principle that the argument presupposes.

18. Astronauts who experience weightlessness frequently get motion sickness. The astronauts see their own motion relative to passing objects, but while the astronauts are weightless their inner ears indicate that their bodies are not moving. The astronauts' experience is best explained by the hypothesis that conflicting information received by the brain about the body's motion causes motion sickness.

Which one of the following, if true, provides the strongest additional support for the hypothesis above?

(A) During rough voyages ship passengers in cabins providing a view of the water are less likely to get motion sickness than are passengers in cabins providing no view.
(B) Many people who are experienced airplane passengers occasionally get motion sickness.
(C) Some automobile passengers whose inner ears indicate that they are moving and who have a clear view of the objects they are passing get motion sickness.
(D) People who have aisle seats in trains or airplanes are as likely to get motion sickness as are people who have window seats.
(E) Some astronauts do not get motion sickness even after being in orbit for several days.

19. Pollen and other allergens can cause cells in the nose to release histamine, a chemical that inflames nasal tissue and causes runny nose, congestion, and sneezing. Antihistamines minimize these allergy symptoms by blocking the action of histamine. In addition, antihistamines have other effects, including drowsiness. However, histamine plays no role in the processes by which colds produce their symptoms.

If the statements above are true, which one of the following must also be true?

(A) Pollen and other allergens do not cause colds.
(B) Colds are more difficult to treat than allergies.
(C) Antihistamines, when taken alone, are ineffective against congestion caused by colds.
(D) The sleeplessness that sometimes accompanies allergies can be effectively treated with antihistamines.
(E) Any effect antihistamines may have in reducing cold symptoms does not result from blocking the action of histamine.

GO ON TO THE NEXT PAGE.

20. A poem is any work of art that exploits some of the musical characteristics of language, such as meter, rhythm, euphony, and rhyme. A novel, though it may be a work of art in language, does not usually exploit the musical characteristics of language. A symphony, though it may be a work of art that exploits the musical characteristics of sounds, rarely involves language. A limerick, though it may exploit some musical characteristics of language, is not, strictly speaking, art.

The statements above, if true, most strongly support which one of the following?

(A) If a creation is neither a poem, nor a novel, nor a symphony, then it is not a work of art.
(B) An example of so-called blank verse, which does not rhyme, is not really a poem.
(C) If a novel exploits meter and rhyme while standing as a work of art, then it is both a novel and a poem.
(D) Limericks constitute a nonartistic type of poetry.
(E) If a symphony does not exploit the musical characteristics of sound, then it is not a work of art.

21. In order to pressure the government of Country S to become less repressive, some legislators in Country R want to ban all exports from R to S. Companies in R that manufacture telecommunication equipment such as telephones and fax machines have argued that exports of their products should be exempted from the ban, on the grounds that it is impossible for a country to remain repressive when telecommunication equipment is widely available to the population of that country.

Which one of the following is an assumption on which the argument given by the manufacturers depends?

(A) The government of S has recently increased the amount of telecommunication equipment it allows to be imported into the country.
(B) The telecommunication equipment that would be imported into S if the exemption were to be granted would not be available solely to top government officials in S.
(C) A majority of the members of R's legislature do not favor exempting telecommunication equipment from the ban on exports to Country S.
(D) Of all exports that could be sent to Country S, telecommunication equipment would be the most effective in helping citizens of S oppose that country's repressive government.
(E) Without pressure from Country R, the government of S would be able to continue repressing its citizens indefinitely.

22. Some people believe that saying that an organization is hierarchical says everything there is to say about how that organization operates. All bureaucratically controlled organizations are hierarchical. Yet the Public Works Department, although bureaucratically controlled, operates quite differently than most other bureaucratically controlled organizations operate.

If the statements above are true, which one of the following must also be true on the basis of them?

(A) The Public Works Department operates more like a nonbureaucratically controlled organization than like a bureaucratically controlled organization.
(B) Any organization that is hierarchical is bureaucratically controlled.
(C) From the fact that a given organization is hierarchical nothing can reliably be concluded about how that organization operates.
(D) Not all hierarchical organizations operate in the same way.
(E) Whether or not an organization is bureaucratically controlled has nothing to do with how that organization operates.

23. Research indicates that 90 percent of extreme insomniacs consume large amounts of coffee. Since Tom drinks a lot of coffee, it is quite likely that he is an extreme insomniac.

Which one of the following most accurately describes a flaw in the argument's reasoning?

(A) It fails to acknowledge the possibility that Tom is among the 10 percent of people who drink large amounts of coffee who are not extreme insomniacs.
(B) It fails to consider the possible contribution to extreme insomnia of other causes of insomnia besides coffee.
(C) It relies on evidence that does not indicate the frequency of extreme insomnia among people who drink large amounts of coffee.
(D) It draws an inference about one specific individual from evidence that describes only the characteristics of a class of individuals.
(E) It presumes without warrant that drinking coffee always causes insomnia.

GO ON TO THE NEXT PAGE.

24. Folklorist: Oral traditions are often preferable to written ones. Exclusive dependence on speech improves the memory; literate populations grow sluggish in recall, running to written sources whenever they need information. Because writing has no limits, it can proliferate to the point where writer and reader both become confused. Since oral traditions are dependent on memory, what is useless and irrelevant is quickly eradicated.

Which one of the following principles, if valid, most helps to justify the folklorist's argumentation?

(A)   Accuracy in communication breeds mental self-reliance.
(B)   Literate populations need to make efforts to communicate efficiently.
(C)   Tradition is of greater value than accumulation of knowledge.
(D)   Economy of expression is to be preferred over verbosity.
(E)   Ideas that cannot be discussed clearly should not be discussed at all.

25. When interviewing job candidates, personnel managers not only evaluate a candidate's work experience and educational background but also inquire about hobbies. Personnel managers try to justify these inquiries by noting that the enthusiasm someone shows for a hobby may well carry over to enthusiasm for a job. But such enthusiasm may also indicate that the candidate is less concerned with work than with play. Therefore personnel managers should not inquire about a candidate's hobbies.

The argument is flawed because it overlooks each of the following possibilities EXCEPT:

(A)   A candidate's involvement in particular hobbies may indicate a capacity to make long-term commitments.
(B)   Candidates who have no hobbies may pretend that they have one when asked in an interview.
(C)   Inquiries about a hobby may put candidates at ease, eliciting more honest responses about important questions.
(D)   Having certain kinds of hobbies may indicate that a candidate has good organizational skills.
(E)   Personnel managers may make better choices among candidates if they are not restricted from asking particular types of questions.

26. Researcher: The vast majority of a person's dreams bear no resemblance whatsoever to real events that follow the dreams. Thus, it is unreasonable to believe that one has extrasensory perception solely on the basis of having had several vivid dreams about events that happen after the dreams.

Which one of the following arguments is most similar in its reasoning to the argument above?

(A)   It is unreasonable to believe that a new drug cures heart disease when it is tested, albeit successfully, on only a few patients. Most new drugs require testing on large numbers of patients before they are considered effective.
(B)   Many people who undergo surgery for ulcers show no long-term improvement. So it is unreasonable to believe that surgery for ulcers is effective, even though ulcer surgery benefits many people as well.
(C)   Even though many cancer patients experience remissions without drinking herbal tea, it is unreasonable to believe that not drinking herbal tea causes such remissions. Several factors are known to be relevant to cancer remission.
(D)   A number of people who die prematurely take aspirin. But it is unreasonable to conclude that aspirin is dangerous. Most people who take aspirin do not die prematurely.
(E)   A significant number of children raised near power lines develop cancer. So it is unreasonable to deny a connection between living near power lines and developing cancer, even though many people living near power lines never develop cancer.

S T O P

IF YOU FINISH BEFORE TIME IS CALLED, YOU MAY CHECK YOUR WORK ON THIS SECTION ONLY.
DO NOT WORK ON ANY OTHER SECTION IN THE TEST.

SECTION II

Time—35 minutes

24 Questions

Directions: Each group of questions in this section is based on a set of conditions. In answering some of the questions, it may be useful to draw a rough diagram. Choose the response that most accurately and completely answers each question and blacken the corresponding space on your answer sheet.

Questions 1–6

During a period of seven consecutive days—from day 1 through day 7—seven investors—Fennelly, Gupta, Hall, Jones, Knight, López, and Moss—will each view a building site exactly once. Each day exactly one investor will view the site. The investors must view the site in accordance with the following conditions:

   Fennelly views the site on day 3 or else day 5.
   López views the site on neither day 4 nor day 6.
   If Jones views the site on day 1, Hall views the site on day 2.
   If Knight views the site on day 4, López views the site on day 5.
   Gupta views the site on the day after the day on which Hall views the site.

1. Which one of the following could be the order in which the investors view the site, from day 1 through day 7 ?

    (A)   Hall, Gupta, Fennelly, Moss, Knight, López, Jones
    (B)   Hall, Gupta, López, Fennelly, Moss, Knight, Jones
    (C)   López, Gupta, Hall, Moss, Fennelly, Jones, Knight
    (D)   López, Jones, Fennelly, Knight, Hall, Gupta, Moss
    (E)   López, Jones, Knight, Moss, Fennelly, Hall, Gupta

2. If Jones views the site on day 1, which one of the following investors must view the site on day 4 ?

    (A)   Fennelly
    (B)   Gupta
    (C)   Knight
    (D)   López
    (E)   Moss

3. If Knight views the site on day 4 and Moss views the site on some day after the day on which Jones views the site, which one of the following must be true?

    (A)   Jones views the site on day 1.
    (B)   Jones views the site on day 2.
    (C)   Jones views the site on day 6.
    (D)   Moss views the site on day 2.
    (E)   Moss views the site on day 6.

4. If Hall views the site on day 2, which one of the following is a complete and accurate list of investors any one of whom could be the investor who views the site on day 4 ?

    (A)   Knight
    (B)   Moss
    (C)   Jones, Moss
    (D)   Knight, Moss
    (E)   Jones, Knight, Moss

5. If Hall views the site on the day after the day Knight views the site and if Fennelly views the site on the day after the day López views the site, then Jones must view the site on day

    (A)   1
    (B)   2
    (C)   3
    (D)   4
    (E)   5

6. If the day on which Gupta views the site and the day on which López views the site both come at some time before the day on which Fennelly views the site, which one of the following is an investor who could view the site on day 3 ?

    (A)   Fennelly
    (B)   Gupta
    (C)   Jones
    (D)   Knight
    (E)   Moss

GO ON TO THE NEXT PAGE.

Questions 7–12

A zoo's reptile house has a straight row of exactly five consecutive habitats—numbered 1 through 5 from left to right—for housing exactly seven reptiles—four snakes and three lizards. Five of the reptiles are female and two are male. The reptiles must be housed as follows:

No habitat houses more than two reptiles.

No habitat houses both a snake and a lizard.

No female snake is housed in a habitat that is immediately next to a habitat housing a male lizard.

7. Which one of the following could be a complete and accurate matching of habitats to reptiles?

(A) 1: two female snakes; 2: one male snake; 3: one female lizard; 4: one male snake, one female lizard; 5: one female lizard

(B) 1: empty; 2: two female snakes; 3: two female lizards; 4: two male snakes; 5: one female lizard

(C) 1: one female snake, one male snake; 2: two female snakes; 3: one male lizard; 4: one female lizard; 5: one female lizard

(D) 1: two male snakes; 2: empty; 3: one female lizard; 4: one female lizard; 5: two female snakes, one female lizard

(E) 1: one female snake, one male snake; 2: one female snake, one male snake; 3: one male lizard; 4: one female lizard; 5: one female lizard

8. If habitat 2 contains at least one female snake and habitat 4 contains two male lizards, then which one of the following could be true?

(A) Habitat 3 contains two reptiles.
(B) Habitat 5 contains two reptiles.
(C) Habitat 1 contains a female lizard.
(D) Habitat 2 contains a female lizard.
(E) Habitat 5 contains a female lizard.

9. Which one of the following must be true?

(A) At least one female reptile is alone in a habitat.
(B) At least one male reptile is alone in a habitat.
(C) At least one lizard is alone in a habitat.
(D) At least one lizard is male.
(E) At least one snake is male.

10. Which one of the following CANNOT be the complete housing arrangement for habitats 1 and 2?

(A) 1: one female snake, one male snake; 2: one male snake

(B) 1: one male lizard; 2: one male snake

(C) 1: two female lizards; 2: one female snake

(D) 1: one male snake; 2: empty

(E) 1: empty; 2: one female lizard

11. If habitat 3 is empty, and no snake is housed in a habitat that is immediately next to a habitat containing a snake, then which one of the following could be false?

(A) All snakes are housed in even-numbered habitats.
(B) None of the lizards is male.
(C) No snake is alone in a habitat.
(D) No lizard is housed in a habitat that is immediately next to a habitat containing a lizard.
(E) Exactly one habitat contains exactly one reptile.

12. If all the snakes are female and each of the lizards has a habitat to itself, then which one of the following habitats CANNOT contain any snakes?

(A) habitat 1
(B) habitat 2
(C) habitat 3
(D) habitat 4
(E) habitat 5

GO ON TO THE NEXT PAGE.

Questions 13–19

Exactly seven film buffs—Ginnie, Ian, Lianna, Marcos, Reveka, Viktor, and Yow—attend a showing of classic films. Three films are shown, one directed by Fellini, one by Hitchcock, and one by Kurosawa. Each of the film buffs sees exactly one of the three films. The films are shown only once, one film at a time. The following restrictions must apply:

Exactly twice as many of the film buffs see the Hitchcock film as see the Fellini film.
Ginnie and Reveka do not see the same film as each other.
Ian and Marcos do not see the same film as each other.
Viktor and Yow see the same film as each other.
Lianna sees the Hitchcock film.
Ginnie sees either the Fellini film or the Kurosawa film.

13. Which one of the following could be an accurate matching of film buffs to films?

   (A)   Ginnie: the Hitchcock film; Ian: the Kurosawa film; Marcos: the Hitchcock film
   (B)   Ginnie: the Kurosawa film; Ian: the Fellini film; Viktor: the Fellini film
   (C)   Ian: the Hitchcock film; Reveka: the Kurosawa film; Viktor: the Fellini film
   (D)   Marcos: the Kurosawa film; Reveka: the Kurosawa film; Viktor: the Kurosawa film
   (E)   Marcos: the Hitchcock film; Reveka: the Hitchcock film; Yow: the Hitchcock film

14. Each of the following must be false EXCEPT:

   (A)   Reveka is the only film buff to see the Fellini film.
   (B)   Reveka is the only film buff to see the Hitchcock film.
   (C)   Yow is the only film buff to see the Kurosawa film.
   (D)   Exactly two film buffs see the Kurosawa film.
   (E)   Exactly three film buffs see the Hitchcock film.

15. Which one of the following could be a complete and accurate list of the film buffs who do NOT see the Hitchcock film?

   (A)   Ginnie, Marcos
   (B)   Ginnie, Reveka
   (C)   Ginnie, Ian, Reveka
   (D)   Ginnie, Marcos, Yow
   (E)   Ginnie, Viktor, Yow

16. If exactly one film buff sees the Kurosawa film, then which one of the following must be true?

   (A)   Viktor sees the Hitchcock film.
   (B)   Ginnie sees the Fellini film.
   (C)   Marcos sees the Fellini film.
   (D)   Ian sees the Fellini film.
   (E)   Reveka sees the Hitchcock film.

17. Which one of the following must be true?

   (A)   Ginnie sees a different film than Ian does.
   (B)   Ian sees a different film than Lianna does.
   (C)   Ian sees a different film than Viktor does.
   (D)   Ian, Lianna, and Viktor do not all see the same film.
   (E)   Ginnie, Lianna, and Marcos do not all see the same film.

18. If Viktor sees the same film as Ginnie does, then which one of the following could be true?

   (A)   Ginnie sees the Fellini film.
   (B)   Ian sees the Hitchcock film.
   (C)   Reveka sees the Kurosawa film.
   (D)   Viktor sees the Hitchcock film.
   (E)   Yow sees the Fellini film.

19. Each of the following could be a complete and accurate list of the film buffs who see the Fellini film EXCEPT:

   (A)   Ginnie, Ian
   (B)   Ginnie, Marcos
   (C)   Ian, Reveka
   (D)   Marcos, Reveka
   (E)   Viktor, Yow

GO ON TO THE NEXT PAGE.

Questions 20–24

Six cars are to be arranged in a straight line, and will be numbered 1 through 6, in order, from the front of the line to the back of the line. Each car is exactly one color: two are green, two are orange, and two are purple. The arrangement of cars is restricted as follows:

No car can be the same color as any car next to it in line.
Either car 5 or car 6 must be purple.
Car 1 cannot be orange.
Car 4 cannot be green.

20. The cars in which one of the following pairs CANNOT be the same color as each other?

   (A)   cars 1 and 4
   (B)   cars 1 and 5
   (C)   cars 3 and 5
   (D)   cars 3 and 6
   (E)   cars 4 and 6

21. If car 2 is the same color as car 4, then which one of the following statements must be true?

   (A)   Car 1 is purple.
   (B)   Car 2 is orange.
   (C)   Car 3 is green.
   (D)   Car 5 is purple.
   (E)   Car 6 is green.

22. If car 4 is purple, which one of the following must be true?

   (A)   Car 1 is orange.
   (B)   Car 2 is green.
   (C)   Car 3 is orange.
   (D)   Car 5 is green.
   (E)   Car 6 is purple.

23. Which one of the following statements must be false?

   (A)   Car 2 is green.
   (B)   Car 4 is orange.
   (C)   Car 5 is purple.
   (D)   Car 6 is orange.
   (E)   Car 6 is green.

24. If one of the two orange cars is replaced by a third green car, and if the arrangement of cars in line must conform to the same restrictions as before, then which one of the following is a complete and accurate list of the cars each of which must be green?

   (A)   car 1
   (B)   car 3
   (C)   car 5
   (D)   car 1, car 3
   (E)   car 1, car 3, car 5

S T O P

IF YOU FINISH BEFORE TIME IS CALLED, YOU MAY CHECK YOUR WORK ON THIS SECTION ONLY.
DO NOT WORK ON ANY OTHER SECTION IN THE TEST.

SECTION III

Time—35 minutes

26 Questions

<u>Directions:</u> Each passage in this section is followed by a group of questions to be answered on the basis of what is <u>stated</u> or <u>implied</u> in the passage. For some of the questions, more than one of the choices could conceivably answer the question. However, you are to choose the <u>best</u> answer; that is, the response that most accurately and completely answers the question, and blacken the corresponding space on your answer sheet.

The expansion of mass media has led to an explosion in news coverage of criminal activities to the point where it has become virtually impossible to find citizens who are unaware of the details of crimes
(5) committed in their communities. Since it is generally believed that people who know the facts of a case are more likely than those who do not to hold an opinion about the case, and that it is more desirable to empanel jurors who do not need to set aside personal prejudices
(10) in order to render a verdict, empaneling impartial juries has proven to be a daunting task in North American courts, particularly in trials involving issues or people of public interest.

Judges rely on several techniques to minimize
(15) partiality in the courtroom, including moving trials to new venues and giving specific instructions to juries. While many judges are convinced that these techniques work, many critics have concluded that they are ineffective. Change of venue, the critics argue, cannot
(20) shield potential jurors from pretrial publicity in widely reported cases. Nor, they claim, can judges' instructions to juries to ignore information learned outside the courtroom be relied upon; one critic characterizes such instruction as requiring of jurors
(25) "mental contortions which are beyond anyone's power to execute."

The remedy for partiality most favored by judges is voir dire, the questioning of potential jurors to determine whether they can be impartial. But critics
(30) charge that this method, too, is unreliable for a number of reasons. Some potential jurors, they argue, do not speak out during voir dire (French for "to speak the truth") because they are afraid to admit their prejudices, while others confess untruthfully to having
(35) prejudices as a way of avoiding jury duty. Moreover, some potential jurors underestimate their own knowledge, claiming ignorance of a case when they have read about it in newspapers or discussed it with friends. Finally, the critics argue, judges sometimes
(40) phrase questions in ways that indicate a desired response, and potential jurors simply answer accordingly.

These criticisms have been taken seriously enough by some countries that rely on juries, such as Canada
(45) and Great Britain, that they have abandoned voir dire except in unusual circumstances. But merely eliminating existing judicial remedies like voir dire does not really provide a solution to the problem of impartiality. It merely recognizes that the mass media
(50) have made total ignorance of criminal cases among

jurors a virtual impossibility. But if a jury is to be truly impartial, it must be composed of informed citizens representative of the community's collective experience; today, this experience includes exposure to
(55) mass media. Impartiality does not reside in the mind of any one juror; it instead results from a process of deliberation among the many members of a panel of informed, curious, and even opinionated people.

1. Which one of the following most accurately expresses the main point of the passage?

(A) Due to the expansion of mass media, traditional methods for ensuring the impartiality of jurors are flawed and must be eliminated so that other methods can be implemented.

(B) Criticisms of traditional methods for ensuring the impartiality of jurors have led some countries to abandon these methods entirely.

(C) Of the three traditional methods for ensuring the impartiality of jurors, voir dire is the most popular among judges but is also the most flawed.

(D) Voir dire is ineffective at ensuring impartiality due to the latitude it offers potential jurors to misrepresent their knowledge of the cases they are called to hear.

(E) Due to the expansion of mass media, solving the problem of minimizing partiality in the courtroom requires a redefinition of what constitutes an impartial jury.

2. One critic characterizes judges' instructions as requiring "mental contortions" (line 25) most likely because of a belief that jurors cannot be expected to

(A) deliberate only on what they learn in a trial and not on what they knew beforehand

(B) distinguish between pretrial speculation and the actual facts of a case

(C) hear about a case before trial without forming an opinion about it

(D) identify accurately the degree of prior knowledge they may possess about a case

(E) protect themselves from widely disseminated pretrial publicity

GO ON TO THE NEXT PAGE.

3. The primary purpose of the third paragraph is to

   (A) propose a new method of ensuring impartiality
   (B) describe criticisms of one traditional method of ensuring impartiality
   (C) argue against several traditional methods of ensuring impartiality
   (D) explain why judges are wary of certain methods of ensuring impartiality
   (E) criticize the views of those who believe judges to be incapable of ensuring impartiality

4. With which one of the following statements would the author be most likely to agree?

   (A) Flaws in *voir dire* procedures make it unlikely that juries capable of rendering impartial decisions can be selected.
   (B) Knowledge of a case before it goes to trial offers individual jurors the best chance of rendering impartial decisions.
   (C) Jurors who bring prior opinions about a case to their deliberations need not decrease the chance of the jury's rendering an impartial decision.
   (D) Only juries consisting of people who bring no prior knowledge of a case to their deliberations are capable of rendering truly impartial decisions.
   (E) People who know the facts of a case are more opinionated about it than those who do not.

5. The passage suggests that a potential benefit of mass-media coverage on court cases is that it will

   (A) determine which facts are appropriate for juries to hear
   (B) improve the ability of jurors to minimize their biases
   (C) strengthen the process by which juries come to decisions
   (D) change the methods judges use to question potential jurors
   (E) increase potential jurors' awareness of their degree of bias

6. Which one of the following principles is most in keeping with the passage's argument?

   (A) Jurors should put aside their personal experiences when deliberating a case and base their decision only on the available information.
   (B) Jurors should rely on their overall experience when deliberating a case even when the case was subject to mass-media exposure before trial.
   (C) Jurors should make every effort when deliberating a case to ignore information about the case that they may have learned from the mass media.
   (D) Jurors should be selected to hear a case based on their degree of exposure to mass-media coverage of the case before trial.
   (E) Jurors should be selected to hear a case based on their capacity to refrain from reading or viewing mass-media coverage of the case while the trial is in progress.

7. Of the following, the author's primary purpose in writing the passage most likely is to

   (A) search for compromise between proponents and critics of *voir dire*
   (B) call attention to the effects of mass media on court proceedings
   (C) encourage judges to find new ways to ensure impartial jurors
   (D) debate critics who find fault with current *voir dire* procedures
   (E) argue for a change in how courts address the problem of impartiality

GO ON TO THE NEXT PAGE.

Personal names are generally regarded by European thinkers in two major ways, both of which deny that names have any significant semantic content. In philosophy and linguistics, John Stuart Mill's
(5) formulation that "proper names are meaningless marks set upon . . . persons to distinguish them from one another" retains currency; in anthropology, Claude Lévi-Strauss's characterization of names as being primarily instruments of social classification has been
(10) very influential. Consequently, interpretation of personal names in societies where names have other functions and meanings has been neglected. Among the Hopi of the southwestern United States, names often refer to historical or ritual events in order both to place
(15) individuals within society and to confer an identity upon them. Furthermore, the images used to evoke these events suggest that Hopi names can be seen as a type of poetic composition.

Throughout life, Hopis receive several names in a
(20) sequence of ritual initiations. Birth, entry into one of the ritual societies during childhood, and puberty are among the name-giving occasions. Names are conferred by an adult member of a clan other than the child's clan, and names refer to that name giver's clan,
(25) sometimes combining characteristics of the clan's totem animal with the child's characteristics. Thus, a name might translate to something as simple as "little rabbit," which reflects both the child's size and the representative animal.
(30) More often, though, the name giver has in mind a specific event that is not apparent in a name's literal translation. One Lizard clan member from the village of Oraibi is named Lomayayva, "beautifully ascended." This translation, however, tells nothing
(35) about either the event referred to—who or what ascended—or the name giver's clan. The name giver in this case is from Badger clan. Badger clan is responsible for an annual ceremony featuring a procession in which masked representations of spirits
(40) climb the mesa on which Oraibi sits. Combining the name giver's clan association with the receiver's home village, "beautifully ascended" refers to the splendid colors and movements of the procession up the mesa. The condensed image this name evokes—a typical
(45) feature of Hopi personal names—displays the same quality of Western Apache place names that led one commentator to call them "tiny imagist poems."

Hopi personal names do several things simultaneously. They indicate social relationships—but
(50) only indirectly—and they individuate persons. Equally important, though, is their poetic quality; in a sense they can be understood as oral texts that produce aesthetic delight. This view of Hopi names is thus opposed not only to Mill's claim that personal names
(55) are without inherent meaning but also to Lévi-Strauss's purely functional characterization. Interpreters must understand Hopi clan structures and linguistic practices in order to discern the beauty and significance of Hopi names.

8. Which one of the following statements most accurately summarizes the passage's main point?

(A) Unlike European names, which are used exclusively for identification or exclusively for social classification, Hopi names perform both these functions simultaneously.

(B) Unlike European names, Hopi names tend to neglect the functions of identification and social classification in favor of a concentration on compression and poetic effects.

(C) Lacking knowledge of the intricacies of Hopi linguistic and tribal structures, European thinkers have so far been unable to discern the deeper significance of Hopi names.

(D) Although some Hopi names may seem difficult to interpret, they all conform to a formula whereby a reference to the name giver's clan is combined with a reference to the person named.

(E) While performing the functions ascribed to names by European thinkers, Hopi names also possess a significant aesthetic quality that these thinkers have not adequately recognized.

9. The author most likely refers to Western Apache place names (line 46) in order to

(A) offer an example of how names can contain references not evident in their literal translations

(B) apply a commentator's characterization of Western Apache place names to Hopi personal names

(C) contrast Western Apache naming practices with Hopi naming practices

(D) demonstrate that other names besides Hopi names may have some semantic content

(E) explain how a specific Hopi name refers subtly to a particular Western Apache site

10. Which one of the following statements describes an example of the function accorded to personal names under Lévi-Strauss's view?

(A) Some parents select their children's names from impersonal sources such as books.

(B) Some parents wait to give a child a name in order to choose one that reflects the child's looks or personality.

(C) Some parents name their children in honor of friends or famous people.

(D) Some family members have no parts of their names in common.

(E) Some family names originated as identifications of their bearers' occupations.

GO ON TO THE NEXT PAGE.

11. The primary function of the second paragraph is to

(A)   present reasons why Hopi personal names can be treated as poetic compositions

(B)   support the claim that Hopi personal names make reference to events in the recipient's life

(C)   argue that the fact that Hopis receive many names throughout life refutes European theories about naming

(D)   illustrate ways in which Hopi personal names may have semantic content

(E)   demonstrate that the literal translation of Hopi personal names often obscures their true meaning

12. Based on the passage, with which one of the following statements about Mill's view would the author of the passage be most likely to agree?

(A)   Its characterization of the function of names is too narrow to be universally applicable.

(B)   It would be correct if it recognized the use of names as instruments of social classification.

(C)   Its influence single-handedly led scholars to neglect how names are used outside Europe.

(D)   It is more accurate than Lévi-Strauss's characterization of the purpose of names.

(E)   It is less relevant than Lévi-Strauss's characterization in understanding Hopi naming practices.

13. It can be inferred from the passage that each of the following features of Hopi personal names contributes to their poetic quality EXCEPT:

(A)   their ability to be understood as oral texts

(B)   their use of condensed imagery to evoke events

(C)   their capacity to produce aesthetic delight

(D)   their ability to confer identity upon individuals

(E)   their ability to subtly convey meaning

14. The author's primary purpose in writing the passage is to

(A)   present an anthropological study of Hopi names

(B)   propose a new theory about the origin of names

(C)   describe several competing theories of names

(D)   criticize two influential views of names

(E)   explain the cultural origins of names

GO ON TO THE NEXT PAGE.

Homing pigeons can be taken from their lofts and transported hundreds of kilometers in covered cages to unfamiliar sites and yet, when released, be able to choose fairly accurate homeward bearings within a
(5) minute and fly home. Aside from reading the minds of the experimenters (a possibility that has not escaped investigation), there are two basic explanations for the remarkable ability of pigeons to "home": the birds might keep track of their outward displacement (the
(10) system of many short-range species such as honeybees); or they might have some sense, known as a "map sense," that would permit them to construct an internal image of their environment and then "place" themselves with respect to home on some internalized
(15) coordinate system.

The first alternative seems unlikely. One possible model for such an inertial system might involve an internal magnetic compass to measure the directional leg of each journey. Birds transported to the release site
(20) wearing magnets or otherwise subjected to an artificial magnetic field, however, are only occasionally affected. Alternately, if pigeons measure their displacement by consciously keeping track of the direction and degree of acceleration and deceleration of
(25) the various turns, and timing the individual legs of the journey, simply transporting them in the dark, with constant rotations, or under complete anesthesia ought to impair or eliminate their ability to orient. These treatments, however, have no effect. Unfortunately, no
(30) one has yet performed the crucial experiment of transporting pigeons in total darkness, anesthetized, rotating, and with the magnetic field reversed all at the same time.

The other alternative, that pigeons have a "map
(35) sense," seems more promising, yet the nature of this sense remains mysterious. Papi has posited that the map sense is olfactory: that birds come to associate odors borne on the wind with the direction in which the wind is blowing, and so slowly build up an olfactory
(40) map of their surroundings. When transported to the release site, then, they only have to sniff the air en route and/or at the site to know the direction of home. Papi conducted a series of experiments showing that pigeons whose nostrils have been plugged are poorly
(45) oriented at release and home slowly.

One problem with the hypothesis is that Schmidt-Koenig and Phillips failed to detect any ability in pigeons to distinguish natural air (presumably laden with olfactory map information) from pure, filtered air.
(50) Papi's experimental results, moreover, admit of simpler, nonolfactory explanations. It seems likely that the behavior of nostril-plugged birds results from the distracting and traumatic nature of the experiment. When nasal tubes are used to bypass the olfactory
(55) chamber but allow for comfortable breathing, no disorientation is evident. Likewise, when the olfactory epithelium is sprayed with anesthetic to block smell-detection but not breathing, orientation is normal.

15. Which one of the following best states the main idea of the passage?

(A) The ability of pigeons to locate and return to their homes from distant points is unlike that of any other species.

(B) It is likely that some map sense accounts for the homing ability of pigeons, but the nature of that sense has not been satisfactorily identified.

(C) The majority of experiments on the homing ability of pigeons have been marked by design flaws.

(D) The mechanisms underlying the homing ability of pigeons can best be identified through a combination of laboratory research and field experimentation.

(E) The homing ability of pigeons is most likely based on a system similar to that used by many short-range species.

16. According to the passage, which one of the following is ordinarily true regarding how homing pigeons "home"?

(A) Each time they are released at a specific site they fly home by the same route.

(B) When they are released they take only a short time to orient themselves before selecting their route home.

(C) Each time they are released at a specific site they take a shorter amount of time to orient themselves before flying home.

(D) They travel fairly long distances in seemingly random patterns before finally deciding on a route home.

(E) Upon release they travel briefly in the direction opposite to the one they eventually choose.

GO ON TO THE NEXT PAGE.

17. Which one of the following experiments would best test the "possibility" referred to in line 6?

   (A) an experiment in which the handlers who transported, released, and otherwise came into contact with homing pigeons released at an unfamiliar site were unaware of the location of the pigeons' home

   (B) an experiment in which the handlers who transported, released, and otherwise came into contact with homing pigeons released at an unfamiliar site were asked not to display any affection toward the pigeons

   (C) an experiment in which the handlers who transported, released, and otherwise came into contact with homing pigeons released at an unfamiliar site were asked not to speak to each other throughout the release process

   (D) an experiment in which all the homing pigeons released at an unfamiliar site had been raised and fed by individual researchers rather than by teams of handlers

   (E) an experiment in which all the homing pigeons released at an unfamiliar site were exposed to a wide variety of unfamiliar sights and sounds

18. Information in the passage supports which one of the following statements regarding the "first alternative" (line 16) for explaining the ability of pigeons to "home"?

   (A) It has been conclusively ruled out by the results of numerous experiments.

   (B) It seems unlikely because there are no theoretical models that could explain how pigeons track displacement.

   (C) It has not, to date, been supported by experimental data, but neither has it been definitively ruled out.

   (D) It seems unlikely in theory, but recent experimental results show that it may in fact be correct.

   (E) It is not a useful theory because of the difficulty in designing experiments by which it might be tested.

19. The author refers to "the system of many short-range species such as honeybees" (lines 9–11) most probably in order to

   (A) emphasize the universality of the ability to home

   (B) suggest that a particular explanation of pigeons' homing ability is worthy of consideration

   (C) discredit one of the less convincing theories regarding the homing ability of pigeons

   (D) criticize the techniques utilized by scientists investigating the nature of pigeons' homing ability

   (E) illustrate why a proposed explanation of pigeons' homing ability is correct

20. Which one of the following, if true, would most weaken Papi's theory regarding homing pigeons' homing ability?

   (A) Even pigeons that have been raised in several different lofts in a variety of territories can find their way to their current home when released in unfamiliar territory.

   (B) Pigeons whose sense of smell has been partially blocked find their way home more slowly than do pigeons whose sense of smell has not been affected.

   (C) Even pigeons that have been raised in the same loft frequently take different routes home when released in unfamiliar territory.

   (D) Even pigeons that have been transported well beyond the range of the odors detectable in their home territories can find their way home.

   (E) Pigeons' sense of smell is no more acute than that of other birds who do not have the ability to "home."

21. Given the information in the passage, it is most likely that Papi and the author of the passage would both agree with which one of the following statements regarding the homing ability of pigeons?

   (A) The map sense of pigeons is most probably related to their olfactory sense.

   (B) The mechanism regulating the homing ability of pigeons is most probably similar to that utilized by honeybees.

   (C) The homing ability of pigeons is most probably based on a map sense.

   (D) The experiments conducted by Papi himself have provided the most valuable evidence yet collected regarding the homing ability of pigeons.

   (E) The experiments conducted by Schmidt-Koenig and Phillips have not substantially lessened the probability that Papi's own theory is correct.

GO ON TO THE NEXT PAGE.

Freud's essay on "The Uncanny" can be said to have defined, for our century, what literary criticism once called the Sublime. This apprehension of a beyond or of a dæmonic—a sense of transcendence—
(5) appears in literature or life, according to Freud, when we feel that something uncanny is being represented, or conjured up, or at least intimated. Freud locates the source of the uncanny in our tendency to believe in the "omnipotence of thought," that is, in the power of our
(10) own or of others' minds over the natural world. The uncanny is, thus, a return to animistic conceptions of the universe, and is produced by the psychic defense mechanisms Freud called repression.

It would have seemed likely for Freud to find his
(15) literary instances of the uncanny, or at least some of them, in fairy tales, since as much as any other fictions they seem to be connected with repressed desires and archaic forms of thought. But Freud specifically excluded fairy tales from the realm of the uncanny.
(20) "Who would be so bold," Freud asks, "as to call it an uncanny moment, for instance, when Snow White opens her eyes once more?" Why not? Because, he goes on to say, in those stories everything is possible, so nothing is incredible, and, therefore, no conflicts in
(25) the reader's judgment are provoked. Thus Freud, alas, found fairy tales to be unsuited to his own analysis.

However, the psychoanalyst Bruno Bettelheim, with a kind of wise innocence, has subjected fairy tales to very close, generally orthodox, and wholly reductive
(30) Freudian interpretations. Bettelheim's book, although written in apparent ignorance of the vast critical traditions of interpreting literary romance, is nevertheless a splendid achievement, brimming with useful ideas and insights into how young children read
(35) and understand.

Bruno Bettelheim's major therapeutic concern has been with autistic children, so inevitably his interpretive activity is directed against a child's tendency to withdraw defensively or abnormally.
(40) According to Bettelheim, a child's desperate isolation, loneliness, and inarticulate anxieties are addressed directly by fairy tales. By telling the child such stories themselves, parents strengthen the therapeutic effect of fairy tales, for in the telling, parents impart to the child
(45) their approval of the stories.

But why should fairy tales, in themselves, be therapeutic? Bettelheim's answer depends on the child's being an interpreter: "The fairy tale is therapeutic because children find their own solutions,
(50) through contemplating what the story seems to imply about their inner conflicts at this moment in their lives." Bettelheim proceeds on the basis of two complementary assumptions: that children will interpret a story benignly, for their own good; and that
(55) Freudian interpretations will yield an accurate account of children's interpretations. The child, questing for help, and the analyst, attempting to find helpful patterns in the stories, thus read alike, though in different vocabularies.

22. According to the author, Bettelheim believes that fairy tales help troubled children by

(A) creating fantasy worlds into which they can escape

(B) helping them find solutions to their own problems

(C) providing a means of communication with their parents

(D) showing them other problems worse than their own

(E) solving their problems for them

23. According to the passage, Bettelheim believes that parents' telling fairy tales to troubled children strengthens the tales' therapeutic effect because

(A) most troubled children do not read independently

(B) most children believe whatever their parents tell them

(C) the parents' telling the stories imparts to the children the parents' sanction of the tales

(D) the parents can help the children interpret the stories according to the parents' belief

(E) the parents can reassure the children that the tales are imaginary

GO ON TO THE NEXT PAGE.

24. It can be inferred from the passage that Freud believed that in fairy tales, "nothing is incredible" (line 24) because, in his view,

    (A)   fairy tales can be read and understood even by young children
    (B)   everything in fairy tales is purely imaginary
    (C)   fairy tales are so fantastic that in them nothing seems out of the ordinary
    (D)   it is uncanny how the patterns of fairy tales fit our unconscious expectations and wishes
    (E)   the reader represses those elements of fairy tales which might conflict with his or her judgment

25. According to the passage, Bettelheim believes that when children interpret a story benignly, they

    (A)   find in fairy tales answers to their own needs
    (B)   do not associate fairy tales with the uncanny
    (C)   do not find underlying meanings in fairy tales
    (D)   are aware that fairy tales are fictions
    (E)   are reassured by parental approval

26. Which one of the following best describes the author's attitude toward Bettelheim's work?

    (A)   approving of Bettelheim's rejection of orthodox and reductive Freudian interpretations of fairy tales
    (B)   appalled at Bettelheim's ignorance of the critical traditions of interpreting literary romance
    (C)   unimpressed with Bettelheim's research methods
    (D)   skeptical of Bettelheim's claim that fairy tales are therapeutic
    (E)   appreciative of Bettelheim's accomplishment and practical insights

S T O P

IF YOU FINISH BEFORE TIME IS CALLED, YOU MAY CHECK YOUR WORK ON THIS SECTION ONLY.
DO NOT WORK ON ANY OTHER SECTION IN THE TEST.

SECTION IV

Time—35 minutes

25 Questions

<u>Directions:</u> The questions in this section are based on the reasoning contained in brief statements or passages. For some questions, more than one of the choices could conceivably answer the question. However, you are to choose the <u>best</u> answer; that is, the response that most accurately and completely answers the question. You should not make assumptions that are by commonsense standards implausible, superfluous, or incompatible with the passage. After you have chosen the best answer, blacken the corresponding space on your answer sheet.

1. Politician: Governments should tax any harmful substance that is available to the general public at a level that the tax would discourage continued use of the substance.

    Which one of the following is an application of the politician's principle of taxation?

    (A)   The tax on products containing sugar is raised in an effort to raise revenue to be applied to the health costs resulting from the long-term use of these products.

    (B)   The tax on certain pain relievers that, even though harmful, are available over the counter is raised, since studies have shown that the demand for these products will not be affected.

    (C)   The tax on a pesticide that contains an organic compound harmful to human beings is raised to give people an incentive to purchase pesticides not containing the compound.

    (D)   The tax on domestically produced alcoholic beverages is not raised, since recent studies show that the tax would have a negative impact on the tourist industry.

    (E)   The tax on products that emit fluorocarbons, substances that have proven to be harmful to the earth's ozone layer, is lowered to stimulate the development of new, less environmentally harmful ways of using these substances.

2. The average cable television company offers its customers 50 channels, but new fiber-optic lines will enable telephone companies to provide 100 to 150 television channels to their customers for the same price as cable companies charge for 50. Therefore, cable companies will be displaced by the new television services offered by telephone companies within a few years.

    Which one of the following, if true, most helps to strengthen the argument?

    (A)   The initial cost per household of installing new fiber-optic television service will exceed the current cost of installing cable television service.

    (B)   The most popular movies and programs on channels carried by cable companies will also be offered on channels carried by the fiber-optic lines owned by the telephone companies.

    (C)   Cable television companies will respond to competition from the telephone companies by increasing the number of channels they offer.

    (D)   Some telephone companies own cable companies in areas other than those in which they provide telephone services.

    (E)   The new fiber-optic services offered by telephone companies will be subject to more stringent governmental programming regulations than those to which cable companies are now subject.

GO ON TO THE NEXT PAGE.

3. A just government never restricts the right of its citizens to act upon their desires except when their acting upon their desires is a direct threat to the health or property of other of its citizens.

Which one of the following judgments most closely conforms to the principle cited above?

(A) A just government would not ban the sale of sports cars, but it could prohibit unrestricted racing of them on public highways.

(B) An unjust government would abolish many public services if these services did not require compulsory labor.

(C) A just government would provide emergency funds to survivors of unavoidable accidents but not to survivors of avoidable ones.

(D) A just government would not censor writings of Shakespeare, but it could censor magazines and movies that criticize the government.

(E) An unjust government would incarcerate one of its citizens even though it had been several years since that citizen harmed someone.

4. Mayor: Citing the severity of the city's winters, the city road commissioner has suggested paving our roads with rubberized asphalt, since the pressure of passing vehicles would cause the rubber to flex, breaking up ice on roads and so making ice removal easier and less of a strain on the road-maintenance budget. However, rubberized asphalt is more expensive than plain asphalt and the city's budget for building and maintaining roads cannot be increased. Therefore, the commissioner's suggestion is not financially feasible.

Which one of the following is assumed by the mayor's argument?

(A) Using rubberized asphalt to pave roads would not have any advantages besides facilitating the removal of ice on roads.

(B) The severity of winters in the region in which the city is located does not vary significantly from year to year.

(C) It would cost more to add particles of rubber to asphalt than to add particles of rubber to other materials that are used to pave roads.

(D) Savings in the cost of ice removal would not pay for the increased expense of using rubberized asphalt to pave roads.

(E) The techniques the city currently uses for removing ice from city roads are not the least expensive possible, given the type of road surface in place.

5. Ticks attach themselves to host animals to feed. Having fed to capacity, and not before then, the ticks drop off their host. Deer ticks feeding off white-footed mice invariably drop off their hosts between noon and sunset, regardless of time of attachment. White-footed mice are strictly nocturnal animals that spend all daytime hours in their underground nests.

Which one of the following conclusions can be properly drawn from the statements above?

(A) Deer ticks all attach themselves to white-footed mice during the same part of the day, regardless of day of attachment.

(B) Deer ticks sometimes drop off their hosts without having fed at all.

(C) Deer ticks that feed off white-footed mice drop off their hosts in the hosts' nests.

(D) White-footed mice to which deer ticks have attached themselves are not aware of the ticks.

(E) White-footed mice are hosts to stable numbers of deer ticks, regardless of season of the year.

6. Monarch butterflies spend the winter hibernating on trees in certain forests. Local environmental groups have organized tours of the forests in an effort to protect the butterflies' habitat against woodcutters. Unfortunately, the tourists trample most of the small shrubs that are necessary to the survival of any monarch butterflies that fall off the trees. Therefore, the tour groups themselves are endangering the monarch butterfly population.

Which one of the following would it be most useful to know in evaluating the argument?

(A) the amount of forest land suitable for monarch butterfly hibernation that is not currently used by monarch butterflies for hibernation

(B) the amount of wood cut each year by woodcutters in forests used by monarch butterflies for hibernation

(C) the amount of plant life trampled by the tourists that is not necessary to the survival of monarch butterflies

(D) the proportion of the trees cut down by the woodcutters each year that are cut in the forests used by monarch butterflies for hibernation

(E) the proportion of hibernating monarch butterflies that fall off the trees

GO ON TO THE NEXT PAGE.

7. If you know a lot about history, it will be easy for you to impress people who are intellectuals. But unfortunately, you will not know much about history if you have not, for example, read a large number of history books. Therefore, if you are not well versed in history due to a lack of reading, it will not be easy for you to impress people who are intellectuals.

The argument's reasoning is flawed because the argument overlooks the possibility that

(A) many intellectuals are not widely read in history
(B) there are people who learn about history who do not impress intellectuals
(C) it is more important to impress people who are not intellectuals than people who are intellectuals
(D) there are other easy ways to impress intellectuals that do not involve knowing history
(E) people who are not intellectuals can be impressed more easily than people who are intellectuals

8. People always seem to associate high prices of products with high quality. But price is not necessarily an indicator of quality. The best teas are often no more expensive than the lower-quality teas.

Which one of the following, if true, does most to explain the apparent counterexample described above?

(A) Packaging and advertising triple the price of all teas.
(B) Most people buy low-quality tea, thus keeping its price up.
(C) All types of tea are subject to high import tariffs.
(D) Low-quality teas are generally easier to obtain than high-quality teas.
(E) The price of tea generally does not vary from region to region.

9. The only physical factor preventing a human journey to Mars has been weight. Carrying enough fuel to propel a conventional spacecraft to Mars and back would make even the lightest craft too heavy to be launched from Earth. A device has recently been invented, however, that allows an otherwise conventional spacecraft to refill the craft's fuel tanks with fuel manufactured from the Martian atmosphere for the return trip. Therefore, it is possible for people to go to Mars in a spacecraft that carries this device and then return.

Which one of the following is an assumption on which the argument depends?

(A) The amount of fuel needed for a spacecraft to return from Mars is the same as the amount of fuel needed to travel from Earth to Mars.
(B) The fuel manufactured from the Martian atmosphere would not differ in composition from the fuel used to travel to Mars.
(C) The device for manufacturing fuel from the Martian atmosphere would not take up any of the spaceship crew's living space.
(D) A conventional spacecraft equipped with the device would not be appreciably more expensive to construct than current spacecraft typically are.
(E) The device for manufacturing fuel for the return to Earth weighs less than the tanks of fuel that a conventional spacecraft would otherwise need to carry from Earth for the return trip.

10. Unplugging a peripheral component such as a "mouse" from a personal computer renders all of the software programs that require that component unusable on that computer. On Fred's personal computer, a software program that requires a mouse has become unusable. So it must be that the mouse for Fred's computer became unplugged.

The argument is most vulnerable to which one of the following criticisms?

(A) It contains a shift in the meaning of "unusable" from "permanently unusable" to "temporarily unusable."
(B) It treats an event that can cause a certain result as though that event is necessary to bring about that result.
(C) It introduces information unrelated to its conclusion as evidence in support of that conclusion.
(D) It attempts to support its conclusion by citing a generalization that is too broad.
(E) It overlooks the possibility that some programs do not require a peripheral component such as a mouse.

GO ON TO THE NEXT PAGE.

Questions 11–12

P: Complying with the new safety regulations is useless. Even if the new regulations had been in effect before last year's laboratory fire, they would not have prevented the fire or the injuries resulting from it because they do not address its underlying causes.

Q: But any regulations that can potentially prevent money from being wasted are useful. If obeyed, the new safety regulations will prevent some accidents, and whenever there is an accident here at the laboratory, money is wasted even if no one is injured.

11. A point at issue between P and Q is whether

   (A) last year's fire resulted in costly damage to the laboratory

   (B) accidents at the laboratory inevitably result in personal injuries

   (C) the new safety regulations address the underlying cause of last year's fire

   (D) it is useful to comply with the new safety regulations

   (E) the new safety regulations are likely to be obeyed in the laboratory

12. Q responds to P's position by

   (A) extending the basis for assessing the utility of complying with the new regulations

   (B) citing additional evidence that undermines P's assessment of the extent to which the new regulations would have prevented injuries in last year's laboratory fire

   (C) giving examples to show that the uselessness of all regulations cannot validly be inferred from the uselessness of one particular set of regulations

   (D) showing that P's argument depends on the false assumption that compliance with any regulations that would have prevented last year's fire would be useful

   (E) pointing out a crucial distinction, overlooked by P, between potential benefits and actual benefits

13. Historian: The ancient Greeks failed to recognize that, morally, democracy is no improvement over monarchy. It is wrong for an individual to have the power to choose the course of action for a government, so it is no less wrong to grant this power to society, which is just a collection of individuals.

The pattern of flawed reasoning in the argument above is most similar to that in which one of the following?

   (A) There is no point in trying to find someone else to solve that problem. If Robin cannot solve it, then none of Robin's friends would be able to solve it.

   (B) We should not pick Hank for the relay team. He has not won a race all season, so there is no reason to expect him to help the relay team win.

   (C) Laws that contain exemptions for some individuals based on no relevant consideration are fundamentally immoral. If it is wrong for a given person to commit an act, then it is wrong for anyone else in similar circumstances to commit the act.

   (D) There is no point in asking the club to purchase tents and make them available for use by club members. No member of the club can afford one of those tents, so the club is unable to afford any either.

   (E) Agreeing with all of the other members of society does not guarantee that one is correct about an issue. With many topics it is possible for society to be mistaken and hence every individual in society to be likewise mistaken.

GO ON TO THE NEXT PAGE.

14. In 1712 the government of Country Y appointed a censor to prohibit the publication of any book critical of Country Y's government; all new books legally published in the country after 1712 were approved by a censor. Under the first censor, one half of the book manuscripts submitted to the censor were not approved for publication. Under the next censor, only one quarter of the book manuscripts submitted were not approved, but the number of book manuscripts that were approved was the same under both censors.

If the statements in the passage are true, which one of the following can be properly concluded from them?

(A) More books critical of Country Y's government were published before the appointment of the first censor than after it.

(B) The first censor and the second censor prohibited the publication of the same number of book manuscripts.

(C) More book manuscripts were submitted for approval to the first censor than to the second.

(D) The second censor allowed some book manuscripts to be published that the first censor would have considered critical of Country Y's government.

(E) The number of writers who wrote unpublished manuscripts was greater under the first censor than under the second.

15. It is often said that beauty is subjective. But this judgment has to be false. If one tries to glean the standard of beauty of earlier cultures from the artistic works they considered most beautiful, one cannot but be impressed by its similarity to our own standard. In many fundamental ways, what was considered beautiful in those cultures is still considered beautiful in our own time.

Which one of the following statements, if true, most weakens the argument?

(A) Few contemporary artists have been significantly exposed to the art of earlier cultures.

(B) The arts held a much more important place in earlier cultures than they do in our culture.

(C) Our own standard of beauty was strongly influenced by our exposure to works that were considered beautiful in earlier cultures.

(D) Much of what passes for important artistic work today would not be considered beautiful even by contemporary standards.

(E) In most cultures art is owned by a small social elite.

16. Nutrition education in schools once promoted daily consumption of food from each of the "four food groups": milk, meat, fruit and vegetables, and breads and cereals. This recommendation was, however, dangerous to health.

Each of the following, if true, provides support for the critique above EXCEPT:

(A) The division into four groups gave the impression that an equal amount of each should be consumed, but milk and meat tend to contain fats that promote heart disease and cancer and should be eaten in lesser amounts.

(B) The omission of fish, which contains beneficial oils, from the names of groups in the list gave the erroneous impression that it is less healthy as a food than is red meat.

(C) A healthy diet should include the consumption of several different fruits and vegetables daily, but the recommendation was often interpreted as satisfied by the consumption of a single serving of a fruit or vegetable.

(D) The recommendation that some food from the fruit and vegetable group be consumed daily constituted a reminder not to neglect this group, which provides needed vitamins, minerals, and fiber.

(E) Encouraging the daily consumption of some product from each of the four food groups gave the impression that eating in that manner is sufficient for a healthy diet, but eating in that manner is consistent with the overconsumption of sweets and fats.

GO ON TO THE NEXT PAGE.

17. The Green Ensemble, a nonprofit theater group, has always been financially dependent on contributions from corporations and would have been forced to disband this year if any of its corporate sponsors had withdrawn their financial support. But the Green Ensemble has not only been able to continue in operation throughout the year, but has recently announced its schedule for next year.

Which one of the following is a conclusion that can be properly drawn from the information above?

(A) None of the Green Ensemble's corporate sponsors withdrew their financial support of the group this year.
(B) Earlier this year the Green Ensemble found other sources of funding for next year, making the group less dependent on corporations for financial support.
(C) During this year corporate funding for the Green Ensemble has been steadily increasing.
(D) This year corporate funding was the source of more than half of the Green Ensemble's income.
(E) Corporate funding for nonprofit theater groups like the Green Ensemble has recently increased.

18. Book publishers have traditionally published a few books that they thought were of intrinsic merit even though these books were unlikely to make a profit. Nowadays, however, fewer of these books are being published. It seems, therefore, that publishers now, more than ever, are more interested in making money than in publishing books of intrinsic value.

Which one of the following statements, if true, most seriously weakens the argument?

(A) Book publishers have always been very interested in making money.
(B) There has been a notable decline in the quality of books written in recent years.
(C) In the past, often books of intrinsic value would unexpectedly make a sizable profit.
(D) There have always been authors unwilling to be published unless a profit is guaranteed.
(E) In recent years, profits in the book publishing industry have been declining.

19. Most people feel that they are being confused by the information from broadcast news. This could be the effect of the information's being delivered too quickly or of its being poorly organized. Analysis of the information content of a typical broadcast news story shows that news stories are far lower in information density than the maximum information density with which most people can cope at any one time. So the information in typical broadcast news stories is poorly organized.

Which one of the following is an assumption that the argument requires in order for its conclusion to be properly drawn?

(A) It is not the number of broadcast news stories to which a person is exposed that is the source of the feeling of confusion.
(B) Poor organization of information in a news story makes it impossible to understand the information.
(C) Being exposed to more broadcast news stories within a given day would help a person to better understand the news.
(D) Most people can cope with a very high information density.
(E) Some people are being overwhelmed by too much information.

20. Art historian: Robbins cannot pass judgment on Stuart's art. While Robbins understands the art of Stuart too well to dismiss it, she does not understand it well enough to praise it.

The art historian's argument depends on the assumption that

(A) in order to pass judgment on Stuart's art, Robbins must be able either to dismiss it or to praise it
(B) if art can be understood well, it should be either dismissed or praised
(C) in order to understand Stuart's art, Robbins must be able to pass judgment on it
(D) Stuart's art can be neither praised nor dismissed
(E) if Robbins understands art well, she will praise it

GO ON TO THE NEXT PAGE.

Questions 21–22

Words like "employee," "payee," and "detainee" support the generalization, crudely stated, that words with the ending *-ee* designate the person affected in the specified way by an action performed by someone else. The word "absentee" seems to be a direct counterexample: it ends in *-ee*, yet, if it makes sense here to speak of an action at all—that of absenting oneself, perhaps—the word can refer to the person who actually performs that action. Clearly, however, putting forward the following resolves the impasse: if a word with the ending *-ee* refers to one party in a two-party transaction, it refers to the party at which the other party's action is directed.

21. The argument does which one of the following in dealing with the counterexample it offers?

(A) provides additional support for the original generalization in part by showing that the supposed force of the counterexample derives from a misanalysis of that example

(B) dismisses the counterexample on the grounds that its force, compared to the weight of the supporting evidence, is insignificant

(C) concedes that the proposed counterexample is an exception to the generalization but maintains the generalization on the grounds that all generalizations have exceptions

(D) narrows the scope of the generalization at issue in such a way that the putative counterexample is no longer relevant

(E) shows how replacing the notion of being affected in the specified way by an action with that of having someone's action directed at oneself reveals the counterexample to be spurious

22. The reasoning in the argument could have remained unchanged in force and focus if which one of the following had been advanced as a counterexample in place of the word "absentee"?

(A) honoree
(B) appointee
(C) nominee
(D) transferee
(E) escapee

23. Much of today's literature is inferior: most of our authors are intellectually and emotionally inexperienced, and their works lack both the intricacy and the focus on the significant that characterize good literature. However, Hypatia's latest novel is promising; it shows a maturity, complexity, and grace that far exceeds that of her earlier works.

Which one of the following statements is most strongly supported by the information in the passage?

(A) Much of today's literature focuses less on the significant than Hypatia's latest novel focuses on the significant.

(B) Much of today's literature at least lacks the property of grace.

(C) Hypatia's latest novel is good literature when judged by today's standards.

(D) Hypatia's latest novel is clearly better than the majority of today's literature.

(E) Hypatia's latest novel has at least one property of good literature to a greater degree than her earlier works.

GO ON TO THE NEXT PAGE.

24. Scientists, puzzled about the development of penicillin-resistant bacteria in patients who had not been taking penicillin, believe they have found an explanation. The relevant group of patients have dental fillings made of mercury-containing amalgam, and the bacteria the patients develop are immune to mercury poisoning. Scientists have concluded that the genes causing resistance to penicillin are closely bundled on the chromosomes of bacteria with the gene that produces immunity to mercury poisoning. Exposure to the mercury kills off bacteria that lack the relevant immunity gene, and leaves room for those that possess both the mercury-immunity gene and the penicillin-resistance gene to flourish.

Which one of the following most accurately characterizes the role played in the passage by the unstated assumption that some patients who take penicillin develop bacteria with an immunity to penicillin?

(A) It is a hypothesis that is taken by the scientists to be conclusively proven by the findings described in the passage.

(B) It is a generalization that, if true, rules out the possibility that some people who do not take penicillin develop bacteria resistant to it.

(C) It is a point that, in conjunction with the fact that some patients who do not take penicillin develop penicillin-resistant bacteria, generates the problem that prompted the research described in the passage.

(D) It is the tentative conclusion of previous research that appears to be falsified by the scientists' discovery of the mechanism by which bacteria become resistant to mercury poisoning.

(E) It is a generalization assumed by the scientists to conclusively prove that the explanation of their problem case must involve reference to the genetic makeup of the penicillin-resistant bacteria.

25. All any reporter knows about the accident is what the press agent has said. Therefore, if the press agent told every reporter everything about the accident, then no reporter knows any more about it than any other reporter. If no reporter knows any more about the accident than any other reporter, then no reporter can scoop all of the other reporters. However, the press agent did not tell every reporter everything about the accident. It follows that some reporter can scoop all of the other reporters.

The argument's reasoning is flawed because the argument fails to recognize that which one of the following is consistent with the facts the argument presents?

(A) The press agent did not tell everything about the accident to any reporter.

(B) Even if some reporter knows more about the accident than all of the other reporters, that reporter need not scoop any other reporter.

(C) Some reporter may have been told something about the accident that the reporter tells all of the other reporters.

(D) The press agent may not know any more about the accident than the most knowledgeable reporter.

(E) No reporter knows any more about the accident than any other reporter.

S T O P

IF YOU FINISH BEFORE TIME IS CALLED, YOU MAY CHECK YOUR WORK ON THIS SECTION ONLY.
DO NOT WORK ON ANY OTHER SECTION IN THE TEST.

Acknowledgment is made to the following sources from which material has been adapted for use in this test booklet: Newton N. Minow and Fred H. Cate, "The Search for Justice: Is Impartiality Really Possible?" ©1992 by the Society for the Advancement of Education.

Peter Whiteley, "Hopuutungwni: 'Hopi Names' as Literature." ©1992 by the Smithsonian Institution.

LSAT® Writing Sample Topic

Directions: The scenario presented below describes two choices, either one of which can be supported on the basis of the information given. Your essay should consider both choices and argue for one over the other, based on the two specified criteria and the facts provided. There is no "right" or "wrong" choice: a reasonable argument can be made for either.

A local television station is deciding which of two comparably priced films to purchase for a public interest program. Both films are about homelessness, which has recently become a serious problem in the medium-sized city where the station is located. Write an argument in support of purchasing one of the films rather than the other based on the following considerations:

- The station desires to preserve its reputation for serious reporting.
- The station desires to increase the size and diversity of its viewing audience.

Patsy: Portrait of a Homeless Woman, a thirty minute color movie, is a dramatic portrayal of the life of Patsy Harper. Named after Patsy Cline, she left her home in a small industrial town seeking stardom. While a teenager, Patsy achieved phenomenal success in the country music industry, but mental illness destroyed her career and she lived on the streets for the next two decades. Her recent recovery was worldwide news. The movie stars a popular talk-show host who is outspoken about the concerns of homeless people. The result is a heart-rending depiction of the realities of homelessness.

Can't Go Home, a one-hour black-and-white documentary film, explores the issue of homeless people in today's cities. The film received positive reviews in the several medium-sized cities in which it played last year. *Can't Go Home* features narrated documentary footage interspersed with short interviews with homeless people of every imaginable description in diverse urban settings. The film also includes interviews with local and federal agency leaders discussing the social and financial causes of homelessness. *Can't Go Home* is an eye opening, revealing, and well-paced overview of a deep social problem.

Directions:

1. Use the Answer Key on the next page to check your answers.

2. Use the Scoring Worksheet below to compute your raw score.

3. Use the Score Conversion Chart to convert your raw score into the 120-180 scale.

Scoring Worksheet

1. Enter the number of questions you answered correctly in each section.

                                **Number
                                Correct**

    SECTION I . . . . . . _____
    SECTION II . . . . . _____
    SECTION III . . . . . _____
    SECTION IV . . . . . _____

2. Enter the sum here: _____
                        This is your Raw Score.

Conversion Chart

For Converting Raw Score to the 120-180 LSAT Scaled Score
LSAT Form 8LSS38

Reported Score	Raw Score Lowest	Raw Score Highest
180	97	101
179	95	96
178	94	94
177	93	93
176	92	92
175	91	91
174	90	90
173	88	89
172	87	87
171	86	86
170	85	85
169	83	84
168	82	82
167	81	81
166	79	80
165	78	78
164	76	77
163	75	75
162	73	74
161	72	72
160	70	71
159	69	69
158	67	68
157	65	66
156	64	64
155	62	63
154	60	61
153	59	59
152	57	58
151	55	56
150	54	54
149	52	53
148	50	51
147	49	49
146	47	48
145	45	46
144	44	44
143	42	43
142	41	41
141	39	40
140	37	38
139	36	36
138	34	35
137	33	33
136	32	32
135	30	31
134	29	29
133	28	28
132	26	27
131	25	25
130	24	24
129	23	23
128	22	22
127	21	21
126	20	20
125	19	19
124	18	18
123	17	17
122	16	16
121	—*	—*
120	0	15

*There is no raw score that will produce this scaled score for this form.

SECTION I

1.	B	8.	B	15.	A	22.	D
2.	D	9.	A	16.	D	23.	C
3.	D	10.	E	17.	B	24.	D
4.	A	11.	B	18.	A	25.	B
5.	C	12.	E	19.	E	26.	D
6.	C	13.	C	20.	C		
7.	C	14.	B	21.	B		

SECTION II

1.	E	8.	E	15.	C	22.	E
2.	E	9.	C	16.	A	23.	A
3.	C	10.	D	17.	E	24.	D
4.	C	11.	A	18.	B		
5.	D	12.	C	19.	E		
6.	B	13.	D	20.	A		
7.	B	14.	A	21.	B		

SECTION III

1.	E	8.	E	15.	B	22.	B
2.	A	9.	B	16.	B	23.	C
3.	B	10.	E	17.	A	24.	C
4.	C	11.	D	18.	C	25.	A
5.	C	12.	A	19.	B	26.	E
6.	B	13.	D	20.	D		
7.	E	14.	D	21.	C		

SECTION IV

1.	C	8.	B	15.	C	22.	E
2.	B	9.	E	16.	D	23.	E
3.	A	10.	B	17.	A	24.	C
4.	D	11.	D	18.	B	25.	E
5.	C	12.	A	19.	A		
6.	E	13.	D	20.	A		
7.	D	14.	C	21.	D		

The Official LSAT PrepTest

28

- June 1999
- Form 0LSS41

The sample test that follows consists of four sections corresponding to the four scored sections of the June 1999 LSAT.

SECTION I

Time—35 minutes

26 Questions

Directions: The questions in this section are based on the reasoning contained in brief statements or passages. For some questions, more than one of the choices could conceivably answer the question. However, you are to choose the best answer; that is, the response that most accurately and completely answers the question. You should not make assumptions that are by commonsense standards implausible, superfluous, or incompatible with the passage. After you have chosen the best answer, blacken the corresponding space on your answer sheet.

1. A student has taken twelve courses and received a B in a majority of them. The student is now taking another course and will probably, given her record, receive a B in it.

   Each of the following, if true, strengthens the argument EXCEPT:

   (A) The student previously studied alone but is receiving help from several outstanding students during the present course.
   (B) The twelve courses together covered a broad range of subject matter.
   (C) The student previously studied in the library and continues to do so.
   (D) The student received a B in all but one of the twelve courses.
   (E) The current course is a continuation of one of the twelve courses in which the student received a B.

2. If the government increases its funding for civilian scientific research, private patrons and industries will believe that such research has become primarily the government's responsibility. When they believe that research is no longer primarily their responsibility, private patrons and industries will decrease their contributions toward research. Therefore, in order to keep from depressing the overall level of funding for civilian scientific research, the government should not increase its own funding.

   Which one of the following is an assumption on which the argument relies?

   (A) Governments should bear the majority of the financial burden of funding for civilian scientific research.
   (B) Any increase in government funding would displace more private funding for civilian scientific research than it would provide.
   (C) Private donations toward research are no longer welcomed by researchers whose work receives government funding.
   (D) Civilian scientific research cannot be conducted efficiently with more than one source of funding.
   (E) Funding for civilian scientific research is currently at the highest possible level.

3. For any given ticket in a 1000-ticket lottery, it is reasonable to believe that that ticket will lose. Hence, it is reasonable to believe that no ticket will win.

   Which one of the following exhibits flawed reasoning most similar to the flawed reasoning in the argument above?

   (A) It is reasonable to believe for any randomly drawn playing card that it will not be an ace, so it is reasonable to believe that an ace will never be drawn.
   (B) When the chances of a certain horse winning the race are 999 out of 1000, it is reasonable to believe that that horse will win. So it is reasonable to believe that no one other than that horse can win.
   (C) It is unreasonable to believe that 1000 consecutive coin flips will turn up heads, so it is reasonable to believe that this never happens.
   (D) It is reasonable to believe that if the most recent flip of a given coin was tails, the next flip will be heads. So if a coin has turned up tails the last 1000 times it was flipped, it is reasonable to believe that it will turn up heads the next time it is flipped.
   (E) For any given group of five-year-old children, the average height is one meter, so it is reasonable to believe that if Pat is five years old, she is exactly one meter tall.

GO ON TO THE NEXT PAGE.

4. Dental researcher: Filling a cavity in a tooth is not a harmless procedure: it inevitably damages some of the healthy parts of the tooth. Cavities are harmful only if the decay reaches the nerves inside the tooth, and many cavities, if left untreated, never progress to that point. Therefore, dentists should not fill a cavity unless the nerves inside the tooth are in imminent danger from that cavity.

Which one of the following principles, if valid, most strongly supports the researcher's reasoning?

(A)   Dentists should perform any procedure that is likely to be beneficial in the long term, but only if the procedure does not cause immediate damage.

(B)   Dentists should help their patients to prevent cavities rather than waiting until cavities are present to begin treatment.

(C)   A condition that is only potentially harmful should not be treated using a method that is definitely harmful.

(D)   A condition that is typically progressive should not be treated using methods that provide only temporary relief.

(E)   A condition that is potentially harmful should not be left untreated unless it can be kept under constant surveillance.

5. The number of codfish in the North Atlantic has declined substantially as the population of harp seals has increased from two million to more than three million. Some blame the seal for the shrinking cod population, but cod plays a negligible role in the seal's diet. It is therefore unlikely that the increase in the seal population has contributed significantly to the decline in the cod population.

Which one of the following, if true, most seriously weakens the argument?

(A)   People who fish for cod commercially are inconvenienced by the presence of large numbers of seals near traditional fishing grounds.

(B)   Water pollution poses a more serious threat to cod than to the harp seal.

(C)   The harp seal thrives in water that is too cold to support a dense population of cod.

(D)   Cod feed almost exclusively on capelin, a fish that is a staple of the harp seal's diet.

(E)   The cod population in the North Atlantic began to decline before the harp-seal population began to increase.

Hospital auditor: The Rodríguez family stipulated that the funds they donated to the neurological clinic all be used to minimize patients' suffering. The clinic administration is clearly violating those terms, since it has allocated nearly one fifth of those funds for research into new diagnostic technologies, instead of letting that money flow directly to its patients.

Clinic administrator: But the successful development of new technologies will allow early diagnosis of many neurological disorders. In most cases, patients who are treated in the early stages of neurological disorders suffer far less than do patients who are not treated until their neurological disorders reach advanced stages.

6. Which one of the following is the main point at issue between the hospital auditor and the clinic administrator?

(A)   whether early treatment of many neurological disorders lessens the suffering associated with those disorders rather than completely eliminating such suffering

(B)   whether the patients being treated at the neurological clinic are currently receiving adequate treatment for the neurological disorders from which they suffer

(C)   whether the Rodríguez family clearly stipulated that the funds they donated to the neurological clinic be used to minimize patients' suffering

(D)   whether the neurological clinic is adhering strictly to the conditions the Rodríguez family placed on the allocation of the funds they donated to the clinic

(E)   whether the Rodríguez family anticipated that some of the funds they donated to the neurological clinic would be used to pay for research into new diagnostic technologies

7. The clinic administrator responds to the hospital auditor by doing which one of the following?

(A)   demonstrating that the hospital auditor's conclusion, though broadly correct, stands in need of a minor qualification

(B)   showing that the hospital auditor's argument fails to separate what is the case from what ought to be the case

(C)   reminding the hospital auditor that, in the case at issue, being told what to do is tantamount to being told how to do it

(D)   arguing that, in assessing the severity of a violation, the reasoning motivating the violation needs to be considered

(E)   reinterpreting a key phrase in the hospital auditor's argument so as to undermine an assumption underlying that argument

8. Generally speaking, if the same crop is sown in a field for several successive years, growth in the later years is poorer than growth in the earlier years, since nitrogen in the soil becomes depleted. Even though alfalfa is a nitrogen-fixing plant and thus increases the amount of nitrogen in the soil, surprisingly, it too, if planted in the same field year after year, grows less well in the later years than it does in the earlier years.

Which one of the following, if true, most helps to explain the similarity described above between alfalfa and non-nitrogen-fixing plants?

(A)   Some kinds of plants grow more rapidly and are more productive when they are grown among other kinds of plants rather than being grown only among plants of their own kind.

(B)   Alfalfa increases the amount of nitrogen in the soil by taking nitrogen from the air and releasing it in a form that is usable by most kinds of plants.

(C)   Certain types of plants, including alfalfa, produce substances that accumulate in the soil and that are toxic to the plants that produce those substances.

(D)   Alfalfa increases nitrogen in the soil in which it grows only if a certain type of soil bacteria is present in the soil.

(E)   Alfalfa is very sensitive to juglone, a compound that is exuded from the leaves of black walnut trees.

9. Political commentators see recent policies of the government toward Country X as appeasement, pure and simple. This view is fundamentally mistaken, for polls show that most people disagree with the political commentators' assessment of government policies toward Country X.

The reasoning in the argument is questionable because

(A)   the term "policies" is used ambiguously in the argument

(B)   the political commentators discussed in the passage are not identified

(C)   a claim is inferred to be false merely because a majority of people believe it to be false

(D)   the claim that the political commentators are mistaken is both a premise and a conclusion in the argument

(E)   it is assumed that what is true of persons individually is true of a country as a whole

10. It is a principle of economics that a nation can experience economic growth only when consumer confidence is balanced with a small amount of consumer skepticism.

Which one of the following is an application of the economic principle above?

(A)   Any nation in which consumer confidence is balanced with a small amount of consumer skepticism will experience economic growth.

(B)   Any nation in which the prevailing attitude of consumers is not skepticism will experience economic growth.

(C)   Any nation in which the prevailing attitude of consumers is either exclusively confidence or exclusively skepticism will experience economic growth.

(D)   Any nation in which the prevailing attitude of consumers is exclusively confidence will not experience economic growth.

(E)   Any nation in which consumer skepticism is balanced with a small amount of consumer confidence will experience economic growth.

11. Sharks have a higher ratio of cartilage mass to body mass than any other organism. They also have a greater resistance to cancer than any other organism. Shark cartilage contains a substance that inhibits tumor growth by stopping the development of a new blood network. In the past 20 years, none of the responses among terminal cancer patients to various therapeutic measures has been more positive than the response among those who consumed shark cartilage.

If the claims made above are true, then each of the following could be true EXCEPT:

(A)   No organism resists cancer better than sharks do, but some resist cancer as well as sharks.

(B)   The organism most susceptible to cancer has a higher percentage of cartilage than some organisms that are less susceptible to cancer.

(C)   The substance in shark cartilage that inhibits tumor growth is found in most organisms.

(D)   In the past 20 years many terminal cancer patients have improved dramatically following many sorts of therapy.

(E)   Some organisms have immune systems more efficient than a shark's immune system.

GO ON TO THE NEXT PAGE.

Questions 12–13

People who say that Dooney County is flat are clearly wrong. On flat land, soil erosion by water is not a problem. Consequently, farmers whose land is flat do not build terraces to prevent erosion. Yet I hear that the farms in Dooney County are dotted with terraces.

12. The author's conclusion in the passage depends on the assumption that

    (A)   the only cause of soil erosion is water
    (B)   there are terraces on farmland in Dooney County which were built to prevent soil erosion
    (C)   terraces of the kind found on farmland in Dooney County have been shown to prevent soil erosion
    (D)   on flat land there is no soil erosion
    (E)   the only terraces in Dooney County are on farmland

13. The reasoning in the passage is most similar to that in which one of the following?

    (A)   If we paint the room white, it will get smudged, and we will have to paint it again soon. Therefore, we should paint it dark blue.
    (B)   People with children need more space than those without children. Yet people with no children can usually afford bigger houses.
    (C)   People who get a lot of exercise have no trouble falling asleep; hence, people who get a lot of exercise do not use medication to help them fall asleep. Jack is taking many kinds of medication, so he must not be getting a lot of exercise.
    (D)   If I go grocery shopping when I am hungry, I buy snack foods and cannot resist eating them. Therefore, I cannot lose weight.
    (E)   People who have many friends tend to go out often, so they need cars. Therefore, if Joe wants to have many friends, he must buy a car.

14. The axis of Earth's daily rotation is tilted with respect to the plane of its orbit at an angle of roughly 23 degrees. That angle can be kept fairly stable only by the gravitational influence of Earth's large, nearby Moon. Without such a stable and moderate axis tilt, a planet's climate is too extreme and unstable to support life. Mars, for example, has only very small moons, tilts at wildly fluctuating angles, and cannot support life.

If the statements above are true, which one of the following must also be true on the basis of them?

    (A)   If Mars had a sufficiently large nearby moon, Mars would be able to support life.
    (B)   If Earth's Moon were to leave Earth's orbit, Earth's climate would be unable to support life.
    (C)   Any planet with a stable, moderate axis tilt can support life.
    (D)   Gravitational influences other than moons have little or no effect on the magnitude of the tilt angle of either Earth's or Mars's axis.
    (E)   No planet that has more than one moon can support life.

GO ON TO THE NEXT PAGE.

15. The town of Springhill frequently must declare a water emergency, making it temporarily unlawful to use water for such nonessential purposes as car washing. These emergencies could be avoided if Springhill would introduce permanent economic incentives for water conservation. Actually, Springhill discourages conservation because each household pays a modest monthly flat fee for any amount of water below a certain usage threshold, and a substantial per-liter rate only after the threshold is reached.

Which one of the following, if true, most strengthens the argument?

(A) The Springhill authorities do a poor job of enforcing its water emergency laws and many people break the laws without incurring a penalty.

(B) The town council of Springhill recently refused to raise the threshold.

(C) The threshold is kept at a high enough level to exceed the water requirements of most households in Springhill.

(D) The threshold is not as high in Springhill as it is in neighboring towns.

(E) The threshold remains at the predetermined level specified by law until a change is approved by the Springhill town council.

16. Poppy petals function to attract pollinating insects. The pollination of a poppy flower triggers the release into that flower of a substance that causes its petals to wilt within one or two days. If the flower is not pollinated, the substance will not be released and the petals will remain fresh for a week or longer, as long as the plant can nourish them. Cutting an unpollinated poppy flower from the plant triggers the release into the flower of the same substance whose release is triggered by pollination.

The statements above, if true, most strongly support which one of the following?

(A) Pollinating insects are not attracted to wilted poppy flowers.

(B) Even if cut poppies are given all necessary nutrients, their petals will tend to wilt within a few days.

(C) Flowers of all plants release the substance that causes wilting when they are cut, although the amount released may vary.

(D) The pollen on pollinated poppy flowers prevents their petals from absorbing the nutrients carried to them by their stems.

(E) Poppy plants are unable to draw nutrients from soil or water after the substance that causes wilting has been released.

17. When a community opens a large shopping mall, it often expects a boost to the local economy, and in fact a large amount of economic activity goes on in these malls. Yet the increase in the local economy is typically much smaller than the total amount of economic activity that goes on in the mall.

Which one of the following, if true, most helps to explain the discrepancy described above?

(A) When large shopping malls are new they attract a lot of shoppers but once the novelty has worn off they usually attract fewer shoppers than does the traditional downtown shopping district.

(B) Most of the money spent in a large shopping mall is spent by tourists who are drawn specifically by the mall and who would not have visited the community had that mall not been built.

(C) Most of the jobs created by large shopping malls are filled by people who recently moved to the community and who would not have moved had there been no job offer in the community.

(D) Most of the money spent in a large shopping mall is money that would have been spent elsewhere in the same community had that mall not been built.

(E) Most of the jobs created by the construction of a large shopping mall are temporary, and most of the permanent jobs created are low paying.

GO ON TO THE NEXT PAGE.

18. Essayist: The way science is conducted and regulated can be changed. But we need to determine whether the changes are warranted, taking into account their price. The use of animals in research could end immediately, but only at the cost of abandoning many kinds of research and making others very expensive. The use of recombinant DNA could be drastically curtailed. Many other restrictions could be imposed, complete with a system of fraud police. But such massive interventions would be costly and would change the character of science.

Which one of the following most accurately expresses the main conclusion of the essayist's argument?

(A) We should not make changes that will alter the character of science.
(B) If we regulate science more closely, we will change the character of science.
(C) The regulation of science and the conducting of science can be changed.
(D) The imposition of restrictions on the conduct of science would be very costly.
(E) We need to be aware of the impact of change in science before changes are made.

19. The postmodern view involves the rejection of modern assumptions about order and the universality of truth. The grand theories of the modern era are now seen as limited by the social and historical contexts in which they were elaborated. Also, the belief in order has given way to a belief in the importance of irregularity and chaos. It follows that we inhabit a world full of irregular events, and in which there are no universal truths.

The argument's reasoning is questionable because the argument

(A) infers that something is the case because it is believed to be the case
(B) uses the term "universal" ambiguously
(C) relies on the use of emotional terms to bolster its conclusion
(D) uses the term "order" ambiguously
(E) fails to cite examples of modern theories that purport to embody universal truths

20. If the economy is weak, then prices remain constant although unemployment rises. But unemployment rises only if investment decreases. Fortunately, investment is not decreasing.

If the statements above are true, then which one of the following must be false?

(A) Either the economy is weak or investment is decreasing.
(B) If unemployment rises, then prices remain constant.
(C) The economy is weak only if investment decreases.
(D) Either the economy is weak or prices are remaining constant.
(E) Either unemployment is rising or the economy is not weak.

21. Psychologist: Some astrologers claim that our horoscopes completely determine our personalities, but this claim is false. I concede that identical twins—who are, of course, born at practically the same time—often do have similar personalities. However, birth records were examined to find two individuals who were born 40 years ago on the same day and at exactly the same time—one in a hospital in Toronto and one in a hospital in New York. Personality tests revealed that the personalities of these two individuals are in fact different.

Which one of the following is an assumption on which the psychologist's argument depends?

(A) Astrologers have not subjected their claims to rigorous experimentation.
(B) The personality differences between the two individuals cannot be explained by the cultural differences between Toronto and New York.
(C) The geographical difference between Toronto and New York did not result in the two individuals having different horoscopes.
(D) Complete birth records for the past 40 years were kept at both hospitals.
(E) Identical twins have identical genetic structures and usually have similar home environments.

GO ON TO THE NEXT PAGE.

22. Under the influence of today's computer-oriented culture, publishing for children has taken on a flashy new look that emphasizes illustrations and graphic design; the resulting lack of substance leads to books that are short-lived items covering mainly trendy subjects. The changes also include more humorous content, simplification of difficult material, and a narrower focus on specific topics.

Which one of the following is most strongly supported by the information above?

(A) The inclusion of humorous material and a narrower focus detract from the substance of a children's book.
(B) The substance of a children's book is important to its longevity.
(C) Children of the computer generation cannot concentrate on long, unbroken sections of prose.
(D) Children judge books primarily on the basis of graphic design.
(E) The lack of substance of a children's book is unlikely to be important to its popularity.

23. Further evidence of a connection between brain physiology and psychological states has recently been uncovered in the form of a correlation between electroencephalograph patterns and characteristic moods. A study showed that participants who suffered from clinical depression exhibited less left frontal lobe activity than right, while, conversely, characteristically good-natured participants exhibited greater left lobe activity. Thus one's general disposition is a result of the activity of one's frontal lobe.

Each of the following, if true, weakens the argument EXCEPT:

(A) Many drugs prescribed to combat clinical depression act by causing increased left lobe activity.
(B) Excessive sleep, a typical consequence of clinical depression, is known to suppress left lobe activity.
(C) Frontal lobe activity is not subject to variation the way general disposition is.
(D) Earlier studies indicated that frontal lobe activity and emotive states are both caused by activity in the brain's limbic system.
(E) Social interaction of the kind not engaged in by most clinically depressed people is known to stimulate left lobe activity.

24. We ought to pay attention only to the intrinsic properties of a work of art. Its other, extrinsic properties are irrelevant to our aesthetic interactions with it. For example, when we look at a painting we should consider only what is directly presented in our experience of it. What is really aesthetically relevant, therefore, is not what a painting symbolizes, but what it directly presents to experience.

The conclusion follows logically if which one of the following is added to the premises?

(A) What an artwork symbolizes involves only extrinsic properties of that work.
(B) There are certain properties of our experiences of artworks that can be distinguished as symbolic properties.
(C) Only an artwork's intrinsic properties are relevant to our aesthetic interactions with it.
(D) It is possible in theory for an artwork to symbolize nothing.
(E) An intrinsic property of an artwork is one that relates the work to itself.

GO ON TO THE NEXT PAGE.

25. McKinley: A double-blind study, in which neither the patient nor the primary researcher knows whether the patient is being given the drug being tested or a placebo, is the most effective procedure for testing the efficacy of a drug. But we will not be able to perform such a study on this new drug, since the drug will have various effects on the patients' bodies, which will make us aware of whether the patients are getting the drug or a placebo.

Engle: You cannot draw that conclusion at this point, for you are assuming you know what the outcome of the study will be.

Engle's statement indicates that he is most likely interpreting McKinley's remarks to be

(A) presuming that a double-blind study is the only effective way to test new drugs
(B) denying that the drug will be effective
(C) presuming that the placebo will produce no effects whatever on the patients' bodies
(D) referring to the drug's therapeutic effects rather than to any known side effects
(E) based on a confusion about when a drug is efficacious

26. Modern navigation systems, which are found in most of today's commercial aircraft, are made with low-power circuitry, which is more susceptible to interference than the vacuum-tube circuitry found in older planes. During landing, navigation systems receive radio signals from the airport to guide the plane to the runway. Recently, one plane with low-power circuitry veered off course during landing, its dials dimming, when a passenger turned on a laptop computer. Clearly, modern aircraft navigation systems are being put at risk by the electronic devices that passengers carry on board, such as cassette players and laptop computers.

Which one of the following, if true, LEAST strengthens the argument above?

(A) After the laptop computer was turned off, the plane regained course and its navigation instruments and dials returned to normal.
(B) When in use all electronic devices emit electromagnetic radiation, which is known to interfere with circuitry.
(C) No problems with navigational equipment or instrument dials have been reported on flights with no passenger-owned electronic devices on board.
(D) Significant electromagnetic radiation from portable electronic devices can travel up to eight meters, and some passenger seats on modern aircraft are located within four meters of the navigation systems.
(E) Planes were first equipped with low-power circuitry at about the same time portable electronic devices became popular.

S T O P

IF YOU FINISH BEFORE TIME IS CALLED, YOU MAY CHECK YOUR WORK ON THIS SECTION ONLY.
DO NOT WORK ON ANY OTHER SECTION IN THE TEST.

SECTION II

Time—35 minutes

23 Questions

Directions: Each group of questions in this section is based on a set of conditions. In answering some of the questions, it may be useful to draw a rough diagram. Choose the response that most accurately and completely answers each question and blacken the corresponding space on your answer sheet.

Questions 1–5

Six racehorses—K, L, M, N, O, and P—will be assigned to six positions arranged in a straight line and numbered consecutively 1 through 6. The horses are assigned to the positions, one horse per position, according to the following conditions:

K and L must be assigned to positions that are separated from each other by exactly one position.
K and N cannot be assigned to positions that are next to each other.
N must be assigned to a higher-numbered position than M.
P must be assigned to position 3.

1. Which one of the following lists an acceptable assignment of horses to positions 1 through 6, respectively?

   (A)   K, L, P, M, N, O
   (B)   M, K, P, L, N, O
   (C)   M, N, K, P, L, O
   (D)   N, O, P, K, M, L
   (E)   O, M, P, L, N. K

2. Which one of the following is a complete and accurate list of the positions any one of which can be the position to which K is assigned?

   (A)   1, 2
   (B)   2, 3
   (C)   2, 4
   (D)   2, 4, 5
   (E)   2, 4, 6

3. Which one of the following CANNOT be true?

   (A)   K is assigned to position 2.
   (B)   L is assigned to position 2.
   (C)   M is assigned to position 1.
   (D)   M is assigned to position 5.
   (E)   O is assigned to position 2.

4. Which one of the following must be true?

   (A)   Either K or else L is assigned to position 2.
   (B)   Either K or else L is assigned to position 4.
   (C)   Either M or else N is assigned to position 2.
   (D)   Either M or else N is assigned to position 5.
   (E)   Either M or else O is assigned to position 6.

5. Which one of the following CANNOT be true?

   (A)   L and N are assigned to positions that are next to each other.
   (B)   M and K are assigned to positions that are next to each other.
   (C)   M and O are assigned to positions that are next to each other.
   (D)   L and N are assigned to positions that are separated from each other by exactly one position.
   (E)   M and P are assigned to positions that are separated from each other by exactly one position.

GO ON TO THE NEXT PAGE.

Questions 6–12

To prepare for fieldwork, exactly four different researchers—a geologist, a historian, a linguist, and a paleontologist—will learn at least one and at most three of four languages—Rundi, Swahili, Tigrinya, and Yoruba. They must learn the languages according to the following specifications:

Exactly one researcher learns Rundi.
Exactly two researchers learn Swahili.
Exactly two researchers learn Tigrinya.
Exactly three researchers learn Yoruba.
Any language learned by the linguist or paleontologist is not learned by the geologist.
Any language learned by the geologist is learned by the historian.

6. Which one of the following could be true?

    (A)   The linguist learns three languages—Rundi, Swahili, and Tigrinya.
    (B)   The linguist learns three languages—Swahili, Tigrinya, and Yoruba.
    (C)   The historian learns three languages—Rundi, Swahili, and Tigrinya.
    (D)   The historian learns three languages—Swahili, Tigrinya, and Yoruba.
    (E)   The paleontologist learns three languages—Rundi, Swahili, and Tigrinya.

7. If the linguist learns three of the languages, then which one of the following must be true?

    (A)   The linguist learns Tigrinya.
    (B)   The linguist learns Rundi.
    (C)   The linguist learns Swahili.
    (D)   The paleontologist learns Rundi.
    (E)   The paleontologist learns Swahili.

8. Each of the following could be true of the researcher who learns Rundi EXCEPT:

    (A)   The researcher also learns Tigrinya but not Swahili.
    (B)   The researcher learns neither Tigrinya nor Swahili.
    (C)   The researcher also learns Tigrinya but not Yoruba.
    (D)   The researcher also learns both Tigrinya and Yoruba.
    (E)   The researcher also learns Yoruba but not Tigrinya.

9. Each of the following could be a complete and accurate list of the researchers who learn both Swahili and Yoruba EXCEPT:

    (A)   the historian
    (B)   the paleontologist
    (C)   the historian, the linguist
    (D)   the historian, the paleontologist
    (E)   the linguist, the paleontologist

10. If the geologist learns exactly two of the languages, then which one of the following could be true?

    (A)   The paleontologist learns Rundi.
    (B)   The paleontologist learns Swahili.
    (C)   The historian learns Rundi.
    (D)   The paleontologist learns exactly three of the languages.
    (E)   The historian learns exactly two of the languages.

11. Which one of the following must be true?

    (A)   Fewer of the languages are learned by the historian than are learned by the paleontologist.
    (B)   Fewer of the languages are learned by the geologist than are learned by the historian.
    (C)   Fewer of the languages are learned by the geologist than are learned by the linguist.
    (D)   Fewer of the languages are learned by the paleontologist than are learned by the linguist.
    (E)   Fewer of the languages are learned by the paleontologist than are learned by the historian.

12. If exactly two of the languages are learned by the historian, then which one of the following must be true?

    (A)   The paleontologist does not learn Rundi.
    (B)   The geologist does not learn Swahili.
    (C)   The linguist does not learn Rundi.
    (D)   The historian does not learn Rundi.
    (E)   The paleontologist does not learn Swahili.

GO ON TO THE NEXT PAGE.

Questions 13–18

During three days—Monday through Wednesday—a health officer will inspect exactly six buildings—three hotels: Grace, Jacaranda, and Lido; and three restaurants: Seville, Vesuvio, and Zeno. Each day, exactly two buildings are inspected: one in the morning and one in the afternoon. Inspections must occur according to the following conditions:

Hotels are not inspected on Wednesday.
Grace is inspected at some time before Jacaranda.
Grace is not inspected on the same day as Seville.
If Zeno is inspected in the morning, Lido is also inspected in the morning.

13. Which one of the following could be the order in which the buildings are inspected, listed in order from Monday morning through Wednesday afternoon?

(A) Grace, Seville, Jacaranda, Lido, Vesuvio, Zeno
(B) Grace, Vesuvio, Zeno, Jacaranda, Lido, Seville
(C) Lido, Jacaranda, Grace, Vesuvio, Zeno, Seville
(D) Lido, Seville, Grace, Jacaranda, Zeno, Vesuvio
(E) Zeno, Grace, Jacaranda, Lido, Seville, Vesuvio

14. Which one of the following could be the buildings inspected in the mornings, listed in order from Monday through Wednesday?

(A) Grace, Jacaranda, Zeno
(B) Jacaranda, Vesuvio, Seville
(C) Lido, Jacaranda, Vesuvio
(D) Seville, Jacaranda, Vesuvio
(E) Seville, Lido, Zeno

15. Which one of the following is a pair of buildings that, if inspected on the same day as each other, must be inspected on Monday?

(A) Grace and Jacaranda
(B) Grace and Vesuvio
(C) Jacaranda and Lido
(D) Lido and Seville
(E) Lido and Vesuvio

16. If Grace is inspected on Tuesday, which one of the following could be the buildings inspected in the afternoons, listed in order from Monday through Wednesday?

(A) Lido, Jacaranda, Vesuvio
(B) Lido, Jacaranda, Zeno
(C) Lido, Vesuvio, Zeno
(D) Seville, Grace, Vesuvio
(E) Seville, Jacaranda, Lido

17. If Seville is inspected on Monday morning, which one of the following must be true?

(A) Grace is inspected on Tuesday afternoon.
(B) Jacaranda is inspected on Monday afternoon.
(C) Lido is inspected on Tuesday morning.
(D) Vesuvio is inspected on Wednesday morning.
(E) Zeno is inspected on Wednesday morning.

18. If Grace is inspected on Monday morning and Zeno is inspected on Wednesday morning, which one of the following must be true?

(A) Jacaranda is inspected before Lido is inspected.
(B) Jacaranda is inspected after Lido is inspected.
(C) Jacaranda is inspected after Seville is inspected.
(D) Lido is inspected before Seville is inspected.
(E) Lido is inspected before Vesuvio is inspected.

GO ON TO THE NEXT PAGE.

Questions 19–23

Morrisville's town council has exactly three members: Fu, Gianola, and Herstein. During one week, the council members vote on exactly three bills: a recreation bill, a school bill, and a tax bill. Each council member votes either for or against each bill. The following is known:

    Each member of the council votes for at least one of the bills and against at least one of the bills.

    Exactly two members of the council vote for the recreation bill.

    Exactly one member of the council votes for the school bill.

    Exactly one member of the council votes for the tax bill.

    Fu votes for the recreation bill and against the school bill.

    Gianola votes against the recreation bill.

    Herstein votes against the tax bill.

19. Which one of the following statements could be true?

    (A)   Fu and Gianola vote the same way on the tax bill.

    (B)   Gianola and Herstein vote the same way on the recreation bill.

    (C)   Gianola and Herstein vote the same way on the school bill.

    (D)   Fu votes for one of the bills and Gianola votes for two of the bills.

    (E)   Fu votes for two of the bills and Gianola votes for two of the bills.

20. If the set of members of the council who vote against the school bill is the same set of members who vote against the tax bill, then which one of the following statements must be true?

    (A)   Fu votes for the tax bill.

    (B)   Gianola votes for the recreation bill.

    (C)   Gianola votes against the school bill.

    (D)   Herstein votes against the recreation bill.

    (E)   Herstein votes against the school bill.

21. If Gianola votes for the tax bill, then which one of the following statements could be true?

    (A)   Fu and Gianola each vote for exactly one bill.

    (B)   Gianola and Herstein each vote for exactly one bill.

    (C)   Fu votes for exactly two bills.

    (D)   Gianola votes for the recreation bill.

    (E)   Herstein votes against the recreation bill.

22. If Gianola votes for exactly two of the three bills, which one of the following statements must be true?

    (A)   Fu votes for the tax bill.

    (B)   Gianola votes for the recreation bill.

    (C)   Gianola votes for the school bill.

    (D)   Gianola votes against the tax bill.

    (E)   Herstein votes for the school bill.

23. If one of the members of the council votes against exactly the same bills as does another member of the council, then which one of the following statements must be true?

    (A)   Fu votes for the tax bill.

    (B)   Gianola votes for the recreation bill.

    (C)   Gianola votes against the school bill.

    (D)   Gianola votes for exactly one bill.

    (E)   Herstein votes for exactly one bill.

S T O P

IF YOU FINISH BEFORE TIME IS CALLED, YOU MAY CHECK YOUR WORK ON THIS SECTION ONLY.
DO NOT WORK ON ANY OTHER SECTION IN THE TEST.

SECTION III

Time—35 minutes

26 Questions

Directions: The questions in this section are based on the reasoning contained in brief statements or passages. For some questions, more than one of the choices could conceivably answer the question. However, you are to choose the best answer; that is, the response that most accurately and completely answers the question. You should not make assumptions that are by commonsense standards implausible, superfluous, or incompatible with the passage. After you have chosen the best answer, blacken the corresponding space on your answer sheet.

1. Flavonoids are a common component of almost all plants, but a specific variety of flavonoid in apples has been found to be an antioxidant. Antioxidants are known to be a factor in the prevention of heart disease.

   Which one of the following can be properly inferred from the passage?

   (A) A diet composed largely of fruits and vegetables will help to prevent heart disease.
   (B) Flavonoids are essential to preventing heart disease.
   (C) Eating at least one apple each day will prevent heart disease.
   (D) At least one type of flavonoid helps to prevent heart disease.
   (E) A diet deficient in antioxidants is a common cause of heart disease.

2. A number of Grandville's wealthiest citizens have been criminals. So, since it is of utmost importance that the Grandville Planning Committee be composed solely of individuals whose personal standards of ethics are beyond reproach, no wealthy person should be appointed to that committee.

   The argument is most vulnerable to the criticism that it

   (A) confuses a result with something that is sufficient for bringing about that result
   (B) mistakes a temporal relationship for a causal relationship
   (C) assumes that because a certain action has a certain result the person taking that action intended that result
   (D) judges only by subjective standards something that can be readily evaluated according to objective standards
   (E) generalizes on the basis of what could be exceptional cases

3. Birds startled by potential predators generally try to take cover in nearby vegetation. Yet many birds that feed at bird feeders placed in suburban gardens are killed when, thus startled, they fly away from the vegetation in the gardens and into the windowpanes of nearby houses.

   Which one of the following, if true, most helps to explain the anomalous behavior of the birds that fly into windowpanes?

   (A) Predator attacks are as likely to occur at bird feeders surrounded by dense vegetation as they are at feeders surrounded by little or no vegetation.
   (B) The bird feeders in some suburban gardens are placed at a considerable distance from the houses.
   (C) Large birds are as likely as small birds to fly into windowpanes.
   (D) Most of the birds startled while feeding at bird feeders placed in suburban gardens are startled by loud noises rather than by predators.
   (E) The windowpanes of many houses clearly reflect surrounding vegetation.

4. Raising the humidity of a room protects furniture, draperies, and computers from damage caused by excessively dry air. Further, it can make people feel warmer, helps the body's defenses against viruses, and alleviates some skin rashes.

   Each of the following is supported by the information above EXCEPT:

   (A) Humidity can be bad for computers.
   (B) A room can be too dry for the optimal maintenance of its furnishings.
   (C) Dry air can feel cooler than humid air of the same temperature.
   (D) Increased humidity can be beneficial to the skin.
   (E) The human immune system can benefit from humidity.

GO ON TO THE NEXT PAGE.

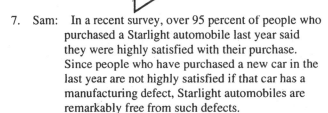

Questions 5–6

Jane: Television programs and movies that depict violence among teenagers are extremely popular. Given how influential these media are, we have good reason to believe that these depictions cause young people to engage in violent behavior. Hence, depictions of violence among teenagers should be prohibited from movies and television programs, if only in those programs and movies promoted to young audiences.

Maurice: But you are recommending nothing short of censorship! Besides which, your claim that television and movie depictions of violence cause violence is mistaken: violence among young people predates movies and television by centuries.

5. Maurice's attempted refutation of Jane's argument is vulnerable to criticism on which one of the following grounds?

(A) It presupposes that an unpopular policy cannot possibly achieve its intended purpose.

(B) It confuses a subjective judgment of private moral permissibility with an objective description of social fact.

(C) It rules out something as a cause of a current phenomenon solely on the ground that the phenomenon used to occur without that thing.

(D) It cites purported historical facts that cannot possibly be verified.

(E) It relies on an ambiguity in the term "violence" to justify a claim.

6. Which one of the following, if true, most strengthens Jane's argument?

(A) The most violent characters depicted in movies and on television programs are adult characters who are portrayed by adult actors.

(B) The movies that have been shown to have the most influence on young people's behavior are those that are promoted to young audiences.

(C) The people who make the most profits in the movie and television industry are those who can successfully promote their work to both young and old audiences.

(D) Many adolescents who engage in violent behavior had already displayed such behavior before they were exposed to violence in movies.

(E) Among the producers who make both movies and television programs, many voluntarily restrict the subject matter of films directed toward young audiences.

7. Sam: In a recent survey, over 95 percent of people who purchased a Starlight automobile last year said they were highly satisfied with their purchase. Since people who have purchased a new car in the last year are not highly satisfied if that car has a manufacturing defect, Starlight automobiles are remarkably free from such defects.

Tiya: But some manufacturing defects in automobiles become apparent only after several years of use.

Which one of the following most accurately describes how Tiya's response is related to Sam's argument?

(A) It argues that Sam's conclusion is correct, though not for the reasons Sam gives.

(B) It provides evidence indicating that the survey results Sam relies on in his argument do not accurately characterize the attitudes of those surveyed.

(C) It offers a consideration that undermines the support Sam offers for his conclusion.

(D) It points out that Sam's argument presupposes the truth of the conclusion Sam is defending.

(E) It presents new information that implies that Sam's conclusion is false.

8. Some environmentalists question the prudence of exploiting features of the environment, arguing that there are no economic benefits to be gained from forests, mountains, or wetlands that no longer exist. Many environmentalists claim that because nature has intrinsic value it would be wrong to destroy such features of the environment, even if the economic costs of doing so were outweighed by the economic costs of not doing so.

Which one of the following can be logically inferred from the passage?

(A) It is economically imprudent to exploit features of the environment.

(B) Some environmentalists appeal to a noneconomic justification in questioning the defensibility of exploiting features of the environment.

(C) Most environmentalists appeal to economic reasons in questioning the defensibility of exploiting features of the environment.

(D) Many environmentalists provide only a noneconomic justification in questioning the defensibility of exploiting features of the environment.

(E) Even if there is no economic reason for protecting the environment, there is a sound noneconomic justification for doing so.

GO ON TO THE NEXT PAGE.

9. Market research traditionally entails surveying consumers about why they buy and use particular products and brands. Observational research—actually watching consumers shopping and interacting with products—is now increasingly used by market researchers to supplement surveys. Market researchers claim that observational research yields information about consumer behavior that surveys alone cannot provide.

Which one of the following, if true, provides the strongest support for the market researchers' claim?

(A) Even consumers who are unable to explain their preference for or rejection of particular brands reveal which brands they are considering by picking up and putting down products while they are shopping.

(B) Market researchers find that consumers are almost always willing to participate in observational research for which the consumer is paid by the hour.

(C) Consumers are becoming increasingly self-conscious about their buying habits, and some consumers have stopped buying some items that they normally used to buy.

(D) Market researchers say they find data collection more enjoyable in observational research than in survey research, because observational research requires more creative judgment on their part.

(E) Consumers are more likely to respond to oral surveys than they are to respond to written questionnaires.

10. Laura: Harold is obviously lonely. He should sell his cabin in the woods and move into town. In town he will be near other people all the time, so he will not be lonely any more.

Ralph: Many very lonely people live in towns. What is needed to avoid loneliness is not only the proximity of other people but also genuine interaction with them.

Ralph responds to Laura by pointing out that

(A) something needed for a certain result does not necessarily guarantee that result

(B) what is appropriate in one case is not necessarily appropriate in all cases

(C) what is logically certain is not always intuitively obvious

(D) various alternative solutions are possible for a single problem

(E) a proposed solution for a problem could actually worsen that problem

11. A rise in the percentage of all 18-year-olds who were recruited by the armed services of a small republic between 1980 and 1986 correlates with a rise in the percentage of young people who dropped out of high school in that republic. Since 18-year-olds in the republic are generally either high school graduates or high school dropouts, the correlation leads to the conclusion that the republic's recruitment rates for 18-year-olds depend substantially on recruitment rates for high school dropouts.

Which one of the following statements, if true, most weakens the argument?

(A) A larger number of 18-year-old high school graduates were recruited for the republic's armed services in 1986 than in 1980.

(B) Many of the high-technology systems used by the republic's armed services can be operated only by individuals who have completed a high school education.

(C) Between 1980 and 1986 the percentage of high school graduates among 18-year-olds recruited in the republic rose sharply.

(D) Personnel of the republic's armed services are strongly encouraged to finish their high school education.

(E) The proportion of recruits who had completed at least two years of college education was greater in 1986 than in 1980.

12. Letter to the Editor: Your article on effective cockroach control states that vexone is effective against only one of the more than 4,000 cockroach species that infest North America: the German cockroach. In actuality, vexone has been utilized effectively for almost a decade against all of the species that infest North America. In testing our product, Roach Ender, which contains vexone, we have conducted many well-documented studies that prove this fact.

Each of the following statements conflicts with the letter writer's view EXCEPT:

(A) Vexone is effective against only two species of cockroach that infest North America.

(B) Not all of the major species of cockroach that infest North America can be controlled by Roach Ender.

(C) Every species of cockroach that infests North America can be controlled by vexone.

(D) The cockroach infestations that have been combated with vexone have not included all of the cockroach species that infest North America.

(E) Roach Ender was tested against exactly 4,000 cockroach species that infest North America.

GO ON TO THE NEXT PAGE.

13. A recent study concludes that prehistoric birds, unlike modern birds, were cold-blooded. This challenges a widely held view that modern birds descended from warm-blooded birds. The conclusion is based on the existence of growth rings in prehistoric birds' bodily structures, which are thought to be found only in cold-blooded animals. Another study, however, disputes this view. It concludes that prehistoric birds had dense blood vessels in their bones, which suggests that they were active creatures and therefore had to be warm-blooded.

Which one of the following, if true, would most help to resolve the dispute described above in favor of one party to it?

(A) Some modern warm-blooded species other than birds have been shown to have descended from cold-blooded species.

(B) Having growth rings is not the only physical trait of cold-blooded species.

(C) Modern birds did not evolve from prehistoric species of birds.

(D) Dense blood vessels are not found in all warm-blooded species.

(E) In some cold-blooded species the gene that is responsible for growth rings is also responsible for dense blood vessels.

14. If citizens do not exercise their right to vote, then democratic institutions will crumble and, as a consequence, much valuable social cohesion will be lost. Of course, one person's vote can only make an imperceptible difference to the result of an election, but one must consider the likely effects of large numbers of people failing to vote. An act or omission by one person is not right if such an act or omission done by large numbers of people would be socially damaging. Organized society would be impossible if theft were common, though a single dishonest act on the part of a single person is likely to have an insignificant effect upon society.

Which one of the following most accurately expresses the main conclusion of the argument?

(A) People in a democracy should not neglect to vote.

(B) Dishonest acts and failure to vote are equally damaging.

(C) There is a risk that individual antisocial acts will be imitated by others.

(D) A single person's vote or wrongful act can in fact make a great deal of difference.

(E) Large-scale dishonesty and neglect of public duty will be destructive of democratic and other societies.

15. Human beings have cognitive faculties that are superior to those of other animals, and once humans become aware of these, they cannot be made happy by anything that does not involve gratification of these faculties.

Which one of the following statements, if true, most calls into question the view above?

(A) Certain animals—dolphins and chimpanzees, for example—appear to be capable of rational communication.

(B) Many people familiar both with intellectual stimulation and with physical pleasures enjoy the latter more.

(C) Someone who never experienced classical music as a child will usually prefer popular music as an adult.

(D) Many people who are serious athletes consider themselves to be happy.

(E) Many people who are serious athletes love gourmet food.

16. Historian: We can learn about the medical history of individuals through chemical analysis of their hair. It is likely, for example, that Isaac Newton's psychological problems were due to mercury poisoning; traces of mercury were found in his hair. Analysis is now being done on a lock of Beethoven's hair. Although no convincing argument has shown that Beethoven ever had a venereal disease, some people hypothesize that venereal disease caused his deafness. Since mercury was commonly ingested in Beethoven's time to treat venereal disease, if researchers find a trace of mercury in his hair, we can conclude that this hypothesis is correct.

Which one of the following is an assumption on which the historian's argument depends?

(A) None of the mercury introduced into the body can be eliminated.

(B) Some people in Beethoven's time did not ingest mercury.

(C) Mercury is an effective treatment for venereal disease.

(D) Mercury poisoning can cause deafness in people with venereal disease.

(E) Beethoven suffered from psychological problems of the same severity as Newton's.

GO ON TO THE NEXT PAGE.

17. In 1992, a major newspaper circulated throughout North America paid its reporters an average salary that was much lower than the average salary paid by its principal competitors to their reporters. An executive of the newspaper argued that this practice was justified, since any shortfall that might exist in the reporters' salaries is fully compensated by the valuable training they receive through their assignments.

Which one of the following, if true about the newspaper in 1992, most seriously undermines the justification offered by the executive?

(A) Senior reporters at the newspaper earned as much as reporters of similar stature who worked for the newspaper's principal competitors.

(B) Most of the newspaper's reporters had worked there for more than ten years.

(C) The circulation of the newspaper had recently reached a plateau, after it had increased steadily throughout the 1980s.

(D) The union that represented reporters at the newspaper was different from the union that represented reporters at the newspaper's competitors.

(E) The newspaper was widely read throughout continental Europe and Great Britain as well as North America.

18. The human brain and its associated mental capacities evolved to assist self-preservation. Thus, the capacity to make aesthetic judgments is an adaptation to past environments in which humans lived. So an individual's aesthetic judgments must be evaluated in terms of the extent to which they promote the survival of that individual.

Which one of the following is a principle that would, if valid, provide the strongest justification for the reasoning above?

(A) All human adaptations to past environments were based on the human brain and its associated mental capacities.

(B) Human capacities that do not contribute to the biological success of the human species cannot be evaluated.

(C) If something develops to serve a given function, the standard by which it must be judged is how well it serves that function.

(D) Judgments that depend on individual preference or taste cannot be evaluated as true or false.

(E) Anything that enhances the proliferation of a species is to be valued highly.

19. On a certain day, nine scheduled flights on Swift Airlines were canceled. Ordinarily, a cancellation is due to mechanical problems with the airplane scheduled for a certain flight. However, since it is unlikely that Swift would have mechanical problems with more than one or two airplanes on a single day, some of the nine cancellations were probably due to something else.

The argument depends on which one of the following assumptions?

(A) More than one or two airplanes were scheduled for the nine canceled flights.

(B) Swift Airlines has fewer mechanical problems than do other airlines of the same size.

(C) Each of the canceled flights would have been longer than the average flight on Swift Airlines

(D) Swift Airlines had never before canceled more than one or two scheduled flights on a single day.

(E) All of the airplanes scheduled for the canceled flights are based at the same airport.

GO ON TO THE NEXT PAGE.

20. Game show host: Humans are no better than apes at investing, that is, they do not attain a better return on their investments than apes do. We gave five stock analysts and one chimpanzee $1,350 each to invest. After one month, the chimp won, having increased its net worth by $210. The net worth of the analyst who came in second increased by only $140.

Each of the following describes a flaw in the game show host's reasoning EXCEPT:

(A) A conclusion is drawn about apes in general on the basis of an experiment involving one chimpanzee.

(B) No evidence is offered that chimpanzees are capable of understanding stock reports and making reasoned investment decisions.

(C) A broad conclusion is drawn about the investment skills of humans on the basis of what is known about five humans.

(D) Too general a conclusion is made about investing on the basis of a single experiment involving short-term investing but not long-term investing.

(E) No evidence is considered about the long-term performance of the chimpanzee's portfolio versus that of the analysts' portfolios.

21. If the law punishes littering, then the city has an obligation to provide trash cans. But the law does not punish littering, so the city has no such obligation.

Which one of the following exhibits a flawed pattern of reasoning most similar to that in the argument above?

(A) If today is a holiday, then the bakery will not be open. The bakery is not open for business. Thus today is a holiday.

(B) Jenny will have lots of balloons at her birthday party. There are no balloons around yet, so today is not her birthday.

(C) The new regulations will be successful only if most of the students adhere to them. Since most of the students will adhere to those regulations, the new regulations will be successful.

(D) In the event that my flight had been late, I would have missed the committee meeting. Fortunately, my flight is on time. Therefore, I will make it to the meeting.

(E) When the law is enforced, some people are jailed. But no one is in jail, so clearly the law is not enforced.

22. Researcher: The role of chemicals called pheromones in determining the sexual behavior of some animals is well documented. But, even though humans also produce these chemicals, it is clear that psychological factors have taken over this role in us. Whereas for animals these behaviors are involuntary, which is a clear sign of chemical control, humans, by virtue of their free will, choose how they behave, and thus psychological factors take over. So pheromones are merely a vestige of our evolutionary past.

The researcher's argument requires the assumption that

(A) whatever does not have a chemical explanation must have a purely psychological one

(B) voluntary action cannot have a chemical explanation

(C) free will can be found only in humans

(D) voluntary action cannot have an evolutionary explanation

(E) there is a psychological explanation for the continuing presence of pheromones in humans

GO ON TO THE NEXT PAGE.

23. Ethicist: It is widely believed that it is always wrong to tell lies, but this is a rule almost no one fully complies with. In fact, lying is often the morally appropriate thing to do. It is morally correct to lie when telling the truth carries the reasonable expectation of producing considerable physical or psychological harm to others.

Which one of the following most closely conforms to the principle the ethicist endorses?

(A) When Juan asked Judy if the movie they were going to was *North by Northwest*, Judy said yes, though she knew that *Persona* was playing instead. This was the only way Juan would see the film and avoid losing an opportunity for an aesthetically pleasing experience.

(B) A daughter asked her father which candidate he supported, McBride or Chang. Though in fact he preferred Chang, the father responded by saying he preferred McBride, in order to avoid discussion.

(C) A husband told his wife he felt ready to go on a canoe trip, though he had recently had severe chest pains; his wife had determined a year ago that they would go on this trip, so to ask to cancel now would be inconvenient.

(D) A young boy asked his mother if she loved his older sister more than she loved him. The mother said she loved them both to the same degree, even though it was not true.

(E) A friend invited Jamal to a party, but Jamal was afraid that he might see his ex-wife and her new husband there. To spare himself emotional pain, as well as the embarrassment of telling his friend why he did not want to go, Jamal falsely claimed he had to work.

24. Surviving seventeenth-century Dutch landscapes attributed to major artists now equal in number those attributed to minor ones. But since in the seventeenth century many prolific minor artists made a living supplying the voracious market for Dutch landscapes, while only a handful of major artists painted in the genre, many attributions of seventeenth-century Dutch landscape paintings to major artists are undoubtedly erroneous.

Which one of the following, if true, most strengthens the argument?

(A) Technically gifted seventeenth-century Dutch landscape artists developed recognizable styles that were difficult to imitate.

(B) In the workshops of major seventeenth-century artists, assistants were employed to prepare the paints, brushes, and other materials that the major artists then used.

(C) In the eighteenth century, landscapes by minor seventeenth-century artists were often simply thrown away or else destroyed through improper storage.

(D) Seventeenth-century art dealers paid minor artists extra money to leave their landscapes unsigned so that the dealers could add phony signatures and pass such works off as valuable paintings.

(E) More seventeenth-century Dutch landscapes were painted than have actually survived, and that is true of those executed by minor artists as well as of those executed by major artists.

GO ON TO THE NEXT PAGE.

25. The interstitial nucleus, a subregion of the brain's hypothalamus, is typically smaller for male cats than for female cats. A neurobiologist performed autopsies on male cats who died from disease X, a disease affecting no more than .05 percent of male cats, and found that these male cats had interstitial nuclei that were as large as those generally found in female cats. Thus, the size of the interstitial nucleus determines whether or not male cats can contract disease X.

Which one of the following statements, if true, most seriously weakens the argument?

(A) No female cats have been known to contract disease X, which is a subtype of disease Y.

(B) Many male cats who contract disease X also contract disease Z, the cause of which is unknown.

(C) The interstitial nuclei of female cats who contract disease X are larger than those of female cats who do not contract disease X.

(D) Of 1,000 autopsies on male cats who did not contract disease X, 5 revealed interstitial nuclei larger than those of the average male cat.

(E) The hypothalamus is known not to be causally linked to disease Y, and disease X is a subtype of disease Y.

26. It is common to respond to a person who is exhorting us to change our behavior by drawing attention to that person's own behavior. This response, however, is irrational. Whether or not someone in fact heeds his or her own advice is irrelevant to whether that person's advice should be heeded.

Which one of the following arguments is most similar in its reasoning to the argument above?

(A) Other countries argue that if we are serious about disarming we should go ahead and disarm to show our good intentions, but this is irrational, for we could make the same argument about them.

(B) My neighbor urges me to exercise, but I see no good reason to do so; despite his strenuous exercise, he has failed to exhibit any real benefits from it.

(C) When one country accuses another country of violating human rights standards, the accused country can reduce the damage to its reputation by drawing attention to the human rights record of its accuser because this tactic distracts critical attention.

(D) One should not dismiss the philosopher's argument that matter does not exist by pointing out that the philosopher acts as though matter exists. People's actions have no effect on the strength of their arguments.

(E) We should not be too severe in our condemnation of the salesperson; we have all lied at one point or another. It is irrational to condemn a person for wrongs committed by everybody.

S T O P

IF YOU FINISH BEFORE TIME IS CALLED, YOU MAY CHECK YOUR WORK ON THIS SECTION ONLY.
DO NOT WORK ON ANY OTHER SECTION IN THE TEST.

SECTION IV

Time—35 minutes

26 Questions

Directions: Each passage in this section is followed by a group of questions to be answered on the basis of what is stated or implied in the passage. For some of the questions, more than one of the choices could conceivably answer the question. However, you are to choose the best answer; that is, the response that most accurately and completely answers the question, and blacken the corresponding space on your answer sheet.

Some Native American tribes have had difficulty establishing their land claims because the United States government did not recognize their status as tribes; therefore during the 1970s some Native Americans
(5) attempted to obtain such recognition through the medium of U.S. courts. In presenting these suits, Native Americans had to operate within a particular sphere of U.S. government procedure, that of its legal system, and their arguments were necessarily
(10) interpreted by the courts in terms the law could understand: e.g., through application of precedent or review of evidence. This process brought to light some of the differing perceptions and definitions that can exist between cultures whose systems of discourse are
(15) sometimes at variance.

In one instance, the entire legal dispute turned on whether the suing community—a group of Mashpee Wampanoag in the town of Mashpee, Massachusetts— constituted a tribe. The area had long been occupied by
(20) the Mashpee, who continued to have control over land use after the town's incorporation. But in the 1960s, after an influx of non-Mashpee people shifted the balance of political power in the town, the new residents were able to buy Mashpee-controlled land
(25) from the town and develop it for commercial or private use. The Mashpee's 1976 suit claimed that these lands were taken in violation of a statute prohibiting transfers of land from any tribe of Native Americans without federal approval. The town argued that the Mashpee
(30) were not a tribe in the sense intended by the statute and so were outside its protection. As a result, the Mashpee were required to demonstrate their status as a tribe according to a definition contained in an earlier ruling: a body of Native Americans "governing themselves
(35) under one leadership and inhabiting a particular territory."

The town claimed that the Mashpee were not self-governing and that they had no defined territory: the Mashpee could legally be self-governing, the town
(40) argued, only if they could show written documentation of such a system, and could legally inhabit territory only if they had precisely delineated its boundaries and possessed a deed to it. The Mashpee marshaled oral testimony against these claims, arguing that what the
(45) town perceived as a lack of evidence was simply information that an oral culture such as the Mashpee's would not have recorded in writing. In this instance, the disjunction between U.S. legal discourse and Mashpee culture—exemplified in the court's inability
(50) to "understand" the Mashpee's oral testimony as

documentary evidence—rendered the suit unsuccessful. Similar claims have recently met with greater success, however, as U.S. courts have begun to acknowledge that the failure to accommodate differences in
(55) discourse between cultures can sometimes stand in the way of guaranteeing the fairness of legal decisions.

1. Which one of the following most completely and accurately expresses the main point of the passage?

(A) Land claim suits such as the Mashpee's establish that such suits must be bolstered by written documentation if they are to succeed in U.S. courts.

(B) Land claim suits such as the Mashpee's underscore the need for U.S. courts to modify their definition of "tribe."

(C) Land claim suits such as the Mashpee's illustrate the complications that can result when cultures with different systems of discourse attempt to resolve disputes.

(D) Land claim suits such as the Mashpee's point out discrepancies between what U.S. courts claim they will recognize as evidence and what forms of evidence they actually accept.

(E) Land claim suits such as the Mashpee's bring to light the problems faced by Native American tribes attempting to establish their claims within a legal system governed by the application of precedent.

GO ON TO THE NEXT PAGE.

2. According to the passage, the Mashpee's lawsuit was based on their objection to

(A) the increase in the non-Mashpee population of the town during the 1960s
(B) the repeal of a statute forbidding land transfers without U.S. government approval
(C) the loss of Mashpee control over land use immediately after the town's incorporation
(D) the town's refusal to recognize the Mashpee's deed to the land in dispute
(E) the sale of Mashpee-controlled land to non-Mashpee residents without U.S. government approval

3. The author's attitude toward the court's decision in the Mashpee's lawsuit is most clearly revealed by the author's use of which one of the following phrases?

(A) "operate within a particular sphere" (lines 7–8)
(B) "continued to have control" (line 20)
(C) "required to demonstrate" (line 32)
(D) "precisely delineated its boundaries" (line 42)
(E) "failure to accommodate" (line 54)

4. Based on the passage, which one of the following can most reasonably be said to have occurred in the years since the Mashpee's lawsuit?

(A) The Mashpee have now regained control over the land they inhabit.
(B) Native American tribes have won all of their land claim suits in U.S. courts.
(C) U.S. courts no longer abide by the statute requiring federal approval of certain land transfers.
(D) U.S. courts have become more likely to accept oral testimony as evidence in land claim suits.
(E) U.S. courts have changed their definition of what legally constitutes a tribe.

5. The passage is primarily concerned with

(A) evaluating various approaches to solving a problem
(B) illuminating a general problem by discussing a specific example
(C) reconciling the differences in how two opposing sides approach a problem
(D) critiquing an earlier solution to a problem in light of new information
(E) reinterpreting an earlier analysis and proposing a new solution to the problem

GO ON TO THE NEXT PAGE.

Long after the lava has cooled, the effects of a major volcanic eruption may linger on. In the atmosphere a veil of fine dust and sulfuric acid droplets can spread around the globe and persist for years.
(5) Researchers have generally thought that this veil can block enough sunlight to have a chilling influence on Earth's climate. Many blame the cataclysmic eruption of the Indonesian volcano Tambora in 1815 for the ensuing "year without a summer" of 1816—when parts
(10) of the northeastern United States and southeastern Canada were hit by snowstorms in June and frosts in August.

The volcano-climate connection seems plausible, but, say scientists Clifford Mass and David Portman, it
(15) is not as strong as previously believed. Mass and Portman analyzed global temperature data for the years before and after nine volcanic eruptions, from Krakatau in 1883 to El Chichón in 1982. In the process they tried to filter out temperature changes caused by the cyclic
(20) weather phenomenon known as the El Niño–Southern Oscillation, which warms the sea surface in the equatorial Pacific and thereby warms the atmosphere. Such warming can mask the cooling brought about by an eruption, but it can also mimic volcanic cooling if
(25) the volcano happens to erupt just as an El Niño–induced warm period is beginning to fade.

Once El Niño effects had been subtracted from the data, the actual effects of the eruptions came through more clearly. Contrary to what earlier studies had
(30) suggested, Mass and Portman found that minor eruptions have no discernible effect on temperature. And major, dust-spitting explosions, such as Krakatau or El Chichón, cause a smaller drop than expected in the average temperature in the hemisphere (Northern or
(35) Southern) of the eruption—only half a degree centigrade or less—with a correspondingly smaller drop in the opposite hemisphere.

Other researchers, however, have argued that even a small temperature drop could result in a significant
(40) regional fluctuation in climate if its effects were amplified by climatic feedback loops. For example, a small temperature drop in the northeastern U.S. and southeastern Canada in early spring might delay the melting of snow, and the unmelted snow would
(45) continue to reflect sunlight away from the surface, amplifying the cooling. The cool air over the region could, in turn, affect the jet stream. The jet stream tends to flow at the boundary between cool northern air and warm southern air, drawing its power from the
(50) sharp temperature contrast and the consequent difference in pressure. An unusual cooling in the region could cause the stream to wander farther south than normal, allowing more polar air to come in behind it and deepen the region's cold snap. Through such a
(55) series of feedbacks a small temperature drop could be blown up into a year without a summer.

6. Which one of the following most accurately expresses the main idea of the passage?

(A) The effect of volcanic eruptions on regional temperature is greater than it was once thought to be.
(B) The effect of volcanic eruptions on regional temperature is smaller than the effect of volcanic eruptions on global temperature.
(C) The effect of volcanic eruptions on global temperature appears to be greater than was previously supposed.
(D) Volcanic eruptions appear not to have the significant effect on global temperature they were once thought to have but might have a significant effect on regional temperature.
(E) Researchers tended to overestimate the influence of volcanic eruptions on global temperature because they exaggerated the effect of cyclical weather phenomena in making their calculations.

7. Not taking the effects of El Niño into account when figuring the effect of volcanic eruptions on Earth's climate is most closely analogous to not taking into account the

(A) weight of a package as a whole when determining the weight of its contents apart from the packing material
(B) monetary value of the coins in a pile when counting the number of coins in the pile
(C) magnification of a lens when determining the shape of an object seen through the lens
(D) number of false crime reports in a city when figuring the average annual number of crimes committed in that city
(E) ages of new immigrants to a country before attributing a change in the average age of the country's population to a change in the number of births

8. The passage indicates that each of the following can be an effect of the El Niño phenomenon EXCEPT:

(A) making the cooling effect of a volcanic eruption appear to be more pronounced than it actually is
(B) making the cooling effect of a volcanic eruption appear to be less pronounced than it actually is
(C) increasing atmospheric temperature through cyclic warming of equatorial waters
(D) initiating a feedback loop that masks cooling brought about by an eruption
(E) confounding the evidence for a volcano-climate connection

GO ON TO THE NEXT PAGE.

9. Which one of the following most accurately characterizes what the author of the passage means by a "minor" volcanic eruption (line 30)?

   (A) an eruption that produces less lava than either Krakatau or El Chichón did

   (B) an eruption that has less of an effect on global temperature than either Krakatau or El Chichón did

   (C) an eruption whose effect on regional temperature can be masked by conditions in the hemisphere of the eruption

   (D) an eruption that introduces a relatively small amount of debris into the atmosphere

   (E) an eruption that causes average temperature in the hemisphere of the eruption to drop by less than half a degree centigrade

10. To which one of the following situations would the concept of a feedback loop, as it is employed in the passage, be most accurately applied?

    (A) An increase in the amount of decaying matter in the soil increases the amount of nutrients in the soil, which increases the number of plants, which further increases the amount of decaying matter in the soil.

    (B) An increase in the number of wolves in an area decreases the number of deer, which decreases the grazing of shrubs, which increases the amount of food available for other animals, which increases the number of other animals in the area.

    (C) An increase in the amount of rain in an area increases the deterioration of the forest floor, which makes it harder for wolves to prey on deer, which increases the number of deer, which gives wolves more opportunities to prey upon deer.

    (D) An increase in the amount of sunlight on the ocean increases the ocean temperature, which increases the number of phytoplankton in the ocean, which decreases the ocean temperature by blocking sunlight.

    (E) An increase in the number of outdoor electric lights in an area increases the number of insects in the area, which increases the number of bats in the area, which decreases the number of insects in the area, which decreases the number of bats in the area.

11. The author of the passage would be most likely to agree with which one of the following hypotheses?

    (A) Major volcanic eruptions sometimes cause average temperature in the hemisphere of the eruption to drop by more than a degree centigrade.

    (B) Major volcanic eruptions can induce the El Niño phenomenon when it otherwise might not occur.

    (C) Major volcanic eruptions do not directly cause unusually cold summers.

    (D) The climatic effects of minor volcanic eruptions differ from those of major eruptions only in degree.

    (E) El Niño has no discernible effect on average hemispheric temperature.

12. The information in the passage provides the LEAST support for which one of the following claims?

    (A) Major volcanic eruptions have a discernible effect on global temperature.

    (B) The effect of major volcanic eruptions on global temperature is smaller than was previously thought.

    (C) Major volcanic eruptions have no discernible effect on regional temperature.

    (D) Minor volcanic eruptions have no discernible effect on temperature in the hemisphere in which they occur.

    (E) Minor volcanic eruptions have no discernible effect on temperature in the hemisphere opposite the hemisphere of the eruption.

13. The primary purpose of the last paragraph of the passage is to

    (A) describe how the "year without a summer" differs from other examples of climatic feedback loops

    (B) account for the relatively slight hemispheric cooling effect of a major volcanic eruption

    (C) explain how regional climatic conditions can be significantly affected by a small drop in temperature

    (D) indicate how researchers are sometimes led to overlook the effects of El Niño on regional temperature

    (E) suggest a modification to the current model of how feedback loops produce changes in regional temperature

GO ON TO THE NEXT PAGE.

Recently, a new school of economics called steady-state economics has seriously challenged neoclassical economics, the reigning school in Western economic decision making. According to the neoclassical model,
(5) an economy is a closed system involving only the circular flow of exchange value between producers and consumers. Therefore, no noneconomic constraints impinge upon the economy and growth has no limits. Indeed, some neoclassical economists argue that
(10) growth itself is crucial, because, they claim, the solutions to problems often associated with growth (income inequities, for example) can be found only in the capital that further growth creates.

Steady-state economists believe the neoclassical
(15) model to be unrealistic and hold that the economy is dependent on nature. Resources, they argue, enter the economy as raw material and exit as consumed products or waste; the greater the resources, the greater the size of the economy. According to these
(20) economists, nature's limited capacity to regenerate raw material and absorb waste suggests that there is an optimal size for the economy, and that growth beyond this ideal point would increase the cost to the environment at a faster rate than the benefit to
(25) producers and consumers, generating cycles that impoverish rather than enrich. Steady-state economists thus believe that the concept of an ever growing economy is dangerous, and that the only alternative is to maintain a state in which the economy remains in
(30) equilibrium with nature. Neoclassical economists, on the other hand, consider nature to be just one element of the economy rather than an outside constraint, believing that natural resources, if depleted, can be replaced with other elements—i.e., human-made
(35) resources—that will allow the economy to continue with its process of unlimited growth.

Some steady-state economists, pointing to the widening disparity between indices of actual growth (which simply count the total monetary value of goods
(40) and services) and the index of environmentally sustainable growth (which is based on personal consumption, factoring in depletion of raw materials and production costs), believe that Western economies have already exceeded their optimal size. In response
(45) to the warnings from neoclassical economists that checking economic growth only leads to economic stagnation, they argue that there are alternatives to growth that still accomplish what is required of any economy: the satisfaction of human wants. One of
(50) these alternatives is conservation. Conservation—for example, increasing the efficiency of resource use through means such as recycling—differs from growth in that it is qualitative, not quantitative, requiring improvement in resource management rather than an
(55) increase in the amount of resources. One measure of the success of a steady-state economy would be the degree to which it could implement alternatives to growth, such as conservation, without sacrificing the ability to satisfy the wants of producers and consumers.

14. Which one of the following most completely and accurately expresses the main point of the passage?

(A) Neoclassical economists, who, unlike steady-state economists, hold that economic growth is not subject to outside constraints, believe that nature is just one element of the economy and that if natural resources in Western economies are depleted they can be replaced with human-made resources.

(B) Some neoclassical economists, who, unlike steady-state economists, hold that growth is crucial to the health of economies, believe that the solutions to certain problems in Western economies can thus be found in the additional capital generated by unlimited growth.

(C) Some steady-state economists, who, unlike neoclassical economists, hold that unlimited growth is neither possible nor desirable, believe that Western economies should limit economic growth by adopting conservation strategies, even if such strategies lead temporarily to economic stagnation.

(D) Some steady-state economists, who, unlike neoclassical economists, hold that the optimal sizes of economies are limited by the availability of natural resources, believe that Western economies should limit economic growth and that, with alternatives like conservation, satisfaction of human wants need not be sacrificed.

(E) Steady-state and neoclassical economists, who both hold that economies involve the circular flow of exchange value between producers and consumers, nevertheless differ over the most effective way of guaranteeing that a steady increase in this exchange value continues unimpeded in Western economies.

15. Based on the passage, neoclassical economists would likely hold that steady-state economists are wrong to believe each of the following EXCEPT:

(A) The environment's ability to yield raw material is limited.

(B) Natural resources are an external constraint on economies.

(C) The concept of unlimited economic growth is dangerous.

(D) Western economies have exceeded their optimal size.

(E) Economies have certain optimal sizes.

GO ON TO THE NEXT PAGE.

16. According to the passage, steady-state economists believe that unlimited economic growth is dangerous because it

(A) may deplete natural resources faster than other natural resources are discovered to replace them
(B) may convert natural resources into products faster than more efficient resource use can compensate for
(C) may proliferate goods and services faster than it generates new markets for them
(D) may create income inequities faster than it creates the capital needed to redress them
(E) may increase the cost to the environment faster than it increases benefits to producers and consumers

17. A steady-state economist would be LEAST likely to endorse which one of the following as a means of helping a steady-state economy reduce growth without compromising its ability to satisfy human wants?

(A) a manufacturer's commitment to recycle its product packaging
(B) a manufacturer's decision to use a less expensive fuel in its production process
(C) a manufacturer's implementation of a quality-control process to reduce the output of defective products
(D) a manufacturer's conversion from one type of production process to another with greater fuel efficiency
(E) a manufacturer's reduction of output in order to eliminate an overproduction problem

18. Based on the passage, a steady-state economist is most likely to claim that a successful economy is one that satisfies which one of the following principles?

(A) A successful economy uses human-made resources in addition to natural resources.
(B) A successful economy satisfies human wants faster than it creates new ones.
(C) A successful economy maintains an equilibrium with nature while still satisfying human wants.
(D) A successful economy implements every possible means to prevent growth.
(E) A successful economy satisfies the wants of producers and consumers by using resources to spur growth.

19. In the view of steady-state economists, which one of the following is a noneconomic constraint as referred to in line 7?

(A) the total amount of human wants
(B) the index of environmentally sustainable growth
(C) the capacity of nature to absorb waste
(D) the problems associated with economic growth
(E) the possibility of economic stagnation

20. Which one of the following most accurately describes what the last paragraph does in the passage?

(A) It contradicts the ways in which the two economic schools interpret certain data and gives a criterion for judging between them based on the basic goals of an economy.
(B) It gives an example that illustrates the weakness of the new economic school and recommends an economic policy based on the basic goals of the prevailing economic school.
(C) It introduces an objection to the new economic school and argues that the policies of the new economic school would be less successful than growth-oriented economic policies at achieving the basic goal an economy must meet.
(D) It notes an objection to implementing the policies of the new economic school and identifies an additional policy that can help avoid that objection and still meet the goal an economy must meet.
(E) It contrasts the policy of the prevailing economic school with the recommendation mentioned earlier of the new economic school and shows that they are based on differing views on the basic goal an economy must meet.

21. The passage suggests which one of the following about neoclassical economists?

(A) They assume that natural resources are infinitely available.
(B) They assume that human-made resources are infinitely available.
(C) They assume that availability of resources places an upper limit on growth.
(D) They assume that efficient management of resources is necessary to growth.
(E) They assume that human-made resources are preferable to natural resources.

GO ON TO THE NEXT PAGE.

As one of the most pervasive and influential popular arts, the movies feed into and off of the rest of the culture in various ways. In the United States, the star system of the mid-1920s—in which actors were
(5) placed under exclusive contract to particular Hollywood film studios—was a consequence of studios' discovery that the public was interested in actors' private lives, and that information about actors could be used to promote their films. Public relations
(10) agents fed the information to gossip columnists, whetting the public's appetite for the films—which, audiences usually discovered, had the additional virtue of being created by talented writers, directors, and producers devoted to the art of storytelling. The
(15) important feature of this relationship was not the benefit to Hollywood, but rather to the press; in what amounted to a form of cultural cross-fertilization, the press saw that they could profit from studios' promotion of new films.
(20)   Today this arrangement has mushroomed into an intricately interdependent mass-media entertainment industry. The faith by which this industry sustains itself is the belief that there is always something worth promoting. A vast portion of the mass media—
(25) television and radio interviews, magazine articles, even product advertisements—now does most of the work for Hollywood studios attempting to promote their movies. It does so not out of altruism but because it makes for good business: If you produce a talk show
(30) or edit a newspaper, and other media are generating public curiosity about a studio's forthcoming film, it would be unwise for you not to broadcast or publish something about the film, too, because the audience for your story is already guaranteed.
(35)   The problem with this industry is that it has begun to affect the creation of films as well as their promotion. Choices of subject matter and actors are made more and more frequently by studio executives rather than by producers, writers, or directors. This
(40) problem is often referred to simply as an obsession with turning a profit, but Hollywood movies have almost always been produced to appeal to the largest possible audience. The new danger is that, increasingly, profit comes only from exciting an
(45) audience's curiosity about a movie instead of satisfying its desire to have an engaging experience watching the film. When movies can pull people into theaters instantly on the strength of media publicity rather than relying on the more gradual process of word of mouth
(50) among satisfied moviegoers, then the intimate relationship with the audience—on which the vitality of all popular art depends—is lost. But studios are making more money than ever by using this formula, and for this reason it appears that films whose appeal is
(55) due not merely to their publicity value but to their ability to affect audiences emotionally will become increasingly rare in the U.S. film industry.

22. The passage suggests that the author would be most likely to agree with which one of the following statements?

(A) The Hollywood films of the mid-1920s were in general more engaging to watch than are Hollywood films produced today.

(B) The writers, producers, and directors in Hollywood in the mid-1920s were more talented than are their counterparts today.

(C) The Hollywood film studios of the mid-1920s had a greater level of dependence on the mass-media industry than do Hollywood studios today.

(D) The publicity generated for Hollywood films in the mid-1920s was more interesting than is the publicity generated for these films today.

(E) The star system of the mid-1920s accounts for most of the difference in quality between the Hollywood films of that period and Hollywood films today.

23. According to the author, the danger of mass-media promotion of films is that it

(A) discourages the work of filmmakers who attempt to draw the largest possible audiences to their films

(B) discourages the critical review of the content of films that have been heavily promoted

(C) encourages the production of films that excite an audience's curiosity but that do not provide satisfying experiences

(D) encourages decisions to make the content of films parallel the private lives of the actors that appear in them

(E) encourages cynicism among potential audience members about the merits of the films publicized

24. The phrase "cultural cross-fertilization" (line 17) is used in the passage to refer to which one of the following?

(A) competition among different segments of the U.S. mass media

(B) the interrelationship of Hollywood movies with other types of popular art

(C) Hollywood film studios' discovery that the press could be used to communicate with the public

(D) the press's mutually beneficial relationship with Hollywood film studios

(E) interactions between public relations agents and the press

GO ON TO THE NEXT PAGE.

25. Which one of the following most accurately describes the organization of the passage?

   (A)   description of the origins of a particular aspect of a popular art; discussion of the present state of this aspect; analysis of a problem associated with this aspect; introduction of a possible solution to the problem

   (B)   description of the origins of a particular aspect of a popular art; discussion of the present state of this aspect; analysis of a problem associated with this aspect; suggestion of a likely consequence of the problem

   (C)   description of the origins of a particular aspect of a popular art; analysis of a problem associated with this aspect; introduction of a possible solution to the problem; suggestion of a likely consequence of the solution

   (D)   summary of the history of a particular aspect of a popular art; discussion of a problem that accompanied the growth of this aspect; suggestion of a likely consequence of the problem; appraisal of the importance of avoiding this consequence

   (E)   summary of the history of a particular aspect of a popular art; analysis of factors that contributed to the growth of this aspect; discussion of a problem that accompanied the growth of this aspect; appeal for assistance in solving the problem

26. The author's position in lines 35–47 would be most weakened if which one of the following were true?

   (A)   Many Hollywood studio executives do consider a film's ability to satisfy moviegoers emotionally.

   (B)   Many Hollywood studio executives achieved their positions as a result of demonstrating talent at writing, producing, or directing films that satisfy audiences emotionally.

   (C)   Most writers, producers, and directors in Hollywood continue to have a say in decisions about the casting and content of films despite the influence of studio executives.

   (D)   The decisions made by most Hollywood studio executives to improve a film's chances of earning a profit also add to its ability to satisfy moviegoers emotionally.

   (E)   Often the U.S. mass media play an indirect role in influencing the content of the films that Hollywood studios make by whetting the public's appetite for certain performers or subjects.

S T O P

IF YOU FINISH BEFORE TIME IS CALLED, YOU MAY CHECK YOUR WORK ON THIS SECTION ONLY.
DO NOT WORK ON ANY OTHER SECTION IN THE TEST.

Acknowledgment is made to the following sources from which material has been adapted for use in this test booklet:

Jonathan Betz-Zall, "Balancing Quality and Relevance: Selecting Series Biographies for Children about Women and People of Color." © 1993 by Greenwood Publishing Group, Inc.

Herman E. Daly, "The Perils of Free Trade." © 1993 by Scientific American, Inc.

Louis Menand, "That's Entertainment." © 1993 by The New Yorker Magazine, Inc.

Gerald Torres and Kathryn Milun, "Translating Yonnondio by Precedent and Evidence: The Mashpee Indian Case. " © 1990 by Duke Law Journal.

LSAT® Writing Sample Topic

Directions: The scenario presented below describes two choices, either one of which can be supported on the basis of the information given. Your essay should consider both choices and argue for one over the other, based on the two specified criteria and the facts provided. There is no "right" or "wrong" choice: a reasonable argument can be made for either.

Dorchester University has a vacancy for a fine arts librarian. Write an argument in support of hiring one of the two candidates described below, taking into account the following considerations:

- Dorchester wants to publicize in the community at large its collection of early Asian musical instruments and its recently donated collection of related artwork;
- Dorchester needs to raise money to improve and update its entire fine arts program, including its museum.

Xiang Chen, who holds an undergraduate degree in music, was born and raised in China; he speaks fluent English, Mandarin, Cantonese, Hindi and Japanese and has lived throughout Asia. He has been translating ancient Chinese texts for a major library over the past year. Two years ago, Mr. Chen served as art consultant to the Japanese Consulate as it began its collection of contemporary Asian sculpture. An accomplished musician, he has studied piano with the well-known composer Mei-Ying Liang. Mr. Chen, who often performs in benefit concerts, suggests a chamber music series, featuring Dorchester's collection of early Asian instruments, to raise funds.

Elise Bogart received a master's degree in library science ten years ago. She has completed the coursework for a master's degree in ethnomusicology and is finishing her thesis, which analyzes the work of four Asian composers. Ms. Bogart worked as assistant fine arts librarian for two years at a prestigious museum of contemporary art, and before that was the head librarian for six years at Connor & Doud, a major law firm. After persuading the firm to begin an art collection, she organized a gala opening exhibit, which featured contemporary local artists. Four years ago, during her tenure as president of a community service organization, Ms. Bogart organized about fifty other volunteers and ran a successful scholarship fund-raising drive.

Directions:

1. Use the Answer Key on the next page to check your answers.

2. Use the Scoring Worksheet below to compute your raw score.

3. Use the Score Conversion Chart to convert your raw score into the 120-180 scale.

Scoring Worksheet

1. Enter the number of questions you answered correctly in each section.

	Number Correct
SECTION I	_____
SECTION II	_____
SECTION III	_____
SECTION IV	_____

2. Enter the sum here: _____
   This is your Raw Score.

Conversion Chart

For Converting Raw Score to the 120-180 LSAT Scaled Score
LSAT Form 0LSS41

Reported Score	Raw Score Lowest	Raw Score Highest
180	99	101
179	98	98
178	97	97
177	96	96
176	95	95
175	94	94
174	93	93
173	91	92
172	90	90
171	89	89
170	88	88
169	86	87
168	85	85
167	83	84
166	82	82
165	80	81
164	78	79
163	77	77
162	75	76
161	73	74
160	71	72
159	70	70
158	68	69
157	66	67
156	64	65
155	63	63
154	61	62
153	59	60
152	57	58
151	56	56
150	54	55
149	52	53
148	50	51
147	49	49
146	47	48
145	45	46
144	44	44
143	42	43
142	41	41
141	39	40
140	38	38
139	36	37
138	35	35
137	33	34
136	32	32
135	30	31
134	29	29
133	28	28
132	26	27
131	25	25
130	24	24
129	22	23
128	21	21
127	20	20
126	19	19
125	18	18
124	17	17
123	16	16
122	14	15
121	—*	—*
120	0	13

*There is no raw score that will produce this scaled score for this form.

SECTION I

1.	A	8.	C	15.	C	22.	B
2.	B	9.	C	16.	B	23.	A
3.	A	10.	D	17.	D	24.	A
4.	C	11.	A	18.	E	25.	D
5.	D	12.	B	19.	A	26.	E
6.	D	13.	C	20.	A		
7.	E	14.	B	21.	C		

SECTION II

1.	B	8.	C	15.	B	22.	C
2.	E	9.	B	16.	B	23.	E
3.	E	10.	A	17.	D		
4.	B	11.	B	18.	D		
5.	C	12.	D	19.	D		
6.	D	13.	D	20.	E		
7.	B	14.	C	21.	A		

SECTION III

1.	D	8.	B	15.	B	22.	B
2.	E	9.	A	16.	B	23.	D
3.	E	10.	A	17.	B	24.	D
4.	A	11.	C	18.	C	25.	E
5.	C	12.	C	19.	A	26.	D
6.	B	13.	E	20.	B		
7.	C	14.	A	21.	D		

SECTION IV

1.	C	8.	D	15.	A	22.	A
2.	E	9.	D	16.	E	23.	C
3.	E	10.	A	17.	B	24.	D
4.	D	11.	C	18.	C	25.	B
5.	B	12.	C	19.	C	26.	D
6.	D	13.	C	20.	D		
7.	E	14.	D	21.	B		

LSAT® PREP TOOLS

The Official LSAT SuperPrep II™

SuperPrep II contains everything you need to prepare for the LSAT—a guide to all three LSAT question types, three actual LSATs, explanations for all questions in the three practice tests, answer keys, writing samples, and score-conversion tables, plus invaluable test-taking instructions to help with pacing and timing. *SuperPrep* has long been our most comprehensive LSAT preparation book, and *SuperPrep II* is even better. The practice tests in *SuperPrep II* are PrepTest 62 (December 2010 LSAT), PrepTest 63 (June 2011 LSAT), and one test that has never before been disclosed.

With this book you can

- Practice on genuine LSAT questions

- Review explanations for right and wrong answers

- Target specific categories for intensive review

- Simulate actual LSAT conditions

LSAC sets the standard for LSAT prep—and *SuperPrep II* raises the bar!

Available at your favorite bookseller.

LSAC.org

General Directions for the LSAT Answer Sheet

The actual testing time for this portion of the test will be 2 hours 55 minutes. There are five sections, each with a time limit of 35 minutes. The supervisor will tell you when to begin and end each section. If you finish a section before time is called, you may check your work on that section **only;** do not turn to any other section of the test book and do not work on any other section either in the test book or on the answer sheet.

There are several different types of questions on the test, and each question type has its own directions. **Be sure you understand the directions for each question type before attempting to answer any questions in that section.**

Not everyone will finish all the questions in the time allowed. Do not hurry, but work steadily and as quickly as you can without sacrificing accuracy. You are advised to use your time effectively. If a question seems too difficult, go on to the next one and return to the difficult question after completing the section. **MARK THE BEST ANSWER YOU CAN FOR EVERY QUESTION. NO DEDUCTIONS WILL BE MADE FOR WRONG ANSWERS. YOUR SCORE WILL BE BASED ONLY ON THE NUMBER OF QUESTIONS YOU ANSWER CORRECTLY.**

ALL YOUR ANSWERS MUST BE MARKED ON THE ANSWER SHEET. Answer spaces for each question are lettered to correspond with the letters of the potential answers to each question in the test book. After you have decided which of the answers is correct, blacken the corresponding space on the answer sheet. **BE SURE THAT EACH MARK IS BLACK AND COMPLETELY FILLS THE ANSWER SPACE.** Give only one answer to each question. If you change an answer, be sure that all previous marks are **erased completely.** Since the answer sheet is machine scored, incomplete erasures may be interpreted as intended answers. **ANSWERS RECORDED IN THE TEST BOOK WILL NOT BE SCORED.**

There may be more question numbers on this answer sheet than there are questions in a section. Do not be concerned, but be certain that the section and number of the question you are answering matches the answer sheet section and question number. Additional answer spaces in any answer sheet section should be left blank. Begin your next section in the number one answer space for that section.

LSAC takes various steps to ensure that answer sheets are returned from test centers in a timely manner for processing. In the unlikely event that an answer sheet is not received, LSAC will permit the examinee either to retest at no additional fee or to receive a refund of his or her LSAT fee. **THESE REMEDIES ARE THE ONLY REMEDIES AVAILABLE IN THE UNLIKELY EVENT THAT AN ANSWER SHEET IS NOT RECEIVED BY LSAC.**

Score Cancellation

Complete this section only if you are absolutely certain you want to cancel your score. **A CANCELLATION REQUEST CANNOT BE RESCINDED. IF YOU ARE AT ALL UNCERTAIN, YOU SHOULD NOT COMPLETE THIS SECTION.**

To cancel your score from this administration, you **must:**

A. fill in both ovals here ...... ○ ○
AND
B. read the following statement. Then sign your name and enter the date.
YOUR SIGNATURE ALONE IS NOT SUFFICIENT FOR SCORE CANCELLATION. BOTH OVALS ABOVE MUST BE FILLED IN FOR SCANNING EQUIPMENT TO RECOGNIZE YOUR REQUEST FOR SCORE CANCELLATION.

I certify that I wish to cancel my test score from this administration. I understand that my request is irreversible and that my score will not be sent to me or to the law schools to which I apply.

_____
Sign your name in full

_____
Date

FOR LSAC USE ONLY ●

HOW DID YOU PREPARE FOR THE LSAT?
(Select all that apply.)

Responses to this item are voluntary and will be used for statistical research purposes only.

○ By studying the free sample questions available on LSAC's website.
○ By taking the free sample LSAT available on LSAC's website.
○ By working through official LSAT *PrepTests*, *ItemWise*, and/or other LSAC test prep products.
○ By using LSAT prep books or software **not** published by LSAC.
○ By attending a commercial test preparation or coaching course.
○ By attending a test preparation or coaching course offered through an undergraduate institution.
○ Self study.
○ Other preparation.
○ No preparation.

CERTIFYING STATEMENT

Please write the following statement. Sign and date.

I certify that I am the examinee whose name appears on this answer sheet and that I am here to take the LSAT for the sole purpose of being considered for admission to law school. I further certify that I will neither assist nor receive assistance from any other candidate, and I agree not to copy, retain, or transmit examination questions in any form or discuss them with any other person.

_____
_____
_____
_____
_____
_____
_____
_____
_____
_____

SIGNATURE: _____   TODAY'S DATE: ___/___/___
                                                                      MONTH DAY YEAR

SCANTRON® EliteView™ EM-295665-1:654321

INSTRUCTIONS FOR COMPLETING THE BIOGRAPHICAL AREA ARE ON THE BACK COVER OF YOUR TEST BOOKLET.
USE ONLY A NO. 2 OR HB PENCIL TO COMPLETE THIS ANSWER SHEET. DO NOT USE INK.

A

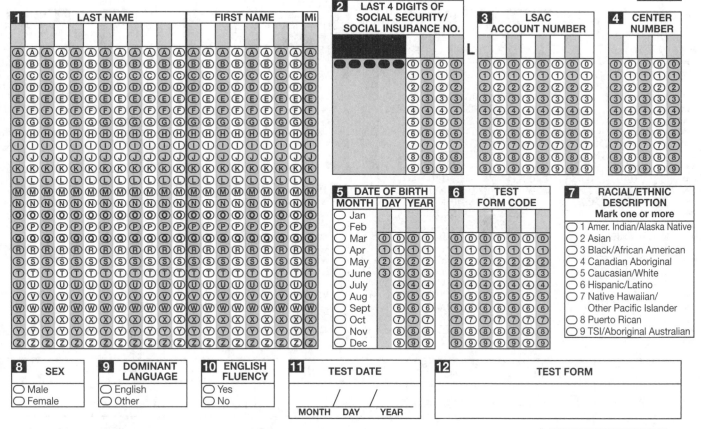

1 LAST NAME — FIRST NAME — MI

2 LAST 4 DIGITS OF SOCIAL SECURITY/ SOCIAL INSURANCE NO.

3 LSAC ACCOUNT NUMBER

4 CENTER NUMBER

5 DATE OF BIRTH — MONTH DAY YEAR

6 TEST FORM CODE

7 RACIAL/ETHNIC DESCRIPTION
Mark one or more
- 1 Amer. Indian/Alaska Native
- 2 Asian
- 3 Black/African American
- 4 Canadian Aboriginal
- 5 Caucasian/White
- 6 Hispanic/Latino
- 7 Native Hawaiian/ Other Pacific Islander
- 8 Puerto Rican
- 9 TSI/Aboriginal Australian

8 SEX
- Male
- Female

9 DOMINANT LANGUAGE
- English
- Other

10 ENGLISH FLUENCY
- Yes
- No

11 TEST DATE
/ /
MONTH DAY YEAR

12 TEST FORM

Law School Admission Test

Mark one and only one answer to each question. Be sure to fill in completely the space for your intended answer choice. If you erase, do so completely. Make no stray marks.

13 TEST BOOK SERIAL NO.

SECTION 1
1 A B C D E
2 A B C D E
3 A B C D E
4 A B C D E
5 A B C D E
6 A B C D E
7 A B C D E
8 A B C D E
9 A B C D E
10 A B C D E
11 A B C D E
12 A B C D E
13 A B C D E
14 A B C D E
15 A B C D E
16 A B C D E
17 A B C D E
18 A B C D E
19 A B C D E
20 A B C D E
21 A B C D E
22 A B C D E
23 A B C D E
24 A B C D E
25 A B C D E
26 A B C D E
27 A B C D E
28 A B C D E
29 A B C D E
30 A B C D E

SECTION 2
1 A B C D E
2 A B C D E
3 A B C D E
4 A B C D E
5 A B C D E
6 A B C D E
7 A B C D E
8 A B C D E
9 A B C D E
10 A B C D E
11 A B C D E
12 A B C D E
13 A B C D E
14 A B C D E
15 A B C D E
16 A B C D E
17 A B C D E
18 A B C D E
19 A B C D E
20 A B C D E
21 A B C D E
22 A B C D E
23 A B C D E
24 A B C D E
25 A B C D E
26 A B C D E
27 A B C D E
28 A B C D E
29 A B C D E
30 A B C D E

SECTION 3
1 A B C D E
2 A B C D E
3 A B C D E
4 A B C D E
5 A B C D E
6 A B C D E
7 A B C D E
8 A B C D E
9 A B C D E
10 A B C D E
11 A B C D E
12 A B C D E
13 A B C D E
14 A B C D E
15 A B C D E
16 A B C D E
17 A B C D E
18 A B C D E
19 A B C D E
20 A B C D E
21 A B C D E
22 A B C D E
23 A B C D E
24 A B C D E
25 A B C D E
26 A B C D E
27 A B C D E
28 A B C D E
29 A B C D E
30 A B C D E

SECTION 4
1 A B C D E
2 A B C D E
3 A B C D E
4 A B C D E
5 A B C D E
6 A B C D E
7 A B C D E
8 A B C D E
9 A B C D E
10 A B C D E
11 A B C D E
12 A B C D E
13 A B C D E
14 A B C D E
15 A B C D E
16 A B C D E
17 A B C D E
18 A B C D E
19 A B C D E
20 A B C D E
21 A B C D E
22 A B C D E
23 A B C D E
24 A B C D E
25 A B C D E
26 A B C D E
27 A B C D E
28 A B C D E
29 A B C D E
30 A B C D E

SECTION 5
1 A B C D E
2 A B C D E
3 A B C D E
4 A B C D E
5 A B C D E
6 A B C D E
7 A B C D E
8 A B C D E
9 A B C D E
10 A B C D E
11 A B C D E
12 A B C D E
13 A B C D E
14 A B C D E
15 A B C D E
16 A B C D E
17 A B C D E
18 A B C D E
19 A B C D E
20 A B C D E
21 A B C D E
22 A B C D E
23 A B C D E
24 A B C D E
25 A B C D E
26 A B C D E
27 A B C D E
28 A B C D E
29 A B C D E
30 A B C D E

14 PLEASE PRINT INFORMATION

LAST NAME

FIRST NAME

DATE OF BIRTH

SCANTRON® EliteView™ EM-295665-1:654321

INSTRUCTIONS FOR COMPLETING THE BIOGRAPHICAL AREA ARE ON THE BACK COVER OF YOUR TEST BOOKLET.
USE ONLY A NO. 2 OR HB PENCIL TO COMPLETE THIS ANSWER SHEET. DO NOT USE INK.

1 LAST NAME / **FIRST NAME** / **MI**

2 LAST 4 DIGITS OF SOCIAL SECURITY/ SOCIAL INSURANCE NO.

3 LSAC ACCOUNT NUMBER

4 CENTER NUMBER

5 DATE OF BIRTH

MONTH	DAY	YEAR
○ Jan		
○ Feb		
○ Mar		
○ Apr		
○ May		
○ June		
○ July		
○ Aug		
○ Sept		
○ Oct		
○ Nov		
○ Dec		

6 TEST FORM CODE

7 RACIAL/ETHNIC DESCRIPTION
Mark one or more

- ○ 1 Amer. Indian/Alaska Native
- ○ 2 Asian
- ○ 3 Black/African American
- ○ 4 Canadian Aboriginal
- ○ 5 Caucasian/White
- ○ 6 Hispanic/Latino
- ○ 7 Native Hawaiian/ Other Pacific Islander
- ○ 8 Puerto Rican
- ○ 9 TSI/Aboriginal Australian

8 SEX
- ○ Male
- ○ Female

9 DOMINANT LANGUAGE
- ○ English
- ○ Other

10 ENGLISH FLUENCY
- ○ Yes
- ○ No

11 TEST DATE
/ /
MONTH DAY YEAR

12 TEST FORM

=== **Law School Admission Test** ===

Mark one and only one answer to each question. Be sure to fill in completely the space for your intended answer choice. If you erase, do so completely. Make no stray marks.

13 TEST BOOK SERIAL NO.

SECTION 1

1 Ⓐ Ⓑ Ⓒ Ⓓ Ⓔ
2 Ⓐ Ⓑ Ⓒ Ⓓ Ⓔ
3 Ⓐ Ⓑ Ⓒ Ⓓ Ⓔ
4 Ⓐ Ⓑ Ⓒ Ⓓ Ⓔ
5 Ⓐ Ⓑ Ⓒ Ⓓ Ⓔ
6 Ⓐ Ⓑ Ⓒ Ⓓ Ⓔ
7 Ⓐ Ⓑ Ⓒ Ⓓ Ⓔ
8 Ⓐ Ⓑ Ⓒ Ⓓ Ⓔ
9 Ⓐ Ⓑ Ⓒ Ⓓ Ⓔ
10 Ⓐ Ⓑ Ⓒ Ⓓ Ⓔ
11 Ⓐ Ⓑ Ⓒ Ⓓ Ⓔ
12 Ⓐ Ⓑ Ⓒ Ⓓ Ⓔ
13 Ⓐ Ⓑ Ⓒ Ⓓ Ⓔ
14 Ⓐ Ⓑ Ⓒ Ⓓ Ⓔ
15 Ⓐ Ⓑ Ⓒ Ⓓ Ⓔ
16 Ⓐ Ⓑ Ⓒ Ⓓ Ⓔ
17 Ⓐ Ⓑ Ⓒ Ⓓ Ⓔ
18 Ⓐ Ⓑ Ⓒ Ⓓ Ⓔ
19 Ⓐ Ⓑ Ⓒ Ⓓ Ⓔ
20 Ⓐ Ⓑ Ⓒ Ⓓ Ⓔ
21 Ⓐ Ⓑ Ⓒ Ⓓ Ⓔ
22 Ⓐ Ⓑ Ⓒ Ⓓ Ⓔ
23 Ⓐ Ⓑ Ⓒ Ⓓ Ⓔ
24 Ⓐ Ⓑ Ⓒ Ⓓ Ⓔ
25 Ⓐ Ⓑ Ⓒ Ⓓ Ⓔ
26 Ⓐ Ⓑ Ⓒ Ⓓ Ⓔ
27 Ⓐ Ⓑ Ⓒ Ⓓ Ⓔ
28 Ⓐ Ⓑ Ⓒ Ⓓ Ⓔ
29 Ⓐ Ⓑ Ⓒ Ⓓ Ⓔ
30 Ⓐ Ⓑ Ⓒ Ⓓ Ⓔ

SECTION 2

1 Ⓐ Ⓑ Ⓒ Ⓓ Ⓔ
2 Ⓐ Ⓑ Ⓒ Ⓓ Ⓔ
3 Ⓐ Ⓑ Ⓒ Ⓓ Ⓔ
4 Ⓐ Ⓑ Ⓒ Ⓓ Ⓔ
5 Ⓐ Ⓑ Ⓒ Ⓓ Ⓔ
6 Ⓐ Ⓑ Ⓒ Ⓓ Ⓔ
7 Ⓐ Ⓑ Ⓒ Ⓓ Ⓔ
8 Ⓐ Ⓑ Ⓒ Ⓓ Ⓔ
9 Ⓐ Ⓑ Ⓒ Ⓓ Ⓔ
10 Ⓐ Ⓑ Ⓒ Ⓓ Ⓔ
11 Ⓐ Ⓑ Ⓒ Ⓓ Ⓔ
12 Ⓐ Ⓑ Ⓒ Ⓓ Ⓔ
13 Ⓐ Ⓑ Ⓒ Ⓓ Ⓔ
14 Ⓐ Ⓑ Ⓒ Ⓓ Ⓔ
15 Ⓐ Ⓑ Ⓒ Ⓓ Ⓔ
16 Ⓐ Ⓑ Ⓒ Ⓓ Ⓔ
17 Ⓐ Ⓑ Ⓒ Ⓓ Ⓔ
18 Ⓐ Ⓑ Ⓒ Ⓓ Ⓔ
19 Ⓐ Ⓑ Ⓒ Ⓓ Ⓔ
20 Ⓐ Ⓑ Ⓒ Ⓓ Ⓔ
21 Ⓐ Ⓑ Ⓒ Ⓓ Ⓔ
22 Ⓐ Ⓑ Ⓒ Ⓓ Ⓔ
23 Ⓐ Ⓑ Ⓒ Ⓓ Ⓔ
24 Ⓐ Ⓑ Ⓒ Ⓓ Ⓔ
25 Ⓐ Ⓑ Ⓒ Ⓓ Ⓔ
26 Ⓐ Ⓑ Ⓒ Ⓓ Ⓔ
27 Ⓐ Ⓑ Ⓒ Ⓓ Ⓔ
28 Ⓐ Ⓑ Ⓒ Ⓓ Ⓔ
29 Ⓐ Ⓑ Ⓒ Ⓓ Ⓔ
30 Ⓐ Ⓑ Ⓒ Ⓓ Ⓔ

SECTION 3

1 Ⓐ Ⓑ Ⓒ Ⓓ Ⓔ
2 Ⓐ Ⓑ Ⓒ Ⓓ Ⓔ
3 Ⓐ Ⓑ Ⓒ Ⓓ Ⓔ
4 Ⓐ Ⓑ Ⓒ Ⓓ Ⓔ
5 Ⓐ Ⓑ Ⓒ Ⓓ Ⓔ
6 Ⓐ Ⓑ Ⓒ Ⓓ Ⓔ
7 Ⓐ Ⓑ Ⓒ Ⓓ Ⓔ
8 Ⓐ Ⓑ Ⓒ Ⓓ Ⓔ
9 Ⓐ Ⓑ Ⓒ Ⓓ Ⓔ
10 Ⓐ Ⓑ Ⓒ Ⓓ Ⓔ
11 Ⓐ Ⓑ Ⓒ Ⓓ Ⓔ
12 Ⓐ Ⓑ Ⓒ Ⓓ Ⓔ
13 Ⓐ Ⓑ Ⓒ Ⓓ Ⓔ
14 Ⓐ Ⓑ Ⓒ Ⓓ Ⓔ
15 Ⓐ Ⓑ Ⓒ Ⓓ Ⓔ
16 Ⓐ Ⓑ Ⓒ Ⓓ Ⓔ
17 Ⓐ Ⓑ Ⓒ Ⓓ Ⓔ
18 Ⓐ Ⓑ Ⓒ Ⓓ Ⓔ
19 Ⓐ Ⓑ Ⓒ Ⓓ Ⓔ
20 Ⓐ Ⓑ Ⓒ Ⓓ Ⓔ
21 Ⓐ Ⓑ Ⓒ Ⓓ Ⓔ
22 Ⓐ Ⓑ Ⓒ Ⓓ Ⓔ
23 Ⓐ Ⓑ Ⓒ Ⓓ Ⓔ
24 Ⓐ Ⓑ Ⓒ Ⓓ Ⓔ
25 Ⓐ Ⓑ Ⓒ Ⓓ Ⓔ
26 Ⓐ Ⓑ Ⓒ Ⓓ Ⓔ
27 Ⓐ Ⓑ Ⓒ Ⓓ Ⓔ
28 Ⓐ Ⓑ Ⓒ Ⓓ Ⓔ
29 Ⓐ Ⓑ Ⓒ Ⓓ Ⓔ
30 Ⓐ Ⓑ Ⓒ Ⓓ Ⓔ

SECTION 4

1 Ⓐ Ⓑ Ⓒ Ⓓ Ⓔ
2 Ⓐ Ⓑ Ⓒ Ⓓ Ⓔ
3 Ⓐ Ⓑ Ⓒ Ⓓ Ⓔ
4 Ⓐ Ⓑ Ⓒ Ⓓ Ⓔ
5 Ⓐ Ⓑ Ⓒ Ⓓ Ⓔ
6 Ⓐ Ⓑ Ⓒ Ⓓ Ⓔ
7 Ⓐ Ⓑ Ⓒ Ⓓ Ⓔ
8 Ⓐ Ⓑ Ⓒ Ⓓ Ⓔ
9 Ⓐ Ⓑ Ⓒ Ⓓ Ⓔ
10 Ⓐ Ⓑ Ⓒ Ⓓ Ⓔ
11 Ⓐ Ⓑ Ⓒ Ⓓ Ⓔ
12 Ⓐ Ⓑ Ⓒ Ⓓ Ⓔ
13 Ⓐ Ⓑ Ⓒ Ⓓ Ⓔ
14 Ⓐ Ⓑ Ⓒ Ⓓ Ⓔ
15 Ⓐ Ⓑ Ⓒ Ⓓ Ⓔ
16 Ⓐ Ⓑ Ⓒ Ⓓ Ⓔ
17 Ⓐ Ⓑ Ⓒ Ⓓ Ⓔ
18 Ⓐ Ⓑ Ⓒ Ⓓ Ⓔ
19 Ⓐ Ⓑ Ⓒ Ⓓ Ⓔ
20 Ⓐ Ⓑ Ⓒ Ⓓ Ⓔ
21 Ⓐ Ⓑ Ⓒ Ⓓ Ⓔ
22 Ⓐ Ⓑ Ⓒ Ⓓ Ⓔ
23 Ⓐ Ⓑ Ⓒ Ⓓ Ⓔ
24 Ⓐ Ⓑ Ⓒ Ⓓ Ⓔ
25 Ⓐ Ⓑ Ⓒ Ⓓ Ⓔ
26 Ⓐ Ⓑ Ⓒ Ⓓ Ⓔ
27 Ⓐ Ⓑ Ⓒ Ⓓ Ⓔ
28 Ⓐ Ⓑ Ⓒ Ⓓ Ⓔ
29 Ⓐ Ⓑ Ⓒ Ⓓ Ⓔ
30 Ⓐ Ⓑ Ⓒ Ⓓ Ⓔ

SECTION 5

1 Ⓐ Ⓑ Ⓒ Ⓓ Ⓔ
2 Ⓐ Ⓑ Ⓒ Ⓓ Ⓔ
3 Ⓐ Ⓑ Ⓒ Ⓓ Ⓔ
4 Ⓐ Ⓑ Ⓒ Ⓓ Ⓔ
5 Ⓐ Ⓑ Ⓒ Ⓓ Ⓔ
6 Ⓐ Ⓑ Ⓒ Ⓓ Ⓔ
7 Ⓐ Ⓑ Ⓒ Ⓓ Ⓔ
8 Ⓐ Ⓑ Ⓒ Ⓓ Ⓔ
9 Ⓐ Ⓑ Ⓒ Ⓓ Ⓔ
10 Ⓐ Ⓑ Ⓒ Ⓓ Ⓔ
11 Ⓐ Ⓑ Ⓒ Ⓓ Ⓔ
12 Ⓐ Ⓑ Ⓒ Ⓓ Ⓔ
13 Ⓐ Ⓑ Ⓒ Ⓓ Ⓔ
14 Ⓐ Ⓑ Ⓒ Ⓓ Ⓔ
15 Ⓐ Ⓑ Ⓒ Ⓓ Ⓔ
16 Ⓐ Ⓑ Ⓒ Ⓓ Ⓔ
17 Ⓐ Ⓑ Ⓒ Ⓓ Ⓔ
18 Ⓐ Ⓑ Ⓒ Ⓓ Ⓔ
19 Ⓐ Ⓑ Ⓒ Ⓓ Ⓔ
20 Ⓐ Ⓑ Ⓒ Ⓓ Ⓔ
21 Ⓐ Ⓑ Ⓒ Ⓓ Ⓔ
22 Ⓐ Ⓑ Ⓒ Ⓓ Ⓔ
23 Ⓐ Ⓑ Ⓒ Ⓓ Ⓔ
24 Ⓐ Ⓑ Ⓒ Ⓓ Ⓔ
25 Ⓐ Ⓑ Ⓒ Ⓓ Ⓔ
26 Ⓐ Ⓑ Ⓒ Ⓓ Ⓔ
27 Ⓐ Ⓑ Ⓒ Ⓓ Ⓔ
28 Ⓐ Ⓑ Ⓒ Ⓓ Ⓔ
29 Ⓐ Ⓑ Ⓒ Ⓓ Ⓔ
30 Ⓐ Ⓑ Ⓒ Ⓓ Ⓔ

14 PLEASE PRINT INFORMATION

LAST NAME

FIRST NAME

DATE OF BIRTH

● Ⓑ

INSTRUCTIONS FOR COMPLETING THE BIOGRAPHICAL AREA ARE ON THE BACK COVER OF YOUR TEST BOOKLET.
USE ONLY A NO. 2 OR HB PENCIL TO COMPLETE THIS ANSWER SHEET. DO NOT USE INK.

1 LAST NAME / FIRST NAME / MI

2 LAST 4 DIGITS OF SOCIAL SECURITY/ SOCIAL INSURANCE NO.

3 LSAC ACCOUNT NUMBER

4 CENTER NUMBER

5 DATE OF BIRTH
MONTH | DAY | YEAR
Jan, Feb, Mar, Apr, May, June, July, Aug, Sept, Oct, Nov, Dec

6 TEST FORM CODE

7 RACIAL/ETHNIC DESCRIPTION
Mark one or more
- 1 Amer. Indian/Alaska Native
- 2 Asian
- 3 Black/African American
- 4 Canadian Aboriginal
- 5 Caucasian/White
- 6 Hispanic/Latino
- 7 Native Hawaiian/ Other Pacific Islander
- 8 Puerto Rican
- 9 TSI/Aboriginal Australian

8 SEX
- Male
- Female

9 DOMINANT LANGUAGE
- English
- Other

10 ENGLISH FLUENCY
- Yes
- No

11 TEST DATE
/ /
MONTH DAY YEAR

12 TEST FORM

Law School Admission Test

Mark one and only one answer to each question. Be sure to fill in completely the space for your intended answer choice. If you erase, do so completely. Make no stray marks.

13 TEST BOOK SERIAL NO.

SECTION 1
1–30 A B C D E

SECTION 2
1–30 A B C D E

SECTION 3
1–30 A B C D E

SECTION 4
1–30 A B C D E

SECTION 5
1–30 A B C D E

14 PLEASE PRINT INFORMATION
LAST NAME
FIRST NAME
DATE OF BIRTH

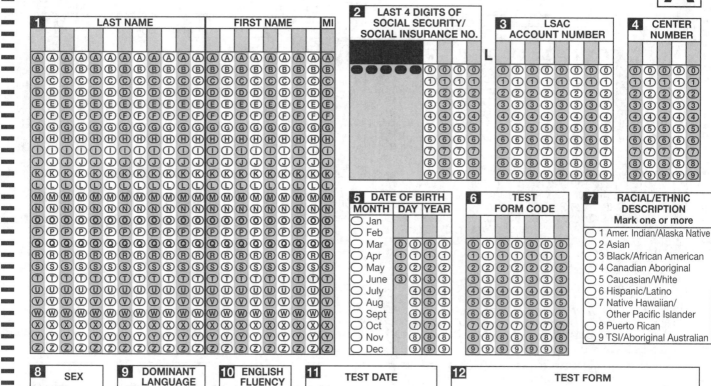

Law School Admission Test

Mark one and only one answer to each question. Be sure to fill in completely the space for your intended answer choice. If you erase, do so completely. Make no stray marks.

SCANTRON® EliteView™ EM-295665-1:654321

INSTRUCTIONS FOR COMPLETING THE BIOGRAPHICAL AREA ARE ON THE BACK COVER OF YOUR TEST BOOKLET.
USE ONLY A NO. 2 OR HB PENCIL TO COMPLETE THIS ANSWER SHEET. DO NOT USE INK.

1 LAST NAME | FIRST NAME | MI

2 LAST 4 DIGITS OF SOCIAL SECURITY/ SOCIAL INSURANCE NO.

3 LSAC ACCOUNT NUMBER

4 CENTER NUMBER

5 DATE OF BIRTH

MONTH	DAY	YEAR
Jan		
Feb		
Mar		
Apr		
May		
June		
July		
Aug		
Sept		
Oct		
Nov		
Dec		

6 TEST FORM CODE

7 RACIAL/ETHNIC DESCRIPTION
Mark one or more
- 1 Amer. Indian/Alaska Native
- 2 Asian
- 3 Black/African American
- 4 Canadian Aboriginal
- 5 Caucasian/White
- 6 Hispanic/Latino
- 7 Native Hawaiian/ Other Pacific Islander
- 8 Puerto Rican
- 9 TSI/Aboriginal Australian

8 SEX
- Male
- Female

9 DOMINANT LANGUAGE
- English
- Other

10 ENGLISH FLUENCY
- Yes
- No

11 TEST DATE
/ /
MONTH DAY YEAR

12 TEST FORM

Law School Admission Test

Mark one and only one answer to each question. Be sure to fill in completely the space for your intended answer choice. If you erase, do so completely. Make no stray marks.

13 TEST BOOK SERIAL NO.

SECTION 1 | SECTION 2 | SECTION 3 | SECTION 4 | SECTION 5

(questions 1–30, each with answer choices A B C D E)

14 PLEASE PRINT INFORMATION

LAST NAME

FIRST NAME

DATE OF BIRTH

© 2014 BY LAW SCHOOL ADMISSION COUNCIL.
ALL RIGHTS RESERVED. PRINTED IN USA.

INSTRUCTIONS FOR COMPLETING THE BIOGRAPHICAL AREA ARE ON THE BACK COVER OF YOUR TEST BOOKLET.

USE ONLY A NO. 2 OR HB PENCIL TO COMPLETE THIS ANSWER SHEET. DO NOT USE INK.

SCANTRON® EliteView™ EM-295665-1:654321

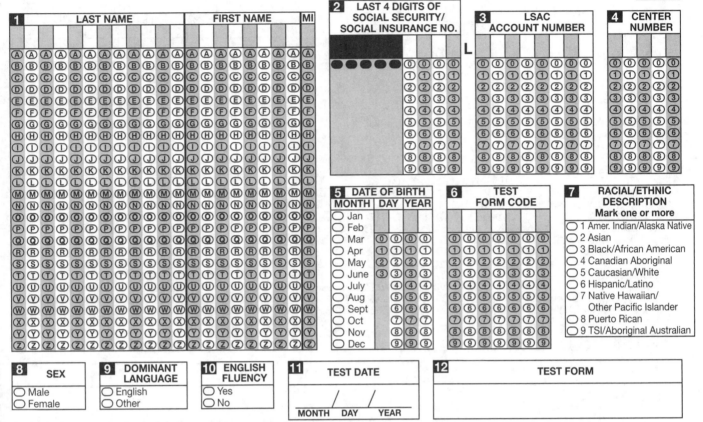

Law School Admission Test

Mark one and only one answer to each question. Be sure to fill in completely the space for your intended answer choice. If you erase, do so completely. Make no stray marks.

INSTRUCTIONS FOR COMPLETING THE BIOGRAPHICAL AREA ARE ON THE BACK COVER OF YOUR TEST BOOKLET.
USE ONLY A NO. 2 OR HB PENCIL TO COMPLETE THIS ANSWER SHEET. DO NOT USE INK.

A

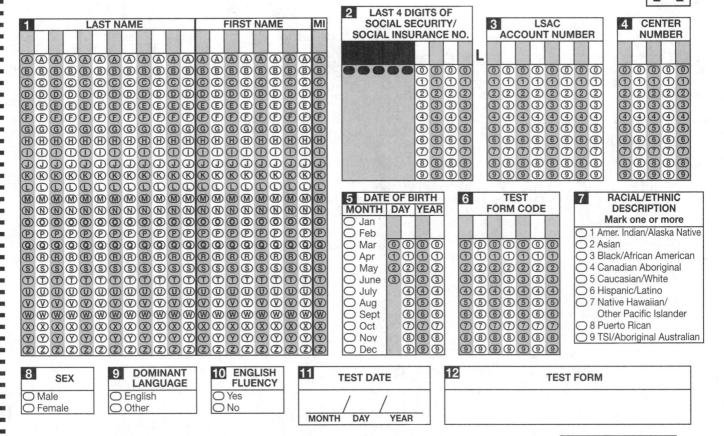

8 SEX
- ○ Male
- ○ Female

9 DOMINANT LANGUAGE
- ○ English
- ○ Other

10 ENGLISH FLUENCY
- ○ Yes
- ○ No

11 TEST DATE
MONTH / DAY / YEAR

12 TEST FORM

Law School Admission Test

Mark one and only one answer to each question. Be sure to fill in completely the space for your intended answer choice. If you erase, do so completely. Make no stray marks.

13 TEST BOOK SERIAL NO.

SECTION 1	SECTION 2	SECTION 3	SECTION 4	SECTION 5
1 Ⓐ Ⓑ Ⓒ Ⓓ Ⓔ	1 Ⓐ Ⓑ Ⓒ Ⓓ Ⓔ	1 Ⓐ Ⓑ Ⓒ Ⓓ Ⓔ	1 Ⓐ Ⓑ Ⓒ Ⓓ Ⓔ	1 Ⓐ Ⓑ Ⓒ Ⓓ Ⓔ
2 Ⓐ Ⓑ Ⓒ Ⓓ Ⓔ	2 Ⓐ Ⓑ Ⓒ Ⓓ Ⓔ	2 Ⓐ Ⓑ Ⓒ Ⓓ Ⓔ	2 Ⓐ Ⓑ Ⓒ Ⓓ Ⓔ	2 Ⓐ Ⓑ Ⓒ Ⓓ Ⓔ
3 Ⓐ Ⓑ Ⓒ Ⓓ Ⓔ	3 Ⓐ Ⓑ Ⓒ Ⓓ Ⓔ	3 Ⓐ Ⓑ Ⓒ Ⓓ Ⓔ	3 Ⓐ Ⓑ Ⓒ Ⓓ Ⓔ	3 Ⓐ Ⓑ Ⓒ Ⓓ Ⓔ
4 Ⓐ Ⓑ Ⓒ Ⓓ Ⓔ	4 Ⓐ Ⓑ Ⓒ Ⓓ Ⓔ	4 Ⓐ Ⓑ Ⓒ Ⓓ Ⓔ	4 Ⓐ Ⓑ Ⓒ Ⓓ Ⓔ	4 Ⓐ Ⓑ Ⓒ Ⓓ Ⓔ
5 Ⓐ Ⓑ Ⓒ Ⓓ Ⓔ	5 Ⓐ Ⓑ Ⓒ Ⓓ Ⓔ	5 Ⓐ Ⓑ Ⓒ Ⓓ Ⓔ	5 Ⓐ Ⓑ Ⓒ Ⓓ Ⓔ	5 Ⓐ Ⓑ Ⓒ Ⓓ Ⓔ
6 Ⓐ Ⓑ Ⓒ Ⓓ Ⓔ	6 Ⓐ Ⓑ Ⓒ Ⓓ Ⓔ	6 Ⓐ Ⓑ Ⓒ Ⓓ Ⓔ	6 Ⓐ Ⓑ Ⓒ Ⓓ Ⓔ	6 Ⓐ Ⓑ Ⓒ Ⓓ Ⓔ
7 Ⓐ Ⓑ Ⓒ Ⓓ Ⓔ	7 Ⓐ Ⓑ Ⓒ Ⓓ Ⓔ	7 Ⓐ Ⓑ Ⓒ Ⓓ Ⓔ	7 Ⓐ Ⓑ Ⓒ Ⓓ Ⓔ	7 Ⓐ Ⓑ Ⓒ Ⓓ Ⓔ
8 Ⓐ Ⓑ Ⓒ Ⓓ Ⓔ	8 Ⓐ Ⓑ Ⓒ Ⓓ Ⓔ	8 Ⓐ Ⓑ Ⓒ Ⓓ Ⓔ	8 Ⓐ Ⓑ Ⓒ Ⓓ Ⓔ	8 Ⓐ Ⓑ Ⓒ Ⓓ Ⓔ
9 Ⓐ Ⓑ Ⓒ Ⓓ Ⓔ	9 Ⓐ Ⓑ Ⓒ Ⓓ Ⓔ	9 Ⓐ Ⓑ Ⓒ Ⓓ Ⓔ	9 Ⓐ Ⓑ Ⓒ Ⓓ Ⓔ	9 Ⓐ Ⓑ Ⓒ Ⓓ Ⓔ
10 Ⓐ Ⓑ Ⓒ Ⓓ Ⓔ	10 Ⓐ Ⓑ Ⓒ Ⓓ Ⓔ	10 Ⓐ Ⓑ Ⓒ Ⓓ Ⓔ	10 Ⓐ Ⓑ Ⓒ Ⓓ Ⓔ	10 Ⓐ Ⓑ Ⓒ Ⓓ Ⓔ
11 Ⓐ Ⓑ Ⓒ Ⓓ Ⓔ	11 Ⓐ Ⓑ Ⓒ Ⓓ Ⓔ	11 Ⓐ Ⓑ Ⓒ Ⓓ Ⓔ	11 Ⓐ Ⓑ Ⓒ Ⓓ Ⓔ	11 Ⓐ Ⓑ Ⓒ Ⓓ Ⓔ
12 Ⓐ Ⓑ Ⓒ Ⓓ Ⓔ	12 Ⓐ Ⓑ Ⓒ Ⓓ Ⓔ	12 Ⓐ Ⓑ Ⓒ Ⓓ Ⓔ	12 Ⓐ Ⓑ Ⓒ Ⓓ Ⓔ	12 Ⓐ Ⓑ Ⓒ Ⓓ Ⓔ
13 Ⓐ Ⓑ Ⓒ Ⓓ Ⓔ	13 Ⓐ Ⓑ Ⓒ Ⓓ Ⓔ	13 Ⓐ Ⓑ Ⓒ Ⓓ Ⓔ	13 Ⓐ Ⓑ Ⓒ Ⓓ Ⓔ	13 Ⓐ Ⓑ Ⓒ Ⓓ Ⓔ
14 Ⓐ Ⓑ Ⓒ Ⓓ Ⓔ	14 Ⓐ Ⓑ Ⓒ Ⓓ Ⓔ	14 Ⓐ Ⓑ Ⓒ Ⓓ Ⓔ	14 Ⓐ Ⓑ Ⓒ Ⓓ Ⓔ	14 Ⓐ Ⓑ Ⓒ Ⓓ Ⓔ
15 Ⓐ Ⓑ Ⓒ Ⓓ Ⓔ	15 Ⓐ Ⓑ Ⓒ Ⓓ Ⓔ	15 Ⓐ Ⓑ Ⓒ Ⓓ Ⓔ	15 Ⓐ Ⓑ Ⓒ Ⓓ Ⓔ	15 Ⓐ Ⓑ Ⓒ Ⓓ Ⓔ
16 Ⓐ Ⓑ Ⓒ Ⓓ Ⓔ	16 Ⓐ Ⓑ Ⓒ Ⓓ Ⓔ	16 Ⓐ Ⓑ Ⓒ Ⓓ Ⓔ	16 Ⓐ Ⓑ Ⓒ Ⓓ Ⓔ	16 Ⓐ Ⓑ Ⓒ Ⓓ Ⓔ
17 Ⓐ Ⓑ Ⓒ Ⓓ Ⓔ	17 Ⓐ Ⓑ Ⓒ Ⓓ Ⓔ	17 Ⓐ Ⓑ Ⓒ Ⓓ Ⓔ	17 Ⓐ Ⓑ Ⓒ Ⓓ Ⓔ	17 Ⓐ Ⓑ Ⓒ Ⓓ Ⓔ
18 Ⓐ Ⓑ Ⓒ Ⓓ Ⓔ	18 Ⓐ Ⓑ Ⓒ Ⓓ Ⓔ	18 Ⓐ Ⓑ Ⓒ Ⓓ Ⓔ	18 Ⓐ Ⓑ Ⓒ Ⓓ Ⓔ	18 Ⓐ Ⓑ Ⓒ Ⓓ Ⓔ
19 Ⓐ Ⓑ Ⓒ Ⓓ Ⓔ	19 Ⓐ Ⓑ Ⓒ Ⓓ Ⓔ	19 Ⓐ Ⓑ Ⓒ Ⓓ Ⓔ	19 Ⓐ Ⓑ Ⓒ Ⓓ Ⓔ	19 Ⓐ Ⓑ Ⓒ Ⓓ Ⓔ
20 Ⓐ Ⓑ Ⓒ Ⓓ Ⓔ	20 Ⓐ Ⓑ Ⓒ Ⓓ Ⓔ	20 Ⓐ Ⓑ Ⓒ Ⓓ Ⓔ	20 Ⓐ Ⓑ Ⓒ Ⓓ Ⓔ	20 Ⓐ Ⓑ Ⓒ Ⓓ Ⓔ
21 Ⓐ Ⓑ Ⓒ Ⓓ Ⓔ	21 Ⓐ Ⓑ Ⓒ Ⓓ Ⓔ	21 Ⓐ Ⓑ Ⓒ Ⓓ Ⓔ	21 Ⓐ Ⓑ Ⓒ Ⓓ Ⓔ	21 Ⓐ Ⓑ Ⓒ Ⓓ Ⓔ
22 Ⓐ Ⓑ Ⓒ Ⓓ Ⓔ	22 Ⓐ Ⓑ Ⓒ Ⓓ Ⓔ	22 Ⓐ Ⓑ Ⓒ Ⓓ Ⓔ	22 Ⓐ Ⓑ Ⓒ Ⓓ Ⓔ	22 Ⓐ Ⓑ Ⓒ Ⓓ Ⓔ
23 Ⓐ Ⓑ Ⓒ Ⓓ Ⓔ	23 Ⓐ Ⓑ Ⓒ Ⓓ Ⓔ	23 Ⓐ Ⓑ Ⓒ Ⓓ Ⓔ	23 Ⓐ Ⓑ Ⓒ Ⓓ Ⓔ	23 Ⓐ Ⓑ Ⓒ Ⓓ Ⓔ
24 Ⓐ Ⓑ Ⓒ Ⓓ Ⓔ	24 Ⓐ Ⓑ Ⓒ Ⓓ Ⓔ	24 Ⓐ Ⓑ Ⓒ Ⓓ Ⓔ	24 Ⓐ Ⓑ Ⓒ Ⓓ Ⓔ	24 Ⓐ Ⓑ Ⓒ Ⓓ Ⓔ
25 Ⓐ Ⓑ Ⓒ Ⓓ Ⓔ	25 Ⓐ Ⓑ Ⓒ Ⓓ Ⓔ	25 Ⓐ Ⓑ Ⓒ Ⓓ Ⓔ	25 Ⓐ Ⓑ Ⓒ Ⓓ Ⓔ	25 Ⓐ Ⓑ Ⓒ Ⓓ Ⓔ
26 Ⓐ Ⓑ Ⓒ Ⓓ Ⓔ	26 Ⓐ Ⓑ Ⓒ Ⓓ Ⓔ	26 Ⓐ Ⓑ Ⓒ Ⓓ Ⓔ	26 Ⓐ Ⓑ Ⓒ Ⓓ Ⓔ	26 Ⓐ Ⓑ Ⓒ Ⓓ Ⓔ
27 Ⓐ Ⓑ Ⓒ Ⓓ Ⓔ	27 Ⓐ Ⓑ Ⓒ Ⓓ Ⓔ	27 Ⓐ Ⓑ Ⓒ Ⓓ Ⓔ	27 Ⓐ Ⓑ Ⓒ Ⓓ Ⓔ	27 Ⓐ Ⓑ Ⓒ Ⓓ Ⓔ
28 Ⓐ Ⓑ Ⓒ Ⓓ Ⓔ	28 Ⓐ Ⓑ Ⓒ Ⓓ Ⓔ	28 Ⓐ Ⓑ Ⓒ Ⓓ Ⓔ	28 Ⓐ Ⓑ Ⓒ Ⓓ Ⓔ	28 Ⓐ Ⓑ Ⓒ Ⓓ Ⓔ
29 Ⓐ Ⓑ Ⓒ Ⓓ Ⓔ	29 Ⓐ Ⓑ Ⓒ Ⓓ Ⓔ	29 Ⓐ Ⓑ Ⓒ Ⓓ Ⓔ	29 Ⓐ Ⓑ Ⓒ Ⓓ Ⓔ	29 Ⓐ Ⓑ Ⓒ Ⓓ Ⓔ
30 Ⓐ Ⓑ Ⓒ Ⓓ Ⓔ	30 Ⓐ Ⓑ Ⓒ Ⓓ Ⓔ	30 Ⓐ Ⓑ Ⓒ Ⓓ Ⓔ	30 Ⓐ Ⓑ Ⓒ Ⓓ Ⓔ	30 Ⓐ Ⓑ Ⓒ Ⓓ Ⓔ

14 PLEASE PRINT INFORMATION

LAST NAME

FIRST NAME

DATE OF BIRTH

● Ⓑ

INSTRUCTIONS FOR COMPLETING THE BIOGRAPHICAL AREA ARE ON THE BACK COVER OF YOUR TEST BOOKLET.
USE ONLY A NO. 2 OR HB PENCIL TO COMPLETE THIS ANSWER SHEET. DO NOT USE INK.

1 LAST NAME · FIRST NAME · MI

(Grid of bubbles A–Z for each letter position)

2 LAST 4 DIGITS OF SOCIAL SECURITY/SOCIAL INSURANCE NO.
L
(Bubbles 0–9)

3 LSAC ACCOUNT NUMBER
(Bubbles 0–9)

4 CENTER NUMBER
(Bubbles 0–9)

5 DATE OF BIRTH

MONTH	DAY	YEAR
○ Jan		
○ Feb		
○ Mar	0 0	0 0
○ Apr	1 1	1 1
○ May	2 2	2 2
○ June	3 3	3 3
○ July	4 4	4 4
○ Aug	5 5	5 5
○ Sept	6 6	6 6
○ Oct	7 7	7 7
○ Nov	8 8	8 8
○ Dec	9 9	9 9

6 TEST FORM CODE
(Bubbles 0–9)

7 RACIAL/ETHNIC DESCRIPTION
Mark one or more
- ○ 1 Amer. Indian/Alaska Native
- ○ 2 Asian
- ○ 3 Black/African American
- ○ 4 Canadian Aboriginal
- ○ 5 Caucasian/White
- ○ 6 Hispanic/Latino
- ○ 7 Native Hawaiian/Other Pacific Islander
- ○ 8 Puerto Rican
- ○ 9 TSI/Aboriginal Australian

8 SEX
- ○ Male
- ○ Female

9 DOMINANT LANGUAGE
- ○ English
- ○ Other

10 ENGLISH FLUENCY
- ○ Yes
- ○ No

11 TEST DATE
MONTH / DAY / YEAR

12 TEST FORM

Law School Admission Test

Mark one and only one answer to each question. Be sure to fill in completely the space for your intended answer choice. If you erase, do so completely. Make no stray marks.

13 TEST BOOK SERIAL NO.
(Bubbles A–T and 0–9)

SECTION 1 — questions 1–30, choices A B C D E
SECTION 2 — questions 1–30, choices A B C D E
SECTION 3 — questions 1–30, choices A B C D E
SECTION 4 — questions 1–30, choices A B C D E
SECTION 5 — questions 1–30, choices A B C D E

14 PLEASE PRINT INFORMATION

LAST NAME

FIRST NAME

DATE OF BIRTH

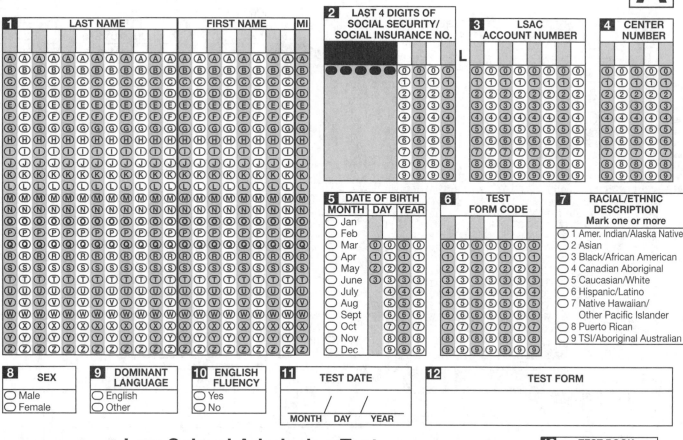

SCANTRON EliteView™ EM-295665-1:654321

INSTRUCTIONS FOR COMPLETING THE BIOGRAPHICAL AREA ARE ON THE BACK COVER OF YOUR TEST BOOKLET.
USE ONLY A NO. 2 OR HB PENCIL TO COMPLETE THIS ANSWER SHEET. DO NOT USE INK.

A

1 LAST NAME / FIRST NAME / MI

2 LAST 4 DIGITS OF SOCIAL SECURITY/ SOCIAL INSURANCE NO.

3 LSAC ACCOUNT NUMBER

4 CENTER NUMBER

5 DATE OF BIRTH
MONTH | DAY | YEAR
Jan, Feb, Mar, Apr, May, June, July, Aug, Sept, Oct, Nov, Dec

6 TEST FORM CODE

7 RACIAL/ETHNIC DESCRIPTION
Mark one or more
1 Amer. Indian/Alaska Native
2 Asian
3 Black/African American
4 Canadian Aboriginal
5 Caucasian/White
6 Hispanic/Latino
7 Native Hawaiian/ Other Pacific Islander
8 Puerto Rican
9 TSI/Aboriginal Australian

8 SEX
Male
Female

9 DOMINANT LANGUAGE
English
Other

10 ENGLISH FLUENCY
Yes
No

11 TEST DATE
MONTH / DAY / YEAR

12 TEST FORM

═══ Law School Admission Test ═══

Mark one and only one answer to each question. Be sure to fill in completely the space for your intended answer choice. If you erase, do so completely. Make no stray marks.

13 TEST BOOK SERIAL NO.

SECTION 1 | **SECTION 2** | **SECTION 3** | **SECTION 4** | **SECTION 5**

(Questions 1–30, each with answer choices A B C D E)

14 PLEASE PRINT INFORMATION

LAST NAME

FIRST NAME

DATE OF BIRTH

© 2014 BY LAW SCHOOL ADMISSION COUNCIL.
ALL RIGHTS RESERVED. PRINTED IN USA.

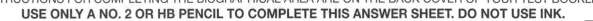

SCANTRON® EliteView™ EM-295665-1:654321

INSTRUCTIONS FOR COMPLETING THE BIOGRAPHICAL AREA ARE ON THE BACK COVER OF YOUR TEST BOOKLET.
USE ONLY A NO. 2 OR HB PENCIL TO COMPLETE THIS ANSWER SHEET. DO NOT USE INK.

1 LAST NAME   FIRST NAME   MI

(Grid A–Z bubbles for Last Name, First Name, and MI)

2 LAST 4 DIGITS OF SOCIAL SECURITY/ SOCIAL INSURANCE NO.

3 LSAC ACCOUNT NUMBER

L

4 CENTER NUMBER

(Number grids 0–9)

5 DATE OF BIRTH

MONTH	DAY	YEAR
○ Jan		
○ Feb		
○ Mar		
○ Apr		
○ May		
○ June		
○ July		
○ Aug		
○ Sept		
○ Oct		
○ Nov		
○ Dec		

(Number grids 0–9 for Day and Year)

6 TEST FORM CODE

(Number grids 0–9)

7 RACIAL/ETHNIC DESCRIPTION
Mark one or more

○ 1 Amer. Indian/Alaska Native
○ 2 Asian
○ 3 Black/African American
○ 4 Canadian Aboriginal
○ 5 Caucasian/White
○ 6 Hispanic/Latino
○ 7 Native Hawaiian/ Other Pacific Islander
○ 8 Puerto Rican
○ 9 TSI/Aboriginal Australian

8 SEX
○ Male
○ Female

9 DOMINANT LANGUAGE
○ English
○ Other

10 ENGLISH FLUENCY
○ Yes
○ No

11 TEST DATE
_____ / _____ / _____
MONTH   DAY   YEAR

12 TEST FORM

═══ Law School Admission Test ═══

Mark one and only one answer to each question. Be sure to fill in completely the space for your intended answer choice. If you erase, do so completely. Make no stray marks.

13 TEST BOOK SERIAL NO.

(Grid A–T and 0–9)

SECTION 1 — 1–30 Ⓐ Ⓑ Ⓒ Ⓓ Ⓔ
SECTION 2 — 1–30 Ⓐ Ⓑ Ⓒ Ⓓ Ⓔ
SECTION 3 — 1–30 Ⓐ Ⓑ Ⓒ Ⓓ Ⓔ
SECTION 4 — 1–30 Ⓐ Ⓑ Ⓒ Ⓓ Ⓔ
SECTION 5 — 1–30 Ⓐ Ⓑ Ⓒ Ⓓ Ⓔ

14 PLEASE PRINT INFORMATION

LAST NAME
_____

FIRST NAME
_____

DATE OF BIRTH
_____

● Ⓑ